75th Anniversary

Beta Sigma Phi

A COOKBOOK CELEBRATING
75 YEARS OF LIFE, LEARNING AND FRIENDSHIP

EDITORIAL STAFF

Executive Editor	Paul Stansberry
Managing Editor	Mary Cummings
Project Editor	Anna Watson
Editorial Consultant	Georgia Brazil
Award Selection Judges	Paul Stansberry, Ron Hartman
Art Director	Steve Newman
Illustrator	Barbara Ball
Book Design	Travis Rader
Production Design	Jessie Anglin, Sara Anglin
Test Kitchen	Sue Hartman, Martha Hodge, Julie Otto, Lequida Slate, Lisa Viator

© Favorite Recipes® Press, A Division of Heritage House, Inc. 2005
P.O. Box 305141, Nashville, Tennessee 37230

ISBN: 0-87197-521-1

Manufactured in the United States of America

First Printing 2005

Contents

Dear Friends,

Here we are 75 years later in the journey of Beta Sigma Phi – and what a wonderful trip it has been.

 I can remember as a young boy, conversations in our home about the beginning of Beta Sigma Phi. We were thrilled about the 25th and 50th anniversaries and here we are at another milestone.

But enough about the past, we must look to the future of your organization. It is my heartfelt hope that women today need Beta Sigma Phi more than ever. I like to think of the organization as a safe haven from the hustle and bustle of the world, where a member will find only The Good, The True, and The Beautiful.

At the beginning of this cookbook, you will find some special recipes of my mother, Dorothy Ross. You will find

Bill and Marilyn Ross

one of my favorite recipes, as well as one of my brother Jack's. You will also find two selections from Marilyn Ross. I want to share these recipes with all Beta Sigma Phis, young and old.

My very best to you as your family and chapter gather for the enjoyment of these wonderful recipes.

Your friend,

Bill Ross

Walter W. Ross, III

P.S. By the purchase of this cookbook, you have allowed the members of Beta Sigma Phi to raise money for worthy causes and contribute to their favorite charities.

Dorothy Ross's Recipes

SMALL DEVIL'S FOOD CAKE
Yield: 9 servings

1 cup all-purpose flour
1 cup sugar
1 egg
1/2 cup buttermilk or 1/2 cup milk
  plus 1 tablespoon vinegar

1/2 cup boiling water
1 teaspoon baking soda
1 teaspoon vanilla extract
2 ounces bittersweet chocolate,
  melted

Butter Cream Frosting
1 ounce bittersweet chocolate,
  melted

Combine the flour and sugar in a bowl and mix well. Whisk the egg and buttermilk in a small bowl. Pour the egg mixture into the flour mixture, stirring to combine. Stir in the water, baking soda and vanilla. Add 2 ounces chocolate, stirring until smooth. Pour the mixture into a greased 8x8-inch baking pan. Bake at 350 degrees for 35 minutes or until it tests done. Cool on a wire rack. When cool, frost with the Butter Cream Frosting and drizzle with 1 ounce melted chocolate.

Butter Cream Frosting

1/2 cup (1 stick) butter, softened
16 ounces confectioners' sugar

Pinch of salt
4 to 5 tablespoons hot coffee

1 1/2 teaspoons vanilla extract

Cream the butter in a mixing bowl. Add the confectioner's sugar gradually. Beat at medium speed for 2 to 3 minutes or until smooth. Add the salt and mix well. Stir in the coffee 1 tablespoon at time until it reaches spreading consistency. Beat at medium speed until fluffy. Stir in the vanilla. Spread the frosting over the Devil's Food Cake.

GUMDROP COOKIES
Yield: 3 to 4 dozen

1 cup shortening
1 cup granulated sugar
1 cup packed brown sugar
2 eggs
1 teaspoon vanilla extract

1 cup coconut
1 cup chopped gumdrops
1 cup chopped pecans
2 cups rolled oats
2 cups all-purpose flour

1 teaspoon baking soda
1 teaspoon baking powder
1/2 teaspoon salt

Cream the shortening and sugars together in a large mixing bowl. Add the eggs, 1 at a time, mixing thoroughly after each addition. Stir in the vanilla. Fold in the coconut, gumdrops and pecans and mix well. Combine the oats, flour, baking soda, baking powder and salt in a bowl and mix well. Add the dry ingredients into the gumdrop mixture, stirring to combine. Drop by teaspoonfuls, 2 inches apart, onto a greased baking sheet. Bake at 350 degrees for 10 to 12 minutes or until golden brown.

Bill's Favorite Recipe

BARBECUED SPARERIBS
Yield: 24 servings

12 pounds spareribs
1 cup chopped onion
4 garlic cloves, minced
$1/4$ cup vegetable oil
1 quart tomato puree

$1/2$ cup lemon juice
$1/2$ cup vinegar
$1/2$ cup packed brown sugar
1 tablespoon salt
1 tablespoon dry mustard

1 tablespoon Tabasco
8 bay leaves
$3/4$ cup all-purpose flour
$3/4$ cup packed brown sugar

Cut the spareribs into serving size pieces and arrange in several large baking pans. Bake at 300 degrees for 1 hour or just until beginning to brown; drain. Sauté the onion and garlic in the oil in a large skillet just until tender. Add the tomato puree, lemon juice, vinegar, $1/2$ cup brown sugar, salt, mustard, Tabasco and bay leaves, stirring to combine. Bring to a boil over high heat. Spoon $1/2$ of the sauce over the spareribs and cook for $1 1/2$ hours longer, basting with sauce frequently. Combine the flour and $3/4$ cup brown sugar in a bowl and mix well. Sprinkle the flour mixture over the ribs, and bake for 30 more minutes or until done.

Jack's Favorite Recipe

TOMATO ASPIC AND SHRIMP REMOULADE
Yield: 8 servings

2 (3-ounce) packages
    unflavored gelatin
1 cup cold water
2 cups tomato juice

2 teaspoons onion juice
2 teaspoons vinegar or lemon juice
1 teaspoon salt
Pinch of pepper

$1/2$ teaspoon hot red pepper sauce
Pinch sugar
1 cup chopped cooked artichoke hearts
Shrimp Remoulade

Sprinkle the gelatin over the water in a bowl; stir and soak for 5 minutes. Bring the tomato juice to a boil in a saucepan over high heat. Pour the hot tomato juice over the gelatin mixture, stirring until the gelatin has dissolved. Add the onion juice, vinegar, salt, pepper, hot sauce and sugar and mix well. Fold in the artichoke hearts. Pour the mixture into a ring mold. Chill, in the refrigerator, until firm. Unmold the aspic onto a large platter. Fill the center with the Shrimp Remoulade. Garnish with avocados, tomatoes, egg slices and mayonnaise.

Shrimp Remoulade

1 cup Dijon mustard
$1/2$ cup ketchup
$3/4$ cup vegetable oil

$1/2$ cup vinegar
$1/2$ cup finely chopped onion
$1/2$ cup finely chopped celery

$1/2$ cup finely chopped green pepper
$1 1/2$ pounds shrimp, peeled,
    deveined and cooked

Combine the Dijon mustard, ketchup, oil, vinegar, onion, celery and green pepper in bowl and mix well. Place the shrimp in the marinade. Cover and marinate in the refrigerator for 1 hour or longer; drain. Serve with the Tomato Aspic.

Marilyn Ross's Recipes

Pear Salad with Raspberry Cream
Yield: 8 servings

Bill and I enjoy this, especially at holiday time!

3/4 cup sour cream
1/4 cup raspberry preserves
3 tablespoons red wine vinegar
1/8 teaspoon Dijon mustard
4 firm, ripe pears

2 tablespoons lemon juice
1 small head Bibb lettuce, torn
1 small head romaine lettuce, torn
1/2 cup (2 ounces) freshly grated
  Parmesan cheese

6 strips bacon, crisp-cooked and
  crumbled
1/2 cup fresh raspberries

Whisk the sour cream, raspberry preserves, red wine vinegar and Dijon mustard in a small bowl; set aside. Rinse the pears and cut them into quarters. Brush the pears with lemon juice. Arrange the lettuce on 4 plates. Top each with 4 pear slices; and drizzle with the dressing. Sprinkle with the Parmesan cheese, bacon, and raspberries.

Sugar and Spice Muffins
Yield: 12 servings

This is a long time favorite of my family and sorority family, too!

1 3/4 cups all-purpose flour
1 1/2 teaspoon baking powder
1/2 teaspoon salt
1/2 teaspoon nutmeg

1/3 cup vegetable oil
3/4 cup sugar
1 egg
3/4 cup milk

1/3 cup butter
1/4 cup sugar
1 teaspoon cinnamon

Sift the flour, baking powder, salt and nutmeg together into a bowl. Beat the oil, sugar, egg and milk in a mixing bowl at medium speed until smooth. Add the oil mixture to the dry ingredients, stirring to combine. Fill greased miniature muffin cups 2/3 full of batter. Bake at 350 degrees for 12 minutes. Remove from the pans immediately. Melt the butter in a small saucepan. Combine 1/4 cup sugar and cinnamon in a small bowl and mix well. Dip the hot muffins in the melted butter and roll in the cinnamon-sugar mixture.

Appetizers

MARINATED VEGETABLE ANTIPASTO

2 heads cauliflower,
  broken into florets
3 green bell peppers,
  sliced
2 pounds carrots, sliced
1 bunch celery, sliced
1 pound button
  mushrooms, sliced
1/2 cup extra-virgin
  olive oil

1 cup vegetable oil
3 cups tarragon vinegar
1/2 to 3/4 cup sugar
3 garlic cloves, minced
1 tablespoon mustard
1 tablespoon salt
2 teaspoons tarragon
  leaves
Pepper to taste

Combine the cauliflower, bell peppers, carrots, celery and mushrooms in a large bowl and mix well. Combine the olive oil, vegetable oil, vinegar, sugar, garlic, mustard, salt, tarragon leaves and pepper in a small bowl and blend well. Pour the dressing over the vegetable mixture and toss gently to coat. Chill, covered, for 24 hours. Drain the vegetables well before serving. Serve the antipasto on a platter lined with red leaf lettuce. Yield: 50 servings.

Sheila Bryson, Epsilon Omicron
Deridder, Louisiana

MEAT AND CHEESE ANTIPASTO SQUARES

2 (8-count) cans
  crescent rolls
4 ounces sliced pepperoni
4 ounces Swiss cheese,
  sliced
4 ounces sliced salami
4 ounces provolone
  cheese, sliced

4 ounces sliced ham
1 (12-ounce) jar sweet
  red peppers, drained
4 eggs, beaten
3 tablespoons grated
  Parmesan cheese

Unroll 1 can of crescent rolls and press the dough in a greased 9×13-inch baking dish. Layer the pepperoni, Swiss cheese, salami, provolone cheese and ham on top of the dough. Top with the sweet red peppers. Combine the eggs and Parmesan cheese in a medium bowl and mix well. Pour half of the egg mixture on top of the layered ingredients. Unroll the other can of crescent rolls and place the dough on top of the layered ingredients. Pour the remaining egg mixture over the top of the dough. Cover the pan with foil. Bake at 350 degrees for 30 minutes or until the egg mixture has set. Remove the foil and bake for 15 minutes longer. Let stand until cool. Cut into 2-inch squares. Squares may be served hot or cold. Yield: 2 dozen squares.

Valerie Krzemienski, Eta Rho
Beaver Falls, Pennsylvania

BACON AND APRICOT WRAPS

1 pound sliced bacon
1 (14-ounce) package
  dried apricots

1/2 cup whole almonds
1/4 cup apple jelly
2 tablespoons soy sauce

Cut each bacon slice into 3 strips. Fold 1 apricot around each almond. Wrap a bacon strip around each apricot bundle and secure with a wooden pick. Place finished wraps in 2 ungreased 10×15-inch baking pans. Bake at 375 degrees for 25 minutes or until the bacon is crisp, turning once. Remove the wraps to paper towels to drain. Combine the jelly and soy sauce in a small saucepan. Cook over low heat for 5 minutes or until smooth, stirring frequently. Serve the wraps with the warm sauce for dipping. Yield: 4 1/2 dozen wraps.

Debbi Wallin, Xi Lambda Theta
Sebastopol, California

ASPARAGUS PUFFS

1 egg, beaten
8 ounces cream cheese,
  softened
1 loaf white bread,
  crusts trimmed
4 ounces Gorgonzola
  cheese crumbles

1 (15-ounce) can
  asparagus spears,
  drained
1/2 stick butter, melted

Combine the egg and cream cheese in a medium bowl and mix well. Spread the cream cheese mixture on each piece of bread. Sprinkle with Gorgonzola cheese crumbles. Place 1 asparagus spear on each piece of bread and roll as for a jelly roll. Place rolls seam down in a 10×15-inch baking pan. Brush with the melted butter. Freeze for 2 to 3 hours. Remove from the freezer and cut each roll with a sharp knife into 4 sections. Bake at 400 degrees for 15 to 20 minutes or until golden brown. Puffs may be refrozen before baking, if desired. Yield: 80 puffs.

Carlene Dockery
Blairsville, Georgia

FRIED ASPARAGUS AND HAM SWIRLS

8 teaspoons mustard
12 ounces sliced ham
12 ounces sliced Swiss
  cheese
1 (15-ounce) can
  asparagus spears,
  drained

2 eggs, beaten
1 cup bread crumbs
Vegetable oil for frying

Spread 1/2 teaspoon of the mustard on each slice of ham. Top each slice with 1 slice of the cheese. Place 1 asparagus spear on top. Roll as for a jelly roll and secure with a wooden pick. Dip each roll in the beaten egg and coat with the bread crumbs. Place the rolls in a 10×15-inch pan. Chill for 1 hour. Heat the oil to 350 degrees in a deep fryer. Fry the rolls for 1 minute or until golden brown. Remove the rolls from the oil using a slotted spoon; drain on paper towels. Cut each roll into 3 pieces before serving. Yield: 4 dozen swirls.

Barbara LaChapelle, Xi Epsilon Pi
Fayetteville, Georgia

SPICY BACON BREADSTICKS

25 slices bacon
25 hard breadsticks
1/2 cup packed brown
  sugar

2 teaspoons cayenne
  pepper

Wrap 1 slice of bacon around the length of each breadstick. Combine the brown sugar and cayenne pepper in a small bowl and mix well. Remove the brown sugar mixture to a plate. Roll each bacon breadstick in the brown sugar mixture. Place finished breadsticks on a baking sheet. Bake at 350 degrees for 10 to 15 minutes or until the sugar is caramelized and the bacon is crisp. Serve warm. Yield: 25 breadsticks.

Mary Riggio, Preceptor Alpha Eta
DuQuoin, Illinois

TRADITIONAL BRUSCHETTA

1 1/2 cups chopped Roma
  tomatoes
2 tablespoons chopped
  red onion
1 large garlic clove,
  minced
2 tablespoons chopped
  fresh basil
1/2 tablespoon olive oil
1/2 teaspoon red wine
  vinegar

1/4 teaspoon salt
Freshly ground pepper
  to taste
1 1/2 tablespoons
  olive oil
1/4 teaspoon garlic salt
1 loaf crusty Italian
  bread or baguette,
  cut into 1-inch slices

Combine the tomatoes, onion, garlic and basil in a medium bowl and mix well. Add 1/2 tablespoon olive oil, vinegar, salt and pepper and toss to coat. Chill, covered, for at least 1 hour. Combine 1 1/2 tablespoons olive oil and garlic salt in a small bowl and blend well. Brush both sides of the bread slices with the olive oil mixture and place on a baking sheet. Broil for 1 1/2 to 2 minutes on each side or until the bread is brown. Serve with the tomato mixture on the side. Yield: 12 servings.

Lisa Sevick, Kappa Lambda
Kansas City, Missouri

LAYERED BRUSCHETTA

1 1/2 cups chopped Roma
  tomatoes
1 large garlic clove,
  minced
1 1/2 cups (6 ounces)
  crumbled feta cheese

1 1/2 cups chopped
  Spanish olives
2 tablespoons olive oil
1 baguette, sliced and
  toasted

Combine the tomatoes and garlic in a small bowl and mix well. Place a small circular mold in the center of a serving plate. Place the feta cheese in the mold. Layer with the Spanish olives and the tomato mixture. Drizzle with the olive oil. Unmold and serve with the baguette slices. Garnish with greens. Yield: 4 servings.

Laura Hannan, Xi Eta Theta
Wamego, Kansas

❖ MIXED OLIVE BRUSCHETTA

The little extra effort is well worth the raves that you will receive from family and friends when you serve this appetizer.

1 cup pitted kalamata olives	1/2 cup chopped stuffed green olives
3/4 cup oil-pack sun-dried tomatoes, drained	2 tablespoons chopped fresh basil
1/4 cup capers	2 garlic cloves, minced
3/4 teaspoon oregano	1 baguette, cut into 1/2-inch slices
2/3 cup olive oil	1/2 cup olive oil
3 Roma tomatoes, seeded and chopped	3/4 cup crumbled feta cheese
1/2 cup chopped red onion	

Combine the kalamata olives, sun-dried tomatoes, capers, oregano and 2/3 cup olive oil in a food processor or blender and purée. Remove to a medium bowl and fold in the tomatoes, onion, green olives, basil and garlic. Brush the bread slices with 1/2 cup olive oil and place in a 10×15-inch baking pan. Broil for 3 minutes on each side or until golden brown. Spread the toast with the olive mixture and sprinkle with the feta cheese. Yield: 8 servings.

Vickie Thomas, Nu Master
Weiser, Idaho

EGGPLANT AND TOMATO BRUSCHETTA

2 tablespoons olive oil	2 tablespoons red wine vinegar
1 small onion, chopped	2 tablespoons sugar
1 large celery rib, chopped	1/2 teaspoon salt
1 (14-ounce) can diced tomatoes, drained	1/4 teaspoon pepper
1 cup canned crushed tomatoes	2 tablespoons olive oil
2 tablespoons capers	1 large eggplant, chopped
1/2 cup pitted green olives, halved	2 tablespoons olive oil
	1 baguette, sliced and toasted

Heat 2 tablespoons olive oil in a large heavy saucepan over medium heat. Add the onion and celery. Cook, covered, for 10 minutes or until the vegetables are tender, stirring frequently. Add the diced and crushed tomatoes, capers, olives, vinegar, sugar, salt and pepper and mix well. Bring the mixture to a boil. Lower the heat and simmer, covered, for 20 minutes. Heat 2 tablespoons olive oil in a large skillet over medium heat. Add half of the eggplant and cook for 10 minutes or until tender, stirring occasionally. Remove to a bowl. Add 2 tablespoons olive oil to the skillet and repeat the process with the remaining eggplant. Combine the tomato mixture and cooked eggplant in a bowl and mix well. Chill, covered, until ready to serve. Serve with slices of toasted baguette. Yield: 6 to 8 servings.

Anne Aho, Florida Xi Delta
The Villages, Florida

BRIE PIZZA

1/4 cup (1/2 stick) butter	2 tablespoons olive oil
6 sweet onions, thinly sliced	8 ounces Brie cheese, rind removed and cut into small pieces
16 ounces baking mix	1/3 cup sliced almonds
1 1/4 cups warm water (120 to 130 degrees)	

Melt the butter in a large skillet over high heat. Add the onions and sauté until transparent. Remove from the heat. Combine the baking mix, warm water and olive oil in a medium bowl and mix well until a dough forms. Remove the dough to a greased bowl, turning to coat the surface. Let rise, covered, for 5 minutes. Roll the dough into a 14-inch circle on a lightly floured surface and place on a greased pizza pan. Top with the onions and Brie. Sprinkle with the almonds. Bake at 400 degrees for 18 to 20 minutes or until the cheese is bubbly. Yield: 8 servings.

Karen Head, Xi Phi
Council Bluffs, Iowa

CHEDDAR CHEESE SHORTBREAD

2 1/2 cups all-purpose flour	1/2 teaspoon Worcestershire sauce
1 teaspoon paprika	2 cups (8 ounces) shredded Cheddar cheese
1 teaspoon salt	
1 cup (2 sticks) butter, softened	
1/2 teaspoon Tabasco sauce	

Combine the flour, paprika and salt in a medium bowl and mix well. Cream the butter in a mixing bowl until light and fluffy. Add the Tabasco sauce, Worcestershire sauce and cheese and mix well. Add the flour mixture to the butter mixture in 3 batches, mixing well after each addition. Remove the dough when it begins to form a ball and divide into halves on a lightly floured surface. Roll each piece of dough into a 1 1/2-inch-thick log. Wrap each log in plastic wrap. Chill for 1 hour. Remove the plastic wrap and slice the logs into 1-inch-thick rounds. Place the rounds on an ungreased baking sheet. Bake at 350 degrees for 20 minutes or until golden brown. Serve with red pepper jelly. Yield: 6 dozen rounds.

Donna O'Neil, Laureate Alpha Zeta
Trenton, Ontario, Canada

TERIYAKI CHICKEN WINGS

1/2 cup molasses
1 cup water
1 tablespoon
   Worcestershire sauce
1/2 cup soy sauce
2 tablespoons honey
1 tablespoon dried
   onion

1 tablespoon dried
   garlic
2 tablespoons brown
   sugar
2 1/2 to 3 dozen chicken
   wings or drumettes,
   cooked

Combine the molasses, water, Worcestershire sauce, soy sauce and honey in a bowl and blend well. Add the onion, garlic and brown sugar and mix well. Place the chicken in a 9×13-inch baking dish. Pour the teriyaki sauce over the chicken, turning to coat. Bake at 350 degrees for 40 minutes or until the sauce has been absorbed, turning occasionally. Yield: 12 servings.

Patty DeGrasse, Preceptor Gamma
Pueblo, Colorado

HAM AND CHICKEN ROLLS

1/4 cup mayonnaise
2 tablespoons sour
   cream
1/2 teaspoon chopped
   fresh savory, or
   1/4 teaspoon dried
   savory

1 cup minced cooked
   chicken
1 tablespoon each minced
   olives, red bell pepper,
   onion and celery
Salt and pepper to taste
16 thin slices ham

Combine the mayonnaise, sour cream and savory in a bowl and blend well. Fold in the chicken, olives, bell pepper, onion and celery. Place 1 tablespoon of the mayonnaise mixture in the center of each ham slice. Roll as for a jelly roll and secure with a wooden pick. Garnish with red bell pepper rings or parsley. Yield: 4 servings.

Marie Glaves, Beta Kappa Master
Dunnville, Ontario, Canada

CUCUMBER BOATS WITH CHICKEN AND SHRIMP SALAD

3 cucumbers, halved
   lengthwise
1/2 cup mayonnaise
2 tablespoons lemon
   juice
2 tablespoons tomato
   sauce
1 tablespoon chili sauce
1/2 cup chopped cooked
   chicken

1/2 cup chopped cooked
   shrimp
1 celery rib, minced
2 tablespoons chopped
   fresh parsley
1 tablespoon chopped
   fresh chives
Salt and pepper
   to taste

Scoop out and discard the seeds from the cucumber halves. Combine the mayonnaise, lemon juice, tomato sauce and chili sauce in a bowl and blend well. Add the chicken, shrimp, celery, parsley, chives, salt and pepper and mix well. Spoon the mixture into the cucumber halves. Serve immediately. Yield: 6 servings.

Kay O'Donnell-Hill, Preceptor Pi
Coon Rapids, Minnesota

CRANBERRY COCKTAIL MEATBALLS

3 pounds ground beef
3 eggs, beaten
1 envelope onion
   soup mix
1 cup bread crumbs
1 1/2 cups chili sauce

1 1/2 cups water
2 cups sauerkraut
2 cups cranberry sauce
1 cup packed brown
   sugar

Combine the ground beef, eggs, onion soup mix and bread crumbs in a large bowl and mix well. Shape the mixture into 1-inch balls. Arrange the meatballs in an ungreased shallow baking dish. Bake at 350 degrees for 20 to 30 minutes or until cooked through. Drain well. Mix the remaining ingredients in a medium bowl. Pour the sauce over the meatballs and return to the oven. Continue to bake for 1 1/2 hours. Yield: 5 dozen meatballs.

Sharon Elliott, Laureate Kappa
New Glasgow, Nova Scotia, Canada

SAUERKRAUT AND SAUSAGE BALLS

8 ounces bulk pork
   sausage
1/4 cup minced onion
1 (14-ounce) can
   sauerkraut, drained
   and snipped
2 tablespoons bread
   crumbs
3 ounces cream cheese,
   softened

2 tablespoons fresh
   parsley
1/2 teaspoon mustard
1/4 teaspoon garlic salt
1/8 teaspoon pepper
1/4 cup all-purpose flour
2 eggs, beaten
1/4 cup milk
3/4 cup bread crumbs

Brown the sausage and onion in a skillet over medium heat; drain well. Add the sauerkraut and 2 tablespoons bread crumbs and mix well. Stir in the cream cheese, parsley, mustard, garlic salt and pepper. Remove to a bowl. Chill, covered, for 1 to 2 hours. Shape the sausage mixture into 3/4-inch balls. Coat with the flour. Combine the eggs and milk in a small bowl and blend well. Dip the sausage balls in the egg mixture and coat with the bread crumbs. Fry the sausage balls in hot oil for 2 to 3 minutes or bake at 350 degrees for 7 to 10 minutes or until golden brown. Yield: 12 servings.

Dee Carter, Laureate Epsilon Beta-Online Alpha
Wooster, Ohio

VEGGIE-STUFFED MUSHROOMS

1 pound mushrooms
1/2 cup minced broccoli
1/4 cup minced carrot
1 tablespoon minced
  onion
1 cup seasoned croutons,
  crushed

1/2 cup (2 ounces)
  shredded Cheddar
  cheese
1/8 teaspoon salt
2 tablespoons butter or
  margarine, melted

Remove the stems from the mushrooms and chop enough stems to equal 1/4 cup. Combine the chopped stems, broccoli, carrot and onion in a bowl and mix well. Add the croutons, cheese and salt and mix well. Add the butter and mix well. Place the mushroom caps on a greased baking sheet. Spoon the vegetable mixture into the mushroom caps. Bake at 400 degrees for 15 to 20 minutes or until light golden brown. Serve warm. Yield: 12 servings.

Diane Martin, Xi Zeta Mu
Borger, Texas

SPICY CRAB-STUFFED MUSHROOMS

1 (6-ounce) can crab
  meat, drained and
  flaked
1 tablespoon lemon
  juice
1/2 cup whipped cream
  cheese
1/2 teaspoon onion
  powder
1/4 cup (1 ounce) grated
  Parmesan cheese

1 fresh jalapeño chile,
  minced
4 pieces bacon, crisp-
  cooked and crumbled
1/4 cup (1/2 stick) butter
1 teaspoon minced garlic
12 to 15 mushrooms,
  stems removed

Place the crab meat in a bowl and sprinkle with the lemon juice. Add the cream cheese and mix well. Add the onion powder and Parmesan cheese and mix well. Fold in the jalapeño and bacon. Melt the butter in a 9×13-inch baking dish. Sprinkle with the garlic. Spoon the crab mixture into the mushroom caps and place in the dish. Bake, covered, at 400 degrees for 20 minutes or until heated through. Spoon the melted butter over the mushrooms before serving. Yield: 12 servings.

Kay Black, Zeta Nu
Sherman, Texas

HAM-STUFFED MUSHROOMS

1 pound mushrooms
1/4 cup olive oil
1/4 cup minced onion
1 garlic clove, minced
4 ounces chopped ham
2 tablespoons grated
  Parmesan cheese

1/2 cup bread crumbs
1 egg, beaten
1/2 teaspoon oregano
1/2 teaspoon salt
Dash of pepper

Remove the stems from the mushrooms and chop enough stems to equal 1/2 cup. Heat the olive oil in a skillet over low heat. Add the mushroom caps and toss to coat. Remove immediately and set aside. Add the chopped mushroom stems, onion and garlic to the skillet and cook for 10 minutes, stirring frequently. Remove from the heat and stir in the remaining ingredients. Spoon into the mushroom caps and place on a greased baking sheet. Bake at 325 degrees for 30 minutes or until heated through. Yield: 12 servings.

Diane Christianson, Tau Tau
Napoleon, Missouri

CHICKEN-STUFFED MUSHROOMS

This is my children's favorite appetizer. We have it for all the holiday dinners and nearly any occasion when we need an appetizer.

1 pound mushrooms
1 tablespoon butter
3 tablespoons chopped
  onion
1 (4-ounce) can chicken
1 tablespoon mustard

2 teaspoons
  Worcestershire sauce
1/4 cup bread crumbs
Grated Parmesan cheese
  to taste
Paprika to taste

Remove the stems from the mushrooms and chop enough stems to equal 3 tablespoons. Simmer the mushroom caps in water to cover in a heavy saucepan for 5 minutes; drain. Melt the butter in a skillet over high heat. Add the onion and chopped mushroom stems. Cook for several minutes or until the vegetables are tender, stirring frequently. Stir in the next 4 ingredients. Stuff the mushroom caps with the chicken mixture and sprinkle with Parmesan cheese and paprika. Bake at 350 degrees for 15 to 20 minutes or until heated through. Yield: 12 servings.

Carolyn Powell, Laureate Iota
Raleigh, North Carolina

MARINATED OLIVES AND ANCHOVIES

1 (6-ounce) can pitted
  black olives, drained
1 garlic clove, halved
1/3 cup red wine
  vinegar
2 tablespoons olive oil
1/2 teaspoon oregano

1 (2-ounce) can anchovy
  fillets, drained and
  chopped
1 (2-ounce) jar pimentos,
  drained and chopped
1/2 cup chopped fresh
  parsley

Place the olives and garlic in a large bowl. Mix the next 5 ingredients in a bowl. Pour over the olive mixture. Chill, covered, for 6 to 10 hours. Drain, discarding the garlic. Pour the olive mixture into a serving bowl. Sprinkle with the parsley. Yield: 8 servings.

Esther Williams, Alpha Master
Dayton, Nevada

CHEESY OLIVE PUFFS

2 cups (8 ounces) shredded sharp Cheddar cheese
1 cup all-purpose flour
1/2 teaspoon paprika
1 stick (1/2 cup) butter, softened
1 (3-ounce) jar Spanish olives

Combine the cheese, flour, paprika and butter in a bowl and mix until a dough forms. Shape 1 teaspoonful of the dough at a time into a ball and press in the center to make a deep depression. Place 1 olive in the depression. Shape the dough around the olive to fully cover. Place on a greased baking sheet. Bake at 400 degrees for 15 minutes or until golden brown. Yield: 3 to 4 dozen.

Bernice Hart, Xi Gamma Eta
Paris, Tennessee

POTATO PUFFS

1/2 cup water
1/2 cup milk
1 tablespoon dried onion
2 tablespoons butter or margarine
1/2 teaspoon salt
11/3 cups instant mashed potatoes
2 eggs, beaten
Vegetable oil for frying

Combine the water, milk, onion, butter and salt in a heavy saucepan over medium heat and bring to a boil, stirring frequently. Remove from the heat and stir in the potatoes. Cool completely. Add the eggs and mix well. Heat 1/2-inch vegetable oil in a skillet over medium-high heat. Drop the potato mixture by teaspoonfuls into the skillet. Fry for 1 1/2 to 2 minutes on each side or until puffed and golden brown. Serve with sour cream or ranch dressing for dipping. Yield: 2 dozen puffs.

Golda Williamson, Sigma Mu
Simpson, Illinois

QUILTERS' CUPS

Quilters are known for their sharing and generosity. These cups are easy to serve and to share with friends.

1 (5-count) package flaky biscuits
1 1/2 cups chopped sliced smoked turkey or any deli meat
1 teaspoon minced onion
1/2 teaspoon garlic powder
3/4 cup (3 ounces) shredded Cheddar cheese or other cheese
2 tablespoons spicy mustard
1/4 cup mayonnaise
1/4 cup chopped black olives
1/4 cup chopped green bell pepper
1 to 2 dashes of Tabasco sauce
Salt and pepper to taste

Separate each biscuit into 2 layers. Place each layer in a greased muffin cup. Flatten and stretch the dough, pressing it up the sides of the cups. Combine the remaining ingredients in a bowl and mix well. Divide the mixture evenly among the 10 muffin cups. Bake at 375 degrees for 25 minutes or until brown on top. Yield: 10 servings.

Dyanna Lawson, Laureate Eta Iota
Aledo, Texas

STEAMED PORK DUMPLINGS

2 cups chopped cabbage
2 pounds ground pork
1 cup grated carrots
3 to 4 green onions, chopped
2 eggs, beaten
1 teaspoon grated fresh ginger
2 packages gyoza wraps
Sesame oil for frying
1/3 cup water
Soy Sauce Dip

Soak the cabbage in salted water in a bowl for 5 minutes; drain. Combine the cabbage, pork, carrots, green onions, eggs and ginger in a large bowl and mix well. Place 1 teaspoon of the pork mixture in the center of a gyoza wrap. Fold the wrap in half, sealing with a small amount of water. Repeat the procedure using the remaining pork mixture and gyoza wraps. Heat the sesame oil in a large skillet over medium heat. Add the dumplings and cook for several minutes or until brown. Add 1/3 cup water. Steam, covered, for 5 to 10 minutes or until the pork is cooked. Remove the dumplings from the skillet with a slotted spoon. Serve warm with Soy Sauce Dip. Yield: 40 servings.

SOY SAUCE DIP

1/2 cup soy sauce
1/2 teaspoon sesame oil
1/3 cup water
2 teaspoons rice vinegar
1 teaspoon sugar
1/2 teaspoon grated fresh ginger
1 green onion, chopped

Combine the soy sauce, sesame oil, water and vinegar in a small bowl and mix well. Whisk in the sugar and ginger. Add the green onion and mix well.

Nancy Purkey, Pi Iota
Overland Park, Kansas

*Karen Danner, Laureate Eta Beta, Mission Viejo, California, prepares **Deviled Eggs** by slicing 12 hard-cooked eggs into halves lengthwise. She scoops out the egg yolks with a spoon into a bowl, reserving the egg whites and adds 1/2 teaspoon salt, 2 tablespoons dry mustard, a dash of cayenne pepper, one 5-ounce can chunk lean ham and mayonnaise to taste. After mixing well, she spoons the egg yolk mixture into the egg whites. The deviled eggs are covered and chilled until serving time.*

PEPPERONI CHEESE PUFFS

1¼ cups water	2 tablespoons minced
⅓ cup shortening	fresh parsley
1½ cups all-purpose	¾ cup (3 ounces) grated
flour	Parmesan cheese or
4 eggs	Romano cheese
¾ cup minced pepperoni	⅛ teaspoon garlic
⅛ teaspoon pepper	powder

Combine the water and shortening in a large heavy saucepan. Cook over medium heat until the mixture comes to a boil, stirring frequently. Add the flour, stirring vigorously. Cook until the mixture forms a ball, stirring constantly. Remove from the heat and cool for 10 minutes. Add the eggs 1 at a time, stirring well with a wooden spoon after each addition. Stir in the remaining ingredients. Drop by rounded teaspoonfuls onto greased baking sheets. Bake at 450 degrees for 15 to 17 minutes or until golden brown. Serve warm. Yield: 48 servings.

Betsie Chilton, Alpha Rho
Hanover, Indiana

SAUSAGE CRESCENT ROLL SLICES

1 pound bulk pork	1 egg white, lightly
sausage	beaten
8 ounces cream cheese,	Poppy seeds for
softened	sprinkling
2 (8-count) cans crescent	
rolls	

Brown the sausage in a skillet, stirring until crumbly; drain. Add the cream cheese and mix well. Cool completely. Unroll 1 can of crescent roll dough. Separate into 2 rectangles, pressing the perforations to seal. Repeat the procedure with the remaining can of crescent roll dough. Divide the sausage mixture evenly between the 2 pieces of dough, spreading lengthwise. Roll as for a jelly roll. Place on an ungreased baking sheet with the seam side down. Brush with the egg white and sprinkle with poppy seeds. Bake at 350 degrees for 25 minutes or until brown. Cut into ¾-inch slices. Freezes well. Yield: 30 slices.

Mary Prehm, Xi Gamma Eta
Paris, Tennessee

CRESCENT YUMMIES

1 pound bulk pork	8 ounces cream cheese,
sausage	softened
1 to 2 jalapeño chiles,	1 (8-count) can crescent
seeded and diced	rolls

Brown the sausage in a skillet, stirring until crumbly; drain. Combine the sausage, jalapeños and cream cheese in a bowl and mix well. Unroll the crescent roll dough and separate into triangles. Spread 1 tablespoon of the cream cheese mixture over the wide end of each triangle. Roll up and place on a baking sheet. Bake at 350 degrees for 13 to 15 minutes or until golden brown. Serve warm. Yield: 8 servings.

Betty J. Wilken, Laureate Beta Omicron
Derby, Kansas

GAME DAY SMOKIES

1 (8-count) can crescent	½ cup grape jelly
rolls	½ cup yellow mustard
1 (16-ounce) package	
cocktail franks	

Unroll the crescent roll dough. Separate into 2 rectangles, pressing perforations to seal. Cut the dough into ½-inch-wide strips. Wrap each strip around a frank. Place on an ungreased baking sheet. Bake at 350 degrees for 15 to 20 minutes or until golden brown. Combine the jelly and mustard in a bowl and mix well. Microwave for 3 to 5 minutes, stirring occasionally. Serve the franks with the jelly mixture for dipping. Yield: 16 servings.

Mary Pritchard, Xi Sigma Delta
The Woodlands, Texas

PEPPERONI CRESCENT BAKE

2 (8-count) cans crescent	16 ounces shredded
rolls	mozzarella cheese
6 eggs, beaten	6 tablespoons grated
8 ounces sliced	Parmesan or Romano
pepperoni, chopped	cheese

Unroll 1 can of crescent rolls. Separate the dough into 2 rectangles, pressing the perforations to seal in a greased 9×13-inch baking pan. Combine the remaining ingredients in a bowl and mix well. Spread the egg mixture over the dough. Unroll 1 can of crescent roll dough and cut into ½-inch strips. Arrange lattice-fashion over the egg mixture. Bake at 325 degrees for 40 to 45 minutes or until golden brown. Yield: 24 servings.

Marlene Pape, Michigan Alpha Alpha Master
Battle Creek, Michigan

SAUSAGE AND CHEESE STARS

1 pound bulk pork	1 cup ranch salad
sausage, browned	dressing
and drained	½ cup chopped red bell
1½ cups (6 ounces) each	pepper
shredded Cheddar	1 package won ton
cheese and Monterey	wrappers
Jack cheese	Vegetable oil
1 cup sliced black olives	

Mix the first 6 ingredients in a bowl. Press 1 won ton wrapper into each of 4 to 5 dozen greased muffin cups. Brush with vegetable oil. Bake at 350 degrees for 5 minutes or until golden brown; cool. Remove to a baking sheet. Fill with the sausage mixture and bake for 5 minutes or until bubbly. Yield: 4 to 5 dozen stars.

Jerri Bloechl, Preceptor Rho
Merrill, Wisconsin

SAUSAGE-STUFFED JALAPEÑOS

20 to 30 jalapeño chiles	*8 to 12 ounces bulk Italian sausage*
1 pound bulk ground chorizo	*10 ounces crumbled blue cheese*

Cut the jalapeños lengthwise into halves, splitting the stem between the 2 halves. Seed the jalapeños. Brown the chorizo and Italian sausage in a skillet over medium-high heat, stirring until crumbly; drain. Add the blue cheese and mix well. Fill the jalapeño halves with the sausage mixture. Grill over medium-low heat for 10 minutes or until heated through but still firm. Yield: 40 to 60 appetizers.

Linda Morris, Alpha Iota
American Falls, Idaho

FRIED CRAB ROLLS

2 cups crab meat	*1 loaf white bread, sliced and crusts removed*
1 onion, minced	
Ketchup to moisten	
1/2 teaspoon hot red pepper sauce	*1 egg, beaten*
	2 cups bread crumbs
Salt and pepper to taste	*Vegetable oil for frying*

Combine the crab meat, onion, ketchup, hot sauce, salt and pepper in a heavy saucepan. Cook over low heat for 10 minutes, stirring frequently. Flatten a slice of bread with a rolling pin. Place 1 teaspoon of the crab mixture in the center of the bread and roll as for a jelly roll. Dip in the egg and coat with the bread crumbs. Heat the vegetable oil in a deep fryer and fry the crab rolls until golden brown. Yield: 20 to 25 rolls.

Patricia S. Barker
Tampa, Florida

SPICY CRAB PUFFS

6 English muffins, halved	*1/2 cup mayonnaise*
1 (5-ounce) can crab meat	*2 teaspoons dry Chinese hot mustard*
1 celery rib, minced	
1 (4-ounce) can sliced black olives	*1/2 large sweet onion, minced*
8 ounces Swiss cheese, cubed	*Salt and pepper to taste*
	Paprika to taste

Place the top halves of the English muffins on a baking sheet. Broil for 3 to 4 minutes or until light brown. Combine the crab meat, celery, olives, cheese, mayonnaise, hot mustard, onion, salt and pepper in a bowl and mix well. Spread 1 1/2 tablespoons of the crab mixture over the bottom (uncooked) halves of the English muffins. Sprinkle with paprika. Broil for 4 to 5 minutes or until brown and bubbly. Top with the muffin tops. Yield: 6 servings.

Donna Lee Anderson, Preceptor Psi
Battle Ground, Washington

CREAMY CRAB CANAPÉS

1 (10-ounce) package frozen cream puff shells, thawed	*Dash of pepper*
	Dash of garlic salt
	1 1/2 cups crab meat
8 ounces cream cheese, softened	*1 cup chopped peeled cucumber*
1 tablespoon horseradish	*1/2 cup chopped celery*
1/2 teaspoon lemon juice	*1 (2-ounce) jar pimentos, chopped*
1/4 teaspoon onion salt	

Cook the cream puff shells using the package directions. Combine the cream cheese, horseradish, lemon juice, onion salt, pepper and garlic salt in a medium bowl and mix well. Fold in the crab meat, cucumber, celery and pimentos. Fill the cream puff shells with the mixture. Yield: 8 servings.

Georgine Wasley, Preceptor Nu Delta
Nevada City, California

CRAWFISH BREAD

24 frozen yeast rolls, thawed	*Dash of Tabasco sauce*
	1/2 teaspoon jalapeño sauce
8 ounces cream cheese, softened	
2 cups (8 ounces) shredded Cheddar cheese	*1 cup cooked and peeled crawfish tails*
	1 (4-ounce) can chopped green chiles, drained

Follow package instructions to let yeast rolls rise. Combine the cream cheese, Cheddar cheese, Tabasco sauce and jalapeño sauce in a bowl and mix well. Fold in the crawfish tails and 1/2 to 3/4 of the green chiles. (Reserve the remainder for a separate use.) Make a small hole in the middle of each roll using a knife or finger. Place 1 tablespoon of the crawfish mixture in the indentation. Pinch the dough around the mixture to enclose. Allow the rolls to finish rising. Bake on a greased baking sheet at 375 degrees for 12 to 15 minutes or until golden brown. Yield: 24 servings.

Cathy Robb, Preceptor Alpha Beta
Harvey, Louisiana

SHRIMP COCKTAIL

5 pounds cooked shrimp, peeled	2 cups chopped avocado
1/2 cup lime juice	2 cups chopped celery
1 cup clamato juice	2 cucumbers, peeled and chopped
1 cup vegetable juice cocktail	Chili sauce to taste
1 cup chopped onion	Tabasco sauce to taste
4 cups shredded lettuce	Salt to taste

Place the shrimp in a bowl. Add the lime juice, clamato juice and vegetable juice cocktail and toss to coat the shrimp. Chill, covered, for at least 12 hours. Add the onion, lettuce, avocado, celery and cucumbers and mix well. Season with the chili sauce, Tabasco sauce and salt and mix well. Serve chilled with crackers. Yield: 25 to 30 servings.

Sylvia Maack, Beta Mu
Lawrence, Kansas

SHRIMP PICO DE GALLO

6 to 8 Roma tomatoes, chopped	1 jalapeño chile, seeded and chopped
3 to 4 green onions, chopped	2 garlic cloves, crushed
1/2 small red onion, chopped	1/2 cup chopped cilantro
Juice of 1 lemon	1 cup clamato juice
1 (7-ounce) can chopped green chiles	Salt and pepper to taste
	1 pound cooked shrimp, peeled

Combine the first 11 ingredients in a bowl and mix well. Chill, covered, for at least 5 hours. Add shrimp and toss just before serving. Yield: 5 to 6 servings.

Cheryl Kramer, Alpha Master
Kalama, Washington

TROUT CAKES

8 trout fillets (fresh or frozen)	1 box sweet corn muffin mix
1 egg, beaten	Olive oil for frying
1 tablespoon flour	

Place the trout in a greased baking dish. Bake at 350 degrees for 10 to 15 minutes or until the skin removes easily, turning once. (Fish will only be partially cooked.) Remove the skin. Remove the fish from the bone along the lateral line of the fish. Combine the trout, egg and flour in a bowl and mix well. Shape into small patties. Coat with the corn muffin mix. Fry in olive oil for several minutes on each side or until golden brown. Yield: 6 to 8 servings.

Susan Goldizen, Preceptor Zeta
Stephens City, Virginia

COQUILLES ST. JACQUES

2 tablespoons butter	1/8 teaspoon pepper
1 pound mushrooms	3 tablespoons butter
Juice of 1 lemon	3 tablespoons flour
1 pound scallops	1 cup light cream
1 cup dry white wine	1 (10-ounce) package frozen puff pastry shells, thawed
1/4 teaspoon thyme	
1 bay leaf	
1/2 teaspoon salt	3/4 cup bread crumbs

Melt 2 tablespoons butter in a large skillet over high heat. Add the mushrooms and sprinkle with the lemon juice. Sauté until the mushrooms are tender. Reduce the heat. Add the scallops, wine, thyme, bay leaf, salt and pepper and mix well. Simmer, covered, for 10 minutes. Remove from the heat and drain, reserving 1 cup of broth. Melt 3 tablespoons butter in a skillet over medium heat. Add the flour and cook until thickened, stirring constantly. Add the reserved broth and cream and cook for several minutes or until thickened, stirring constantly. Remove from the heat. Add the scallop mixture and mix well. Spoon into the buttered puff pastry shells and top with the bread crumbs. Bake at 400 degrees for 10 minutes or until brown. Yield: 8 servings.

Judy Livingston, Xi Epsilon Alpha
Paonia, Colorado

STEAK SKEWERS WITH BLOODY MARY SAUCE

1 tablespoon extra-virgin olive oil	1 cup tomato sauce
1 small onion, minced	1 heaping tablespoon horseradish
1/2 cup vodka	Salt and pepper to taste
2 tablespoons Worcestershire sauce	2 tablespoons extra-virgin olive oil
2 teaspoons hot red pepper sauce	1 1/3 pounds sirloin beef, cut into 2-inch pieces

Heat 1 tablespoon olive oil in a small saucepan over medium heat. Add the onions and sauté for 5 minutes or until tender. Add the vodka and cook until the mixture is reduced by half, stirring constantly. Add the Worcestershire sauce, hot sauce, tomato sauce and horseradish and mix well. Bring the mixture to a boil, stirring frequently. Add the salt and pepper and remove from the heat. Heat 2 tablespoons olive oil in a skillet over high heat. Add the sirloin and cook for 2 minutes on each side or until brown. Place the sirloin on 6-inch skewers, allowing 2 pieces per skewer. Serve with the sauce for dipping. Yield: 6 servings.

Barb Munger, Preceptor Alpha Zeta
Newcastle, Wyoming

Dips & Spreads

CREAMY DIP FOR BAGELS

2 cups (16 ounces)
   mayonnaise
8 ounces cream cheese,
   softened

1/4 cup beef bouillon
1/2 cup minced onion
12 bagels, halved

Blend the mayonnaise and cream cheese in a mixing bowl. Add the bouillon and mix well. Fold in the onion. Chill, covered, for at least 30 minutes. Toast the bagels and cut into bite-size pieces. Serve with the dip. Yield: 24 servings.

Angela Folks, Upsilon Gamma
Wooster, Ohio

BLACK BEAN DIP

1 (16-ounce) jar salsa
3 green onions, chopped
1 (15-ounce) can black
   beans, rinsed and
   drained

1 (6-ounce) can black
   olives, chopped
1 cup (4 ounces)
   shredded Cheddar
   cheese

Combine the salsa, onions, black beans and olives in a bowl and mix well. Chill, covered, overnight. Fold in the cheese just before serving. Yield: 16 servings.

Perry Raye Graef, Xi Lambda Tau
Blairstown, Missouri

CREAMY BROCCOLI DIP

3/4 cup sour cream
1 (16-ounce) bottle
   ranch salad dressing
8 ounces Parmesan
   cheese, grated
6 ounces chopped
   cashews

1 cup sunflower seeds
2 bunches broccoli
   florets, chopped
1 green bell pepper,
   chopped
1 red bell pepper,
   chopped

Combine the sour cream and salad dressing in a large bowl and blend well. Add the cheese, cashews and sunflower seeds and mix well. Fold in the broccoli and the green and red bell peppers. Chill, covered, for at least 3 hours. Serve with cocktail bread or crackers. Yield: 24 servings.

Linda Humphrey, Xi Beta Epsilon
Woodward, Oklahoma

CREAMY BROCCOLI AND BEEF DIP

1 pound lean ground
   beef
1 (11-ounce) can
   condensed broccoli
   cheese soup
1 (11-ounce) can
   condensed cream of
   chicken soup

4 ounces Velveeta cheese
1 teaspoon garlic
   powder
1 (4-ounce) can chopped
   green chiles, drained
1 (10-ounce) package
   frozen chopped
   broccoli

Brown the ground beef in a skillet, stirring until crumbly; drain. Stir in the broccoli cheese soup, cream of chicken soup, Velveeta cheese, garlic powder and green chiles. Add the frozen broccoli and simmer until the broccoli is tender. Serve warm with tortilla chips. Yield: 12 servings.

Honoria McClanahan, Xi Beta Iota
Gallup, New Mexico

For an easy party dip, Cheryl Allmen-Vinnedge, Xi Iota Zeta, San Jose, California, prepares **Pesto Baked Brie**. *She warms the Brie for 10 minutes in the oven or 2 to 4 minutes in the microwave, transfers it to a serving platter and tops with pesto sauce. She serves it with crackers.*

ASIAGO CHEESE DIP

1 round loaf bread	1 (14-ounce) can
2 cups (8 ounces) grated	artichoke hearts,
Asiago cheese	drained and chopped
2 cups mayonnaise	2 garlic cloves, minced

Hollow out the center of the bread to create a bread bowl. Combine the cheese, mayonnaise, artichoke hearts and garlic in a bowl and mix well. Place the mixture in the bread bowl. Cover with foil. Bake at 350 degrees for 45 minutes. Remove the foil and bake for 15 additional minutes. Tear the hollowed-out bread into bite-size pieces. Yield: 32 servings.

Lyn Turnbull, Xi Epsilon Phi
Oakville, Ontario, Canada

CHEESE FONDUE

A friend gave me this recipe after I received three fondue pots as wedding gifts. I serve it on New Year's Eve. It is as delicious today as it was thirty-four years ago.

2 cups (8 ounces)	2 tablespoons all-
shredded Swiss	purpose flour
cheese	1 (12-ounce) can of lager
2 cups (8 ounces)	beer
shredded Cheddar	1 envelope onion
cheese	soup mix

Combine the Swiss cheese, Cheddar cheese and flour in a medium bowl and mix well. Combine the beer and soup mix in a saucepan and mix well. Cook over medium-high heat until the mixture comes to a boil. Gradually add the cheese mixture, stirring constantly. Add additional beer if the mixture becomes too thick. Remove to a fondue pot to serve. Serve with bread cubes and sliced apples. Yield: 4 servings.

Mary Arena, Psi Chi
Danville, California

MUSHROOM AND CHEESE DIP

2 tablespoons margarine	1/2 teaspoon seasoned
3 cups sliced mushrooms	salt
1 cup chopped onion	1/2 teaspoon dill
1/2 teaspoon minced	1/2 teaspoon pepper
garlic	1 1/2 cups (6 ounces)
8 ounces cream cheese,	shredded Monterey
softened	Jack cheese
1/2 cup mayonnaise	

Melt the margarine in a heavy saucepan over medium heat. Add the mushrooms, onion and garlic and mix well. Cook, stirring often, for 20 minutes or until the mushrooms are brown. Remove from the heat and add the cream cheese, mayonnaise, seasoned salt, dill and pepper and mix well. Add the cheese and mix well. Remove to a greased pie plate and bake at 350 degrees for 30 minutes or until bubbly. Serve warm with crackers or bread. Yield: 8 servings.

Gennifer Ediger, Xi Nu
Rosetown, Saskatchewan, Canada

BUFFALO CHICKEN DIP

1 1/2 cups ranch salad	2 to 3 boneless skinless
dressing	chicken breasts,
2/3 cup hot red pepper	cooked and shredded
sauce	2 cups (8 ounces)
16 ounces cream cheese,	shredded Colby-Jack
softened	cheese

Combine the salad dressing, hot sauce and cream cheese in a large heavy saucepan. Cook over medium heat, stirring often, until the cream cheese has melted. Remove from the heat, add the chicken and stir to coat. Pour the chicken mixture into a greased 9×13-inch baking dish. Cover with the cheese. Bake at 350 degrees for 25 minutes or until bubbly. Serve with crackers and celery. Yield: 24 servings.

Tammy Deaver, Gamma Upsilon
Jefferson City, Missouri

CHEESY BUFFALO CHICKEN DIP

8 ounces light cream	1 to 1 1/4 cups hot red
cheese, softened	pepper sauce
3 to 4 boneless	6 ounces blue cheese
skinless chicken	salad dressing
breasts, cooked and	1 cup (4 ounces) shredded
shredded	mozzarella cheese

Spread the cream cheese over the bottom of a greased 9×13-inch baking dish. Combine the chicken and hot sauce in a bowl and mix well. Pour the chicken mixture over the cream cheese. Top with the blue cheese dressing and sprinkle with mozzarella cheese. Bake at 350 degrees for 25 minutes or until bubbly. Serve warm with crackers and crudités. Yield: 8 servings.

Wanda Gacioch, Beta Pi
Dubuque, Iowa

CHICKEN ENCHILADA DIP

8 ounces cream cheese,	1 large jalapeño chile,
softened	minced
1 cup mayonnaise	1 small onion, minced
1 cup (4 ounces)	1 pound boneless
shredded Cheddar	skinless chicken,
cheese	cooked in chicken
6 ounces sour cream	broth and shredded

Blend the first 4 ingredients in a bowl. Add the jalapeño, onion and chicken and mix well. Spoon the mixture into a greased 9×13-inch baking dish. Bake at 350 degrees for 30 minutes or until the sides are light brown. Serve with tortilla chips. Yield: 16 servings.

Freda I. Bush, Preceptor Gamma Kappa
Chesapeake, Virginia

CREAMY CORN DIP

16 ounces cream cheese, softened	2 jalapeño chiles, minced
1 envelope ranch salad dressing mix	1 (2-ounce) can chopped black olives
1/4 cup chopped green bell pepper	1 (15-ounce) can corn, drained

Combine the cream cheese and salad dressing mix in a bowl and blend well. Add the bell pepper, jalapeños, olives and corn and mix well. Chill, covered, for several hours. Serve with corn chips or tortilla chips. Yield: 16 servings.

Ann Bedinghaus, Alpha Gamma Master
Hutchinson, Kansas

CREAMY CUCUMBER DIP

3 large cucumbers, peeled, seeded and chopped	3/4 cup mayonnaise
	1/2 cup chopped onion
	1 teaspoon garlic salt
8 ounces cream cheese, softened	2 to 3 teaspoons pepper

Combine all the ingredients in a bowl and mix well. Chill, covered, for several hours. Serve with ridged potato chips. Yield: 16 servings.

Bev Schmeidler, Xi Iota Beta
Hays, Kansas

LAYERED CHILI-CHEESE DIP

16 ounces cream cheese, softened	1 small onion, chopped
1 (12-ounce) bottle chili sauce	3/4 cup (3 ounces) shredded mozzarella cheese
6 ounces Canadian bacon, crisp-cooked and chopped	3/4 cup (3 ounces) shredded Cheddar cheese
1 small green bell pepper, chopped	

Spread the cream cheese in a round 12-inch baking pan. Layer with the chili sauce. Sprinkle with the remaining ingredients. Chill, covered, for several hours. Serve with corn chips. Yield: 16 servings.

Barbara Peterson, Preceptor Delta Upsilon
Webster City, Iowa

HOT REUBEN DIP

8 ounces cream cheese, softened	1 cup drained sauerkraut
1/2 cup sour cream	1 cup (4 ounces) shredded Swiss cheese
2 tablespoons ketchup	
8 ounces chopped cooked corned beef	2 tablespoons minced onion

Blend the cream cheese, sour cream and ketchup in a mixing bowl. Add the corned beef, sauerkraut, cheese and onion and mix well. Spoon the mixture into a greased 9×13-inch baking dish. Bake, covered, at 375 degrees for 30 minutes. Remove the cover and bake 5 minutes longer or until bubbly. Yield: 12 servings.

Willene White, Xi Beta Omega
Valdosta, Georgia

AVOCADO SALSA

1 (16-ounce) can corn, drained	1/3 cup olive oil
	1/4 cup lemon juice
1 (16-ounce) can olives, drained and chopped	3 tablespoons white wine vinegar
1 red bell pepper, chopped	2 teaspoons cilantro
	1/2 teaspoon salt
1 small onion, chopped	1/2 teaspoon pepper
5 garlic cloves, minced	4 avocados, chopped

Combine the corn, olives, bell pepper, onion and garlic in a large bowl and mix well. Add the olive oil, lemon juice, vinegar, cilantro, salt and pepper and toss to coat the vegetables. Chill, covered, overnight. Add the avocado just before serving. Serve with tortilla chips. Yield: 48 servings.

Joyce Reich, Preceptor Alpha Lambda
Auburn, Nebraska

❖ AVOCADO AND SHRIMP SALSA

1/4 cup ketchup	1/4 cup chopped onion
1/4 cup lime juice	1/2 cup chopped tomato
1 to 2 teaspoons hot red pepper sauce	1/4 cup chopped fresh cilantro
1 pound cooked shrimp, peeled	2 avocados, chopped

Combine the ketchup, lime juice and hot sauce in a large bowl and mix well. Add the shrimp, onion, tomato and cilantro and mix well. Chill, covered, for 2 to 4 hours. Add the avocados just before serving. Serve with tortilla chips and lime wedges. Yield: 8 servings.

Lilli (Gigi) Inness, Xi Gamma Alpha
Norfolk, Nebraska

SIMPLE SALSA

This is so easy to make. I also use it in casseroles, meat loaf, and combine it with sour cream for a tangy dip.

8 tomatoes, chopped
1/2 cup chopped green
  onions
1/4 cup chopped green
  bell pepper

2 tablespoons chopped
  fresh oregano
Salt and pepper to taste
3 tablespoons sugar

Combine the tomatoes, green onions and bell pepper in a large bowl and mix well. Add the oregano, salt, pepper and sugar and mix well. Serve with tortilla chips. Yield: 8 servings.

Chari Stanley, Pi Master
Firth, Nebraska

SPICY SALSA

6 to 8 Roma tomatoes,
  chopped
1 large onion, chopped
1/4 teaspoon minced
  garlic

1 to 2 jalapeño chiles
1/4 cup white vinegar
Chopped fresh cilantro
  to taste
1 teaspoon salt

Combine the tomatoes, onion, garlic and jalapeños in a food processor and process to the desired consistency. Add the vinegar, cilantro and salt and mix well. Remove to a bowl and serve with tortilla chips. Yield: 8 servings.

Sharon Mandigo, Xi Alpha Pi
Houston, Texas

CHEESY CHILI DIP

1 (15-ounce) can chili
  with beans
1 (16-ounce) jar salsa
8 ounces cream cheese,
  softened

2 cups (8 ounces)
  shredded Cheddar
  cheese or other
  shredded cheese

Pour the chili in a greased 9×13-inch baking dish. Combine the salsa and cream cheese in a medium bowl and mix well. Pour the salsa mixture over the chili. Sprinkle the shredded cheese over the top. Bake at 375 degrees for 20 minutes or until the cheese has melted. Serve with tortilla chips. Yield: 16 servings.

Cheryl Bennett, Preceptor Tau
Slater, South Carolina

*Maurita R. Meehan, Preceptor Tau, Sheridan, Wyoming, prepares **Mango Salsa** by combining chopped fresh mango, tomato, cucumber, red bell pepper, jalapeño chile and cilantro in a bowl. She adds lime juice, orange juice and sea salt and mixes well. Chopped avocado is stirred in just before serving.*

FRUIT SALSA

1 cup chopped fresh fruit
  (apples, peaches,
  plums or other fruit)
2 tablespoons chopped
  red onion
2 tablespoons chopped
  fresh cilantro

2 teaspoons apple cider
  vinegar
1/8 teaspoon salt
1/4 teaspoon hot red
  pepper sauce

Combine the fruit, onion, cilantro, vinegar, salt and hot sauce in a bowl and mix well. Serve with chips or as a topping for grilled chicken. Yield: 8 servings.

Joani Gent, Nu Lambda
Ames, Iowa

ORANGE AND RASPBERRY SAUCE

1 cup chopped mandarin
  orange segments
1 cup chopped red onion
3 teaspoons lime juice

1/2 cup raspberry
  chipotle sauce
1/2 bunch fresh cilantro,
  chopped

Combine the orange segments, onion, lime juice, chipotle sauce and cilantro in a bowl and mix well. Serve with tortilla chips. Yield: 8 servings.

Sharon Ryen, Preceptor Alpha Chi
Sugar Land, Texas

PEACH SALSA

1 (16-ounce) can peaches,
  drained and chopped
4 Roma tomatoes,
  chopped
2 tablespoons canned
  chopped jalapeño
  chiles

4 green onions, chopped
1 tablespoon olive oil
1 tablespoon lime juice
1 tablespoon honey
1/4 teaspoon salt
1/4 teaspoon pepper

Mix the peaches, tomatoes, jalapeños and onions in a bowl. Add the olive oil, lime juice, honey, salt and pepper and mix well. Chill, covered, for up to 3 days. Serve with tortilla chips. Yield: 12 servings.

Correna Vaughn
Poplar Bluff, Missouri

SEVEN-LAYER SEAFOOD DIP

8 ounces cream cheese,
  softened
1/2 cup sour cream
1/4 cup mayonnaise
1 (6-ounce) can shrimp
  or crab, drained
1 cup cocktail sauce

2 cups (8 ounces)
  shredded mozzarella
  cheese
1 green bell pepper,
  chopped
3 green onions, chopped
1 tomato, chopped

Combine the cream cheese, sour cream and mayonnaise in a bowl and blend well. Spread the mixture in a round 12-inch pan. Layer with the shrimp and cocktail sauce. Sprinkle with the cheese. Top with the bell pepper, onions and tomato. Chill, covered, until ready to serve. Serve with tortilla chips or assorted crackers. Yield: 8 to 10 servings.

Margaret Rae, Gamma Master
Yorkton, Saskatchewan, Canada

SPINACH DIP

16 ounces cream cheese,
   softened
2 (10-ounce) packages
   frozen creamed
   spinach, thawed
2 teaspoons garlic
   powder
2 cups (8 ounces)
   shredded Havarti or
   Swiss cheese
1 (6-ounce) jar artichoke
   hearts, drained and
   chopped

Beat the cream cheese in a mixing bowl until fluffy. Add the spinach, garlic powder, cheese and artichoke hearts and mix well. Pour the mixture into a greased baking dish and bake at 350 degrees for 30 minutes or until bubbly. Serve with corn chips. Yield: 16 servings.

Diana Grotewiel, Kappa Upsilon
Warner Robins, Georgia

CREAMY SPINACH AND ARTICHOKE DIP

1 (14-ounce) can
   artichoke hearts,
   drained and chopped
1 (10-ounce) package
   frozen spinach,
   thawed, drained and
   squeezed dry
1/2 cup (2 ounces) grated
   Parmesan cheese
1/2 cup sour cream
1 cup (4 ounces)
   shredded mozzarella
   cheese
1/2 cup mayonnaise
3 ounces cream cheese,
   softened
1 teaspoon garlic salt
1/4 cup grated Parmesan
   cheese

Combine the artichoke hearts, spinach, 1/2 cup Parmesan cheese, sour cream, mozzarella cheese, mayonnaise, cream cheese and garlic salt in a large bowl and mix well. Pour the mixture into a greased 1-quart baking dish. Sprinkle with 1/4 cup Parmesan cheese. Bake at 350 degrees for 15 to 20 minutes or until bubbly. Serve with tortilla chips. Yield: 16 servings.

Donna Vance-Nase, Delta Gamma
Corpus Christi, Texas

CURRIED MANGO DIP

8 ounces light cream
   cheese, softened
1 tablespoon curry
   powder
1 tablespoon cumin
1/4 cup mango chutney

Combine the cream cheese, curry, cumin and chutney in a medium bowl and mix well. Garnish with jalapeño jelly, dried blueberries, toasted pine nuts or chopped green onions. Serve with an assortment of crackers. Yield: 8 servings.

Joan Pacholko, Xi Kappa
Calvary, Alberta, Canada

SWEET CREAMY DIP FOR APPLES

8 ounces cream cheese,
   softened
1/2 cup packed brown
   sugar
1/4 cup granulated sugar
1 teaspoon vanilla
   extract
7 ounces chocolate-
   covered toffee bits

Combine the cream cheese, brown sugar, granulated sugar and vanilla in a medium bowl and beat until fluffy. Fold in the chocolate-covered toffee bits. Serve with sliced tart apples. Yield: 8 servings.

Shirley J. Bird, Xi Alpha Nu
Eureka Springs, Arkansas

CREAMY CHOCOLATE DIP

2 (4-ounce) packages
   sugar-free chocolate
   instant pudding mix
2 cups milk
8 ounces whipped
   topping
8 ounces cream cheese,
   softened
1 stick butter, softened
1/2 teaspoon vanilla
   extract
3/4 cup miniature
   chocolate chips
3/4 cup minced pecans

Combine the instant pudding mix and milk in a medium bowl and whisk until blended. Add the whipped topping and mix well. Combine the cream cheese, butter and vanilla in a mixing bowl and beat until fluffy. Add the pudding mixture and mix well. Fold in the chocolate chips and pecans. Chill, covered, for at least 1 hour. Serve with graham crackers. Yield: 32 servings.

Glendel Warren, Preceptor Phi
Mount Vernon, Illinois

CREAMY KAHLÚA DIP FOR FRUIT

8 ounces cream cheese,
   softened
3/4 cup packed brown
   sugar
1 cup sour cream
1/4 cup Kahlúa
8 ounces whipped
   topping

Combine the cream cheese, brown sugar, sour cream and Kahlúa in a bowl and mix well. Fold in the whipped topping. Serve with strawberries, pineapple, apple slices and other fresh fruit. Yield: 15 servings.

Shirley Bigletti, Omega Theta
Fort Myers, Florida

BAKED BRIE WITH CARAMELIZED ONIONS

1 tablespoon butter or margarine	1 tablespoon water
1 large sweet onion, thinly sliced	1 (8-ounce) round Brie cheese
1 tablespoon brown sugar	

Melt the butter in a skillet over medium heat. Add the onion and sprinkle with the brown sugar and 1 tablespoon water. Cook over low heat for 35 minutes or until the onion is tender and caramelized. Place the Brie in a shallow baking dish. Bake at 350 degrees for 10 to 15 minutes or until softened. Top with the onion mixture. Serve warm with bagel chips. Yield: 8 servings.

Bev Kearns, Laureate Gamma Upsilon
Selah, Washington

CANDIED PECAN BRIE

1/4 cup (1/2 stick) butter	1 tablespoon water
1/4 cup packed dark brown sugar	1/4 cup chopped pecans
2 teaspoons light corn syrup	1 (16-ounce) round Brie cheese, cut into 8 wedges

Melt the butter in a large heavy saucepan over medium-low heat. Add the brown sugar, corn syrup and 1 tablespoon water and mix well. Simmer, stirring frequently, for 3 minutes. Add the pecans and remove from heat. Place the Brie wedges on a serving platter. Spoon 1 teaspoon of the pecan mixture over each wedge. Serve with crackers. Yield: 8 servings.

Diane Sackman, Tau Lambda
Parkland, Florida

KAHLÚA AND PECAN BRIE

3 tablespoons brown sugar	3/4 cup toasted pecans
3 tablespoons Kahlúa	1 (14-ounce) round Brie cheese

Combine the brown sugar and Kahlúa, stirring to mix. Stir in the pecans. Cut the top off the Brie. Place the Brie in a microwave-safe dish. Pour the Kahlúa mixture over the Brie. Microwave on High for 1 minute or until the cheese is soft. Yield: 10 servings.

Sylvia Doyle, Alpha Master
Lancaster, Pennsylvania

NUT-GLAZED BRIE

1/4 cup packed brown sugar	1 tablespoon brandy
1/4 cup chopped pecans	1 (16-ounce) round Brie cheese

Combine the brown sugar, pecans and brandy in a small bowl and mix well. Chill, covered, for at least 24 hours. (Mixture will keep in the refrigerator for up to 1 week.) Place the Brie in a baking dish and bake at 500 degrees for 4 to 5 minutes or until softened. Spread the sugar mixture evenly over the Brie. Bake for an additional 2 to 3 minutes or until the sugar melts. Serve warm with apple slices, pear slices and crackers. Yield: 16 to 20 servings.

Mary Kay Simms, Laureate Beta
Beach Park, Illinois

CREAMY CARROT LOG

2 carrots, shredded	1/4 teaspoon crushed oregano
4 ounces light cream cheese, softened	1/4 cup Grape Nuts cereal, crushed
3 tablespoons grated Parmesan cheese	

Combine the carrots, cream cheese, Parmesan cheese and oregano in a mixing bowl and mix well. Chill, covered, for at least 1 hour. Shape the cheese mixture into a 7-inch long log. Roll in the crushed cereal to coat. Serve with cucumber slices. Yield: 5 servings.

Jacqueline Kozarevic, Laureate Delta Upsilon
Barberton, Ohio

THREE-CHEESE LOG

8 ounces cream cheese, softened	1 cup (4 ounces) crumbled blue cheese
2 cups (8 ounces) shredded Cheddar cheese	1/3 cup sherry
	1 cup minced pecans

Combine the cream cheese, Cheddar cheese, blue cheese and sherry in a blender or food processor and mix well. Shape the mixture into a log. Roll the log in the pecans. Serve with crackers. Yield: 20 servings.

Margaret L. Schmalz, Alpha Phi Master
Sarasota, Florida

CHOCOLATE CHIP CHEESE BALL

8 ounces cream cheese, softened	2 tablespoons brown sugar
1 stick butter, softened	3/4 cup miniature chocolate chips
1/4 teaspoon vanilla extract	3/4 cup minced pecans
3/4 cup confectioners' sugar	

Combine the cream cheese, butter and vanilla in a mixing bowl and beat until fluffy. Gradually add the confectioners' sugar and brown sugar, mixing well after each addition. Fold in the chocolate chips. Chill, covered, for 2 hours. Shape the cream cheese mixture into a ball. Chill, wrapped in plastic wrap, for at least 1 hour. Roll the ball in pecans before serving. Serve with chocolate graham crackers. Yield: 16 servings.

Margie Fluhr
Dubuque, Iowa

PINEAPPLE CHEESE BALL

16 ounces cream cheese, softened	**1 (8-ounce) can crushed pineapple, drained**
1/4 cup chopped green onion	**1 tablespoon seasoned salt**
1/4 cup chopped green bell pepper	**1 cup chopped pecans**

Combine the cream cheese, green onion, bell pepper, pineapple and seasoned salt in a bowl and mix well. Chill, covered, overnight. Shape the cheese mixture into a ball and roll in pecans. Serve with crackers. Yield: 16 servings.

Peggy Gallant, Preceptor Beta Iota
Dalton, Georgia

TROPICAL FRUIT BALL

16 ounces cream cheese, softened	**2/3 cup sugar**
1 (12-ounce) package dried fruit, chopped	**1 (8-ounce) can crushed pineapple, drained and juice reserved**
1 cup flaked coconut (optional)	**1 cup minced pecans**

Combine the cream cheese, dried fruit, coconut, sugar and pineapple in a bowl and mix well. If the mixture becomes too hard to stir, add a tablespoon of the reserved pineapple juice. Freeze, covered, for 20 minutes. Shape the mixture into 2 balls and roll in pecans. Serve with crackers or gingersnap cookies. Yield: 16 servings.

Kay Price, Eta Nu
Theodore, Alabama

VANILLA PECAN CHEESE BALL

16 ounces cream cheese, softened	**2 cups toasted chopped pecans**
1 (3-ounce) package vanilla instant pudding mix	

Place the cream cheese in a mixing bowl and beat until light and fluffy. Add the vanilla pudding mix and mix well. Stir in 1 cup of the pecans. Shape the cream cheese mixture into a ball and roll in the remaining pecans. Serve with graham crackers. Yield: 20 servings.

Arlene Fox, Preceptor Iota Iota
Houston, Texas

CHICKEN CURRY BALL

1/2 boneless skinless chicken breast, cooked and shredded	**2 tablespoons chopped chutney**
3/4 cup sliced almonds	**8 ounces cream cheese, softened**
1 tablespoon curry powder	**1/3 cup mayonnaise**
	Sliced almonds

Combine the chicken, almonds, curry powder and chutney in a food processor and process until mixed well. Stir in the cream cheese and the mayonnaise. Chill, covered, for several hours. Shape into a ball and roll in almonds. Serve with wheat crackers. Yield: 16 servings.

Lucy Ude, Alpha Delta Omicron
Bonne Terre, Missouri

TURKEY CHEESE BALL

This is a great way to get rid of leftovers after Thanksgiving or Christmas. It is easy to make and very tasty!

2 cups ground leftover turkey	**1/2 pound bacon, crisp-cooked and crumbled**
1 (8-ounce) carton sour cream	**Dried parsley flakes**
1 (4-ounce) package crumbled blue cheese	

Combine the turkey with the sour cream, blue cheese and crisp bacon in a large bowl and mix well. Shape into a ball and coat with parsley flakes. Wrap the cheese ball in plastic wrap. Refrigerate for at least 1 hour. Serve with crackers. Yield: 8 servings.

Marsha Pool
Malakoff, Texas

SAUERKRAUT CHEESE BALL

2 1/2 cups finely chopped sauerkraut	**1/2 cup bread crumbs**
2 cups (8 ounces) shredded Cheddar cheese	**1/4 cup mayonnaise-style salad dressing**
2 tablespoons chopped onion	**1 teaspoon salt**
3 tablespoons chopped green bell pepper	**1 tablespoon sugar**
	8 ounces cream cheese, softened

Combine the sauerkraut, Cheddar cheese, onion, bell pepper, bread crumbs, salad dressing, salt and sugar in a bowl and mix well. Shape the mixture into a ball and coat with an even layer of cream cheese. Serve with crackers. Yield: 16 servings.

Eileen Hanson, Epsilon Master
Duluth, Minnesota

ZESTY CHEESE BALL

8 ounces cream cheese, softened	1 tablespoon parsley
1/3 cup shredded American cheese	2 tablespoons minced green bell pepper
1/3 cup shredded Cheddar cheese	2 tablespoons minced pimentos
1/3 cup shredded sharp Cheddar cheese	2 tablespoons fajita seasoning
1 tablespoon chives	Chopped pecans

Mix the cream cheese, American cheese and Cheddar cheeses in a bowl. Add the next 5 ingredients and mix well. Shape the mixture into a ball and roll in pecans. Serve with crackers. Yield: 16 servings.

Cheryl Gibson-Salgado, Preceptor Epsilon Zeta
Spearman, Texas

OLIVE AND CHEESE BALL

8 ounces cream cheese, softened	Dash of Worcestershire sauce
1 (4-ounce) package blue cheese	1 (12-ounce) jar chopped olives, drained
8 ounces sharp pasteurized cheese spread	

Combine the cream cheese, blue cheese and cheese spread in a bowl and mix well. Add the Worcestershire sauce and mix well. Shape the cheese mixture into a ball and roll to coat in olives. Yield: 12 servings.

Cathy Willmann, Laureate Beta Upsilon
Hartford City, Indiana

ALMOND PINECONE

Though it's fast and easy to make, the presentation is beautiful. I make it every year for my family and friends during the holidays.

8 ounces cream cheese, softened	1 tablespoon chopped onion
1/2 cup mayonnaise	1/2 teaspoon dill weed
5 bacon slices, crisp-cooked, drained and crumbled	1/8 teaspoon pepper
	1 1/4 cups whole almonds, toasted

Combine the cream cheese and mayonnaise in a bowl and mix well. Add the bacon, onion, dill weed and pepper and mix well. Cover and chill overnight. Form the cheese mixture into two large pinecone shapes and place on a large serving platter. Press the almonds all over the cheese at slight angles in overlapping rows until all of the cheese is covered.

Garnish with real or artificial pine sprigs. Serve with crackers. Yield: 12 appetizer servings.

Ellen F. Boyd, Preceptor Alpha Zeta
Elmira, New York

SPICY CHEESE LOG

32 ounces Velveeta cheese	1 cup mayonnaise
1/2 cup (2 ounces) shredded sharp Cheddar cheese	5 ounces horseradish
	5 drops of Tabasco sauce
	Dash of garlic salt

Melt the Velveeta cheese in a large heavy saucepan over medium-low heat. Add the Cheddar cheese, mayonnaise, horseradish, Tabasco sauce and garlic salt and cook, stirring constantly, until well blended. Pour the mixture into a mold and chill, covered, until set. Serve with crackers. Yield: 32 servings.

Mabelgene Lenfers, Chi Master
Newburgh, Indiana

CRAN-HORSERADISH SPREAD

2 cups cranberries	1/3 cup minced onion
1/2 cup sugar	1/2 teaspoon salt
2 tablespoons horseradish	8 ounces cream cheese, softened

Combine the cranberries, sugar, horseradish, onion and salt in a bowl and mix well. Chill, covered, for several hours. Place the block of cream cheese in a serving dish. Pour the cranberry mixture over the cream cheese. Serve with crackers. Yield: 8 servings.

Margaret N. Poston, Laureate Delta Gamma
Tampa, Florida

GARLIC CHEESE SPREAD

16 ounces cream cheese, softened	1 tablespoon garlic salt
1 cup mayonnaise	2 (14-ounce) cans artichoke hearts, drained and chopped
1/2 cup (2 ounces) grated Parmesan cheese	2 cups shredded sharp Cheddar cheese
1 teaspoon garlic powder	

Combine the cream cheese, mayonnaise, Parmesan cheese, garlic powder and garlic salt in a bowl and mix well. Add the artichoke hearts and Cheddar cheese and mix well. Chill, covered, until ready to serve. Serve with breadsticks or crackers. Yield: 32 servings.

Annette Simmons, Delta Iota
Higginsville, Missouri

CHICKEN LIVER PÂTÉ

16 ounces chicken livers, cooked and chopped
4 large onions, minced
2 tablespoons lemon juice
2 teaspoons salt
1/4 teaspoon pepper
4 hard-cooked eggs, chopped
1/2 cup (1 stick) butter, melted

Combine the livers, onions, lemon juice, salt, pepper, eggs and butter in a bowl and mix well. Remove the mixture to a pâté mold. Chill, covered, until ready to serve. Serve with crackers. Yield: 16 servings.

Dorothy Gray, Laureate Alpha Lambda
Portland, Oregon

SMOKED OYSTER SPREAD

16 ounces cream cheese, softened
1/4 cup chopped green onions
2 tablespoons mayonnaise
2 teaspoons Worcestershire sauce
1 tablespoon lemon juice
1/4 teaspoon onion powder
1/2 teaspoon hot red pepper sauce
2 (4-ounce) cans smoked oysters, drained, chopped

Beat the cream cheese in a mixing bowl until smooth. Add the onions, mayonnaise, Worcestershire sauce, lemon juice, onion powder and hot red pepper sauce and mix well. Stir in the oysters. Chill, covered, for 8 hours or overnight. Serve with crackers. Yield: 16 servings.

Mary Jo Bent, Epsilon Master Mu
Kansas City, Missouri

SALMON MOUSSE

2 packages unflavored gelatin
1 1/2 cups hot water
1 cup yogurt
1 cup low-fat mayonnaise
1 teaspoon onion salt
1 teaspoon dill weed
1 teaspoon hot red pepper sauce
1 (7-ounce) can salmon, drained and flaked
1 cup chopped green onions
1 cup chopped cucumber

Combine the gelatin and hot water in a medium bowl and stir until gelatin has dissolved. Cool completely. Combine the yogurt, mayonnaise, onion salt, dill weed and hot sauce in a large bowl and mix well. Add the cooled gelatin mixture and chill, covered, until partially set. Add the salmon, onions and cucumber to the partially set gelatin. Chill, covered, overnight in a mold. Yield: 16 servings.

Colleen Murray, Xi Epsilon Phi
Oakville, Ontario, Canada

SUN-DRIED TOMATOES OVER GOAT CHEESE

1 cup oil-pack sun-dried tomatoes, chopped
2 tablespoons minced fresh rosemary
1 garlic clove, minced
2 tablespoons olive oil
6 ounces goat cheese

Combine the sun-dried tomatoes, rosemary, garlic and olive oil in a bowl and mix well. Chill, covered, for at least 1 hour. Place the goat cheese in a serving dish. Top with the sun-dried tomato mixture. Serve with toasted pita wedges or crackers. Yield: 8 servings.

Donna Winslow, Xi Lambda Theta
Carthage, Missouri

FETA CHEESE AND SUN-DRIED TOMATO SPREAD

This spread can be prepared in advance. It will keep for up to 5 days in the refrigerator or 6 months in the freezer. You can use a yogurt container for the mold.

6 ounces feta cheese, softened
8 ounces cream cheese, softened
1/4 cup (1/2 stick) unsalted butter, softened, cut into pieces
2 tablespoons dry white wine
1/2 garlic clove, crushed
1/2 shallot, or 3 green onions
White pepper to taste
6 tablespoons minced sun-dried tomatoes
1/4 cup minced fresh parsley
2 tablespoons sesame seeds, toasted
3 green onions

Combine the feta cheese, cream cheese, butter, wine, garlic, shallot and white pepper in a food processor. Process until the ingredients are mixed. Line a two-cup straight-sided mold with plastic wrap. Combine the sun-dried tomatoes, parsley and sesame seeds in a small bowl and mix well. Spread 1/2 of the sun-dried tomato mixture over the bottom of the mold. Layer with 1/2 of the cheese mixture. Repeat the layers with the remaining mixtures. Chill, covered, for 2 hours or until firm. Invert the mold onto a serving plate and remove plastic wrap before serving. Serve with bread or crackers. Yield: 16 servings.

Fran Robbins, Laureate Alpha Iota
Orleans, Ontario, Canada

For a unique take on guacamole, Helen Blower, Theta Pi, Kelowna, British Columbia, Canada, makes **Guacamole Tomatoes** *by mashing 1 avocado with 4 teaspoons lemon juice, 1 teaspoon minced onion, 1 clove of minced garlic and 1/2 teaspoon salt. She stuffs the avocado mixture into hollowed-out cherry tomatoes.*

Snacks & Beverages

GRANOLA

5 cups quick-cooking oats	1 cup wheat germ
1/2 cup vegetable oil	1 cup chopped walnuts
1/2 cup honey	2 cups dried apricots
1/2 cup water	1 cup dates
	1/2 cup sunflower seeds

Place the oats in a large bowl. Mix the oil, honey and water in a small bowl and pour over the oats. Add the wheat germ, walnuts, apricots, dates and sunflower seeds; mix well. Spread the mixture evenly in a 10×15-inch baking pan. Bake at 350 degrees for 30 minutes. Yield: 10 cups.

Sharon L. Nelson, Preceptor Eta Gamma
West Chester, Ohio

CARAMEL CORN

6 quarts popped popcorn	1 cup light corn syrup
1 cup unsalted mixed nuts	4 sticks margarine
1 cup cashews or pecans	4 teaspoons vanilla extract
2 2/3 cups sugar	

Pour the popcorn and nuts into a large roasting pan and mix well. Place the mixture in a 200-degree oven while preparing the sauce. Combine the sugar, syrup and margarine in a large saucepan. Bring to a boil over medium heat. Boil for 8 to 10 minutes or until the mixture changes to a light caramel color, stirring constantly. Remove from the heat and add the vanilla. Pour the mixture over the popcorn, stirring to coat evenly. Pour onto waxed paper. Break into pieces when cooled. Yield: 20 servings.

Mary L. Partridge, Xi Gamma
Miles City, Montana

CRAZY CRUNCH POPCORN

2 quarts popped popcorn	1 cup (2 sticks) butter
1 1/3 cups toasted pecans	1/2 cup light corn syrup
2/3 cup toasted almonds	1 teaspoon vanilla extract
1 1/3 cups sugar	

Combine the popcorn and nuts in a large mixing bowl. Combine the sugar, butter and corn syrup in a 1 1/2-quart saucepan over medium heat. Bring to a boil, stirring constantly. Boil for 8 to 10 minutes or until the mixture turns a light caramel color, stirring occasionally. Remove from the heat. Stir in the vanilla. Pour the warm caramel sauce over the popcorn and nuts and stir to coat well. Spread the mixture over waxed paper. Break apart when cooled. Store in an airtight container. Yield: 20 servings.

Georgia Schaefer, Beta Nu
Joseph, Oregon

SPICED NUTS

3/4 cup packed brown sugar	2 1/2 tablespoons water
3/4 teaspoon salt	1/4 teaspoon nutmeg
1/2 teaspoon allspice	3 cups pecans, walnuts or almonds
1 teaspoon cinnamon	

Combine the first 6 ingredients in a microwave-safe glass dish. Microwave, uncovered, for 80 seconds, stirring halfway through. Add the pecans 1 cup at a time, stirring gently to coat each pecan. Place the pecans in a greased glass dish. Microwave for 3 to 5 minutes or until the syrup is slightly hardened. Spread over waxed paper to cool. Yield: 3 cups.

Colleen J. Ingersoll, Preceptor Alpha Omicron
Pekin, Illinois

SCRAMBLES

2 pounds salted mixed nuts	1 small bag pretzel twists
1 (12-ounce) box wheat Chex cereal	3 cups vegetable oil
1 (12-ounce) box rice Chex cereal	3 tablespoons Worcestershire sauce
1 (12-ounce) box corn Chex cereal	1¹/₂ teaspoons garlic salt
1 (10-ounce) box Cheerios	1¹/₂ teaspoons Lawry's seasoning
1 small bag pretzel sticks	1¹/₂ teaspoons celery salt
	1¹/₂ teaspoons onion salt

Combine the nuts, cereals and pretzels in a large roasting pan and mix well. Whisk the oil, Worcestershire sauce and seasonings in a bowl. Pour the oil and seasonings over the cereal mixture and stir to mix. Bake at 250 degrees for 2 hours, stirring every 15 minutes. Yield: (about) 5 pounds.

Joyce A. Lockwood, Preceptor Kappa Kappa
Fairfield, California

ORIENTAL SNACK MIX

4 cups Crispix cereal	¹/₄ cup (¹/₂ stick) butter, melted
¹/₂ cup honey-roasted peanuts	3 tablespoons teriyaki sauce
¹/₂ cup cashews	1 tablespoon sesame oil
1 (5-ounce) can chow mien noodles	1 teaspoon garlic powder

Combine the cereal, peanuts, cashews and noodles in a large bowl. Combine the butter, teriyaki sauce, sesame oil and garlic powder in a small bowl; mix well. Pour over the cereal mixture, stirring until coated. Spread the mixture in a 9×13-inch baking dish. Bake at 250 degrees for 1 hour, stirring frequently. Yield: (about) 1 gallon.

Holly Crowell, Zeta Kappa
Red Oak, Iowa

SPECIAL OCCASION PARTY MIX

1 (10-ounce) package miniature pretzels	2 cups salted peanuts
1 pound "M & M's" Chocolate Candies	2 (12-ounce) packages vanilla chips
5 cups Cheerios cereal	3 tablespoons vegetable oil
5 cups corn Chex cereal	

Combine the pretzels, "M & M's," cereals and peanuts in a large bowl; set aside. Combine the vanilla chips and oil in a microwave-safe bowl. Microwave on Medium-High for 2 minutes, stirring once. Microwave on High for 10 seconds; stir until smooth. Pour over the cereal mixture and stir to mix. Spread over 3 waxed paper-lined baking sheets. Break apart when cool. Store in an airtight container. Yield: (about) 3 pounds.

Linda Fisher, Preceptor Delta Lambda
Hiawatha, Iowa

PETTY PARTY MIX

4 cups Chex cereal	¹/₄ cup (¹/₂ stick) butter or margarine, melted
2 cups peanuts	2 cups "M & M's" Chocolate Candies
2 cups raisins	
2 cups pretzels	
¹/₂ cup honey	

Combine the cereal, peanuts, raisins and pretzels in a large bowl. Combine the honey and butter in a separate bowl and mix well. Pour over the cereal mixture, stirring to coat. Spread over a baking sheet. Bake at 350 degrees for 10 minutes. Spread the mixture over waxed paper to cool. Pour into a 2-quart bowl. Add the "M & M's" and toss to mix. Yield: 12 cups.

Elena Bennett, Alpha Phi Master
Bakersfield, California

PRETZEL MIX

1 bag pretzels	³/₄ cup vegetable oil
1 box Cheese Nips	3 teaspoons dried dill weed
1 box Wheat Thins	2 teaspoons lemon pepper
1 envelope ranch salad dressing mix	

Combine the pretzels, Cheese Nips and Wheat Thins in a large microwave-safe bowl. Whisk the ranch dressing mix, oil, dill weed and lemon pepper in a separate bowl. Pour over the pretzel mixture. Microwave for 2¹/₂ minutes and stir. Microwave an additional 2¹/₂ minutes. Spread over waxed paper to cool. Yield: (about) 2 pounds.

Marcia Kelly, Laureate Delta Psi
Kansas City, Missouri

SEASONED PRETZELS

1 bottle butter-flavored popping oil	4 pounds pretzel twists
2 envelopes ranch salad dressing mix	¹/₈ teaspoon garlic powder
2 (18-ounce) cans mixed nuts	¹/₂ tablespoon dried dill weed

Combine all the ingredients in a large airtight container, stirring to coat. Let stand overnight. Yield: 5 pounds.

Maggie Kimbler, Preceptor Alpha Delta
Eagan, Minnesota

CHRISTMAS EGGNOG FOR A CROWD

12 pasteurized egg yolks	1 quart half-and-half
1 cup sugar	1 pint heavy cream
1 cup brandy	1 cup apricot brandy
1/2 teaspoon salt	Nutmeg
12 pasteurized egg whites	

Combine the egg yolks and sugar in a mixing bowl; beat until thick and lemon colored. Chill, covered, for several hours. Add the brandy and blend well. Combine the salt and egg whites in a separate bowl and beat until almost stiff. Add the half-and-half to the egg yolk mixture and stir to mix. Fold in the beaten egg whites and the cream. Chill, covered, for 1 hour. Pour into a punch bowl and stir before serving. Sprinkle each serving with nutmeg.
Yield: 30 servings.

Pat McCourry, Preceptor Gamma Theta
Canton, Ohio

HOLIDAY PUNCH

1 quart eggnog	1 quart lemon-lime soda
1 quart mint ice cream	Nutmeg

Pour the eggnog into a chilled punch bowl. Scoop the ice cream into the bowl. Pour the lemon-lime soda slowly into the bowl. Sprinkle with nutmeg.
Yield: 16 servings.

Sara Bee-Gay, President City Council
Chillicothe, Ohio

ROSY CHAMPAGNE PUNCH

2 (16-ounce) cans pitted dark sweet cherries	1/2 cup brandy
1 (12-ounce) can pineapple juice	1/4 teaspoon lemon juice
	2 (4- to 5-quart) bottles Champagne, chilled

Drain the cherries, reserving 2 tablespoons of the syrup. Combine the cherries, pineapple juice, brandy, lemon juice and reserved cherry syrup in a bowl and mix well. Chill, covered, to blend the flavors. Remove just before serving and pour into a punch bowl. Add the Champagne and mix well. Yield: 20 servings.

Marcia Hillock, Preceptor Beta Alpha
North Collins, New York

SUPER PUNCH

1 cup sugar	1 (12-ounce) can frozen pink lemonade, thawed
1 cup warm water	
1 (12-ounce) can frozen orange juice, thawed	1/3 cup grenadine
9 cups water	7 cups ginger ale
1/4 cup lemon juice	Ice

Dissolve the sugar in the warm water in a small bowl; pour into a punch bowl. Add the orange juice, 9 cups water, lemon juice, pink lemonade and grenadine and mix well. Add the ginger ale just before serving. Chill with the ice. Yield: 35 servings.

Nancy Bobick, Laureate Delta
Saskatoon, Saskatchewan, Canada

TROPICAL PUNCH

1 (6-ounce) can frozen lemonade, thawed	1 (46-ounce) can pineapple juice
2 (6-ounce) cans frozen limeade, thawed	4 cups water
	2 (2-liter) bottles ginger ale
1 (6-ounce) can frozen orange juice, thawed	Sherbet of your choice
2 cups Hawaiian punch	

Combine the lemonade, limeade, orange juice, Hawaiian punch, pineapple juice and water in a large punch bowl and mix well. Add the ginger ale and sherbet, stirring until the sherbet is partially melted. Yield: 30 servings.

Marilyn A. Parker, Preceptor Zeta Tau
Sandusky, Ohio

AMARETTO PUNCH

2 cups sugar	2 quarts water
1 quart boiling water	2 cups amaretto or almond-flavored liqueur
1 (46-ounce) can unsweetened pineapple juice	
	2 tablespoons vanilla extract
1 (12-ounce) can frozen orange juice, thawed	1 tablespoon almond extract
1 (6-ounce) can frozen lemonade, thawed	

Dissolve the sugar in the boiling water in a large saucepan. Add the pineapple juice, orange juice, lemonade, water, amaretto, vanilla and almond extract and mix well. Separate the punch into 6 quart-size sealable plastic bags; freeze. Remove as needed. Let stand at room temperature until slushy. Pour into a pitcher to serve. Yield: 6 servings.

Debra L. Rotundo, Preceptor Zeta
Stephens City, Virginia

AMARETTO SLUSHIES

1 (750-ml) bottle amaretto	1 (12-ounce) can frozen pineapple or orange juice, thawed
1 (12-ounce) can frozen raspberry lemonade, thawed	
	8 cups water
1/2 cup sugar	1 (2-liter) bottle lemon-lime soda

Combine the amaretto, lemonade, sugar, pineapple juice and water in 2 freezer-safe pitchers. Freeze for 24 hours, stirring after 12 hours. Remove from the freezer. Add the soda, stirring to a slushy consistency. Garnish with orange slices or cherries.
Yield: 25 servings.

Leesa Wood Calvi, Xi Alpha Beta Gamma
Canyon, Texas

CHOCOLATE PUNCH

1½ quarts water
½ cup instant chocolate
 drink mix
½ cup sugar
¼ cup instant coffee
 granules
½ gallon vanilla ice
 cream
½ gallon chocolate ice
 cream

Bring the water to a boil in a large saucepan; remove from the heat. Add the chocolate drink mix, sugar and coffee granules and stir until dissolved. Cover and chill. Pour the punch into a punch bowl 30 minutes before serving. Add the ice cream to the punch, stirring until the ice cream is partially melted.
Yield: 25 servings.

Niki Cloud, Xi Lambda Theta
Carthage, Missouri

SPARKLING BERRIES AND LIME PUNCH

1 (16-ounce) package
 frozen berry medley,
 thawed
2 (33.8-ounce) bottles
 lemon or lime
 sparkling water
4 cups cran-raspberry
 juice
1 lime, sliced
1 lemon, sliced
1 quart ice cubes

Combine the berries, sparkling water and cran-raspberry juice in a punch bowl and mix well. Add the lime slices, lemon slices and ice cubes; serve immediately. Yield: 16 servings.

Joyce Symank, Laureate Eta Alpha
Valley Mills, Texas

SUNNY WEDDING PUNCH

1 (6-ounce) can frozen
 lemonade, thawed
1 (6-ounce) can frozen
 orange juice, thawed
½ teaspoon almond
 extract
½ cup lemon juice
2 cups pineapple juice
1 (12-ounce) can apricot
 nectar
1 (1-quart) bottle
 lemon-lime soda or
 ginger ale
Sherbet or fruit-filled ice
 ring (optional)

Prepare the lemonade and orange juice in a large punch bowl using the package directions; mix well. Add the almond extract, lemon juice, pineapple juice

and apricot nectar and stir to mix. Add the soda just before serving. Drop in scoops of sherbet or float an ice ring in the punch bowl, if desired.
Yield: 30 servings.

Joella Toppi, Omega Master
Brerton, Washington

GRAPEFRUIT MARGARITAS

3 cups ruby red
 grapefruit juice
2 cups tequila
1 cup triple sec
1 grapefruit

Combine the grapefruit juice, tequila and triple sec in a pitcher and mix well. Chill, covered, for 1 hour. Cut the grapefruit into 12 slices. Add 6 slices to the pitcher. Dip the wet rims of 6 margarita glasses in sugar or salt. Serve the margaritas on the rocks with a slice of grapefruit for garnish. Yield: 6 servings.

Mary Kent, Beta Phi
Crete, Nebraska

FRESH PEACH DAIQUIRI

2 peaches, sliced
1 (3-ounce) can frozen
 lemonade, thawed
6 ounces water
6 ounces rum
1 tablespoon sugar
8 to 10 ice cubes

Place the peaches in a blender. Add the lemonade, water, rum, sugar and ice cubes; blend quickly. Serve immediately. Yield: 4 servings.

Sara Daniels, Preceptor Beta Theta
Morehead City, North Carolina

CHI-CHI'S SLUSH

1 fifth of vodka
1 (12-ounce) can frozen
 lemonade, thawed
1 (46-ounce) can
 pineapple juice
1 (16-ounce) can cream
 of coconut
1 (2-liter) lemon-lime
 soda

Combine the vodka, lemonade, pineapple juice and cream of coconut in a large freezer-safe bowl; mix well. Freeze, covered, until frozen. Scoop the frozen mixture into glasses. Add the soda to taste.
Yield: 10 servings.

Jo Prusha, Preceptor Gamma
Omaha, Nebraska

Patricia Reece, Omicron Beta, Ripon, California, makes **Cranberry Slush** *by combining 48 ounces cran-apple juice, one thawed 6-ounce can limeade, one 6-ounce can water and 2 cups Southern Comfort in a freezer-safe pitcher and freezes overnight. She scoops the mixture into glasses to serve.*

FESTIVE SANGRIA

1 gallon pinot noir
2 quarts lemon-lime
 soda
2 quarts orange soda

4 large oranges, sliced
2 large lemons, sliced
Sugar or sweetener
 to taste

Combine the wine, lemon-lime soda and orange soda in a large container and mix well. Chill or freeze, covered, until the mixture is slushy. Pour the mixture into a punch bowl. Garnish with the orange slices and lemon slices. Stir in sugar. Yield: 2 gallons.

Anita Jemison, Xi
Ridgeland, Mississippi

MULLED WINE

4 apples
36 whole cloves
4-inch piece fresh
 gingerroot, peeled

4 cinnamon sticks
2 cups orange juice
2 bottles dry red wine
1/2 cup sugar

Press 8 cloves into each apple and place the apples in a large stockpot. Add the gingerroot, cinnamon sticks, orange juice and 1 bottle of red wine; mix well. Allow the mixture to stand, covered, for 12 hours or overnight. Add the sugar and remaining wine and bring to a boil. Serve immediately, reserving the fruit for additional batches. Yield: 15 servings.

Yvonne Wiegand, Preceptor Xi Kappa
Brea, California

RITUAL FROZEN WINE PUNCH

1 bottle semisweet
 white wine
1 (48-ounce can)
 pineapple juice
1 (36-ounce) bottle
 apple juice

1 (36-ounce) bottle
 white grape juice
1/2 (2-liter) bottle citrus
 soda
2 tablespoons lemon
 juice

Combine the white wine, pineapple juice, apple juice, white grape juice, citrus soda and lemon juice in a large bowl and mix well. Pour into 1-quart freezer containers; freeze until slushy. Refreeze any leftovers. Variation: Substitute sparkling wine for the white wine and white cranberry-peach juice for the white grape juice. Substitute red wine for the white wine, cranberry juice for the apple juice and white grape and lemon-lime soda for the citrus soda. Substitute sparkling grape juice for the wine for nonalcoholic punch. Yield: 28 servings.

June Reasons, Preceptor Beta Theta
New Bern, North Carolina

CHAI TEA MIX

1 cup nonfat dry milk
 powder
1 cup powdered
 nondairy creamer
1 cup French vanilla-
 flavored nondairy
 creamer
2 1/2 cups sugar
1 1/2 cups unsweetened
 instant tea granules

2 teaspoons ground
 ginger
2 teaspoons ground
 cinnamon
1 teaspoon each ground
 cloves, cardamom,
 nutmeg and allspice
1/4 teaspoon white
 pepper

Combine all the ingredients in a large bowl and mix well. Blend the mixture, 1 cup at a time, in a blender until of the consistency of fine powder. Stir 2 heaping tablespoons of the mixture into a mug of hot water to serve. Yield: 60 servings.

Deborah Wensel, Preceptor Beta Epsilon
Kane, Pennsylvania

ORANGE SPICED TEA

4 cups water
2 cups sugar or
 sweetener
2 sticks cinnamon
4 whole cloves
5 individual tea bags or
 1 family-size tea bag

1 (6-ounce) can frozen
 orange juice, thawed
3 (6-ounce) cans water
2 cups pineapple juice
Juice of 2 lemons
4 cups water

Combine the first 4 ingredients in a large saucepan. Boil for 5 minutes. Remove from the heat and add the tea bags; steep for 15 minutes. Combine the orange juice, water, pineapple juice and lemon juice in a gallon jar. Remove the tea bags and spices from the tea; pour the tea into the juice mixture. Add 4 cups of water and mix well. Yield: 1 gallon.

Yvonne F. Kennedy, Preceptor Omicron Epsilon
Kilgore, Texas

SPICED TEA

3 quarts water
1 stick cinnamon
1 teaspoon whole cloves
2 1/2 teaspoons black tea,
 or 5 individual tea
 bags

Juice of 3 oranges
Juice of 1 1/2 lemons
1 cup sugar

Pour the water into a large saucepan. Place the cinnamon and cloves in a cloth bag in the water and bring to a boil. Add the tea, reduce the heat and steep. Add the orange juice, lemon juice and sugar; mix well. Serve while hot. Yield: 5 servings.

Paula Keicer, Preceptor Epsilon Alpha
Dale City, Virginia

Fruit Salads

FRUIT SALAD WITH LIME ZEST

2 Granny Smith apples,
  chopped
1 cup seedless red grape
  halves
1 (11-ounce) can
  mandarin oranges,
  drained
1¹/2 cups miniature
  marshmallows
³/4 cup French vanilla
  yogurt
Grated zest of 1 lime
2 tablespoons chopped
  pecans

Combine the apples, grapes, oranges, marshmallows, yogurt and lime zest in a bowl. Add the oranges and toss to combine. Sprinkle the pecans over the top. Yield: 4 to 6 servings.

Paula Clemmons, Alpha Mu Psi
Morse, Texas

DATE AND APPLE WALDORF SALAD

1 orange, peeled and
  sectioned
2 cups chopped peeled
  apples
¹/2 cup chopped dates
¹/2 cup chopped celery
¹/3 cup chopped walnuts
1 tablespoon sugar
1 tablespoon orange
  juice
¹/4 cup mayonnaise or
  mayonnaise-style
  salad dressing
³/4 cup whipped topping
Lettuce leaves

Combine the orange, apples, dates, celery and walnuts in a bowl. Whisk the sugar, orange juice and mayonnaise together in a bowl. Fold in the whipped topping. Add the mayonnaise mixture to the fruit mixture, stirring to combine. Serve over lettuce. Yield: 6 servings.

Lydia Cook, Epsilon Master
Fenton, Michigan

STRAWBERRY SUPREME SALAD

³/4 cup sugar
8 ounces cream cheese,
  softened
1 (20-ounce) can crushed
  pineapple, drained
1 (10-ounce) package
  frozen strawberries,
  thawed
2 bananas, chopped
1 (16-ounce) package
  whipped topping
³/4 cup chopped nuts
  (optional)

Cream the sugar and cream cheese in a large mixing bowl. Fold in the pineapple, strawberries, bananas, whipped topping and nuts. Spoon the mixture into a freezer-proof serving dish. Freeze, covered, until firm. Let stand for 45 minutes to thaw before serving. Yield: 20 servings.

Roylene Phillips, Laureate Beta Delta
Olathe, Kansas

CRANBERRY RELISH

1 small Gala apple,
  peeled and chopped
¹/2 teaspoon lemon juice
1 (6-ounce) package
  cranberry or
  raspberry gelatin
1¹/2 cups hot water
¹/2 cup chopped pecans
2 (11-ounce) cans
  mandarin oranges
2 (16-ounce) cans whole
  cranberries in sauce

Toss the apple with the lemon juice in a bowl to prevent browning. Dissolve the gelatin in the hot water in a bowl. Add the pecans, mandarin oranges, cranberries and apple. Chill, covered, for 8 to 12 hours or until thickened. Yield: 10 cups.

Linda Koch, Xi Beta Mu
Port Royal, Virginia

CRANBERRY SALAD

1 (12-ounce) package cranberries	1 teaspoon grated orange zest
1/2 cup water	1 cup chopped peeled Golden Delicious apple
3/4 cup orange juice	
1 1/4 cups sugar	
1 teaspoon ginger	1 cup walnuts, chopped

Combine the cranberries, water, orange juice and sugar in a large saucepan. Bring to a boil. Simmer for 15 minutes or until thickened, stirring frequently. Let stand to cool. Stir in the ginger, orange zest, apple and walnuts. Spoon into a serving dish and chill, covered, until serving time. Yield: 15 servings.

Sally Burns, Preceptor Delta Delta
Olathe, Kansas

WINEBERRY SALAD

1 cup cranberry juice	1 cup whole cranberry sauce
1 (3-ounce) package raspberry gelatin	
1/4 cup sugar	1 cup chilled whipped cream
3/4 cup sangria	1/2 cup chopped pecans

Microwave the cranberry juice in a microwave-safe bowl for 2 to 3 minutes or until boiling. Dissolve the gelatin in the juice. Add the sugar and sangria and mix well. Chill for 1 hour. Fold in the cranberry sauce, whipped cream and pecans. Spoon the mixture into a 6-cup mold. Chill for 3 to 4 hours or until set. Unmold onto a serving plate. Yield: 8 servings.

Cheryll Stewart, Laureate Zeta Tau
Palm Coast, Florida

SPICED PEACH SALAD

1 (29-ounce) can peach halves	3 tablespoons white vinegar
1 tablespoon whole cloves	2 cups water
4 cinnamon sticks	1 (6-ounce) package peach gelatin
1/2 cup sugar	

Drain the peaches, reserving the liquid in a 2-cup liquid measuring cup. Tie the cloves and cinnamon sticks in cheesecloth. Combine with the sugar, vinegar and water in a medium saucepan. Bring to a boil. Simmer for 10 minutes. Remove from the heat and discard the spices. Dissolve the gelatin in the sugar mixture, stirring constantly. Add enough water to the reserved peach liquid to measure 2 cups. Stir the peach juice into the gelatin mixture. Chill until slightly thickened. Slice the peaches thinly and fold into the gelatin. Spoon the gelatin into a 2-quart glass bowl. Chill until firm. Yield: 8 to 12 servings.

Cindy Johnson, Laureate Omega
Bartlett, Tennessee

PRETZEL GELATIN SALAD

3 cups coarsely crushed pretzels	8 ounces cream cheese, softened
1 1/4 cups (2 1/2 sticks) butter, melted	1 cup confectioners' sugar
1/4 cup plus 3 tablespoons granulated sugar	2 (6-ounce) packages strawberry gelatin
1 (8-ounce) container whipped topping	2 cups boiling water
	2 (10-ounce) packages frozen strawberries

Combine the pretzels, butter and granulated sugar in a medium bowl. Spread evenly in a greased 9×13-inch baking pan. Bake at 400 degrees for 8 minutes. Cool completely. Blend the whipped topping, cream cheese and confectioners' sugar in a mixing bowl. Spread evenly over the pretzel mixture. Dissolve the gelatin in the water. Add the unthawed strawberries and stir until the mixture begins to thicken. Pour over the cream cheese mixture. Chill until set. Cut into squares to serve. Yield: 12 servings.

Helen French, Xi Iota Omega
Florissant, Missouri

CHERRY LEMONADE GELATIN SALAD

1 (21-ounce) can cherry pie filling	3 ounces cream cheese, softened
1 (3-ounce) package cherry gelatin	1 (8-ounce) container whipped topping
1 cup boiling water	1 (8-ounce) can crushed pineapple
1 (3-ounce) package lemon gelatin	2 1/2 cups miniature marshmallows
1 cup boiling water	

Spread the cherry pie filling over the bottom of a 9×9-inch glass baking pan. Dissolve the cherry gelatin in 1 cup boiling water. Pour over the pie filling and stir until mixed. Chill, covered, for 3 hours or until set. Dissolve the lemon gelatin in 1 cup boiling water, stirring constantly. Add the cream cheese and stir until melted. Fold in the whipped topping. Stir in the pineapple and marshmallows. Pour over the prepared layer. Chill, covered, for 3 hours or until set. Yield: 16 to 20 servings.

Stephanie Robie, Alpha Eta Mu
Ennis, Texas

Vegetable Salads

WARM PEAR AND GREEN BEAN SALAD

2 tablespoons extra-
  virgin olive oil
1/2 teaspoon salt
1/4 teaspoon pepper
2 pounds green beans,
  trimmed
2 tablespoons extra-
  virgin olive oil
1/2 teaspoon salt
1/4 teaspoon pepper
4 pears, cored and cut
  into eighths
1 teaspoon sugar

2 tablespoons sherry
  vinegar
1 teaspoon Dijon
  mustard
1/2 teaspoon minced
  garlic
1/4 cup extra-virgin olive
  oil
1/4 teaspoon salt
1/4 teaspoon pepper
1/2 cup chopped toasted
  hazelnuts, pecans or
  walnuts

Whisk 2 tablespoons olive oil, 1/2 teaspoon salt and 1/4 teaspoon pepper in a large bowl. Add the green beans and toss to mix. Spread the green beans in a single layer in a greased baking pan. Whisk 2 tablespoons olive oil, 1/2 teaspoon salt and 1/4 teaspoon pepper in a large bowl. Add the pears and toss to mix. Spread the pears in a single layer in another baking pan. Sprinkle the pears with the sugar. Bake the green beans and pears at 400 degrees for 30 minutes. Bake the pears for 15 minutes longer. Whisk the vinegar, Dijon mustard and garlic together in a small bowl. Add 1/4 cup olive oil in a thin stream, whisking constantly. Stir in 1/4 teaspoon salt and 1/4 teaspoon pepper. Toss the green beans, pears, dressing and hazelnuts together in a salad bowl. Serve immediately. Yield: 8 servings.

Debbie Cain, Laureate Theta Phi
The Woodlands, Texas

MANGO PEPPER SALAD

This salad is fresh, light, low in fat, zesty, and so colorful to display. For serving at Christmastime, use only red and green bell peppers.

2 or 3 ripe mangoes,
  peeled and chopped
1 each red, green, yellow
  and orange bell
  pepper, chopped

Chopped fresh cilantro
  (optional)
Juice of 1 lime
Lemon pepper to taste

Combine the mangoes, bell peppers, cilantro, lime juice and lemon pepper in a large bowl and mix well. Yield: 6 servings.

Heather Greenwald, Epsilon Rho
Unionville, Ontario, Canada

FRESH VEGETABLE SALAD

1 cup low-fat sour
  cream
1/2 cup low-fat
  mayonnaise
Pinch of dill weed
1 head cauliflower, cut
  into bite-size pieces
1 bunch broccoli, cut
  into bite-size pieces

1 bell pepper, cut into
  bite-size pieces
1 bunch green onions,
  cut into bite-size
  pieces
1 cup finely chopped
  celery

Mix the sour cream, mayonnaise and dill weed in a large bowl. Add the vegetables and mix well. Chill, covered, for 8 to 12 hours before serving. Yield: 6 to 8 servings.

Joyce Matheny-Eisenmann, Preceptor Nu
Murfreesboro, Tennessee

CRUNCHY PEA SALAD

1 (16-ounce) package
   frozen peas, thawed
1 cup chopped
   cauliflower
1 cup finely chopped
   celery
1 cup finely chopped
   green bell pepper
1 cup slivered almonds

1/4 cup sliced green
   onions
1 cup ranch salad
   dressing
1/2 cup sour cream
1/2 teaspoon dill weed
1/4 teaspoon salt
1/8 teaspoon pepper

Combine the peas, cauliflower, celery, bell pepper, almonds and green onions in a large salad bowl and mix well. Combine the salad dressing, sour cream, dill weed, salt and pepper in a small bowl and mix well. Pour the dressing over the vegetable mixture and toss gently to combine. Chill until serving time. Serve over lettuce if desired. Yield: 6 to 8 servings.

Elaine C. Olson, Chi Master
Lake Havasu City, Arizona

CUCUMBER SALAD

2 1/4 pounds cucumbers,
   peeled, halved
   lengthwise and sliced
2 tablespoons fine sea
   salt
3 tablespoons chopped
   fresh dill weed

1/4 cup sour cream
1 tablespoon white
   vinegar
Freshly ground pepper
   to taste

Toss the cucumbers and salt together in a large bowl. Let stand at room temperature for 30 minutes. Drain and rinse the cucumbers under cold running water. Drain in a colander for 10 minutes longer. Press the cucumbers with paper towels to remove as much liquid as possible. Combine the cucumbers, dill weed, sour cream and vinegar in a large bowl and mix well. Season with pepper. Refrigerate, covered, for 1 to 24 hours. Serve cold. Yield 4 to 6 servings.

Janet Meyers, Laureate Eta Eta
Twentynine Palms, California

CUCUMBER AND ONION SALAD

3 large cucumbers,
   peeled
3 Vidalia onions
1 cup water
3/4 cup vegetable oil
1/3 cup sugar

1/4 cup cider vinegar
1 teaspoon tarragon
3/4 teaspoon salt
1/2 teaspoon white or
   black pepper

Cut the cucumbers and onions into 1/4-inch-thick slices. Combine the remaining ingredients in a small saucepan and bring to a boil, stirring occasionally. Boil for 3 minutes. Place the cucumbers and onions in

a large bowl. Pour the hot dressing over the vegetables. Refrigerate, covered, for up to 2 weeks. Serve cold. Yield: 6 to 8 servings.

Marilyn Borras, Preceptor Alpha Zeta
Stafford, Virginia

WATERMELON AND CUCUMBER SALAD

This salad is both tart and sweet, with an intriguing bite from the red pepper. It's a delicious and beautiful summer salad for any occasion.

1/4 cup white vinegar
1/4 cup sugar
1/4 teaspoon crushed red
   pepper
4 cucumbers, peeled,
   halved lengthwise
   and seeded

Salt to taste
8 cups cubed seeded
   watermelon
1/2 teaspoon salt

Combine the vinegar, sugar and red pepper in a small saucepan and bring to a boil. Boil for 1 minute. Slice the cucumbers and toss with salt in a large bowl. Let stand at room temperature for 30 minutes. Press the cucumbers with paper towels to remove any excess liquid. Toss the watermelon and 1/2 teaspoon salt together in a large bowl. Add the cucumbers and vinegar mixture and toss gently to combine. Serve chilled or at room temperature. Yield: 8 cups.

Norma Jean Jones, Epsilon Master
Broken Arrow, Oklahoma

GRILL-SIDE GARDEN SALAD

2 tomatoes, seeded and
   chopped
1 zucchini, diced
1 cup frozen whole
   kernel corn
1/3 cup thinly sliced
   green onions
1 small avocado,
   chopped
1/3 to 1/2 cup picante
   sauce

2 tablespoons vegetable
   oil
2 tablespoons chopped
   fresh cilantro
1 tablespoon lemon
   juice or lime juice
3/4 teaspoon garlic salt
1/4 teaspoon ground
   cumin

Combine the tomatoes, zucchini, corn, green onions and avocado in a large bowl. Combine the remaining ingredients in a small bowl and stir to mix. Pour the picante sauce mixture over the vegetables and toss gently. Refrigerate, covered, for 3 to 4 hours, stirring occasionally. Serve chilled or at room temperature. Yield: 4 servings.

Margi Klein, Sigma Lambda
Placerville, California

CARROT SALAD

3½ cups shredded
  carrots
1½ cups miniature
  marshmallows
1 (20-ounce) can
  pineapple tidbits,
  drained
2 cups pecan pieces

1 cup golden raisins
1 cup shredded coconut
1 (6-ounce) jar
  maraschino cherries,
  drained and chopped
1 cup mayonnaise
1 (16-ounce) container
  whipped topping

Mix all the ingredients in a large bowl. Cover and chill thoroughly. Yield: 16 to 24 servings.

Barbara Oller, Preceptor Nu
Orlando, Florida

MARINATED GARDEN TOMATOES

12 large tomatoes, cut
  into wedges
1 cup thinly sliced
  green onions
½ cup finely chopped
  fresh parsley, or
  2 tablespoons dried
  parsley
⅔ cup olive oil or

canola oil

Layer the tomatoes and green onions in a 9×13-inch serving dish. Whisk the remaining ingredients together in a small bowl. Pour the marinade over the tomato mixture. Chill, covered, for 2 to 12 hours. Yield: 20 servings.

Phyllis Paine, Psi Master
Mount Pleasant, Iowa

WILTED LETTUCE SALAD

2 bunches leaf lettuce,
  torn into bite-size
  pieces
⅓ cup chopped green
  onions
4 slices bacon, chopped

¼ cup vinegar
¼ teaspoon salt
⅛ teaspoon pepper
2 teaspoons sugar
2 hard-cooked eggs,
  sliced

Place the lettuce and green onions in a large salad bowl. Cook the bacon in a skillet over medium heat until crisp. Remove the bacon with a slotted spoon, reserving the drippings. Add the vinegar, salt, pepper and sugar to the reserved drippings in the skillet and bring to a boil. Pour the hot vinegar mixture over the lettuce and green onions. Toss for 1 to 2 minutes or until the lettuce wilts. Add the bacon and the eggs and toss gently to combine. Serve immediately. Yield: 8 servings.

Carolyn Powell, Laureate Iota
Raleigh, North Carolina

CHICAGO BACON SALAD

8 to 10 thick slices
  bacon, cut into 1-inch
  pieces
4 slices dry white bread,
  cut into 1-inch pieces
4 garlic cloves, minced
½ cup balsamic vinegar
2 tablespoons fresh
  lemon juice
1½ tablespoons herb
  mustard or Dijon
  mustard

1 tablespoon finely
  chopped chives
2 tablespoons tarragon
½ cup olive oil
½ cup corn oil or
  vegetable oil
Salt and pepper to taste
1 bunch lettuce and/or
  spinach, torn into
  bite-size pieces
¾ cup crumbled blue
  cheese

Cook the bacon in a skillet over medium heat until crisp. Remove with a slotted spoon, reserving the drippings. Drain the bacon on paper towels. Add the bread to the bacon drippings in the skillet and cook until crisp and brown. Remove with a slotted spoon. Whisk the garlic, vinegar, lemon juice and mustard together in a bowl. Add the chives and tarragon and mix well. Add the olive oil and corn oil gradually, whisking constantly to combine. Season with salt and pepper. Toss the lettuce, cheese, bacon and bread together in a large salad bowl. Toss the salad with the vinaigrette and serve immediately. Yield: 4 or 5 servings.

Griff Jappé, Laureate Delta Xi
Lehigh Acres, Florida

TWENTY-FOUR-HOUR SALAD

This salad looks and tastes great, and any leftovers taste good up to four days later.

1 head lettuce, torn
1 cup sliced onion
1 cup sliced celery
1 can sliced water
  chestnuts, drained
1 (10-ounce) package
  frozen peas, thawed
2 cups mayonnaise
1 teaspoon sugar
½ teaspoon salt

¼ teaspoon pepper
1 cup (4 ounces)
  shredded mozzarella
  cheese
½ cup (2 ounces) grated
  Parmesan cheese
Tomato wedges or
  cherry tomatoes
Bacon bits

Layer the lettuce, onion, celery, water chestnuts and peas in the order given in a 9×13-inch serving dish. Spread a mixture of the mayonnaise and sugar over the top, sealing to the edge. Sprinkle with the salt and pepper. Layer the mozzarella cheese and Parmesan cheese over the top. Chill, covered, for 24 hours. Top with the tomatoes and bacon bits to serve.

Lenora Tarnow, Gamma Theta Master
League City, Texas

COUNTRY SALAD

1 head lettuce, shredded
1 tomato, chopped
1/2 onion, chopped
2 cups (8 ounces) shredded Cheddar cheese
1/2 green bell pepper, chopped
1 carrot, shredded
3 or 4 hard-cooked eggs, chopped
Ranch salad dressing

Toss the lettuce, tomato, onion, cheese, bell pepper, carrot and eggs in a large serving bowl. Serve immediately with ranch salad dressing. Yield: 6 servings.

Doris Menter, Laureate Mu
Douglas, Wyoming

GREEK SALAD

1/3 cup extra-virgin olive oil
3 tablespoons white wine vinegar
2 tablespoons lemon juice
1 1/2 teaspoons chopped fresh oregano
1 teaspoon sugar
1/2 teaspoon dried oregano
1 garlic clove, minced
1/4 teaspoon pepper
1/2 cucumber, sliced
3 Roma tomatoes, chopped
1/2 cup finely chopped black olives
1/2 cup crumbled feta cheese
1 head romaine lettuce, chopped
1/3 cup thinly sliced red onion

Whisk the olive oil, vinegar, lemon juice, chopped oregano, sugar, dried oregano, garlic and pepper together in a bowl. Combine the remaining ingredients in a large bowl and mix well. Pour the dressing over the lettuce mixture and toss to combine. Yield: 4 to 6 servings.

Gina Fegler, Beta Kappa
Boise, Idaho

GREEK PEASANT SALAD

1/2 red onion, chopped
1 cup sliced pitted black olives
1 green bell pepper, chopped
1 red bell pepper, chopped
2 tomatoes, chopped
1 cucumber, chopped
1 cup cubed feta cheese
6 tablespoons extra-virgin olive oil
1 teaspoon oregano
Juice of 1 lemon
Black pepper to taste

Combine the first 7 ingredients in a salad bowl and mix well. Whisk the olive oil, oregano, lemon juice and pepper together in a small bowl. Pour the dressing over the salad and toss gently to combine. Serve immediately. Yield: 6 servings.

Carol Reusch, Laureate Alpha Nu
Mississauga, Ontario, Canada

SPRING SALAD

2 heads romaine lettuce, torn into bite-size pieces
8 to 10 radishes, thinly sliced
12 cherry tomatoes
1 red onion, sliced and separated
1 (8-ounce) can mandarin oranges, drained
2/3 cup drained pineapple tidbits
8 to 12 strawberries, quartered
8 ounces feta cheese, crumbled
1/2 cup chopped walnuts
Croutons
Raspberry Salad Dressing

Combine the lettuce, radishes, tomatoes, onion, oranges, pineapple, strawberries, cheese, walnuts and croutons in a salad bowl. Add the Raspberry Salad Dressing just before serving. Toss and serve. Yield: 6 servings.

RASPBERRY SALAD DRESSING

1 cup raspberry vinegar
1/2 cup vegetable oil
1 to 4 tablespoons sugar

Place the vinegar, vegetable oil and sugar in a jar with a tight-fitting lid. Seal and shake vigorously to combine. Let stand for 1 to 2 hours. Shake again before serving.

Bertie Farabee, Laureate Beta Kappa
Haysville, Kansas

MANDARIN ORANGE SALAD

1/2 cup slivered almonds
3 tablespoons sugar
3/4 cup vegetable oil
6 tablespoons tarragon vinegar
3/4 teaspoon Tabasco sauce
6 tablespoons sugar
1 1/2 teaspoons salt
Dash of pepper
1 head romaine lettuce, torn into bite-size pieces
1 cup chopped celery
2 green onions, chopped
1 (11-ounce) can mandarin oranges, drained

Cook the almonds and sugar in a small skillet, stirring constantly until the sugar dissolves and the almonds are coated with sugar. Cool completely. Combine the oil, vinegar, Tabasco sauce, sugar, salt and pepper a blender container and process until mixed. Cover and chill thoroughly. Combine the lettuce, celery, green onions and oranges in a salad bowl. Add the almonds and desired amount of dressing at serving time. Toss and serve. Yield: 6 to 8 servings.

Beth Ezel, Zeta Zi
Algona, Iowa

CHAMPAGNE MANDARIN SALAD

1 bunch bok choy,
  chopped
1 red onion, chopped
1 (15-ounce) can
  mandarin oranges,
  drained

4 ounces blue cheese,
  crumbled
1/2 cup chopped pecans
1/2 cup Champagne salad
  dressing

Place the bok choy, onion, oranges, cheese and pecans in a salad bowl. Pour the salad dressing over the bok choy mixture. Toss gently to mix. Yield: 12 servings.

Sharon Donahue, Laureate Alpha Alpha
Wausau, Wisconsin

MANDARIN ORANGE AND RICE NOODLE TOSSED SALAD

1 head lettuce, torn into
  bite-size pieces
1 head romaine lettuce,
  torn into bite-size
  pieces
1 small onion, thinly
  sliced
1 (11-ounce) can
  mandarin oranges,
  drained

1 cup chopped celery
1 cup prepared rice
  noodles
1/4 cup vegetable oil
2 tablespoons sugar
2 tablespoons vinegar
1 tablespoon chopped
  fresh parsley

Combine the lettuce, onion, oranges, celery and rice noodles in a salad bowl and mix well. Whisk the oil, sugar, vinegar and parsley together in a small bowl. Pour the dressing over the salad. Toss gently to combine. Yield: 10 to 12 servings.

Jean Holeczy, Exemplar Preceptor
Spring Hill, Kansas

STRAWBERRY AND ORANGE TOSSED SALAD

1 (10-ounce) package
  romaine lettuce
1 (8-ounce) can
  mandarin oranges,
  drained
1 cup sliced fresh
  strawberries

1/3 cup thinly sliced red
  onion
1/2 cup chopped walnuts
  or pecans
Poppy seed salad
  dressing

Combine the lettuce, oranges, strawberries, onion and walnuts in a salad bowl. Pour the salad dressing over the salad. Toss and serve. Yield: 4 to 6 servings.

Judy Charron, Preceptor Eta
Lincoln, Illinois

STRAWBERRIES AND ROMAINE WITH POPPY SEED DRESSING

1 head romaine lettuce,
  torn into bite-size
  pieces
1 quart strawberries,
  sliced
1 small sweet onion,
  sliced

1/2 cup mayonnaise
2 tablespoons red wine
  vinegar
1/3 cup sugar
1/4 cup milk
1 tablespoon poppy
  seeds

Combine the lettuce, strawberries and onion in a large salad bowl and mix well. Combine the remaining ingredients in a jar with a tight-fitting lid. Seal and shake vigorously to mix. Add the dressing to the salad and toss well. Yield: 6 to 8 servings.

Marie Shaughnessy, Preceptor Beta Phi
Centennial, Colorado

BLUEBERRY SALAD

1 (10-ounce) package
  romaine lettuce
1 cup blueberries
1/2 cup cashews, chopped
8 ounces Monterey Jack
  cheese, cubed
1 tablespoon prepared
  mustard

2 tablespoons vinegar
3/4 cup vegetable oil
1/3 cup honey
1/2 teaspoon salt
2 to 3 teaspoons poppy
  seeds

Combine the lettuce, blueberries, cashews and cheese in a salad bowl. Whisk the mustard, vinegar, oil, honey, salt and poppy seeds together in a small bowl. Pour the dressing over the salad and toss to mix. Yield: 4 to 6 servings.

Olga Clarice, Preceptor Eta Phi
Satellite Beach, Florida

APPLE AND SWISS SPINACH SALAD

3/4 cup olive oil
1/3 cup cider vinegar
1 teaspoon salt
1 1/2 teaspoons dry
  mustard
1 1/2 teaspoons poppy
  seeds
3/4 cup sugar
1 (10-ounce) bag baby
  spinach leaves

1 head lettuce, torn into
  bite-size pieces
3 Granny Smith apples,
  finely chopped
1 cup slivered almonds
1 cup (4 ounces)
  shredded Swiss
  cheese

Place the first 6 ingredients in a jar with a tight-fitting lid. Seal and shake vigorously to combine. Combine the spinach, lettuce, apples, almonds and cheese in a salad bowl. Add the dressing. Toss and serve. Yield: 10 to 12 servings.

Becky Kneedy, Beta Mu
Macomb, Illinois

WINTER SALAD

This salad is easy to make and is a refreshing change from regular green salads. The red pears are available in winter.

3 tablespoons red wine vinegar	2 small heads radicchio, torn into bite-size pieces
2 teaspoons Dijon mustard	2 bunches arugula, torn into bite-size pieces
1/2 teaspoon salt	1/2 cup toasted pecans
1/2 teaspoon pepper	6 ounces Parmesan cheese, shaved
1/3 cup extra-virgin olive oil	
3 red pears, cut into wedges	
2 small heads Belgian endive, chopped	

Whisk the vinegar, mustard, salt and pepper together in a salad bowl. Add the olive oil slowly, whisking constantly. Add the pears and toss gently to coat. Add the endive, radicchio and arugula. Toss gently. Top with the pecans and cheese and serve.
Yield: 10 servings.

Jean Jewell, Beta Nu Master
Burlington, Ontario, Canada

NORTHWEST AUTUMN SALAD

1 head red leaf lettuce, torn into bite-size pieces	1/2 cup vegetable oil
1 head romaine lettuce, torn into bite-size pieces	2 tablespoons finely chopped green onions
2 Fuji apples, cut into thin wedges	1 tablespoon maple syrup
3/4 cup Glazed Pecans	1/4 cup cider vinegar
3/4 cup crumbled feta cheese	2 tablespoons fresh lemon juice
	1/4 teaspoon salt
	1/4 teaspoon pepper

Place the red leaf lettuce and romaine lettuce in a salad bowl. Layer the apples over the lettuce. Top with the pecans and cheese. Place the oil, green onions, maple syrup, vinegar, lemon juice, salt and pepper in a jar with a tight-fitting lid. Seal and shake vigorously to combine. Add the dressing just before serving. Toss and serve. Yield: 6 to 8 servings.

GLAZED PECANS

1/4 cup (1/2 stick) butter	1 teaspoon salt
2 tablespoons water	1 pound pecan halves
1/4 cup light corn syrup	

Combine the butter, water, corn syrup and salt in a medium saucepan and bring to a boil. Add the pecans and stir to coat. Spread the pecans on a foil-lined baking sheet. Bake at 250 degrees for 1 hour, stirring every 10 minutes. Cool completely.

Terri Blane, Xi Alpha Rho
Wenatchee, Washington

ARTICHOKE SPINACH SALAD

This salad is easy and delicious. If you're in a hurry, don't make the dressing. Use Italian dressing—it contains similar ingredients and works well.

12 cups torn fresh spinach	8 slices bacon, crisp-cooked and crumbled
8 green onions, chopped	1/2 cup cider vinegar
8 ounces fresh mushrooms, sliced	1/2 cup sugar
1 (8-ounce) can water chestnuts, drained and sliced	1/2 teaspoon salt
	1/2 teaspoon dry mustard
1 (6-ounce) jar marinated artichoke hearts, drained and quartered	1 teaspoon grated onion
	1 cup vegetable oil
	6 hard-cooked eggs, sliced (optional)
	Cherry tomatoes (optional)

Combine the spinach, green onions, mushrooms, water chestnuts, artichoke hearts and bacon in a salad bowl. Place the vinegar, sugar, salt, mustard and onion in a blender container and process until smooth. Add the oil in a fine stream, processing constantly. Drizzle the dressing over the salad. Top with the eggs and tomatoes if desired. Toss and serve.
Yield: 12 servings.

Elaine Sills, Beta Gamma Master
El Paso, Texas

❖ SPINACH SALAD WITH CARAMELIZED ONION DRESSING

2 sweet onions, sliced	1 (10-ounce) bag baby spinach
3 shallots, sliced	1 (14-ounce) can artichoke hearts, drained
2 tablespoons butter	
6 tablespoons brown sugar	
1/2 cup plus 1 tablespoon balsamic vinegar	4 ounces gorgonzola cheese, crumbled
2 cups grape tomatoes	

Sauté the onions and shallots in the butter over medium heat for 20 minutes or until golden. Add the brown sugar and cook for 10 minutes or until the onions are caramelized. Stir in the vinegar and cook for 5 more minutes. Combine the tomatoes, spinach and artichoke hearts in a salad bowl. Spoon the hot dressing over the salad. Top with the cheese. Serve immediately. Yield: 8 servings.

Mary Elizabeth Reinhart, Gamma Master
Milwaukee, Wisconsin

LUSCIOUS SPINACH SALAD

3 or 4 hard-cooked eggs, sliced	1 onion, chopped
8 slices crisp-cooked bacon, crumbled	1 cup vegetable oil
1 (20-ounce) can bean sprouts, drained	1/3 cup ketchup
	1/4 cup vinegar
	3/4 cup sugar
2 (10-ounce) bags spinach	1 teaspoon Worcestershire sauce

Combine the eggs, bacon, bean sprouts and spinach in a salad bowl. Place the onion, oil, ketchup, vinegar, sugar and Worcestershire in a jar with a tight-fitting lid. Seal and shake vigorously to combine. Add the dressing to the salad just before serving. Toss and serve. Yield: 18 to 20 servings.

Karen Dobbins, Preceptor Lambda Alpha
Laurie, Missouri

SPINACH SALAD WITH MUSTARD VINAIGRETTE

1/2 cup vinegar	1 head red leaf lettuce, torn into bite-size pieces
1 cup vegetable oil	
1 small onion, finely chopped	
1 1/3 cups sugar	1 (8-ounce) package garlic-flavored croutons
1 teaspoon salt	
1 teaspoon celery seeds	
1 tablespoon dry mustard	1 pound bacon, crisp-cooked and crumbled
1 pound baby spinach	5 hard-cooked eggs, finely chopped

Whisk the vinegar, oil, onion, sugar, salt, celery seed and mustard together in a bowl. Refrigerate, covered, for 8 to 12 hours. Combine the spinach, lettuce, croutons, bacon and eggs in a salad bowl. Refrigerate 1 to 8 hours. Bring the dressing to a boil in a saucepan over medium heat or in the microwave. Pour the dressing over the salad. Toss and serve immediately. Yield: 8 to 10 servings.

Ginger Schneider, Preceptor Beta Omicron
Rolla, Missouri

SPINACH AND ORANGE SALAD

10 cups torn spinach	1/2 cup sliced red onion
2 cups orange sections	1 cup fat-free Italian salad dressing
1 cup crumbled feta cheese	

Combine the spinach, orange, cheese and onion in a salad bowl. Add the dressing just before serving. Toss and serve. Yield: 10 servings.

Karen C. Wall, Kappa Upsilon
Bonaire, Georgia

MAPLE LEAF SPINACH AND STRAWBERRY SALAD

1/2 cup vegetable oil	2 (10-ounce) bags baby spinach
1/3 cup white wine vinegar	
2 to 3 tablespoons maple syrup	1 small red onion
	1 pint strawberries, sliced
1 tablespoon Dijon mustard	2/3 cup salted sunflower seeds
1/2 teaspoon salt	

Whisk the oil, vinegar, maple syrup, mustard and salt together in a small bowl. Combine the spinach, onion and strawberries in a salad bowl. Top with the sunflower seeds. Add the dressing and toss to combine. Serve immediately. Yield: 6 servings.

Nancy McDonald, Laureate Alpha Iota
Ottawa, Ontario, Canada

SPINACH PECAN SALAD

This salad was made by my newly married daughter for a special Mother's Day dinner. Needless to say, I had to get the recipe from her!

1/2 cup chopped pecans	2 pears, peeled and chopped (optional)
1/2 cup dried cranberries	
1/4 cup (1/2 stick) butter	Raspberry vinaigrette salad dressing
1 (10-ounce) package baby spinach or spring mix lettuce	

Sauté the pecans and dried cranberries in the butter in small skillet. Place the spinach and pears in a salad bowl. Top with the pecan mixture. Add the salad dressing just before serving. Toss and serve. Yield: 4 to 6 servings.

Linda Daniels, Laureate Tau
Leawood, Kansas

SPANISH SLAW

1 (16-ounce) bag coleslaw mix	1 (16-ounce) bottle Italian salad dressing
1 red bell pepper, cut into small strips	Salt
6 or 7 green chiles, cut into small strips	White pepper to taste
	Black pepper to taste
1 small onion, minced	Celery seed to taste

Combine the coleslaw, bell pepper, chiles and onion in a large bowl. Add the salad dressing and seasonings. Toss to mix. Refrigerate, covered, up to 8 hours. Toss and serve. Yield: 6 to 8 servings.

Linda Darnell, Delta Omega
Albuquerque, New Mexico

SAUERKRAUT SALAD

2 cups sugar	1 (22-ounce) jar
1 cup vegetable oil	sauerkraut
1 cup vinegar	2 cups chopped celery
1/2 teaspoon pepper	1 cup shredded carrots
1 (32-ounce) jar	1 cup chopped sweet
sauerkraut	onion

Combine the sugar, oil, vinegar and pepper in a saucepan over medium-high heat. Cook, stirring occasionally, until the sugar dissolves. Combine the sugar mixture with the sauerkraut, celery, carrots and onion in a large bowl. Refrigerate, covered, for 8 to 12 hours. Yield: 12 servings.

Verna L. Creech, Preceptor Beta Sigma
Tillamook, Oregon

FIVE-VEGETABLE SLAW

3 cups shredded cabbage	1/2 cup fat-free sour
5 plum tomatoes, seeded	cream
and chopped	1/4 cup reduced-fat
1 cup broccoli florets,	mayonnaise
cut into small pieces	1 tablespoon cider
1 cup cauliflower	vinegar
florets, cut into small	3/4 teaspoon salt
pieces	1/4 teaspoon pepper
1/2 cup chopped red onion	

Combine the cabbage, tomatoes, broccoli, cauliflower and onion in a large bowl. Combine the sour cream, mayonnaise, vinegar, salt and pepper in a small bowl; whisk until smooth. Pour the sour cream mixture over the cabbage mixture and mix well. Cover and chill thoroughly. Yield: 6 servings.

Gloria Cobb, Alpha Alpha
Decatur, Alabama

BEST BARBECUE COLESLAW

2 (10-ounce) packages	1/2 cup mayonnaise
finely shredded	1/4 cup milk
cabbage	1/4 cup buttermilk
1 carrot, grated	2 1/2 tablespoons lemon
1/2 cup sugar	juice
1/4 teaspoon salt	1 1/2 tablespoons vinegar
1/8 teaspoon pepper	

Combine the cabbage and carrot in a large bowl. Combine the sugar, salt, pepper, mayonnaise, milk, buttermilk, lemon juice and vinegar in a bowl; whisk until smooth. Pour the mayonnaise mixture over the cabbage mixture and stir well. Refrigerate, covered, for 2 hours. Yield: 8 to 10 servings.

Susan H. Lincoln, Mu Omega
Perry, Florida

CRANBERRY AND WALNUT COLESLAW

1 cup coarsely chopped	1/2 cup thinly sliced red
walnuts	onion
1 cup dried cranberries	1/3 cup red wine vinegar
2 cups thinly sliced red	or cider vinegar
cabbage	1/3 cup vegetable oil
2 cups thinly sliced	1/3 cup sugar
green cabbage	1 teaspoon celery seeds

Combine the walnuts, cranberries, cabbage and onion in a large bowl. Combine the vinegar, oil, sugar and celery seeds in a bowl; whisk until smooth. Pour the vinegar mixture over the cabbage mixture and stir well. Refrigerate, covered, for 3 hours. Stir and drain all liquid before serving. Yield: 8 to 10 servings.

Janice Crissup, Preceptor Alpha Upsilon
Lawrenceville, Georgia

FOUR-MONTH CABBAGE SALAD

8 cups chopped cabbage	2 cups cider vinegar
4 onions, chopped	1 teaspoon salt
1 green bell pepper,	1/4 teaspoon turmeric
chopped	(optional)
1 red bell pepper,	2 1/2 cups sugar
chopped	1 teaspoon celery seeds
1 (7-ounce) jar	1 1/2 teaspoons mustard
pimentos, chopped	seeds

Combine the cabbage, onions, peppers and pimentos in a large bowl and mix well. Combine the vinegar, salt, turmeric, sugar, celery seeds and mustard seeds in a saucepan and bring to a boil. Pour the hot vinegar mixture over the cabbage mixture and stir well. Cool to room temperature. Refrigerate, covered, for 24 hours before serving. Store in the refrigerator for up to 4 months. Yield: 24 servings.

Janet McGrath, Preceptor Delta Zeta
Manitou Beach, Michigan

NUTTY NEVADA SLAW

This slaw is delicious and very popular. If you prepare it for an event, do not stir the ingredients until serving time.

1 (2-ounce) package	2 packages ramen
slivered almonds	noodles, crumbled
2 tablespoons sesame	6 tablespoons sugar
seeds	1 teaspoon salt
1 tablespoon butter	1 teaspoon pepper
1 (16-ounce) bag	6 tablespoons rice
coleslaw mix	vinegar or white
8 green onions, thinly	vinegar
sliced	1/4 cup vegetable oil

Brown the almonds and sesame seeds in the butter in a small skillet. Cool completely. Combine the coleslaw and onions with the almond mixture in a salad bowl. Sprinkle the noodles over the coleslaw mixture. Combine the sugar, salt, pepper, vinegar and oil in a small bowl and mix well. Pour the dressing over the slaw and toss to mix. Serve immediately. Yield: 10 servings.

Cheryl Brown, Preceptor Alpha Omega
Mandeville, Louisiana

BIRD'S NEST SALAD

The longer this salad stands the better. It will keep in the refrigerator for up to one week.

2 (3-ounce) packages
   ramen noodles,
   crumbled
1/4 cup sunflower seeds
1 (2-ounce) package
   slivered almonds

1/2 bunch green onions
1 cup vegetable oil
1/4 tablespoon soy sauce
3/4 cup sugar
1 (16-ounce) bag
   broccoli coleslaw mix

Combine the noodles, sunflower seeds and almonds in a baking pan. Bake at 325 degrees for 20 minutes or until toasted. Combine the seasoning packets from the ramen noodles, green onions, oil, soy sauce and sugar in a salad bowl. Add the coleslaw mix and toss to combine. Top with noodle mixture and mix well. Refrigerate, covered, for 8 to 12 hours. Stir and serve. Yield: 10 servings.

Lucille Davis, Laureate Xi
Nashville, Tennessee

CHINESE COLESLAW

1 cup slivered almonds
2 (3-ounce) packages
   chicken-flavor ramen
   noodles, crumbled
1/4 cup sugar
1 cup vegetable oil
6 tablespoons red wine
   vinegar

2 teaspoons salt
1 head cabbage, finely
   chopped, or
   1 (16-ounce) bag
   coleslaw mix
1/4 cup sesame seeds
4 green onions, chopped

Place the almonds in a large baking pan. Bake at 350 degrees for 5 to 8 minutes or until toasted. Cool completely. Combine the sugar, oil, red wine vinegar, salt and 1 seasoning packet from the ramen noodles in a jar with a tight-fitting lid. Seal and shake vigorously to combine. Toss the cabbage, sesame seeds and almonds together in a salad bowl. Add the onions and noodles and mix well. Pour the dressing over the salad just before serving. Yield: 10 servings.

Pat Moody, Laureate Tau
Clovis, New Mexico

SUMI SLAW

1/4 cup rice vinegar
2 tablespoons balsamic
   vinegar
1 teaspoon salt
1 teaspoon pepper
1 cup olive oil
1/4 cup sugar, or
   equivalent sugar
   substitute
1/4 cup toasted almonds
1/4 cup sesame seeds

1 cup halved green
   grapes
1 head of cabbage,
   chopped, or
   1 (16-ounce) bag
   coleslaw mix
8 green onions, chopped
2 (3-ounce) packages
   ramen noodles,
   crumbled

Combine the rice vinegar, balsamic vinegar, salt, pepper, oil and sugar in a jar with a tight-fitting lid. Seal and shake vigorously to combine. Toss the almonds, sesame seeds, grapes, cabbage and onions together in a salad bowl. Pour the dressing over the salad and mix well. Add the ramen noodles just before serving. Mix well. Yield: 6 to 10 servings.

Thomasine Morris
Miami, Florida

CRANOCCOLI SALAD

1 bunch of broccoli,
   chopped
1/2 cup sunflower seeds
1 cup dried cranberries
1/2 cup raisins
1/2 cup finely chopped
   celery

12 ounces bacon, crisp-
   cooked and crumbled
1 small red onion, thinly
   sliced
1 cup mayonnaise
1/3 cup sugar
1 teaspoon cider vinegar

Toss the first 7 ingredients together in a salad bowl. Whisk the mayonnaise, sugar and vinegar in a small bowl. Pour over the salad and toss. Chill, covered, for 1 hour. Yield: 6 servings.

Gurli Lockerman, Alpha Lambda Master
Palm Springs, California

BROCCOLI SALAD

1 large bunch broccoli,
   separated into florets
1 small red onion,
   chopped
10 to 12 slices bacon,
   crisp-cooked and
   crumbled

1 cup raisins
3 tablespoons vinegar
1/3 cup mayonnaise
1/3 cup sugar

Toss the broccoli, onion, bacon and raisins together in a salad bowl. Whisk the vinegar, mayonnaise and sugar together in a small bowl. Pour the dressing over the salad and mix well. Chill for 1 hour before serving. Yield: 6 to 8 servings.

Sandra Spear, Upsilon
Tobaccoville, North Carolina

BROCCOLI AND ALMOND SALAD

4 cups broccoli florets
1 cup chopped celery
2/3 cup toasted slivered almonds
1 cup halved seedless green grapes
1 cup halved seedless red grapes
1/2 cup chopped green onions
1 cup mayonnaise
1/3 cup sugar
1 tablespoon vinegar
8 slices bacon, crisp-cooked and crumbled

Toss the broccoli, celery, almonds, grapes and green onions together in a salad bowl. Whisk the mayonnaise, sugar and vinegar together in a small bowl. Pour the mayonnaise mixture over the broccoli mixture and mix well. Top with the bacon.
Yield: 8 servings.

Sherry Burrell, Preceptor Rho
Waterloo, Iowa

BROCCOLI WALDORF SALAD

I grew up in a large farm family. My mother doubled or tripled this recipe and prepared it ahead of time.

6 cups broccoli florets
1 large apple, chopped
1 cup seedless grapes
1/2 cup chopped pecans
1/2 cup mayonnaise-type salad dressing
1/4 cup sugar
2 tablespoons vinegar

Toss the broccoli, apple, grapes and pecans together in a salad bowl. Whisk the salad dressing, sugar and vinegar together in a small bowl. Pour the dressing over the salad and mix well. Refrigerate, covered, for 8 to 12 hours. Yield: 6 servings.

Naomi E. Golden, Alpha Nu Master
Van Buren, Ohio

FAVORITE BROCCOLI AND CAULIFLOWER SALAD

1 bunch broccoli, cut into bite-size pieces
1 head cauliflower, cut into bite-size pieces
1 cup cashews
1 cup golden raisins
1/2 onion, finely chopped
1 1/2 tablespoons sugar
1 cup mayonnaise-type salad dressing
1 tablespoon cider vinegar
2 teaspoons milk
6 slices bacon, crisp-cooked and crumbled

Toss the first 5 ingredients together in a salad bowl. Whisk the sugar, salad dressing, vinegar and milk together in a small bowl. Pour the dressing over the salad and mix well. Refrigerate, covered, for 8 to 12 hours for best flavor. Stir in the bacon just before serving. Yield: 15 to 20 servings.

Patsy Bratton, Laureate Alpha Mu
Angola, Indiana

FRESH CAULIFLOWER AND BACON SALAD

8 ounces bacon, crisp-cooked and crumbled or 1 (3-ounce) jar bacon bits
1 (1-ounce) package ranch salad dressing mix
1 cup mayonnaise or mayonnaise-type salad dressing
1 head cauliflower, cut into bite-size pieces
1 small head lettuce, chopped
1/4 cup Italian salad dressing (optional)
Chopped broccoli (optional)

Combine the bacon, salad dressing mix and mayonnaise in a small bowl and mix well. Pour the bacon mixture over a combination of the cauliflower and lettuce in a salad bowl and mix well. Add the Italian salad dressing and broccoli if desired and mix well. Refrigerate, covered, for 8 to 12 hours.
Yield: 12 servings.

Lynda Runyon, Kappa Chi
Woodstock, Georgia

TOMATO ASPIC

1 (5-ounce) can tomato juice cocktail
3 1/4 cups tomato juice
2 ribs celery, chopped
10 green onions, chopped
1/4 cup chopped green olives
1 tablespoon sugar
1 teaspoon salt
1 teaspoon Worcestershire sauce
1/2 teaspoon unflavored gelatin
1/2 cup cold water
2 tablespoons lemon juice
2 tablespoons olive juice

Combine the tomato juice cocktail, tomato juice, celery, onions, olives, sugar, salt and Worcestershire sauce in a large saucepan. Bring to a boil. Remove from the heat. Soften the gelatin in the water. Add the softened gelatin to the tomato juice mixture and mix well. Stir in the lemon juice and olive juice. Spoon the aspic into individual molds or an 8x8-inch dish. Chill until set. Yield: 8 servings.

Valerie Johnson, Xi Alpha Nu
Baker, Montana

HOT POTATO SALAD

6 cups chopped cooked potatoes
1/2 cup chopped celery
1/2 cup chopped green onions
1 dill pickle, chopped
1 teaspoon celery seed
1 cup mayonnaise
1/3 cup vinegar
1 teaspoon dry mustard
1 teaspoon sugar
1 teaspoon salt

Combine the potatoes, celery, onions, pickle and celery seed in a large bowl. Whisk the mayonnaise, vinegar, mustard, sugar and salt together in a small bowl. Pour the mayonnaise mixture over the potato mixture and toss gently to mix. Place the salad over hot water in a double boiler. Cook for 25 to 35 minutes. Yield: 6 to 8 servings.

Beverly Schwab, Laureate Omega
Memphis, Tennessee

GERMAN POTATO SALAD

5 large potatoes, cooked, peeled and chopped	1/4 cup vegetable oil
1/4 onion, chopped	1/2 teaspoon dried parsley
1 teaspoon salt	1 beef bouillon cube
1/4 teaspoon pepper	1/2 cup boiling water
1/4 cup vinegar	

Combine the potatoes, onion, salt, pepper, vinegar, oil and parsley in a large bowl. Toss gently to mix. Dissolve the bouillon cube in the water. Stir into the potato mixture. Yield: 6 to 8 servings.

Margot Peverley, Preceptor Chi
Rawlins, Wyoming

OVERNIGHT GERMAN POTATO SALAD

1 tablespoon salt	1/2 cup (scant) vegetable oil
1 teaspoon sugar	
1/4 teaspoon pepper	3/4 cup warm water
1/4 teaspoon celery seeds	3 pounds small potatoes, cooked, peeled and chopped
1 small onion, finely chopped	
1 to 2 teaspoons dried parsley	1 tablespoon mayonnaise
1/2 cup (scant) cider vinegar	

Whisk the salt, sugar, pepper, celery seeds, onion, parsley, cider vinegar, oil and water together in a large bowl. Add the potatoes and stir gently. Marinate, covered, at room temperature for 8 to 12 hours. Add the mayonnaise and toss gently. Serve immediately. Yield: 6 to 8 servings.

Janice Reisch, Laureate Alpha Rho
Worthington, Ohio

BEST POTATO SALAD AROUND

5 pounds potatoes, chopped	4 1/2 tablespoons relish
12 hard-cooked eggs	4 cups mayonnaise
2 1/4 tablespoons prepared mustard	1 cup sugar
	Salt and pepper to taste

Place the potatoes and water to cover in a large stockpot. Boil until almost fork-tender. Drain well. Shred

the potatoes and eggs in a food processor. Combine the potatoes, eggs, mustard, relish, mayonnaise, sugar, salt and pepper in a large bowl and mix well. Refrigerate, covered, for 8 to 12 hours. Yield: 16 servings.

Carol Fielder, Laureate Kappa
Beatrice, Nebraska

OKLAHOMA CAVIAR

1 (16-ounce) can white hominy, drained	1 or 2 jalapeño chiles, chopped (optional)
2 (16-ounce) cans black-eyed peas, rinsed and drained	1/2 cup chopped broccoli (optional)
4 or 5 green onions, chopped	1/2 cup chopped carrots (optional)
1 or 2 garlic cloves, chopped	1/2 cup chopped cauliflower (optional)
1/2 small onion, chopped	1/2 cup chopped celery (optional)
2 or 3 tomatoes, chopped, or 1 (16-ounce) can diced tomatoes, drained	1 (8-ounce) bottle Italian salad dressing

Combine the hominy, black-eyed peas, green onions, garlic, onion, tomatoes, jalapeño, broccoli, carrots, cauliflower and celery in a large bowl. Add the salad dressing and mix well. Refrigerate, covered, until serving time. Yield: 6 to 8 servings.

Sharon Rutherford, Alpha Omicron Theta
Alvarado, Texas

BLACK-EYED SUSAN SALAD

1 (15-ounce) can black-eyed peas, rinsed and drained	2 tablespoons finely chopped onion
1 (10-ounce) package frozen corn kernels, thawed	1/2 cup finely chopped celery
	1/4 cup cider vinegar
1 small green bell pepper, finely chopped	2 tablespoons Worcestershire sauce
	1/4 cup vegetable oil
1 small red bell pepper, finely chopped	1 tablespoon sugar
	1/2 teaspoon garlic salt
	1/8 teaspoon salt

Combine the black-eyed peas, corn, bell peppers, onion and celery in a large bowl. Whisk the cider vinegar, Worcestershire sauce, oil, sugar, garlic salt and salt together in a bowl. Pour the vinegar mixture over the corn mixture and mix well. Refrigerate, covered, for 3 to 4 hours. Yield: 6 to 8 servings.

Darlene Ebeling, Xi Beta Epsilon
Woodward, Oklahoma

CONFETTI SALAD

1 (30-ounce) can black beans, rinsed and drained	1 avocado, finely chopped
1 cup corn kernels	1/4 cup lime juice
2 cups halved grape or cherry tomatoes	2 teaspoons grated lime zest
	1/4 teaspoon salt

Toss the beans, corn, tomatoes, avocado, lime juice, lime zest and salt together in a large salad bowl. Serve immediately or refrigerate, covered, for 8 to 12 hours and serve cold. Yield: 12 servings.

Kathleen J. Shafer, Xi Theta Eta
Mifflinburg, Pennsylvania

BLACK BEAN AND CORN SALAD

1 (16-ounce) can black beans, rinsed and drained	1 cup sliced zucchini (optional)
1 cup thawed frozen corn kernels	1/4 cup olive oil
1 tomato, chopped	1 1/2 tablespoons lime juice
1/2 cup sliced green onions	1/2 teaspoon salt
1/2 cup chopped green bell pepper	1 cup (4 ounces) shredded cheese

Toss the beans, corn, tomato, green onions, bell pepper and zucchini together in a large salad bowl. Whisk the olive oil, lime juice and salt together in a small bowl. Pour the olive oil mixture over the bean mixture and toss to combine. Refrigerate, covered, until serving time. Sprinkle with the cheese just before serving. Yield: 8 servings.

Mary S. Beamer, Xi Delta Xi
Oakridge, Oregon

LEBANESE TABOULI

1/2 cup bulgur wheat	2 tomatoes, finely chopped
3 bunches parsley, finely chopped	2/3 cup olive oil
2 bunches green onions, finely chopped	1/2 cup lemon juice
1 small yellow onion, finely chopped	Salt and pepper to taste
	Romaine lettuce leaves

Rinse the bulgur wheat in cold water. Drain well. Toss the bulgur wheat, parsley, green onions, yellow onion, tomatoes, olive oil, lemon juice, salt and pepper together in a large salad bowl. Serve over lettuce leaves. Yield: 12 to 15 servings.

Barbara Lindsey, Xi Omicron Lambda
Blythe, California

TABOULI WITH RICE

2 (6-ounce) packages wild rice, prepared	1/3 cup extra-virgin olive oil
1 (1/2-ounce) jar parsley flakes	Chopped celery to taste
1 (3-ounce) jar dry minced onions	Chopped green bell pepper to taste
3/4 cup lemon juice	Chopped red bell pepper to taste

Toss the cooled rice, parsley, onions, lemon juice, olive oil, celery and bell peppers together in a large salad bowl. Refrigerate, covered, for 8 to 12 hours. Yield: 20 servings.

Linda J. Gemuend, Beta Delta
New Smyrna Beach, Florida

SANTA FE SALAD

This salad says "Southwest" and is good served with grilled chicken breasts.

1 large avocado, finely chopped	6 cups torn lettuce leaves
1/2 cup sour cream	2 large tomatoes, finely chopped
3 tablespoons fresh lemon juice	1 cup (4 ounces) shredded Cheddar cheese
1 tablespoon minced shallots	1/2 cup sliced black olives
1 tablespoon white wine or water	1 cup crushed tortilla chips
1/4 teaspoon hot sauce	
2 large avocados, sliced	
1 tablespoon lemon juice	

Place the finely chopped avocado, sour cream, 3 tablespoons lemon juice, shallots, wine and hot sauce in a blender container and process until smooth. Pour the avocado mixture into a bowl. Refrigerate, covered, for 3 hours. Place the sliced avocados in a large bowl. Sprinkle with 1 tablespoon lemon juice and toss gently. Layer the lettuce, tomatoes, cheese and olives over the avocado. Refrigerate, covered, until chilled. Pour the dressing over the salad and toss gently to coat. Garnish with the tortilla chips. Serve immediately. Yield: 6 to 8 servings.

Gloria F. Mendiola, Alpha Omicron
Roswell, New Mexico

Bonnie Miller, Preceptor Xi Nu, Los Banos, California, prepares **Spinach Salad** *by combining one 6-ounce bag spinach, 1 chopped large Bartlett pear, and 1/3 cup crumbled blue cheese in a salad bowl. She then adds balsamic vinaigrette salad dressing and tosses to combine. The salad should be served immediately.*

Main Dish Salads

DRIED CRANBERRY CHICKEN SALAD

6 (8-ounce) cans
  chopped cooked
  chicken, drained
1 (8-ounce) package
  dates, chopped
1 (6-ounce) package
  dried cranberries
1 cup mayonnaise
1 cup chopped celery
1 cup chopped walnuts
Old Bay seasoning to
  taste

Combine the chicken, dates, dried cranberries, mayonnaise, celery, walnuts and Old Bay seasoning in a large bowl. Mix well. Refrigerate, covered, for 8 to 12 hours. Yield: 10 to 12 servings.

Diann C. Walters, Delta Kappa
Ellisville, Mississippi

ALMOND CHICKEN SALAD

6 tablespoons sugar
2 teaspoons salt
1/4 teaspoon black
  pepper
1/4 cup vinegar
1/4 cup vegetable oil
2 tablespoons lemon
  juice
1 tablespoon chopped
  fresh gingerroot
3 skinless boneless
  chicken breasts
1 1/2 heads lettuce, cut
  into bite-size pieces
3 green onions, chopped
1/4 cup sesame seeds
1 (2-ounce) package
  sliced almonds
1 cucumber, sliced

Whisk the sugar, salt, pepper, vinegar, oil and lemon juice together in a small bowl. Refrigerate, covered, for 8 to 12 hours. Add the gingerroot and mix well. Place the chicken in a baking dish. Bake at 350 degrees for 30 minutes or until cooked through. Chop or shred the chicken. Toss the chicken, lettuce, green onions, sesame seeds, almonds and cucumber together in a large bowl. Pour the dressing over the salad and mix well. Yield: 6 servings.

Deanie Binsfield, Alpha Chi Master
Spokane, Washington

PECAN CHICKEN SALAD WITH GRAPES

1/2 teaspoon curry
  powder
1 tablespoon vegetable
  oil
2 teaspoons minced
  candied gingerroot
2 tablespoons wine
  vinegar
2 tablespoons soy sauce
2 tablespoons finely
  chopped onion
1 1/4 cups mayonnaise
4 chicken breasts,
  cooked and chopped
1/2 cup sliced water
  chestnuts
1/2 cup seedless green
  grapes
1/2 cup chopped pecans
1/2 cup finely chopped
  celery
Lettuce leaves
Sliced pineapple
Sliced avocado
Sliced hard-cooked eggs
Paprika to taste

Heat the curry powder in the oil in a small skillet over medium heat until fragrant. Whisk the oil mixture together with the gingerroot, wine vinegar, soy sauce, onion and mayonnaise in a large bowl. Add the chicken, water chestnuts, grapes, pecans and celery. Refrigerate, covered, until chilled. Serve over lettuce leaves with pineapple, avocado and eggs. Sprinkle with paprika. Yield: 18 servings.

Dianna Mathis, Xi Alpha Kappa
Guymon, Oklahoma

GLORIFIED CHICKEN SALAD

1/2 cup red wine vinegar	1/2 cup bacon bits
2 teaspoons dry mustard	1/2 cup sunflower seeds
1/2 cup finely chopped red onion	2 cups (8 ounces) shredded mozzarella cheese
1 cup sugar	
1/2 cup canola oil	1 1/2 cups (6 ounces) grated Parmesan cheese
2 (10-ounce) bags mixed salad greens	
3 or 4 chopped cooked chicken breasts	Dried cherries or dried cranberries

Whisk the vinegar, mustard, onion and sugar together in a small bowl. Add the oil gradually, whisking constantly. Toss the salad greens, chicken, bacon bits, sunflower seeds, mozzarella cheese, Parmesan cheese and cherries together in a large salad bowl. Pour the dressing over the salad just before serving. Yield: 8 to 10 servings.

Sharon Rustemeyer, Xi Mu Iota
Salisbury, Missouri

WILD RICE CHICKEN SALAD

2 (6-ounce) jars marinated artichokes	2 celery ribs, thinly sliced
2 (6-ounce) boxes long grain and wild rice mix, prepared	5 green onions, chopped
	1 (2-ounce) can sliced black olives
4 cups chopped cooked chicken	1 cup mayonnaise
1 red bell pepper, chopped	1 1/2 teaspoons curry powder
	Lettuce leaves

Drain the artichokes, reserving 1/2 cup liquid. Combine the artichokes, rice, chicken, bell pepper, celery, green onions and olives in a large bowl. Whisk the reserved liquid together with the mayonnaise and curry powder in a small bowl. Pour over the rice mixture and mix well. Refrigerate, covered, for 4 to 8 hours. Serve over lettuce leaves.
Yield: 6 to 10 servings.

Patricia A. Siron, Laureate Gamma Mu
Mexico, Missouri

HAWAIIAN CURRY CHICKEN DELIGHT

3 cups chopped cooked chicken	1/2 cup macadamias, crushed
1 cup chopped celery	1 cup mayonnaise
1 tart apple, chopped	2 teaspoons curry powder
1 (11-ounce) can mandarin oranges, drained and chopped	1 teaspoon salt
	Lettuce leaves

Combine the chicken and the next 7 ingredients in a large bowl. Mix well. Refrigerate, covered, for 2 hours. Serve over lettuce leaves. Yield: 6 servings.

Patricia R. Conrath, Alpha Lambda
Cheney, Washington

CURRY CHICKEN CROISSANTS

1/2 cup mayonnaise	1/2 cup chopped walnuts
2 tablespoons sour cream	1/3 cup finely chopped celery
3/4 teaspoon curry powder	2 tablespoons grated onion
1/8 teaspoon Cajun seasoning	4 to 6 croissants, halved
2 1/2 cups chopped cooked chicken	Lettuce leaves

Whisk the mayonnaise, sour cream, curry powder and Cajun seasoning together in a small bowl. Chop the chicken in a food processor fitted with a steel blade. Combine the chicken, walnuts, celery and onion in a large bowl. Add the mayonnaise mixture and mix well. Refrigerate, covered, for 1 hour. Spread the chicken salad over the bottom halves of the croissants. Top with the lettuce and the top halves of the croissants. Yield: 4 to 6 servings.

Joanna Remley, Delta Epsilon
Northwood, Ohio

❖ CHICKEN CAESAR SALAD WRAPS

2 boneless skinless chicken breast halves	4 cups thinly sliced romaine lettuce
2 garlic cloves, minced	3/4 cup seasoned croutons
1/4 cup chopped red onion	1/2 cup fat-free Caesar salad dressing
1/4 cup chopped black olives	6 (8-inch) reduced-fat flour tortillas
1/4 cup chopped red bell pepper	
1/4 cup grated Parmesan cheese	

Sauté the chicken and garlic in a nonstick skillet over medium heat for 5 minutes each side or until the chicken is cooked through. Remove the chicken from the skillet and let cool. Cut into 1/4-inch-thick strips. Toss the chicken, onion, olives, bell pepper, cheese, lettuce, croutons and salad dressing together in a large bowl. Spoon 3/4 cup of the chicken mixture onto each tortilla. Roll to enclose the filling. Cut each wrap into halves. Yield: 6 servings.

Zonna F. Craig, Laureate Theta Eta
Livingston, Texas

ORIENTAL DUCK SALAD

1 duckling	1/2 to 1 tablespoon
1 onion	toasted sesame seeds
2 teaspoons garlic	1 (8-ounce) can sliced
powder	water chestnuts,
2 teaspoons rosemary or	drained (optional)
herbes de Provence	Oriental Sauce
2 (5-ounce) bags spring	
mix salad greens	

Preheat the oven to 400 degrees. Rinse the duck and pat dry. Place the onion inside the duck. Cut a criss-cross pattern into the duck skin and rub with the garlic powder and rosemary. Place the duck in a roasting pan in the hot oven and decrease the heat to 375 degrees. Bake for 2 hours or until a meat thermometer inserted into the thickest portion of the duck registers 180 degrees. Cool completely. Remove the skin and fat and place in a large skillet over low heat. Cook until the fat melts and the skin is crisp. Drain the fat and reserve the skin. Shred the duck meat. Toss the duck meat, salad greens, sesame seeds and water chestnuts together in a large salad bowl. Top with the reserved duck skin and the Oriental Sauce.
Yield: 4 to 6 servings.

ORIENTAL SAUCE

1 (7-ounce) jar hoisin	2 tablespoons chopped
sauce	fresh gingerroot
1/2 cup rice vinegar	2 teaspoons toasted
1/2 teaspoon ground	sesame seeds
ginger	11/2 teaspoons sugar

Bring the hoisin sauce, vinegar, ground ginger, gingerroot, sesame seeds and sugar to a boil in small saucepan, stirring constantly. Reduce the heat and simmer for 4 minutes. Cool completely.

Cathy Robb, Preceptor Alpha Beta
Harvey, Louisiana

SHRIMP AND ORZO SALAD

16 ounces orzo	2 teaspoons lemon juice
8 ounces peeled cooked	Dash of salt
medium shrimp	Dadh of black pepper
2 ribs celery, sliced	Dash of cayenne pepper
1 large tomato, finely	1/2 cup mayonnaise
chopped	Old Bay seasoning to
1/2 cup frozen peas,	taste
thawed and blanched	Lettuce leaves

Prepare the orzo using the package instructions. Toss the orzo, shrimp, celery, tomato, peas, lemon juice, salt, black pepper, cayenne pepper, mayonnaise and Old Bay seasoning together in a large salad bowl. Chill thoroughly. Serve over lettuce leaves.
Yield: 6 to 8 servings.

Carole Knapp, Preceptor Omega
Beaufort, South Carolina

ROAST BEEF SALAD

1 head romaine lettuce,	3 large tomatoes,
torn into bite-size	chopped
pieces	1 avocado, chopped
2 cups chopped cooked	1 cup Italian salad
roast beef	dressing
1 onion, chopped	

Toss all the ingredients together in a large salad bowl.
Yield: 4 servings.

Barbara Karakas, Laureate Gamma Theta
Alta Loma, California

❖ SALPICON

2 flank steaks or	1 (4-ounce) can
briskets	tomatoes with green
Salt and pepper to taste	chiles
2 tablespoons vegetable	2 to 4 jalapeño chiles,
oil	chopped
2 cups water	3 tablespoons jalapeño
1 tablespoon salt	liquid (from jarred
1 (1-ounce) packages	jalapeño chiles)
garlic salad dressing	3/4 cup chopped sweet
mix	onions
1/3 cup vegetable oil	8 ounces Monterey Jack
1/3 cup olive oil	cheese, cut into cubes
1/3 cup red wine vinegar	2 tomatoes, chopped
1/4 cup fresh lemon juice	1 avocado, finely
or lime juice	chopped

Season the beef with salt and pepper. Brown the beef in 2 tablespoons vegetable oil in a large heavy skillet over medium heat. Add the water and 1 tablespoon salt. Cover and bring to a boil. Reduce the heat and simmer for 11/2 hours or until fork tender. Cool completely. Slice across the grain and shred with a fork. Whisk the salad dressing mix, 1/3 cup vegetable oil, olive oil and wine vinegar together in a small bowl. Pour over the beef in a large bowl and toss to coat. Refrigerate, covered, for 8 hours. Combine the lemon juice, tomatoes with green chiles, jalapeño chiles and jalapeño liquid in a small bowl; mix well. Let stand for 30 minutes at room temperature. Toss the onions, cheese, tomatoes, avocado, beef, salad dressing mixture and jalapeño mixture together in a large salad bowl. Serve with warm corn tortillas.
Yield: 6 to 8 servings.

Anne Elmore-Devinny, Laureate Beta Psi
Orlando, Florida

MY TACO SALAD

An organization I belong to demands that I bring this salad to our annual spring luncheon. If I take anything else the members don't hesitate to let me know how disappointed they are.

1 pound ground beef	2 large tomatoes, finely
1 large onion, chopped	chopped
1 envelope taco	1 (3-ounce) can pitted
seasoning	black olives, drained
1 (3-ounce) can diced	16 ounces Cheddar
green chiles, drained	cheese, shredded
1 (15-ounce) can kidney	1/2 (15-ounce) bag corn
beans, rinsed and	chips, coarsely
drained	crushed

Brown the ground beef with the chopped onion in a skillet, stirring until the ground beef is crumbly. Stir in the taco seasoning. Drain well. Toss the ground beef mixture, green chiles, kidney beans, chopped tomatoes, black olives, half the Cheddar cheese and half the crushed corn chips in a large salad bowl. Top with the remaining Cheddar cheese and crushed corn chips. Serve immediately.
Yield: 10 to 12 servings.

Barbara R. Wright, Gamma Master
Woodland, California

MARINATED PASTA SALAD

12 ounces bow tie pasta,	4 bunches green onions,
cooked and drained	white parts only,
1 tablespoon olive oil	chopped
2 bunches asparagus,	2 teaspoons oregano
trimmed and	2 teaspoons basil
blanched	1/2 cup red wine vinegar
4 cups chopped	2 tablespoons sugar
tomatoes or cherry	
tomatoes	

Combine the pasta and olive oil in a large bowl and stir gently. Refrigerate, covered, until chilled. Cut the asparagus into bite-size pieces. Toss the pasta, tomatoes, green onions, oregano and basil together in a large salad bowl. Whisk the wine vinegar and sugar together in a small bowl. Pour the vinegar mixture over the pasta mixture and toss gently. Add the asparagus just before serving and toss gently.
Yield: 8 servings.

Mary Lou Loatsch, Preceptor Gamma Sigma
Quincy, Illinois

SHRIMP AND PASTA SALAD

16 ounces macaroni	1 (32-ounce) package
1 red bell pepper,	frozen cooked shrimp,
chopped	thawed
1 green bell pepper,	1 (6-ounce) can whole
chopped	black olives, drained
1 (8-ounce) package	Mayonnaise to taste
cheese cubes	Salt and pepper to taste

Prepare the pasta using the package directions. Cool completely. Toss the pasta and the remaining ingredients together in a large salad bowl. Refrigerate, covered, until chilled. Yield: 25 servings.

Carolyn Blankenship, Iota Mu
Nacogdoches, Texas

PASTA SALAD WITH SQUASH, TOMATOES, BASIL AND PINE NUTS

4 zucchini or summer	1/2 cup chopped fresh
squash	basil
1 tablespoon kosher salt	2 tablespoons balsamic
16 ounces farfalle pasta	vinegar
5 tablespoons extra-	1/4 cup pine nuts, lightly
virgin olive oil,	toasted
divided	Grated Parmesan cheese
3 garlic cloves, minced	Salt and pepper to taste
1/2 teaspoon red pepper	
flakes	
1 pint grape tomatoes,	
halved	

Cut the zucchini into halves lengthwise and crosswise into 1/2-inch slices. Combine the zucchini and kosher salt in a large bowl. Toss to mix. Spoon into a colander set over a bowl. Let stand for 30 minutes. Spread the zucchini on paper towels and pat dry and remove the salt with a paper towel. Cook the pasta al dente using the package directions; drain. Heat 1 tablespoon of the olive oil in a large skillet over high heat. Add 1/2 the zucchini and sauté for 5 to 7 minutes or until golden brown all over and slightly charred. Remove to a plate. Repeat the process with 1 tablespoon olive oil and the remaining zucchini. Add 1 tablespoon of the olive oil, garlic and red pepper flakes to the skillet. Sauté for 10 seconds. Add the remaining 2 tablespoons olive oil, cooked zucchini, tomatoes, basil, vinegar and pine nuts. Toss to mix. Add the pasta and cheese. Season with salt and pepper. Toss to mix. Serve chilled or at room temperature. Yield: 4 to 6 servings.

Kelli Hamilton, Phi
Grand Junction, Colorado

TORTELLINI SALAD

1/4 cup chopped fresh parsley	Dash of nutmeg
3 tablespoons chopped fresh basil, or 2 teaspoons dried basil	1 (5-ounce) package cheese tortellini
1/3 cup olive oil	4 ounces feta cheese, crumbled
1 tablespoon Italian salad dressing	1/2 cup pitted black olives, halved
	1 tomato, chopped

Whisk the parsley, basil, olive oil, salad dressing and nutmeg together in a small bowl. Prepare the pasta using the package directions. Cool completely. Toss the dressing, pasta, cheese, olives and tomato together in a large salad bowl. Serve chilled or at room temperature. Yield: 5 or 6 servings.

Kay Donaldson, Kappa Lambda
Edenton, North Carolina

RAINBOW SALAD

2 boneless skinless chicken breast halves, chopped	1/4 cup shredded carrot
	1/4 cup black olives
1 tablespoon butter or olive oil	2 tablespoons finely chopped sweet onion
12 ounces rainbow rotelle	1/2 cup Cheddar cheese cubes
1/2 cup finely chopped tomato	Salt and pepper to taste
1/2 cup finely chopped green bell pepper	1/4 cup Italian salad dressing

Sauté the chicken in the butter in a skillet over medium heat until cooked through. Cool completely. Prepare the pasta using the package directions. Cool completely. Toss the chicken, pasta, tomato, bell pepper, carrot, olives, onion, cheese, salt and pepper together in a large salad bowl. Refrigerate, covered, for 30 minutes. Pour the salad dressing over the pasta mixture and toss to mix. Yield: 8 servings.

Janie Overbeck, Xi Alpha Beta Eta
Seminole, Texas

Yvonne Upson, Xi Alpha Alpha, Sparks, Nevada, makes **Spinach Salad Isabella** *by tearing 1 pound fresh spinach leaves and 1 small head radicchio into bite size pieces. She then tosses the torn spinach and radicchio with 1 shredded carrot in a large bowl. The salad is covered and chilled. Just before serving, the salad is tossed with 1/2 cup Italian dressing and sprinkled with 2 cups seasoned croutons.*

CORN BREAD SALAD

1 cup sugar	2 (15-ounce) cans pinto beans, rinsed and drained
2/3 cup vegetable oil	
2/3 cup ketchup	2 (15-ounce) cans whole kernel corn, drained
2/3 cup vinegar	
2 teaspoons minced onion	2 green bell peppers, finely chopped
1 teaspoon salt	4 large tomatoes, chopped
1 teaspoon pepper	
4 (6-ounce) packages yellow corn bread mix	1 red onion, chopped
1 (10-ounce) can green chiles, drained and chopped	4 cups (16 ounces) shredded Cheddar cheese

Whisk the first 7 ingredients together in a bowl. Refrigerate, covered, for 8 to 12 hours. Prepare the corn bread using the package directions, stirring the chiles into the batter before baking. Cool completely and cut into 2-inch squares. Place the corn bread squares in a large salad bowl. Layer with the beans, corn, bell peppers, tomatoes and onion. Sprinkle the layers with the cheese. Toss before serving. Serve with the dressing. Yield: 20 servings.

Connie Leetsch, Gamma Zeta Master
Abilene, Texas

EAST TEXAS CORN BREAD SALAD

1 (8-ounce) package Mexican corn bread mix	1/2 cup chopped green onions
2 (16-ounce) cans whole kernel corn, drained	10 slices bacon, crisp-cooked and crumbled
2 (15-ounce) cans pinto beans, rinsed and drained	2 cups (8 ounces) shredded Cheddar cheese
1 (15-ounce) can black beans, rinsed and drained	1 cup sour cream
	1 cup mayonnaise
3 tomatoes, chopped	1 package ranch salad dressing mix
1 each red and green bell pepper, chopped	1/2 cup picante sauce
	1 small head romaine lettuce, shredded

Prepare the corn bread using the package directions. Cool completely and crumble. Toss the corn, beans, tomatoes, bell peppers, onions, bacon and cheese together in a large bowl. Mix the next 4 ingredients in a bowl. Layer half the corn bread, lettuce and corn mixture in a large serving dish. Top with half the dressing. Repeat the layers and top with the remaining dressing. Refrigerate, covered, for 2 hours. Yield: 20 to 22 servings.

Opal Stewart, Preceptor Omicron Epsilon
Kilgore, Texas

CHILI CORN BREAD SALAD

This is a great recipe to use as the main course for a ladies luncheon. It's a make-ahead recipe that give the hostess free time to get ready.

1 (8-ounce) package corn
  bread mix
1 (4-ounce) can chopped
  green chiles
1/8 teaspoon ground
  cumin
1/8 teaspoon oregano
1 cup mayonnaise
1 cup sour cream
1 package ranch salad
  dressing mix
1 (15-ounce) can pinto
  beans, rinsed and
  drained

2 (15-ounce) cans whole
  kernel corn, drained
3 tomatoes, chopped
1 cup chopped green bell
  pepper
1 cup chopped green
  onions
10 slices bacon, crisp-
  cooked and crumbled
2 cups (8 ounces)
  shredded Cheddar
  cheese

Prepared the corn bread mix using the package directions, stirring the undrained chiles, cumin and oregano into the batter before baking. Pour the batter into an 8×8-inch baking dish. Bake at 400 degrees for 20 to 25 minutes. Cool completely. Combine the mayonnaise, sour cream and salad dressing mix in a bowl. Crumble half the corn bread into a 9×13-inch dish. Layer with half the beans, mayonnaise mixture, corn, tomatoes, bell pepper, onions, bacon and cheese. Repeat the layers. Refrigerate, covered, for 2 hours. Yield: 12 to 16 servings.

Nova Bergschneider, Xi Lambda Tau
Urich, Missouri

HOT BACON SALAD DRESSING

4 slices bacon, cut into
  1-inch pieces
1 cup granulated sugar
1/2 cup packed brown
  sugar
1/2 cup vinegar

1/2 cup water
2 eggs
1 teaspoon salt
1/2 teaspoon dry mustard
1 tablespoon
  all-purpose flour

Cook the bacon in a skillet over medium heat until crisp. Remove the bacon with a slotted spoon. Drain most of the drippings. Whisk the granulated sugar, brown sugar, vinegar, water, eggs, salt, mustard and flour together in a bowl until smooth. Pour the sugar mixture into the skillet with the reserved drippings. Cook, stirring constantly, until thickened. Add the bacon and mix well. Serve as a dressing over lettuce. Yield: 8 servings.

Mary Elizabeth Arnold, Alpha Epsilon Master
Lebanon, Pennsylvania

ZESTY SALAD DRESSING

2/3 cup sugar
1/4 cup vinegar
1 teaspoon salt
1/4 teaspoon minced
  garlic
1 cup vegetable oil

2 teaspoons prepared
  mustard
1/2 teaspoon pepper
1/2 onion, finely chopped
Celery seeds to taste
  (optional)

Combine all the ingredients in a blender and process until smooth. Yield: 2 cups.

Sandi Keim, Laureate Epsilon Beta
Wooster, Ohio

TOMATO SOUP SALAD DRESSING

1 cup vegetable oil
1 cup sugar
1 cup vinegar
1 teaspoon salt
1 teaspoon paprika

1 teaspoon dry mustard
1/2 teaspoon pepper
1 (10-ounce) can tomato
  soup

Combine all the ingredients in a jar with a tight-fitting lid. Seal and shake well. Refrigerate until serving. Yield: 4 cups.

June A. Strohacker, Preceptor Omega
El Paso, Texas

PEPPER CREAM SALAD DRESSING

1 cup mayonnaise
2 tablespoons water
1/2 teaspoon lemon juice
3/4 teaspoon
  Worcestershire sauce
3/4 teaspoon dry mustard

1 tablespoon freshly
  ground pepper
3/4 teaspoon garlic salt
1/3 cup freshly grated
  Parmesan cheese

Process all the ingredients in a food processor until smooth. Refrigerate, covered, for 1 hour. Serve over lettuce and fresh vegetable salad. Yield: 1 1/2 cups.

Kathleen Conway, Preceptor Chi
Rawlins, Wyoming

CREAMY BASIL SALAD DRESSING

1 cup loosely packed
  fresh basil
1 1/2 tablespoons chopped
  shallots or scallions
2 tablespoons balsamic
  vinegar

3/4 teaspoon salt
1/4 teaspoon pepper
2 tablespoons
  mayonnaise
6 tablespoons extra-
  virgin olive oil

Combine all the ingredients in a blender and process until smooth. Refrigerate, covered, for 24 hours. Serve over sliced tomatoes or spinach salad. Yield 1 1/2 cups.

Nancy C. Holden-Smith, Laureate Beta
Lincoln, Delaware

Soups

CANTALOUPE SOUP

1 cantaloupe, peeled
1 (6-ounce) can frozen
 orange juice, thawed
1¹/2 cups cold water
1 tablespoon lemon or
 lime juice
Pinch of nutmeg
Pinch of cinnamon

Cut the cantaloupe into 2-inch chunks and place in a blender. Add the orange juice, water, lemon juice, nutmeg and cinnamon and process until smooth. Chill until ready to serve. Yield: 4 servings.

Ione Fitzgerald, Lambda Lambda
Redford, Michigan

CRAB AND CORN BISQUE

4 cups frozen corn,
 thawed
3 cups water
1¹/2 fish bouillon cubes
2 chicken bouillon cubes
2 cups finely minced
 onions
2 tablespoons seafood
 seasoning
¹/2 teaspoon white
 pepper
¹/4 teaspoon cayenne
 pepper
1 teaspoon salt
¹/4 teaspoon celery
 powder
3 tablespoons parsley
 flakes
1 cup (¹/2 stick) butter
¹/2 cup all-purpose flour
5 cups milk
1 pound crab meat

Purée 1 cup of the corn in a blender. Add to the remaining 3 cups of corn in a large Dutch oven. Add 1 cup of the water and cook on medium heat for 15 minutes. Dissolve the bouillon cubes in the remaining water in a small bowl. Add the bouillon mixture, onions, seafood seasoning, white pepper and cayenne pepper, salt, celery powder and parsley to the Dutch oven and mix well. Cook for 30 to 45 minutes. Melt the butter in a small saucepan and add the flour, making a paste. Add the flour mixture to the corn mixture and blend well. Add the milk, gradually, stirring constantly. Add the crab meat, reduce the heat and simmer for 2 hours. Yield: 8 servings.

Brenda S. Dupre, Laureate Upsilon
Mobile, Alabama

CRAB BISQUE

6 tablespoons butter
¹/4 cup finely chopped
 onion
¹/4 cup finely chopped
 green bell pepper
1 scallion, chopped
2 tablespoons parsley
¹/2 cup sliced fresh
 mushrooms
2 tablespoons
 all-purpose flour
1 cup milk
1 teaspoon salt
¹/8 teaspoon white
 pepper
Dash of Tabasco sauce
1 cup half-and-half
1¹/2 cups cooked crab
 meat
3 tablespoons dry sherry

Melt ¹/4 cup of the butter in a skillet. Add the onion, bell pepper, scallion, parsley and mushrooms and sauté until the onion is tender. Heat the remaining 2 tablespoons butter in a large saucepan and add the flour. Add the milk and cook until thickened, stirring constantly. Add the salt, pepper and Tabasco sauce and mix well. Add the sautéed vegetables and half-and-half; bring to a boil, stirring constantly. Reduce the heat, add the crab meat and simmer for 5 minutes. Stir in the sherry just before serving. Yield: 4 servings.

Marna Randall, Alpha Nu Master
Tucson, Arizona

LOW-FAT CRAB BISQUE

1/2 cup finely shredded carrots	*4 (5-ounce) cans evaporated milk*
1/4 cup finely chopped onion	*2 to 3 cups imitation crab meat*
1/2 cup finely chopped celery	*1/4 cup dry sherry*
1/4 cup (1/2 stick) butter or margarine	*1/3 cup finely chopped parsley*
3 tablespoons all-purpose flour	*Dash of ground red pepper*
2 (10-ounce) cans low-fat chicken broth	*Black pepper to taste*

Sauté the carrots, onion and celery in the butter in a skillet over medium heat until the vegetables are tender. Reduce the heat and add the flour, stirring until smooth. Cook for 1 minute, stirring constantly. Add the broth gradually, and cook until thickened, stirring constantly. Add the evaporated milk, crab meat and sherry and stir well. Cook until thoroughly heated. Add the parsley and red and black pepper and stir well. Yield: 10 to 12 cups.

Delores Bartholomew, Xi Phi Upsilon
Mariposa, California

EASY SHRIMP BISQUE

1 (10-ounce) can cream of shrimp soup	*1 cup cooked baby shrimp*
1 (10-ounce) can tomato bisque soup	*Old Bay seasoning to taste*
2 1/2 cups milk	
1 cup (4 ounces) shredded Cheddar cheese	

Combine the soups and milk in a medium saucepan and blend until smooth. Add the cheese gradually, stirring until melted. Add the shrimp and heat thoroughly. Season with Old Bay seasoning.
Yield: 4 servings.

Rose-Marie Gross, Xi Eta Chi
Cogan Station, Pennsylvania

MUSHROOM BISQUE

1 pound mushrooms	*1 cup heavy cream*
7 tablespoons butter	*1 teaspoon salt*
1 quart chicken broth	*1/2 teaspoon white pepper*
1 onion, chopped	*Dash of Tabasco sauce*
6 tablespoons all-purpose flour	*2 tablespoons dry sherry*
3 cups milk	

Remove the stems from 6 of the mushrooms. Slice the caps and sauté in 1 tablespoon of the butter in a skillet. Remove and reserve for garnish. Chop the remaining mushrooms in a food processor. Add the mushrooms, broth and onion to the skillet and simmer, covered, for 30 minutes. Melt the remaining 6 tablespoons butter in a saucepan. Add the flour and whisk until smooth. Pour the milk into a separate saucepan and bring to a boil. Add the milk to the flour mixture, whisking until combined. Cook until thickened and add the cream. Combine the sauce and mushroom mixture and mix well. Season with the salt, pepper and Tabasco sauce. Add the sherry before serving, stirring well. Garnish with the reserved mushrooms. Yield: 8 servings.

Carolyn Powell, Laureate Iota
Raleigh, North Carolina

TOMATO BISQUE

1 cup water	*1 large tomato, peeled and chopped*
1 tablespoon chicken bouillon granules or 3 bouillon cubes	*1/4 cup (1/2 stick) butter*
1 (8-ounce) can diced tomatoes	*2 tablespoons all-purpose flour*
1 tablespoon chopped onion	*1 cup cream or half-and-half*
1/2 cup chopped celery	*1 tablespoon sugar*

Combine the water, bouillon, canned tomatoes, onion and celery in a medium saucepan. Cover and simmer for 20 minutes. Place the mixture into a blender and blend until smooth. Cook the chopped tomato and 2 tablespoons of the butter in the same saucepan for 5 minutes. Add the remaining butter and stir in the flour. Add the cream and sugar and mix well. Add the blended mixture and heat thoroughly. Yield: 4 servings.

Diane Almy, Xi Delta Eta
Delta, Colorado

CHEDDAR CHOWDER

2 cups water	*1/4 cup (1/2 stick) butter*
2 cups diced potatoes	*1/4 cup all-purpose flour*
1/2 cup chopped carrots	*2 cups milk*
1/2 cup chopped celery	*2 cups (8 ounces) finely shredded Cheddar cheese*
1/4 cup chopped onion	
1/4 teaspoon black pepper	*1 cup cubed ham*
1 teaspoon salt	

Combine the first 7 ingredients in a large stockpot. Bring the mixture to a boil and boil for 10 to 12 minutes. Melt the butter in a saucepan and add the flour, stirring until smooth. Add the milk slowly and cook until thickened. Add the cheese and stir until melted. Add the sauce and ham to the stockpot and heat thoroughly. Yield: 6 servings.

Jan Gorath, Xi Kappa
Austin, Minnesota

BARBARA BUSH'S CLAM CHOWDER

3 slices bacon	1 cup cubed potatoes
1/2 cup chopped onion	1 1/2 cups milk
1 (7-ounce) can minced clams, reserving liquid	1 (10-ounce) cream of celery soup
	Dash of black pepper

Fry the bacon in a skillet until crisp; remove to a plate and crumble. Sauté the onion in the bacon drippings and drain. Add the clam liquid and potatoes. Cover and cook on low heat for 15 minutes or until the potatoes are tender. Add the clams and next 3 ingredients and heat thoroughly. Season with pepper. Yield: 2 servings.

Louise G. Taylor, Zeta Master
Danville, Kentucky

HEARTY CLAM CHOWDER

4 slices bacon, chopped	2 (8-ounce) bottles clam juice
3 celery ribs, chopped	
2 carrots, chopped	1 1/2 cups water
1 onion, chopped	1 sprig fresh thyme
2 large potatoes, peeled and cubed	1 teaspoon salt
	1/2 teaspoon pepper
4 (6-ounce) cans minced clams	1 1/2 cups milk
	1/3 cup all-purpose flour

Cook the bacon in a Dutch oven for 4 minutes or until almost crisp. Add the celery, carrots and onion and cook for 5 minutes, stirring frequently. Add the next 7 ingredients and mix well. Bring to a boil and reduce the heat. Simmer, uncovered, for 20 minutes. Blend the milk and flour in a bowl. Stir into the chowder and simmer for 10 minutes or until thickened, stirring often. Remove the thyme before serving. Yield: 10 1/2 cups.

Karla LaPlante, Kappa Upsilon
Bonaire, Georgia

CORN CHOWDER

1 cup (2 sticks) butter	1 garlic clove, minced
1 small carrot, finely chopped	1/2 cup all-purpose flour
	3 cups whole kernel corn
1 celery rib, finely chopped	2 cups chicken stock
	2 cups half-and-half
1 small onion, finely chopped	Salt and black pepper to taste

Melt 1 stick of the butter in a saucepan over medium heat. Add the carrot, celery, onion and garlic and sauté for 2 minutes. Add the flour and stir until light brown and set aside. Combine the corn and stock in a separate saucepan and bring to a boil. Reduce the heat and simmer for 10 minutes. Add the corn mixture to the flour mixture gradually, whisking constantly to prevent lumps. Return to the heat and bring to a boil. Heat the half-and-half in a small saucepan and add to the soup. Add the remaining butter, salt and pepper before serving, stirring well to combine. Yield: 10 servings.

Gina Marie Aleo, Laureate Epsilon Zeta
Wilkes-Barre, Pennsylvania

GROUND BEEF CHOWDER

2 potatoes, peeled and diced	1 pound lean ground beef, browned and drained
2 carrots, peeled and diced	
	1 (10-ounce) can beef stock
1 onion, peeled and chopped	1 (10-ounce) can tomato soup
2 celery ribs, chopped	
1/2 green bell pepper, chopped	1/2 teaspoon salt
	Black pepper to taste
2 1/2 cups water	

Combine the first 6 ingredients in a large saucepan. Bring to a boil, cover and cook for 10 minutes or until the vegetables are tender. Add the remaining ingredients to the vegetables. Bring to a boil, reduce the heat and simmer for 20 minutes. Yield: 6 servings.

Anna Shail, Laureate Gamma Tau
Barrie, Ontario, Canada

ZUCCHINI GARDEN CHOWDER

1 onion, chopped	1 teaspoon lemon juice
2 zucchini, chopped	1 (14-ounce) can diced tomatoes
2 tablespoons minced fresh parsley	
	1 (12-ounce) can evaporated milk
1 teaspoon dried basil	
1/3 cup butter or margarine	1 (10-ounce) package frozen corn, thawed
1/3 cup all-purpose flour	1/4 cup grated Parmesan cheese (optional)
1 teaspoon salt	
1/2 teaspoon black pepper	2 cups (8 ounces) shredded Cheddar cheese
3 cups water	
3 chicken bouillon cubes	Pinch of sugar

Sauté the first 4 ingredients in the butter in a Dutch oven. Stir in the flour, salt and pepper and mix well. Stir in the water gradually. Add the bouillon and lemon juice and mix well. Bring the mixture to a boil and cook for 2 minutes, stirring constantly. Add the tomatoes, evaporated milk and corn and return to a boil. Reduce the heat, cover and simmer for 5 minutes. Add the cheeses and sugar, stirring until the cheeses are melted. Yield: 8 to 10 servings.

Carol Bennett, Alpha Rho Zeta
Cross Plains, Texas

SHRIMP GUMBO

6 slices bacon	1 teaspoon MSG
1/4 pound salt pork	2 bay leaves
1/2 cup all-purpose flour	4 drops of hot red
1 cup chopped celery	pepper sauce
1/2 cup Worcestershire	2 (10-ounce) packages
sauce	frozen sliced okra
1/2 teaspoon basil	1 pound peeled
1 teaspoon black pepper	uncooked shrimp
1/2 cup chopped parsley	1 pound beef sausage,
2 (14-ounce) cans stewed	casings removed and
tomatoes	sliced
1 (13-ounce) can chicken	1/8 to 1/4 teaspoon gumbo
broth	filé

Cook the bacon and salt pork in a large stockpot until the bacon is crisp. Crumble the bacon and set aside. Remove the salt pork. Add the flour gradually and stir until the mixture is medium brown. Stir in the next 11 ingredients. Cook for 20 minutes. Add the shrimp and sausage. Cover and simmer for 15 minutes. Stir in the gumbo filé just before serving.
Yield: 6 servings.

Mary Edmond
Channelview, Texas

QUICK CHILI

1 pound ground beef	1 teaspoon salt
1 green bell pepper,	4 teaspoons chili
chopped	powder
1/2 cup chopped onion	1/8 teaspoon black
1 (10-ounce) can tomato	pepper
soup	Dash of cayenne pepper
2 tablespoons taco	1 (15-ounce) can pinto
seasoning	beans (optional)

Brown the ground beef in a skillet, stirring until crumbly; drain. Remove to a plate and keep warm. Add the green pepper and onion to the same skillet and sauté until tender. Add the beef and the remaining ingredients. Bring to a boil. Cover and simmer for 10 minutes. Yield: 6 servings.

Vivian Wilburn
Richardson, Texas

CHUNKY PORK CHILI

1 (12-ounce) pork	1 (14-ounce) can beef
tenderloin, cubed	broth
2 teaspoons cumin	1 (14-ounce) can diced
2 teaspoons chili powder	tomatoes, drained
1 tablespoon oil	1 (4-ounce) can chopped
1 small onion, chopped	green chiles
2 to 3 garlic cloves,	3 (16-ounce) can pinto
minced	beans, drained, rinsed

Combine the tenderloin, cumin and chili powder in a bowl and stir to coat. Heat the oil in a skillet, add the pork and cook until brown. Add the onion and garlic and sauté until the onion is tender. Add the broth, tomatoes and chiles and bring to a boil. Add the beans and simmer, uncovered, for 5 minutes. Top each serving with sour cream, if desired.
Yield: 6 to 8 servings.

Carol Grider, Mu Theta
Salina, Kansas

CHILI FOR A CROWD

3 pounds round steak,	2 cups hot salsa
cut into 1/2-inch cubes	2 (28-ounce) cans diced
1/4 cup olive oil	tomatoes
2 large onions, chopped	1 (28-ounce) can kidney
4 red bell peppers,	beans, drained
seeded and chopped	1 (28-ounce) can pinto
4 jalapeño chiles, seeded	beans, drained
and chopped	1 (28-ounce) can black
6 tablespoons chili	beans, drained
powder	1 (8-ounce) package
1 tablespoon cumin	frozen corn, thawed
1 teaspoon salt	

Brown the steak in half the olive oil in a skillet; remove to a Dutch oven. Sauté the onion in the remaining oil in the skillet until tender. Add the bell peppers and jalapeños and continue to cook until they begin to brown. Stir in the chili powder, cumin and salt and cook for 2 minutes. Add to the Dutch oven. Add the salsa, tomatoes, beans and corn and stir well. Cover and bake at 350 degrees for 2 hours or until the steak is tender and the flavors are blended. Yield: 15 to 20 servings.

Jane Hall, Xi Iota Zeta
San Jose, California

MEXICAN CHICKEN SOUP

1 whole chicken, cooked	4 (4-ounce) cans diced
1 cup chopped onion	green chiles
1 teaspoon cumin	1/2 cup chopped fresh
2 garlic cloves, minced	cilantro or parsley
2 tablespoons vegetable	2 tablespoons chopped
oil	fresh oregano
2 (46-ounce) cans	1 (13-ounce) package
chicken broth	tortilla chips,
2 (10-ounce) can	crushed
tomatoes with green	2 cups (8 ounces)
chiles	shredded Monterey
1 (28-ounce) can crushed	Jack or Cheddar
tomatoes	cheese
1 (46-ounce) can tomato	
juice	

Shred the chicken finely, discarding the skin and bones. Cook the onion, cumin and garlic in the oil in a skillet until the onion is tender. Add the broth, tomatoes with green chiles, crushed tomatoes, tomato juice, green chiles, cilantro and oregano; bring to a boil, reduce the heat and simmer, covered, for 20 minutes. Stir in the chicken. Cook until heated through. Place ½ cup tortilla chips in each bowl. Ladle the soup over the chips and top with the cheese. Yield: 8 servings.

Trina Jackson, Beta Eta
Hamlin, West Virginia

WHITE CHILI

1 large onion, chopped
2 garlic cloves, minced
1 tablespoon oil
2 (4-ounce) cans
   chopped green chiles
1 tablespoon cumin
1½ teaspoons oregano
¼ teaspoon ground
   cloves
¼ teaspoon cayenne
   pepper

4 to 6 cups chicken
   broth
3 (16-ounce) cans white
   beans or cannellini
4 cups diced cooked
   chicken
Salt and black pepper
   to taste

Sauté the onion and garlic in the oil in a skillet for 5 minutes or until the onion is tender. Add the green chiles, cumin, oregano, cloves and cayenne pepper and mix well. Add the broth, beans and chicken and simmer for at least 1 hour. Season with salt and pepper. Serve with shredded cheese and/or sour cream, if desired. Yield: 8 servings.

Ruth Schwanebeck, Kappa Master
Knoxville, Iowa

TAMALE SOUP

The more you reheat this soup, the better it gets.

1 pound ground beef
2 cups chopped onions
1½ cups chopped green
   bell peppers
1 (14-ounce) can stewed
   tomatoes with green
   chiles
1 (28-ounce) can pinto
   beans
1 (28-ounce) black beans

1 (14-ounce) can cream-
   style corn
1 (14-ounce) can beef
   broth
1 (14-ounce) can
   hominy, drained
2 (15-ounce) cans beef
   tamales in chili
   sauce, cut into 1-inch
   pieces

Brown the ground beef with the onions and bell peppers in a Dutch oven, stirring until the ground beef is crumbly; drain. Add the tomatoes, beans, corn, broth and hominy and bring to a boil. Reduce the heat and

simmer, uncovered, for 45 minutes, stirring occasionally. Stir in the tamale pieces and cook until heated through. Yield: 8 servings.

Felisha Crawford, Xi Alpha Chi
Frederick, Oklahoma

TACO SOUP

2 pounds ground turkey
   or beef
1 onion, chopped
1 (15-ounce) can each
   black beans, kidney
   beans and pinto
   beans
1 (15-ounce) can each
   white and yellow
   hominy

1 (10-ounce) can
   tomatoes with green
   chiles
1 envelope ranch salad
   dressing mix
1 envelope taco
   seasoning
1 (46-ounce) can chicken
   broth

Brown the ground turkey in a large skillet, stirring until crumbly; drain. Add the onion and sauté until the onion is tender. Combine the beans, hominy, tomatoes with green chiles, ranch dressing mix, taco seasoning and broth in a large stockpot and mix well. Add the turkey or beef mixture and mix well. Simmer for 2 hours. Variation: Substitute two 15-ounce cans whole kernel corn for the hominy. Yield: 12 servings.

Claudia Ash, Laureate Gamma Xi
Monett, Missouri

SANTA FE TACO SOUP

1 (4-pound) chicken
1 small onion, chopped
1 envelope taco
   seasoning mix
1 envelope ranch salad
   dressing mix
2 (15-ounce) cans pinto
   beans
2 (15-ounce) cans kidney
   beans

2 (15-ounce) cans diced
   tomatoes
2 (10-ounce) cans
   tomatoes with green
   chiles
1 (16-ounce) can whole
   kernel corn
1 (4-ounce) can chopped
   green chiles
2 teaspoons salt

Boil the chicken in a large saucepan, reserving the broth. Skin, debone, and chop the cooked chicken. Combine the chicken, onion, taco seasoning mix, ranch dressing mix, beans, tomatoes and corn in a large stockpot and mix well. Add 2 cups of the reserved broth, green chiles and salt and mix well. Simmer for 20 to 30 minutes. Serve over tortilla chips, sprinkle with shredded cheese and top with sour cream and avocado slices, if desired. Yield: 12 servings.

Jenny King, Preceptor Beta Tau
Dallas, Texas

CHICKEN TORTILLA SOUP

I love to make a pot of this delicious soup, have a bowl, then freeze the rest in containers with 1 to 2 servings. It is wonderful on a chilly Wyoming day to have this handy soup as close as the freezer.

1/2 green bell pepper	3 chicken breasts, cooked
1/2 onion	in 6 cups water,
3 celery ribs	drained and liquid
1/2 pound baby carrots	reserved
1/4 cup chopped cilantro	3 tablespoons all-
1 1/2 teaspoons garlic salt	purpose flour
1 teaspoon chili powder	1 (10-ounce) can
1 teaspoon cumin	tomatoes with green
3/4 teaspoon black pepper	chiles
3/4 cup (1 1/2 sticks) butter	1 (14-ounce) can whole
1 (12-count) package	kernel corn
6-inch corn tortillas	Grated Cheddar cheese

Place the bell pepper, onion, celery and carrots in a food processor and process until medium fine. Combine the garlic salt, chili powder, cumin and black pepper in a small bowl and add to the chopped vegetables. Melt half the butter in a large skillet and add the vegetables and spice mixture. Sauté until the vegetables are tender, stirring frequently. Cut up the tortillas and add to the vegetables and continue to sauté until the tortillas are soft. Add the reserved cooking liquid and mix well. Melt the remaining 3/4 stick butter and combine with the flour in a small bowl; add to the vegetables. Add the chicken, tomatoes and corn and simmer for 30 to 40 minutes. Serve with the grated cheese. Yield: 8 to 10 servings.

Shirley Nordquist, Eta Masters
Laramie, Wyoming

TORTILLA SOUP

1 (10-ounce) can tomato	3 chicken breasts,
soup	cooked and cubed
2 (10-ounce) cans	1 (4-ounce) can chopped
Cheddar cheese	green chiles
soup	Shredded cheese
2 to 3 cups chicken	Tortilla chips
broth	

Combine the soups, broth and chicken in a large stockpot and cook over medium heat, stirring occasionally. Simmer for 1 hour. Pour into bowls and top with the shredded cheese and tortilla chips. Yield: 8 servings.

Connie Allen, Eta Masters
Sioux Falls, South Dakota

TORTILLA SOUP WITH AVOCADO AND CILANTRO

2 teaspoons ghee or	1 teaspoon marjoram
olive oil	1 1/2 cups chopped
2 corn tortillas, cut into	carrots
strips	1/2 cup chopped green
1 cup chopped leeks or	bell pepper
red onion	1/4 cup diced roasted red
1 tablespoon turmeric	bell pepper
1 teaspoon black pepper	1 cup whole kernel corn
Pinch of red pepper	4 cups vegetable stock
flakes	1/4 cup chopped cilantro
1 teaspoon chili powder	1 cup sautéed shrimp
1 tablespoon cumin	1 cup chopped avocado
1 teaspoon coriander	

Heat 1 teaspoon of the ghee in a large skillet over medium-high heat. Layer the tortilla strips evenly in the skillet; sauté until crisp and remove to paper towels. Heat the remaining ghee in a stock pot. Add the leeks, turmeric, black pepper, red pepper flakes, chili powder, cumin, coriander and marjoram and sauté for 3 to 4 minutes. Add the carrots and sauté for 3 minutes. Add the green and red pepper and corn, reduce the heat and simmer for 4 to 5 minutes. Add 1/4 cup of the vegetable stock and cook until the carrots are tender. Add the remaining stock, bring to a boil and boil for 4 to 5 minutes. Add the cilantro and shrimp and mix well. Divide the avocado into bowls and ladle the soup over the avocado. Garnish with the tortilla strips. Yield: 4 to 6 servings.

Monique LeBlanc, Gamma Phi
Stratford, Ontario, Canada

BAKED OLIVE MINESTRONE

1 1/2 pounds lean stew	1 1/2 cups sliced carrots
meat, cut into 1/4-inch	1 1/2 to 2 teaspoons
cubes	Italian seasoning
1 cup chopped onion	1 (16-ounce) can
1 1/2 teaspoons minced	chopped tomatoes
garlic	1 (15-ounce) can kidney
1 scant teaspoon salt	beans
1/4 teaspoon black	1 (6-ounce) can black
pepper	pitted olives, drained,
2 tablespoons olive oil	reserving liquid
3 (10-ounce) cans beef	1 1/2 cups shell macaroni,
broth	uncooked
2 (10-ounce) cans water	2 cups sliced zucchini

Combine the beef, onion, garlic, salt and pepper in a Dutch oven. Add the oil, stirring to coat the meat. Bake, uncovered, at 400 degrees for 40 minutes or until brown, stirring occasionally. Reduce the heat to 350 degrees. Add the broth, water, carrots and Italian seasoning. Cover and bake for 1 hour. Stir in the tomatoes, beans, olives, 1 cup of the reserved olive liquid and macaroni. Sprinkle the zucchini on top and bake for 1 hour or until the macaroni is cooked. Serve with Parmesan cheese. Yield: 3½ to 4 quarts.

Judy Glorioso, Eta Theta
Plant City, Florida

FAT-FREE MINESTRONE

1 onion, chopped	*1 (6-ounce) tomato paste*
4 garlic cloves, minced	*3 to 4 potatoes, peeled*
2 tablespoons fat-free	*and cubed*
chicken broth	*½ cup uncooked*
8 cups chicken broth	*macaroni*
2 cups water	*3 celery ribs, chopped*
1 cup lima beans	*1¼ cups chopped carrots*
1 teaspoon oregano	*1 small zucchini,*
1 teaspoon rosemary	*chopped*
1 (14-ounce) can	*½ cup peas*
chopped tomatoes	*¼ teaspoon parsley*

Simmer the onion and garlic in the 2 tablespoons broth in a large saucepan. Add the 8 cups broth, water, lima beans, oregano and rosemary and mix well. Bring to a boil. Reduce the heat and simmer for 20 minutes. Add the next 6 ingredients and mix well. Simmer for 10 minutes. Add the zucchini and peas and mix well. Simmer for 5 minutes. Add the salt, pepper and parsley; mix well and simmer for 2 to 3 minutes. Yield: 10 servings.

Barbara Shopek, Omega Preceptor
Cynthiana, Kentucky

MINESTRONE

2 teaspoons olive oil	*¾ cup chopped celery*
¾ cup chopped onion	*½ teaspoon dried basil*
1 (14-ounce) can diced	*¼ teaspoon salt*
tomatoes	*¼ teaspoon dried*
3 cups chicken broth	*oregano*
2 cups chopped zucchini	*⅛ teaspoon black*
1 cup chopped carrots	*pepper*
1 cup cannellini beans,	*1 garlic clove, minced*
drained	*¼ cup uncooked ditalini*

Heat the oil in a Dutch oven over medium-high heat. Add the onion and sauté for 4 minutes. Add the tomatoes, broth, zucchini, carrots, beans, celery, basil, salt, oregano, pepper and garlic and mix well. Bring to a boil. Reduce the heat and simmer, covered, for 25 minutes. Add the pasta. Simmer, covered, for 10 minutes. Yield: 4 servings.

Eileen Martel, Preceptor Gamma Alpha
Fairfax, Virginia

PASTA FAGIOLI

1 pound lean ground	*5 (12-ounce) cans*
beef	*vegetable juice*
1 small onion, chopped	*cocktail*
2 carrots, julienned	*1 tablespoon vinegar*
3 celery ribs, thinly	*1½ teaspoons salt*
sliced	*1 teaspoon oregano*
2 garlic cloves, minced	*1 teaspoon basil*
2 (14-ounce) cans	*½ teaspoon black*
tomatoes	*pepper*
1 (15-ounce) can kidney	*½ teaspoon thyme*
beans	*¼ cup uncooked ditali*
1 (15-ounce) Great	
Northern beans	

Brown the ground beef with the onion in a skillet, stirring until the ground beef is crumbly; drain. Add the carrots, celery and garlic and sauté until the vegetables are almost tender. Add the tomatoes, beans, vegetable juice cocktail, vinegar, salt, oregano, basil, pepper and thyme and mix well. Simmer for 30 to 45 minutes or until the vegetables are tender. Cook the pasta according to the package directions; drain and add to the soup mixture just before serving. Yield: 12 to 15 servings.

Jenny Harding, Xi Pi Delta
New Braunfels, Texas

SLOW-COOKER PASTA FAGIOLI

1 pound ground beef	*½ teaspoon black*
1 onion, chopped	*pepper*
1 (15-ounce) can Great	*½ teaspoon marjoram*
Northern beans	*¼ teaspoon cayenne*
1 celery rib, chopped	*pepper*
2 garlic cloves, minced	*¼ teaspoon hot red*
2 (14-ounce) cans beef	*pepper sauce*
broth	*1 teaspoon basil*
2 (14-ounce) cans whole	*3 cups cooked pasta*
tomatoes	

Brown the ground beef with the onion in a skillet, stirring until the ground beef is crumbly; drain. Combine the beef mixture, beans, celery, garlic, broth, tomatoes, pepper, marjoram, cayenne pepper, hot sauce and basil in a slow cooker. Add the pasta to the slow cooker and mix well. Cook on Low for 8 to 10 hours or on High for 4 to 5 hours. Yield: 12 servings.

Kathy Benzel, Alpha Alpha
Torrington, Wyoming

ITALIAN SAUSAGE SOUP WITH TORTELLINI

1 pound Italian sausage, casings removed and sliced
1 cup chopped onion
2 garlic cloves, minced
5 cups beef broth
1/2 cup water
1/2 cup dry white wine
2 cups chopped tomatoes
1 cup sliced carrots
1/2 teaspoon basil
1/2 teaspoon oregano
1 (8-ounce) can tomato sauce
1 1/2 cups shredded zucchini
3 tablespoons chopped parsley
1 green bell pepper, chopped
8 ounces meat or cheese tortellini
Grated Parmesan cheese

Combine the sausage, onion, garlic, broth, water and wine in a large stockpot and mix well. Add the next 8 ingredients and mix well. Simmer for several hours or until the flavors are blended. Add the tortellini 30 minutes before serving. Top each serving with grated Parmesan cheese. Yield: 8 servings.

Peggy Bartholomaus, Xi Kappa
Corvallis, Oregon

BEEF MUSHROOM BARLEY SOUP

1 pound stew meat, cut into 1-inch cubes
1 onion, chopped
2 teaspoons vegetable oil
1 pound mushrooms, sliced
6 cups beef broth
1/2 cup barley
Salt and pepper to taste

Brown the meat and onion in 1 teaspoon of the oil in a skillet, drain and set aside. Sauté the mushrooms in the remaining oil in the skillet and add the beef mixture. Add the broth and barley, bring to a boil, reduce the heat and simmer, covered, for 1 hour. Add salt and pepper to taste. Yield: 8 to 10 servings.

Marjorie Swiger, Alpha Alpha Master
Bridgeport, Ohio

MAIN COURSE CABBAGE SOUP

1 pound ground beef
1 large onion, chopped
2 celery ribs, chopped
2 tablespoons vegetable oil
2 teaspoons salt
1/4 teaspoon black pepper
2 tablespoons brown sugar
1 (28-ounce) can tomatoes
6 cups hot water
4 beef bouillon cubes
2 to 4 chile peppers, seeded and chopped
3 tablespoons chopped parsley
1/2 green bell pepper, chopped
2 cups diced potatoes
2 cups chopped carrots
1 small head cabbage, chopped

Brown the ground beef with the onion in a large stockpot, stirring until crumbly; drain. Add the next 13 ingredients and mix well. Simmer, uncovered, for 1 hour, stirring occasionally. Add the cabbage. Simmer, covered, for 1 hour. Add 1 to 2 cups water if the soup is too thick. Yield: 12 servings.

Ginette Hunter, Xi Theta
Niagara Falls, Ontario, Canada

BORSCHT

8 to 10 cups water
1 pound beef brisket or soup bone
2 onions, sliced
2 celery ribs, chopped
4 to 6 beets, julienned
4 carrots, thinly sliced
1 small head cabbage, chopped
1 bay leaf
1 teaspoon salt
2 beets, coarsely grated
1 (6-ounce) can tomato paste
2 tablespoons vinegar
2 tablespoons sugar
Salt and black pepper to taste

Combine the water, beef, onions, celery, julienned beets, carrots, cabbage, bay leaf and 1 teaspoon salt in a large stockpot. Mix well and simmer for 2 hours. Add the grated beets, tomato paste, vinegar, sugar and salt and pepper. Mix well and simmer for 30 minutes. Garnish with fresh dill and sour cream and serve with dark rye bread. Yield: 12 servings.

Lois Scott, Laureate Alpha Phi
Brantford, Ontario, Canada

CHEESEBURGER SOUP

1 pound ground beef
1 cup chopped onion
1 cup diced celery
4 cups diced potatoes
3/4 cup shredded carrots
2 teaspoons basil
1 tablespoon parsley
1/4 cup (1/2 stick) butter
1/4 cup all-purpose flour
3 (15-ounce) cans chicken broth
1 1/4 pounds low-fat Velveeta cheese, cubed
2 cups milk
1/2 teaspoon salt
Black pepper to taste
1/3 cup marsala

Brown the ground beef with the onion in a skillet, stirring until crumbly; drain. Combine the beef mixture, celery, potatoes, carrots, basil and parsley in a large stockpot and bring to a boil. Reduce the heat. Cover and simmer for 15 minutes or until the vegetables are tender. Melt the butter in a separate saucepan and stir in the flour. Add the chicken broth. Add the flour mixture to the vegetables slowly and bring to a boil, boiling for 5 minutes. Reduce the heat and add the cheese, milk, salt and pepper, cooking until the cheese melts. Add the wine and simmer. Yield: 8 servings.

Kim Downs, Preceptor Delta Tau
St. Charles, Iowa

STUFFED SWEET PEPPER SOUP

1 pound ground beef
2 quarts water
1 quart tomato juice
3 medium red or green
  bell peppers, diced
1½ cups chili sauce
1 cup uncooked long
  grain rice

2 celery ribs, diced
1 large onion, diced
2 tablespoons browning
  sauce (optional)
3 chicken bouillon cubes
2 garlic cloves, minced
½ teaspoon salt

Brown the beef in a Dutch oven, stirring until crumbly; drain. Add the water, tomato juice, bell peppers, chili sauce, rice, celery, onion, browning sauce, bouillon, garlic and salt and mix well. Bring to a boil, reduce the heat and simmer, uncovered, for 1 hour or until the rice is tender. Yield: 16 servings.

Sonja Leavitt, Laureate Beta Tau
Elwood, Indiana

HOMEMADE CHEESE SOUP

4 to 5 medium potatoes,
  peeled and diced
1 cup chopped celery
1 cup chopped onion
1 (16-ounce) package
  frozen mixed
  vegetables, thawed
1½ quarts water

4 chicken bouillon cubes
1 (10-ounce) can cooked
  chicken
2 (10-ounce) cans cream
  of chicken soup
1 pound Velveeta cheese,
  cubed

Combine the potatoes, celery, onion, California medley, water and bouillon in a Dutch oven. Bring to a boil and boil until the vegetables are tender. Add the chicken and soup and simmer for 30 minutes. Add the cheese just before serving, stirring until the cheese is melted. Yield: 6 to 8 servings.

Addie Miller, Preceptor Beta Gamma
Sharpsburg, Georgia

COME TOGETHER SOUP

2 tablespoons extra-
  virgin olive oil
¼ cup finely chopped
  onion
2 garlic cloves, minced
2 (15-ounce) cans white
  beans, drained
1½ cups torn fresh
  spinach

2 carrots, sliced
1 tablespoon all-
  purpose flour
1½ cups cooked,
  chopped chicken
3 cups chicken broth
Salt and pepper to taste
2 tablespoons sour
  cream (optional)

Heat the olive oil in a small Dutch oven and add the onion and garlic. Sauté until the onion is tender and add the beans, spinach, carrots and flour, stirring to coat lightly. Cook on medium heat for 3 minutes, stir-

ring occasionally. Add the chicken, stirring gently and add the broth. Season with the salt and pepper and simmer for 30 minutes. Add the sour cream just before serving and mix well. Yield: 6 to 8 servings.

Jane E. Morrow, Xi Epsilon Rho
Macomb, Illinois

PORK SOUP

3 pounds pork neck and
  shoulder bones
2 tablespoons vegetable
  oil
1 bay leaf
1 tablespoon fennel seed
1 tablespoon whole
  cumin
1 tablespoon celery seed
2 garlic cloves
3 onions, peeled

4 carrots, coarsely
  chopped
4 potatoes, chopped
4 celery ribs, coarsely
  chopped
½ cup lime juice
1 (15-ounce) can
  vegetable broth
1 tablespoon honey
Salt to taste

Brown the pork in the oil in a skillet and drain on paper towels. Tie the pork, bay leaf, fennel seed, cumin, celery seed and garlic in a cheese cloth and place in a slow cooker. Add the onion, carrots, potatoes and celery and mix well. Add the lime juice and broth and cook on Low for 8 to 12 hours or on High for 5 hours. Remove from the heat 30 minutes before serving. Remove the cheese cloth and discard the bones and spices. Add the meat to the soup. Add the honey and salt and cook on low until ready to serve. Yield: 3 to 5 servings.

Betsy Heilman, Xi Zeta Lambda
Reston, Virginia

CARIBBEAN HAM AND BLACK BEAN SOUP

½ cup chopped onion
2 cups chicken stock
1 cup diced ham
1 (15-ounce) can black
  beans
1 (14-ounce) can
  tomatoes with green
  chiles

1 cup corn kernels
2 tablespoons hot red
  pepper sauce
¼ teaspoon salt
¼ teaspoon cumin
⅛ teaspoon ginger

Sauté the onion in a saucepan over medium heat for 2 to 3 minutes or until the onion is tender-crisp. Add the stock, ham, beans, tomatoes with green chiles, corn, hot sauce, salt, cumin and ginger and mix well. Bring to a boil, reduce the heat and simmer for 15 minutes, stirring occasionally. Yield: 4 servings.

Anita Wilson, Omega Master
Mansfield, Ohio

CREAM OF WILD RICE SOUP

1 large onion, finely diced	8 cups chicken broth
1 celery rib, finely diced	3 cups cooked wild rice
1 cup finely diced ham	Salt and white pepper to taste
1 carrot, finely diced	
1/2 cup (1 stick) butter	1 cup light cream or half-and-half
1 cup all-purpose flour	

Combine the onion, celery, ham and carrot in the butter in a large stockpot and cook for 3 to 4 minutes. Stir in the flour gradually until blended. Add the chicken broth slowly, stirring until blended. Bring to a boil; reduce the heat and simmer, uncovered, for 30 minutes. Add the rice and season with the salt and pepper. Add the cream and heat thoroughly.
Yield: 10 to 12 servings.

Edie Loewen, Laureate Iota
Minnetonka, Minnesota

FRIENDSHIP POTATO SOUP

5 pounds potatoes, peeled and sliced	1 quart half-and-half
2 bunches green onions, chopped	1/2 teaspoon garlic powder
1 small onion, chopped	1 1/2 teaspoons salt
1/2 cup (1 stick) butter	1 1/2 teaspoons black pepper
4 (12-ounce) cans evaporated milk	1 1/2 pounds ham, chopped

Boil the potatoes in large saucepan until tender; drain. Mash 1 cup of the potatoes and return to the saucepan. Sauté the onions in the butter in a skillet until the onions are tender. Add the onion mixture and the next 5 ingredients to the mashed potatoes and mix well. Add the ham and the remaining potatoes; simmer for 20 minutes. Yield: 20 servings.

Nina Jones, Xi Tau
Northport, Alabama

POTATO SAUSAGE SOUP

1/2 pound pork sausage	2 cups water
1 (16-ounce) package frozen hash brown potatoes, thawed	1 (10-ounce) can cream of celery soup
1 large onion, diced	1 (10-ounce) can cream of chicken soup
1 (14-ounce) can chicken broth	2 cups milk

Brown the sausage in a large Dutch oven, stirring until crumbly; drain. Add the potatoes, onion, broth and water and bring to a boil. Reduce the heat. Simmer, covered, for 30 minutes. Add the soups and milk and cook until heated through, stirring often.
Yield: 4 to 6 servings.

Lynda L. Evans, Laureate Theta Eta
Livingston, Texas

FIFTEEN-BEAN SOUP

1 package 15-bean soup beans	1 to 2 tablespoons chili powder
1 pound smoked sausage, cut into small pieces	3 tablespoons lemon juice
1 large onion, chopped	2 garlic cloves, minced
1 (15-ounce) can chopped tomatoes	Ham packet from the soup beans
1 (15-ounce) can crushed tomatoes	Salt and black pepper to taste

Place the beans in a large Dutch oven, cover with water and soak overnight. Drain the beans, add 2 quarts water and the sausage and bring to a boil. Reduce the heat and simmer, uncovered, for 2 to 2 1/2 hours. Add the onion, tomatoes, chili powder, lemon juice and garlic and simmer for 30 minutes. Add the ham packet contents and salt and pepper and simmer for 5 minutes. Cover and let sit for 2 to 3 hours. Reheat before serving. Yield: 15 to 20 servings.

Jo Ann Kidd, Xi Alpha Xi
Bessemer, Alabama

BROCCOLI CHEESE SOUP

1 1/2 pounds broccoli, separated into florets	3/4 teaspoon salt
1 pint half-and-half	1/2 teaspoon black pepper
2 cups water	1/2 cup cornstarch
1 pound Velveeta cheese, cut into chunks	1 cup cold water

Steam the broccoli in a steamer until the broccoli is tender. Combine the half-and-half and water in a large microwave-safe bowl. Add the cheese, salt and pepper and microwave until the cheese is melted. Add the broccoli and mix well. Combine the cornstarch and water in a small bowl. Add to the cheese mixture and heat until the soup thickens, stirring occasionally. Yield: 10 servings.

Beth Singleton, Beta
Nacogdoches, Texas

CARROT AND CILANTRO SOUP

1 tablespoon butter	Pinch of grated nutmeg
1 onion, finely chopped	1 tablespoon chopped cilantro
1 garlic clove, minced	
1 1/2 pounds carrots, coarsely chopped	1/2 cup heavy cream
1 3/4 pints vegetable stock	Salt and black pepper to taste

Melt the butter in a saucepan and sauté the onion and garlic until the onion is tender. Add the carrots, stock and nutmeg and cover. Bring to a boil, reduce the heat and simmer until the vegetables are tender. Remove from the heat and purée the vegetables in a blender. Return the soup to a separate saucepan and add the cilantro and cream. Season with the salt and pepper. Garnish each serving with a sprinkle of fresh cilantro on top. Yield: 6 servings.

Claire Swinhoe, Preceptor Beta
Los Alamos, New Mexico

CAULIFLOWER SOUP

3 small onions, chopped	1/2 teaspoon crushed
2 garlic cloves, minced	basil or dill
1/4 cup (1/2 stick) butter	1/2 teaspoon dry mustard
3/4 cup chopped celery	5 cups chicken stock
1 head cauliflower,	1 1/2 cups milk
separated into florets	Salt and white pepper
2 potatoes, peeled and	to taste
chopped	2 cups (8 ounces)
3 carrots, peeled and	shredded
sliced	Cheddar cheese

Sauté the onions and garlic in the butter in a saucepan until the onions are tender. Add the celery and sauté for 2 minutes. Add the cauliflower, potatoes, carrots, basil, dry mustard and stock and cook until the vegetables are tender. Purée with a hand-held mixer. Add the milk, salt and white pepper and cheese and heat just until the soup is thoroughly heated. Yield: 12 servings.

Kathy Smith, Laureate Alpha Sigma
Tilbury, Ontario, Canada

PARSNIP SOUP

Superb and unusual!

1 pound parsnips,	3 cups cold water
peeled, sliced and	1/4 teaspoon grated
quartered	nutmeg
1 cup chopped celery	1 teaspoon salt
1/4 cup (1/2 stick) butter	Black pepper to taste
3 cups chicken stock	1/3 cup chopped parsley
3 tablespoons	Parmesan cheese, grated
all-purpose flour	

Sauté the parsnips and celery in the butter in a stockpot. Cover and cook over medium heat for 10 minutes. Add the stock and stir well. Place 1 cup of the mixture into a blender. Add the flour, 1 cup of the cold water, nutmeg and salt and purée. Pour the mixture back into the stockpot and add the remaining water. Heat, uncovered, for 5 minutes and season with the salt and pepper. Place 1 cup of the soup into

a blender and blend well. Pour back into the stockpot and heat thoroughly. Top each serving with grated Parmesan cheese. Yield: 6 to 8 servings.

Janet Hamilton, Preceptor Alpha Beta
Kalamazoo, Michigan

PINK SOUP

6 slices bacon	1 (10-ounce) can
1 onion, chopped	tomatoes with green
2 potatoes, diced	chiles
5 cups water	2 cups uncooked elbow
1 tablespoon salt	macaroni
1 tablespoon black	2 cups half-and-half
pepper	
1 (28-ounce) can diced	
tomatoes	

Sauté the bacon and onion in a stockpot until the onion is tender. Add the potatoes, water, salt, pepper, diced tomatoes and tomatoes with green chiles and bring to a boil. Reduce the heat and simmer for 15 minutes. Add the macaroni. Cook, covered, stirring frequently until the macaroni is tender. Remove from the heat and stir in the half-and-half.
Yield: 6 to 8 servings.

Suzanne Thompson, Xi Alpha Zeta
Bentonville, Arkansas

BOURBON AND BUTTERNUT SQUASH SOUP

2 tablespoons butter	1 1/2 quarts chicken stock
1 large onion, coarsely	1/4 cup bourbon
chopped	1 bay leaf
1 large butternut	Salt and black pepper
squash, peeled,	to taste
seeded and cut into	Lemon juice to taste
1-inch chunks	1/4 cup heavy cream

Melt the butter in a large stockpot and add the onion, stirring to coat. Cover and simmer for 10 minutes. Add the squash, stock, bourbon and bay leaf and bring to a boil. Reduce the heat and simmer, uncovered, for 30 to 40 minutes or until the squash is tender. Strain the mixture, reserving the liquid and discarding the bay leaf. Transfer the squash and onion to a blender and process until smooth. Return to the stockpot and add the reserved broth. Cook over medium heat for 10 to 15 minutes, stirring occasionally, until the soup thickens to a light cream consistency. Add the salt, pepper and lemon juice and mix well. Add the cream just before serving. Yield: 8 to 10 servings.

Marlene Blankenship, Laureate Alpha
Beckley, West Virginia

MUSHROOM SOUP

1/4 cup (1/2 stick) butter
3 green onions, chopped
2 cups sliced mushrooms
1/4 cup chopped celery
1/4 cup all-purpose flour
2/3 cup water

2 cups chicken broth
1/4 teaspoon dry mustard
2 cups half-and-half
Salt and black pepper
   to taste

Melt the butter in a large saucepan and sauté the green onions, mushrooms and celery for 15 minutes or until the vegetables are tender. Combine the flour and water in a small bowl, stirring constantly to prevent lumping and set aside. Add the broth, dry mustard and half-and-half to the vegetable mixture. Add the flour mixture and simmer until the mixture thickens, stirring often. Garnish each serving with fresh parsley. Yield: 6 servings.

Sheila Saunders, Epsilon Sigma
Ville Platte, Louisiana

LOADED POTATO SOUP

4 to 6 potatoes, peeled
   and chopped
Garlic salt to taste
1 teaspoon onion
   salt
1/2 cup bacon bits
Salt and black pepper
   to taste
1 (10-ounce) can cream
   of chicken soup

1 cup chopped celery or
   1 can cream of celery
   soup
1 (10-ounce) can cream
   of mushroom soup
   (optional)
1/3 cup butter
8 ounces Velveeta cheese
1 (15-ounce) can carrots,
   drained (optional)

Boil the potatoes in water to cover in a large saucepan. Add the garlic salt, onion salt, bacon bits, salt and pepper when the potatoes are tender. Simmer over low heat, stirring occasionally. Stir in the soups and celery. Add the butter, Velveeta and carrots and simmer, stirring often, until thickened. Yield: 4 to 6 servings.

Joyce Schoening, Alpha Omega
Ledbetter, Kentucky

SLOW-COOKER POTATO SOUP

10 to 12 potatoes, peeled
   and chopped
1 (8-ounce) container
   French onion dip
1/2 cup (1 stick)
   margarine
2 (10-ounce) cans cream
   of chicken soup
2 cups milk

1 pound bacon
1 onion, chopped
Salt and black pepper
   to taste
Milk
2 cups (8 ounces)
   shredded Swiss
   cheese

Parboil the potatoes in a saucepan and drain. Combine the onion dip, margarine, soup and the 2 cups of the milk in a slow cooker. Fry the bacon in a skillet until crisp. Remove the bacon and crumble. Sauté the onion in the drippings. Add the onion, potatoes, 1/2 of the bacon, salt and pepper to the slow cooker. Add enough milk to nearly fill the slow cooker and cook on Low for 8 hours. Add the cheese and remaining bacon and stir well. Yield: 10 servings.

Debbie Bailey, Preceptor Gamma Tau
Jacksonville, Florida

GERMAN TOMATO SOUP

1 onion, chopped
1 leek, chopped
1 shallot, chopped
3 red bell peppers,
   chopped

4 tomatoes, chopped
1/4 cup (1/2 stick) butter
1 cup chicken broth
Dash of seasoned salt
1 cup heavy cream

Sauté the onion, leek, shallot, bell peppers and tomatoes in the butter in a skillet until the vegetables are tender. Cool the vegetables slightly and purée in a blender. Pour the mixture into a saucepan and add the broth, seasoned salt and cream and simmer for 30 minutes. Yield: 6 servings.

Bette Kochsiek, Laureate Iota Rho
Palm Desert, California

ROASTED VEGETABLE SOUP

1 bulb fennel, chopped
1 red onion, chopped
1 sweet potato, chopped
1 red bell pepper,
   chopped
1 small zucchini,
   chopped
1 small yam, chopped
Parsnip, chopped
   (optional)
1/4 cup olive oil

4 cups vegetable stock
2 tablespoons paprika
2 tablespoons ginger
1 teaspoon cumin
Roasted garlic to taste
2 teaspoons coriander
1/4 teaspoon nutmeg
Pinch of salt
2 tablespoons balsamic
   vinegar

Place the fennel, red onion, sweet potato, bell pepper, zucchini, yam and parsnip in a roasting pan and drizzle with the olive oil. Roast at 425 degrees for 1 hour. Combine the stock, paprika, ginger, cumin, coriander, nutmeg, salt and balsamic vinegar in a saucepan and bring to a boil. Reduce the heat and simmer for 20 minutes. Add the vegetables and cook for 20 minutes. Purée using a hand mixer and serve. Garnish with chopped parsley and green onions. Yield: 6 servings.

Lavinia Switzer, Preceptor Beta Iota
Queshel, British Columbia, Canada

Meats

❖ GRILLED TRI-TIP ROAST WITH TEQUILA MARINADE AND CHERRY TOMATO RELISH

¹/₂ cup fresh lime juice	*2 teaspoons cumin*
¹/₂ cup chopped fresh	*2 teaspoons dried*
cilantro	*oregano*
¹/₂ cup olive oil	*1 teaspoon freshly*
¹/₃ cup soy sauce	*ground pepper*
¹/₄ cup tequila	*2 (2-pound) beef loin*
7 garlic cloves, finely	*tri-tip roasts,*
chopped	*trimmed*
2 teaspoons grated	*Cherry Tomato Relish*
lime zest	

Whisk together the lime juice, cilantro, olive oil, soy sauce, tequila, garlic, lime zest, cumin, oregano and pepper in a medium bowl. Pierce the tri-tip roasts all over using a small sharp knife. Place the meat in a sealable plastic bag. Pour the marinade over the steaks. Seal and refrigerate at least 2 hours, or overnight, turning the bag occasionally. Remove the meat and discard the marinade. Grill the meat over hot coals for 10 minutes per side or until the meat has reached the desired doneness. Remove the roasts to a cutting board; let stand for 10 minutes before carving. Slice against the grain into thin strips. Serve with Cherry Tomato Relish. Yield: 8 servings.

CHERRY TOMATO RELISH

¹/₄ cup balsamic vinegar	*4 green onions, finely*
³/₄ cup olive oil	*chopped*
4 teaspoons chopped	*4 cups halved cherry*
fresh oregano	*tomatoes*
2 tablespoons diced	*Salt and pepper to taste*
mild chilies	

Whisk together the vinegar and olive oil in a medium bowl. Add the oregano, chilies, green onions and tomatoes. Toss to coat. Season with salt and pepper to taste.

Lynn Gustin, Alpha Zeta
Missoula, Montana

STUFFED STEAK ROLLS

3 pounds round steak	*¹/₂ cup vegetable oil*
2 cups fresh bread	*3 tablespoons chopped*
crumbs	*fresh parsley*
³/₄ teaspoon seasoned	*1 teaspoon salt*
salt	*1 teaspoon pepper*
1¹/₂ teaspoons garlic	*1 (10-ounce) can*
powder	*mushroom soup*
1 teaspoon Greek	*1 (4-ounce) can sliced*
seasoning	*black olives*
1 cup chopped fresh	*1 (4-ounce) can*
mushrooms	*mushrooms*

Cut the steaks into 8 pieces. Combine the bread crumbs, seasoned salt, garlic powder, Greek seasoning, 1 cup mushrooms, oil, parsley, salt and pepper in a large bowl and mix well. Cover the steaks with the seasoning mixture. Roll the steaks and secure with a toothpick. Place the steak rolls seam side down in a greased large heavy baking pan. Bake at 350 degrees for 30 minutes. Combine the mushroom soup, black olives and canned mushrooms in a bowl and mix well. Add the juices from the meat. Pour the mixture over the steaks. Return the steaks to the oven for 15 more minutes or until warm. Yield: 8 servings.

Diane Evrard, Gamma Pi
Cleveland, Mississippi

GARLIC-ROASTED CHATEAUBRIAND WITH COGNAC-MUSTARD SAUCE

2 (2- to 2¹/₂-pound) beef tenderloins, trimmed	2 tablespoons cognac
	2 tablespoons Dijon mustard
4 garlic cloves, finely chopped	3 tablespoons minced fresh parsley
3 tablespoons olive oil	¹/₂ cup (1 stick) butter, cut into 8 pieces
1 tablespoon butter	
4 green onions, minced	Salt and freshly ground pepper to taste
2 cups beef broth	

Cut ³/₄-inch-deep slits in the tenderloins. Insert the garlic in the slits. Brush the tenderloins with 2 tablespoons of the olive oil. Brown all sides of the tenderloins in the remaining 1 tablespoon of olive oil in a large skillet over medium-high heat. Remove the tenderloins from the skillet and place on a rack in a large roasting pan. Roast the tenderloins at 450 degrees for 30 to 40 minutes or until a meat thermometer inserted in the thickest portion of the meat reaches 140 degrees for rare, 160 degrees for medium or until done to taste. Cut the tenderloins in ¹/₂-inch slices and cover with aluminum foil to keep warm. Melt 1 tablespoon of butter in the reserved skillet. Add the onions and sauté until tender. Drain the fat from the roasting pan. Set the roasting pan over high heat and stir in the broth, scraping up the brown bits. Add the broth to the onions and boil until reduced by half. Add the cognac and boil for one minute. Reduce the heat to low and whisk in the Dijon mustard. Stir in the parsley, then whisk in the butter one piece at a time. Season with salt and pepper to taste. Arrange the tenderloin slices on a serving platter. Pour the sauce over the tenderloin. Yield: 12 servings.

Majorie Kubr, Laureate Zeta
Fremont, Nebraska

MARINATED BEEF TENDERLOIN

1 (5- to 6-pound) beef tenderloin, trimmed	1 teaspoon soy sauce
	¹/₃ cup Burgundy or other dry red wine
2 (16-ounce) bottles zesty Italian salad dressing	1 garlic clove, minced
	¹/₂ teaspoon lemon-pepper seasoning
¹/₃ cup meat and vegetable marinade	

Place the meat in a sealable plastic bag. Combine the salad dressing, meat and vegetable marinade, soy sauce, Burgundy, garlic and lemon-pepper marinade in a bowl and mix well. Pour the marinade over the meat. Seal and refrigerate for 8 hours, turning occasionally. Remove the tenderloin, discarding the marinade. Grill the tenderloin, covered with the grill lid, over high heat for 3 minutes. Turn and cook for 3 minutes longer. Reduce the heat to low. Cook, covered, for 12 minutes or until a meat thermometer inserted in thickest portion registers 140 degrees for rare, 160 degrees for medium or until done to taste. Let stand for 15 minutes before carving.
Yield: 10-12 servings.

Jenny Poole, Preceptor Mu
Lexington, Kentucky

TERIYAKI TENDERLOIN

1 (2-pound) beef tenderloin	¹/₄ cup soy sauce
	2 tablespoons brown sugar
¹/₂ cup dry sherry	
2 tablespoons onion soup mix	2 tablespoons water

Place the meat in a sealable plastic bag. Combine the sherry, soup mix, soy sauce and brown sugar in a bowl and mix well. Pour the marinade over the meat. Seal and refrigerate for 8 to 24 hours, turning occasionally. Remove the meat, reserving the marinade, and place on a rack in a roasting pan. Bake at 425 degrees for 50 minutes or until a meat thermometer inserted in the thickest portion registers 140 degrees for rare, 160 degrees for medium or until done to taste, basting occasionally with half of the marinade. Slice against the grain into thin strips. Bring the remaining half of the marinade to a boil. Add the water and stir well. Pour the sauce over the tenderloin strips to serve. Yield: 6 to 8 servings.

Terry Meredith, Xi Beta Upsilon
Delta, British Columbia, Canada

SPICY WINE BEEF ROAST

1 (3- to 4-pound) beef roast	¹/₄ cup dry red wine
Salt and pepper to taste	2 tablespoons plus 2 teaspoons Dijon mustard
1 small onion, chopped	
1 envelope brown gravy mix	1 teaspoon Worcestershire sauce
1 cup water	¹/₈ teaspoon garlic powder
¹/₄ cup ketchup	

Season the roast with salt and pepper. Place the roast in a slow cooker. Combine the remaining ingredients in a bowl and mix well. Pour the sauce over the roast. Cover and cook on Low for 8 hours or until tender. Remove the roast and slice. Serve the sauce over the roast, if desired. Yield: 10 to 12 servings.

Clara Murphy, Laureate Gamma
Dalhart, Texas

MARINATED FLANK STEAK

1 envelope meat marinade	1/3 cup bourbon
1/2 cup soy sauce	1/3 cup water
1/2 cup Worcestershire sauce	1/3 cup red wine vinegar or cider vinegar
	2 flank steaks

Combine the marinade, soy sauce, Worcestershire sauce, bourbon, water and vinegar in a bowl and mix well. Pour the mixture into a sealable plastic bag. Add the steaks; seal and marinate in the refrigerator for 6 to 8 hours. Remove the steaks and marinade to a 9×13-inch baking pan. Bake, uncovered, at 350 degrees for 20 to 25 minutes on each side or until tender and cooked through. Yield: 8 to 10 servings.

Eleanor H. Redican, Preceptor Gamma Delta
Burke, Virginia

DILLED POT ROAST

1 teaspoon dill weed	3 tablespoons all-purpose flour
1 teaspoon salt	
1/4 teaspoon pepper	1/4 cup cold water
1 (2- to 2 1/2-pound) boneless chuck roast	1 cup sour cream
1 tablespoon cider vinegar	1/2 teaspoon browning sauce (optional)
1 teaspoon dill weed	Hot cooked rice

Combine 1 teaspoon dill weed, salt and pepper in a small bowl. Sprinkle over both sides of the roast. Place the roast in a 3-quart slow cooker. Add the vinegar and enough water to cover. Cover and cook on Low for 7 to 8 hours or until the meat is tender. Remove the roast and keep warm. Combine 1 teaspoon dill and flour in a small bowl. Stir in 1/4 cup cold water until smooth. Add the mixture gradually into the slow cooker, stirring constantly. Cover and cook on High for 30 minutes or until the sauce is thickened. Stir in the sour cream and browning sauce. Serve the sauce with sliced roast and rice. Yield: 6 to 8 servings.

Delma Chesshir, Laureate Iota Alpha
Dallas, Texas

POT ROAST WITH A FLAIR

1 (3-pound) boneless lean chuck roast	1 (14-ounce) can Italian-style tomatoes
Salt and pepper to taste	2 tablespoons cornstarch
6 ounces fresh mushrooms, sliced	1/2 cup cold water
1 onion, sliced	

Season the roast with salt and pepper. Place the roast on a large piece of heavy duty foil in a 9×13-inch baking pan. Cover the roast with the mushrooms and onion. Pour the tomatoes over the roast. Dissolve the cornstarch in the cold water in a small bowl, stirring well. Pour the cornstarch over the roast. Fold the foil securely. Bake at 350 degrees for 2 to 2 1/2 hours or until done. Yield: 4 to 6 servings.

Rosemarie Wilson, Laureate Phi
Germantown, Maryland

ROCKY MOUNTAIN BRISKET WITH BARBECUE SAUCE

1 1/2 teaspoons salt	1 (4-pound) beef brisket
1 1/2 teaspoons pepper	2 tablespoons liquid smoke
2 tablespoons chili powder	Barbecue Sauce
1 teaspoon crushed bay leaves	

Combine the salt, pepper, chili powder and bay leaves in a small bowl and mix well. Coat the brisket completely with the liquid smoke and sprinkle with the seasoning mixture. Place the brisket, fat side up, in a large roasting pan. Bake, covered, at 325 degrees for 4 hours or until done. Scrape off the seasonings and cut the brisket into very thin slices across the grain. Pour the hot Barbecue Sauce over the meat to serve. Yield: 6 servings.

BARBECUE SAUCE

3 tablespoons brown sugar	1/4 cup Worcestershire sauce
1 (14-ounce) bottle ketchup	2 teaspoons celery seeds
1/2 cup water	6 tablespoons butter
2 tablespoons liquid smoke	1/4 teaspoon cayenne pepper
1 tablespoon dry mustard	Salt and pepper to taste

Combine all the ingredients in a medium saucepan. Bring to a boil, stirring occasionally. Boil for 10 minutes.

Polly Jo Wick, Xi Delta Eta
Austin, Colorado

Linda Weir, Epsilon Alpha, Garland, Texas, prepares **French Beef Bake** *by browning 2 pounds cubed round steak in 1/4 cup butter. The meat is drained and the butter is discarded. The meat is placed in a large casserole and combined with 1 envelope dry onion soup mix, 1 cup dry red wine, and 1 1/4 cups water. She covers and bakes the casserole at 350 degrees for 2 hours. The braised meat is served over noodles or rice.*

ROUND STEAK STRIPS

1 pound round steak, cut into strips	6 tablespoons tomato sauce
Salt and pepper to taste	4 heaping teaspoons prepared mustard
1/3 cup all-purpose flour	
4 cubes beef bouillon	4 teaspoons Worcestershire sauce
2 cups warm water	
1 1/3 cups sour cream	

Season the steak with salt and pepper and dredge in the flour. Brown both sides of the steak in a nonstick skillet over medium heat. Drain and return the steak to the skillet over low heat. Dissolve the bouillon cubes in the warm water in a small bowl, stirring to combine. Pour the bouillon over the steak. Combine the sour cream, tomato sauce, mustard and Worcestershire sauce in a bowl and mix well. Pour the tomato mixture over the steak. Simmer in the skillet until the meat is tender, stirring occasionally. Yield: 6 to 8 servings.

Sharon J. Simon, Gamma Zeta
Mobridge, South Dakota

SWISS STEAK IN SOUR CREAM

1 (3-pound) round steak, 2 inches thick	1/2 cup sour cream
Salt and pepper to taste	2 tablespoons shredded Swiss cheese
1/3 cup all-purpose flour	3/4 teaspoon paprika
2 tablespoons shortening	1/2 to 1 cup water
	1 onion, sliced

Season the steak with salt and pepper and dredge in the flour. Brown both sides of the steak in the shortening in a large skillet over medium-high heat until cooked through. Mix the sour cream, cheese, paprika and water in a bowl. Add the mixture to the skillet and stir until melted. Add the onion to the skillet; cover and simmer for 2 hours or until tender. Yield: 4 servings.

Diane Domaschko, Preceptor Alpha
South Charleston, West Virginia

SPECIAL SWISS STEAK

Prepared mustard	6 tablespoons vinegar
1 (4-pound) round steak, tenderized	1/2 green bell pepper, chopped
1/3 cup all-purpose flour	1 teaspoon dried parsley flakes
1/4 cup vegetable oil	
1/2 cup chopped onion	1/4 cup packed brown sugar
1 (8-ounce) can tomato sauce	2 teaspoons salt
3/4 cup water	1/8 teaspoon pepper
1 (10-ounce) can tomato soup	2 teaspoons Worcestershire sauce

Spread the mustard over the steak. Dredge the steak in the flour. Brown both sides of the steak in the oil in a large skillet over medium-high heat until done; remove the steak to a Dutch oven. Sauté the onion in the same skillet until tender; discard excess fat. Combine the remaining ingredients in a bowl and mix well. Add the sauce to the onion, stirring to combine. Pour the onion mixture over the steak. Cover and simmer over low heat for 2 hours or until tender. Yield: 6 to 8 servings.

Louise Goode, Xi Alpha Lambda
Sedan, Kansas

BEEF BOURGUIGNON

3 pounds lean beef cubes	1 teaspoon dried thyme
1/4 cup olive oil	1 cup beef broth
3 tablespoons all-purpose flour	1 cup dry red wine
	1 cup sliced mushrooms
1 1/2 teaspoons salt	2 small onions, chopped
1 teaspoon pepper	

Sauté the beef in the olive oil in a skillet over medium-high heat until browned. Stir in the flour, salt, pepper and thyme and mix well. Spoon the beef mixture into a 2-quart casserole. Add the beef broth and wine and stir to combine. Bake, covered, at 325 degrees for 2 hours. Add the mushrooms and onions and bake an additional 30 minutes or until the vegetables are tender. Yield: 6 to 8 servings.

Susan L. Hodge, Delta Master
Rapid City, South Dakota

BURGUNDY BEEF STEW

1 (1 1/2-pound) lean boneless round steak	6 carrots, peeled and cut in 1-inch pieces
1 tablespoon olive oil	2 onions, quartered
1/2 teaspoon dried thyme	8 ounces mushrooms, quartered
2 large garlic cloves, minced	6 tablespoons cornstarch
3 cups Burgundy	6 tablespoons water
6 ounces tomato paste	1/4 cup chopped fresh parsley
2 bay leaves	
4 cups beef broth	1/2 teaspoon salt
3/4 cup water	1/2 teaspoon pepper
1 1/2 pounds red potatoes, quartered	

Trim the fat from the steak and cut into 1-inch pieces. Coat a large Dutch oven with nonstick cooking spray; add the olive oil. Brown the steak pieces in the oil over medium heat, stirring frequently; drain. Wipe the drippings from the pan. Coat the pan again with cooking spray. Add the steak pieces, thyme and garlic. Stir in the wine, tomato paste and bay leaves and mix well. Bring to a boil. Reduce heat and simmer, covered, for 1½ hours or until the steak is tender. Add the next 6 ingredients and simmer for an additional 20 minutes or until the vegetables are tender. Dissolve the cornstarch in 6 tablespoons water. Add the cornstarch mixture and parsley to the Dutch oven and mix well. Simmer for 2 to 3 minutes or until thickened. Season with the salt and pepper. Remove the bay leaves before serving. Yield: 12 servings.

Bea Glassco, Laureate Theta Eta
Coldspring, Texas

POT ROAST STEW

1 (2- to 3-pound) pot roast, fat trimmed	½ package baby carrots
2 to 3 tablespoons vegetable oil	5 or 6 potatoes, quartered
2 cups hot water	1 (10-ounce) can beef broth
½ teaspoon salt	½ cup water
¼ teaspoon pepper	1 tablespoon all-purpose flour
4 carrots, finely chopped	½ cup water
4 ribs celery, finely chopped	1 envelope brown gravy mix
½ onion, finely chopped	
2 tablespoons butter	

Cut the roast into ¾-inch cubes. Heat the oil in a Dutch oven over medium heat. Brown the roast in the hot oil for 10 to 15 minutes, turning frequently. Add 2 cups hot water, the salt and pepper and mix well. Bring to a boil. Reduce the heat to low; cover and simmer for 2 hours. Sauté the carrots, celery and onion in the butter in a skillet over medium heat until tender. Add the vegetable mixture to the roast. Cut the baby carrots in half. Add the baby carrots and potatoes to the stew. Cover and bring to a boil. Add the beef broth and ½ cup water. Cover and cook over medium-high heat for 30 minutes, stirring occasionally. Stir the flour into ½ cup water. Add the flour mixture and gravy mix to the stew and stir to mix well. Simmer for 10 minutes, stirring occasionally. Yield: 6 to 8 servings.

Laurie Gordon, Delta Gamma
Crofton, Maryland

BEEF STROGANOFF

2 pounds beef stew meat	¾ teaspoon pepper
1 cup chopped onion	8 ounces cream cheese, cubed
1 (10-ounce) can golden mushroom soup	2 cups sour cream
1 (10-ounce) can cream of onion soup	16 ounces egg noodles, cooked and drained
1 (8-ounce) can sliced mushrooms, drained	Chopped fresh parsley (optional)

Mix the first 6 ingredients in a 3- to 6-quart slow cooker. Cook, covered, on Low for 8 to 10 hours. Add the cream cheese about 15 minutes before serving and stir until melted. Stir in the sour cream. Serve over the noodles. Garnish with parsley. Yield: 8 servings.

Janet Howell, Alpha Zeta Master
Holland, Michigan

HUNGARIAN GOULASH

1 pound beef cubes	¾ teaspoon cider vinegar
2 onions, minced	6 tablespoons ketchup
¼ teaspoon dry mustard	1 cup water
1¼ teaspoons paprika	3 tablespoons all-purpose flour
2 tablespoons brown sugar	½ cup water
1¼ teaspoons (or less) salt	1 (6-ounce) package egg noodles, cooked and drained
3 tablespoons Worcestershire sauce	

Brown the beef on all sides in a large heavy skillet over medium-high heat. Add the onions and stir well. Combine the dry mustard, paprika, brown sugar and salt in a bowl and mix well. Combine the Worcestershire sauce, vinegar and ketchup in a separate bowl and mix well. Add the ketchup mixture to the dry mustard mixture and mix well. Add the sauce to the meat. Stir in 1 cup water. Cover and cook over low heat for 2½ hours or until the meat is tender. Blend the flour with ½ cup water and add to the meat mixture. Stir until thickened. Serve the meat mixture over the noodles. Yield: 8 servings.

Carolyn Woelfle, Laureate Beta Nu
Harrison, Ohio

BUL-GO-KEE

1 (1-pound) top sirloin	½ teaspoon finely chopped onion
1 tablespoon sesame oil	1 green onion, finely chopped
2 tablespoons soy sauce	Hot cooked rice
2 tablespoons water	
1 tablespoon sugar	
1 teaspoon sesame seeds	
1 teaspoon finely chopped garlic	

Cut the sirloin into thin slices. Combine the sesame oil, soy sauce, water, sugar, sesame seeds, garlic, onion and green onion in a bowl and mix well. Add the meat and toss to coat. Cover and let stand at room temperature for 30 minutes to 1 hour. Brown the meat in a large skillet over high heat until done. Serve over rice. Yield: 4 servings.

Betty Turkle, Laureate Beta Kappa
Haysville, Kansas

BULGOGIE

1/4 cup sesame oil	5 garlic cloves, minced
5 tablespoons brown sugar	2 pounds sirloin steak, cut into thin strips
3 tablespoons granulated sugar	1 large onion, halved and thinly sliced
1 tablespoon garlic powder	1 carrot, julienned
7 tablespoons soy sauce	1 green bell pepper, julienned
1/2 teaspoon pepper	1 small bunch green onions, diced
1/4 cup sesame seeds	

Whisk the sesame oil, brown sugar, granulated sugar, garlic powder, soy sauce, pepper, sesame seeds and garlic in a small bowl. Pour the mixture into a large sealable plastic bag. Add the sirloin strips, onion, carrot, and bell pepper to the bag with the marinade. Seal the bag and refrigerate overnight. Cook the mixture in small batches in a large skillet over high heat for 5 minutes or until done. Garnish with the green onions. Yield: 6 to 8 servings.

Faye Walker, Chi Master
Moyock, North Carolina

MANDARIN BEEF STIR-FRY

1 cup orange juice	1 onion, quartered
1/2 cup soy sauce	1 green bell pepper, cut in thin strips
2 tablespoons Worcestershire sauce	1 cup sliced fresh mushrooms
1 teaspoon garlic powder	2 tablespoons vegetable oil
1/4 teaspoon ground ginger	1 (11-ounce) can mandarin oranges, drained
1 (1-pound) beef round steak, cut into thin strips	2 tablespoons cornstarch
2 cups snow peas	Hot cooked rice

Combine the orange juice, soy sauce, Worcestershire sauce, garlic powder and ginger in a bowl and mix well. Reserve 1/2 of the marinade for another use. Pour the remaining marinade into a sealable plastic bag. Add the steak to the bag; seal and refrigerate for 15 minutes. Stir-fry the snow peas, onion, bell pepper and mushrooms in the oil in a large skillet for 2 minutes. Remove the vegetables and keep warm. Drain the steak, discarding the marinade. Stir-fry the steak in the skillet over medium-high heat until done. Combine the oranges and the reserved marinade and add to the meat; stir until mixed. Add the cornstarch and stir until smooth. Bring to a boil and cook for 2 minutes or until thickened, stirring constantly. Serve over steamed rice. Yield: 6 servings.

Sandra E. Moody, Preceptor Eta Sigma
Trinity, Florida

SAUCY BARBECUE BEEF SANDWICHES

1 (2 1/2- to 3-pound) chuck roast	2 tablespoons white vinegar
2 tablespoons butter	1 cup water
1 onion, chopped	3 tablespoons Worcestershire sauce
2 tablespoons brown sugar	1/2 cup sliced mushrooms
1/4 cup lemon juice	Salt and pepper to taste
1/2 teaspoon dry mustard	Rolls
1/2 cup diced celery	

Place the roast in a covered deep baking pan. Bake at 350 degrees for 2 hours or until tender. Bone and shred the roast. Simmer the roast in the butter in a large Dutch oven. Add the onion, brown sugar, lemon juice, dry mustard and celery and mix well. Add the vinegar, water, Worcestershire sauce, mushrooms, salt and pepper; stir to combine. Simmer, covered, for 1 1/2 to 2 hours. Serve on the rolls. Yield: 10 to 12 servings.

T. Lynn Moerke, Preceptor Upsilon
Franklin, Wisconsin

REUBEN LOAF

2 1/2 cups all-purpose flour	1/4 cup Thousand Island salad dressing
1 tablespoon sugar	1 (12-ounce) can corned beef, sliced
1 teaspoon salt	4 ounces Swiss cheese, thinly sliced
1 package rapid rise yeast	1 (8-ounce) can sauerkraut, drained
1 cup hot water (125 to 130 degrees)	1 egg white, beaten
1 tablespoon margarine	Caraway seeds
1 cup or less flour	

Mix 2 1/2 cups flour, sugar, salt and yeast in a large bowl. Stir in the hot water and the margarine. Add 1 cup flour gradually, stirring until a soft dough forms. Knead the dough on a floured surface for 4 minutes, adding additional flour if necessary. Roll the dough into a 10×14-inch rectangle. Place the dough on a greased baking sheet. Spread the dressing down the center. Arrange layers of the corned beef, cheese slices and sauerkraut over the dressing. Cut each side into 1-inch-wide diagonal strips. Fold alternately over the center to enclose the filling. Cover the dough with a damp cloth. Place the baking sheet over a pan of very hot water for 15 minutes or until the dough rises. Brush the dough with the egg white and sprinkle with caraway seeds. Bake at 400 degrees for 25 minutes. Serve warm. Yield: 8 to 10 servings.

Wanda Blake, Laureate Alpha Epsilon
Lewisburg, West Virginia

REUBEN CASSEROLE

1 cup sour cream	1 loaf dry rye bread
1 onion, chopped	8 ounces shredded Swiss
1 (16-ounce) can	cheese
sauerkraut, drained	1/4 cup (1/2 stick) butter
1 (12-ounce) can corned	
beef, sliced	

Mix the sour cream, onion and sauerkraut together in a bowl. Spoon the mixture into a 9×13-inch baking dish. Arrange the corned beef over the sauerkraut mixture. Crumble the bread in a food processor or tear by hand. Spread the bread crumbs over the casserole and sprinkle with cheese. Melt the butter and drizzle over the casserole. Bake at 350 degrees for 30 to 35 minutes or until brown and bubbling. Yield: 8 servings.

Helen L. Newlin, Laureate Delta Delta
Oak Grove, Missouri

CORNED BEEF CASSEROLE

1 (8-ounce) package	1 (10-ounce) can cream
wide noodles	of chicken soup
1 (6-ounce) can corned	1 (12-ounce) can
beef	evaporated milk
1 small onion, diced	2 tablespoons butter,
4 ounces cubed American	melted
cheese	2 cups cornflakes
1 (10-ounce) can cream	
of mushroom soup	

Cook the noodles using the package directions; drain. Break the beef in small pieces with a spoon in a large mixing bowl. Add the onion, cheese, soups and evaporated milk, stirring to combine. Add the noodles and mix well. Spoon the mixture into a 9×13-inch baking dish. Combine the butter and cornflakes in a medium bowl. Sprinkle the cornflake mixture over the casserole. Bake at 350 degrees for 45 minutes or until bubbling and browned. Yield: 12 to 15 servings.

Earlita Kahler, Preceptor Psi
Fort Dodge, Iowa

AFRICAN CHOP SUEY

1 pound ground beef	1 (10-ounce) can chicken
1 cup chopped celery	with rice soup
1 cup chopped onion	1 (10-ounce) can cream
1 small green bell	of mushroom soup
pepper, diced	2 teaspoons soy sauce
1 cup boiling water	1/2 cup uncooked rice
1 chicken bouillon cube	1 to 2 cups crushed
1 cup boiling water	potato chips

Brown the ground beef, celery, onion and bell pepper in 1 cup boiling water, stirring constantly. Remove from the heat. Dissolve the bouillon cube in 1 cup boiling water. Add the bouillon liquid, soups and soy sauce and mix well. Add the rice to the mixture and stir to combine. Spoon the mixture into a baking dish. Bake at 350 degrees for 30 minutes. Stir in the chips and bake an additional 30 minutes. Yield: 4 to 6 servings.

Linda Hymes, Xi Delta Psi
Redford, Michigan

BELIZEAN BEEF ON SPICED POTATOES

1 pound ground beef	2 large baking potatoes,
1 (14-ounce) can zesty	unpeeled
diced tomatoes,	Caribbean jerk
drained	seasoning to taste
1 1/2 teaspoons minced	1/2 cup plain yogurt
garlic	3/4 teaspoon minced
1 teaspoon Caribbean	garlic
jerk seasoning	1/2 teaspoon Caribbean
Salt and pepper to taste	jerk seasoning

Brown the ground beef in a large nonstick skillet, stirring until crumbly; drain. Set aside 1 tablespoon of the tomatoes. Add the remaining tomatoes, 1 1/2 teaspoons garlic and 1 teaspoon jerk seasoning to the beef and mix well. Bring to a boil and reduce the heat. Cover and simmer for 8 minutes, stirring occasionally. Season with salt and pepper to taste. Cut the potatoes lengthwise into 1/4-inch slices. Pierce the potatoes in several places with a fork and dip them in cold water. Arrange the potatoes on a nonstick baking pan and sprinkle lightly with salt, pepper and jerk seasoning. Broil 6 inches from the heat source for 10 to 12 minutes, turning once. Spoon the beef mixture over the potatoes. Combine the yogurt, the reserved 1 tablespoon tomatoes, 3/4 teaspoon garlic, 1/2 teaspoon jerk seasoning, salt and pepper in a bowl and mix well. Spoon the yogurt topping over the beef mixture. Serve warm. Yield: 4 servings.

Valerie McArdle, Alpha Alpha Master
Grants Pass, Oregon

ZESTY SANDWICHES

10 pounds ground beef	*2 cups dried onions*
1 tablespoon salt	*2 cups water*
10 tablespoons chili	*1 (106-ounce) can*
powder	*ketchup*
1 teaspoon cumin	*Buns*

Cook the ground beef with the salt, chili powder, cumin, onions and water in a Dutch oven over low heat, stirring until the ground beef is crumbly but not browned; drain. Add the ketchup and cook over low heat for 1 hour, stirring frequently. Serve on buns. Yield: 20 to 25 servings.

Dawn K. Graham, Upsilon Gamma
Wooster, Ohio

LAZY MAN'S CABBAGE ROLLS

2 pounds lean ground	*2 (10-ounce) cans*
beef	*tomato soup*
1 onion, chopped	*Salt and pepper to taste*
6 cups cooked rice	*1 large cabbage, chopped*

Brown the ground beef with the onion in a medium skillet, stirring until the ground beef is crumbly; drain. Add the rice, 1 1/3 cans of soup, the salt and pepper to the beef and mix well. Layer the cabbage and beef 1/2 at a time in a greased baking dish, ending with the beef. Pour the remaining 2/3 can of soup over the top. Bake at 350 degrees for 1 hour. Yield: 6 servings.

Beverley Adams, Laureate Alpha Theta
Coquitlam, British Columbia, Canada

CHEESEBURGER CASSEROLE

1 1/2 pounds lean ground	*1 cup all-purpose flour*
beef	*1/2 teaspoon salt*
1 teaspoon minced	*1 1/2 teaspoons baking*
onion	*powder*
1 (4-ounce) can sliced	*2 tablespoons*
mushrooms, drained	*shortening*
1 (10-ounce) can tomato	*3 cups plus 1 teaspoon*
soup	*milk*
1/2 cup water	*8 (3/4-inch) cubes*
1 cup frozen peas	*American cheese*
1 carrot, grated	

Brown the ground beef with the onion and mushrooms in a large skillet, stirring until the ground beef is crumbly; drain. Add the soup, water, peas and carrot to the ground beef and mix well. Spoon the mixture into a 1 1/2-quart casserole. Sift together the flour, salt and baking powder in a medium bowl. Cut in the shortening until crumbly. Add the milk to the flour mixture and stir until the dough clings together. Knead the dough on a lightly floured surface 12 times. Divide the dough into 8 rounds; wrap each round around 1 cheese cube. Press to seal. Place the biscuits on top of the casserole. Bake the casserole at 425 degrees for 25 to 30 minutes or until the biscuits are golden brown. Yield: 8 servings.

Florence Helle
Luverne, Minnesota

GREEK HAMBURGER

2 tablespoons butter or	*1/4 cup finely sliced green*
margarine, melted	*onions*
3/4 cup crushed	*1/4 cup chopped fresh*
stuffing mix	*parsley*
1 egg, beaten	*1/4 cup chopped almonds*
1 (4-ounce) can	*1 teaspoon lemon juice*
mushroom pieces,	*2 pounds ground beef*
drained	*1 teaspoon salt*
1/3 cup beef broth	

Combine the butter, stuffing mix, egg, mushrooms, broth, onions, parsley, almonds and lemon juice in a large bowl and mix well; set aside. Combine the beef and salt in a bowl and mix well. Shape the beef into 2 large patties. Place the stuffing mixture on 1 patty. Place the second patty on top of the stuffing mixture. Seal the edges and place in a grill press. Grill the patty over medium heat for 15 to 20 minutes on each side. Remove the patty to a serving platter and cut into wedges to serve. Yield: 6 to 8 servings.

Pat Geyer, Preceptor Gamma Mu
Rochester, Michigan

SPECIAL OCCASION LASAGNA

4 ounces ground beef or	*1 (10-ounce) package*
ground turkey	*lasagna noodles*
12 ounces Italian sausage,	*3 cups cottage cheese*
casings removed	*2 eggs, beaten*
1 1/2 teaspoons garlic salt	*1 teaspoon salt*
1 tablespoon parsley	*1/2 teaspoon pepper*
flakes	*2 tablespoons parsley*
1 1/2 teaspoons basil	*flakes*
1/2 teaspoon oregano	*1/4 cup (1 ounce)*
1/2 teaspoon salt	*Parmesan cheese*
1 (20-ounce) can	*4 cups (16 ounces)*
tomatoes	*shredded mozzarella*
1 (6-ounce) can tomato	*cheese*
paste	

Brown the ground beef and sausage together in a large skillet, stirring until crumbly; drain. Add the garlic salt, 1 tablespoon parsley, the basil, oregano, 1/2 teaspoon salt, tomatoes and tomato paste to the meat and stir to combine. Simmer, uncovered, for

1 hour, stirring occasionally. Cook the noodles using the package directions; drain. Combine the cottage cheese, eggs, 1 teaspoon salt, pepper, 2 tablespoons parsley and Parmesan cheese in a medium bowl and mix well. Layer the noodles, meat sauce, cottage cheese mixture and mozarella cheese alternately in a greased 9×13-inch baking dish until all the ingredients are used, ending with the mozzarella cheese. Bake, covered, at 375 degrees for 30 minutes. Yield: 8 to 12 servings.

Beverly Jordan, Xi Delta Eta
Delta, Colorado

CRAZY MIXED-UP PIZZA

1 pound ground beef	2/3 cup tomato sauce
3/4 teaspoon salt	1 cup (4 ounces)
1/4 teaspoon garlic salt	shredded mozzarella
1/2 cup chopped green	cheese
olives	Hamburger buns

Brown the ground beef in a large skillet, stirring until crumbly; drain. Add the salt, garlic salt, green olives and tomato sauce to the beef. Simmer over low heat for 15 minutes. Stir in the mozzarella cheese until melted. Serve on buns. Yield: 6 servings.

Lisa Weant, Eta Zeta
Ponca City, Oklahoma

SPAGHETTI PIZZA

7 ounces spaghetti	2 garlic cloves, minced
1/2 cup milk	1 teaspoon Italian
1 egg, lightly beaten	seasoning
8 ounces ground beef	1/4 teaspoon pepper
1 green bell pepper,	1 (7-ounce) can
chopped	mushrooms, drained
1 onion, chopped	2 cups (8 ounces)
1 (15-ounce) can tomato	shredded mozzarella
sauce	cheese

Prepare the spaghetti using the package directions; drain. Remove the spaghetti to a medium bowl. Stir in the milk and egg and mix well. Pour the spaghetti mixture into a 9×13-inch baking dish. Brown the ground beef in a large skillet, stirring until crumbly; drain. Add the bell pepper and onion and cook until tender. Add the tomato sauce, garlic, Italian seasoning and pepper, stirring to combine. Simmer the beef mixture for 5 minutes. Pour the beef mixture over the spaghetti. Top with the mushrooms and cheese. Bake at 350 degrees for 20 minutes. Yield: 8 servings.

Charlene Schilling, Xi Epsilon Epsilon
Evansville, Indiana

THE BEST-EVER SPAGHETTI SAUCE

1 pound ground beef	1/4 cup fresh or dried
1 large green bell pepper,	parsley
chopped	1 (6-ounce) can tomato
1 large onion,	paste
chopped	3/4 cup water
1 teaspoon salt	1 (14-ounce) can tomato
1/2 teaspoon pepper	purée
1 teaspoon dried	1 (28-ounce) jar
oregano	spaghetti sauce
1 teaspoon Italian	1 cup water
seasoning	1/4 cup (1 ounce) grated
1 teaspoon minced	Parmesan cheese
garlic	

Brown the ground beef in a skillet, stirring until crumbly; drain. Remove the ground beef to a stockpot. Cook the bell pepper and onion in the stockpot over medium heat for 15 minutes. Add the salt, pepper, oregano, Italian seasoning, garlic and parsley to the onion mixture, stirring to combine. Stir in the tomato paste and 3/4 cup water and mix well. Add the tomato purée and spaghetti sauce. Rinse the spaghetti sauce jar with 1 cup water; add to the stockpot and mix well. Stir in the Parmesan cheese and simmer for 1 hour. Yield: 1 quart.

Charlotte Cumings, Zeta Sigma
Fairfield Bay, Arkansas

PIZZA CASSEROLE

1 1/2 pounds ground beef	1/2 teaspoon garlic salt
1 cup chopped onion	1/4 teaspoon oregano
1 (5-ounce) package	2 cups (8 ounces)
macaroni and cheese	shredded mozzarella
2 (10-ounce) cans pizza	cheese
sauce	1 cup pepperoni

Brown the ground beef with the onion in a medium skillet, stirring until the ground beef is crumbly; drain. Prepare the macaroni and cheese using the package directions. Combine the pizza sauce, garlic salt and oregano in a large bowl and mix well. Add the meat and macaroni to the pizza sauce mixture and mix well. Spoon half of the beef mixture into a 9×13-inch greased baking dish. Layer 1 cup of the cheese over the beef mixture. Pour the remaining beef mixture over the cheese. Sprinkle with the remaining cup of cheese and top with the pepperoni. Bake at 350 degrees for 10 to 15 minutes. Yield: 8 servings.

Irene Cureton, Eta Eta
Fredericktown, Maryland

APPLESAUCE MEATBALLS

2 pounds ground beef	*2 tablespoons vegetable*
1 cup applesauce	*oil*
1 cup soft bread crumbs	*1 celery rib, thinly sliced*
2 eggs, beaten	*1 green bell pepper, diced*
1 teaspoon salt	*1 carrot, thinly sliced*
1/4 teaspoon pepper	*1 small onion, diced*
All-purpose flour	*2 cups tomato juice*

Combine the first 6 ingredients in a medium bowl and mix well. Shape into 1-inch balls. Dredge the meatballs in the flour, shaking off the excess. Brown the meatballs in the oil in a large skillet; drain. Remove the meatballs to a large baking dish. Add the celery, bell pepper, carrot, onion and tomato juice to the reserved skillet. Bring to a boil over high heat. Pour the sauce over the meatballs. Bake, covered, at 350 degrees for 40 minutes. Yield: 8 to 10 servings.

Shirley Rader, Beta Kappa Sigma
Hilltop Lakes, Texas

NIPPY MEATBALLS

1 pound ground beef	*1 teaspoon salt*
1/2 cup dry bread crumbs	*Pepper to taste*
1/4 cup minced onion	*1 teaspoon*
1/4 cup milk	*Worcestershire sauce*
1 egg, lightly beaten	*1 (12-ounce) bottle chili*
2 teaspoons minced	*sauce*
parsley	*11/4 cups grape jelly*

Combine the first 9 ingredients in a large bowl and mix well. Shape into 1-inch balls. Place the meatballs on a rack in a broiler pan. Bake at 350 degrees for 10 minutes, turning to brown all sides. Heat the chili sauce in a large skillet over medium heat. Add the grape jelly and cook until melted, stirring constantly. Add the meatballs to the jelly mixture. Simmer, uncovered, for 30 minutes. Yield: 4 to 6 servings.

Myrna Schroder, Upsilon Nu
Stover, Missouri

REUBEN MEATBALLS

1 egg, lightly beaten	*2 cups sauerkraut,*
1 small onion,	*drained*
minced	*11/2 teaspoons caraway*
2/3 cup soft bread crumbs	*seeds*
1/4 cup minced parsley	*1 (10-ounce) can cream*
1/2 teaspoon salt	*of mushroom soup*
1/2 teaspoon pepper	*1/2 cup Thousand Island*
1 cup cooked rice	*salad dressing*
11/2 pounds lean	*1/4 cup (1 ounce)*
ground beef	*shredded Swiss cheese*

Combine the first 6 ingredients in a large bowl. Stir in the rice and mix well. Crumble the beef over the rice mixture and stir to mix well. Shape the mixture into 15 meatballs. Place the meatballs in an ungreased 9×13-inch baking dish. Bake at 350 degrees for 15 to 20 minutes; drain. Layer the sauerkraut over the meatballs and sprinkle with the caraway seeds. Mix the soup and dressing together and spread over the top. Bake, covered, at 350 degrees for 35 to 45 minutes or until done. Sprinkle with Swiss cheese. Bake for 10 minutes or until the cheese melts. Yield: 6 servings.

Helga Stremel, Delta Chi
Hays, Kansas

MEAT LOAF

3 slices bread	*1/2 teaspoon pepper*
1 pound ground sausage	*3 tablespoons chili*
2 pounds ground beef	*sauce*
1 small onion, minced	*1 egg, lightly beaten*
1 tablespoon salt	

Process the bread slices in a food processor until crumbled. Combine the bread crumbs, sausage and ground beef in a large bowl and mix well. Add the onion, salt, pepper and chili sauce and mix well. Add the egg, stirring until combined. Divide the mixture into 2 portions and press into two 5×9-inch loaf pans. Bake at 350 degrees for 11/2 hours or until cooked through. Yield: 6 to 8 servings. Yield: 12 servings.

Barbara Vogt, Xi Gamma Mu
Carmel, Indiana

SWEET AND SOUR MEAT LOAF

1 egg, beaten	*2 tablespoons onion*
2 tablespoons ketchup	*soup mix*
2 tablespoons prepared	*1 pound ground beef*
mustard	*1/4 cup granulated sugar*
1/4 teaspoon salt	*2 tablespoons brown*
1/4 teaspoon pepper	*sugar*
1/2 cup dry bread crumbs	*3 tablespoons ketchup*
1/4 cup packed brown	*2 to 3 tablespoons cider*
sugar	*vinegar*

Combine the first 8 ingredients in a large bowl and mix well. Crumble the ground beef over the mixture and stir to combine. Shape into an oval loaf in a shallow baking dish. Bake, covered, at 350 degrees for 1 hour. Combine the granulated sugar, 2 tablespoons brown sugar, the remaining ketchup and the vinegar in a bowl. Pour the sugar mixture over the loaf. Bake for an additional 15 to 30 minutes or until cooked through. Yield: 8 servings.

Sheryl Augustine, Laureate Alpha
Pueblo West, Colorado

MEAT LOAF WELLINGTON

1 (10-ounce) can beef gravy	1 egg
1½ cups cubed day-old bread	1 teaspoon salt
	2 pounds ground beef
¼ cup chopped onion	1 (8-count) can crescent rolls

Combine ¼ cup gravy, bread cubes, onion, egg and salt in a medium bowl. Crumble the ground beef over the mixture and mix well. Press the mixture into a greased 9×5-inch loaf pan. Bake, uncovered, at 375 degrees for 1 hour or until cooked through. Remove the loaf from the pan to a paper towel to drain. Place the loaf on a greased 9×13-inch baking pan. Unroll the crescent roll dough and press to seal perforations. Cover the top and sides of the meat loaf with the dough and trim the excess. Bake for an additional 10 to 15 minutes or until the pastry is golden brown. Heat the remaining gravy and serve with the loaf. Yield: 6 to 8 servings.

Ruth Ann Carlisle, Preceptor Zeta Upsilon
Richardson, Texas

MEXICAN MEAT LOAF

Vegetable cooking spray	1 small onion, chopped
1½ pounds ground beef	1 (16-ounce) can tomato sauce
1½ pounds ground turkey	3 cups crushed nacho cheese chips
1 (1-ounce) packet taco seasoning mix	

Coat a foil-lined 9×13-baking dish with vegetable cooking spray. Combine the ground beef, ground turkey, seasoning mix, onion, tomato sauce and chips in a large bowl and mix well. Shape into a loaf in the prepared baking dish. Bake at 350 degrees for 1 hour or until cooked through. Yield: 8 to 10 servings.

Sandy Jackson, Xi Delta Sigma
Brunswick, Georgia

*Becky Allen, Laureate Kappa Nu, Mission Viejo, California, makes **Slow-Cooked Beef Burritos** by rubbing a 2-pound London Broil roast with one 1-ounce packet of taco seasoning. She places the meat in a slow cooker with 1 chopped onion, 1 tablespoon white distilled vinegar and one 4-ounce can diced green chilies. The meat is covered and cooked on Low for 9 hours. Once cooked, the meat is removed from the slow cooker and shredded with forks, then recombined with the cooking liquid. The meat is served with tortillas and cilantro, chopped onion, shredded cheese, or jalapeño peppers.*

ENCHILADAS

2 pounds ground beef	2 cups sour cream
1 large onion, diced	4 cups (16 ounces) shredded Monterey Jack cheese
1 (16-ounce) can refried beans	
1 (10-count) package tortillas	1 (2-ounce) can olives (optional)
1 (28-ounce) can enchilada sauce	Green onions, chopped (optional)

Brown the ground beef a large skillet, stirring until crumbly; drain. Add the onion and beans to the ground beef and mix well. Lightly coat the tortillas with the enchilada sauce using a pastry brush. Spoon 3 tablespoons of the ground beef mixture onto each tortilla. Add 2 heaping teaspoons of sour cream on top of the meat. Sprinkle 3 tablespoons cheese over the sour cream and loosely roll the tortillas. Place the rolled tortillas, seam side down, in a 9×13-inch baking dish. Pour the remaining enchilada sauce over the tortillas. Bake at 325 degrees for 30 minutes. Sprinkle the remaining cheese over the tortillas and bake an additional 5 minutes. Garnish with olives and green onions, if desired. Yield: 6 servings.

Beatrice Louise Thiel
Redding, California

ENCHILADA CASSEROLE

1½ pounds ground beef	½ teaspoon pepper
1 cup chopped onion	1 cup water
1½ teaspoons cumin	2 cups taco sauce
1½ teaspoons garlic salt	12 corn tortillas
4 teaspoons chili powder	1 cup sour cream
1½ teaspoons salt	4 cups (16 ounces) shredded Monterey Jack cheese

Brown the ground beef with the onion in a large skillet, stirring until crumbly; drain. Add the cumin, garlic salt, chili powder, salt, pepper and water and mix well. Simmer the mixture for 10 minutes. Spread ½ cup of the taco sauce in the bottom of a 9×13-greased baking dish. Cover the sauce with 6 tortillas. Top the tortillas with ½ cup of sauce. Layer the sauce with the meat. Add the sour cream and spread evenly. Add ½ of the cheese and top with the remaining 6 tortillas. Add the remaining taco sauce and top with the remaining cheese. Bake, covered, at 375 degrees for 40 minutes. Yield: 8 to 10 servings.

Stephanie Smith, Pi Upsilon
Odessa, Missouri

GREEN ENCHILADA CASSEROLE

1 to 1½ pounds ground
    beef
1 small onion
1 (10-ounce) can cream
    of mushroom soup
1 cup water

4 (7-ounce) cans green
    chilies
18 small flour tortillas
2 cups (8 ounces) grated
    Mexican cheese

Brown the ground beef with the onion in a large skillet, stirring until crumbly; drain. Add the mushroom soup, water and chiles and mix well. Simmer for 5 minutes. Layer ⅓ of the tortillas, ⅓ of the meat mixture and ⅓ of the cheese in a greased 9×13-inch baking dish. Repeat layers until all ingredients are used, ending with the cheese. Bake at 350 degrees for 30 to 35 minutes or until cooked through. Yield: 8 to 10 servings.

Nona Akins, Preceptor Beta Iota
Tunnel Hill, Georgia

MEXICAN CASSEROLE

2 pounds ground beef
1 small onion, minced
1 (8-ounce) can tomato
    sauce
1 envelope taco
    seasoning
½ to 1 cup sour
    cream

½ cup (2 ounces)
    shredded mozzarella
    cheese
1 (8-count) can crescent
    rolls
½ cup (1 stick) butter,
    melted
Parmesan cheese, grated

Brown the ground beef in a large skillet, stirring until crumbly; drain. Add the onion, tomato sauce and taco seasoning and mix well. Spoon the meat mixture into a 9×13-inch baking dish. Combine the sour cream and mozzarella cheese in a bowl and mix well. Spread the sour cream mixture over the meat. Place the unrolled rectangles of crescent rolls on top of cheese mixture. Pour the butter over the casserole. Sprinkle with Parmesan cheese. Bake at 350 degrees for 10 to 15 minutes or until the rolls are golden brown. Yield: 8 to 10 servings.

Nancy Whetstone, Xi Alpha Omicron
Elkhart, Indiana

MEXICAN PIZZA

1 pound ground beef
1 (16-ounce) can refried
    beans
1 (15-inch) pizza crust
¼ cup mayonnaise
1 envelope taco
    seasoning
1½ cups (6 ounces)
    grated Cheddar cheese

1½ cups shredded lettuce
1½ cups chopped
    tomatoes
1 (4-ounce) can slice
    olives, drained
1 cup chopped ham

Brown the beef in a skillet, stirring until crumbly; drain. Spread the beans over the pizza crust. Spread the mayonnaise over the beans. Add the taco seasoning to the beef and stir to combine. Spread the beef mixture over the mayonnaise. Sprinkle the cheese over the pizza. Bake at 350 degrees for 20 to 30 minutes or until the cheese melts. Top the pizza with layers of lettuce, tomatoes, olives and ham before serving. Yield: 4 to 5 servings.

Melanie Carroll, Xi Delta Mu
Madras, Oregon

TACORITOS

1 pound ground beef
2 tablespoons
    all-purpose flour
1 (14½-ounce) can
    stewed tomatoes
1 (4-ounce) can diced
    green chilies
1 cup water
Salt and pepper to taste
½ teaspoon cumin

1 (16-ounce) can refried
    beans
4 flour tortillas
¼ head lettuce, shredded
1 tomato, chopped
1 small onion, chopped
2 cups (8 ounces)
    shredded Cheddar
    cheese

Brown the beef in a skillet, stirring until crumbly; drain. Remove half of the ground beef to a plate and keep warm. Add the flour, stewed tomatoes, chilies, water, salt, pepper and cumin to the remaining beef in the skillet. Simmer for 10 minutes. Spread an even layer of beans on each tortilla. Sprinkle the reserved beef over the beans. Add layers of lettuce, tomato, onion, cheese and 1 tablespoon of the meat sauce on each tortilla. Roll each tortilla and place seam side down in a medium baking dish. Pour the remaining sauce over the tortillas. Sprinkle with the remaining cheese. Bake, covered, at 350 degrees for 15 minutes. Yield: 4 servings.

Jackie Nielson, Xi Delta Tau
Dove Creek, Colorado

SKILLET TAMALE PIE

1 pound ground beef
1 onion, chopped
2 (14-ounce) cans stewed
    chopped tomatoes
1 cup cornmeal
1 cup water
1 teaspoon salt

1 tablespoon chili
    powder or taco
    seasoning
1 (15-ounce) can black
    pitted olives, drained
Grated cheese (optional)

Brown the beef in a large skillet, stirring until crumbly; drain. Add the onion to the meat and cook until onion turns transparent, stirring frequently. Add the tomatoes and bring to a simmer, stirring frequently. Combine the cornmeal and water in a small bowl to make a thick paste. Add the cornmeal paste to the beef gradually, stirring well after each addition. Add the salt and chili powder and mix well. Add additional water as needed to prevent sticking. Cover and simmer until the cornmeal is fully cooked. Add the olives and stir to combine. Simmer another 3 to 4 minutes or until heated through. Top with grated cheese, if desired. Yield: 6 servings.

Bettie Killgore, Laureate Iota Mu
Santa Cruz, California

TAMALE PIE

1 cup Masa flour	1/2 cup frozen corn,
1/2 teaspoon salt	thawed
1 tablespoon vegetable	1 (10-ounce) can
oil	chopped tomatoes
1 cup water	1/3 cup black olives,
1 pound ground beef	chopped
1/2 onion, chopped	2 tablespoons
1 garlic clove, crushed	all-purpose flour
1 teaspoon chili powder	3/4 cup (3 ounces) Colby-
1/2 teaspoon salt	Jack cheese, grated
1/3 cup chopped green or	
red bell pepper	

Combine the flour, salt, oil and water in a bowl and mix well. Press the mixture into a greased 9-inch pie plate. Bake at 375 degrees for 5 to 10 minutes. Brown the beef in a large skillet, stirring until crumbly; drain. Add the next 8 ingredients and mix well. Cook for 3 to 5 minutes and add the flour, stirring to combine. Spoon the beef mixture into the prepared crust. Bake at 375 degrees for 20 to 25 minutes. Sprinkle with the cheese and bake for 5 minutes longer or until the cheese melts. Let stand for 5 to 10 minutes before serving. Yield: 6 servings.

Sandra Moore, Preceptor Alpha Phi
Jerome, Idaho

CITY CHICKEN

2 pounds lean veal	1/2 cup all-purpose flour
12 to 15 (6-inch) wooden	Salt and pepper to taste
skewer sticks	1/2 cup bacon drippings

Slice the veal into thin 1-inch strips. Soak the skewers in water for 10 minutes. Weave the veal onto skewers, leaving the end clear for handling. Combine the flour, salt and pepper in a small bowl. Roll the veal skewers in the flour mixture to coat, shaking off any excess. Working in batches, brown the veal on all sides in the bacon drippings in an iron skillet over high heat; set aside. Return the veal to the skillet and add water to cover. Simmer, covered, for 1 hour. Serve immediately. Yield 4 to 6 servings.

Joanna Wills-Bernard, Preceptor Beta Sigma
Oklahoma City, Oklahoma

OSSO BUCCO

3 onions, sliced	Thyme to taste
1/4 cup vegetable oil	Basil to taste
2 carrots, sliced	Pinch of grated lemon
3 ribs celery, chopped	zest
Salt and pepper to taste	2 tablespoons tomato
1/2 cup all-purpose flour	paste
6 to 8 (1-inch-thick) veal	1/2 cup white wine
shanks	1 cup chicken stock
3 tablespoons oil	Grated lemon zest and
1 bay leaf	chopped fresh parsley
2 garlic cloves, crushed	

Sauté the onions in 1/4 cup oil in a skillet over medium heat until tender. Remove the onion to a large Dutch oven. Sauté the carrots and celery in the same skillet until tender; add to the onions. Combine the salt, pepper and flour in a bowl and mix well. Coat the veal shanks in the flour, shaking off any excess. Brown the veal shanks in 3 tablespoons oil in the skillet. Place the veal shanks on top of the vegetables in the Dutch oven, standing upright. Add the bay leaf, garlic, thyme, basil and lemon zest. Combine the tomato paste, wine and chicken stock in a bowl. Pour the mixture over the meat and bring to a boil. Reduce the heat and simmer, covered, for 4 hours. Remove the bay leaf and sprinkle with lemon rind and parsley before serving. Serve with risotto.
Yield: 4 to 6 servings.

Ann Jung, Xi Epsilon Rho
Unionville, Ontario, Canada

VEAL POT ROAST

1/2 cup all-purpose flour	1/8 teaspoon sweet basil
1 teaspoon salt	1/8 teaspoon oregano
1/4 teaspoon celery salt	1 (4-pound) veal roast
1/4 teaspoon pepper	3 tablespoons vegetable
1 teaspoon dry mustard	oil
1/2 teaspoon paprika	3/4 cup water
1 teaspoon garlic	2 tablespoons cider
powder	vinegar
1/4 teaspoon ground	1 onion, sliced
ginger	1/2 teaspoon
1/8 teaspoon thyme	Worcestershire sauce

Combine the first 11 ingredients in a small bowl and mix well. Rub the roast with the seasoned flour. Brown the roast in hot oil in a Dutch oven over medium-high heat. Reduce the heat and add the water, vinegar, onion and Worcestershire sauce, stirring to combine. Cover and simmer for 1 hour (about 15 minutes per pound) or until tender. Add water as needed during cooking. Yield: 10 to 12 servings.

Lorraine Fenton, Xi Omicron
Whitinsville, Massachusetts

VENISON CASSEROLE

1 pound ground venison	2 (10-ounce) cans
4 to 5 potatoes, sliced	vegetable beef soup
1 onion, sliced	1 (10-ounce) can cream
1/2 cup (1 stick) butter,	of mushroom soup
cut into pieces	Salt and pepper to taste

Brown the venison in a skillet, stirring until crumbly; drain. Arrange the potatoes in a greased 2-quart casserole dish and top with the onion. Sprinkle the butter over the onion and top with the venison. Combine the soups in a bowl and mix well. Pour the soups over the meat; season with salt and pepper to taste. Bake at 350 degrees for 45 minutes or until the potatoes are tender. Yield: 8 servings.

Nora Kelley, Xi Beta Chi
Rockford, Alabama

VENISON PEPPER STEAK

1 pound venison steak	2 small green bell
1 tablespoon paprika	peppers, cut in strips
2 tablespoons butter	2 tablespoons cornstarch
2 garlic cloves, minced	1/4 cup water
1 (14-ounce) can beef	2 tablespoons soy sauce
broth	2 tomatoes, cut into
1 cup sliced green onion	eighths

Cut the steaks into 1/2-inch strips. Sprinkle with paprika and let stand for 10 minutes. Brown the steak strips in the butter in a large skillet. Stir in the garlic and broth and mix well. Simmer, covered, for 30 to 45 minutes or until the meat is tender. Stir in the green onions and bell peppers. Combine the cornstarch, water and soy sauce in a small bowl and mix well. Add the cornstarch mixture to the meat, stirring to combine. Cook until the liquid is clear and thickened, stirring constantly. Add the tomatoes, stirring gently, and cook until heated through. Serve over hot cooked rice. Yield: 4 to 6 servings.

Jane Owen, Xi Xi
Lynchburg, Virginia

VENISON SCALOPPINI

3 pounds venison,	5 bouillon cubes
pounded to 1/4 inch	2 (11-ounce) cans
thick	tomato juice
1/4 cup all-purpose flour	1 to 11/2 cups dry white
Salt and pepper to taste	wine
1 tablespoon butter	1 teaspoon chopped
3 tablespoons olive oil	rosemary
1 red onion, chopped	1 tablespoon chopped
1 teaspoon garlic	parsley
powder	8 ounces fresh
2 cups water	mushrooms, sliced

Cut the venison into thin strips. Combine the flour, salt and pepper and mix well. Dredge the venison in the flour, shaking off any excess. Heat the butter and olive oil in a large skillet over medium heat. Brown the venison slowly on both sides in the hot butter and oil. Remove the venison and keep warm. Add the onion and garlic powder to the skillet and cook over low heat for 5 minutes. Remove the onion to a heavy Dutch oven. Add the water, bouillon, tomato juice and wine to the Dutch oven and cook for 10 minutes, stirring constantly. Add the rosemary, parsley, mushrooms and venison. Cook over low heat for 1 hour, stirring occasionally.
Yield: 8 servings.

Shirley Ceccon, Preceptor Omicron Eta
Orland, California

PORK TENDERLOIN EN CROUTE WITH CRANBERRY PORT SAUCE

2 (1-pound) pork	1 egg, lightly beaten
tenderloins	1 tablespoon water
8 slices prosciutto	Cranberry Port Sauce
Dijon mustard	
8 (7×7-inch) puff	
pastries, thawed	

Cut the tenderloins in eight 3-inch pieces. Wrap 1 slice prosciutto around each tenderloin. Spread the Dijon mustard on each tenderloin roll. Place each tenderloin on a pastry square. Bring the sides of the pastry together, seal, and fold the ends into a triangle. Place the rolls on a baking sheet lined with parchment paper. Slice a small opening in each pastry. Whisk the egg and water together in a small bowl. Brush each roll with the egg wash. Bake the rolls at 425 degrees for 40 minutes or until the meat thermometer registers 160 degrees. Serve with the Cranberry Port Sauce. Yield: 8 servings.

CRANBERRY PORT SAUCE

2 tablespoons butter	2 cups chicken broth
11/2 cups chopped onions	2 cups cranberry juice
5 garlic cloves, minced	cocktail
4 teaspoons grated	2 cups fresh cranberries
orange zest	1/2 cup sugar
11/2 teaspoons dried sage	1/2 cup Port
leaves	1 tablespoon cornstarch
2 teaspoons thyme	Salt and pepper to taste

Melt the butter in a skillet over medium heat. Add the onions and sauté until soft. Add the garlic, orange zest, sage and thyme and mix well. Cook for 1 minute. Add the broth and cranberry juice, stirring to combine. Simmer for 10 minutes or until reduced by half. Strain the sauce into a heavy saucepan. Add the cranberries and sugar to the saucepan and boil for 6 to 8 minutes or until the berries pop. Whisk the Port and the cornstarch together in a small bowl. Add the Port mixture to the sauce, stirring to combine. Boil until the sauce thickens. Season with salt and pepper.

Delma Waller, Laureate Delta Lambda
Waterloo, Ontario, Canada

❖ CHIPOTLE PORK TENDERLOIN

1 (2-pound) pork tenderloin, trimmed	*1 tablespoon garlic powder*
1 cup olive oil	*1 tablespoon curry powder*
1 tablespoon oregano	*1 (7-ounce) jar chipotle salsa*
1 tablespoon thyme	
1 tablespoon garlic powder	*1 cup packed brown sugar*
Salt and pepper to taste	*1 cup vinegar*
1 cup ketchup	
1 cup soy sauce	

Place the meat in a sealable plastic bag. Combine the olive oil, oregano, thyme, 1 tablespoon garlic powder, salt and pepper in a small bowl and mix well. Pour the marinade over the meat. Seal and refrigerate for 8 hours, turning occasionally. Remove the tenderloin, discarding the marinade. Grill the tenderloin, covered with the grill lid, over high heat for 3 minutes. Turn and cook for 3 minutes longer. Place the meat in a 9×13-inch baking dish. Combine the ketchup, soy sauce, 1 tablespoon garlic powder, curry powder, salsa, brown sugar and vinegar in a medium bowl and mix well. Pour the sauce over the meat, reserving ³/4 cup of sauce. Bake at 350 degrees for 30 to 45 minutes or until the meat thermometer registers 160 degrees. Serve with the reserved sauce. Yield: 8 servings.

Joyce Cooper, Preceptor Omicron Rho
Bedford, Texas

PORK TENDERLOIN WITH MUSTARD SAUCE

2 pork tenderloins	*1/2 teaspoon ground ginger*
1/2 cup soy sauce	
1/4 cup sherry	*1/2 teaspoon hot water*
1/2 cup ketchup	*1/2 cup toasted sesame seeds (optional)*
1/2 cup sugar	
2 garlic cloves, crushed	*Mustard Sauce*
1/2 teaspoon salt	

Bake the tenderloins in a baking dish at 275 degrees for 1 hour or until tender. Pour off the drippings. Combine the soy sauce, sherry, ketchup, sugar, garlic and salt in a small bowl and mix well. Dissolve the ginger in the hot water in a separate bowl, stirring

into a paste. Add the ginger paste to the sherry sauce, stirring to combine. Pour the sauce over the tenderloins. Return to the oven and bake for 1 hour longer, basting frequently with the sauce. Remove from the oven and let stand, basting frequently. Roll the tenderloins in toasted sesame seeds if desired. Slice the tenderloin in 1-inch slices and serve with the Mustard Sauce. Yield: 8 to 10 servings.

MUSTARD SAUCE

²/3 cup sour cream	*1/2 teaspoon hot water*
²/3 cup mayonnaise	*1¹/2 teaspoons vinegar*
1 tablespoon minced green onions	*Salt and pepper to taste*
1 tablespoon dry mustard	

Combine the sour cream, mayonnaise and green onions in a medium bowl and mix well. Dissolve the dry mustard in the hot water and mix well. Add the mustard paste to the mayonnaise sauce, stirring to combine. Stir in the vinegar; season with salt and pepper to taste. Yield: 1¹/2 cups.

Peg Espy, Preceptor Chi
Rawlins, Wyoming

PECAN-ENCRUSTED PORK WITH PEACHES

2 tablespoons tarragon leaves	*1 pound boneless pork tenderloin, trimmed*
1 tablespoon packed brown sugar	*1 cup finely chopped pecans*
1 tablespoon honey	*2 onions, coarsely chopped*
2 garlic cloves, minced	
2 teaspoons olive oil	*2 (15-ounce) cans peach slices, drained*
1 teaspoon salt	
1 teaspoon pepper	

Combine the tarragon, brown sugar, honey and garlic in a food processor. Cover and process until the mixture forms a thick paste. Add 1 teaspoon of the olive oil. Cover and process until the mixture is well blended. Add the remaining teaspoon of olive oil, if necessary, until the mixture is a spreadable consistency. Rub the tenderloin with the salt and pepper. Rub the tarragon mixture over the tenderloin. Roll the tenderloin in the pecans until all sides are evenly coated. Place the onions and peaches in a foil-lined 9×13-inch baking dish. Top with the tenderloin. Bake, covered, at 400 degrees for 50 minutes. Uncover and bake for an additional 10 minutes or until the meat thermometer registers 160 degrees. Yield: 4 servings.

Janice F. Huerter, Xi Alpha Gamma Alpha
Conroe, Texas

DATE-STUFFED PORK LOIN

1 (2- to 3-pound) pork loin	Pepper to taste
1 cup whole dates	1/2 pound sliced bacon
1/2 teaspoon garlic powder	1 envelope brown gravy mix
1/2 teaspoon onion powder	1 tablespoon olive oil
	1 to 2 teaspoons all-purpose flour

Cut a slit down the center of the pork loin, being careful not to cut through. Stuff the slit with dates. Combine the garlic powder, onion powder and pepper in a small bowl. Rub the seasonings over the pork loin. Cover the pork loin and refrigerate for 2 to 3 hours. Place the pork loin in a 9×13-inch baking dish and bring to room temperature. Cover the pork loin with bacon slices and bake at 325 degrees until a meat thermometer inserted into the loin registers 160 degrees. Prepare the brown gravy in a medium bowl using the package directions. Add the olive oil, flour and pork drippings to the gravy and mix well. Serve the gravy with the pork loin.
Yield: 4 to 6 servings.

Nancy E. Clapp, Preceptor Xi Sigma
Houston, Texas

TOMATO-BASIL STUFFED PORK

1/2 pound pork tenderloin	2 tablespoons raspberry walnut vinaigrette dressing
4 slices plum tomato	
1 teaspoon basil	Vegetable cooking spray
1/8 teaspoon pepper	1 teaspoon vegetable oil
3 tablespoons bread crumbs	
1 tablespoon grated Parmesan cheese	

Cut the tenderloin in half lengthwise. Cut each piece in half crosswise. Place each of the 4 cutlets between plastic wrap and flatten to 1/8 inch thick, using a meat mallet. Place 2 tomato slices on 2 cutlets. Top each tomato with basil and pepper. Top each with the remaining cutlet, pressing edges together to seal. Combine the bread crumbs and cheese. Brush both sides with the dressing and dredge in the bread-crumb mixture. Coat a medium skillet with cooking spray and add the oil. Cook the cutlets in the oil over medium heat for 5 minutes on each side or until cooked through. Yield: 2 servings.

Florence Marie Short, Preceptor Alpha Epsilon
Melbourne, Florida

PORK CHOP SURPRISE

6 slices bacon	2 tomatoes, sliced 1/2 inch thick
6 (11/2-inch-thick) pork chops	1 green bell pepper, sliced 1/4 inch thick
Salt and pepper to taste	6 slices American cheese
1 onion, sliced 1/4 inch thick	

Place 1 slice bacon on the work surface. Place 1 pork chop on the bacon. Season the chop with salt and pepper. Layer 1 slice onion, 1 slice tomato and 1 slice bell pepper over the chop. Bring the ends of bacon over the chop and secure with a toothpick. Repeat the process with the remaining pork chops. Grill over hot coals for 15 minutes or until the meat thermometer registers 160 degrees. Remove the chops to a serving platter and immediately place 1 slice of cheese over each chop to melt. Yield: 6 servings.

Carla McDaniel, Preceptor Delta
Centralia, Illinois

PORK ROAST WITH FRUIT COMPOTE

2 tablespoons all-purpose flour	2/3 cup orange juice
1 regular size oven cooking bag	1 (21/2- to 3-pound) pork loin roast, boneless
1/2 teaspoon ground cinnamon	1/4 teaspoon thyme
1/2 cup plum or raspberry preserves	1/2 teaspoon salt
	1/4 teaspoon pepper
	Fruit Compote

Place the flour in the cooking bag and lay in a 9×13-inch baking dish. Combine the cinnamon, preserves and orange juice in a bowl and mix well. Add the preserve mixture to the cooking bag. Rub the pork roast with thyme, salt and pepper. Place the pork roast in the cooking bag, fat side up. Close the bag with a nylon tie and make 6 (1-inch) slits in the bag. Bake at 350 degrees for 11/2 hours or until the meat thermometer registers 160 degrees. Let stand before carving. Serve with the Fruit Compote.
Yield: 8 servings.

FRUIT COMPOTE

3 apples	1/2 teaspoon cinnamon
1 cup orange juice	11/2 cups raisins
1 (16-ounce) can pineapple chunks	1/3 cup minute tapioca
1/4 teaspoon ground cloves	1 (14-ounce) can mandarin oranges
1/4 teaspoon ground ginger	3 bananas, sliced
	1/2 cup pecans (optional)

Peel, core and cut the apples in wedges. Simmer the apples in orange juice and the juice from the pineapple chunks in a medium saucepan. Add the cloves, ginger, cinnamon and raisins to the apple mixture and stir well. Add the tapioca to the fruit mixture and simmer until the liquid starts to thicken. Add the pineapple, mandarin oranges and bananas, mixing well. Pour the mixture in a 9×13-inch baking dish. Bake at 350 degrees for 20 minutes. Serve with the roast. Yield: 10 to 12 servings.

Ellen Rawls, Laureate Delta Iota
Manchester, Missouri

PORK ROAST WITH MUSHROOMS

1 (3- to 4-pound) blade roast	1 teaspoon parsley
1 tablespoon vegetable oil	1 teaspoon bay leaf
1 onion, chopped	1 teaspoon basil
2 garlic cloves, minced	1/2 teaspoon thyme
3 ribs celery, chopped	Salt and pepper to taste
1 pound fresh mushrooms, sliced	2 beef bouillon cubes
	2 cups water

Brown the roast in the oil in a large skillet over medium heat. Remove the roast to a Dutch oven. Sauté the onion, garlic and celery in the skillet until tender. Add the vegetable mixture to the roast. Add the mushrooms, parsley, bay leaf, basil, thyme, salt and pepper to the Dutch oven and mix well. Dissolve the bouillon cubes in the water and add to the Dutch oven. Bake, covered, at 350 degrees for 3 1/2 hours. Yield: 6 servings.

Wendy Ellis, Delta Epsilon
Rupert, Idaho

PORK MEDALLIONS WITH OLIVE-CAPER SAUCE

1 pound pork tenderloin, trimmed	1/2 cup fat-free, low-sodium chicken broth
1/2 teaspoon salt	1/2 cup chopped, pitted Kalamata olives
1/2 teaspoon pepper	2 tablespoons capers
1/4 cup all-purpose flour	2 tablespoons chopped flat-leaf fresh parsley
1 tablespoon olive oil	
1/2 cup dry white wine	

Cut the pork crosswise into 8 pieces. Pound each slice 1/4-inch thick between sheets of waxed paper. Sprinkle both sides of the pork slices with salt and pepper. Pour the flour in a shallow bowl. Dredge the pork slices in the flour, shaking off the excess. Heat 1 1/2 teaspoons of the olive oil in a nonstick skillet over medium-high heat. Add half of the pork and cook for 2 minutes on each side or until cooked through. Remove the pork from the pan and keep warm. Repeat the procedure with the remaining 1 1/2 teaspoons oil and pork. Return all of the pork slices to the pan. Add the wine and broth; bring to a boil. Stir in the olives and capers and cook for 4 minutes or until the pork is cooked through. Sprinkle with the parsley to serve. Yield: 4 servings.

Chyrl Gemberling, Preceptor Theta
Selinsgrove, Pennsylvania

PORK PARMESAN

1 pound pork tenderloin	1 cup sliced mushrooms
1 egg, lightly beaten	1 onion, thinly sliced
2 tablespoons water	2 garlic cloves, minced
1/4 cup fine bread crumbs	1 cup tomato sauce
1/4 cup (1 ounce) grated Parmesan cheese	1/4 teaspoon oregano
1/2 teaspoon salt	6 slices mozzarella cheese
1/8 teaspoon pepper	
1 tablespoon vegetable oil	

Cut the pork into 4-inch cubes. Pound the cubes to 1/2-inch thickness between sheets of waxed paper. Whisk the egg and water together in a small bowl; set aside. Combine the bread crumbs, Parmesan cheese, salt and pepper in a bowl and mix well. Coat the pork in the egg mixture and dip in the bread crumbs. Brown the pork in the oil in a large skillet. Remove to a large baking dish. Sauté the mushrooms, onion and garlic in the skillet over medium heat until tender, stirring frequently. Add the tomato sauce and oregano and mix well. Simmer for 5 minutes, stirring occasionally. Pour the sauce over the pork and top with the slices of mozzarella cheese. Bake at 350 degrees for 1 to 1 1/2 hours or until the pork is cooked through. Yield: 4 servings.

Valdean Fremont, Xi Theta Gamma
Petawawa, Ontario, Canada

BARBEQUE PORK CHOPS

6 pork chops	1 dash Tabasco sauce
1/4 cup ketchup	1/4 teaspoon chili powder
1/2 cup water	1 tablespoon brown sugar
2 tablespoons vinegar	
1/2 teaspoon salt	

Place the pork chops in a roasting pan. Combine the ketchup, water, vinegar, salt, Tabasco, chili powder and brown sugar in a bowl and mix well. Pour the sauce over the pork chops. Bake at 350 degrees for 1 hour or until the pork chops are cooked through. Yield: 6 servings.

Irma Ford, Rho Master
Drumheller, Alberta, Canada

PORK CHOPS WITH CORN SALSA

1 teaspoon vegetable oil	1 (10-ounce) can corn,
1/4 teaspoon salt	drained
1/4 teaspoon pepper	1 cup salsa
4 (1-inch-thick) center-	Chopped fresh cilantro
cut bone-in pork	
chops	

Heat the oil in a large nonstick skillet over medium-high heat. Sprinkle the skillet with the salt and pepper. Add the pork chops and cook for 5 to 6 minutes on each side or until done. Remove the chops to a serving platter and keep warm. Sauté the corn in the same skillet for 2 to 3 minutes. Remove the skillet from the heat and stir in the salsa. Pour the corn mixture over the chops. Garnish with cilantro.
Yield: 4 servings.

Sandra Childs, Laureate Lambda
Wichita, Kansas

ITALIAN PORK CHOPS AND RICE

4 (5-ounce) pork chops	3 cups Italian-style
1/2 cup all-purpose flour	stewed tomatoes
1 cup sliced onion	1 teaspoon Italian
1 cup diced green bell	seasoning
pepper	Pepper to taste
1/2 cup uncooked long	
grain white rice	

Dredge the pork chops in the flour, shaking off the excess. Arrange the pork chops on a rack in a broiler pan. Broil 2 inches from the heat source for 4 minutes on each side or until browned. Remove the pork chops to a 9×13-inch baking pan. Top the pork chops with the onions, bell pepper and rice. Pour the tomatoes over the pork. Sprinkle with the Italian seasoning and pepper. Bake, covered, at 350 degrees for 1 to 1 1/2 hours or until the pork chops are cooked through. Yield: 4 servings.

Joan Boucher, Xi Xi Iota
Lake Placid, Florida

OVEN-FRIED PORK CHOPS

2 tablespoons pineapple	1/3 cup bread crumbs
juice	1/4 teaspoon Italian
1 tablespoon soy sauce	seasoning
1/4 teaspoon ginger	1/4 teaspoon paprika
1/8 teaspoon garlic	Garlic powder to taste
powder	4 (5-ounce) center-cut
1 large egg white	pork chops

Whisk the pineapple juice, soy sauce, ginger, garlic powder and egg white in a medium bowl. Combine the bread crumbs, Italian seasoning, paprika and garlic powder in a medium bowl and mix well. Coat the pork chops with the juice mixture and then the breadcrumb mixture. Bake the pork chops on a broiler pan coated with cooking spray at 350 degrees for 50 minutes, turning after 25 minutes.
Yield: 4 servings.

Nancy Taylor, Xi Master
Decatur, Illinois

PORK CHOPS IN WINE SAUCE

1 teaspoon sage	4 (1-inch-thick)
1 teaspoon rosemary	center-cut pork chops
2 garlic cloves, minced	2 tablespoons butter
1 teaspoon salt	1 tablespoon peanut oil
Fresh ground pepper	1/2 cup dry white wine
to taste	1/4 cup dry white wine

Combine the sage, rosemary, garlic, salt and pepper in a small bowl and mix well. Rub the seasonings on both sides of the pork chops. Melt the butter and oil in a large skillet and brown the chops on both sides. Remove the pork chops and pour off the drippings from the skillet, reserving a small amount. Add 1/2 cup of wine to the skillet and bring to a boil over high heat. Return the chops to the skillet, cover, and reduce the heat. Simmer the pork chops for 25 to 30 minutes or until cooked through. Remove the pork chops to a heated plate. Add the remaining 1/4 cup of wine to the skillet and boil until reduced by half. Pour the wine sauce over the chops.
Yield: 4 servings.

Gay Grimm, Beta Sigma Phi
Danville, California

SLOW COOKER BARBECUE RIBS

4 pounds country-style	1/2 cup orange juice
ribs	1 tablespoon steak
2 teaspoons salt	sauce
1 onion, chopped	1 teaspoon coarse
1 cup packed brown	ground pepper
sugar	1 teaspoon minced
1 cup apple butter	garlic
1 cup ketchup	1/2 teaspoon
1/2 cup lemon juice	Worcestershire sauce

Cut the ribs apart, if necessary, and trim. Sprinkle 1 teaspoon of salt evenly over the ribs and set aside. Combine the remaining 1 teaspoon of salt and the remaining ingredients in a bowl and mix well. Pour half of the sauce in a 5-quart slow cooker. Place the ribs in the slow cooker. Pour the remaining sauce over the ribs. Cover and cook on Low for 8 to 10 hours or on for High 6 to 7 hours.
Yield: 6 to 8 servings.

Karen Hamilton, Laureate Phi
Monroe, Louisiana

BARBECUED RIBS

3 pounds spare ribs
2 onions, thinly sliced
1/2 cup ketchup
1/4 teaspoon Tabasco
   sauce

1 1/2 teaspoons salt
1/8 teaspoon chili
   powder
1 cup water

Place 1/2 of the ribs in the bottom of a large roasting pan. Cover the ribs with 1/2 of the onions. Combine the remaining ingredients in a bowl and mix well. Pour 1/2 of the sauce over the ribs and onions. Add another layer of ribs, onions and sauce. Bake, covered, at 350 degrees for 2 hours or until tender. Yield: 6 to 8 servings.

Betty Lee DeBrosse, Delta Kappa Master
Corpus Christi, Texas

SPARERIBS BURGUNDY

3 pounds spare ribs
Salt and pepper to taste
1/2 cup chopped onions
3 large red cooking
   apples

1/2 cup chili sauce
1/2 cup Burgundy
3 tablespoons brown
   sugar
1/2 cup Burgundy

Wipe the spare ribs with a damp cloth and sprinkle with salt and pepper. Place the ribs in a roasting pan and cover with the onions. Peel and core the apples and cut in half lengthwise. Place the apples around the ribs. Combine the chili sauce and 1/2 cup of wine in a bowl and mix well. Pour the wine sauce over the ribs and the apples. Sprinkle the apples with the brown sugar. Bake, covered, at 450 degrees for 1 hour. Uncover and pour in 1/2 cup of wine. Bake, uncovered, for 15 minutes. Yield: 4 to 6 servings.

Sally McFarland, Laureate Alpha Lambda
Gresham, Oregon

HAWAIIAN SPARERIBS

1 slab spareribs
1 (2-inch) piece fresh
   gingerroot, peeled
   and sliced

3/4 cup sugar
1/2 cup soy sauce
1 cup ketchup

Place the spareribs and the ginger in a stockpot full of boiling water. Boil for 1 hour; let cool. Combine the sugar, soy sauce and ketchup in a small bowl and mix well. Pour the sauce into a sealable plastic bag. Add the ribs to the bag and seal. Marinate in the refrigerator for 1 hour, turning the bag occasionally. Remove the ribs and discard the marinade. Grill over low heat for 1 to 1 1/2 hours or until tender. Yield: 2 to 4 servings.

Paula S. Franklin, Xi Gamma Epsilon
Columbus, Georgia

PORK AND APPLES

1 1/2 pounds boneless
   pork, cubed
1 tablespoon vegetable
   oil
4 cups water
1 tablespoon chicken
   bouillon granules
1 teaspoon thyme
1/4 teaspoon pepper

1 bay leaf
10 to 12 small red
   potatoes, quartered
4 medium tart apples
2 tablespoons cold
   water
2 tablespoons
   cornstarch

Brown the pork in the oil in a Dutch oven. Add the water, bouillon, thyme, pepper and bay leaf to the Dutch oven and mix well. Bring to a boil over high heat. Reduce heat; cover and let simmer for 1 1/2 to 2 hours or until the pork is nearly cooked through. Add the potatoes; cover and cook for an additional 15 minutes. Peel the apples and cut in wedges. Add the apples to the Dutch oven; cover and cook for 10 to 12 minutes or until tender-crisp. Remove the bay leaf. Combine the cornstarch and cold water in a small bowl and stir until smooth. Add the cornstarch mixture to the pork and bring to a boil. Cook, stirring constantly, for 2 minutes or until thickened. Serve with hot rolls. Yield: 6 to 8 servings.

Joyce Boor, Theta Master
Great Bend, Kansas

CREPES ENSENADA

12 ham slices
4 cups (16 ounces) cubed
   Monterey Jack cheese
1 (14-ounce) can whole
   green chiles, drained
12 flour tortillas
1/2 cup (1 stick) butter
1/2 cup all-purpose flour

1 tablespoon prepared
   mustard
1 teaspoon salt
4 cups milk
3 cups (12 ounces)
   shredded sharp
   Cheddar cheese
Paprika to taste

Place 1 ham slice, 2 to 3 cubes of Monterey Jack cheese and 1 tablespoon green chiles in the center of each tortilla. Roll the tortillas around the filling and place seam side down in a greased 9×13-inch baking dish. Melt the butter in a medium saucepan over medium heat. Stir in the flour, mustard and salt and mix well. Add the milk, stirring constantly, and cook until the sauce thickens. Remove from the heat. Add the Cheddar cheese and stir until melted. Pour the Cheddar cheese sauce over the rolled tortillas. Sprinkle with the paprika. Bake, uncovered, at 350 degrees for 45 minutes. Yield: 10 to 12 servings.

Mary Peterson, Xi Alpha Sigma
Burnsville, Minnesota

❖ HAM AND ARTICHOKE LASAGNA

1 cup shredded carrots
1 (8-ounce) can sliced
   mushrooms, drained
5 green onions, chopped
2 tablespoons olive oil
1/4 cup dry sherry
1/2 cup heavy cream
2 pounds boneless
   hickory-smoked ham,
   cut in 1-inch cubes
2 (14-ounce) cans
   quartered artichoke
   hearts, drained

1 (24-ounce) container
   small curd cottage
   cheese
2 eggs, beaten
1/2 cup (2 ounces) grated
   Parmesan cheese
1 teaspoon basil
8 ounces lasagna
   noodles
3 cups (12 ounces)
   shredded mozzarella
   cheese

Sauté the carrots, mushrooms and onions in the oil in a large skillet over medium-high heat until tender. Stir in the sherry and cook for 2 minutes. Stir in the cream and cook for an additional 2 minutes or until slightly thickened. Remove from the heat and stir in the ham cubes and artichokes. Combine the cottage cheese, eggs, Parmesan cheese and basil in a medium bowl and mix well. Prepare the noodles using the package directions; drain. Layer the noodles, ham mixture, cottage cheese mixture and mozzarella cheese 1/3 at a time in a greased 9×13-inch baking dish, ending with the mozzarella cheese. Bake, covered, at 350 degrees for 45 minutes. Uncover and bake for 15 minutes longer or until light brown on top. Let stand for 15 minutes before serving.
Yield: 8 to 10 servings.

Sandi Davison, Laureate Gamma Upsilon
Kansas City, Missouri

HAM BALLS

The late Bonnie Gjelde is credited for this scrumptious recipe.

1 1/2 pounds ground ham
1 1/2 pounds ground pork
2 1/4 cups soft bread
   crumbs
3 eggs, beaten
1 1/2 cups milk
2 (6-ounce) cans
   pineapple slices

1 1/8 cups packed brown
   sugar
4 1/2 tablespoons vinegar
1/2 cup pineapple juice
1/4 teaspoon dry mustard
Maraschino cherries

Combine the ham, pork, bread crumbs, eggs and milk in a large bowl and mix well. Shape into balls, using 1/2 cup of meat mixture per meatball. Line the bottom of a baking sheet with pineapple slices. Place 1 meatball on each pineapple slice. Combine the brown sugar, vinegar, pineapple juice and dry mustard in a small bowl and mix well. Pour the sauce over the meatballs. Bake, uncovered, at 325 degrees

for 45 minutes, basting occasionally with the sauce. Top each with a cherry before serving.
Yield: 10 servings.

Jane Williams, Phi Master
Joseph, Oregon

HAM LOAF

1 pound ground ham
2 pounds ground
   pork
1 cup cracker crumbs
1 egg, beaten
1 teaspoon onion
   soup mix

1 cup milk
6 tablespoons brown
   sugar
1/2 cup ketchup
2 teaspoons dry
   mustard

Combine the ham, pork, cracker crumbs, egg, milk and onion soup mix in a large bowl and mix well. Press the mixture into a large loaf pan. Combine the brown sugar, ketchup and dry mustard in a small bowl. Pour the sauce over the meat. Bake the loaf at 350 degrees for 1 1/2 hours or until done.
Yield: 8 to 10 servings.

Maretta Grindeland, Preceptor Omicron Tau
Hallettsville, Texas

BAKED HAM AND CHEESE CASSEROLE

2 cups macaroni
1 cup celery, diced
2 cups (8 ounces) sharp
   Cheddar cheese cubes
2 cups milk
2 tablespoons Wondra
   flour
2 tablespoons diced
   onion

2 tablespoons diced
   green bell pepper
1 teaspoon salt
2 cups diced cooked
   ham
Grated Parmesan
   cheese
Bread crumbs

Place the macaroni and the celery in a stockpot full of boiling water. Cook until the macaroni is tender; drain. Combine the Cheddar cheese and milk in a medium saucepan over medium heat. Cook until the cheese melts, stirring constantly. Stir in the flour and cook until thickened. Add the onion, bell pepper and salt and mix well. Alternate layers of the macaroni, cheese sauce, ham and Parmesan cheese in a greased 3-quart casserole dish until all ingredients are used. Top with the Parmesan cheese and bread crumbs. Bake at 350 degrees for 1 hour. Yield: 6 servings.

Elaine M. Wilson, Laureate Beta
Warwick, Rhode Island

HAM AND POTATO AU GRATIN

4 cups cubed cooked
   potatoes
2 cups diced cooked ham
1 (4-ounce) can sliced
   mushrooms, drained
1/4 cup (1/2 stick)
   margarine

1/4 cup all-purpose flour
1 cup milk
1/2 cup (2 ounces)
   shredded Colby cheese
1/2 cup sour cream
3/4 cup buttered bread
   crumbs

Layer the potatoes, ham and mushrooms in a shallow 2-quart casserole. Melt 1/4 cup margarine in a medium saucepan. Stir in the flour, blending thoroughly. Add the milk slowly and cook until thickened, stirring constantly. Fold in the cheese and sour cream. Pour the cheese sauce over the casserole. Sprinkle the bread crumbs over the casserole. Bake at 350 degrees for 35 minutes. Yield: 6 to 8 servings.

Jane Chapman, Gamma Nu
Brestow, Oklahoma

CREAMY HAM AND SCALLOPED POTATOES

3 pounds potatoes,
   peeled and sliced
1 cup (4 ounces)
   Cheddar cheese
1/2 cup chopped onion
1 (10-ounce) can cream
   of mushroom soup

1 cup diced ham
3/4 cup water
1/2 teaspoon garlic
   powder
1/4 teaspoon salt
1/4 teaspoon pepper

Combine all the ingredients in a slow cooker. Cover and cook on High for 4 hours. Yield: 6 servings.

Joei Cullan, Delta Gamma
Hemingford, North Carolina

BAKE CABBAGE JAMBALAYA

1 cup uncooked rice,
   soaked and drained
1 pound ground beef
1 onion, chopped
1 pound smoked
   sausage, cut in pieces
1 head cabbage, chopped

Chili powder to taste
1/3 cup vegetable oil
1/2 teaspoon Tabasco
   sauce
1 (8-ounce) can tomatoes
   with green chiles

Brown the ground beef with the onion and sausage in a skillet, stirring until the ground beef is crumbly; drain. Combine the ground beef mixture and the remaining ingredients in a large bowl. Spoon the mixture into a greased 9×13-inch baking dish. Bake, covered, at 300 degrees for 2 hours, stirring halfway through the cooking time. Yield: 6 to 8 servings.

Gina Smith, Xi Delta Tau
Jonesboro, Louisiana

CAJUN JAMBALAYA

1/2 cup bacon drippings
1 pound smoked
   sausage, diced
1/2 pound crisp-cooked
   bacon, crumbled
2 cups julienned chicken
2 large onions, chopped
1 green bell pepper,
   chopped
6 ribs celery, chopped
4 garlic cloves, minced
3 cups long grain rice
2 cups beef broth

2 (8-ounce) cans
   tomatoes with green
   chilies
2 teaspoons Kitchen
   Bouquet
1/2 teaspoon thyme
2 teaspoons chili
   powder
Salt and pepper to taste
Cayenne pepper to taste
2 pounds peeled shrimp
12 green onions, sliced
1/2 cup minced parsley

Melt the bacon drippings in a large Dutch oven over high heat. Fry the sausage and bacon in the bacon drippings for 8 minutes, stirring constantly. Add the chicken and cook until done. Add the onions, bell pepper, celery and garlic, stirring to combine. Reduce the heat to medium-high and cook until the vegetables are tender. Add the rice and cook for 5 minutes, stirring constantly. Add the broth, tomatoes with green chiles, Kitchen Bouquet, thyme and chili powder, stirring to combine. Bring the mixture slowly to a boil. Season with the salt, pepper and cayenne pepper to taste. Cover and simmer for 1 hour. Add the shrimp, green onions and parsley 5 minutes before serving. Cover and simmer until the shrimp turn pink. Serve with buttered French bread.
Yield: 10 to 12 servings.

Linda Hill Mizell, Kappa Lambda
Bogalusa, Louisiana

CHALUPAS

2 (6-ounce) cans pinto
   beans, drained
1 (2-pound) pork roast
7 cups water
1/2 cup chopped onion
2 garlic cloves, minced
1 tablespoon salt
2 tablespoons chili
   powder

1 tablespoon cumin
1 teaspoon oregano
1 (4-ounce) can chopped
   green chiles
Toppings such as corn
   chips, tomato,
   avocado, onion,
   lettuce, Cheddar
   cheese, salsa

Combine the beans, roast, water, onion, garlic, salt, chili powder, cumin, oregano and green chilies in a large Dutch oven. Cover and simmer for 5 hours or until the roast is done. Uncover and cook for an additional 30 minutes. Shred the meat and serve with toppings. Yield: 6 servings.

Linda Miles, Preceptor Gamma Iota
Colorado Springs, Colorado

CANADIAN PORK PIE

2 cups all-purpose flour	1 onion, chopped
1 teaspoon salt	1 garlic clove, chopped
2/3 cup plus 2	1/2 cup water
tablespoons	1 1/2 teaspoons salt
shortening	(optional)
1 egg, lightly beaten	1/2 teaspoon thyme
2 to 3 tablespoons cold	1/4 teaspoon ground sage
water	1/4 teaspoon pepper
1 pound ground pork	1/8 teaspoon ground
1/2 pound ground beef	cloves

Combine the flour and salt in a medium bowl. Cut in the shortening until crumbly. Whisk the egg and water in a small bowl. Add the egg mixture to the flour mixture and stir until moistened. Shape the dough into a ball. Divide the dough in half and shape into 2 flattened rounds. Chill, wrapped in plastic wrap, for 30 minutes or longer. Combine the pork, beef, onion, garlic, water, salt, thyme, sage, pepper and cloves in a large saucepan; stir well. Bring to a boil, stirring constantly. Reduce the heat, stirring until the ground beef is crumbly; drain. Remove the pastry rounds from the refrigerator. Roll each round into an 11-inch circle on a lightly floured surface. Fit 1 pastry circle into a 9-inch pie plate. Spoon the meat mixture into the pastry-lined pie plate. Top with the remaining pastry, sealing edges and cutting slits in the center. Cover the edge of the pie with foil. Bake at 425 degrees for 35 to 40 minutes, removing the foil during the last 15 minutes of baking. Let stand for 10 minutes before serving. Yield: 8 to 10 servings.

Karen Swanberg, Xi Mu Gamma
Cement City, Michigan

CHEESE AND PORK BAKE

1 1/2 pounds lean ground	1 cup cottage cheese
pork	1 tablespoon minced
4 cups cooked noodles	onion
8 ounces cream cheese,	1 (16-ounce) can tomato
softened	sauce
1/4 cup sour cream	

Brown the pork in a large skillet, stirring until crumbly; drain. Layer half of the noodles in a greased 7×11-inch baking dish. Combine the cream cheese, sour cream, cottage cheese and onion in a medium bowl and mix well. Spread the cheese mixture over the noodles. Top with the remaining half of the noodles. Pour the meat over the noodles. Pour the tomato sauce over the casserole. Bake at 350 degrees for 45 minutes. Yield: 8 servings.

Roberta Hersom, Mu Mu
Emmetsburg, Idaho

SAUSAGE-RICE CASSEROLE

1 pound ground sausage	1 (13-ounce) can
1 onion, minced	mushroom pieces and
1 green bell pepper,	stems
minced	1 teaspoon thyme
1 (4-ounce) jar	1 teaspoon marjoram
pimentos, diced	1 package wild rice

Brown the sausage in a large skillet, stirring until crumbly; drain. Return to the skillet over low heat. Sauté the onion and bell pepper in a separate skillet until tender. Add the onion mixture to the sausage, stirring to combine. Add the pimentos, mushrooms, thyme and marjoram to the sausage and mix well. Prepare the rice using the package directions. Combine the rice and the sausage mixture and mix well. Spoon the mixture into a large baking dish and bake at 350 degrees for 30 minutes. Yield: 6 to 8 servings.

Audrey Guinn, Phi Master
Arlington, Texas

GERMAN LASAGNA

3/4 cup (1 1/2 sticks) butter	2 eggs
3/4 cup all-purpose flour	1 (12-ounce) container
1 tablespoon beef	small curd cottage
bouillon	cheese
2 teaspoons onion salt	1 teaspoon pepper
1 teaspoon pepper	9 lasagna noodles,
2 1/4 cups milk	cooked
1 (14-ounce) can chicken	1 (16-ounce) jar
broth	sauerkraut, drained
1 pound kielbasa	2 cups shredded
sausage, cubed	Monterey Jack cheese

Melt the butter in a large saucepan. Stir in the flour, bouillon, onion salt and 1 teaspoon pepper until smooth. Stir in the milk and broth gradually. Bring to a boil. Cook for 2 minutes or until thickened, stirring constantly. Add the sausage and cook until heated through, stirring frequently. Combine the eggs, cottage cheese and 1 teaspoon pepper in a bowl and mix well. Spread 1 cup of the sausage mixture in a greased 9×13-inch baking dish. Layer the sausage with 3 noodles, 1/3 of the sausage mixture, 1/2 of the cottage cheese mixture and the sauerkraut and 3/4 cup of Monterey Jack cheese. Repeat the layers and top with the remaining noodles and sausage mixture. Bake, covered, at 350 degrees for 50 to 60 minutes or until bubbly. Sprinkle with the remaining 1/2 cup Monterey Jack cheese and bake for 10 more minutes or until the cheese melts. Let stand for 15 minutes before serving. Yield: 10 to 12 servings.

Estelle D. Seachrist, Preceptor Theta
Webster, Massachusetts

Poultry

BRUSCHETTA CHICKEN

1¹/₂ pounds boneless
  skinless chicken
  breasts
1 teaspoon basil
1 cup (4 ounces)
  shredded mozzarella
  cheese

1 (14-ounce) can diced
  tomatoes
1 (6-ounce) package
  stuffing mix for
  chicken
¹/₂ cup water
2 garlic cloves, minced

Rinse the chicken and pat dry. Cut into bite-size pieces. Place in a 9×13-inch baking dish. Sprinkle with the basil and cheese. Combine the tomatoes, stuffing mix, water and garlic in a large bowl, stirring just until the stuffing is moist. Spoon over the chicken. Bake at 400 degrees for 30 minutes or until heated through. Yield: 6 servings.

Margaret I. Budney, Preceptor Eta Phi
Indian Harbor Beach, Florida

LINGUIÇA CHICKEN

Linguiça is a garlicky Portuguese sausage and can be found in many supermarkets.

8 ounces linguiça, sliced
2 tablespoons olive oil
4 boneless skinless
  chicken breasts
1 teaspoon salt
¹/₂ teaspoon pepper
1 onion, minced

1 green bell pepper,
  chopped
1 (14-ounce) can diced
  tomatoes
2 garlic cloves, minced
¹/₄ teaspoon sugar

Brown the sausage in the olive oil in a large skillet. Remove the sausage, leaving the drippings in the skillet. Rinse the chicken and pat dry. Season with the salt and pepper. Sauté in the drippings until brown.

Remove to a baking dish. Cover with the linguiça. Add the onion to the drippings. Cook until translucent. Add the bell pepper. Cook for 2 minutes. Stir in the tomatoes, garlic and sugar. Cook for 3 minutes longer. Pour over the chicken and linguiça. Bake, covered, at 375 degrees for 45 minutes.
Yield: 4 servings.

Dorothy Vieira
Leesburg, Florida

GARLIC CHICKEN MARBELLA

I like to impress company with this dish. The sweet fruit, garlic, and olives give the impression it's a complicated dish, but it's really quick and easy.

8 bone-in chicken
  breasts
1¹/₂ cups pitted prunes
1 cup garlic-stuffed
  Spanish olives
¹/₂ cup drained capers
¹/₂ cup olive oil
¹/₂ cup red wine vinegar

1 head garlic, minced
2 tablespoons oregano
4 bay leaves
Salt and pepper to taste
1 cup packed dark
  brown sugar
1¹/₂ cups white wine

Rinse the chicken and pat dry. Place in one layer in a large shallow baking dish. Combine the prunes, olives, capers, olive oil, vinegar, garlic, oregano, bay leaves, salt and pepper in a large bowl and mix well. Pour over the chicken. Marinate, covered, in the refrigerator for 8 to 10 hours. Sprinkle the brown sugar over the chicken. Pour the wine around the chicken. Bake at 350 degrees for 45 minutes. Discard the bay leaves. Serve with rice. Yield: 8 servings.

Kathryn Daly, Xi Alpha Omega
Banner, Wyoming

ORANGE THYME CHICKEN

4 boneless skinless
   chicken breasts
1/2 cup freshly squeezed
   orange juice
2 tablespoons olive oil

2 tablespoons honey
1 tablespoon fresh
   thyme leaves
Salt and pepper to taste

Rinse the chicken and pat dry. Place in a shallow baking dish. Combine the orange juice, olive oil, honey, thyme, salt and pepper in a bowl and mix well. Pour over the chicken. Marinate, covered, in the refrigerator for 8 to 10 hours, turning once. Bake at 350 degrees for 30 minutes or until cooked through, basting occasionally with the marinade. Yield: 6 servings.

Dana Lovins, Xi Nu Lambda
Dexter, Missouri

BAKED REUBEN CHICKEN

8 boneless skinless
   chicken breasts
1/4 teaspoon salt
1/8 teaspoon pepper
2 cups sauerkraut

1 1/4 cups Russian
   dressing
4 to 6 slices Swiss cheese
1 tablespoon chopped
   fresh parsley

Rinse the chicken and pat dry. Place in a large nonstick baking pan. Sprinkle with the salt and pepper. Rinse the sauerkraut; drain. Layer the sauerkraut, Russian dressing and cheese over the chicken. Bake at 350 degrees for 1 hour or until the chicken is forktender. Sprinkle with the parsley. Yield: 8 servings.

Debbie Meegan, Preceptor Beta Phi
Lemont Furnace, Pennsylvania

SCAMPI-STYLE CHICKEN

2 to 3 pounds boneless
   skinless chicken
   breasts
1/2 cup (1 stick) butter or
   margarine
2 whole scallions,
   minced

3 garlic cloves, minced
1 tablespoon chopped
   fresh parsley
1/2 tablespoon fresh
   dill weed or oregano
1/2 teaspoon salt
1/2 teaspoon pepper

Rinse the chicken and pat dry. Cut into 3-inch pieces. Place in a 9×13-inch baking dish. Melt the butter in a saucepan over low heat. Add the scallions, garlic, parsley, dill weed, salt and pepper. Cook over low heat for 2 minutes. Pour over the chicken. Bake at 350 degrees for 10 to 15 minutes. Turn the chicken. Bake for 15 minutes longer. Broil for 3 to 4 minutes or until the chicken is browned. Serve over rice or angel hair pasta. Yield: 6 servings.

Mary Dunworth, Xi Alpha Beta
Coldwater, Michigan

POLYNESIAN CHICKEN

6 chicken breasts, or
   other pieces
1 1/2 teaspoons seasoning
   salt
1/2 cup all-purpose flour
1/2 cup (1 stick)
   margarine, melted

1 (20-ounce) can
   pineapple chunks
2 tablespoons lemon
   juice
1 tablespoon cornstarch
1 tablespoon soy sauce
Chopped parsley

Rinse the chicken and pat dry. Sprinkle with the seasoning salt and coat with the flour. Place in a baking pan coated with nonstick cooking spray. Brush with the margarine. Bake at 350 degrees for 50 minutes. Drain the pineapple chunks over a 1-cup measure. Add enough water to fill the cup. Combine the pineapple juice, lemon juice, cornstarch and soy sauce in a saucepan and mix well. Cook over medium heat until the juice is clear and thickened, stirring constantly. Stir in the pineapple chunks. Pour over the chicken. Bake, covered, at 350 degrees for 10 minutes. Garnish with parsley. Serve with rice and a tossed salad. Yield: 6 servings.

Joan McKay, Mu Master
Kelowna, British Columbia, Canada

CARROT CHICKEN

4 to 6 boneless skinless
   chicken breasts
2 tablespoons butter
1/2 teaspoon garlic
   powder
3 to 4 carrots, thinly
   sliced

2 (4-ounce) cans
   mushroom stems
   and pieces, drained
2 (10-ounce) cans cream
   of chicken soup
1/2 cup white wine
1/2 cup sour cream

Rinse the chicken and pat dry. Sauté in the butter in a skillet until brown, sprinkling with the garlic powder while cooking. Combine the carrots, mushrooms, soup, wine and sour cream in a large bowl and mix well. Pour over the chicken. Simmer, covered, for 25 to 35 minutes or until the chicken and carrots are tender. Serve with rice. Yield: 4 to 6 servings.

Pat Scharch, Beta Epsilon
Madison, Wisconsin

CHICKEN WITH SPICY FRUIT

4 boneless skinless
   chicken breasts
1 1/4 cups unsweetened
   pineapple juice
1/4 cup dried cranberries
1/2 to 1/4 teaspoon
   crushed red pepper

2 garlic cloves, minced
1/4 cup reduced-sugar
   strawberry fruit
   spread
1 teaspoon cornstarch
2 green onions, thinly
   sliced

Rinse the chicken and pat dry. Combine the next 4 ingredients in a large skillet. Add the chicken. Bring to a boil. Reduce the heat and simmer, covered, for 15 minutes or until the chicken is cooked through. Remove the chicken to a serving dish. Bring the liquid in the skillet to a boil. Reduce the heat and simmer for 5 to 7 minutes or until reduced to 3/4 cup. Combine the fruit spread and cornstarch in a small bowl. Stir into the skillet. Cook for 1 minute or until thickened, stirring constantly. Spoon over the chicken. Sprinkle with the green onions. Yield: 4 servings.

Marcia Carter, Theta
Vincennes, Indiana

GENERAL TSAO'S CHICKEN

The chicken is stir-fried rather than deep-fried in this traditional dish. You'll love the great Asian flavor.

1 pound boneless skinless chicken breasts	2 tablespoons cornstarch
2 teaspoons peanut oil	2 tablespoons sugar
2 scallions, chopped	2 tablespoons low-sodium soy sauce
2 garlic cloves, minced	1 tablespoon white wine vinegar
1/2 teaspoon red pepper flakes	1/2 teaspoon ginger
3/4 cup chicken broth	2 cups cooked rice

Rinse the chicken and pat dry. Cut into 2-inch pieces. Heat the peanut oil in a large skillet over medium-high heat. Add the scallions, garlic and red pepper flakes. Stir-fry for 2 minutes. Add the chicken and stir-fry for 5 minutes or until browned. Whisk the chicken broth, cornstarch, sugar, soy sauce, vinegar and ginger together in a bowl. Add to the skillet. Cook for 3 minutes or until the sauce thickens and the chicken is cooked through. Serve over the rice. Yield: 4 servings.

Janet Tweed, Laureate Phi
Victoria, British Columbia, Canada

RED PEPPER CHICKEN

1 pound chicken tenders	1 cup hot water
1/2 teaspoon salt	1 (15-ounce) can diced tomatoes, drained
1/8 teaspoon pepper	1 tablespoon cornstarch
Vegetable oil	1/4 cup water
1 large red bell pepper, chopped	2 tablespoons soy sauce
1 chicken bouillon cube	

Rinse the chicken and pat dry. Cut into bite-size pieces. Season with the salt and pepper. Sauté in oil in a skillet until the chicken turns white. Add the bell pepper. Cook for 2 to 3 minutes. Dissolve the bouillon cube in the hot water and add to the skillet. Bring

to a boil. Reduce the heat and simmer, covered, for 40 minutes. Add the tomatoes. Combine the cornstarch, 1/4 cup water and soy sauce in a bowl and mix well. Add to the skillet. Bring to a boil. Reduce the heat and simmer for 1 minute, stirring constantly. Serve over rice. Yield: 4 servings.

Jan Roden, Rho Master
Odessa, Texas

CHICKEN ROULADES

6 boneless skinless chicken breasts	6 ounces feta cheese
6 tablespoons sun-dried tomato pesto	2 tablespoons butter
	1 tablespoon olive oil
2 tablespoons chopped fresh basil	1/2 cup chicken broth
	1/4 cup sun-dried tomato pesto

Rinse the chicken and pat dry. Pound into 1/4-inch thickness. Top each chicken breast with 1 tablespoon sun-dried tomato pesto, 1 teaspoon basil and 1 ounce feta cheese. Roll up to enclose the filling and secure with wooden picks. Heat the butter and olive oil in a large skillet. Add the chicken. Cook for 10 to 12 minutes or until the chicken is cooked through and the filling is still moist, turning frequently. Remove to a serving dish. Discard all but 1 tablespoon of the drippings. Add the chicken broth and 1/4 cup sun-dried tomato pesto. Cook until the liquid is reduced by half. Remove the wooden picks from the rolls. Slice the rolls on the diagonal into 1/2-inch pieces. Spoon 1 tablespoon of the sauce over each serving. Yield: 6 servings.

Fran Gaskell, Xi Mu
Edmonton, Alberta, Canada

FLAMING CHICKEN SATAY

4 boneless skinless chicken breasts	2 tablespoons salt
1/2 cup lemon juice	1 tablespoon red pepper flakes
1/2 cup chunky peanut butter	1 tablespoon ground ginger
5 garlic cloves, minced	1/2 cup chopped fresh parsley (optional)
2 tablespoons sugar	

Rinse the chicken and pat dry. Cut into 1-inch cubes. Combine the lemon juice, peanut butter, garlic, sugar, salt, red pepper flakes, ginger and parsley in a sealable plastic bag. Add the chicken. Marinate in the refrigerator for 8 to 10 hours. Thread the chicken onto wooden skewers presoaked in water. Grill over medium-hot coals for 15 minutes or until browned and cooked through, turning occasionally. Yield: 10 servings.

Sharon Brownlee
Goderich, Ontario, Canada

COUSCOUS WITH CHICKEN, SPINACH AND MUSHROOMS

Fresh spinach is great in this dish but you can substitute one 10-ounce package of frozen chopped spinach, thawed and squeezed dry.

3 boneless skinless chicken breasts	1/2 cup sliced fresh mushrooms
1/2 cup chopped onion	2 tablespoons dry white wine or lemon juice
1 garlic clove, minced	
1 tablespoon olive oil	1 (6-ounce) package herbed chicken-flavor couscous mix
1 1/2 cups packed chopped fresh spinach	
1 1/2 cups water	Grated Parmesan cheese

Rinse the chicken and pat dry. Cut into 1/2-inch pieces. Sauté the chicken, onion and garlic in the olive oil in a skillet for 3 to 4 minutes or until the chicken is no longer pink. Add the spinach, water, mushrooms, wine and the seasonings included in the couscous mix. Bring to a boil. Stir in the couscous; cover and remove from the heat. Let stand for 5 minutes. Fluff lightly with a fork. Sprinkle with cheese. Yield: 4 servings.

Janice DiBeneditto, Theta Master
Waterbury, Connecticut

CHICKEN MANICOTTI

This dish is time-consuming but worth it. I made it for my future husband when we were dating. He was really impressed and thought I always cooked like this.

8 manicotti shells	2 tablespoons butter, melted
1 (10-ounce) can creamy chicken mushroom soup	1/2 teaspoon chicken-flavored bouillon granules
1/2 cup sour cream	
2 cups chopped cooked chicken	1/4 cup warm water
1 (4-ounce) can sliced mushrooms, drained	1 cup (4 ounces) shredded Cheddar cheese
1/4 cup chopped onion	

Cook the manicotti shells using the package directions, omitting the salt; drain. Combine the soup and sour cream in a bowl and mix well. Combine 1/2 of the soup mixture with the chicken in a bowl. Spoon the chicken mixture into the manicotti shells. Place the shells in a greased 8×12-inch baking dish. Sauté the mushrooms and onion in the butter in a skillet until tender. Dissolve the bouillon granules in the water in a measuring cup. Stir into the remaining soup mixture. Add the soup mixture to the mushroom mixture and stir well. Spoon over the manicotti. Bake at 350 degrees for 15 minutes. Sprinkle with the cheese. Bake for 5 minutes longer. Yield: 4 to 6 servings.

Lisa McGinnis, Alpha Epsilon Omega
O'Fallon, Missouri

CHICKEN AND BROCCOLI ALFREDO

This homemade version of Alfredo sauce is quick, easy, and much tastier than the kind you buy.

8 ounces linguini	1 can low-fat cream of mushroom soup
1 cup broccoli florets	
1 pound boneless skinless chicken breasts, cubed	1/2 cup (2 ounces) freshly grated Parmesan cheese
2 tablespoons butter	1/4 teaspoon freshly ground black pepper
1/2 cup milk	

Cook the linguini using the package directions, adding the broccoli to the cooking water for the last 4 minutes of cooking time; drain. Sauté the chicken in the butter in a large skillet until brown. Add the milk, soup, cheese, pepper and linguini mixture. Cook until heated through. Serve with additional Parmesan cheese. Yield: 4 servings.

Mary Schmidt, Preceptor Delta Upsilon
Woolstock, Iowa

CHICKEN CREPES

1/2 cup (1 stick) butter	2 handfuls fresh spinach
1 cup chopped onion	1 cup (4 ounces) shredded Colby cheese
1/2 cup chopped red bell pepper	
1 cup chopped zucchini	1 cup all-purpose flour
1 teaspoon salt	1/2 cup (1 stick) butter, melted
1 teaspoon pepper	
1 teaspoon chipotle spice	1/2 cup water
	1/2 cup milk
3 to 4 cups chopped cooked chicken	1 egg
	Salt to taste
1 cup heavy cream	Shredded cheese

Melt 1/2 cup butter in a skillet over medium heat. Add the onion and stir-fry for 2 to 3 minutes. Add the bell pepper, then the zucchini, stir-frying each for 2 to 3 minutes. Combine the salt, pepper and chipolte spice and add to the skillet. Add the chicken, heavy cream, spinach and cheese, mixing well after each addition. Cook for 7 minutes or until the cheese melts and the ingredients are heated through. Combine the flour, 1/2 cup butter, water, milk, egg and salt in a mixing bowl. Beat for 2 minutes. Cook the crepes in a crepe maker until golden brown. Spoon 1/3 cup of the filling on each crepe; roll up tightly. Place the crepes seam side down in a baking dish and sprinkle with shredded cheese. Broil until the cheese is melted. Serve immediately. Yield: 10 to 12 crepes

Anita Brown, Preceptor Xi Zeta
Abilene, Texas

CHICKEN SALAD WITH NORTH AFRICAN SPICES

This dish offers a unique combination of flavors and colors. It's great for potluck suppers and can be served as a main dish or salad.

3 cups chopped cooked chicken
1 cup chick-peas, drained
1/2 cup each sliced green and red bell pepper
1/2 cup chopped red onion
1/4 cup chopped fresh parsley
1 (2-ounce) can sliced black olives, drained
1 cup plain nonfat yogurt
2 teaspoons lemon juice
1 teaspoon caraway seeds
1/2 teaspoon cumin
1/2 teaspoon coriander
1/4 teaspoon salt
1/4 teaspoon crushed red pepper
1/4 teaspoon black pepper

Combine the chicken, chick peas, bell peppers, red onion, parsley and olives in a salad bowl. Combine the yogurt, lemon juice, caraway seeds, cumin, coriander, salt, red pepper and black pepper in a small bowl and mix well. Add to the salad and toss to coat. Yield: 5 servings.

Claudia S. Byers, Xi Gamma Xi
Corvallis, Oregon

QUICK-AND-EASY SOUTHWEST QUICHE

You can pick up the ingredients for this simple quiche in the dairy case and Mexican food aisle of your grocery store. Serve with hash browns.

1 unbaked (9-inch) pie shell
1 (6-ounce) package Southwest chicken strips
3 ounces cream cheese, softened
1 (4-ounce) can diced green chiles
1 1/2 cups (6 ounces) shredded Mexican-blend cheese
4 eggs
1 1/2 cups half-and-half
1/2 teaspoon salt
1/4 teaspoon pepper
3 drops Tabasco sauce
Salsa for garnish

Bake the pie shell at 350 degrees for 7 minutes. Cut the chicken strips and cream cheese into bite-size cubes. Spread in the pie shell. Layer the chiles and cheese over the top. Beat the eggs with the half-and-half, salt, pepper and Tabasco sauce. Pour over the cheese. Bake at 350 degrees for 40 minutes or until a knife inserted in the center comes out clean. Cool slightly. Serve with salsa. Yield: 6 servings.

Patty Ruddell-Willbanks, Preceptor Phi
Chandler, Arizona

CHICKEN BARBECUE

Turkey works just as well in this yummy quick barbecue recipe, which came to me from my mother-in-law. It freezes and reheats well too.

1 green bell pepper, chopped
2 tablespoons minced onion
1 cup (2 sticks) butter
2 cups ketchup
2/3 cup chicken broth
1/3 cup vinegar
1/3 cup sugar
1/3 teaspoon Worcestershire sauce
1/8 teaspoon Tabasco sauce
5 cups chopped cooked chicken

Sauté the bell pepper and onion in the butter in a skillet until tender. Add the ketchup, chicken broth, vinegar, sugar, Worcestershire sauce and Tabasco sauce. Bring to a boil. Reduce the heat and simmer for 10 minutes. Add the chicken. Simmer for 20 minutes, stirring occasionally. Serve the chicken and sauce on buns. Yield: 6 to 8 servings.

Viola McBride, Upsilon Master
Raymore, Missouri

CHICKEN AND ARTICHOKE PIZZA

My husband and I love to visit the Old Market District in Omaha, Nebraska. This is my attempt to duplicate a pizza from one of the restaurants there.

1 prepared pizza crust
Olive oil
1 cup Alfredo sauce
1 1/2 cups artichoke hearts, chopped
1 cup chopped fresh spinach
1 cup sliced fresh mushrooms
2 cups chopped cooked chicken
Basil to taste
1 1/2 cups (6 ounces) shredded pizza cheese
1/2 cup (2 ounces) grated Parmesan cheese

Brush the pizza crust with olive oil. Spread with the Alfredo sauce. Top with the artichoke hearts, spinach, mushrooms, chicken and basil. Sprinkle the pizza cheese and Parmesan cheese over the top. Bake at 425 degrees for 15 to 18 minutes or until the cheese is melted and the crust is crisp. Yield: 3 to 4 servings.

Deborah A. Patton, Xi Eta Sigma
Gowrie, Iowa

CHICKEN CURRY CASSEROLE

4 boneless skinless
    chicken breasts
1 (14-ounce) can chicken
    broth
1 package curry-
    flavored rice
1 (16-ounce) can French-
    style green beans
1 (8-ounce) can sliced
    water chestnuts
    (optional)
1 (4-ounce) can sliced
    mushrooms
    (optional)
1 (2-ounce) jar pimento
    (optional)
1 onion, finely chopped
1 (10-ounce) can cream
    of celery soup
1 cup mayonnaise

Rinse the chicken. Add water to the chicken broth to make 2½ cups liquid. Combine the chicken and chicken broth in a saucepan. Bring to a boil. Reduce the heat and simmer for 15 minutes or until the chicken is just partially cooked. Remove the chicken; chop into bite-size pieces. Add the rice to the broth. Cook for 5 minutes. Drain the green beans, water chestnuts, mushrooms and pimento. Add to the rice mixture with the chicken, soup, and mayonnaise and mix well. Pour into a greased 9×13-inch casserole. Bake, uncovered, for 40 minutes or until bubbly. Let stand for 5 to 10 minutes before serving. Yield: 10 to 12 servings.

Linda Davis, Preceptor Gamma Tau
Jacksonville, Florida

LOW-FAT HOT CHICKEN SALAD

2 (13-ounce) cans
    chicken breast in
    water
3½ cups cooked rice
2 cups (8 ounces)
    shredded cheese (may
    be low-fat)
1 (10-ounce) can low-fat
    cream of celery soup
1 (10-ounce) can low-fat
    cream of chicken
    soup
1 (8-ounce) can sliced
    water chestnuts
¾ cup low-fat
    mayonnaise
1 cup chopped celery
1 tablespoon diced
    onion
Salt and pepper to taste
1½ cups stuffing mix
½ cup (1 stick) light
    margarine, melted

Drain the chicken. Combine the chicken, rice, cheese, soups, water chestnuts, mayonnaise, celery, onion, salt and pepper in a bowl and mix well. Pour into a 9×13-inch baking pan coated with nonstick cooking spray. Combine the stuffing mix and margarine in a small bowl and mix well. Spread over the rice mixture. Bake, covered, at 350 degrees for 30 minutes. Bake, uncovered, for 15 minutes longer. Cut into squares to serve. Yield: 12 to 15 servings.

Katy Kiene, Laureate Gamma Kappa
Janesville, Iowa

POPPY SEED CHICKEN CASSEROLE

4 boneless skinless
    chicken breasts
1⅓ cups uncooked
    instant brown rice
1 cup chicken broth
1 cup sour cream
1 (10-ounce) can cream
    of mushroom soup
1 (10-ounce) can cream
    of chicken soup
1 tablespoon poppy
    seeds
¼ cup chopped onion
2 cups (8 ounces)
    shedded mozzarella
    cheese
40 butter crackers,
    crushed
½ cup (1 stick) butter,
    melted

Cook the chicken; cut into bite-size pieces. Combine the chicken and rice in a 9 x 13-inch baking dish. Pour the chicken broth over the top. Combine the sour cream, soups, poppy seeds and onion in a bowl and mix well. Spread over the chicken mixture. Layer the cheese and crushed crackers over the top. Drizzle with the melted butter. Bake at 350 degrees for 35 to 40 minutes. Yield: 8 to 10 servings.

Lee Howell, Preceptor Alpha Tau
Buda, Texas

SQUASH CHICKEN CASSEROLE

I created this dish to use the frozen squash and tomatoes from my large garden crop. To sweeten the tomatoes, I heat them with ¼ cup sugar in the microwave before adding them to the casserole.

4 boneless skinless
    chicken breasts
Salt
½ cup dried split peas
3 yellow squash, sliced
3 large tomatoes,
    chopped
1 (10-ounce) can cream
    of celery soup
1 garlic clove, minced
1 teaspoon onion
    powder
1 teaspoon poultry
    seasoning
½ teaspoon saffron
    (optional)
Pepper and Italian
    seasoning to taste
1 cup (4 ounces)
    shredded Monterey
    Jack or Colby cheese
¼ cup bread crumbs
¼ cup quick-cooking
    oats

Cook the chicken in boiling salted water in a saucepan until tender; cut into bite-size pieces. Cook the split peas in boiling salted water in a saucepan until slightly softened; drain. Combine the chicken, split peas and the next 10 ingredients in a bowl and mix well. Pour into a greased 9×13-inch baking dish. Combine the cheese, bread crumbs and oats in a small bowl. Sprinkle over the casserole. Bake at 350 degrees for 30 minutes or until heated through. Yield: 6 to 8 servings.

Nancy Chipukites, Xi Iota
Cushing, Oklahoma

ITALIAN SLOW-COOKER CHICKEN

1 onion, sliced
4 boneless skinless
  chicken breasts
1/2 cup all-purpose flour
Salt and pepper to taste
1 (26-ounce) jar
  spaghetti sauce
1 cup sour cream
1 (4-ounce) can sliced
  mushrooms

1 teaspoon chopped
  garlic
3 sprigs fresh rosemary
1/2 teaspoon oregano
Dash of garlic salt
1/2 cup (2 ounces)
  shredded mozzarella
  cheese

Spread the onion slices in a slow cooker. Rinse the chicken and pat dry. Season the flour with salt and pepper. Coat the chicken with the flour and place over the onion slices. Combine the spaghetti sauce, sour cream, mushrooms, garlic, rosemary, oregano and garlic salt in a bowl and mix well. Pour over the chicken. Top with the cheese. Cook on Low for 6 to 8 hours. Serve with noodles or spaghetti.
Yield: 4 servings.

Marcia Osloond, Theta Master
Reno, Nevada

CHICKEN PARISIENNE

1 (3-pound) chicken,
  cut up
6 chicken breasts
Salt and pepper to taste
1 (10-ounce) can cream
  of mushroom soup

1 (4-ounce) can
  mushrooms, drained
1/4 cup dry white wine or
  chicken broth
1 cup sour cream
1/4 cup all-purpose flour

Rinse the chicken and pat dry. Place in a slow cooker. Season with salt and pepper. Combine the soup, mushrooms and wine in a bowl and mix well. Pour over the chicken. Cook on Low for 7 to 9 hours or on High for 3 to 4 hours. Remove the chicken. Stir the sour cream and flour together in a small bowl. Stir into the sauce in the slow cooker. Cook until heated through. Serve the chicken and sauce over rice or noodles. Yield: 6 to 8 servings.

Sandy Thompson, Laureate Delta Psi
Blue Springs, Missouri

BARBECUED WILD DUCK

1/2 cup ketchup
1/2 cup chopped onion
1/4 cup (1/2 stick) butter
  or margarine
5 teaspoons lemon juice
1 tablespoon brown
  sugar

1 tablespoon
  Worcestershire sauce
1 teaspoon salt
2 (1-pound) wild ducks,
  cut into halves

Combine the first 7 ingredients in a saucepan. Bring to a boil. Reduce the heat and simmer, covered, for 5 minutes. Rinse the ducks and pat dry. Place in a 9×13-inch baking dish. Bake, covered, at 350 degrees for 2 hours or until tender, basting with the sauce during the last 30 minutes of baking time. Yield: 4 servings.

Faye A. Magers, Alpha Upsilon Master
Chester, Illinois

HEAVENLY HENS

6 Cornish game hens
Salt and pepper to taste
1 tablespoon minced
  shallots
1 tablespoon minced
  canned mushrooms

2 tablespoons olive oil
1 tablespoon Catawba
  wine (optional)
3 cups cooked wild rice
Melted butter or
  olive oil

Rinse the hens and pat dry. Season them inside and out with salt and pepper. Sauté the shallots and mushrooms in the olive oil in a large skillet until tender. Stir in the wine and rice. Spoon the rice mixture into the hen cavities. Place in a shallow roasting pan. Drizzle with a little butter or olive oil. Bake at 400 degrees for 1 hour or until browned and cooked through, basting often with the pan drippings.
Yield: 6 servings.

Louise F. Borchelt, Preceptor Gamma Omicron
Cape Girardeau, Missouri

DEEP-FRIED TURKEY

To determine the exact amount of oil to heat in your turkey fryer, place the turkey in the empty fryer and fill it with water to cover the bird. Remove the turkey and mark the water line. Empty the water and refill to the mark with oil.

1 (10-pound) turkey
2 tablespoons House
  Seasoning

2 tablespoons dry rub
3 to 5 gallons peanut oil

Rinse the turkey and pat dry. Coat all sides with the House Seasoning and dry rub. Let stand until the turkey reaches room temperature. Heat the peanut oil to 350 degrees in a turkey fryer. Submerge the turkey completely in the hot oil. Fry for 3 minutes per pound plus 5 minutes. Remove the turkey; drain on paper towels. Yield: 6 to 8 servings.

HOUSE SEASONING

1 cup salt
1/4 cup pepper

1/4 cup garlic powder

Combine the salt, pepper and garlic powder in an airtight container. Store for up to 6 months.

Rhonda Biggs, Xi Lambda Theta
Dallas, Texas

❖ GRILLED CHILES RELLENOS

6 large poblano chiles
1 pound ground turkey
2 teaspoons olive oil
1/2 onion, chopped
1/2 red bell pepper, finely
 chopped
2 garlic cloves, crushed
2 jalapeño chiles, finely
 chopped
1/2 cup chopped cilantro
1 teaspoon ground
 cumin
1/2 cup salsa
3 cups (12 ounces)
 shredded Monterey
 Jack cheese
Salt and pepper to taste

Cut the poblano chiles lengthwise to form a boat shape; discard the seeds. Brown the turkey in the olive oil in a skillet, stirring until crumbly. Add the onion, bell pepper, garlic, jalapeño chiles, cilantro and cumin. Cook until the vegetables are tender. Stir in the salsa. Cook until heated through. Stir in 2 cups of the cheese, salt and pepper. Spoon the turkey mixture into the chiles and top with the remaining cheese. Place on the least hot part of a grill heated to medium-high. Grill until the chiles are tender and the cheese is browned and bubbly. Serve immediately. Yield: 6 servings.

Mickey Roberts, Xi Gamma Kappa
Shirley, Arkansas

TURKEY LOAF WITH MUSHROOM GRAVY

1/2 cup fat-free sour
 cream
3 egg whites
1/4 cup low-fat milk
1/2 cups fine dry bread
 crumbs
1/4 cup finely chopped
 onion
2 tablespoons snipped
 fresh parsley
1 tablespoon
 Worcestershire sauce
1 tablespoon Dijon
 mustard
1/4 teaspoon salt
1/4 teaspoon pepper
11/2 pounds ground
 turkey
1 (10-ounce) can
 reduced-fat cream of
 mushroom soup
1/2 cup fat-free sour
 cream

Combine 1/2 cup sour cream, egg whites, milk, bread crumbs, onion, parsley, Worcestershire sauce, Dijon mustard, salt and pepper in a large bowl and mix well. Add the turkey and mix thoroughly. Press into a 5×9-inch loaf pan. Bake at 350 degrees for 11/4 hours or to 170 degrees on a meat thermometer. Cool for 10 minutes before removing from the pan. Combine the soup and 1/2 cup sour cream in a small saucepan. Cook just until heated through, stirring constantly. Serve with the turkey loaf along with mashed potatoes and green beans. Yield: 6 servings.

Debbie Dirkes, Xi Epsilon Gamma
Kirkland, Washington

TURKEY LOAF

This recipe is a favorite of my son who has type 2 diabetes. I try to make meals that will keep his weight up and his insulin level low and this healthy dish works well. Vary it by adding Italian or Mexican seasonings, chopped mushrooms, olives, or japapeño chiles.

1 pound ground turkey
2 eggs, beaten
1/2 cup quick-cooking
 oats
1/2 cup ketchup
1/4 cup chopped onion
1/4 cup chopped green
 bell pepper
1/4 teaspoon sage
1 teaspoon
 Worcestershire sauce
1/4 teaspoon garlic
 powder
1/4 teaspoon dried
 parsley
1/4 teaspoon salt
1/4 teaspoon pepper

Combine the turkey, eggs, oats, ketchup, onion, bell pepper, sage, Worcestershire sauce, garlic powder, parsley, salt and pepper in a large bowl and mix well. Press into a 5×9-inch baking pan coated with nonstick cooking spray. Bake at 350 degrees for 30 to 40 minutes or until a wooden pick inserted in the center comes out clean. Cool slightly before removing from the pan. Freeze and reheat in the microwave if desired. Yield: 4 to 6 servings.

Sandra Cox, Xi Alpha Mu
Reno, Nevada

HOT TURKEY SALAD

3 to 4 cups chopped
 cooked turkey
2 cups diced celery
1 small onion,
 diced
1 (8-ounce) can sliced
 water chestnuts
1 (15-ounce) can cream
 of chicken soup
3/4 cup mayonnaise
3 hard-cooked eggs,
 chopped
1 teaspoon minced garlic
1/2 cup (1 stick) butter or
 margarine
1 package plain or
 flavored croutons
11/2 cups (6 ounces)
 shredded Cheddar
 cheese

Combine the turkey, celery, onion, water chestnuts, soup, mayonnaise and eggs in a large bowl and mix well. Spoon into a 9×13-inch baking dish coated with nonstick cooking spray. Sauté the garlic in the butter in a large skillet. Add the croutons and stir until the butter is absorbed. Spread over the turkey mixture. Bake at 350 degrees for 45 to 50 minutes. Remove from the oven. Top with the cheese and let stand until the cheese is melted. Yield: 12 to 16 servings.

Becky Abbott, Laureate Beta Upsilon
Hartford City, Indiana

Seafood

DELICIOUS LINGUINI WITH RED CLAM SAUCE

I created this recipe for a great Lenten meal. Serve this with a small salad and garlic toast. It's delicious!

1/4 cup (1/2 stick) butter	1 (31-ounce) jar garden-
1 garlic clove, minced	style pasta sauce
2 (6-ounce) cans	Salt and pepper to taste
chopped clams	16 ounces linguini
1/2 cup chopped parsley	Grated Romano cheese
3 tablespoons olive oil	

Melt the butter in a large heavy-bottomed skillet over medium heat. Sauté the garlic in the butter for 1 to 2 minutes or until soft but not brown. Add the clams, parsley and olive oil to the skillet, stirring to combine. Add the pasta sauce and simmer for 10 minutes; season with salt and pepper. Cook the linguini in a large stockpot of boiling water using the package directions; drain. Place the linguini in a large serving bowl and pour the clam sauce on top. Serve with grated Romano cheese. Yield: 6 to 8 servings.

Debbie Meegan, Preceptor Beta Phi
Lemon Furnace, Pennsylvania

ASPARAGUS CRAB AU GRATIN

1 (10-ounce) package	2 tablespoons
frozen asparagus	all-purpose flour
1 (6-ounce) can crab	1 cup milk
meat, drained and	1/2 teaspoon dry mustard
shells removed	1/2 teaspoon salt
1/2 cup (2 ounces)	1/8 teaspoon pepper
shredded Cheddar	2 teaspoons lemon juice
cheese	1 cup soft bread crumbs
2 tablespoons butter	2 tablespoons butter

Thaw the asparagus using the package directions and drain. Layer the asparagus, crab meat and cheese in a greased 1-quart baking dish. Melt 2 tablespoons butter in a small saucepan. Add the flour and stir until smooth. Add the milk, dry mustard, salt and pepper and bring to a boil. Boil for 2 minutes or until thickened, stirring constantly. Remove the pan from the heat and stir in the lemon juice. Pour the sauce over the asparagus and crab meat. Toss the bread crumbs with 2 tablespoons melted butter in a medium bowl. Sprinkle the buttered bread crumbs on top of the sauce. Bake at 350 degrees for 30 minutes. Yield: 4 to 6 servings.

Iris Hendershot, Iota Lambda
Warfordsberg, Pennsylvania

BAKED CRAB SALAD

1 cup flaked crab meat	1 teaspoon minced
1 cup soft bread crumbs	onion
1 cup heavy cream	1 cup chopped celery
1 1/2 cups mayonnaise	1/2 teaspoon salt
6 hard-cooked eggs,	1/2 cup quartered
chopped	blanched almonds
1 tablespoon minced	1/2 cup buttered bread
parsley	crumbs

Stir the crab meat, bread crumbs and heavy cream together in a large bowl and mix well. Add the mayonnaise, eggs, parsley, onion, celery and salt, stirring to combine. Spoon the mixture into a greased casserole and top with the almonds and buttered bread crumbs. Bake at 350 degrees for 30 minutes. Yield: 8 to 10 servings.

June M. Kelly, Beta Master
Mill Creek, Washington

CRAB MEAT CASSEROLE

1 pound lump crab meat, drained and shells removed	1 tablespoon minced onion
1 cup white bread cubes	1 teaspoon chopped parsley
1 cup half-and-half	1/2 teaspoon salt
1 1/2 cups mayonnaise	1/2 teaspoon pepper
4 hard-cooked eggs, chopped	3/4 cup buttered cracker crumbs

Combine the crab meat, bread cubes, half-and-half and mayonnaise in a large bowl and mix well. Add the eggs, onion, parsley, salt and pepper, stirring to combine. Spoon the mixture into a greased 9x9-inch baking dish and sprinkle with the cracker crumbs. Bake at 350 degrees for 40 minutes. Yield: 9 servings.

Linda Faye Lemon, Delta Master
Salem, Virginia

CRAB CAKES

1 egg, lightly beaten	1 or 2 drops of Worcestershire sauce
1 teaspoon dry mustard	
1 teaspoon chopped parsley	1 (16-ounce) can lump crab meat, drained and shells removed
3 tablespoons melted butter	
1 tablespoon mayonnaise	1 1/2 cups bread crumbs

Combine the egg, dry mustard, parsley, butter, mayonnaise and Worcestershire sauce in a large bowl and mix well. Stir in the crab meat gently. Add 1/2 cup bread crumbs and mix just until combined. Shape the mixture into 6 crab cakes and place on a baking sheet. Dip the crab cakes into the remaining 1 cup of bread crumbs, turning to coat on all sides. Broil 6 inches from the heat source, or pan-fry in 2 to 4 tablespoons vegetable oil for 4 minutes per side or until golden brown. Yield: 6 servings.

Jane Neville
Ellicott City, Maryland

CRAB FETTUCCINI

6 ounces fettuccini	1 cup half-and-half
3 tablespoons olive oil	Pepper to taste
1/2 cup (1 stick) butter	1/2 cup (2 ounces) grated Parmesan cheese, or to taste
2 garlic cloves, minced	
1 pound fresh lump crab meat, drained and shells removed	
	Sprig of parsley, for garnish

Cook the fettuccini al dente in boiling water using the package directions; drain. Toss the pasta in the olive oil in a large bowl and set aside. Heat the butter in a large saucepan. Add the garlic and sauté for 1 minute. Stir in the crab meat, half-and-half and pepper and let simmer for 3 minutes or until slightly thickened. Add the cheese and cook until heated through, stirring constantly. Pour the sauce over the pasta in a large bowl, tossing to combine. Add more cheese, if desired. Garnish with a sprig of parsley. Yield: 2 servings.

Jean McDonough, Kappa Chi
Woodstock, Georgia

CRAB PIE

1/2 cup mayonnaise	7 ounces fresh lump crab meat, drained and shells removed
2 tablespoons all-purpose flour	
2 eggs, beaten	1/4 cup chopped green onions
1/2 cup milk	
2 tablespoons vermouth	1 (10-inch) unbaked pie shell
2 cups (8 ounces) Swiss cheese, shredded	

Combine the mayonnaise, flour, eggs, milk and vermouth in a medium-sized bowl and mix well. Add the cheese, crab meat and green onions and stir to combine. Pour the mixture into the pie shell. Bake at 350 degrees for 30 to 40 minutes.
Yield: 6 to 8 servings.

Ometta Murray, Xi Omicron Iota
Sachse, Texas

TWICE-BAKED CRAB MEAT POTATOES

6 baking potatoes, washed and oiled	1 (6-ounce) can crab meat, drained and shells removed
1/2 cup (1 stick) butter	
1/4 cup milk	Salt and pepper to taste
1/2 cup sour cream	1 cup (4 ounces) shredded sharp Cheddar cheese
1 green bell pepper, diced	
6 green onions, diced	

Place the potatoes on an oven rack and bake at 400 degrees for 1 hour or until done. Set the potatoes on a cooling rack to cool slightly. Cut the tops off the potatoes and scoop the centers into a bowl; place the potato shells on a baking sheet. Combine the potatoes, butter, milk, and sour cream in a medium bowl and beat with an electric mixer until light and fluffy. Add the bell pepper, green onions, crab meat, salt and pepper, stirring to combine. Spoon the potato mixture into the potato shells and sprinkle with the cheese. Bake at 350 degrees for 15 minutes.
Yield: 6 servings.

Carole Nichols, Beta Master
Wilmington, Ohio

CRAWFISH CASSEROLE

2 (6-ounce) packages
saffron rice mix
1 onion, finely chopped
1 bell pepper, finely
chopped
1/2 cup (1 stick) butter
1 (12-ounce) package
frozen crawfish

1 (10-ounce) can
Mexican-style
tomatoes
1 (10-ounce) can cream
of mushroom soup
4 cups (16 ounces)
shredded Cheddar
cheese

Prepare the rice using the package directions. Sauté the onion and bell pepper in the butter in a large skillet over medium heat for 4 to 5 minutes or until softened. Add the crawfish and tomatoes and simmer for 10 minutes. Stir in the soup and the rice. Pour the mixture into a 9×13-inch baking dish and sprinkle with the cheese. Bake at 350 degrees for 20 to 25 minutes or until the cheese melts. Yield: 6 servings.

Regina Keyser, Alpha Phi
Natchitoches, Louisiana

CRAYFISH PIE

When my grandchildren visit me in New Orleans, this is a must-have. It is a very easy recipe to change and add to. For example, I usually add a little more pepper and Tabasco sauce. Sometimes, I add salsa instead of the tomato sauce to give it extra "kick." I also add two tablespoons of sherry or brandy when adding the cream. To make this less fattening, use margarine in place of butter and milk in place of the cream.

1/2 cup (1 stick) butter
1 large onion, chopped
2 garlic cloves, minced
1/2 green bell pepper,
chopped
1/2 cup chopped celery
1 (10-ounce) can cream
of celery soup
1 pound crayfish tails
1/4 cup minced fresh
parsley

4 teaspoons tomato
sauce
1/2 cup seasoned bread
crumbs
1 teaspoon salt
1/2 teaspoon black pepper
1 egg, beaten
1 cup heavy cream
2 frozen (10-inch)
deep-dish pie shells,
thawed

Melt the butter in a large skillet over medium heat. Sauté the onion, garlic, bell pepper and celery in the butter until soft. Add the soup, crayfish tails, parsley and tomato sauce, stirring to combine. Simmer over low heat for 10 minutes. Turn off the heat and add the next 4 ingredients, stirring constantly. Stir in the cream. Spoon the mixture into 1 pie shell and cover with the other pie shell. Crimp the edges of the pie shells together and cut 3 slits in the top shell. Bake at 350 degrees for 40 to 50 minutes. Yield: 8 servings.

Barbara Toups, Laureate Alpha
New Orleans, Louisiana

BAKED FISH AND ANGEL HAIR PASTA

2 tablespoons olive oil
1 onion, finely chopped
2 garlic cloves, finely
chopped
1/2 cup dry white wine
1 (15-ounce) can diced
tomatoes
3 tablespoons chopped
fresh parsley

2 pounds cod or
haddock, rinsed and
patted dry
Salt and pepper to taste
2 tablespoons butter
8 ounces angel hair
pasta, cooked and
drained

Heat the olive oil in a large skillet over medium heat. Add the onion and garlic and sauté for 5 minutes or until soft but not brown. Add the wine and let simmer for 1 minute; add the tomatoes and bring to a boil. Remove from the heat and stir in the parsley. Season the fish on both sides with salt and pepper. Spread a small amount of the sauce in a shallow 9×13-inch baking dish and arrange the fish in a single layer on top. Pour the remaining sauce over the fish. Bake at 350 degrees for 15 to 18 minutes or until the fish is firm and opaque. Cut the fish into 4 pieces and place on individual serving plates. Top each with a few spoonfuls of sauce. Stir the butter into the remaining sauce and toss with the pasta in a large serving bowl. Mound the pasta beside the fish and serve. Yield: 4 servings.

Jean Poynor, Xi Alpha Nu
Eureka Springs, Arizona

FISH ROLL-UPS

1/3 cup butter or
margarine
1/3 cup lemon juice
2 teaspoons chicken
bouillon
1 teaspoon Tabasco
sauce
1 cup cooked rice

1 (10-ounce) package
frozen chopped
broccoli, thawed
1 cup (4 ounces) shredded
Cheddar cheese
8 (6-ounce) firm fish
fillets
Paprika for garnish

Melt the butter in a small saucepan over medium heat. Add the lemon juice, bouillon and Tabasco sauce and mix well. Cook over low heat until the bouillon dissolves, stirring constantly; set aside. Combine the rice, broccoli, cheese and 1/4 cup of the lemon butter sauce in a medium bowl and mix well. Divide the broccoli mixture equally among the fillets on a clean work surface. Roll up the fish fillets to enclose the filling and place seam side down in a shallow 9×13-inch baking dish. Pour the remaining sauce over the roll-ups. Bake at 375 degrees for 25 minutes. Spoon some sauce over each individual serving; garnish with paprika. Yield: 4 to 6 servings.

Darlene Schelke, Preceptor Alpha Gamma
Las Vegas, Nevada

ISLAND-STYLE POACHED FISH

1 pound mullet or other firm white fish	1 (1-inch) piece fresh gingerroot, grated
1/4 cup minced onion	1/4 cup vegetable oil, heated
1/4 cup minced green onions	2 tablespoons soy sauce

Submerge the fish in a large saucepan of boiling water. Cover the saucepan immediately and turn off the heat. Poach for 15 minutes or until the fish flakes easily with a fork. Using a spatula, carefully remove the fish to a warm platter. Sprinkle the fish with onion, green onions and ginger and drizzle with the warm oil and soy sauce. Yield: 2 to 3 servings.

Juliette Chock, Preceptor Delta
Honolulu, Hawaii

FLOUNDER IN ORANGE SAUCE

1/3 cup sugar-free orange marmalade	1/3 cup sliced onion
2 tablespoons orange juice	4 (4-ounce) flounder fillets
1/4 teaspoon ground ginger	Vegetable cooking spray

Combine the orange marmalade, orange juice and ginger in a small saucepan and mix well. Cook over medium heat until the mixture is heated through and combined, stirring constantly. Remove from the heat and stir in the onion. Place the flounder in a 13x9-inch baking pan sprayed with cooking spray. Spoon the orange mixture over the fish. Bake at 400 degrees for 10 minutes. Yield: 4 servings.

Florence Santarsieri, Xi Mu Eta
Jacksonville, Florida

GRILLED HALIBUT STEAKS

4 (6-ounce) halibut steaks	1/2 cup lime juice
Paprika	1 tablespoon lemon pepper
Extra-virgin olive oil	1 tablespoon garlic powder
1/2 cup (1 stick) melted butter	

Sprinkle the halibut steaks with paprika and drizzle with olive oil; rub the mixture into the steaks. Place the steaks on a baking sheet and set aside. Combine the remaining ingredients in a small bowl. Brush the halibut with some of the butter-lime sauce and place on a grill over hot coals. Grill for 5 to 10 minutes per side, basting frequently with the sauce.
Yield: 2 to 4 servings.

Cindy Johns, Laureate Iota
Raleigh, North Carolina

HALIBUT IN CREAMY WHITE SAUCE

For a lighter sauce, you can use milk instead of half-and-half. This is an easy dish to fix during Lent.

2 (12-ounce) packages frozen halibut steaks, thawed	1/4 teaspoon salt
2 tablespoons all-purpose flour	1/4 cup (1/2 stick) butter
1 tablespoon sugar	1/3 cup dry white wine
	2/3 cup half-and-half
	Lemon wedges

Pat the halibut steaks dry and place in a slow cooker. Combine the flour, sugar and salt in a small bowl and mix well. Melt the butter in a saucepan over medium heat and stir in the flour mixture. Add the wine and half-and-half and cook until thickened, stirring constantly. Increase the heat and boil for 1 minute, stirring constantly. Pour the hot sauce over the fish. Cover and cook on a high setting for 2 1/2 to 3 hours. Serve with lemon wedges. Yield: 4 servings.

Anita Karl, Laureate Zeta
Cheyenne, Wyoming

GRILLED OYSTERS STUFFED WITH SNOW CRAB AND BACON IN A MANGO BARBECUE SAUCE

1/2 pound frozen snow crab meat, thawed and drained	1 tablespoon lemon pepper seasoning
6 slices bacon, crisp-cooked, crumbled	1 tablespoon lemon juice
2 garlic cloves, minced	Dash of hot red pepper sauce
1 small onion, finely chopped	Salt and pepper
1 tablespoon chopped fresh dill weed	16 fresh oysters
	1 mango, peeled, pitted
	1/2 cup barbecue sauce

Combine the crab meat, bacon, garlic, onion, dill weed, lemon pepper seasoning and lemon juice in a large bowl and mix well. Season to taste with hot sauce, salt and pepper. Shuck the oysters over a bowl, using an oyster knife. Strain the oyster liquid into the crab mixture. Remove the oysters from their shells and set aside. Place 1 heaping tablespoon of the crab mixture into each of the 16 half shells. Top each stuffed shell with an oyster. Purée the mango in a food processor until smooth. Add the barbecue sauce and blend well. Top each oyster with 1 tablespoon mango sauce. Arrange the stuffed oysters on a grill screen; place on a grill over hot coals. Close the lid and grill for 10 to 12 minutes or until the mango sauce and stuffing are hot. Remove carefully and serve. Yield: 4 main dish servings or 16 appetizers.

Cecilia Welsh, Xi Xi Eta
Blue Springs, Missouri

CORN AND OYSTER CASSEROLE

2 (10-ounce) cans corn,
  drained
2 (8-ounce) cans whole
  oysters
1 tablespoon sugar
1/2 cup (1 stick)
  margarine, cut
  into pats

8 ounces crackers,
  crumbled
1 (8-ounce) container
  half-and-half
Pepper, to taste
2 teaspoons salt

Spread 1 can of corn in a greased casserole. Layer with 1 can of oysters, 1/2 tablespoon sugar, 1/2 stick of margarine and 4 ounces of the cracker crumbs. Repeat the layering with the remaining corn, oysters, sugar, margarine and cracker crumbs. Pour in the half-and-half carefully, making sure it does not cover the top layer of crumbs. Bake the casserole, covered, at 350 degrees for 1 hour. Uncover and bake for 10 more minutes or until brown. Yield: 8 servings.

Janey Eaton, Preceptor Epsilon Gamma
Topeka, Kansas

HERBED BAKED SALMON

3/4 cup mayonnaise
3/4 cup (3 ounces) grated
  Parmesan cheese
3 tablespoons chopped
  fresh herbs such as
  dill, basil, thyme,
  parsley

6 tablespoons chopped
  green onions
Juice of 1/2 lemon
Salt and pepper to taste
1 (1 1/2 pound) salmon
  fillet

Combine the mayonnaise, cheese, herbs, green onions, lemon juice, salt and pepper in a small bowl and mix well. Place the salmon in a shallow 9×13-inch baking dish. Spread the mayonnaise mixture over the salmon. Bake at 350 degrees for 20 minutes or until the fish flakes easily with a fork. Do not overcook. Yield: 4 servings.

Ellen Jones, Gamma Delta
Middleton, Wisconsin

SALMON IN SCALLION AND GINGER SAUCE

1/3 cup white cooking
  wine
3 tablespoons soy
  sauce
2 teaspoons olive oil
1/4 cup chopped green
  onions

1 teaspoon grated fresh
  gingerroot
1 teaspoon finely
  chopped garlic
2 (6-ounce) salmon
  fillets

Whisk the wine, soy sauce, olive oil, green onions, ginger and garlic in a small bowl. Place the salmon in a 9×13-inch baking dish. Drizzle sauce over the salmon and bake at 375 degrees for 12 to 15 minutes or until the fish flakes easily with a fork. Yield: 2 servings.

Emily Engelbrecht, Delta Iota
Lexington, Missouri

BAKED HONEY-DIJON SALMON

1/2 cup lemon juice
1/2 cup Chablis
2 pounds salmon fillets,
  cut into 8 pieces
1/4 cup (1/2 stick) butter,
  melted
3 tablespoons Dijon
  mustard

1 1/2 tablespoons honey
Salt and pepper to taste
1/4 cup dry bread crumbs
1/4 cup finely chopped
  walnuts or almonds
4 teaspoons chopped
  fresh parsley

Whisk the lemon juice and wine in a small bowl. Place the salmon fillets in a 9×13-inch glass baking dish. Pour the lemon-wine marinade over the salmon. Chill, covered with plastic wrap, for 3 to 4 hours. Whisk the butter, mustard, honey, salt and pepper in a small bowl. Combine the bread crumbs, walnuts and parsley in another bowl and mix well. Brush each fillet with the honey-mustard mixture. Sprinkle the tops of the fillets with the bread crumb mixture. Bake at 375 degrees for 12 to 15 minutes or until the salmon flakes easily with a fork. Yield: 8 servings.

Donna Bagnall, Preceptor Alpha
Sarasota, Florida

BARBECUED SALMON FILLETS

4 (6-ounce) salmon
  fillets
2 tablespoons butter,
  melted
2 tablespoons lemon
  juice
2 tablespoons ketchup
1 tablespoon
  Worcestershire sauce

2 tablespoons minced
  onion
1 tablespoon brown
  sugar
1/2 teaspoon dry mustard
1 teaspoon salt

Place the salmon fillets on a greased, foil-lined baking sheet. Combine the butter, lemon juice, ketchup, Worcestershire sauce, onion, brown sugar, dry mustard and salt in a small saucepan. Warm over low heat, stirring constantly until blended. Remove from the heat and pour the sauce over the salmon fillets. Place the salmon 2 inches from the heat source or on a well-oiled grill rack over hot coals. Cook for 10 to 15 minutes or until the salmon flakes easily with a fork; do not turn. Yield: 4 servings.

Frances Davie, Laureate Alpha
Winnipeg, Manitoba, Canada

❖ SIZZLE SALMON STEAKS

*This is not just an outdoor summer grilling recipe –
I like it even better on my indoor 'health' grill.*

1/4 cup balsamic vinegar	1/2 teaspoon cayenne
1/4 cup chili sauce	pepper
1/4 cup packed light	1/2 teaspoon crushed red
brown sugar	pepper flakes
1 garlic clove, minced	2 (6-ounce) salmon
1 tablespoon chopped	steaks or fillets
fresh parsley	
1 teaspoon grated fresh	
ginger	

Combine the balsamic vinegar, chili sauce, brown
sugar, garlic, parsley, ginger, cayenne pepper and red
pepper flakes in a medium bowl and mix well. Place
the salmon steaks in the marinade and marinate, covered, in the refrigerator for 1 hour. Remove the
salmon steaks from the marinade. Grill over hot coals
on an oiled grill rack for 4 to 5 minutes per side, basting occasionally with the marinade. Yield: 2 servings.

Pamela Thomas, Preceptor Pi
Sturgis, South Dakota

SALMON BURGERS

3 (6-ounce) cans	1 teaspoon salt
boneless pink salmon	1 teaspoon paprika
1 cup Italian seasoned	2 tablespoons vegetable
bread crumbs	oil
1 cup egg substitute	6 English muffins, split
1/3 cup lemon juice	and toasted

Combine the salmon, bread crumbs, egg substitute,
lemon juice, salt and paprika in a medium bowl and
mix well. Shape into 6 patties and place on an
ungreased baking sheet. Heat the vegetable oil in a
large nonstick skillet over medium-high heat. Cook
the salmon patties in batches for 5 minutes per side
or until golden brown. Drain on paper towels. Serve
on toasted English muffin halves with alfalfa sprouts.
Yield: 6 servings.

Barbara Todd
Dearborn, Missouri

SALMON CAKES

2 (15-ounce) cans pink	1 teaspoon black pepper
salmon, drained	2 tablespoons dill weed
20 unsalted saltine	2 cups Italian bread
crackers, crushed	crumbs
1 egg, lightly beaten	1/4 cup vegetable oil

Remove the bones and the skin from the salmon;
place the meat in a medium bowl. Add the crushed
crackers, egg, pepper and dill weed and mix well.

Shape into 8 patties and coat with the bread crumbs.
Heat the oil in a large skillet over medium-high heat.
Fry the patties in batches for 3 to 5 minutes per side
or until golden brown. Drain on paper towels and
serve immediately. Leftovers can be reheated in the
microwave. Yield: 8 servings.

Elaine Penner, Laureate Epsilon Theta
St. Petersburg, Florida

SALMON ALFREDO

2 cups chicken broth	16 ounces angel hair
1 cup white wine	pasta
1 tablespoon	1 (26-ounce) jar Alfredo
peppercorns	sauce
4 (6-ounce) boneless	1 bunch fresh dill weed,
salmon fillets	finely chopped

Combine the chicken broth, wine and peppercorns in
a large skillet and mix well. Bring to a boil over high
heat. Reduce the heat and add the salmon fillets.
Cover and poach for 10 minutes over low heat.
Prepare the pasta in a large stockpot of boiling water
using the package directions; drain. Heat the Alfredo
sauce in a medium saucepan, stirring occasionally.
Mound the pasta onto 4 serving plates. Top with a
salmon fillet, Alfredo sauce and chopped dill weed.
Serve with steamed asparagus. Yield: 4 servings.

Terri Steffes, Preceptor Lambda Epsilon
Jefferson City, Missouri

SALMON PUFF LITE

1 1/2 tablespoons	3 tablespoons lemon
margarine	juice
1/2 cup skim milk	2 teaspoons finely
4 slices low-calorie	chopped onion
bread, torn into	1 teaspoon salt
pieces	1/2 teaspoon pepper
1 (15-ounce) can salmon,	2 egg whites
drained and flaked	Paprika
2 egg yolks	

Combine the margarine, milk and bread in a large
bowl and mix well. Add the salmon, egg yolks,
lemon juice, onion, salt and pepper, stirring to
combine. Beat the egg whites until stiff in a large
clean bowl. Fold the egg whites gently into the
salmon mixture with a spatula. Pour the mixture into
a greased 1 1/2-quart casserole and sprinkle with
paprika. Bake, uncovered, at 350 degrees for 1 hour.
Yield: 6 servings.

Jayne Hornsby, Xi Alpha Xi
Hueytown, Alabama

SEAFOOD AND ARTICHOKE AU GRATIN

1/4 cup (1/2 stick) butter
1/2 pound fresh
   mushrooms, sliced
3 garlic cloves, minced
6 tablespoons minced
   green onions
1/4 cup all-purpose flour
3/4 cup milk
1/2 teaspoon pepper
3 cups (12 ounces)
   grated Romano
   cheese

2/3 cup dry white wine
1 pound shrimp, peeled
   and deveined
2 (8-ounce) cans crab
   meat, drained and
   flaked
1 (14-ounce) can
   artichoke hearts
   packed in water

Melt the butter over medium heat in a large saucepan. Sauté the mushrooms, garlic and green onions in the butter until soft. Remove the pan from the heat and stir in the flour, milk and pepper. Return to the heat and bring to a boil. Add 2 cups of the cheese, stirring to combine. Stir in the wine. Add the shrimp, crab meat and artichoke hearts and mix well. Spoon the mixture into a greased 9×13-inch casserole. Sprinkle the remaining 1 cup of cheese on top. Bake at 350 degrees for 30 minutes. Serve over rice. Yield: 8 servings.

Monica Samson, Chi Omicron
Naperville, Illinois

SEAFOOD CASSEROLE

1 (12-ounce) package
   crab meat, flaked
1 (4-ounce) can shrimp,
   drained
1 1/2 cups chopped celery
1/4 cup chopped green
   bell pepper
1/4 cup chopped green
   onions
1 (4-ounce) jar pimentos

3/4 cup sour cream
1/4 cup mayonnaise
1 tablespoon lemon juice
1/2 teaspoon
   Worcestershire sauce
1/2 teaspoon salt
Dash of pepper
1 cup soft bread crumbs
1 tablespoon butter,
   melted

Combine the crab meat, shrimp, celery, green pepper, green onions and pimentos in a large bowl and mix well. Whisk the sour cream, mayonnaise, lemon juice, Worcestershire sauce, salt and pepper in a small bowl. Add the sour cream mixture to the seafood and vegetables, stirring to combine. Spoon the mixture into a greased 1 1/2-quart baking dish. Toss the bread crumbs with the butter in a small bowl. Sprinkle over the casserole. Bake at 350 degrees for 30 minutes. Yield: 6 to 8 servings.

Audrey C. Nichols, Beta Beta
Bethany, Missouri

CHEESY BAKED PASTA WITH SHRIMP AND SCALLOPS

This is easy to prepare and can be made the night before. If reheating, add a little cream, as it dries out easily. It's a fabulous entertaining recipe.

16 ounces penne
1/4 cup (1/2 stick) butter
4 garlic cloves, crushed
1 (12-ounce) can diced
   tomatoes
1 pound medium shrimp,
   peeled and deveined
1 pound fresh scallops
2 fresh basil leaves,
   chopped
2 cups heavy cream
1/4 cup crumbled
   Gorgonzola cheese

1 cup (4 ounces) grated
   Romano cheese
1/2 cup (2 ounces)
   shredded Fontina
   cheese
2 tablespoons ricotta
   cheese
1 cup (4 ounces) shredded
   Parmesan cheese plus
   more for sprinkling
   on top

Cook the pasta al dente using the package directions; drain. Melt the butter in a large skillet over medium heat. Sauté the garlic, tomatoes, shrimp, scallops and basil in the butter for 5 to 7 minutes or until the shrimp are pink and the scallops are tender. Combine the pasta and the sautéed seafood mixture in a large bowl and mix well. Add the heavy cream, stirring to combine. Stir in the cheeses and mix well. Spoon the mixture into a greased 13×9-inch baking dish and sprinkle with additional Parmesan cheese. Bake at 350 degrees for 45 to 60 minutes or until warmed through. Yield: 8 servings.

Sandra K. Wieland, Tau Beta
Cape Coral, Florida

GRILLED SHRIMP WITH HOT LIME BUTTER

Bamboo skewers
2 pounds large fresh
   shrimp, peeled with
   tails intact and
   deveined

2 cups (4 sticks) butter,
   melted
Juice of 2 limes
1 1/2 teaspoons cayenne
   pepper

Soak the skewers in water for 30 minutes; drain. Thread the shrimp on the skewers. Combine the butter, lime juice and cayenne in a bowl and mix well. Reserve 1 1/2 cups of the lime butter for dipping. Grill the shrimp over medium-hot coals for 2 to 3 minutes per side or until the shrimp are pink, basting with the lime butter occasionally. Serve with the reserved lime butter for dipping. Yield: 4 to 6 servings.

Dolores Bronowski, Preceptor Omega
Lakewood, Colorado

CURRIED SHRIMP

1/4 cup (1/2 stick) butter, melted	3 tablespoons ketchup
1/4 cup all-purpose flour	1/4 cup cooking sherry (optional)
1/2 teaspoon salt	1 1/2 cups shrimp, peeled and deveined
Paprika	
1 teaspoon curry powder	2 cups cooked rice
1 1/2 cups milk	

Combine the butter, flour, salt, paprika and curry powder in a medium saucepan over medium heat, stirring until smooth. Add in the milk gradually and cook until thickened, stirring constantly. Add the ketchup, sherry and shrimp and mix well, cooking until heated through. Serve over the rice.
Yield: 6 servings.

Sarah M. Stephens, Tau Master
Austin, Texas

SHRIMP WITH SNOW PEAS

1/2 cup dry sherry	1 pound snow peas
1/4 teaspoon paprika	Salt to taste
1/4 teaspoon white pepper	1/2 pound mushrooms, sliced
1/2 teaspoon salt	2 tablespoons vegetable oil
1 1/2 pounds large fresh shrimp, peeled and deveined	6 green onions, chopped
1 tablespoon vegetable oil	2 tablespoons cornstarch

Whisk the sherry, paprika, pepper and salt in a large bowl. Add the shrimp and let sit, covered, for 30 minutes. Heat 1 tablespoon of oil in a wok over high heat. Add the snow peas and sprinkle with salt. Cook for 30 seconds, stirring constantly. Add the mushrooms and stir-fry for 30 seconds. Remove the vegetables to a bowl. Heat the additional 2 tablespoons of oil to the wok. Add the onions and the shrimp, reserving the marinade. Stir-fry until the shrimp are pink, about 3 minutes. Stir the cornstarch into the marinade to thicken. Add the vegetables and marinade to the shrimp in the wok, tossing to combine. Cook over low heat until heated through. Serve with steamed rice. Yield: 4 servings.

Jo Anne Rasmussen, Alpha Eta
Shoreacres, Texas

SHRIMP STROGANOFF

1/4 cup minced onion	1 teaspoon butter
1/4 cup (1/2 stick) butter	1 tablespoon all-purpose flour
1 1/2 pounds shrimp, peeled and deveined	1 1/2 cups sour cream
1/2 pound mushrooms, quartered	1 1/4 teaspoons salt
	Pepper to taste

Sauté the onion in the butter in a large skillet over medium heat. Add the shrimp and sauté for 3 to 5 minutes or until the shrimp are pink. Remove the shrimp and onions to a preheated dish and keep warm. Add the mushrooms to the same skillet and sauté in 1 teaspoon of butter over medium heat. Cook for 5 minutes or until the mushrooms are brown. Sprinkle the mushrooms with flour and cook for 2 more minutes. Reduce the heat and stir in the sour cream, salt and pepper. Cook for 2 to 3 minutes. Stir in the shrimp and simmer until the mixture is heated through; do not boil. Yield: 4 servings.

Dottie Viehweg, Laureate Beta Omicron
Prescott Valley, Arizona

SHRIMP ALFREDO

My sisters and I love both seafood and Italian food. This recipe combines both.

16 ounces fettuccine	1 cup milk
1 pound medium shrimp, peeled and deveined	1/2 cup (2 ounces) grated Parmesan cheese
3 garlic cloves, minced	1/2 teaspoon salt
1/2 cup (1 stick) margarine	Dash of pepper
8 ounces cream cheese, cubed	Chopped fresh parsley (optional)

Prepare the fettuccine using the package directions; drain. Sauté the shrimp and garlic in the margarine in a large skillet over medium heat for 3 to 5 minutes or until the shrimp turn pink. Remove to a bowl and keep warm. Combine the cream cheese, milk and Parmesan cheese in the same skillet over medium heat, stirring constantly. Cook until melted and smooth. Stir the shrimp mixture into the sauce. Season with salt and pepper. Pour the sauce over the pasta in a large bowl and toss to combine. Serve immediately, garnished with fresh parsley if desired. Yield: 4 servings.

Rose Throesch, Eta Omega
Pocahontas, Arizona

SHRIMP WITH ASPARAGUS AND MUSHROOMS

1 pound medium shrimp, peeled and deveined	1 (4-ounce) can sliced black olives
Seasoned salt	8 ounces angel hair pasta, cooked and drained
Red pepper flakes	
2 tablespoons extra-virgin olive oil	2 tablespoons extra-virgin olive oil
1 pound fresh asparagus, trimmed and chopped	
8 ounces mushrooms, chopped	

Season the shrimp with seasoned salt and red pepper flakes and let sit for 30 minutes. Heat 2 tablespoons of olive oil in a large skillet over medium heat. Add the shrimp and sauté for 3 minutes or until the shrimp turn pink. Add the asparagus and mushrooms and cook for 10 minutes, stirring occasionally. Add the black olives and simmer for 20 minutes. Serve over the angel hair pasta and drizzle with the additional 2 tablespoons of olive oil. Yield: 4 servings.

Brenda Boudreaux, Beta Omega
New Iberia, Louisiana

CHARDONNAY SHRIMP

1/2 cup (1 stick) margarine	2 1/2 pounds shrimp, peeled and deveined
2 tablespoons minced garlic	1 teaspoon cornstarch
2 (8-ounce) cans tomato sauce	1 tablespoon water
1 cup Chardonnay	3 tablespoons chopped fresh parsley
1 onion, thinly sliced	3 green onions, finely chopped
8 to 10 mushrooms, sliced	8 ounces angel hair pasta, cooked and drained
2 cups heavy cream	

Heat the margarine in a large skillet over medium-high heat. Sauté the garlic in the margarine until softened but not brown. Add the tomato sauce and the Chardonnay, stirring to combine. Add the onion, mushrooms and heavy cream, stirring constantly. Add the shrimp and cook for 15 minutes or until the sauce has thickened and the shrimp have turned pink. Mix the cornstarch with 1 tablespoon of water in a small bowl. Pour the cornstarch slurry into the sauce, stirring until thickened. Remove from the heat and stir in the parsley and green onions. Serve over angel hair pasta. Yield: 6 servings.

Mary Abshire, Beta Lambda
Kaplan, Louisiana

LINGUINE WITH SHRIMP AND BASIL SAUCE

12 ounces linguine	2 cups canned baby shrimp
1/3 cup olive oil	
2 tablespoons chopped fresh basil	1 1/2 cups chopped plum tomatoes
2 teaspoons minced garlic	Salt to taste
Pinch of cayenne pepper	1/4 cup grated Parmesan cheese

Prepare the linguine al dente using the package directions; drain. Heat the olive oil in a large skillet over medium heat. Sauté the basil, garlic and cayenne in the olive oil for 1 minute, stirring constantly. Stir in the shrimp and the tomatoes. Cook for 3 minutes or until the shrimp turn pink; season with salt to taste. Pour the sauce over the pasta in a large bowl and toss to combine. Serve immediately, sprinkled with Parmesan cheese. Yield: 4 servings.

Elisa Maria Wilson, Preceptor Epsilon Theta
Simcore, Ontario, Canada

SHRIMP AND PEPPER PASTA

8 ounces pasta (any kind)	1 cup sliced mushrooms
1/4 cup olive oil	3 garlic cloves, minced
1 pound medium shrimp, peeled and deveined	1 tablespoon dried basil, crumbled
1 green bell pepper, cut into strips	2 medium tomatoes, chopped
1 yellow bell pepper, cut into strips	1 cup picante sauce
	Grated Parmesan cheese

Prepare the pasta al dente using the package directions; drain. Heat the olive oil in a large skillet over medium-high heat. Add the shrimp, bell peppers, mushrooms, garlic and basil. Cook, stirring frequently, for 3 to 4 minutes or until the shrimp turn pink. Stir in the tomatoes and picante sauce; simmer for 2 to 3 minutes. Add the pasta and mix well. Garnish with Parmesan cheese. Yield: 4 to 6 servings.

Deanna Porter, Xi Alpha Beta Gamma
Canyon, Texas

SHRIMP WITH HERBED CHEESE

1 1/2 pounds medium shrimp, peeled and deveined	1 1/2 cups heavy cream
1/4 cup (1/2 stick) butter, melted	2 medium tomatoes, peeled, seeded and chopped
8 mushrooms, cut into quarters	16 ounces fettuccine, cooked and drained
3 green onions, sliced	Salt and pepper to taste
12 ounces herbed cream cheese, cubed	

Sauté the shrimp in the butter in a large skillet over medium-high heat for 3 to 5 minutes. Add the mushrooms and the green onions and sauté for 1 minute. Add the herbed cream cheese and the heavy cream and continue to cook for 2 minutes or until smooth, stirring constantly. Add the tomatoes and the pasta. Cook for an additional 2 minutes until the sauce reaches the desired consistency, stirring frequently. Serve with crusty bread and a salad for a complete meal. Yield: 4 to 6 servings.

Thelma Kenney, Preceptor Gamma Kappa
Virginia Beach, Virginia

GOURMET SHRIMP

My nineteen grandchildren love this dish. They call it "Shrimp Goo." Since my family is so large (40 people), I usually double the recipe twice. Even then, it is gone almost immediately!

2 cups half-and-half
2 cups mayonnaise
3 green onions, minced
1 cup minced fresh
  parsley, plus more
  for garnish
2 cups soft bread crumbs

12 hard-cooked eggs,
  quartered
1¹/2 to 2 pounds boiled
  shrimp, peeled and
  deveined
Paprika for garnish

Combine the half-and-half, mayonnaise, green onions, parsley and bread crumbs in a large bowl and mix well. Add the eggs and shrimp, stirring to combine. Spoon the mixture into a 4-quart casserole dish sprayed with nonstick baking spray. Bake at 300 degrees for 30 to 40 minutes or until heated through; do not overcook. Garnish with paprika and parsley. Serve with mashed potatoes. Yield: 12 servings.

Jeanette E. Felger, Iota Master
New Braunfels, Texas

LOUISIANA SHRIMP CASSEROLE

¹/4 cup (¹/2 stick) butter
1 onion, thinly sliced
³/4 cup thinly sliced
  celery
¹/2 cup chopped green
  bell pepper
¹/4 cup all-purpose
  flour
1¹/2 teaspoons sea salt
1 (15-ounce) can diced

tomatoes

Heat the butter in a large skillet over medium heat. Sauté the onion, celery and green bell pepper in the butter for 5 minutes. Sprinkle the flour and salt over the vegetables and cook until bubbly, stirring to blend. Stir in the tomatoes, shrimp and sherry and bring to a boil. Reduce the heat and simmer, covered, for 10 minutes. Add 1 cup of the cheese and 4 sliced eggs; stir gently to combine. Layer half of the rice, the tomato-shrimp mixture, the other half for the rice and one sliced egg in a 1³/4-quart casserole. Sprinkle with the remaining ³/4 cup of cheese. Bake at 350 degrees for 25 to 30 minutes. Yield: 4 to 6 servings.

I. Joyce Kilback, Laureate Alpha
Nanaimo, British Columbia, Canada

RED SNAPPER STUFFED WITH CRAB MEAT

1 whole red snapper
  (about 7 pounds),
  cleaned
Salt and pepper to taste
Garlic powder to taste
Onion salt to taste
2 pounds fresh crab
  meat, drained and
  shells removed
2 eggs, beaten

1 onion, chopped
20 saltine crackers,
  crushed
6 slices bacon
2 slices lemon
¹/4 teaspoon dried
  dill weed, or
  1 teaspoon chopped
  fresh dill weed

Rinse the snapper and pat dry. Lay the snapper in a large baking pan lined with oiled aluminum foil. Season the inside and outside of the snapper with salt, pepper, garlic powder and onion salt. Make 2 long slits in the side of the snapper facing up. Combine the crab meat, eggs, onion, cracker crumbs, salt and pepper in a large bowl and mix well. Stuff the crab mixture into the cavity of the snapper. If there is extra filling, spoon it onto the baking sheet around the fish. Lay the bacon and lemon slices on top of the fish and sprinkle with the dill weed. Bake, covered with aluminum foil, at 350 degrees for 55 minutes. Uncover and bake for an additional 5 minutes or until browned. Yield: 6 servings.

Robin Cannon, Kappa Upsilon
Bonaire, Georgia

GRILLED SWORDFISH WITH BACON

8 slices bacon
¹/2 cup soy sauce
¹/2 cup olive oil
2 tablespoons lemon
  juice
2 tablespoons minced
  garlic

1 tablespoon grated
  fresh gingerroot
4 (1 inch thick)
  swordfish steaks

Cook the bacon partially for 3 minutes in a skillet over medium-high heat. Drain on paper towels and set aside. Whisk the soy sauce, olive oil, lemon juice, garlic and gingerroot in a small bowl. Arrange the swordfish steaks in a shallow baking dish and pour the marinade on top. Cover with plastic wrap and marinate in the refrigerator for 2 hours. Remove the swordfish steaks from the marinade and wrap each with 2 slices of bacon. Place the steaks in a hinged wire grilling basket. Grill for 8 minutes per side, basting frequently with the marinade. Yield: 4 servings.

Brenda Shawgo, Epsilon Alpha
Canton, Illinois

Meatless Entrées

BEAN LOAF

3 cups cooked white
  beans
1 small onion, finely
  chopped
1 cup bread crumbs
1 cup evaporated milk
1 egg
3 tablespoons
  shortening
1½ teaspoons salt

Mash the beans in a bowl. Add the onion, bread crumbs, evaporated milk, egg, shortening and salt in a bowl. Stir to mix well. Pat into a well greased loaf pan. Bake at 375 degrees for 45 minutes. Serve with ketchup. Yield: 6 to 8 servings.

Dorothy Wilson, Preceptor Eta Omicron
West Sacramento, California

VEGETABLE CURRY

1 cup jasmine rice
1½ cups diced potatoes
2 carrots, sliced
2 cups water
1 (14-ounce) can
  chopped tomatoes
1½ teaspoons curry
  powder
½ teaspoon salt
1 teaspoon minced
  garlic
1 tablespoon grated
  fresh ginger
1 (15-ounce) can red
  beans
2 cups cauliflower
  florets
1 cup green peas
2 cups water
1 tablespoon mustard
  seeds
2 tablespoons lemon
  juice
Pepper to taste

Combine the rice, potatoes, carrots and 2 cups water in a large saucepan. Bring to a boil. Reduce the heat and cover. Simmer for 5 minutes. Stir in the tomatoes, curry powder, salt, garlic and ginger. Simmer for 5 minutes. Stir in the beans, cauliflower, peas and 2 cups water. Simmer for 5 to 10 minutes. Sauté the mustard seeds in a small skillet until they pop. Add to the vegetable mixture. Stir in the lemon juice and season with pepper. Yield: 8 servings.

Elizabeth Scott-Jones, Delta Mu Eta
Riverside, California

EGGPLANT LASAGNA

1 (16-ounce) package
  lasagna noodles
2½ pounds eggplant
Salt
Beaten eggs
All-purpose flour
½ cup olive oil
4 cups marinara sauce
2 cups (8 ounces)
  shredded mozzarella
  cheese
⅔ cup grated Parmesan
  cheese

Cook the noodles using the package directions. Thinly slice the eggplant and place in a colander. Sprinkle with salt and let stand for 20 minutes. Rinse and drain the eggplant. Pat dry with paper towels. Coat the eggplant slices in beaten eggs and dredge in flour. Heat the olive oil in a large skillet. Add the eggplant and fry until light brown on both sides. Remove to paper towels to drain. Arrange a layer of eggplant in a 9x13-inch baking dish. Top with a layer of noodles. Spread some of the marinara sauce over the noodles and sprinkle with some of the mozzarella cheese. Repeat the layers until all of the eggplant, noodles, marinara sauce and mozzarella cheese are used. Sprinkle with the Parmesan cheese. Bake at 350 degrees for 35 to 45 minutes or until bubbly. This can be made ahead and frozen.
Yield: 12 servings.

Mary Ann Pappani, Preceptor Alpha Phi
Jerome, Idaho

EGGPLANT PARMESAN

1 eggplant	1/4 cup grated Parmesan
2 (8-ounce) cans tomato	cheese
sauce	6 ounces sliced
1 teaspoon oregano	mozzarella cheese
1 teaspoon basil	

Peel the eggplant and cut into 1/2-inch slices. Alternate layers of the eggplant, tomato sauce, oregano, basil and Parmesan cheese in a 7×11-inch microwave-safe dish. Microwave, tightly covered, on High for 14 to 16 minutes or until the eggplant is tender. Arrange the slices of mozzarella cheese on top. Microwave on High for 1 to 1 1/2 minutes or until the cheese is beginning to melt. Yield: 4 to 6 servings.

Nancy Fairchild, Preceptor Omega
Las Cruces, New Mexico

ROLLED STUFFED EGGPLANT

1 large eggplant	2 cups (8 ounces)
4 eggs	shredded mozzarella
1/4 cup milk	cheese
4 cups bread crumbs	1/2 cup (2 ounces) grated
2 cups all-purpose flour	Romano cheese
1/2 teaspoon salt	1/2 cup chopped fresh
1/2 teaspoon pepper	parsley
Olive oil for frying	4 cups spaghetti sauce
2 (15-ounce) cartons	
ricotta cheese	

Peel the eggplant and cut into 1/8-inch slices. Beat the eggs and milk in a shallow dish. Mix the bread crumbs, flour, salt and pepper in a shallow dish. Dip the eggplant slices in the egg mixture and coat with the bread crumb mixture, shaking off any excess. Cover the bottom of a large skillet with olive oil and heat until hot but not smoking. Add the eggplant and fry until golden brown on both sides, adding more olive oil if needed. Remove to paper towels to drain. Combine the ricotta cheese, mozzarella cheese, Romano cheese and parsley in a bowl. Stir to mix well. Place 2 tablespoons of the cheese mixture on each eggplant slice and roll up. Spread 1/2 of the spaghetti sauce in a 9x13-inch baking pan. Arrange the eggplant rolls, seam side down, on the sauce. Cover with the remaining sauce. Bake at 350 degrees for 30 minutes or until bubbly.
Yield: 12 to 14 servings.

Beverly Inferrera, Preceptor Beta Upsilon
Wellsville, New York

CORN FRITTATA

2 tablespoons butter	1 1/4 cups (5 ounces)
3 green onions, sliced	finely shredded sharp
3/4 cup canned Mexicorn	Cheddar cheese
8 eggs	Salsa (optional)

Melt the butter in an ovenproof skillet over medium heat. Add the green onions and Mexicorn and sauté for 2 minutes. Beat the eggs in a bowl until foamy. Add to the skillet. Cook for 2 to 3 minutes or until the eggs are partially set, stirring constantly. Stir in the cheese. Place the skillet in a 375-degree oven. Bake for 20 minutes or until puffed and golden brown and the eggs are set. Cut into wedges and serve with salsa. Yield: 4 to 6 servings.

Jeaneen Ritzman, Alpha
Rocklin, California

SPAGHETTI SQUASH FRITTATA

2 pounds spaghetti	8 eggs
squash	1/2 cup cold milk
1 tablespoon vegetable	1/2 teaspoon salt
oil	1/2 teaspoon nutmeg
1/2 cup chopped green	1/2 cup (2 ounces)
onions	shredded Cheddar

Cook the squash in a saucepan of boiling water for 20 to 30 minutes or until tender. Cut the squash in half. Remove and discard the seeds. Scrape out the strands with a fork. Heat the oil in an ovenproof skillet over medium heat. Remove and reserve 1 tablespoon green onions. Add the remaining green onions and squash to the skillet. Cook for 4 to 5 minutes or until hot, stirring occasionally. Beat the eggs, milk, salt and nutmeg in a bowl. Pour over the squash mixture. Cook for 8 to 10 minutes or until the eggs are almost set. Sprinkle with the cheese. Broil 6 inches from the heat source until the cheese melts and the eggs are set. Sprinkle with the reserved green onions and cut into wedges. Yield: 4 to 6 servings.

Carol Zeiss, Delta Tau
St. Peters, Missouri

ALL-DAY MACARONI AND CHEESE

8 ounces elbow	1 (12-ounce) can
macaroni, cooked,	evaporated milk
drained	1 teaspoon salt
3 cups (12 ounces)	1/2 teaspoon pepper
shredded sharp	1 cup (4 ounces)
Cheddar cheese	shredded sharp
1 1/2 cups milk	Cheddar cheese
2 eggs, beaten	

Place the macaroni in a 3½-quart (or larger) slow cooker coated with nonstick cooking spray. Add 3 cups cheese, milk, eggs, evaporated milk, salt and pepper. Stir to mix well. Sprinkle with 1 cup cheese. Cook on Low for 5 to 6 hours or until the mixture is firm and golden brown around the edges. Do not remove the cover or stir during cooking.
Yield: 4 to 6 servings.

Sandra McIntyre, Preceptor Gamma Mu
Waterville, Kansas

MACARONI AND CHEESE

¼ cup (½ stick) butter	*Worcestershire sauce*
3 tablespoons	*Pepper to taste*
all-purpose flour	*8 ounces elbow*
3 cups milk	*macaroni, cooked,*
1 teaspoon salt	*drained*
½ to 1 teaspoon dry	*12 ounces shredded*
mustard	*Cheddar cheese*

Melt the butter in a saucepan. Remove from the heat and add the flour. Stir until smooth. Whisk in the milk. Return the saucepan to the heat and cook until the consistency of thin cream, whisking constantly. Whisk in the salt, dry mustard and a few drops of Worcestershire sauce. Season with pepper. Alternate layers of macaroni and cheese in a greased baking dish, starting with macaroni and ending with a generous layer of cheese. Pour the sauce over the top. Bake at 400 degrees for 30 minutes. Yield: 4 servings.

Ruth Edsall, Xi Alpha
Gardnerville, Nevada

SPICY MACARONI AND CHEESE

1 box macaroni and	*1 teaspoon cumin*
cheese	*¼ teaspoon garlic salt*
1 (16-ounce) can red	*¼ teaspoon cayenne*
kidney beans, drained	*pepper*
2 (10-ounce) cans	*⅓ cup fresh parsley or*
tomatoes with green	*cilantro, chopped*
chiles, drained	*¼ to ½ cup milk*
1 (4-ounce) can chopped	*(optional)*
black olives, drained	*1 cup (4 ounces) shredded*
4 green onions, chopped	*Cheddar cheese*

Prepare the macaroni and cheese using the package directions. Combine the macaroni and cheese and the next 8 ingredients in a large bowl. Stir to mix well. Stir in the milk if the mixture seems dry. Spoon into a greased 8x12-inch baking dish. Sprinkle with the Cheddar cheese. Bake at 350 degrees for 10 to 12 minutes. Yield: 8 to 10 servings.

Pat Tarpley, Alpha Alpha
Decatur, Alabama

CORN AND MAC BAKE

1 (15-ounce) can whole	*1 cup elbow macaroni,*
kernel corn	*uncooked*
1 (15-ounce) can cream-	*½ cup (1 stick)*
style corn	*margarine, cut into*
1 cup (4 ounces)	*pats*
shredded or cubed	
Cheddar cheese	

Mix the whole kernel corn, cream-style corn, cheese and macaroni in a 2-quart baking dish coated with nonstick cooking spray. Arrange the margarine on top. Bake, covered, at 350 degrees for 35 minutes or until bubbly and set. Yield: 8 to 10 servings.

Cheryl Kay H. Gregory, Mu Omega
Perry, Florida

CHILAQUILES

12 corn tortillas, torn	*½ teaspoon chili*
into bite-size pieces	*powder*
2 to 3 tablespoons	*1½ cups (6 ounces)*
vegetable oil	*shredded Cheddar*
1 cup chili sauce	*cheese*
½ cup tomato sauce	*1 green onion, chopped*
½ teaspoon minced	*2 tablespoons chopped*
garlic	*fresh cilantro*
½ teaspoon cumin	

Fry the tortillas in the oil in a large skillet until crisp and light brown. Stir in the next 5 ingredients and reduce the heat to low. Cook, covered, until the liquid is absorbed. Sprinkle with the cheese, green onion and cilantro. Cook, covered, until the cheese melts. Serve immediately. Yield: 4 to 6 servings.

Olga Sarouhan, Preceptor Iota Mu
Huntington Beach, California

CHEESE AND BEAN QUESADILLA ROLL-UPS

8 flour tortillas, warmed	*1 onion, chopped*
1 can refried beans	*½ cup cilantro leaves*
7 ounces shredded	*1 small jar salsa*
Cheddar cheese	

Spread each tortilla with a layer of refried beans. Sprinkle with the cheese, onion and cilantro. Top each with a spoonful of salsa. Roll up tightly. Heat a nonstick skillet over medium heat. Sprinkle with a few drops of water. Add the rolled tortillas. Cook, covered, until light brown and the cheese melts. Remove the quesadillas to a cutting board and slice each diagonally into 4 pieces. Yield: 8 servings.

Maria Colwell, Xi Beta Omega
Valdosta, Georgia

CHILES RELLENOS CASSEROLE

5 small cans whole green chiles	2 tablespoons all-purpose flour
16 ounces Cheddar cheese, shredded	½ teaspoon salt
4 eggs	1 (12-ounce) can evaporated milk

Alternate layers of the green chiles and cheese in a 9x13-inch baking dish coated with nonstick cooking spray. Beat the eggs, flour, salt and evaporated milk in a bowl. Pour over the green chiles and cheese. Bake at 350 degrees for 45 minutes. Yield: 6 to 8 servings.

Connie Childs, Xi Beta Upsilon
Nelson, Missouri

BLACK BEAN TORTILLA PIE

3 tablespoons vegetable oil	½ teaspoon chili powder
½ cup chopped onion	¼ teaspoon cayenne pepper
½ cup chopped green bell pepper	1 (2-crust) refrigerated pie pastry
1 (15-ounce) can black beans, drained and rinsed	2 cups (8 ounces) shredded Cheddar cheese
½ cup salsa	3 (8-inch) flour tortillas

Heat the oil in a large skillet over medium-high heat. Add the onion and bell pepper and sauté until tender. Stir in the black beans, salsa, chili powder and cayenne pepper. Simmer for 7 to 10 minutes, stirring occasionally. Fit 1 pie pastry into a 9-inch pie plate. Spread about ½ cup of the bean mixture over the bottom of the pie shell. Sprinkle with ½ cup of the cheese and top with 1 tortilla. Repeat the layers 2 more times and sprinkle with the remaining ½ cup cheese. Top with the other pie pastry and flute the edges to seal. Cut slits in the top to vent. Bake at 350 degrees for 40 to 50 minutes or until golden brown. Remove to a wire rack and let cool for 10 minutes. Serve with sour cream. Yield: 6 to 8 servings.

Alexis Bullard, Rho
Birmingham, Alabama

OLD WORLD MANICOTTI

12 large manicotti shells	1 (26-ounce) jar spaghetti sauce
2 cups ricotta cheese	
6 tablespoons fresh chopped basil	1 cup (4 ounces) shredded mozzarella cheese
3 cups (12 ounces) shredded mozzarella cheese	½ cup (2 ounces) grated Parmesan cheese

Cook the manicotti using the package directions. Drain; rinse with cold water and drain well. Spread on paper towels. Mix the ricotta cheese, basil and 3 cups mozzarella cheese in a bowl. Stuff the cooked shells with the cheese mixture. Spread 2 cups of the spaghetti sauce in a 9x13-inch baking dish coated with nonstick cooking spray. Arrange the stuffed shells on top. Cover with the remaining spaghetti sauce. Sprinkle with 1 cup mozzarella cheese. Bake at 350 degrees for 15 minutes. Sprinkle with the Parmesan cheese. Bake for 10 minutes longer. Serve immediately. You may use 2 tablespoons dried basil instead of fresh basil and or Romano cheese instead of Parmesan cheese. Yield: 6 servings.

Gussie Kolda, Preceptor Kappa Kappa
Fairfield, California

HEALTHY STUFFED SHELLS

20 jumbo pasta shells	½ cup (2 ounces) shredded mozzarella cheese
1 (10-ounce) package frozen chopped spinach	
2 cups fat-free cottage cheese	1 (26-ounce) jar spaghetti sauce
1 red bell pepper, chopped	½ cup (2 ounces) shredded mozzarella cheese
1 egg white	
1 envelope Italian salad dressing mix	

Cook the pasta shells using the package directions; drain well. Thaw the spinach and drain well. Combine the spinach, cottage cheese, bell pepper, egg white, salad dressing mix and ½ cup mozzarella cheese in a bowl. Stir to mix well. Stuff each shell with 1 heaping tablespoon of the spinach mixture. Spread ½ the spaghetti sauce in a 9x13-inch baking dish. Arrange the stuffed shells on the top. Cover with the remaining spaghetti sauce. Sprinkle with ½ cup mozzarella cheese. Cover with foil. Bake at 400 degrees for 30 to 40 minutes. Yield: 5 servings.

Carita Shoemaker, Chi Master
Lees Summit, Missouri

SOUTHWESTERN TOMATO PASTA

3 to 4 small ripe tomatoes	½ teaspoon chili powder
2 tablespoons extra-virgin olive oil	¼ teaspoon salt
	¼ teaspoon white pepper
3 garlic cloves, minced	Angel hair pasta
3 tablespoons chopped fresh cilantro	Crumbled goat cheese or feta cheese
1 tablespoon fresh lime juice	2 tablespoons pine nuts, toasted

Peel the tomatoes and coarsely chop over a bowl to catch the juice. Add the olive oil, garlic, cilantro, lime juice, chili powder, salt and white pepper to the bowl. Stir to mix well. Cover and let stand for 1 hour. Cook the pasta in a saucepan of boiling water until al dente; drain. Place the cooked pasta on serving plates. Top with the tomato mixture. Sprinkle with goat cheese and the pine nuts. You may add grilled chicken strips or cooked shrimp, if desired. Yield: 3 to 4 servings.

Carolyn S. Mawyer, Preceptor Kappa
Charlottesville, Virginia

LOW-CARB PIZZA

4 ounces cream cheese, softened	2 cups (8 ounces) shredded Italian-style cheese
3 eggs	
1/3 cup heavy cream	1/2 cup favorite spaghetti sauce
1/4 cup (1 ounce) grated Parmesan cheese	1 cup (4 ounces) shredded mozzarella cheese
1/2 teaspoon oregano	
1/4 teaspoon garlic powder	Favorite pizza toppings

Beat the cream cheese and eggs in a bowl until smooth. Stir in the cream, Parmesan cheese, oregano and garlic powder. Spread the Italian-style cheese in an oiled 9x13-inch baking pan. Pour the egg mixture over the cheese. Bake at 375 degrees for 15 minutes. Remove to a wire rack and let cool for 5 minutes. Spread with the spaghetti sauce and sprinkle with the mozzarella cheese. Cover with your favorite pizza toppings. Sprinkle with additional Parmesan cheese, if desired. Bake at 375 degrees for 5 minutes or until bubbly and light brown. Remove to a wire rack and let stand for 10 minutes before cutting. Yield: 6 to 8 servings.

Mary Ellen Pruess, Laureate Beta Lambda
Green Valley, Arizona

❖ GREEK SPINACH PIE

2 eggs	2 green onions, minced
1 (12-ounce) carton small curd cottage cheese	2 (10-ounce) packages frozen chopped spinach
1 cup (4 ounces) crumbled feta cheese	Salt and pepper to taste
3 tablespoons chopped fresh parsley	10 sheets phyllo dough
	1/2 cup (1 stick) butter, melted

Beat the eggs in a bowl. Stir in the cottage cheese, feta cheese, parsley and green onions. Thaw the spinach. Drain and squeeze dry. Add to the egg mixture and season with salt and pepper. Stir to mix well. Cut the

phyllo sheets in half. Place 1/2 of the sheets in a buttered 7x11-inch baking pan, brushing each sheet with melted butter. Spread with the spinach mixture. Top with the remaining phyllo sheets, brushing each sheet with melted butter. Bake at 350 degrees for 40 minutes or until golden brown. Cut into squares to serve. Yield: 6 to 8 servings.

Rosemary Marc-Aurele, Laureate Gamma
Rochester, New Hampshire

CHEESE AND MUSHROOM TART

2 tablespoons olive oil	1/8 teaspoon nutmeg
2 cups thinly sliced onions	1 baked (9-inch) pie shell
8 cups sliced mushrooms	1 tablespoon Dijon mustard
1/2 teaspoon thyme	
1/2 teaspoon salt	1 1/2 cups (6 ounces) shredded fontina cheese
1/2 teaspoon pepper	
3 eggs	
1 cup milk	

Heat the olive oil in a skillet. Add the onions and sauté for 10 minutes or until slightly softened. Add the mushrooms, thyme, salt and pepper. Sauté over high heat for 3 to 5 minutes or until the liquid has evaporated. Remove from the heat and let cool slightly. Beat the eggs, milk and nutmeg in a large bowl. Stir in the mushroom mixture. Brush the bottom of the pie shell with the mustard. Sprinkle with the cheese. Pour the mushroom mixture into the pie shell. Bake at 400 degrees for 20 to 25 minutes or until golden brown and set. Yield: 6 to 8 servings.

Claudia M. Long, Kappa Kappa
Meriden, Kansas

ZUCCHINI AND EGG PUFF

1 cup baking mix	1/2 cup (2 ounces) shredded Cheddar cheese
1/2 cup vegetable oil	
4 eggs, lightly beaten	
3 cups thinly sliced zucchini	2 (4-ounce) cans chopped green chiles
1/2 cup (2 ounces) grated Parmesan cheese	1/3 cup finely chopped onion
	1 tablespoon oregano

Combine the baking mix, oil, eggs, zucchini, Parmesan cheese, Cheddar cheese, green chiles, onion and oregano in a large bowl. Stir to mix well. Pour into a nonstick 9x13-inch baking pan. Bake at 325 degrees for 45 minutes. Serve with fresh fruit. You may add 1/4 cup chopped fresh parsley before baking, if desired. Yield: 9 to 12 servings.

Dottie Sinovic, Laureate Kappa Nu
Mission Viejo, California

Vegetables & Side Dishes

❖ PARMESAN ROASTED ASPARAGUS

1½ pounds asparagus,
trimmed
(about 30 stalks)
2 tablespoons olive oil
½ teaspoon kosher salt

¼ teaspoon freshly
ground pepper
½ cup grated Parmesan
cheese
2 lemons

Arrange the asparagus in a single layer in a shallow 11×13-inch roasting pan. Drizzle with the olive oil, then season with the salt and pepper. Roast at 400 degrees for 15 to 20 minutes or until tender. Sprinkle the asparagus with the Parmesan cheese and roast for 1 more minute or until the cheese is melted. Cut the lemons into 6 wedges each and serve with the asparagus. Yield: 6 servings.

Jackie Ann Nelson, Xi Theta Chi
Chesapeake, Virginia

BROCCOLI WITH BLUE CHEESE SAUCE

1 tablespoon margarine
1 tablespoon all-purpose
flour
½ cup milk
2 teaspoons dry mustard
⅓ cup crumbled blue

cheese
1 (10-ounce) package
frozen broccoli
florets, cooked and
drained

Melt the margarine in a medium-size pan over medium-high heat. Whisk in the flour until smooth. Pour the milk into the flour and margarine mixture and cook until slightly thickened. Add the mustard, blue cheese and salt, stirring until smooth. Add the broccoli and toss with the warm sauce. Cook until the broccoli is heated through. Yield: 4 servings.

Sue Warden, Laureate Alpha Rho
Salem, Virginia

BROCCOLI AND CORN CASSEROLE

1 (10-ounce) package
frozen broccoli cuts
1 (15-ounce) can
creamed corn
1 egg, beaten

½ teaspoon salt
Pepper to taste
½ cup cracker crumbs
¼ cup (½ stick)
margarine, melted

Combine the first 5 ingredients in a bowl. Mix the crackers and margarine in a small bowl until the crackers are well coated with the margarine. Spoon the broccoli mixture into a well greased 2-quart casserole dish. Sprinkle the cracker mixture evenly on top of the casserole. Bake at 425 degrees for 30 to 35 minutes or until light brown. Yield: 4 to 6 servings.

La Verne Morris, Laureate Alpha Zeta
Drumright, Oklahoma

SIMMERED BLACK BEANS

1 pound dried black
beans
1 green bell pepper,
chopped
⅔ cup olive oil
1 large onion, minced
4 garlic cloves, crushed
¼ teaspoon oregano
1 bay leaf

1 tablespoon sugar
2½ quarts water
2 tablespoons vinegar
2 tablespoons white
wine
4 teaspoons salt
½ teaspoon pepper
2 tablespoons olive oil

Sort and rinse the black beans. Soak the black beans and bell pepper in water in a stockpot overnight. Drain the beans and the bell pepper and rinse; set aside. Heat ⅔ cup olive oil in a large stock pot over medium heat. Stir in the onion, garlic, oregano, bay leaf, sugar, black beans and bell pepper. Pour in 2½ quarts of water and bring the mixture to a boil.

Reduce the heat and simmer for 1 hour. Add the vinegar, white wine, salt and pepper. Simmer for 1 hour, or until the beans are soft and the mixture has thickened. Remove and discard the bay leaf. Drizzle with 2 tablespoons of olive oil before serving. Yield: 10 to 15 servings.

Nancy Carol Meyland
Tampa, Florida

HOMEMADE BAKED BEANS

12 slices bacon, chopped
3 onions, chopped
1 (15-ounce) can red
*   kidney beans, drained*
1 (15-ounce) can butter
*   beans, drained*
2 (16-ounce) cans baked
*   beans*
1 teaspoon garlic
*   powder*
1/2 teaspoon dry mustard
1/2 cup packed brown
*   sugar*
1/3 cup cider vinegar
1/4 cup ketchup

Sauté the bacon in a Dutch oven over medium heat until crisp. Drain the bacon, reserving 2 tablespoons of the bacon drippings. Return the Dutch oven to the heat and sauté the onions in the bacon drippings just until tender. Stir in the beans. Add the garlic powder, dry mustard, brown sugar, cider vinegar and ketchup. Stir until all of the ingredients are well combined. Bake, uncovered, at 350 degrees for 60 to 70 minutes or until hot and bubbly. Yield: 12 servings.

Diane Ely, Theta Eta
Florissant, Missouri

NEW ENGLAND BAKED BEANS

2 pounds dried lima
*   beans*
1/2 pound bacon, chopped
1 tablespoon dry
*   mustard*
1 1/2 cups ketchup
1 1/2 cups water
1 1/2 cups packed brown
*   sugar*
1 1/2 tablespoons
*   molasses*
Salt to taste

Sort and rinse the beans. Place the beans in a stockpot and cover with water. Cook for 30 minutes over medium heat. Turn off the heat and let the beans stand in the hot water for 1 1/2 hours; drain. Sauté the bacon in a skillet over medium heat until crisp. Drain the bacon, reserving the bacon drippings, and set aside. Combine the beans, dry mustard, ketchup, water, bacon and bacon drippings in a large slow cooker and mix well. Cover and cook on Low for 10 to 12 hours, or on High for 4 to 6 hours, stirring occasionally. Add the brown sugar, molasses and salt when the beans are tender. Cook until the mixture has a creamy consistency. Yield: 8 to 10 servings.

Mildred Harris, Laureate Epsilon
Belvidere, New Jersey

FOUR-BEAN BAKE

1 cup water
1 pound lean bacon,
*   chopped*
1 large onion, chopped
1 1/4 cups packed light
*   brown sugar*
1 teaspoon salt
*   (optional)*
2 (15-ounce) cans red
*   kidney beans, drained*
2 (15-ounce) cans lima
*   beans, drained*
2 (16-ounce) cans butter
*   beans, drained*
3 (16-ounce) cans pork
*   and beans*

Simmer the water, bacon, and onion in a medium-size saucepan for 10 minutes. Stir the brown sugar into the bacon mixture; set aside. Combine all of the beans in a large bowl and mix well. Stir the bacon mixture into the beans. Pour the mixture into a large glass baking dish. Bake, covered, at 350 degrees for 1 hour. Yield: 20 servings.

Rose Mary Coakes, Laureate Alpha Rho
Marshall, Michigan

BRAISED SWEET AND SOUR CABBAGE

Because of the vinegar content, the cabbage keeps in the refrigerator for 2 to 3 weeks.

1/4 cup (1/2 stick) butter
1/2 cup chopped onion
1/2 head red cabbage,
*   shredded*
1/2 cup red wine vinegar
1/2 cup sugar
2 apples, peeled and
*   chopped*
1/2 teaspoon salt
Pepper to taste

Melt the butter in a large Dutch oven over medium heat. Add the onion and cabbage and sauté until tender. Cover and cook for 5 minutes. Add the vinegar, sugar, apples and salt, stirring to combine. Simmer the cabbage mixture for 30 minutes. Season with salt and pepper to taste. Yield: 4 servings.

Catherine Martin, Laureate Epsilon Epsilon
Lorain, Ohio

SKILLET CABBAGE

1/4 cup olive oil or bacon
*   drippings*
2 large onions, sliced
1 green bell pepper,
*   chopped*
2 cups chopped celery
4 cups shredded cabbage
2 tomatoes, chopped, or
*   1 (16-ounce) can*
*   stewed tomatoes*
2 teaspoons sugar
Salt and pepper to taste

Heat the olive oil in a large cast-iron skillet over medium-high heat. Add the onions, bell pepper, celery, cabbage, tomatoes and sugar; stir until combined. Simmer, covered, for 30 minutes. Season with salt and pepper to taste. Yield: 6 servings.

Margaret Funderburg, Theta Master
Raleigh, North Carolina

FRIED CABBAGE

The pickle juice should enhance but not overpower the flavor of the cabbage.

1 pound bacon, chopped	Garlic powder to taste
1 medium onion, chopped	Salt and pepper to taste
2 heads cabbage, finely chopped	1/2 cup (or more) pickle juice

Fry the bacon until crisp in a large saucepan over medium heat. Remove the bacon with a slotted spoon; drain on paper towels. Sauté the onion in the bacon drippings for 5 to 7 minutes or until tender. Remove the onions with a slotted spoon; set aside. Add the chopped cabbage to the pan with the remaining bacon drippings and fry over medium heat, stirring frequently. Add the garlic powder, salt and pepper, stirring frequently. Stir in the bacon, onions and pickle juice when the cabbage is tender. Yield: 8 to 10 servings.

Sheila Harrington, Beta Kappa Omicron
Coleman, Texas

CABBAGE AND CARROT CASSEROLE

Adding cooked sausage links to this dish will enhance the flavor and turn it into a hearty main dish.

1 large head cabbage, chopped	1 onion, finely chopped
4 to 5 carrots, sliced	1/4 cup sugar
4 celery ribs, sliced	Salt and pepper to taste
	6 tablespoons butter

Combine the cabbage, carrots, celery, onion, sugar, salt and pepper in a large bowl. Place cabbage mixture in a 9×13-inch baking dish. Dot the top of the cabbage mixture with the butter. Cover tightly with foil. Bake at 350 degrees for 1 to 1½ hours or until the cabbage is tender. Yield: 10 to 15 servings.

Sandy Guthrie, Alpha Alpha Master
Wheeling, West Virginia

CALABACITA

1 tablespoon olive oil	1 green bell pepper, chopped (optional)
1 tablespoon butter	
1 small sweet onion, chopped	4 to 5 Roma tomatoes, chopped
2 garlic cloves, minced	1/4 cup sliced black olives (optional)
2 to 3 zucchini, chopped	
2 to 3 crookneck squash, chopped	Salt and pepper to taste

Heat the olive oil and butter in a large skillet over medium heat. Add the onion and sauté until tender. Add the garlic and sauté until tender but not browned. Add the zucchini, crookneck squash and bell pepper. Sauté until the vegetables are tender. Stir in the tomatoes and olives. Season with salt and pepper. Cook until heated through. Serve by itself or over steamed white rice. Add 1 chopped cooked chicken breast or 1 cup chopped cooked beef, if desired. Yield: 4 to 6 servings.

Annette Thivierge, Xi Iota
Lewiston, Idaho

GLAZED JULIENNED CARROTS

1/4 cup water	2 tablespoons margarine, softened
3½ cups julienned carrots (about 1 pound)	
	1/2 teaspoon nutmeg
1/2 teaspoon salt	Chopped fresh mint (optional)
2 tablespoons sugar	

Simmer the water, carrots and salt in a covered saucepan for 10 minutes. Stir in the sugar and margarine. Cook the carrots until glazed and tender. Sprinkle the carrots with the nutmeg and mint, if desired. Yield: 4 to 6 servings.

Linda Lee Wyatt, Laureate Theta Eta
Livingston, Texas

BROCCOLI AND CAULIFLOWER CASSEROLE

1 bunch broccoli	1 (10-ounce) can cream of mushroom soup
1 head cauliflower	
3 cups (12 ounces) shredded sharp Cheddar cheese	1 (3-ounce) can fried onion rings

Steam the broccoli and cauliflower florets for 6 to 8 minutes or until tender-crisp; drain and set aside. Combine the cheese and mushroom soup in a medium saucepan over medium heat; stir until the cheese melts. Place the broccoli and cauliflower into a well greased 9×13-inch baking dish. Pour the mushroom soup mixture over the vegetables. Bake at 350 degrees for 20 to 25 minutes. Sprinkle the casserole with the fried onion rings. Bake for 5 minutes or until lightly browned and crispy. Yield: 6 to 8 servings.

Jean Credle, Kappa Lambda
Edenton, North Carolina

QUICK AND EASY CAULIFLOWER

2 tablespoons water	1 teaspoon dehydrated onion
1 large head cauliflower, core removed	
	Pinch of salt
1/2 cup mayonnaise	1/2 cup (2 ounces) shredded cheese
1 teaspoon prepared mustard	

Place 2 tablespoons of water in a microwave-safe container. Place the cauliflower in the container and cover with plastic wrap; set aside. Combine the mayonnaise, mustard, onion and salt in a bowl and mix well. Microwave the cauliflower on High for 7 minutes. Remove the plastic wrap and spread the mayonnaise mixture over the cauliflower. Place the cauliflower in the microwave and cook for 1 minute. Sprinkle with the cheese and microwave for 1 more minute. Cut the cauliflower into large florets and serve. Yield: 6 servings.

Karen Dobbins, Preceptor Lambda Alpha
Laurie, Missouri

CURRIED CAULIFLOWER

3 cups water	1 (10-ounce) can cream
1/2 teaspoon salt	of chicken soup
1 head cauliflower or	1/3 cup mayonnaise
1 (1-pound) package	1/2 teaspoon curry
frozen cauliflower	powder
florets	1/2 cup bread crumbs
1 cup (4 ounces)	3 tablespoons butter or
shredded Cheddar	margarine, melted
cheese	

Bring the water and salt to a boil in a large saucepan. Add the cauliflower and boil for 8 minutes or until tender-crisp; drain. Combine the cheese, soup, mayonnaise and curry powder in a bowl. Mix the bread crumbs and butter in a small bowl, stirring until combined. Place the cauliflower in a greased 2-quart casserole dish. Pour the soup mixture over the cauliflower. Sprinkle the bread crumb mixture on top of the casserole. Bake at 350 degrees for 30 minutes or until light brown and bubbly. For color, add one 10-ounce package of cooked frozen peas. Yield: 6 to 8 servings.

Janeene Spangler, Alpha Delta Master
Arkansas City, Kansas

CONFETTI CAULIFLOWER

1 head cauliflower	2 tablespoons chopped
2 tablespoons butter	pimento
1/4 cup chopped onion	1 teaspoon chopped
2 tablespoons	parsley
all-purpose flour	1/2 teaspoon instant
1 cup half-and-half	chicken bouillon
1 cup frozen petite peas,	1/2 teaspoon salt
thawed	1/8 teaspoon pepper

Cover the cauliflower with water in a medium saucepan and bring to a boil. Cook until tender-crisp; drain. Melt the butter in a medium saucepan over medium-high heat. Add the onion and sauté until tender. Whisk in the flour. Pour the half-and-half into the onion mixture. Cook until the mixture has thickened, stirring constantly. Add the cauliflower, peas, pimento, parsley, bouillon, salt and pepper and mix well. Pour the cauliflower mixture into a well buttered 1 1/2-quart casserole dish. Bake at 350 degrees for 15 minutes or until bubbly. Yield: 6 to 8 servings.

Joyce Horvath, Preceptor Epsilon Lambda
Wellington, Ohio

GREEN BEAN AND CORN CASSEROLE

1 (16-ounce) can French-style green beans, drained	1/2 cup sour cream
	1/2 cup (2 ounces) shredded Cheddar cheese
1 (16-ounce) can small-kernel corn, drained	Salt and pepper to taste
1 (8-ounce) can sliced water chestnuts, drained	1 1/2 cups cracker crumbs
	1/2 cup toasted almonds
1 onion, chopped	1/4 cup (1/2 stick) butter, melted
1 (10-ounce) can cream of celery soup	

Combine the green beans, corn, water chestnuts and onion in a large bowl and mix well. Add the soup, sour cream, cheese, salt and pepper and stir until well combined; set aside. Mix the cracker crumbs, almonds and butter in a small mixing bowl, stirring to coat evenly. Spoon the green bean mixture into a well greased 2 1/2-quart baking dish. Sprinkle the cracker mixture evenly on top of the casserole. Bake at 350 degrees for 30 to 35 minutes or until lightly browned and bubbly. Yield: 6 to 8 servings.

Julie McCormick, Preceptor Alpha Kappa
Fort Collins, Colorado

CHILE CORN CASSEROLE

1 (4-ounce) can chopped green chiles	1 teaspoon sugar
	1/2 teaspoon salt
1 (17-ounce) can cream-style corn	1/8 teaspoon oregano
	1 tablespoon butter, melted
2 eggs, beaten	
1/2 cup all-purpose flour	

Combine the chiles, corn and eggs in a bowl and mix well. Combine the flour, sugar, salt and oregano in a separate bowl and mix well. Add the dry ingredients to the chile mixture and stir just until combined. Spoon into a well greased 1-quart casserole dish. Drizzle with the melted butter. Bake at 350 degrees for 55 to 60 minutes. Yield: 6 servings.

Mary Johnson, Laureate Beta Upsilon
Chico, California

BAKED CORN CASSEROLE

1 egg, beaten
1/2 cup (1 stick) margarine, melted
1 (15-ounce) can cream-style corn
1 cup sour cream
1 (15-ounce) can whole kernel corn, drained
1 (7-ounce) package corn muffin mix

Combine all the ingredients in a bowl and mix well. Pour into a well greased 2-quart casserole dish. Bake at 350 degrees for 45 minutes. Yield: 6 to 8 servings.

Violet Arnold, Delta Psi
Norwalk, Ohio

FRESH CORN CASSEROLE

To peel the tomatoes, cut an "X" into the bottom of the tomatoes and drop into boiling water for 10 to 30 seconds (depending on ripeness). Remove the tomatoes with a slotted spoon, then immediately plunge into a bowl of ice water for 15 seconds. Skins will slip off easily.

6 ears of corn, husked
1 cup chopped green bell pepper
1/2 cup chopped onion
2 tablespoons bacon drippings
6 slices crisp-cooked bacon, drained and crumbled
1 teaspoon salt
1/8 teaspoon pepper
2 sliced peeled tomatoes

Cut the kernels from the cobs; set aside. Sauté the corn, bell pepper and onion in the bacon drippings in a large skillet over medium-high heat for 5 minutes, stirring constantly. Add the crumbled bacon, salt and pepper to the corn mixture and remove from the heat. Alternate layers of the corn mixture and tomato slices in a greased 2-quart baking dish until all ingredients are used. Bake at 350 degrees for 30 to 40 minutes. Yield: 6 to 8 servings.

Betty Mullis
Tampa, Florida

EGGPLANT SOUFFLÉ

1 large eggplant, peeled
2 cups water
1/2 cup nonfat dry milk
2 cups (8 ounces) shredded sharp Cheddar cheese
2 eggs, beaten
1 cup cracker crumbs
2 teaspoons butter or margarine, melted
1 teaspoon salt
1/8 teaspoon pepper

Cut the eggplant into 1/2-inch cubes. Simmer the eggplant in the water in a large saucepan over medium heat until tender. Drain the eggplant, reserving 1 1/2 cups of the water. Combine the eggplant, reserved water, dry milk, cheese, eggs, cracker crumbs, butter, salt and pepper in a large bowl and mix well. Pour the eggplant mixture into a greased 2-quart baking dish. Bake at 350 degrees for 30 minutes or until a knife inserted in the center comes out clean. Yield: 8 servings.

Marion Catherine Wallace, Laureate Epsilon Phi
Plant City, Florida

FIDDLEHEAD CASSEROLE

Available in the spring and early summer, fiddleheads are the young, tightly-coiled fronds of certain types of ferns.

1 1/2 pounds fiddlehead ferns
2 tablespoons bread crumbs
2 tablespoons grated Parmesan cheese
1 tablespoon butter, melted
2 tablespoons vegetable oil
1 tablespoon vinegar
4 green onions, chopped
1/4 teaspoon salt
1/8 teaspoon pepper

Place the fiddleheads in a medium saucepan and cover with water. Cook until tender; drain and set aside. Combine the bread crumbs, cheese and butter in a small bowl, stirring until well combined; set aside. Combine the fiddleheads, vegetable oil, vinegar, green onions, salt and pepper in a bowl and mix well. Spoon the fiddlehead mixture into a greased baking dish. Sprinkle evenly with the bread crumb mixture. Bake at 350 degrees for 20 minutes. Yield: 6 servings.

Christine Oliver, Xi Psi
Kiersteadville, Nebraska

MUSHROOM CASSEROLE

3 pounds mushrooms, quartered
1/2 cup (1 stick) butter or margarine, melted
1 large onion, chopped
8 ounces Velveeta cheese, thinly sliced
1 (6-ounce) package chicken stuffing mix
2 cups half-and-half

Cook the mushrooms, butter and onion in a covered 5-quart saucepan over low heat for 30 minutes, stirring occasionally. Layer 1/3 of the mushroom mixture and cooking juices, 1/2 of the cheese and 1/2 of the stuffing mix in a greased 2-quart baking dish. Using a slotted spoon, layer with 1/2 of the remaining mushrooms and the remaining stuffing mix. Top with the remaining mushrooms and cheese. Combine the remaining mushroom cooking juices with the half-and-half in a small bowl and mix well. Pour the mixture over the casserole. Bake at 350 degrees for 30 to 40 minutes. Yield: 10 to 12 servings.

Lucy Lutz, Laureate Epsilon
Laurel, Delaware

❖ BAKED PORTABELLO MUSHROOMS

4 portabello mushrooms, stems removed	2¹/₂ tablespoons grated Parmesan cheese
4 teaspoons olive oil	2 tomatoes, sliced
Salt and pepper to taste	¹/₂ teaspoon basil
1 teaspoon garlic powder	¹/₂ teaspoon oregano
	8 ounces mozzarella cheese, sliced

Place the portabello mushrooms top side down in a well greased baking dish. Drizzle the mushrooms with the olive oil. Sprinkle each mushroom with the salt, pepper, garlic powder, and Parmesan cheese. Place 2 tomato slices on each mushroom. Sprinkle the tomatoes with the basil and oregano. Place the mozzarella cheese over the tomatoes. Bake at 350 degrees for 25 to 30 minutes or until the cheese is light brown. Serve with beef, chicken or pork, or cut into quarters and serve as an appetizer. Yield: 4 servings.

Gerda M. Cote, Epsilon Master
Manchester, New Hampshire

DILLED ONION RINGS

1 cup white vinegar	4 teaspoons salt
¹/₂ cup water	1 teaspoon dill weed
1 cup sugar	2 large onions, sliced

Boil the vinegar, water, sugar, salt and dill weed in a 3-quart saucepan over high heat until the sugar dissolves, stirring constantly. Reduce the heat and add the onions. Simmer for 1 minute. Cool the mixture to room temperature. Pour into a nonreactive container, cover and refrigerate overnight. Yield: 1 quart.

Jan Wallick, Laureate Gamma Alpha
Cashmere, Washington

VIDALIA ONION PIE

1 unbaked (9-inch) deep-dish pie shell	3 tablespoons all-purpose flour
3 cups thinly sliced Vidalia onions	2 eggs, beaten
3 tablespoons butter, melted	¹/₂ cup milk
1 cup sour cream	2 slices crisp-cooked bacon, drained, crumbled
1 teaspoon salt	

Bake the pie shell at 350 degrees for 10 minutes; cool slightly. Sauté the onions in the butter in a skillet over medium-high heat until tender; set aside. Combine the sour cream, salt and flour in a medium bowl and mix well. Stir the eggs and milk into the sour cream mixture until smooth. Spread the onion mixture evenly in the bottom of the pie shell. Pour the sour cream mixture over the onions. Bake at 325 degrees for 30 to 45 minutes or until the center of the pie is firm. Sprinkle the top of the pie with the bacon and serve. Yield: 6 to 8 servings.

Anne Schroeder, Preceptor Alpha Zeta
Appleton, Wisconsin

STUFFED ONIONS

6 Vidalia onions, peeled	Dash of cayenne pepper
2 tablespoons butter	2 tablespoons bread crumbs
¹/₂ each green and red bell peppers, chopped	2 tablespoons butter, melted
¹/₂ cup bread crumbs	Paprika to taste
¹/₂ teaspoon sugar	
1 teaspoon salt	

Cut the tops off of the onions. Scoop out the cores of the onions with a melon-baller. Chop the onion cores and set aside. Place the onions hollowed side up in a large saucepan with 1 inch of water. Simmer, covered, over low heat until fork-tender. Drain the onions and place in a shallow baking dish. Melt 2 tablespoons butter in a skillet over medium heat. Sauté the bell peppers and onion cores in the butter until light brown, stirring constantly. Add the next 5 ingredients to the bell pepper mixture, stirring to combine. Stuff each onion with the bell pepper mixture. Sprinkle with the bread crumbs and drizzle with the melted butter. Broil 4 inches from the heat source until light brown. Sprinkle with paprika and serve. Yield: 6 servings.

Gloria J. Snyder, Alpha Delta Phi
Lowry City, Missouri

FRIED ONION RINGS

4 large onions	¹/₂ tablespoon lemon juice
1 cup all-purpose flour	1 tablespoon shortening, melted
2 teaspoons baking powder	Vegetable oil for frying
¹/₂ teaspoon salt	All-purpose flour for dredging
1 egg	
²/₃ cup water	

Cut the onions into ¹/₄-inch slices and separate into rings. Sift the flour, baking powder and salt into a bowl. Whisk the egg, water, lemon juice and shortening in a small bowl until frothy. Pour the egg mixture into the dry ingredients and stir just until combined. Heat the vegetable oil to 375 degrees in a deep frying pan. Dredge the onion rings in the flour, shaking off the excess. Dip the onion rings in the batter and place gently in the hot oil using tongs. Working in batches, deep-fry the onion rings until golden brown; drain on paper towels. Serve while hot. Yield: 6 servings.

Norma M. Ellis, Gamma Omicron Master
Yureka, California

CARAMEL ONIONS

3 large onions
2 tablespoons butter or
    margarine
3 tablespoons brown

sugar

Cut the onions into thick slices; do not separate into rings. Melt the butter in a large skillet over medium-high heat. Stir in the brown sugar and salt until smooth. Remove from the heat. Place the onion slices over the sugar mixture, cover and cook over low heat for 10 minutes. Turn each onion slice over with a spatula and sprinkle with the parsley. Cook, uncovered, over low heat for 10 minutes.
Yield: 4 to 6 servings.

Marie Geesa, Kappa Alpha
Blairsville, Georgia

❖ VIDALIA ONION CASSEROLE

6 Vidalia onions, thinly
    sliced
1/2 cup (1 stick) butter,
    melted
1 (10-ounce) can cream
    of mushroom soup
1/2 cup milk
1 tablespoon soy sauce
Salt and pepper to taste

1 cup chopped cooked
    chicken breast
    (optional)
1 cup (4 ounces) shredded
    Swiss cheese
Sourdough bread, thinly
    sliced
1/2 cup (2 ounces) grated
    Parmesan cheese

Cook the onions in the butter in a large skillet over low heat just until tender. Combine the soup, milk, soy sauce, salt and pepper in a bowl and mix well. Layer the onions, chicken and Swiss cheese in a 9×13-inch baking pan. Pour the soup mixture over the Swiss cheese layer. Place the bread slices in one layer over the top; sprinkle with the Parmesan cheese. Bake at 350 degrees for 35 to 40 minutes.
Yield: 6 to 8 servings.

Chris Boyd, Laureate Alpha Kappa
Lincoln, Nebraska

CREAMY POTATO CASSEROLE

1 (2-pound) bag frozen
    hash brown potatoes
6 tablespoons (3/4 stick)
    margarine, cut into
    small pieces
Salt and pepper to taste

1 cup heavy cream
2 cups half-and-half
2 cups (8 ounces)
    shredded Cheddar
    cheese

Layer 1/2 of the potatoes in a greased 9×13-inch baking dish. Sprinkle with 1/2 of the margarine pieces, salt and pepper. Repeat layers with the remaining potatoes, margarine, salt and pepper. Pour the cream and half-and-half over the top. Sprinkle with the cheese. Bake, covered, at 325 degrees for 1 hour. Uncover and bake for an additional 30 minutes or until lightly browned. Yield: 12 servings.

Carolyn A. Cunningham, Laureate Beta Gamma
Flint, Texas

SLOW-COOKER CHEESE POTATOES

1 (2-pound) package
    frozen hash brown
    potatoes
1 (10-ounce) can
    Cheddar cheese soup
1 (10-ounce) can cream
    of chicken soup

1 (13-ounce) can
    evaporated milk
1 (3-ounce) can French-
    fried onion rings
Salt and pepper to taste

Combine the potatoes, soups, evaporated milk, 1/2 of the fried onions, salt and pepper in a large bowl and mix well. Pour the potato mixture into a greased slow cooker. Cook on Low for 7 to 9 hours or on High for 3 hours. Top with the remaining onions and serve.
Yield: 6 to 8 servings.

Jeanne Poll, Alpha Iota
Holland, Michigan

CHEESY WALNUT POTATOES

This recipe is a creative twist on an old favorite, Potatoes Au Gratin. It has universal appeal.

1 onion, chopped
2 garlic cloves, minced
1/4 cup (1/2 stick) butter,
    melted
3 tablespoons
    all-purpose flour
21/2 cups milk
3 tablespoons chopped
    fresh sage

1/2 teaspoon seasoned
    salt
6 potatoes, peeled and
    thinly sliced
11/2 cups (6 ounces)
    shredded Cheddar
    cheese
1/2 cup walnuts, coarsely
    chopped

Sauté the onion and garlic in the butter in a medium saucepan over medium-high heat until tender. Whisk in the flour until smooth. Add the milk and cook until the mixture thickens, stirring constantly. Remove from the heat and stir in the sage and salt. Layer 1/2 of the potatoes, 1/2 of the sauce and 1/2 of the cheese in a greased 2-quart baking dish. Layer with the remaining potatoes, sauce and cheese. Bake, covered, at 350 degrees for 40 minutes. Uncover and bake for an additional 15 minutes. Sprinkle the top with the walnuts and bake for 5 minutes longer.
Yield: 8 servings.

Nina Rohlfs, Preceptor Tau
Unadilla, Nebraska

REFRIGERATOR POTATOES

5 pounds potatoes,
  peeled and quartered
6 ounces cream cheese,
  softened
1 cup sour cream

1 teaspoon onion salt
1 teaspoon salt
1/4 teaspoon pepper
2 tablespoons butter or
  margarine

Combine the potatoes with enough water to cover in a saucepan. Bring to a boil. Boil until tender; drain. Mash the potatoes in a large mixing bowl. Beat in the cream cheese until smooth. Add the sour cream, onion salt, salt and pepper; stir until well combined. Spread in a greased 2-quart baking dish. Dot the top with the butter. Bake at 350 degrees for 30 minutes. Refrigerator Potatoes can be refrigerated several days before baking. Yield: 12 servings.

Judy Manning, Xi Eta Omicron
Great Bend, Kansas

STUFFED BAKED POTATOES

3 large baking potatoes
2 teaspoons vegetable
  oil
1/4 cup (1/2 stick) butter
  or margarine
1/2 cup sliced green
  onions
1/2 cup light cream
1/2 cup sour cream

1/2 cup (4 ounces)
  shredded Cheddar
  cheese
1 teaspoon salt
1/2 teaspoon white
  pepper
1/4 cup (1/2 stick) melted
  butter for topping
Paprika to taste

Rub the potatoes with vegetable oil. Pierce each potato with a fork. Place the potatoes on a baking sheet and bake at 400 degrees for 1 hour and 20 minutes or until tender. Melt the butter and sauté the onions in a skillet over medium heat until tender. Cut the potatoes lengthwise into halves. Scoop out the pulp into a bowl, leaving 1/2-inch shells. Mash the pulp. Beat in the light cream and the sour cream until smooth. Fold in the green onions, cheese, salt and pepper. Spoon the potato mixture into each potato shell. Drizzle the tops with the melted butter and sprinkle with the paprika. Place the stuffed potatoes into a 9×13-inch baking pan. Bake at 350 degrees for 30 minutes. Yield: 6 servings.

Melissa Priano, Rho chapter
Coeur d'Alene, Idaho

DIJON-ROASTED NEW POTATOES

1 teaspoon olive oil
2 tablespoons Dijon
  mustard
1 teaspoon paprika
1/4 teaspoon thyme

1/2 teaspoon salt
1/4 teaspoon pepper
11/2 pounds new
  potatoes, quartered

Whisk the first 6 ingredients in a large bowl until combined. Toss the potatoes in the olive oil mixture until coated. Place the potatoes in a greased 9×13-inch baking pan. Bake at 425 degrees for 30 minutes or until tender. Yield: 4 servings.

Michelle Doyle, Xi Omega
Worland, Wyoming

LOADED POTATO FANS

4 large baking potatoes,
  peeled
2 tablespoons butter,
  melted
2 tablespoons grated
  Parmesan cheese
1/4 teaspoon salt
1/8 teaspoon pepper

1/2 teaspoon rosemary,
  crushed
1/2 cup (2 ounces)
  shredded Cheddar
  cheese
1/4 cup real bacon bits
1 green onion, chopped

Cut each potato crosswise into thin slices, cutting to but not through the bottom of the potato. Place the potato fans on a microwave-safe plate and drizzle the potatoes with the butter. Combine the Parmesan cheese, salt, pepper and rosemary in a small bowl. Sprinkle the Parmesan cheese mixture in between each slice and on top of each potato. Microwave, uncovered, on High for 12 to 18 minutes or until tender. Top the potatoes with the Cheddar cheese, bacon and green onions. Microwave for 1 to 2 minutes or until the cheese has melted. Yield: 4 servings.

Mildred Sharp, Kappa Master
McClave, Colorado

SPINACH AND ARTICHOKE CASSEROLE

2 (10-ounce) packages
  frozen chopped
  spinach, thawed and
  drained
1 (14-ounce) can
  artichoke hearts,
  drained and chopped
1/2 cup heavy cream
1/3 cup grated Parmesan
  cheese

1/2 teaspoon salt
1/8 teaspoon coarsely
  ground pepper
8 ounces cream cheese,
  softened
1 cup milk
1/3 cup grated Parmesan
  cheese for the topping

Combine the first 6 ingredients in a mixing bowl. Beat the cream cheese until fluffy in a separate mixing bowl. Add the milk gradually, mixing well. Pour the spinach mixture into a well greased 8×8-inch glass baking dish. Spread the cream cheese mixture over the top. Sprinkle with the remaining cheese. Bake at 350 degrees for 25 to 30 minutes or until golden brown. Yield: 8 servings.

Judy Knight, Epsilon-Alpha
Mesquite, Texas

SPINACH CASSEROLE

2 (10-ounce) packages
 frozen chopped
 spinach, cooked and
 drained
1 cup bread crumbs

1/2 envelope onion
 soup mix
1/4 cup grated Parmesan
 cheese
2 cups sour cream

Combine the spinach, bread crumbs, soup mix, Parmesan cheese and sour cream in a large bowl and mix well. Pour into an 8×8-inch glass baking dish. Bake at 350 degrees for 30 minutes. Yield: 6 servings.

Margaret Wilson, Xi Alpha Eta
Grass Valley, California

AUTUMN BUTTERNUT SQUASH AND APPLE CASSEROLE

3 cups mashed cooked
 butternut squash
1/4 teaspoon salt
Dash white pepper
1/4 cup (1/2 stick) butter
 or margarine
6 cups sliced peeled
 apples
1/4 cup granulated sugar

1 tablespoon brown
 sugar
1/2 cup crushed corn
 flakes
1/2 cup chopped pecans
1/2 cup packed brown
 sugar
2 tablespoons butter,
 melted

Season the butternut squash with the salt and pepper and set aside. Melt 1/4 cup butter in a skillet over medium heat. Add the apples, granulated sugar and 1 tablespoon brown sugar and sauté until tender. Arrange the apples in a single layer in a greased 2-quart baking dish. Spread the squash over the apples. Combine the corn flakes, pecans, 1/2 cup brown sugar and 2 tablespoons melted butter in a small bowl and mix well. Sprinkle the corn flake topping evenly over the squash. Bake at 350 degrees for 30 minutes. Yield: 10 servings.

Marlin Stork, Alpha Master
Springfield, Massachusetts

YELLOW SQUASH CASSEROLE

6 cups sliced yellow
 squash
1/4 cup chopped onion
1 cup sour cream
1 (10-ounce) can cream
 of chicken soup
2 cups herb-seasoned
 stuffing mix

1/2 cup (1 stick)
 margarine
2 cups (8 ounces)
 shredded Cheddar
 cheese

Cook the squash in water to cover in a saucepan just until tender; drain. Combine the squash, onion, sour cream and soup in a large bowl and mix well.

Combine the stuffing mix and margarine in a small bowl; stir until the stuffing mix is well coated. Fold the stuffing mix into the squash mixture. Spoon the mixture into a greased 2-quart baking dish. Sprinkle the top with cheese. Bake at 350 degrees for 30 minutes. Yield: 12 servings.

Susan Hayden, Preceptor Beta Phi
Centennial, Colorado

MEXICAN SQUASH AND CORN (CALABACITA)

3 zucchini squash, cut
 into cubes
1 (15-ounce) can whole-
 kernel corn
2 jalapeño peppers,
 chopped
1 onion, sliced
1 (15-ounce) can cream-
 style corn

1/2 cup (1 stick) butter,
 melted
1 teaspoon garlic salt
2 tablespoons sugar
1/2 teaspoon salt
1/4 teaspoon pepper
1 cup (4 ounces)
 shredded Cheddar
 cheese

Cook the zucchini, whole-kernel corn, jalapeño peppers, and onion in water to cover in a large saucepan until the zucchini is tender; drain. Heat the cream-style corn, butter, garlic salt, sugar, salt and pepper in a separate saucepan over medium heat, stirring constantly. Remove from the heat and add the zucchini mixture; stir until well combined. Pour into a greased 9×13-inch baking dish. Sprinkle the top with the cheese. Bake at 350 degrees for 25 minutes. Yield: 12 servings.

Jan McCrary, Xi Nu Nu
Littlefield, Texas

SUMMER SQUASH CASSEROLE

1/4 cup (1/2 stick) butter
3 yellow squash, cut
 into 1/2-inch slices
1 onion, chopped
1 (10-ounce) can cream
 of mushroom soup

1 (4-ounce) can chopped
 green chiles
1 cup (4 ounces)
 shredded cheese
1 cup cracker crumbs

Melt the butter in a skillet over medium-high heat. Add the squash and onion; sauté just until tender. Mix the soup, chiles and squash mixture in a large bowl; stir until well combined. Pour into a greased 9×13-inch baking pan. Sprinkle the top with the cheese and cracker crumbs. Bake at 350 degrees for 30 minutes. Yield: 8 servings.

Brenda Funk, Xi Delta Tau
Dove Creek, Colorado

SWEET POTATO BALLS

These sweet potato balls are such a holiday tradition that we once got them past airport security when traveling to a holiday family gathering. We got kidded a lot about our little sweet potato "bombs".

6 sweet potatoes,
   cooked and mashed
1/2 cup (1 stick)
   margarine, melted
1 cup packed brown
   sugar

1 cup pecans or walnuts,
   chopped
12 large marshmallows
2 cups crushed corn
   flakes

Combine the sweet potatoes, margarine, brown sugar and pecans in a large bowl and mix well. Form a ball around 1 marshmallow with about 3 tablespoons of the sweet potato mixture. Repeat the process until all the marshmallows are used. Roll the balls in the corn flakes to coat well. Place the balls 1/2 inch apart in a well greased 9×13-inch baking pan. Bake at 350 degrees for 15 minutes. Yield: 12 servings.

Della Biddiscombe, Theta Master
Lewiston, Idaho

ROASTED SWEET POTATOES AND ONIONS

3 tablespoons olive oil
1/4 cup amaretto
1 teaspoon thyme
Salt and pepper to taste
2 large peeled sweet
   potatoes, peeled and
   cut into 1-inch cubes

2 Vidalia onions,
   cut into 1-inch cubes
1/4 cup sliced almonds,
   toasted

Combine the olive oil, liqueur, thyme, salt and pepper in a large bowl and mix well. Toss the potatoes and onions in the olive oil mixture until well coated. Place the potato mixture in a 9×13-inch baking pan. Bake, covered, at 425 degrees for 30 minutes. Remove the cover and bake for 20 minutes. Sprinkle with the almonds and serve. Yield: 8 to 10 servings.

Gladys Weems, Laureate Eta Iota
Highland, California

SWEET POTATO AND APPLE CASSEROLE

3 cups sliced cooked
   sweet potatoes
2 cups thinly sliced
   peeled tart apples
1 cup packed brown
   sugar

1 tablespoon orange zest
1/2 teaspoon cinnamon
Salt and pepper to taste
1/4 cup (1/2 stick)
   margarine

Layer the sweet potatoes and apples alternately in a greased 1 1/2-quart baking dish, sprinkling each layer with the brown sugar, orange zest, cinnamon, salt and pepper. Dot the top with the margarine. Bake at 350 degrees for 1 hour. Yield: 8 servings.

Barbara Lesley, Xi Tau
Northport, Alabama

SWEET POTATO SOUFFLÉ

3 cups mashed cooked
   sweet potatoes
1 cup granulaed sugar
1/2 teaspoon salt
1 egg, beaten
1/2 cup milk
1/2 teaspoon vanilla
   extract

1 cup packed brown
   sugar
1/3 cup flour
1 cup chopped pecans
3 tablespoons butter,
   melted

Combine the sweet potatoes, sugar, salt, egg, milk and vanilla extract in a large bowl and mix well; set aside. Combine the brown sugar, flour, pecans and butter in a small bowl and mix well. Spread the sweet potato mixture into a greased 9×9-inch baking dish. Sprinkle the top with the brown sugar mixture. Bake at 350 degrees for 35 minutes. Yield: 8 to 10 servings.

Carol Urquhart, Eta Omicron
Kingman, Arizona

TOMATO CASSEROLE

1 pound bacon, chopped
1 tablespoon butter,
   melted
1/2 teaspoon seasoned
   salt
1/4 teaspoon garlic salt
2 teaspoons sugar
1/2 cup Pepperidge Farm
   Dressing Mix

5 tomatoes, thickly
   sliced
1 cup thinly sliced
   onions
1 cup (4 ounces)
   shredded Cheddar
   cheese
1/4 teaspoon oregano

Fry the bacon in a skillet over medium-high heat until crisp. Drain the bacon, reserving 1 tablespoon of the drippings. Combine the butter, bacon drippings, seasoned salt, garlic salt and sugar in a bowl and mix well. Alternate layers of dressing mix, tomatoes, onions, butter mixture, cheese and bacon in a greased 2-quart baking dish until all of the ingredients are used. Sprinkle the top with the oregano and additional dressing. Bake at 350 degrees for 30 minutes. Yield: 8 servings.

Barbara King, Xi Delta Sigma
Brunswick, Georgia

TOMATOES ROCKEFELLER

1 (10-ounce) package frozen spinach, cooked and drained	1/2 cup grated Parmesan cheese
1 cup fresh bread crumbs	1 teaspoon thyme
1 green onion, chopped	3/4 teaspoon salt
6 eggs, beaten	1/2 teaspoon minced garlic
3/4 cup (1 1/2 sticks) butter, melted	12 thick tomato slices

Combine the spinach, bread crumbs, onion, eggs, butter and cheese in a large bowl and mix well. Add the thyme, salt and garlic, stirring to combine. Layer the tomato slices in a greased 9×13-inch baking pan. Spread the spinach mixture over the tomatoes. Bake at 350 degrees for 30 minutes. Yield: 12 servings.

Jeanette Haynes, Xi Alpha Nu
Eureka Springs, Arizona

APPLE TURNIP CASSEROLE

1 1/2 cups peeled and sliced apples	1/3 cup packed brown sugar
1/4 cup packed brown sugar	1/3 cup flour
1 large turnip, cooked and mashed	2 tablespoons butter, softened
1/8 teaspoon cinnamon	1/2 teaspoon salt

Combine the apples, brown sugar, turnip and cinnamon in a bowl and mix well. Combine the remaining ingredients in a small bowl, stirring until crumbly. Spread the apple mixture into a greased 2-quart baking dish. Sprinkle the butter mixture over the top. Bake at 350 degrees for 1 hour. Yield: 8 servings.

Mary Lou Rutter, Laureate Epsilon
Brantford, Ontario, Canada

CHEESE-STUFFED ZUCCHINI

4 large zucchini	1 tablespoon chopped parsley
6 ounces mozzarella cheese, chopped	1 garlic clove, minced
1 teaspoon grated Parmesan cheese or Romano cheese	Pinch of nutmeg
	Salt and pepper to taste
1/4 pound fresh mushrooms, sliced and cooked	Seasoned bread crumbs for topping
	2 tablespoons olive oil

Cut off the stem ends of the zucchini. Cut the zucchini lengthwise into halves. Scoop out the pulp, leaving 1/4-inch shells. Chop the pulp and place in a medium bowl. Add the next 7 ingredients; stir until well combined. Spoon the pulp mixture into each shell. Place the zucchini in a greased 9×13-inch baking pan. Sprinkle the tops with the bread crumbs.

Drizzle with the olive oil. Bake, covered, at 350 degrees for 30 minutes. Uncover and bake for 15 minutes or until browned. Yield: 8 servings.

Carole Pipetti, Laureate Zeta Theta
Altoona, Pennsylvania

ZUCCHINI CASSEROLE

3 cups thinly sliced zucchini	1/4 cup oil
	1/2 cup chopped onion
1 1/2 cups (6 ounces) shredded sharp Cheddar cheese	1/2 cup (2 ounces) shredded sharp Cheddar cheese for the topping
1/2 cup baking mix	
2 eggs, beaten	

Combine the zucchini, 1 1/2 cups cheese, baking mix, eggs, oil, and onion in a bowl and mix well. Pour the zucchini mixture into a greased 9×13-inch baking dish. Sprinkle with the remaining 1/2 cup cheese. Bake at 375 degrees for 30 minutes. Yield: 6 to 8 servings.

Cheryl Reynolds, Preceptor Alpha Kappa
Fort Collins, Colorado

ZUCCHINI AND YELLOW SQUASH CASSEROLE

4 zucchini, sliced	1/2 teaspoon garlic powder
3 yellow squash, sliced	
1/2 onion, chopped	1 (8-ounce) package Italian shredded cheese
1 (14-ounce) can Italian stewed tomatoes	
1 teaspoon pepper	

Sauté the zucchini, yellow squash and onion in a nonstick skillet over medium–high heat until light brown. Add the tomatoes, pepper and garlic powder. Simmer, covered, over low heat for 30 minutes. Sprinkle with the cheese; cover and cook until the cheese melts. Yield: 6 to 8 servings.

June Badgett, Zeta Pi
Burleson, Texas

MIXED VEGETABLE CASSEROLE

1 cup chopped onion	1 (8-ounce) can water chestnuts, drained and chopped
1 cup chopped celery	
3 tablespoons butter	
1 cup mayonnaise	1 cup (4 ounces) shredded sharp Cheddar cheese
1/2 cup milk	
2 (10-ounce) packages frozen mixed vegetables, thawed and drained	1 cup cracker crumbs
	1/4 cup (1/2 stick) butter, melted

Sauté the onion and celery in the butter in a skillet over medium heat until tender. Combine the mayonnaise and milk in a large bowl and mix well. Add the vegetables, onion, celery, water chestnuts and cheese, stirring to combine. Mix the crackers and butter in a small bowl until well combined. Spoon the vegetable mixture into a greased 8×10-inch baking dish. Sprinkle the cracker mixture evenly over the top. Bake at 350 degrees for 25 minutes. You may substitute fresh vegetables, steamed tender-crisp, for the frozen vegetables. Yield: 8 servings.

Mary Broughton, Chi Master
Fort Myers, Florida

FRIED APPLES

1/4 cup (1/2 stick) butter	1/2 teaspoon cinnamon
6 Granny Smith apples, quartered	1/4 teaspoon nutmeg
2 McIntosh apples, quartered	2 tablespoons brown sugar
	1 cup water

Melt the butter in a large frying pan over medium-high heat. Fry the apples until lightly browned. Stir in the cinnamon, nutmeg, brown sugar and water. Cook, covered, over low heat until tender. Yield: 6 servings.

Patricia Rose Soard, Theta Psi
Cookeville, Tennessee

PINEAPPLE CASSEROLE

2 (15-ounce) cans pineapple chunks	5 tablespoons flour
2 cups shredded sharp Cheddar cheese	1 cup crushed butter crackers
3/4 cups sugar	1/2 cup (1 stick) butter, melted

Drain the pineapple, reserving 3/4 cup pineapple juice. Combine the pineapple and the cheese in a medium bowl. Combine the sugar and flour in a bowl and mix well. Stir in the pineapple juice until blended. Add the pineapple mixture and stir until combined. Spoon the pineapple mixture into a greased 2-quart baking dish. Sprinkle with the cracker crumbs and drizzle with the butter. Bake at 350 degrees for 30 minutes. Yield: 6 to 8 servings.

Elaine Karsner, Laureate Alpha Beta
Cleveland, Georgia

SQUASH DRESSING

2 cups sliced yellow squash, cooked	1 (10-ounce) can cream of chicken soup
2 cups crumbled corn bread	1/4 cup (1/2 stick) melted margarine
1 onion, chopped	Salt and pepper to taste

Combine the squash, corn bread, onion and soup in a large bowl and mix well. Add the margarine, salt and pepper. Spread the squash mixture into a greased 2-quart baking dish. Bake at 350 degrees for 30 minutes. Yield: 8 to 10 servings.

Janis Halstead, Xi Delta Iota
Tucson, Arizona

SLOW-COOKER DRESSING

1 (8-inch) pan baked corn bread	1 teaspoon pepper
8 slices day-old bread	4 eggs, beaten
1 onion, chopped	2 (14-ounce) cans chicken broth
1 cup chopped celery	2 (10-ounce) cans cream of chicken soup
2 tablespoons sage or poultry seasoning	2 tablespoons margarine
1 teaspoon salt	

Crumble the breads and place in a large mixing bowl. Add the onion, celery, sage, salt and pepper, tossing to combine. Combine the eggs, chicken broth and soup in a medium-size bowl and mix well. Pour the egg mixture into the bread crumbs mixture and stir until well combined. Place into a slow cooker. Dot the top with the margarine. Cook, covered, on High for 2 hours or on Low for 4 hours. Yield: 16 servings.

Melba June Cochran, Laureate Phi
Walnut Ridge, Arizona

YORKSHIRE PUDDING

Serve this with roast beef and gravy. It is my son's favorite birthday dinner forever!

3/4 cup plus 2 tablespoons flour	2 eggs, beaten, at room temperature
1/2 teaspoon salt	1/2 cup water
1/2 cup milk, at room temprature	1/2 cup (1 stick) butter

Sift the flour and salt into a large mixing bowl; set aside. Combine the milk, eggs and water in a small bowl and mix well. Pour the liquid ingredients into the flour mixture. Beat until bubbles appear on the surface. Melt the butter in a 9-inch cast-iron skillet over medium-high heat. Remove the pan from the heat. Pour the batter into the hot pan. Bake at 400 degrees for 20 minutes. Reduce the oven temperature to 350 degrees. Bake for 20 minutes longer or until light brown. Serve immediately. Yield: 6 servings.

Barbara M. Ziegler
Greenville, South Carolina

LUAU RICE

Our chapter has served this at every Luau for the past thirty years. We can't celebrate without it!

1/4 cup (1/2 stick) butter
1/2 cup chopped onion
1 cup chopped celery
1/2 cup chopped green
  bell pepper
1/2 cup chopped
  mushrooms
1 (10-ounce) can cream
  of mushroom soup

1 cup milk
1/2 cup long grain rice
1/2 cup slivered almonds
1/2 teaspoon salt
1/8 teaspoon pepper
1/4 cup chopped parsley

Melt the butter in a skillet over medium-high heat. Sauté the onion, celery, bell pepper and mushrooms until tender, stirring frequently. Stir in the soup, milk, rice, almonds, salt and pepper. Pour into a well-greased 9×13-inch baking pan. Bake, covered, at 350 degrees for 50 minutes. Uncover and sprinkle with parsley. Bake for 10 minutes longer.
Yield: 6 servings.

Kathleen Lewis, Xi Omicron Rho
Willits, California

PINE NUT PILAF

2 tablespoons butter
1/2 cup sliced green
  onions
1 cup long grain rice
1/2 cup pine nuts,
  toasted

1 teaspoon grated lemon
  zest
2 1/2 cups chicken broth
1/4 teaspoon salt
1/4 cup sliced green
  onion tops

Melt the butter in a 3-quart saucepan over medium-high heat. Add the green onions and sauté just until tender. Add the rice, nuts and lemon zest; stir until all the ingredients are well coated with the butter. Stir in the broth and salt. Bring to a boil. Reduce the heat to medium. Simmer, covered, for 14 minutes. Remove from the heat and fluff the rice with a fork. Cover and let stand for 10 minutes. Sprinkle the rice with the green onion tops. Yield: 6 to 8 servings.

Jennifer Cormack, Xi Beta, Phi
Massena, Iowa

RICE PILAF WITH RAISINS

1/4 cup (1/2 stick)
  margarine
1 cup chopped onion
1 garlic clove, minced
1 cup long grain rice
2 cups chicken broth

2 tablespoons chopped
  parsley
1 cup raisins
1/2 teaspoon salt
1/4 teaspoon pepper
1/4 cup pine nuts, toasted

Melt the margarine in a skillet over medium heat. Add the onion and garlic and cook until light brown.

Combine the rice, broth, parsley, raisins, salt and pepper in a mixing bowl. Add the onion and garlic, stirring until well combined. Pour the rice mixture into a 2-quart baking dish. Bake, covered, at 350 degrees for 30 minutes or until the liquid is absorbed. Fluff the rice with a fork. Stir in the pine nuts.
Yield: 8 to 10 servings.

Roslyn Bond, Beta Nu Master
Burlington, Ontario, Canada

RICE AND ZUCCHINI A LA GRECQUE (GREEK STYLE)

1/4 cup olive oil
3 cups chopped onions
1/2 teaspoon thyme
1 bay leaf
1 1/2 pounds zucchini,
  cut into 1/2-inch cubes

1 cup rice
1 cup chicken broth
Salt and pepper to taste

Heat the olive oil in a medium saucepan. Add the onions, thyme and bay leaf. Cook until the onions are tender. Add the zucchini, rice, chicken broth, salt and pepper. Stir until well combined. Bring the mixture to a boil and cook for 30 seconds longer. Pour the rice mixture into a 9×13-inch baking dish. Bake, covered, at 400 degrees for 20 minutes. Remove the bay leaf and serve. Yield: 6 to 8 servings.

Dolores Black, Master Alpha Delta
Bowling Green Ohio

AUTUMN WILD RICE CASSEROLE

3 tablespoons margarine
1 pound fresh
  mushrooms, sliced
3 tablespoons chopped
  green onions
2 (6-ounce) packages
  quick cooking long
  grain rice mix

2 1/2 cups chicken broth
2 cups cream
1 cup dried cherries
3/4 cup chopped pecans
1/2 teaspoon salt
1/4 cup chopped pecans
  for topping

Melt the margarine in a medium saucepan over low heat. Add the mushrooms and green onions and cook for 5 minutes. Stir in the rice, seasoning packets, broth and cream. Add the cherries, 3/4 cup pecans and salt, stirring until well combined. Pour the rice mixture into a 3-quart baking dish. Bake, covered, for 50 minutes at 350 degrees. Remove the cover and sprinkle with the remaining 1/4 cup pecans. Bake for 15 minutes. Let stand for 10 minutes before serving.
Yield: 10 to 12 servings.

Gwen Bogardus, Alpha Master
Council Bluffs, Iowa

Brunch

BACON AND EGG CASSEROLE

1 pound bacon
1/4 cup (1/2 stick) butter
1/4 cup all-purpose flour
1 cup heavy cream
1 cup milk
16 ounces sharp
    Cheddar cheese,
    shredded
1/4 teaspoon thyme
1/4 teaspoon marjoram
1/4 teaspoon basil
18 hard-cooked eggs,
    thinly sliced
1/4 cup chopped
    parsley
Buttered bread crumbs

Cook the bacon in a large skillet until crisp. Remove to paper towels to drain; crumble. Melt the butter in a saucepan. Stir in the flour until smooth. Stir in the cream and milk. Cook until slightly thickened, stirring constantly. Add the cheese, thyme, marjoram and basil. Cook until the cheese melts, stirring frequently. Alternate layers of the bacon, eggs and parsley in a buttered 9×13-inch baking dish. Pour the cheese sauce evenly over the top. Sprinkle with buttered bread crumbs. Bake at 350 degrees for 45 minutes. You may use crushed cornflakes instead of buttered bread crumbs. Yield: 10 to 12 servings.

Synda Prisbrey, Alpha Delta Omicron
Bonne Terre, Missouri

SWISS OVEN OMELET

6 slices bacon
1/2 cup finely chopped
    onion
8 eggs
1 cup milk
1/2 teaspoon salt
1/4 teaspoon pepper
2 tablespoons chopped
    parsley
2 cups (8 ounces)
    shredded
    Swiss cheese

Cook the bacon in a skillet until crisp. Remove to paper towels to drain. Remove all but 1 tablespoon of bacon drippings from the skillet. Add the onion and sauté until tender. Beat the eggs in a large bowl. Beat in the milk, salt and pepper. Stir in the onion and parsley. Pour into a greased 1½-quart baking dish. Top with the cooked bacon slices and the cheese. Bake at 350 degrees for 40 minutes. Let stand for 5 minutes before serving. Yield: 4 servings.

Barbara M. Brock, Preceptor Alpha Pi
Tracy City, Tennessee

CANADIAN BACON BAKE

1/2 cup (1 stick) butter
1/4 cup all-purpose flour
1/2 teaspoon salt
1/8 teaspoon pepper
2 cups milk
1 cup sour cream
2 tablespoons chopped
    parsley
2 ounces sharp Cheddar
    cheese, shredded
8 ounces frozen hash
    brown potatoes,
    thawed
8 eggs, beaten
1 pound sliced Canadian
    bacon

Melt the butter in a 3-quart saucepan. Stir in the flour, salt and pepper until smooth. Stir in the milk. Cook until thickened, stirring constantly. Remove from the heat. Stir in the sour cream, parsley, cheese, potatoes and eggs. Pour into a 9×13-inch baking dish. Top with the Canadian bacon, overlapping the slices. Bake at 350 degrees for 40 minutes. Yield: 8 to 16 servings

Judy Ann Evans, Alpha Beta Master
Fairmont, West Virginia

EASTER BREAKFAST CASSEROLE

8 slices bread	6 eggs, beaten
Butter	3 cups milk
3 cups chopped ham	3/4 teaspoon salt
3 cups (12 ounces)	3/4 teaspoon dry mustard
shredded American	Crushed potato chips
cheese	

Toast the bread and spread with butter. Cut into cubes. Arrange in a buttered 9×13-inch baking pan. Sprinkle with the ham and top with the cheese. Mix the eggs, milk, salt and dry mustard in a bowl. Pour over the cheese. Cover and chill overnight. Sprinkle with the crushed potato chips. Bake at 350 degrees for 1 hour. Let cool for 10 minutes before serving. Yield: 10 servings.

Fran Wicks, Psi Master
Ann Arbor, Michigan

HAM AND EGG CASSEROLE

10 eggs	1 1/2 cups cubed ham
2 cups milk	8 slices bread, cubed
1/2 teaspoon dry mustard	Chopped green bell
1/2 teaspoon salt	pepper
1 cup (4 ounces)	1/2 cup (1 stick)
shredded Cheddar	margarine, melted
cheese	

Beat the eggs in a large bowl. Beat in the milk, dry mustard and salt. Stir in the cheese, ham, bread and bell pepper. Pour into a greased 9×13-inch baking pan. Drizzle the melted margarine over the top. Cover and chill overnight. Bake, uncovered, at 350 degrees for 1 hour. Yield: 10 to 12 servings.

Meleah Sohlers
Council Bluffs, Iowa

HAM AND CHEESE STRATA

1 loaf Texas Toast bread	1/4 cup chopped parsley
Dijon mustard	3 eggs
Softened butter	1 1/2 cups milk
8 slices Black Forest	1/2 cup sour cream
ham, chopped	1/2 teaspoon salt
1 cup (4 ounces) shredded	Dash of Tabasco
Cheddar cheese	sauce

Slice and remove the crusts from the bread. Spread 1 side of each slice with Dijon mustard and spread butter on the other side. Arrange 1/2 the bread slices, buttered side down, in a 9×13-inch baking pan. Sprinkle with 1/2 of the ham, 1/2 of the cheese and 1/2 of the parsley. Top with the remaining bread slices, buttered side up. Sprinkle with the remaining ham, cheese and parsley. Beat the eggs, milk, sour cream, salt and Tabasco in a bowl. Pour evenly over the bread. Dot with butter and cover with foil. Chill overnight. Bake, covered, at 350 degrees for 30 minutes. Uncover and bake for 10 minutes longer. Let stand for 5 minutes before serving.
Yield: 10 to 12 servings.

Pat Flynn, Xi Epsilon Phi
Ancaster, Ontario, Canada

HAM AND MUSHROOM BREAKFAST CASSEROLE

2 to 3 cups cubed	2 cups shredded Cheddar
ham	cheese
8 hard-cooked eggs,	2 teaspoons
sliced	Worcestershire sauce
1 large can mushrooms,	1/2 teaspoon Tabasco
drained	sauce
1 (10 3/4-ounce) can	Garlic salt to taste
condensed cream of	Pepper to taste
celery soup	2 cups seasoned croutons
1 cup sour cream with	3/4 cup (1 1/2 sticks)
chives	butter, melted

Sprinkle the ham in a nonstick 9×13-inch baking pan. Top with the eggs and sprinkle with the mushrooms. Mix the next 5 ingredients in a bowl. Pour over the mushrooms. Season with garlic salt and pepper. Sprinkle with the croutons. Drizzle with the butter. Bake at 350 degrees for 45 to 60 minutes. Let stand for 10 minutes before serving. Yield: 12 servings.

Kathy Jaske Gardner, Omicron Tau
Ottumwa, Iowa

CHEESE AND SAUSAGE CASSEROLE

8 ounces bulk sweet	8 egg yolks
Italian sausage	2/3 cup evaporated milk
2 cups shredded	2 tablespoons
Monterey Jack cheese	all-purpose flour
2 cups shredded Cheddar	1 teaspoon salt
cheese	1/2 teaspoon pepper
1 (10-ounce) can	8 egg whites
tomatoes with green	Sliced tomatoes
chiles	

Brown the sausage in a skillet, stirring until crumbly; drain. Mix the cooked sausage and the next 3 ingredients in a large bowl. Beat the egg yolks, evaporated milk, flour, salt and pepper in a bowl. Stir into the cheese mixture. Beat the egg whites in a bowl until stiff peaks form. Fold into the cheese mixture. Pour into a 9×13-inch baking dish coated with nonstick cooking spray. Bake at 350 degrees for 35 to 40 minutes. Top with sliced tomatoes. Bake for 20 to 25 minutes longer or until a knife inserted in the center comes out clean. Let cool for 10 to 15 minutes. Cut into squares and serve with fresh fruit and rolls.

This casserole may be prepared ahead. Cover and chill. Bake before serving. Yield: 8 to 10 servings.

Patricia E. Beers
The Villages, Florida

CHRISTMAS MORNING SAUSAGE CASSEROLE

1 pound bulk pork sausage	*4 eggs*
	2 cups milk
2 cups (8 ounces) shredded sharp Cheddar cheese	*1/2 teaspoon salt*
	1 teaspoon dry mustard (optional)
8 slices white bread	*Pepper to taste*

Brown the sausage in a skillet, stirring until crumbly; drain. Remove to a bowl and mix with the cheese. Fit the bread in the bottom of a greased 8×12-inch baking dish. Sprinkle with the sausage mixture. Beat the eggs, milk, salt and dry mustard in a bowl. Season with pepper. Pour over the sausage mixture. Cover and chill overnight. Bake, uncovered, at 350 degrees for 30 to 35 minutes. Yield: 8 to 10 servings.

Kandie Andrews, Beta Delta
Elberton, Georgia

BREAKFAST CASSEROLE

8 slices white bread	*Salt and pepper to taste*
12 ounces ground beef	*2 cups (8 ounces) shredded Cheddar cheese*
12 ounces bulk pork sausage	
8 eggs, beaten	*1 (10³/4-ounce) can condensed cream of mushroom soup*
1¹/2 cups milk	
3/4 tablespoon dry mustard	*3/4 cup evaporated milk*

Arrange the bread in a buttered nonstick 9×12-inch baking pan. Brown the ground beef and sausage in a skillet, stirring until crumbly; drain. Sprinkle over the bread. Mix the eggs, milk and dry mustard in a bowl. Season with salt and pepper. Pour over the meat mixture. Sprinkle with the cheese. Cover and chill overnight. Mix the soup and evaporated milk in a bowl. Pour over the layers. Bake, uncovered, at 300 degrees for 1¹/2 to 2 hours. Yield: 8 to 10 servings.

Elizabeth Burton, Beta Mu
Good Hope, Illinois

BREAKFAST BEFORE CASSEROLE

1 pound bulk pork sausage	*1 teaspoon dry mustard (optional)*
6 eggs	*2 slices firm white bread*
2 cups milk	*1 cup (4 ounces) shredded cheese*
1 teaspoon salt	

Brown the sausage in a skillet, stirring until crumbly; drain. Spread the sausage in a 9×13-inch baking dish. Beat the eggs, milk, salt and dry mustard in a bowl. Pour over the sausage. Toast the bread and cut into cubes. Sprinkle the bread over the egg mixture. Top with the cheese. Cover and chill overnight. Bake, uncovered, at 350 degrees for 45 minutes. You may use half-and-half instead of milk. Do not use skim milk. Yield: 6 to 8 servings.

Pauletta Myers, Delta Kappa Master
Corpus Christi, Texas

LINKS AND EGGS CASSEROLE

20 sausage links	*2 cups milk*
8 slices white bread	*1 tablespoon chopped onion*
6 eggs	
1 (10³/4-ounce) can condensed cream of mushroom soup	*12 ounces sharp Cheddar cheese, shredded*

Brown the sausage in a skillet. Remove to paper towels to drain. Tear the bread into bite-size pieces. Beat the eggs and soup in a bowl. Stir in the milk, onion, cheese and bread. Pour into a greased 9×13-inch baking dish. Arrange the sausage on top. Cover and chill overnight. Bake, covered, at 325 degrees for 1 hour. Serve hot. You may add 1 can chopped green chiles to the egg mixture, if desired. Yield: 6 to 8 servings.

Susan LaBarge, Beta Psi
Albuquerque, New Mexico

SAUSAGE AND EGG CASSEROLE

1 pound bulk pork sausage	*2¹/4 cups milk*
8 slices white bread, cubed	*1 (10³/4-ounce) can condensed cream of mushroom soup*
2 cups (8 ounces) shredded extra-sharp Cheddar cheese	*1 (4-ounce) can mushroom pieces, drained*
4 eggs	*1/4 cup milk*
3/4 teaspoon dry mustard	

Brown the sausage in a skillet, stirring until crumbly; drain. Spread the sausage in a 8×12-inch baking dish. Top with the bread and sprinkle with the cheese. Beat the eggs, dry mustard and 2¹/4 cups milk in a bowl. Mix the soup, mushroom pieces and ¹/4 cup milk in a bowl. Add to the egg mixture and stir to mix well. Pour over the cheese layer. Cover and chill overnight or up to 24 hours. Bake, uncovered, at 325 degrees for 1 hour. Yield: 8 to 10 servings.

Theresa "Melinda" Lysinger, Alpha Delta Phi
Lowry City, Missouri

SOUTH-OF-THE-BORDER BREAKFAST ENCHILADAS

1 cup sour cream	6 eggs, lightly beaten
1 (10³/4-ounce) can condensed cream of mushroom soup	1/4 cup cottage cheese
	1 tablespoon chopped parsley
1 (4-ounce) can chopped green chiles	1/4 cup finely chopped green onions
1 cup chunky salsa	12 (8-inch) flour tortillas
1/4 teaspoon cumin	
1/4 teaspoon coriander	1 cup (4 ounces) shredded mild Cheddar cheese
1 pound hot bulk pork sausage	
2 tablespoons butter	1 cup (4 ounces) shredded Monterey Jack cheese

Whisk the sour cream, soup, green chiles, salsa, cumin and coriander in a bowl. Brown the sausage in a large skillet, stirring until crumbly; drain on paper towels. Wipe out the skillet with a paper towel. Melt the butter in the skillet. Stir in the eggs and cottage cheese. Stir in the parsley and green onions. Cook until lightly set. Stir in 2 tablespoons of the sour cream mixture and the sausage. Remove from the heat. Spread the egg mixture on the tortillas and roll up. Spread a small amount of the sour cream mixture in the bottom of a buttered 9×13-inch baking pan. Top with the rolled tortillas in a single layer. Cover with the remaining sour cream mixture. Sprinkle with the Cheddar cheese and Monterey Jack cheese. Bake at 325 degrees for 30 to 45 minutes. Yield: 6 servings.

Sheryl Helm, Xi Lambda Tau
Urich, Missouri

SOUTHWEST SAUSAGE BAKE

1 pound bulk pork sausage	10 eggs
	1/2 cup milk
6 (10-inch) flour tortillas	1/2 teaspoon salt
	1/2 teaspoon garlic powder
4 (4-ounce) cans chopped green chiles, drained	1/2 teaspoon onion salt
	1/2 teaspoon pepper
	1/2 teaspoon cumin
2 cups (8 ounces) shredded Monterey Jack cheese	2 tomatoes, sliced
	Paprika

Brown the sausage in a skillet, stirring until crumbly; drain. Cut the tortillas into 1/2-inch strips. Spread 1/2 of the tortilla strips in a greased 9×13-inch baking pan. Sprinkle with 1/2 of the green chiles, 1/2 of the sausage and 1/2 of the cheese. Repeat the layers. Beat the eggs, milk, salt, garlic powder, onion salt, pepper and cumin in a bowl. Pour over the layers in the baking pan. Sprinkle with paprika. Cover and chill overnight. Let stand at room temperature for 30 min-

utes before baking. Bake, uncovered, at 350 degrees for 50 minutes. Arrange the tomato slices on top. Bake for 10 to 15 minutes longer or until a knife inserted in the center comes out clean. Let stand for 10 minutes. Serve with sour cream and salsa. Yield: 12 servings.

Bette Boggess, Alpha Chi Master
Chattaroy, Washington

CHILE CHEESE SOUFFLÉ

16 ounces shredded Monterey Jack cheese	1 cup evaporated milk
	1 tablespoon all-purpose flour
16 ounces shredded mild Cheddar cheese	1 teaspoon salt
	1/4 teaspoon pepper
1 (8-ounce) can chopped green chiles	4 egg whites
	Tomato slices
4 egg yolks	

Mix the Monterey Jack cheese, Cheddar cheese and green chiles in a bowl. Spread in a soufflé dish. Beat the egg yolks, evaporated milk, flour, salt and pepper in a bowl. Beat the egg whites in a bowl until soft peaks form. Fold in the egg yolk mixture. Pour over the cheese mixture. Press with a fork to submerge the cheese mixture into the egg mixture. Bake at 325 degrees for 30 minutes. Top with tomato slices. Bake for 30 minutes longer or until a knife inserted in the center comes out clean. Yield: 6 to 8 servings.

Kathy Wartinbee, Preceptor Pi
Soldotna, Alaska

❖ MUSHROOM-SPINACH SOUFFLÉ

1 (10-ounce) package frozen chopped spinach	1 cup cottage cheese
	1 cup sour cream
	8 eggs, well beaten
1/4 cup (1/2 stick) butter	1/4 teaspoon nutmeg
8 ounces fresh mushrooms, sliced	Salt and pepper to taste
	1 cup each shredded Monterey Jack and Cheddar cheese
1 small onion, finely chopped	

Thaw the spinach and squeeze dry. Melt the butter in a skillet. Add the mushrooms and onion and sauté until tender. Spread in a 9×13-inch baking dish. Combine the thawed spinach, cottage cheese, sour cream, eggs and nutmeg in a bowl. Season with salt and pepper. Stir to mix well. Pour over the mushroom mixture. Bake at 375 degrees for 40 to 50 minutes or until set. Sprinkle with the Monterey Jack and Cheddar cheeses. Bake until the cheese melts. This can be made 1 day ahead. Cover and chill until ready to bake. Yield: 8 to 10 servings.

Lucille Wanee, Alpha Iota Master
Chio, California

BREAKFAST TACOS

2 pounds chorizo,
  casings removed
1 (4-ounce) can chopped
  green chiles
1 onion, chopped
12 eggs, beaten

Taco shells
Shredded cheese
Sour cream
Picante sauce

Brown the sausage in a skillet, stirring until crumbly; drain. Add the green chiles and onion and sauté until the onion is tender. Stir in the eggs. Cook for 20 minutes, stirring occasionally. Warm the taco shells. Spoon the egg mixture into the taco shells and top with cheese, sour cream and picante sauce.
Yield: 6 servings.

Jeanne Mudge, Pi Omicron
Council Bluffs, Iowa

EGGS RANCHEROS

1/4 cup vegetable oil
2 tablespoons finely
  chopped onion
1 garlic clove, minced
4 green chiles, peeled
  and mashed

1 teaspoon oregano
1 (16-ounce) can tomato
  sauce
1/2 teaspoon salt
8 eggs

Heat the oil in a skillet. Add the onion and sauté until tender. Stir in the next 5 ingredients. Cook over low heat for 4 minutes. Poach the eggs in the tomato sauce mixture until cooked through. Serve with refried beans and warm tortillas.
Yield: 4 to 8 servings.

Christine Soard, Theta Psi
Cookeville, Tennessee

BRUNCH QUICHE CUPS

1 (16-ounce) package
  frozen chopped
  spinach
6 eggs
1/3 cup half-and-half
1/2 cup chopped red bell
  pepper
1 onion, chopped

1 garlic clove, minced
3/4 cup (3 ounces)
  shredded Swiss cheese
3/4 cup (3 ounces) grated
  Parmesan cheese
1 teaspoon kosher salt
1/2 teaspoon cayenne
  pepper

Thaw the spinach and squeeze dry. Combine the eggs and half-and-half in a large bowl. Beat until frothy. Stir in the remaining ingredients. Add the spinach and stir to mix well. Spoon into 12 muffin cups coated with nonstick cooking spray. Bake at 350 degrees for 20 minutes. Let cool in the pan for 5 minutes. Loosen the edges with a sharp knife and remove to a serving platter. Yield: 12 servings.

Karen Whitney, Gamma Tau
Bowie, Maryland

CRUSTLESS QUICHE

3 eggs
1/4 cup baking mix
11/2 cups milk
Salt and pepper to taste
1 cup chopped ham
1 cup sliced mushrooms

1 cup (4 ounces)
  shredded Cheddar
  cheese
1/2 cup chopped onion
Chopped green bell
  pepper

Combine the eggs, baking mix and milk in a blender. Season with salt and pepper. Process at low speed for 30 to 45 seconds or until well mixed. Remove to a bowl. Add the ham, mushrooms, cheese, onion and bell pepper. Stir to mix well. Pour into a greased 9-inch pie plate. Bake at 350 degrees for 40 minutes. Let stand for 10 minutes before cutting.
Yield: 6 to 8 servings.

Kimberly Alderman, Xi Beta Upsilon
Kingsport, Tennessee

BLISSFUL HAM AND GRITS PIE

1/3 cup quick-cooking
  grits
1 cup water
1 cup evaporated milk
3/4 cup (3 ounces)
  shredded Cheddar
  cheese
3/4 cup chopped lean ham

3 eggs, beaten
1 tablespoon chopped
  fresh parsley
1/2 teaspoon dry mustard
1/2 teaspoon hot red
  pepper sauce
1/4 teaspoon salt

Cook the grits in the water in a saucepan according to the package directions; do not add salt to the water. Remove the cooked grits to a bowl. Stir in the remaining ingredients. Spoon into a greased 9-inch pie plate. Bake at 350 degrees for 35 minutes. Let stand for 10 minutes before cutting. Yield: 6 to 8 servings.

Jan Hicky, Alpha Psi
Knoxville, Arkansas

NO-CRUST SPINACH QUICHE

1 (10-ounce) package
  frozen spinach
4 ounces sliced
  mushrooms
1 tablespoon finely
  chopped onion
16 ounces ricotta cheese

1 cup (4 ounces)
  shredded sharp
  Cheddar cheese
7 eggs, lightly beaten
1/4 teaspoon pepper
Dash of salt
Dash of nutmeg

Thaw the spinach and squeeze dry. Combine the spinach and the remaining ingredients in a bowl. Stir to mix well. Pour into a greased 10-inch deep-dish pie plate or 6×10-inch baking dish. Bake at 350 degrees for 1 hour. Yield: 10 to 12 servings.

Nancy Garrett, Eto Rho
Beaver Falls, Pennsylvania

ZUCCHINI CHEESE PIE

1/2 cup (2 ounces) shredded Cheddar cheese	1/2 cup vegetable oil
	1 tablespoon chopped parsley
3 cups shredded zucchini	4 eggs
1 cup baking mix	Salt and pepper to taste

Mix the cheese, zucchini, baking mix, oil and parsley in a bowl. Beat the eggs in a bowl. Season with salt and pepper. Add to the zucchini mixture and stir to mix well. Pour into a greased 9-inch pie plate. Bake at 375 degrees for 40 minutes. Cut into wedges and serve with salad and/or salsa. Yield: 6 to 8 servings

Marion Shand, Alpha Master
Medicine Hat, Alberta, Canada

EASY CHEESY YORKSHIRE PIE WITH ASPARAGUS

2 eggs	1 cup chopped asparagus, cooked
1 cup milk	
1/2 cup all-purpose flour	1/2 cup (2 ounces) shredded Cheddar cheese
1/2 teaspoon salt	
1/2 cup (2 ounces) shredded Cheddar cheese	

Beat the eggs and milk in a bowl. Add the flour and salt. Beat until smooth. Stir in 1/2 cup cheese. Pour into a greased pie plate. Top with the asparagus and sprinkle with 1/2 cup cheese. Bake at 425 degrees for 30 minutes. Yield: 4 servings.

Dani Mains, Preceptor Pi
Sterling, Alaska

HASH BROWN POTATO PIE

5 eggs	1/4 teaspoon hot red pepper sauce
1/2 cup milk	
3 cups frozen hash brown potatoes, thawed	1 cup (4 ounces) shredded sharp Cheddar cheese
	1/3 cup real bacon bits
1/3 cup thinly sliced green onions	1/2 cup (2 ounces) shredded Cheddar cheese
1/2 teaspoon salt	

Beat the eggs and milk in a bowl. Stir in the potatoes, green onions, salt, hot sauce, 1 cup cheese and 1/2 of the bacon bits. Pour into a greased 9-inch pie plate or quiche dish. Bake at 350 degrees for 25 to 30 minutes or until the center is set. Sprinkle with the remaining bacon bits and 1/2 cup cheese. Bake for 3 to 4 minutes longer or until the cheese melts. You may use 1 1/4 cups egg substitute instead of 5 eggs. Yield: 6 servings.

Twila Moots, Xi Beta Iota
Gallup, New Mexico

HASH BROWN QUICHE

3 cups loosely packed frozen shredded hash brown potatoes	1 cup diced ham
	1 cup (4 ounces) shredded cheese
5 1/3 tablespoons butter, melted	2 eggs
	1/2 cup milk
1 cup diced green bell pepper	1/2 teaspoon salt
	1/4 teaspoon pepper

Thaw the potatoes and press between paper towels to remove excess moisture. Press the potatoes over the bottom and up the side of a ungreased 9-inch pie plate. Drizzle with the butter. Bake at 425 degrees for 25 minutes. Remove to a wire rack. Mix the bell pepper, ham and cheese in a bowl. Spread over the potato crust. Beat the eggs, milk, salt and pepper in a bowl. Pour over the ham mixture. Bake at 350 degrees for 25 to 30 minutes or until a knife inserted in the center comes out clean. Let stand for 10 minutes before cutting. Yield: 6 servings.

Diana A. Burge, Preceptor Beta Chi
Niles, Michigan

BACON SWISS QUICHE

4 slices bacon	4 eggs, beaten
1 small onion, chopped	2 cups heavy cream
1 partially baked (9-inch) pie shell	1/2 teaspoon salt
	1/4 teaspoon white pepper
1 cup (4 ounces) cubed Swiss cheese	1/4 teaspoon nutmeg
1/4 cup (1 ounce) grated Parmesan cheese	

Cook the bacon in a skillet until crisp. Drain on paper towels; crumble. Reserve 1 tablespoon of bacon drippings in the skillet. Add the onion and sauté until tender. Spread the onion in the pie shell. Sprinkle with the bacon, Swiss cheese and Parmesan cheese. Combine the remaining ingredients in a bowl. Beat for 1 minute. Pour over the cheese layer in the pie shell. Bake at 450 degrees for 15 minutes. Reduce the heat to 350 degrees. Bake for 35 minutes or until a knife inserted in the center comes out clean. Bake for 10 minutes longer. Yield: 6 servings.

Aliene Gribas, Zeta Master
Havre, Montana

ASPARAGUS PARMESAN QUICHE

1 unbaked (9-inch) pie shell	3 eggs
	1 cup heavy cream
1 bunch young asparagus	1/4 to 1/2 cup (1 to 2 ounces) grated Parmesan cheese
1 teaspoon margarine	
1/2 onion, chopped	Salt and pepper to taste

Bake the pie shell at 450 degrees for 7 to 9 minutes or until light brown. Remove to a wire rack to cool. Wash and trim the asparagus. Cut 2 inches from the tops and cut the stalks into 1-inch pieces. Cook the stalks in a saucepan of lightly salted boiling water for 1 minute. Add the asparagus tops and cook for 3 to 4 minutes. Drain and plunge into ice water; drain well. Remove to paper towels and blot dry. Melt the margarine in a small skillet. Add the onion and sauté for 3 to 5 minutes. Spread the onion in the pie shell. Top with the asparagus. Whisk the eggs, cream and cheese in a bowl. Season with salt and pepper. Pour into the pie shell. Bake at 350 degrees for 30 to 45 minutes. Yield: 6 to 8 servings.

Adrianne Loser, Laureate Beta Omega
Port Orchard, Washington

CRAB QUICHE

2 cups (8 ounces) shredded Cheddar cheese	1 (6-ounce) can fancy white crab meat, drained and flaked
2 tablespoons all-purpose flour	Dash of pepper
4 eggs, lightly beaten	2 to 3 grinds nutmeg
1¹/2 cups skim milk	1 unbaked (9-inch) deep dish pie shell

Combine the cheese and flour in a bowl. Toss to coat. Add the eggs, milk, crab meat, pepper and nutmeg. Stir to mix well. Pour into the pie shell. Bake at 350 degrees for 1 hour. Serve with parfaits made with layers of fresh fruit, plain or vanilla yogurt and granola. Yield: 6 servings.

Scottie Michelle, Laureate Upsilon
Asheboro, North Carolina

HAM AND BROCCOLI QUICHE

1 cup diced ham	¹/4 cup baking mix
1 cup (4 ounces) shredded Cheddar cheese	1¹/2 cups milk
	3 eggs, lightly beaten
¹/2 cup chopped broccoli	¹/2 teaspoon salt
¹/2 cup chopped onion	¹/4 teaspoon pepper
¹/2 cup chopped green bell pepper	¹/8 teaspoon paprika

Sprinkle the ham, cheese, broccoli, onion and bell pepper in a greased 10-inch quiche pan. Whisk the baking mix, milk, eggs, salt and pepper in a bowl. Pour into the quiche pan. Sprinkle with the paprika. Bake at 375 degrees for 30 to 35 minutes or until a knife inserted in the center comes out clean. Yield: 8 servings.

Emma Holbert, Preceptor Alpha Sigma
Knoxville, Tennessee

HAM AND CHEESE QUICHE

1¹/2 cups diced ham	3 eggs, beaten
1 cup (4 ounces) shredded Cheddar cheese	¹/4 teaspoon salt
	¹/8 teaspoon pepper
	¹/8 teaspoon nutmeg
1¹/2 cups milk or heavy cream	1 unbaked (9-inch) pie shell

Mix the ham, cheese, milk, eggs, salt, pepper and nutmeg in a bowl. Pour into the pie shell. Bake at 350 degrees for 30 to 35 minutes. Yield: 6 servings.

Patricia J. Forbes, Preceptor Beta Sigma
Niagara Falls, New York

QUICHE LORRAINE

8 ounces bacon	1 cup heavy cream
1 small onion, chopped	¹/4 cup milk
1 unbaked (9-inch) pie shell	¹/2 teaspoon salt
	¹/2 teaspoon dry mustard
¹/2 cup (2 ounces) shredded Swiss cheese	¹/4 teaspoon black pepper
3 eggs	Dash of cayenne pepper

Cook the bacon in a skillet until crisp. Remove to paper towels to drain; crumble. Remove all but 1 tablespoon of bacon drippings from the skillet. Add the onion and sauté until tender; drain. Sprinkle the bacon in the pie shell. Sprinkle the cheese over the bacon. Top with the onion. Beat the eggs in a bowl. Beat in the remaining ingredients. Pour into the pie shell. Bake at 375 degrees for 45 minutes. Let cool slightly before serving. Yield: 6 to 8 servings.

Shirley A. Rader, Beta Kappa Sigma
Hilltop Lakes, Texas

MEXICAN QUICHE

¹/2 cup all-purpose flour	16 ounces Monterey Jack cheese, shredded
1 teaspoon baking powder	
1 teaspoon salt	¹/2 cup (1 stick) butter or margarine, melted
10 eggs, well beaten	
2 cups cottage cheese	10 drops Tabasco sauce
1 (7-ounce) can chopped green chiles	

Mix the flour, baking powder and salt in a small bowl. Beat the eggs and flour mixture in a large bowl. Add the cottage cheese, green chiles, Monterey Jack cheese, melted butter and Tabasco. Stir to mix well. Pour into a nonstick 9×13-inch baking pan. Bake at 400 degrees for 15 minutes. Reduce the heat to 350 degrees. Bake for 25 minutes. Yield: 8 to 12 servings.

Ann Eddins, Xi Delta Eta
Delta, Colorado

SPINACH QUICHE

1 (10-ounce) package frozen spinach	2 cups half-and-half
1 tablespoon butter or margarine	8 ounces Swiss cheese, shredded
1 small onion, minced	1/2 teaspoon salt
3 eggs	1 unbaked (8-inch) pie shell

Cook the spinach according to the package directions; drain well. Melt the butter in a small skillet. Add the onion and sauté until tender. Beat the eggs in a bowl. Stir in the half-and-half, cheese, salt, spinach and onion. Pour into the pie shell. Bake at 375 degrees for 30 to 35 minutes. You may use one 6-ounce can drained crab meat or cooked chopped broccoli instead of the spinach. Yield: 6 to 8 servings.

Renita Brown, Laureate Lambda
Chelsea, Maine

SHRIMP AND SPINACH QUICHE

1 pound fresh shrimp	2 eggs
1 (10-ounce) package frozen chopped spinach	1 egg yolk
	1 cup milk
1 egg white	2 tablespoons all-purpose flour
1 unbaked (9-inch) pie shell	Salt and pepper to taste
1/2 onion, finely chopped	3/4 cup (3 ounces) shredded Swiss cheese

Cook the shrimp in a saucepan of boiling water until partially cooked. Drain and peel. Chop the shrimp into bite-size pieces. Cook the spinach according to the package directions; drain well. Brush the egg white on the pie shell. Spread the shrimp in the pie shell and sprinkle with the onion. Top with the spinach. Beat the eggs, egg yolk, milk and flour in a bowl. Season with salt and pepper. Pour into the pie shell. Sprinkle with the cheese. Bake at 425 degrees for 15 minutes. Reduce the heat to 300 degrees. Bake for 45 minutes or until a knife inserted in the center comes out clean. Let stand for 10 minutes before serving. Yield: 6 servings.

Yvonne N. Pearrow, Alpha Upsilon Master
St. Augustine, Florida

ZUCCHINI BACON QUICHE

1 (8-count) can refrigerator crescent rolls	2 cups shredded mozzarella cheese
2 teaspoons mustard	2 tablespoons dried parsley flakes
6 slices bacon, chopped	1/2 teaspoon pepper
3 cups thinly sliced zucchini	1/4 teaspoon garlic powder
1 onion, chopped	1/4 teaspoon oregano
2 eggs, beaten	1/4 teaspoon basil

Separate the crescent dough into 8 triangles and arrange in a greased 10-inch pie plate, pressing the seams together to form a pie shell. Spread with the mustard. Cook the bacon in a skillet until crisp. Drain on paper towels. Remove all but 2 tablespoons of bacon drippings from the skillet. Add the zucchini and onion and sauté until tender. Mix the zucchini mixture and the remaining ingredients in a large bowl. Pour into the pie shell. Bake at 375 degrees for 25 to 30 minutes or until a knife inserted in the center comes out clean. Cover the edges of the crust with foil to prevent overbrowning. Yield: 6 to 8 servings.

Bonnie Netjes, Preceptor Gamma Psi
Rock Rapids, Iowa

BREAKFAST PIZZA WITH EXTRA CHEESE

1 pound bulk pork sausage	10 ounces mozzarella cheese, shredded
2 (8-count) cans refrigerator crescent rolls	10 ounces sharp Cheddar cheese, shredded
1 package frozen hash brown potatoes with onions and bell peppers, thawed	5 eggs
	1/3 cup milk
	Salt and pepper to taste

Brown the sausage in a skillet, stirring until crumbly; drain. Unroll the crescent dough and fit in the bottom of a large deep-dish pizza pan, pressing the seams to seal. Sprinkle with the sausage. Spread the potatoes over the sausage. Sprinkle with the mozzarella cheese and Cheddar cheese. Beat the eggs and milk in a bowl. Season with salt and pepper. Pour evenly over the cheese layer. Bake at 350 degrees for 45 minutes. Cut into slices and serve. Yield: 8 servings.

Jaquie Fotheringham, Lambda Master
West Valley City, Utah

BREAKFAST PIZZA WITH BELL PEPPERS

1 pound bulk pork sausage	1/4 cup thinly sliced green onions
1 cup frozen cubed hash brown potatoes	3 cups shredded sharp Cheddar cheese
1 (8-count) can refrigerator crescent rolls	3 eggs, lightly beaten
	3 tablespoons milk
3 tablespoons diced red and green bell pepper	Salt and pepper to taste
	2 tablespoons grated Parmesan cheese

Brown the sausage in a skillet, stirring until crumbly; drain. Thaw the potatoes. Separate the crescent dough into 8 triangles. Press into an ungreased

12-inch deep-dish pizza pan, pressing the dough 1 inch larger than the pan. Fold the edges under and press the seams to seal. Sprinkle with the sausage. Spread the potatoes over the sausage. Sprinkle with the bell pepper and green onions. Top with the Cheddar cheese. Beat the eggs and milk in a bowl. Season with salt and pepper. Pour over the cheese layer. Sprinkle with the Parmesan cheese. Bake at 375 degrees for 20 minutes or until the eggs are set and the crust is golden brown. Yield: 4 servings.

Betty P. Andrews, Beta Lambda
Virginia Beach, Virginia

BREAKFAST PIZZA

1 pound bulk pork sausage	1 cup chopped onions
1 (8-count) can refrigerator crescent rolls	1 cup (4 ounces) shredded Cheddar cheese
1 cup frozen hash brown potatoes, thawed	7 eggs
	½ cup milk
	2 tablespoons grated Parmesan cheese

Brown the sausage in a skillet, stirring until crumbly; drain. Unroll the crescent dough and fit in the bottom of a pizza pan, pressing the seams to seal. Sprinkle with the sausage. Spread the potatoes over the sausage. Sprinkle with the onions and top with the Cheddar cheese. Beat the eggs and milk in a bowl. Pour over the cheese layer. Sprinkle with the Parmesan cheese. Bake at 350 degrees for 25 to 30 minutes. Yield: 8 servings.

Jeri Lynne Strathman, Delta Iota
Higginsville, Missouri

ARTICHOKE-POTATO CASSEROLE

2 cans artichoke hearts	1 package shredded Cheddar cheese
8 potatoes	
1 package brown-and-serve sausage links	2 (10¾-ounce) cans condensed cream of celery soup
2 onions, thinly sliced	
3 carrots, thinly sliced	1 can French-fried onions

Drain the artichokes and chop. Parboil the potatoes in a saucepan of boiling water. Drain and thinly slice. Brown the sausages in a skillet, following the package directions. Drain and slice. Arrange ½ of the artichokes in a 9×13-inch baking dish. Top with ½ of the potatoes, ½ of the sliced onions and ½ of the carrots. Sprinkle with ½ of the cheese. Spread 1 can of the celery soup over the cheese. Repeat the layers. Cover with foil. Bake at 350 degrees for 40 minutes. Sprinkle with the French-fried onions. Bake, uncovered, for 20 minutes longer. Yield: 12 servings.

Terri English, Alpha Omicron Master
Mountlake Terrace, Washington

BREAKFAST HASH BROWN CASSEROLE

1 pound bulk pork sausage	½ teaspoon pepper
1 (16-ounce) bag frozen hash brown potatoes, thawed	½ cup (1 stick) butter or margarine, melted
	8 ounces shredded Cheddar cheese
9 eggs	12 (or more) grape tomatoes, halved
¾ cup milk	
½ teaspoon salt	

Brown the sausage in a skillet, stirring until crumbly; drain. Spread the sausage in a greased 9×13-inch baking dish. Top with the potatoes. Beat the eggs, milk, salt and pepper in a bowl. Pour evenly over the potato layer. Drizzle with the melted butter. Sprinkle with the cheese. Bake at 350 degrees for 1 hour. Arrange the tomatoes on top and serve.
Yield: 8 servings.

Katherine Radford, Xi Gamma Alpha
Waterford, Michigan

SAUSAGE CREPES

1 cup all-purpose flour	6 ounces cream cheese
1½ cups milk	8 ounces sliced fresh mushrooms
2 eggs	
1 tablespoon vegetable oil	1¼ cups sour cream
¼ teaspoon salt	¼ teaspoon garlic salt
18 ounces bulk pork sausage	¼ teaspoon marjoram
	¼ teaspoon dill weed
1 cup chopped onion	½ cup (1 stick) butter, softened
1 cup (4 ounces) shredded Cheddar cheese	½ cup sour cream

Combine the flour, milk, eggs, oil and salt in a bowl. Beat with a rotary beater until smooth. Heat a lightly greased 6-inch skillet until hot. Remove from the heat and add 2 tablespoons of the crepe batter. Tilt the skillet to spread the batter. Return to the heat and cook until lightly browned on the bottom. Invert the skillet over a paper towel to release the crepe. Repeat with the remaining batter, greasing the skillet as needed. Cook the sausage and onion in a skillet, stirring until the sausage is crumbly; drain. Add the next 7 ingredients. Cook until the cheese melts, stirring frequently. Thin with a small amount of milk if the mixture seems dry. Spoon about 2 tablespoons of the sausage mixture onto each crepe and roll up. Arrange in a single layer in a lightly greased shallow baking pan. Mix the butter and ½ cup sour cream in a small bowl until smooth. Spoon over the crepes. Cover with foil. Bake at 375 degrees for 30 minutes.
Yield: 10 servings.

Gloria Richardson, Laureate Theta Nu
Santa Rosa, California

SAUSAGE EN CROÛTE

1 sheet frozen puff pastry	1 large tomato, diced
1 pound bulk pork sausage	1 cup (4 ounces) shredded Swiss cheese
1/2 cup chopped onion	
1/3 cup chopped green bell pepper	3 tablespoons chopped parsley

Thaw the puff pastry for 20 minutes. Brown the sausage in a skillet, stirring until crumbly. Add the onion and bell pepper. Sauté for 5 minutes or until the vegetables are tender. Remove from the heat and drain. Add the tomato, cheese and parsley. Stir lightly to mix. Unfold the pastry on a lightly floured work surface. Roll out to a 10×14-inch rectangle. Spread the sausage mixture on the pastry. Roll up from the long side and pinch the edges to seal. Place on a 10×15-inch baking pan lined with brown paper. Form into a semicircle. Cut slits from the outside edge 2/3 of the way through the roll every 1½ inches. Bend the roll slightly so that the filling shows through the slits. Bake at 425 degrees for 20 minutes or until golden brown. Yield: 8 servings.

Marilyn Haynes, Zeta Sigma
North Platte, Nebraska

SCRAPPLE

1 pound hot bulk pork sausage	2 teaspoons sugar
2 cups cornmeal	5½ cups water
2 cups milk	All-purpose flour
2 teaspoons salt	Vegetable oil for frying

Brown the sausage in a skillet, stirring until crumbly; drain. Mix the cornmeal, milk, salt and sugar in a bowl. Bring the water to a boil in a saucepan. Stir in the cornmeal mixture. Reduce the heat to low and cook until thickened, stirring constantly. Remove from the heat and cover. Let cool for 10 minutes. Stir in the sausage. Pour into 2 greased loaf pans. Cover and chill overnight. Unmold on a work surface and cut into ½-inch slices. Dredge the slices in flour. Fry in hot oil in a skillet until golden brown on both sides. Serve plain or with maple syrup.
Yield: 8 to 10 servings.

Barbara Johns, Xi Theta
Bartlesville, Oklahoma

GRITS CASSEROLE

4 cups water	1/2 cup (1 stick) butter or margarine
1 cup quick-cooking grits	
1½ cups shredded sharp Cheddar cheese	2 or 3 garlic cloves, minced
1/2 cup milk	3 eggs, well beaten

Bring the water to a boil in a saucepan. Stir in the grits and return to a boil. Reduce the heat and cook for 5 minutes, stirring occasionally. Remove from the heat and add the cheese, milk, butter and garlic. Stir for 5 minutes or until the cheese melts. Stir in the eggs. Pour into a lightly greased 2-quart baking dish. Bake at 350 degrees for 1 hour. Yield: 6 servings.

Aileen Irvin Tarver, Theta Master
Raleigh, North Carolina

BREAKFAST BREAD

2 loaves frozen bread dough	16 ounces mozzarella cheese, shredded
1 pound bulk breakfast sausage	1/4 cup (1 ounce) grated Parmesan cheese
4 eggs	Salt and pepper to taste
1 teaspoon garlic powder	

Thaw the bread dough in the refrigerator overnight. Brown the sausage in a skillet, stirring until crumbly. Drain and let cool. Beat the eggs in a bowl. Stir in the sausage, garlic powder, mozzarella cheese and Parmesan cheese. Season with salt and pepper. Flatten the dough on a work surface. Spoon ½ of the sausage mixture down the middle of each loaf. Fold the sides of the dough over the filling and pinch the edges to seal. Spray with nonstick cooking spray and place on a nonstick baking sheet. Bake at 350 degrees for 30 minutes. Remove to a wire rack and let cool for 15 minutes. Cut into slices and serve.
Yield: 16 servings.

Theresa Scannell, Xi Gamma chi
Crosby, Texas

MAKE-IT-EASY HOT CINNAMON ROLLS

My grandmother would be up very early on a Saturday morning. We would wake up to the wonderful smell of hot cinnamon rolls waiting for us. It was a special treat.

2 envelopes dry yeast	Cinnamon-sugar
2 cups warm water	1 cup (2 sticks) butter, melted
1 (2-layer) package yellow cake mix	
2 eggs	1 cup milk or heavy cream
5½ cups (or more) all-purpose flour	2 cups packed brown sugar
Butter or margarine, softened	Chopped nuts

Dissolve the yeast in the warm water in a large bowl. Add the cake mix and eggs and beat well. Stir in the flour until a dough forms. Knead the dough on a floured work surface until smooth and elastic, kneading in more flour if necessary. Remove to a greased bowl and turn to coat. Cover and let rise in a warm place until doubled in bulk. Roll out on a floured work surface to a 12×24-inch or longer rectangle. Spread with softened butter and sprinkle with cinnamon-sugar. Roll up from the long side and pinch the edges to seal. Cut into about 36 slices. Mix 1 cup melted butter, the milk and brown sugar in a bowl. Spread in the bottom of 2 nonstick 9×13-inch baking pans. Sprinkle with chopped nuts. Top with the cinnamon roll slices. Let rise until doubled in bulk. Bake at 350 degrees for 30 minutes. Yield: about 3 dozen rolls.

Joan Petainen, Laureate Delta Eta
Sault Ste. Marie, Ontario, Canada

ALMOND STREUSEL COFFEE CAKE

2 cups all-purpose flour	1/2 teaspoon vanilla
1 teaspoon baking	extract
powder	Streusel (below)
1 teaspoon baking soda	2/3 cup orange juice
1/2 cup (1 stick) butter or	1/2 cup confectioners'
margarine, softened	sugar
1/2 cup granulated sugar	2 1/2 teaspoons orange
3 eggs	juice
1 teaspoon grated	
orange zest	

Mix the flour, baking powder and baking soda in a bowl. Combine the butter and granulated sugar in a large bowl. Beat with an electric mixer at medium speed until light and fluffy. Add the eggs, 1 at a time, beating well after each addition. Beat in the orange zest and vanilla. Beat in the dry ingredients alternately with 2/3 cup orange juice at low speed, beginning and ending with the dry ingredients. Spoon 1/2 of the batter into a greased 9- or 10-inch tube pan. Sprinkle with 1/2 of the Streusel. Cover with the remaining batter and top with the remaining Streusel. Bake at 350 degrees for 30 to 35 minutes or until a wooden pick inserted in the center comes out clean. Remove to a wire rack and let cool. Invert onto a serving plate. Mix the confectioners' sugar and 2 1/2 teaspoons orange juice in a small bowl until smooth. Drizzle over the cake. Yield: 16 servings

STREUSEL TOPPING

1 cup packed brown	3 tablespoons butter or
sugar	margarine, melted
1 cup sliced almonds	1 teaspoon grated
1/4 cup all-purpose flour	orange zest

Mix the brown sugar, almonds and flour in a bowl. Add the melted butter and orange zest and stir until crumbly.

Valla Vee Dunn, Eta Master
Sioux Falls, South Dakota

BLUEBERRY CRUMB CAKE

My mother-in-law, Rusti, gave me this recipe. It was originally in The Joy of Cooking *she received as a young bride. It's no longer in the book. Thank goodness she still has her early edition!*

2 cups all-purpose flour	1 egg
2 teaspoons baking	1/2 cup milk
powder	1 pint fresh blueberries
1/2 teaspoon salt	1/4 cup all-purpose flour
1/4 cup (1/2 stick)	1/2 teaspoon ground
unsalted butter,	cinnamon
softened	1/4 cup (1/2 stick)
3/4 cup sugar	unsalted butter

Sift 2 cups flour, the baking powder and salt together. Combine 1/4 cup butter and the sugar in a large bowl. Beat with an electric mixer until light and fluffy. Beat in the egg and milk. Beat in the dry ingredients gradually. Fold in the blueberries. Spread the batter in a buttered and floured 8×8-inch or 9×9-inch baking pan. Mix 1/4 cup flour and the cinnamon in a bowl. Cut in 1/4 cup butter with a fork until the mixture resembles coarse meal. Sprinkle over the batter. Bake at 375 degrees on the middle rack in the oven for 35 to 45 minutes or until a wooden pick inserted in the center comes out clean. Remove to a wire rack. Serve warm or cooled. Yield: 9 servings.

Clare L. VonderHaar, Preceptor Gamma Alpha
Eugene, Oregon

SOUR CREAM COFFEE CAKE

1/2 cup (1 stick) butter,	1 teaspoon baking soda
softened	1 teaspoon baking
1 cup sugar	powder
2 eggs	1/4 teaspoon salt
1 teaspoon vanilla	1/2 cup chopped walnuts
extract	1/4 cup sugar
1 cup sour cream	1 teaspoon ground
2 cups all-purpose flour,	cinnamon
sifted	

Beat the butter and 1 cup sugar in a bowl until light and fluffy. Beat in the eggs. Beat in the vanilla and sour cream. Sift the next 4 ingredients together. Beat into the butter mixture. Pour 1/2 of the batter into a buttered tube pan. Mix the walnuts, 1/4 cup sugar and the cinnamon in a bowl. Sprinkle 1/2 of the nut mixture over the batter. Top with the remaining batter and nut mixture. Bake at 350 degrees for 45 minutes or until a wooden pick inserted in the center comes out clean. Cool in the pan for 10 to 15 minutes. Remove to a wire rack. Yield: 12 to 16 servings.

Mary E. Krivac, Beta Delta
San Antonio, Texas

HONEY BUN COFFEE CAKE

1 (2-layer) package yellow cake mix	2 cups confectioners' sugar
1 cup sour cream	2 tablespoons butter, softened
2/3 cup vegetable oil	
4 eggs	1/4 cup milk
1 cup packed brown sugar	1 teaspoon vanilla extract
2 tablespoons ground cinnamon	

Combine the cake mix, sour cream, oil and eggs in a large bowl. Stir to mix well. Spread 1/2 of the batter in a greased 9×13-inch baking pan. Mix the brown sugar and cinnamon in a small bowl. Sprinkle over the batter in the pan. Top with the remaining batter. Swirl a knife through the batter. Bake at 350 degrees for 40 minutes or until a wooden pick inserted in the center comes out clean. Remove to a wire rack. Beat the confectioners' sugar, butter, milk and vanilla in a bowl until smooth. Pour 1/2 over the hot cake. Let the cake cool. Pour the remaining confectioners' sugar mixture over the cooled cake. Yield: 15 servings.

Sharon Putnam, Xi Nu Lambda
Dexter, Missouri

PINEAPPLE CHEESECAKE STREUSEL COFFEE CAKE

This is easily adaptable with any flavor cake mix, pudding mix, or type of nut. This is my Aunt Mary's prize-winning recipe in the Brown County, South Dakota State Fair.

1 (2-layer) package pineapple cake mix	1 teaspoon ground cinnamon
1 (3 1/2-ounce) package instant cheesecake pudding mix	1 tablespoon margarine
	1/2 cup chopped pecans
4 eggs	1/2 cup confectioners' sugar
1 cup sour cream	1 1/2 teaspoons milk
1/3 cup vegetable oil	
2 tablespoons brown sugar	

Remove and reserve 2 tablespoons of the cake mix. Combine the remaining cake mix, pudding mix, eggs, sour cream and oil in a large bowl. Beat with an electric mixer for 3 minutes. Pour 1/2 of the batter into a greased bundt pan. Combine the reserved cake mix, brown sugar, cinnamon, margarine and pecans in a bowl. Mix until crumbly. Sprinkle over the batter in the pan. Top with the remaining batter. Bake at 350 degrees for 50 to 60 minutes or until a wooden pick inserted in the center comes out clean. Cool in the pan for 10 to 15 minutes. Remove to a wire rack to cool completely. Mix the confectioners' sugar and milk in a small bowl until smooth. Drizzle over the cooled cake. Yield: 12 servings

Nancy DeMond, Preceptor Mu
Brookings, Oregeon

RASPBERRY CREAM CHEESE COFFEE CAKE

2 1/4 cups all-purpose flour	1 teaspoon almond extract
3/4 cup sugar	8 ounces cream cheese, softened
3/4 cup (1 1/2 sticks) butter	
1/2 teaspoon baking powder	1/4 cup sugar
	1 egg
1/2 teaspoon baking soda	1/2 cup raspberry preserves
1/4 teaspoon salt	
3/4 cup sour cream	1/2 cup sliced almonds
1 egg	

Mix the flour and 3/4 cup sugar in a large bowl. Cut in the butter with a pastry blender or fork until the mixture resembles coarse crumbs. Remove and reserve 1 cup of the crumb mixture. Stir the baking powder, baking soda and salt into the remaining crumb mixture. Add the sour cream, 1 egg and the almond extract and stir to mix well. Pat the mixture over the bottom and 2 inches up the side of a greased and floured 9- or 10-inch springform pan. Beat the cream cheese, 1/4 cup sugar and 1 egg in a bowl until smooth. Pour into the springform pan. Spoon the raspberry preserves evenly over the cream cheese mixture. Stir the reserved crumb mixture and almonds in a small bowl. Sprinkle over the preserves. Bake at 350 degrees for 45 to 55 minutes or until set. Remove to a wire rack and let cool for 15 minutes. Loosen from the side of the pan with a sharp knife and remove the side. Yield: 16 servings.

Susan Heyen, Mu Theta
Paxton, Illinois

FRUIT CREPES

My German mother, Maria Kuhnhenn, loved to cook, and everyone in our family makes these delicious crepes. We eat them for breakfast or dinner.

1 cup milk	Butter-flavored shortening
3 eggs, at room temperature	Fresh fruit or jam
1 cup all-purpose flour	Confectioners' sugar

Beat the milk, eggs and flour in a bowl until smooth. Melt about 1 tablespoon of shortening in a cast-iron or nonstick skillet. Heat until hot. Add 1 ladle of batter. Tilt the skillet to spread the batter. Cook until bubbly on top and golden brown on the bottom. Flip the crepe and cook until golden brown on the other side. Remove to a plate and keep warm. Repeat with the remaining batter, using shortening as needed. Top each crepe with fruit or spread with 1 tablespoon of jam. Roll up and sprinkle with confectioners' sugar. Yield: 10 servings.

Paulette Blackstone, Gamma Alpha Eta
Bella Vista, California

HEALTHY BREAKFAST COOKIES

1½ cups Splenda sweetener	½ cup applesauce
2½ cups rolled oats	½ cup baby food prunes
4 cups all-purpose flour	5 egg whites
1 tablespoon baking soda	½ to 1 cup water
1 teaspoon baking powder	1½ teaspoons vanilla extract
1 teaspoon salt	¾ cup raisins
1½ teaspoons ground cinnamon	½ cup miniature chocolate chips

Mix the first 7 ingredients in a large bowl. Make a well in the center and pour in the applesauce, prunes, egg whites, water and vanilla. Stir until just combined. Stir in the raisins and chocolate chips. Form into golf ball-sized balls with damp hands. Place on a greased cookie sheet and flatten to ½-inch thickness. Bake at 350 degrees for 8 to 10 minutes for a chewy cookie and 10 to 12 minutes for a drier cookie. Remove the cookies to a wire rack to cool. Yield: 14 servings.

Deb Thiems, Delta Gamma
Alliance, Nebraska

HAWAIIAN DOUGHNUTS

2 envelopes dry yeast	8 eggs, beaten
1 cup warm milk	1 cup milk
6 cups all-purpose flour, sifted	Vegetable oil for deep-frying
1 cup sugar	Sugar
1 teaspoon salt	

Dissolve the yeast in 1 cup warm milk. Let stand until bubbly. Mix the flour, 1 cup sugar and salt in a bowl. Beat the eggs and 1 cup milk in a bowl. Stir into the dry ingredients gradually. Stir in the yeast mixture gradually. Stir until smooth. Cover with a damp cloth. Let rise in a warm place for 2 hours or until doubled in bulk. Stir to mix. Heat oil to 350 degrees in a heavy saucepan or deep-fryer. Add the dough by tablespoonfuls. Fry until golden brown on all sides. Drain on paper towels. Roll in sugar and serve warm. Yield: about 8 dozen doughnuts.

Janice Sebring, Xi Nu Nu
Littlefield, Texas

FRENCH BREAKFAST PUFFS

1½ cups sifted all-purpose flour	1 egg
1½ teaspoons baking powder	½ cup milk
½ teaspoon salt	½ cup sugar
¼ teaspoon nutmeg	1 teaspoon ground cinnamon
⅓ cup shortening	6 tablespoons butter, melted
½ cup sugar	

Sift the flour, baking powder, salt and nutmeg together. Beat the shortening and ½ cup sugar in a bowl until light and fluffy. Beat in the egg. Stir in the dry ingredients alternately with the milk. Fill greased muffin cups ⅔ full. Bake at 350 degrees for 20 to 25 minutes or until golden brown. Cool in the pan for 5 minutes. Remove to a wire rack. Mix ½ cup sugar and the cinnamon in a shallow bowl. Dip the puffs in the melted butter and then roll in the cinnamon mixture. Yield: 12 servings.

Gleora Strauss, Laureate Gamma Alpha
Randolph, Kansas

SAVORY ONION SCONES

Great flavor combination—wonderful with chili.

1 tablespoon butter	1 (6-ounce) package golden raisins and dried cherries, chopped
1 cup chopped yellow onion	
2 cups all-purpose flour	
1 tablespoon sugar	1 teaspoon grated orange zest
2 teaspoons baking powder	2 eggs, beaten
½ teaspoon salt	½ cup heavy cream
6 tablespoons butter	2 tablespoons heavy cream
1 cup (4 ounces) finely shredded Cheddar cheese	

Melt 1 tablespoon butter in a skillet. Add the onion and sauté until light brown. Mix the flour, sugar, baking powder and salt in a large bowl. Cut in 6 tablespoons butter with a pastry blender or fork until crumbly. Stir in the onions, cheese, raisins and cherries and orange zest. Mix the eggs and ½ cup cream in a bowl. Add to the flour mixture and stir just until combined. Divide the dough in half and place on a floured work surface. Pat each into an 8-inch circle that is ¾-inch thick. Cut each circle into 6 wedges and arrange the wedges on a lightly greased baking sheet. Brush the tops and sides with 2 tablespoons cream. Bake at 425 degrees for 22 to 28 minutes. Serve warm. Yield: 12 servings.

Fawn Wright, Laureate Omicron
Clear Lake, Minnesota

MAPLE PECAN STICKY BUNS

1 cup chopped pecans	2 tablespoons butter, softened
1/2 cup maple syrup	
2 cups all-purpose flour	1 cup all-purpose flour
1/4 cup granulated sugar	1/4 cup (1/2 stick) butter, softened
1 envelope quick-rising yeast	
	1/2 cup packed light brown sugar
1 teaspoon salt	
1 egg, at room temperature	1 teaspoon ground cinnamon
1 cup very warm water	

Spread the pecans in a greased 9×13-inch baking pan. Drizzle the maple syrup evenly over the pecans. Mix 2 cups flour, the granulated sugar, yeast and salt in a large bowl. Stir in the egg, water and 2 tablespoons butter. Beat until smooth. Stir in 1 cup flour gradually until a soft dough forms. Cover with plastic wrap and let rise in a warm place for 30 minutes or until doubled in bulk. Roll out the dough on a lightly floured surface to a 12×15-inch rectangle. Spread with 1/4 cup butter. Mix the brown sugar and cinnamon in a small bowl. Sprinkle over the dough. Roll up from the 12-inch side and cut into 12 slices. Arrange the slices, cut side down, in the prepared pan. Cover with plastic wrap and let rise in a warm place until doubled in bulk. Bake, uncovered, at 375 degrees for 25 to 30 minutes or until golden brown. Cool in the pan for 1 minute. Invert the buns onto a serving platter. Serve warm. Yield: 12 servings.

Joyce Hyde, Preceptor Eta
Lincoln, Illinois

APPLE-RAISIN SCONES

Breakfast is our favorite meal, especially on the weekends. It brings back special memories of my mom's baking and our togetherness while growing up.

2 1/2 cups all-purpose flour	1/2 cup (1 stick) chilled butter
2 teaspoons baking powder	1 cup diced peeled Granny Smith apple
1/2 teaspoon baking soda	1/2 cup raisins
1/2 teaspoon salt	2/3 cup buttermilk
1/4 cup packed brown sugar	1 tablespoon granulated sugar
1/4 cup granulated sugar	

Mix the flour, baking powder, baking soda, salt, brown sugar and 1/4 cup granulated sugar in a large bowl. Cut in the butter with a pastry blender or fork until crumbly. Stir in the apple and raisins. Add the buttermilk and stir just until combined. Place the dough on an ungreased baking sheet and pat into a 9-inch circle. Cut into 8 wedges. Separate the wedges at least 1/2-inch apart. Sprinkle with 1 tablespoon granulated sugar. Bake at 375 degrees for 25 minutes or until golden brown. Serve warm. Yield: 8 servings.

Candace Hamilton, Laureate Alpha Pi
Westfield, New York

SWEET ROLL DOUGH

2 cups lukewarm water	1/2 cup shortening
1/2 cup sugar	6 cups all-purpose flour
2 teaspoons salt	Softened butter
2 envelopes dry yeast	Brown sugar
2 eggs	Cinnamon

Combine the water, sugar and salt in a saucepan. Cook over low heat until the sugar dissolves, stirring frequently. Remove from the heat and let cool until warm. Beat the yeast, eggs and shortening in a large bowl. Beat in the warm water mixture. Stir in the flour, 2 cups at a time. Turn out the dough onto a lightly floured work surface and knead a few times. Place in a greased bowl and turn to coat. Let rise in a warm place until doubled in bulk. Punch down the dough and let rise until doubled in bulk again. Roll out on a lightly floured work surface and spread with softened butter and sprinkle with a mixture of brown sugar and cinnamon. Roll up and cut into slices. Place the slices in a nonstick 9×13-inch baking pan. Let rise until doubled in bulk. Bake at 375 degrees for 35 minutes. Yield: 12 servings.

Sheila Baccari, Xi Alpha Beta Eta
Seminole, Texas

BLUEBERRY FRENCH TOAST

1 loaf dry white bread	Egg substitute equivalent to 12 eggs
16 ounces light cream cheese	
	2 cups skim milk
1 cup fresh or frozen blueberries	1/3 cup maple syrup
	Blueberry Sauce

Remove the crust from the bread and cut the bread into 1-inch cubes. Spread 1/2 of the bread cubes in a 9×13-inch baking dish coated with nonstick cooking spray. Cut the cream cheese into 1-inch cubes. Sprinkle the cream cheese over the bread in the baking dish. Sprinkle with the blueberries and top with the remaining bread cubes. Beat the egg substitute, milk and maple syrup in a large bowl. Pour over the bread mixture. Cover and chill for 8 hours or overnight. Let stand at room temperature for 30 minutes before baking. Bake, covered, at 350 degrees for 30 minutes. Uncover and bake for 25 to 30 minutes longer or until golden brown and the center is set.

Serve with the Blueberry Sauce spooned over the top. Yield: 8 to 10 servings.

BLUEBERRY SAUCE

1 cup sugar	*1 cup water*
2 tablespoons cornstarch	*1 cup fresh or frozen blueberries*

Mix the sugar and cornstarch in a saucepan. Stir in the water. Bring to a boil over medium heat, stirring constantly. Boil for 3 minutes, stirring constantly. Stir in the blueberries and reduce the heat. Simmer for 8 to 10 minutes or until the blueberries pop.

Cherie Fields, Xi Alpha Theta
Bartlesville, Oklahoma

OVEN-BAKED CARAMEL FRENCH TOAST

1 cup packed brown sugar	*1 1/2 cups milk*
1/2 cup (1 stick) butter	*1 teaspoon vanilla extract*
2 tablespoons light corn syrup	*1 teaspoon nutmeg*
1 cup chopped pecans	*1 1/2 teaspoons ground cinnamon*
12 slices French bread	*1/4 teaspoon salt*
6 eggs	*Caramel Sauce*

Combine the brown sugar, butter and corn syrup in a saucepan. Cook over medium heat until thickened, stirring constantly. Pour into a 9×13-inch baking pan coated with nonstick cooking spray. Sprinkle with 1/2 of the pecans. Top with 1/2 of the bread slices. Sprinkle with the remaining pecans and top with the remaining bread slices. Combine the eggs, milk, vanilla, nutmeg, cinnamon and salt in a blender and process until smooth or beat in a bowl with a rotary beater. Pour over the bread mixture. Cover and chill for 8 hours or overnight. Let stand at room temperature for 30 minutes before baking. Bake, uncovered, at 350 degrees for 40 to 45 minutes or until lightly browned. Drizzle the Caramel Sauce over the top just before serving. Yield: 8 to 10 servings.

CARAMEL SAUCE

1/2 cup packed brown sugar	*1 tablespoon light corn syrup*
1/4 cup (1/2 stick) butter	

Combine the brown sugar, butter and corn syrup in a saucepan. Cook over medium heat until thickened, stirring constantly.

Sally Magin, Preceptor Alpha Zeta
Byron, Minnesota

✤ MORNING FRENCH TOAST

1 cup packed brown sugar	*1 loaf Italian or French bread*
1/2 cup (1 stick) butter, melted	*6 eggs*
1 teaspoon ground cinnamon	*1 1/2 cups milk*
3 tart apples, such as Granny Smith	*1 tablespoon vanilla extract*
1/2 cup sweetened dried cranberries or raisins	*2 teaspoons ground cinnamon*

Mix the brown sugar, butter and 1 teaspoon cinnamon in a 9×13-inch baking dish. Peel, core and thinly slice the apples. Add to the baking dish. Add the cranberries and toss to coat. Spread the fruit mixture evenly in the baking dish. Cut the bread into 1-inch slices. Arrange the bread slices in the dish. Beat the eggs, milk, vanilla and 2 teaspoons cinnamon in a bowl. Pour evenly over the bread. Cover and chill for 4 to 24 hours. Bake, covered, at 375 degrees for 40 minutes. Uncover and bake for 5 minutes longer. Let stand for 5 minutes before serving. Yield: 12 servings.

Marie Bray, Alpha Omega Master
Orlando, Florida

BAKED ORANGE-PECAN FRENCH TOAST

8 (1/2-inch-thick) bread slices	*1/4 cup sugar*
4 eggs	*1/4 teaspoon nutmeg*
2/3 cup orange juice	*1/4 cup (1/2 stick) butter or margarine*
1/3 cup milk	*1/2 cup chopped pecans*
1/2 teaspoon vanilla extract	*Orange Sauce*

Arrange the bread slices in a 10×15-inch baking pan. Beat the next 6 ingredients in a bowl. Pour over the bread slices. Chill, covered, for 2 hours. Melt the butter in a 10×15-inch baking pan in the oven. Arrange the soaked bread slices on top of the melted butter. Bake at 350 degrees for 20 minutes. Sprinkle with the pecans. Bake for 10 minutes longer. Serve with Orange Sauce or maple syrup. Yield: 4 servings.

ORANGE SAUCE

1/2 cup sugar	*1 cup orange juice*
1/2 cup (1 stick) butter	

Combine the sugar, butter and orange juice in a saucepan. Cook over low heat, stirring constantly. Do not boil. Let cool for 10 minutes and serve warm.

Nancy Blake, Laureate Omega
Memphis, Tennessee

ALMOND OMELET PANCAKE

⅓ cup baking mix	1¼ cups milk
¼ cup sugar	¼ teaspoon almond
2 eggs	extract
3 tablespoons sour	¼ cup sliced almonds
cream	Sugar

Mix the baking mix and ¼ cup sugar in a bowl. Add the eggs, sour cream, milk and almond extract. Whisk until blended, the mixture will not be smooth. Stir in ½ of the almonds. Pour into a well buttered 9-inch pie plate. Sprinkle with sugar and the remaining almonds. Bake at 400 degrees for 35 to 40 minutes or until puffed and golden brown. Yield: 5 servings.

Alta Mae Seiler, Alpha Iota Master
Chico, California

APPLE PUFF PANCAKE

6 eggs	¼ teaspoon cinnamon
1½ cups milk	½ cup (1 stick) butter or
1 cup all-purpose flour	margarine
3 tablespoons sugar	2 apples
1 teaspoon vanilla	2 to 3 tablespoons
extract	brown sugar
½ teaspoon salt	

Process the first 7 ingredients in a blender or beat in a bowl until a few lumps remain. Melt the butter in a 12-inch quiche dish or 9×13-inch baking dish in the oven. Core, peel and thinly slice the apples. Spread the apples on top of the melted butter. Bake at 425 degrees until the butter is sizzling but not brown. Pour the batter immediately over the apples. Sprinkle with the brown sugar. Bake at 425 degrees for 20 minutes or until puffed and golden brown. Serve immediately. Yield: 4 to 6 servings.

Mary A. Chamberlain, Laureate Beta Omicron
Fort Myers, Florida

DUTCH BABIES

¼ cup (½ stick) butter	¾ cup milk
3 eggs	¾ cup all-purpose flour

Divide the butter between two 8-inch cake pans. Melt the butter in the oven. Process the eggs in a blender at high speed for 1 minute. Add the milk slowly with the machine running. Add the flour slowly with the machine running. Divide the batter between the 2 hot pans. Bake at 425 degrees for 20 to 25 minutes or until puffed and well browned. Serve with butter, syrup, confectioners' sugar or your favorite fruit jam. Yield: 3 to 6 servings.

Janice Bussey, Preceptor Alpha Upsilon
Lakewood, Washington

EGG FLAPJACKS

My husband makes these for our sorority brunch for our Valentine Queen. It is truly my sisters' favorite.

4 eggs	½ teaspoon salt
1 tablespoon grated	⅛ teaspoon pepper
onion	1⅓ cups shredded sharp
⅓ cup all-purpose flour	Cheddar cheese
1 teaspoon baking	⅓ cup vegetable oil
powder	

Beat the eggs and onion in a bowl. Sift in the flour, baking powder, salt and pepper. Stir to mix well. Stir in the cheese. Heat some of the oil in a skillet. Drop large spoonfuls of the batter into the skillet. Cook until browned on both sides, turning once. Repeat with the remaining batter, adding oil as needed. Serve hot with cranberry sauce, marmalade or sour cream. Yield: 4 servings.

Valerie Smith, Preceptor Alpha
Sherwood, Arkansas

BUTTERMILK PANCAKES

My eighty-eight year-old mother has made these pancakes every Sunday for over sixty years. I look forward to visiting her and getting to have her pancakes.

2 cups buttermilk	1 tablespoon baking
2 eggs, beaten	powder
2 tablespoons vegetable	1 teaspoon baking soda
oil	⅛ teaspoon salt
1 to 1¼ cups	
all-purpose flour	

Whisk the buttermilk, eggs, oil, flour, baking powder, baking soda and salt in a bowl. Ladle spoonfuls of batter onto a hot greased griddle. Cook until browned on both sides, turning once. Yield: 8 to 12 servings.

Janet Walker, Xi Beta Epsilon
Woodward, Oklahoma

LOG CABIN PANCAKES

1 cup cottage cheese	¼ cup vegetable oil
½ cup all-purpose flour	½ teaspoon vanilla
6 eggs	extract
¼ cup milk	

Combine the cottage cheese, flour, eggs, milk, oil and vanilla in a blender. Process until well mixed. Pour ¼ cupfuls of the batter onto a hot greased griddle. Cook until browned on both sides, turning once. Serve with your favorite syrup or jam. Yield: 8 servings.

Pam Smith, Xi Chi
Fallon, Nevada

Breads

ALMOND TEA BREAD

3 cups all-purpose flour
1½ teaspoons baking
   powder
1 teaspoon salt
3 eggs
2¼ cups sugar
1 cup plus 2 tablespoons
   vegetable oil
1½ cups milk

1½ teaspoons vanilla
   extract
1½ teaspoons almond
   extract
1½ teaspoons butter
   flavoring
4½ teaspoons poppy
   seeds
Glaze

Combine the flour, baking powder and salt together in a bowl and mix well. Beat the eggs, sugar and oil in a large bowl. Beat in the dry ingredients alternately with the milk. Stir in the vanilla, almond extract and butter flavoring. Stir in the poppy seeds. Pour into a nonstick bundt pan or 2 nonstick loaf pans. Bake at 350 degrees for 40 to 45 minutes; the bread will be very moist. Cool in the pan for 10 to 15 minutes. Remove to a wire rack to cool. Drizzle the Glaze over the cake. Yield: 12 servings.

ORANGE GLAZE

¾ cup sugar
¼ cup orange juice
½ teaspoon vanilla
   extract

½ teaspoon almond
   extract
½ teaspoon butter
   flavoring

Combine the sugar, orange juice, vanilla, almond extract and butter flavoring in a small saucepan. Cook until the sugar dissolves, stirring frequently. Let cool slightly.

Marlys Werner, Xi Alpha Delta
West Fargo, North Dakota

FRESH APPLE BREAD

2 cups sugar
2 eggs
¾ cup vegetable oil
1 teaspoon salt
1 teaspoon baking soda
¼ teaspoon baking
   powder
1½ teaspoons cinnamon

2 teaspoons vanilla
   extract
2 cups all-purpose flour
4 cups diced peeled
   apples
1½ cups chopped
   walnuts

Whisk the first 8 ingredients in a bowl. Stir in the flour just until combined. Stir in the apples and walnuts. Pour into 2 greased and floured loaf pans. Bake at 350 degrees for 55 to 65 minutes. Cool in the pan for 10 minutes. Remove to a wire rack to cool. Yield: 24 servings.

Susan Holste, Xi Eta Omicron
Great Bend, Kansas

FAVORITE BANANA NUT BREAD

1 cup sugar
½ cup shortening
2 eggs, beaten
3 bananas, mashed
2 cups all-purpose flour
¼ teaspoon baking
   powder

1 teaspoon baking soda
½ cup chopped nuts
2 tablespoons brown
   sugar
¼ cup chopped pecans
   or walnuts
¼ teaspoon cinnamon

Beat the sugar, shortening, eggs and bananas in a bowl. Stir in the next 4 ingredients. Pour into a non-stick loaf pan. Sprinkle with the brown sugar, ¼ cup pecans and the cinnamon. Bake at 350 degrees for 1 hour. Cool in the pan for 10 minutes. Remove to a wire rack to cool. Yield: 12 servings.

Holly Wideman, Xi Zeta
Anthony, Kansas

BANANA NUT BREAD

5¹/₃ tablespoons margarine, softened	¹/₂ cup milk
³/₄ cup packed brown sugar	1¹/₂ cups sifted all-purpose flour
2 eggs	1 teaspoon baking soda
1 cup mashed ripe banana	¹/₂ cup chopped walnuts (optional)

Beat the margarine and brown sugar in a bowl until light and fluffy. Add the eggs, 1 at a time, beating well after each addition. Beat in the banana. Beat in the milk gradually. Add the flour and baking soda and beat for 1 minute. Stir in the walnuts. Pour into a greased loaf pan. Bake at 350 degrees for 65 minutes or until a wooden pick inserted in the center comes out clean. Cool in the pan for 10 minutes. Remove to a wire rack to cool completely. Yield: 12 servings.

Beverly J. Magda, Xi Kappa Sigma
Youngstown, Ohio

CARROT BANANA BREAD

2 cups all-purpose flour	2 eggs
1 teaspoon baking soda	1 cup mashed ripe banana
¹/₂ teaspoon salt	1 cup grated carrot
¹/₂ teaspoon cinnamon	¹/₂ cup chopped pecans
¹/₃ cup vegetable oil	
1 cup sugar	

Combine the flour, baking soda, salt and cinnamon in a bowl and mix well. Beat the oil, sugar and eggs in a large bowl. Stir in the dry ingredients alternately with the banana. Stir in the carrot and pecans. Pour into a greased 5×9-inch loaf pan. Bake at 350 degrees for 55 to 65 minutes or until a wooden pick inserted in the center comes out clean. Cool in the pan for 10 minutes. Remove to a wire rack to cool completely. Yield: 12 servings.

Virginia King, Laureate Nu
Minden, Nevada

BISHOPS BREAD

2 cups all-purpose flour	1 cup sliced maraschino cherries
2 teaspoons baking powder	1 cup miniature chocolate chips
1 teaspoon salt	4 eggs, beaten
1 cup chopped pecans or walnuts	1 cup sugar
1 cup chopped dates	

Combine the flour, baking powder and salt in a large bowl and mix well. Add the pecans, dates, cherries and chocolate chips; toss to mix. Beat the eggs and sugar in a bowl. Add to the fruit mixture and stir to

mix well. Pour into a greased 5×9-inch loaf pan. Bake at 325 degrees for 1 hour and 15 minutes or until a wooden pick inserted in the center comes out clean. Cool in the pan for 10 minutes. Remove to a wire rack to cool completely. Yield: 12 servings.

Jan Kaywood, Laureate Rho
Jackson, Michigan

BLUEBERRY NUT BREAD SUPREME

1 (15-ounce) can blueberries	¹/₄ cup all-purpose flour
2 eggs	¹/₄ cup chopped pecans
¹/₂ cup sour cream	³/₄ teaspoon cinnamon
¹/₄ cup water	¹/₄ teaspoon salt
1 package wild blueberry muffin mix	

Drain and rinse the blueberries. Combine the eggs, sour cream and water in a large bowl and mix well. Add the muffin mix, flour, pecans, cinnamon and salt and stir to mix well. Fold in the blueberries. Grease the bottom of a 5×9-inch loaf pan. Pour in the batter. Bake at 350 degrees for 50 to 55 minutes or until a wooden pick inserted in the center comes out clean. Cool in the pan for 10 minutes. Remove to a wire rack to cool completely. Yield: 6 to 8 servings.

Rosemary E. Collard, Xi Mu Upsilon
Mundelein, Illinois

❖ DELICIOUS BLUEBERRY ZUCCHINI BREAD

3 cups sifted all-purpose flour	1 cup vegetable oil
1 teaspoon baking powder	2 cups sugar
	2 cups grated zucchini
1 teaspoon salt	1 tablespoon vanilla extract
1 tablespoon cinnamon	¹/₂ cup walnuts
Dash of nutmeg	1 to 1¹/₂ cups blueberries
3 eggs	

Combine the flour, baking powder, salt, cinnamon and nutmeg in a bowl and mix well. Beat the eggs in a large bowl. Stir in the oil and sugar. Add the zucchini and vanilla and stir gently. Add the dry ingredients and stir to mix well. Fold in the walnuts and blueberries. Pour into 2 nonstick loaf pans. Bake at 325 degrees for 1 hour or until a wooden pick inserted in the center comes out clean. Cool in the pan for 10 minutes. Remove to a wire rack to cool completely. Yield: 24 servings.

Nancy Auf Der Heide, Pi Iota
Shawnee, Kansas

CHEESE BREAD

2 eggs, lightly beaten	1/4 cup milk
1 cup low-fat plain yogurt	1 tablespoon spicy brown mustard
1 cup (4 ounces) shredded Cheddar cheese	2 1/2 cups self-rising flour
1/2 cup vegetable oil	1 tablespoon sugar
1 cup thinly sliced green onions	1 tablespoon cracked pepper
	1/2 teaspoon baking soda

Combine the eggs, yogurt, cheese, oil, green onions, milk and mustard in a bowl and mix well. Combine the flour, sugar, pepper and baking soda in a large bowl and mix well. Make a well in the center and pour in the egg mixture. Stir just until moistened. Grease the bottom of a 5×9-inch loaf pan. Pour in the batter. Bake at 350 degrees for 45 to 50 minutes or until a wooden pick inserted in the center comes out clean. Cool in the pan for 10 minutes. Remove to a wire rack and let cool for 1 hour. Yield: 12 servings.

Joan K. Smith, Xi Gamma Eta
Alpharetta, Georgia

CRANBERRY BREAD

2 cups all-purpose flour	1 egg, lightly beaten
1 cup sugar	1 teaspoon grated orange zest
1 1/2 teaspoons baking powder	2/3 cup orange juice
1/2 teaspoon salt	1 1/2 cups fresh cranberries, halved
1/4 teaspoon baking soda	1 cup chopped pecans
5 1/3 tablespoons butter	

Combine the flour, sugar, baking powder, salt and baking soda in a large bowl and mix well. Cut in the butter with a pastry blender or fork until the mixture resembles coarse crumbs. Whisk the egg, orange zest and orange juice in a small bowl. Add to the crumb mixture and stir just until moistened. Fold in the cranberries and pecans. Spoon into a greased 5×9-inch loaf pan. Bake at 350 degrees for 60 to 70 minutes or until a wooden pick inserted in the center comes out clean. Cool in the pan for 10 minutes. Remove to a wire rack to cool completely. Yield: 16 servings.

Denzalene T. Conkling, Xi Nu Epsilon
Flagler Beach, Florida

IRISH SODA BREAD

4 cups all-purpose flour	2 teaspoons caraway seeds (optional)
3 heaping teaspoons baking powder	1 egg, beaten
1/2 teaspoon salt	2 cups milk
3 tablespoons sugar	1 tablespoon butter, melted
2 cups raisins	

Combine the flour, baking powder, salt, sugar, raisins and caraway seeds in a large bowl and mix well. Whisk the egg and milk together in a bowl. Add to the flour mixture. Add the melted butter, stirring to combine. Spoon into a buttered and floured 9-inch round baking pan. Cut a cross in the top of the batter. Bake at 350 degrees for 1 hour or until a wooden pick inserted in the center comes out clean. Cool in the pan for 10 minutes. Remove to a wire rack to cool completely. Yield: 9 servings.

Joan Seidel, Theta Gamma
Arkansas City, Kansas

DATE AND WALNUT BREAD

1 cup chopped dates	2 teaspoons salt
2 teaspoons baking soda	2 cups sugar
1 1/2 cups boiling water	2 tablespoons butter, softened
3 1/2 cups all-purpose flour	2 eggs, beaten
1 teaspoon baking powder	1 cup walnuts

Combine the dates and baking soda in a bowl and mix well. Stir in the boiling water. Let stand until cool. Combine the flour, baking powder and salt in a bowl and mix well. Beat the sugar, butter and eggs in a large bowl. Stir in the dry ingredients. Fold in the date mixture and the walnuts. Pour into 4 small non-stick loaf pans. Bake at 350 degrees for 40 minutes. Reduce the heat to 300 degrees. Bake for 15 to 20 minutes or until a wooden pick inserted in the center comes out clean. Cool in the pan for 10 minutes. Remove to a wire rack to cool completely. Yield: 20 servings.

Janet Sowerby, Preceptor Gamma Mu
Auburn Hills, Michigan

MANGO NUT BREAD

1 cup sugar	2 cups all-purpose flour
1/2 cup shortening	1 teaspoon baking soda
2 eggs	1 cup chopped pecans
1 cup mashed ripe mango	2 teaspoons vanilla extract

Beat the sugar and shortening in a large bowl until light and fluffy. Beat in the eggs, mango, flour, baking soda, pecans and vanilla. Pour into 2 greased 3×7-inch loaf pans. Bake at 325 degrees for 1 hour or until a wooden pick inserted in the center comes out clean. Cool in the pan for 10 minutes. Remove to a wire rack to cool completely. Yield: 12 to 14 servings.

Vivian Dekar, Laureate Gamma Upsilon
Fruitland Park, Florida

TEXAS PEACH PECAN BREAD

2 cups all-purpose flour	1¹/₂ cups sugar
2 teaspoons baking powder	2 eggs
¹/₂ teaspoon salt	¹/₄ cup sour cream
¹/₂ teaspoon nutmeg	1 cup mashed, peeled fresh peaches
10²/₃ tablespoons butter, softened	1 cup chopped pecans

Combine the flour, baking powder, salt and nutmeg in a bowl and mix well. Beat the butter and sugar in a large bowl until light and fluffy. Add the eggs and sour cream and beat for 1 to 2 minutes. Stir in the dry ingredients alternately with the peaches. Stir in the pecans. Pour into a greased 5×9-inch loaf pan. Bake at 350 degrees for 50 to 60 minutes or until a wooden pick inserted in the center comes out clean. Cool in the pan for 10 minutes. Remove to a wire rack to cool completely. You may bake this bread in wide-mouth canning jars for round loaves. Yield: 12 servings.

Kay F. Mauer, Delta Kappa Master
Robstown, Texas

POPPY SEED BREAD

3 cups all-purpose flour	3 eggs
1¹/₂ teaspoons baking powder	1¹/₂ teaspoons vanilla extract
¹/₂ teaspoon salt	1¹/₂ teaspoons almond extract
2 tablespoons poppy seeds	1¹/₂ cups milk
2 cups sugar	Glaze
1¹/₂ cups vegetable oil	

Combine the flour, baking powder, salt and poppy seeds in a large bowl and mix well. Beat the sugar, oil, eggs, vanilla and almond extract in a large bowl. Beat in the dry ingredients alternately with the milk, beginning and ending with the dry ingredients. Pour into 2 greased loaf pans. Bake at 350 degrees for 1 hour or until a wooden pick inserted in the center comes out clean. Cool in the pan for 10 minutes. Remove to a wire rack to cool completely. Drizzle with the Glaze. You may bake this bread in 5 small loaf pans for 35 to 40 minutes. Yield: 24 servings.

ORANGE GLAZE

³/₄ cup sugar	¹/₂ teaspoon almond extract
¹/₄ cup orange juice	

Combine the sugar, orange juice and almond extract in a small bowl. Stir until the sugar dissolves.

Peggy Wallis, Delta Master
Pueblo, Colorado

PUMPKIN BREAD

3¹/₂ cups all-purpose flour	¹/₄ teaspoon cloves
3 cups sugar	4 eggs
2 teaspoons baking soda	1 cup corn oil
1¹/₂ teaspoons salt	²/₃ cup water
1 teaspoon cinnamon	2 cups canned pumpkin
1 teaspoon ginger	1 cup chopped pecans
1 teaspoon nutmeg	1 cup chocolate chips

Combine the flour, sugar, baking soda, salt, cinnamon, ginger, nutmeg and cloves in a bowl and mix well. Beat the eggs in a large bowl. Beat in the oil, water and pumpkin. Stir in the dry ingredients gradually. Stir until smooth. Stir in the pecans and chocolate chips. Pour into 3 nonstick loaf pans. Bake at 350 degrees for 1 hour or until a wooden pick inserted in the center comes out clean. Cool in the pan for 10 minutes. Remove to a wire rack to cool completely. Yield: 24 servings.

Bobbie Richards, Xi Beta Iota
Gallup, New Mexico

PUMPKIN CHERRY LOAVES

3 cups all-purpose flour	1¹/₄ cups vegetable oil
2 teaspoons baking soda	3¹/₂ cups sugar
2 teaspoons baking powder	2 cups canned pumpkin
1 teaspoon salt	1 cup raisins
2 teaspoons cinnamon	1 cup chopped glacé cherries
4 eggs	¹/₂ cup walnuts

Sift the flour, baking soda, baking powder, salt and cinnamon together. Beat the eggs in a large bowl. Beat in the oil, sugar and pumpkin. Stir in the dry ingredients. Stir in the raisins, cherries and walnuts. Pour into 2 large or 3 small greased and floured loaf pans. Bake at 325 degrees for 1 hour or until a wooden pick inserted in the center comes out clean. Cool in the pan for 10 minutes. Remove to a wire rack to cool completely. Yield: 24 servings.

Evelyn R. Orr, Alpha Beta Master
Richards Landing, Ontario, Canada

MELT-IN-YOUR-MOUTH PUMPKIN BREAD

2 cups all-purpose flour	1 teaspoon cinnamon
2 cups sugar	¹/₂ teaspoon salt
2 (3-ounce) cans flaked coconut	5 eggs
1 teaspoon baking soda	1¹/₄ cups vegetable oil
	2 cups canned pumpkin

Mix the flour, sugar, coconut, baking soda, cinnamon and salt in a bowl. Beat the eggs in a large bowl. Beat

in the oil and pumpkin. Stir in the flour mixture. Pour into 2 nonstick loaf pans. Bake at 325 degrees for 1 hour or until a wooden pick inserted in the center comes out clean. Cool in the pan for 10 minutes. Remove to a wire rack to cool completely.
Yield: 24 servings.

Beverly Long, Alpha Zeta Alpha
Lowry City, Missouri

PUMPKIN SPICE CANNED BREAD

3¹/₂ cups all-purpose flour	*¹/₂ cup raisins*
2 teaspoons baking soda	*¹/₂ cup chopped nuts*
¹/₂ teaspoon baking powder	*10²/₃ tablespoons margarine, softened*
1 teaspoon salt	*2²/₃ cups sugar*
1 teaspoon cinnamon	*4 eggs*
1 teaspoon nutmeg	*2 cups pumpkin*
1 teaspoon cloves	*²/₃ cup water*

Combine the flour, baking soda, baking powder, salt, cinnamon, nutmeg and cloves in a large bowl and mix well. Stir in the raisins and nuts. Beat the margarine and sugar in a bowl until light and fluffy. Beat in the eggs and water. Add to the dry ingredients and stir gently to mix. Fill greased wide-mouth pint or quart canning jars ¹/₂ full. Bake at 325 degrees for 45 minutes or until a wooden pick inserted in the center comes out clean. Seal the hot jars carefully with 2-piece canning lids. Let cool and check that the lids are sealed. Store in a cool place for up to 1 year. Yield: 8 pints or 4 quarts.

Judy Bespalec, Alpha Theta
Crete, Nebraska

STRAWBERRY NUT BREAD

2 eggs	*1¹/₂ cups all-purpose flour*
1 cup sugar	
¹/₂ cup plus 2 tablespoons vegetable oil	*1 (10-ounce) package frozen strawberries, thawed*
¹/₂ teaspoon salt	
1¹/₂ teaspoons cinnamon	*¹/₂ cup plus 2 tablespoons chopped pecans*
¹/₂ teaspoons baking soda	

Beat the eggs, sugar, oil, salt and cinnamon in a large bowl. Add the baking soda, flour, strawberries and pecans. Stir just until combined. Pour into a greased and floured loaf pan. Bake at 350 degrees for 1 hour or until a wooden pick inserted in the center comes out clean. Cool in the pan for 10 minutes. Remove to a wire rack to cool completely. Yield: 8 to 10 servings.

Deborah K. Ailey, Iota Tau
Pryor, Oklahoma

STRAWBERRY BREAD

2 cups all-purpose flour	*2 cups sugar*
1 teaspoon salt	*1 cup vegetable oil*
1 teaspoon baking soda	*1 teaspoon vanilla extract*
¹/₂ teaspoon baking powder	
1 teaspoon cinnamon	*2 cups crushed strawberries*
3 eggs	

Combine the flour, salt, baking soda, baking powder and cinnamon in a bowl and mix well. Beat the eggs and sugar in a large bowl. Beat in the oil and vanilla. Stir in the dry ingredients. Stir in the strawberries. Pour into 2 greased and floured loaf pans. Bake at 350 degrees for 1 hour or until a wooden pick inserted in the center comes out clean. Cool in the pan for 10 minutes. Remove to a wire rack to cool completely. Yield: 24 servings.

Carole Schweitzer, Xi Zeta Omicron
Osborne, Kansas

SWEET POTATO PECAN BREAD

1¹/₂ cups all-purpose flour, sifted	*2 eggs, lightly beaten*
	¹/₂ cup applesauce
2 teaspoons baking powder	*2 tablespoons milk*
	1 cup mashed cooked sweet potatoes
¹/₄ teaspoon salt	
1 teaspoon mace	*1 cup chopped pecans*
¹/₂ teaspoon cinnamon	*¹/₂ cup chopped dates or raisins*
1 cup sugar	

Combine the flour, baking powder, salt, mace and cinnamon in a large bowl and mix well. Add the sugar, eggs, applesauce and milk and stir just until moistened. Stir in the sweet potatoes, pecans and dates. Grease the bottom of a loaf pan. Pour in the batter. Bake at 325 degrees for 1 hour and 10 minutes or until a wooden pick inserted in the center comes out clean. Cool in the pan for 10 minutes. Remove to a wire rack to cool completely. Yield: 12 servings.

Carol J. Harper, Alpha Delta Phi
Lowry City, Missouri

---

*Darcy Jackson, Eta Xeta, Ponca City, Oklahoma, makes **Beer Bread** by combining 2 cups self-rising flour with 1 cup sugar and 1 can warm beer in a large bowl. She stirs the ingredients until well-blended and pours the mixture into a greased loaf pan. The bread is baked at 325 degrees for 45 minutes. A slit is made in the top of the loaf and it is returned to the oven for 15 minutes. The bread should stand for 30 minutes before serving.*

BEST ZUCCHINI BREAD

3 cups all-purpose flour	3 eggs
1 teaspoon cinnamon	2 cups sugar
1/4 teaspoon nutmeg	1 cup vegetable oil
1 teaspoon salt	3 cups shredded zucchini
1 teaspoon baking soda	2 teaspoons vanilla
1/4 teaspoon baking	extract
powder	1 cup pecans, chopped

Sift the flour, cinnamon, nutmeg, salt, baking soda and baking powder into a large bowl. Beat the eggs in a large bowl. Beat in the sugar. Stir in the oil, zucchini and vanilla. Stir in the dry ingredients. Stir in the pecans. Pour into 2 greased loaf pans. Bake at 325 degrees for 1 hour or until a wooden pick inserted in the center comes out clean. Cool in the pan for 10 minutes. Remove to a wire rack to cool completely. Yield: 24 servings.

Ramona Brunswick, Alpha Lambda Master
Westminster, Colorado

ORANGE ZUCCHINI BREAD

3 cups sifted all-purpose	2 cups sugar
flour	1 cup vegetable oil
1 teaspoon salt	2 teaspoons vanilla
1 teaspoon baking soda	extract
1/4 teaspoon baking	1 cup chopped walnuts
powder	2 cups grated zucchini
1 teaspoon nutmeg	1 tablespoon grated
1/2 teaspoon cinnamon	orange zest
3 eggs	

Sift the flour, salt, baking soda, baking powder, nutmeg and cinnamon into a large bowl. Beat the eggs and sugar in a large bowl until thick and pale yellow. Stir in the oil, vanilla, walnuts, zucchini and orange zest. Stir in the dry ingredients. Pour into 2 nonstick 5×9-inch loaf pans. Bake at 350 degrees for 50 to 60 minutes or until a wooden pick inserted in the center comes out clean. Cool in the pan for 10 minutes. Remove to a wire rack to cool completely. Yield: 20 servings.

Jean McMillan, Beta Delta
Cheney, Washington

BABY BUTTERBALL BISCUITS

2 cups self-rising flour	1 cup sour cream
1 cup (2 sticks) butter or	
margarine	

Place the flour in a bowl. Cut in the butter with a pastry blender or fork until crumbly. Add the sour cream and stir to mix well. Drop by heaping teaspoonfuls into ungreased mini-muffin cups. Bake at

350 degrees for 20 minutes or until firm to the touch; they will not brown. Cool in the pan for 5 minutes. Remove to a wire rack to cool. Yield: 12 to 14 servings.

Sandy Bartholomew, Xi Epsilon Iota
Ballwin, Missouri

BUBBA BEER BISCUITS

4 cups baking mix	2 tablespoons butter,
1/2 cup sugar	melted
1 (12-ounce) can beer	

Combine the baking mix, sugar, beer and melted butter in a bowl. Stir just until moistened. Spoon into greased muffin cups. Bake at 400 degrees for 15 to 20 minutes or until a wooden pick inserted in the center comes out clean. Cool in the pan for 5 minutes. Remove to a wire rack to cool. Yield: 12 servings.

Kathy Verchick, Omega Lambda
Lake City, Florida

MILE-HIGH CHEDDAR BISCUITS

6 cups all-purpose flour	2 teaspoons salt
8 teaspoons baking	1 cup shortening
powder	1 1/2 cups (6 ounces)
1 rounded tablespoon	shredded Cheddar
confectioners' sugar	cheese
2 teaspoons cream	2 cups milk
of tartar	2 eggs, beaten

Sift the flour, baking powder, confectioners' sugar, cream of tartar and salt into a large bowl. Cut in the shortening with a pastry blender or fork until crumbly. Stir in the cheese. Make a well in the center and pour in the milk and eggs. Stir just until combined. Knead the dough briefly on a lightly floured work surface. Roll or pat out to 1-inch thickness. Cut with a 2- to 3-inch biscuit cutter. Arrange the biscuits on an ungreased baking sheet. Bake at 425 degrees for 14 to 15 minutes or until golden brown. Serve warm with your favorite beef stew or chili or topped with honey or homemade jam. Yield: 24 servings.

Karen A. Parenteau, Xi Theta
Minnedosa, Manitoba, Canada

DEVILED HAM SHORTCAKES

2 cups all-purpose flour	3/4 cup milk
1 tablespoon baking	1 (4-ounce) can deviled
powder	ham
1 teaspoon salt	1/4 cup cream or
1/4 cup (about)	evaporated milk
shortening	

Sift the flour, baking powder and salt into a bowl. Cut in the shortening with a pastry blender or fork until crumbly. Stir in the milk just until combined. Knead the dough lightly on a floured work surface. Roll or pat out the dough. Cut 1/2 of the dough with a biscuit cutter and the other 1/2 with a donut cutter. Spread each plain biscuit with 2 teaspoons of deviled ham. Top each with a donut-shaped biscuit and secure with a wooden pick. Arrange with the sides touching on a nonstick baking sheet. Brush with the cream. Bake at 450 degrees for 15 minutes. Serve hot with cheese sauce. You may use creamed asparagus instead deviled ham. Yield: 8 servings.

Wanda E. Dudley, Upsilon Master
Albuquerque, New Mexico

SWEET POTATO BISCUITS

4 cups self-rising flour
3 tablespoons sugar
1/4 teaspoon baking soda
2 cups cooked sweet
  potatoes
1/2 cup (1 stick) butter,
  melted
1 1/4 cups milk

Combine the flour, sugar and baking soda in a large bowl. Purée the cooked sweet potatoes in a food processor or put through a food mill. Combine the sweet potatoes, melted butter and milk in a large bowl and mix well. Stir in the dry ingredients. Shape into a ball. Knead the dough 10 times on a floured work surface. Roll out to 1-inch thickness. Cut with a 2-inch biscuit cutter. Arrange the biscuits on a well greased baking sheet. Bake at 400 degrees for 15 to 20 minutes. Yield: 15 servings

Shannon Barlow, Preceptor Zeta
Beaumont, Texas

BROCCOLI CORN BREAD

1 (10-ounce) package
  frozen chopped
  broccoli
2 (8-ounce) packages
  corn bread mix
4 eggs
1 cup chopped onion
3/4 cup cottage cheese
1/2 cup (1 stick)
  margarine, softened

Thaw the broccoli and drain well. Combine the broccoli, corn bread mix, eggs, onion, cottage cheese and margarine in a large bowl. Stir to mix well. Pour into a 9×13-inch baking pan coated with nonstick cooking spray. Bake at 350 degrees for 35 to 40 minutes or until golden brown. Yield: 12 servings.

Lynette Major, Xi Theta Pi
Levelland, Texas

FANTASTIC CORN BREAD

12 slices bacon
1 (8-ounce) package corn
  bread mix
1 cup shredded sharp
  Cheddar cheese
3 tablespoons hot
  pepper jelly
3 tablespoons butter

Fry the bacon in a large skillet until crisp. Remove to paper towels to drain; crumble. Reserve 2 tablespoons of the bacon drippings. Prepare the corn bread batter using the package directions. Add the bacon, reserved bacon drippings and cheese. Stir to mix well. Pour into a greased 9×13-inch baking pan. Bake using the package directions. Melt the jelly and butter in a small saucepan over low heat, stirring occasionally. Poke holes in the top of the corn bread with a fork. Pour the jelly mixture evenly over the top. Yield: 8 servings.

Claudette Hall, Laureate Sigma
Baton Rouge, Louisiana

TRUCK STOP CORN BREAD

1 2/3 cups sifted all-
  purpose flour
2/3 cup sugar
5 teaspoons baking
  powder
1 teaspoon salt
1 2/3 cups cornmeal
2 eggs, beaten
1 2/3 cups milk
5 1/3 tablespoons
  margarine, melted

Combine the flour, sugar, baking powder and salt in a large bowl. Stir in the cornmeal. Add the eggs and milk and stir until smooth. Add the melted margarine and stir just until combined. Pour into a well buttered 9×13-inch baking pan or greased ovenproof skillet. Bake at 425 degrees for 30 minutes or until a wooden pick inserted in the center comes out clean. Remove to a wire rack to cool. Yield: 15 servings.

Mary Walzel, Xi Kappa Chi
Refugio, Texas

HUSH PUPPIES

1 cup cornmeal mix
1 cup all-purpose flour
1/4 cup sugar
1/4 cup vegetable oil
1 cup milk
1 small onion, minced
Vegetable oil for
  deep-frying

Combine the cornmeal mix, flour, sugar, 1/4 cup oil, milk and onion in a bowl and mix well. Heat the oil in a heavy saucepan or deep-fryer to 375 degrees. Drop the dough by spoonfuls into the hot oil. Fry for 3 to 5 minutes or until golden brown on all sides. Remove to paper towels to drain. Yield: 24 servings.

Patricia Grant, Preceptor Kappa Epsilon
Arlington, Texas

BERRY STREUSEL MUFFINS

1½ cups all-purpose flour	1 cup fresh or frozen berries
2 teaspoons baking soda	¼ cup chopped pecans
½ cup sugar	¼ cup all-purpose flour
1 egg, beaten	¼ cup packed brown sugar
½ cup milk	2 tablespoons butter, softened
½ cup (1 stick) butter, melted	

Combine 1½ cups flour, the baking soda and sugar in a large bowl. Combine the egg, milk and ½ cup melted butter in a bowl and mix well. Add to the dry ingredients and stir just until combined. Stir in the berries. Fill greased muffin cups. Combine the pecans, ¼ cup flour, the brown sugar and 2 tablespoons butter in a bowl, stirring until crumbly. Sprinkle over the muffins. Bake at 375 degrees for 20 minutes or until a wooden pick inserted in the center comes out clean. Cool in the pan for 5 minutes. Remove to a wire rack to cool. Yield: 12 servings.

Cindi Dryden, Beta Omega
Richmond, Kansas

BLUEBERRY OAT MUFFINS

½ cup rolled oats	¼ teaspoon baking soda
½ cup orange juice	½ cup vegetable oil
1½ cups all-purpose flour	1 egg, lightly beaten
½ cup sugar	1 cup fresh or frozen blueberries
1¼ teaspoons baking powder	2 tablespoons sugar
½ teaspoon salt	¼ teaspoon cinnamon

Combine the oats and orange juice in a large bowl. Add the flour, ½ cup sugar, baking powder, salt, baking soda, oil and egg. Stir to mix well. Fold in the blueberries. Fill nonstick muffin cups. Mix 2 tablespoons sugar and cinnamon in a small bowl. Sprinkle over the muffins. Bake at 400 degrees for 18 to 22 minutes or until a wooden pick inserted in the center comes out clean. Cool in the pan for 5 minutes. Remove to a wire rack to cool. Yield: 12 servings.

Ruth Molzan, Xi Epsilon Mu
Leamington, Ontario, Canada

ONE-MONTH BRAN MUFFINS

2 cups rolled oats	1 cup vegetable oil
4 large shredded wheat cereal biscuits	4 cups buttermilk
2 cups All-Bran cereal	4 eggs, beaten
1 cup boiling water	5 cups all-purpose flour
2¼ cups packed brown sugar	5 teaspoons baking soda
	1 tablespoon salt

Combine the oats, shredded wheat and bran cereal in a large bowl. Add the boiling water and stir to mix. Stir in the oil, buttermilk and brown sugar. Stir in the eggs. Combine the flour, baking soda and salt in a bowl and add to the cereal mixture. Stir to mix well. Fill muffin cups coated with nonstick cooking spray. Bake at 400 degrees for 15 to 20 minutes or until a wooden pick inserted in the center comes out clean. Cool in the pan for 5 minutes. Remove to a wire rack to cool. This batter can be stored, covered, in the refrigerator for up to 1 month. Stir well before using. Yield: 36 to 48 servings.

Judy Bartolo, Preceptor Omicron
Las Vegas, Nevada

CARROT PINEAPPLE MUFFINS

1½ cups all-purpose flour	⅔ cup vegetable oil
2 teaspoons baking powder	2 eggs, beaten
1 teaspoon baking soda	1 cup grated carrots
1 teaspoon cinnamon	1 cup crushed pineapple, drained
½ teaspoon salt	1 teaspoon vanilla extract
1 cup sugar	

Combine the flour, baking powder, baking soda, cinnamon and salt in a bowl and mix well. Beat the sugar, oil and eggs in a large bowl. Add the dry ingredients and stir just until combined. Stir in the carrots, pineapple and vanilla. Fill greased muffin cups to the top. Bake at 375 degrees for 20 minutes or until a wooden pick inserted in the center comes out clean. Cool in the pan for 5 minutes. Remove to a wire rack to cool. Yield: 12 servings.

Margaret Kilby, Xi Theta Gamma
Petawawa, Ontario, Canada

MORNING GLORY MUFFINS

4 cups all-purpose flour	1 cup chopped pecans
2½ cups sugar	1 cup flaked coconut
4 teaspoons baking soda	2 tart apples
4 teaspoons cinnamon	6 eggs
1 teaspoon salt	1¾ cups canola oil
4 cups grated carrots	4 teaspoons vanilla extract
1 cup raisins	

Combine the flour, sugar, baking soda, cinnamon and salt in a large bowl. Stir in the carrots, raisins, pecans and coconut. Peel, core and grate the apples. Stir into the flour mixture. Beat the eggs in a bowl. Stir in the canola oil and vanilla. Add to the flour mixture and stir just until moistened. Fill greased muffin cups ¾ full. Bake at 350 degrees for 30 minutes or until a wooden pick inserted in the center comes out clean. Cool in the pan for 5 minutes. Remove to a wire rack to cool. Yield: 30 servings.

Gay Eppinga, Xi Nu Nu
Amherst, Texas

COTTAGE CHEESE MUFFINS

1/3 cup sugar
3 tablespoons butter or
  margarine, softened
1 teaspoon grated
  lemon zest

1/2 cup cottage cheese
1 egg
1 3/4 cups baking mix
1/2 cup milk

Beat the sugar and butter in a bowl until light and fluffy. Beat in the lemon zest and cottage cheese. Add the egg and beat well. Add the baking mix and milk and stir just until moistened. Fill greased mini-muffin cups. Bake at 400 degrees for 20 minutes or until a wooden pick inserted in the center comes out clean. Cool in the pan for 5 minutes. Remove to a wire rack to cool. Yield: 20 servings.

Geneice B. Smith, Xi Nu
Winter Haven, Florida

LEMON POPPY SEED MUFFINS

1 (2-layer) package
  yellow cake mix
4 eggs
1/2 cup vegetable oil
1 cup warm water

2 tablespoons poppy
  seeds
1 (3-ounce) package
  instant lemon
  pudding mix

Beat all the ingredients in a large bowl. Fill nonstick muffin cups 3/4 full. Bake at 350 degrees for 25 minutes or until a wooden pick inserted in the center comes out clean. Cool in the pan for 5 minutes. Remove to a wire rack to cool. Yield: 24 servings.

Pat Geskey, Preceptor Eta
Lincoln, Illinois

DATE ORANGE MUFFINS

1 orange
1/2 cup orange juice
1 egg
1/3 cup vegetable oil
1 cup all-purpose flour
3/4 cup natural bran

3/4 cup sugar
1 teaspoon baking
  powder
1 teaspoon baking soda
1/2 cup finely chopped
  dates

Cut the unpeeled orange into 7 or 8 pieces and remove the seeds. Purée the orange pieces and orange juice in a blender. Add the egg and oil and process until blended. Pour into a large bowl. Combine the next 5 ingredients in a bowl and mix well. Add the dates and toss to coat. Add the date mixture to the orange mixture. Stir just until combined. Fill greased muffin cups 3/4 full. Bake at 400 degrees for 20 minutes or until a wooden pick inserted in the center comes out

clean. Cool in the pan for 5 minutes. Remove to a wire rack to cool. Yield: 12 to 16 servings.

Rhoda Dickson, Beta Xi
Fort Frances, Ontario, Canada

ORANGE CRANBERRY MUFFINS

1 1/2 cups all-purpose
  flour
3/4 cup sugar
1 teaspoon baking soda
1 teaspoon baking
  powder
1/4 teaspoon salt
  (or to taste)

1 orange
1/2 cup orange juice
1 egg, beaten
1/2 cup sweetened dried
  cranberries
1/2 cup (1 stick)
  margarine, softened

Combine the first 5 ingredients in a bowl and mix well. Slice the orange and finely chop. Combine the chopped orange, orange juice, egg, cranberries and margarine in a large bowl. Stir to mix well. Add the dry ingredients and stir just until moistened. Fill muffin cups 3/4 full. Bake at 400 degrees for 15 minutes or until a wooden pick inserted in the center comes out clean. Cool in the pan for 5 minutes. Remove to a wire rack to cool. Yield: 18 servings.

Gayle Butler, Laureate Alpha
Regina, Saskatchewan, Canada

PUMPKIN SPICE CRAN-APPLE MUFFINS

3 cups all-purpose flour
2 teaspoons baking soda
1 teaspoon baking
  powder
1 teaspoon cinnamon
1/2 teaspoon ginger
1/2 teaspoon allspice
4 eggs
2 cups sugar
1/2 cup packed brown
  sugar

1 tablespoon vanilla
  extract
2 cups canned pumpkin
1 cup vegetable oil
1/2 cup water
2 cups chopped peeled
  baking apples
1 1/2 cups fresh or frozen
  cranberries
3/4 cup chopped nuts
  (optional)

Combine the flour, baking soda, baking powder, cinnamon, ginger and allspice in a large bowl and mix well. Combine the eggs, sugar, brown sugar, vanilla, pumpkin, oil and water in a large bowl. Beat with an electric mixer until smooth. Beat in the dry ingredients gradually. Fold in the apples, cranberries and nuts. Fill greased miniature muffin cups. Bake at 350 degrees for 20 to 25 minutes or until a wooden pick inserted in the center comes out clean. Cool in the pan for 5 minutes. Remove to a wire rack to cool. You may bake these in standard muffin cups for 25 to 30 minutes. Yield: 24 servings.

Belinda Hemp, Laureate Delta Phi
Sidney, Ohio

AUTUMN PUMPKIN MUFFINS

3¹/₂ cups all-purpose flour	2 cups canned pumpkin
2 teaspoons baking soda	1 cup canola oil
1 teaspoon baking powder	3 cups sugar
1 teaspoon cinnamon	3 eggs
1 teaspoon nutmeg	1 cup raisins
1 teaspoon cloves	1 cup chopped walnuts
¹/₂ teaspoon salt	Orange Glaze
	Additional chopped walnuts

Combine the first 7 ingredients in a bowl and mix well. Combine the pumpkin, canola oil, sugar and eggs in a large bowl. Beat with an electric mixer until well blended. Beat in the dry ingredients. Stir in the raisins and 1 cup walnuts. Fill muffin cups coated with nonstick cooking spray ³/₄ full. Bake at 350 degrees for 20 to 23 minutes or until a wooden pick inserted in the center comes out clean. Cool in the pan for 15 minutes. Remove to a wire rack to cool. Drizzle the Orange Glaze over the tops and down the sides of the cooled muffins. Sprinkle with chopped walnuts. Yield: 18 servings.

ORANGE GLAZE

1¹/₂ cups confectioners' sugar	6 tablespoons orange juice
1 teaspoon grated orange zest	

Combine the confectioners' sugar, orange zest and orange juice in a bowl and mix well.

Lela Sandrock, Preceptor Alpha Omicron
Pekin, Illinois

PUMPKIN PEANUT BUTTER MUFFINS

3¹/₂ cups all-purpose flour	1³/₄ cups buttermilk
2 cups sugar	1 cup canned pumpkin
1¹/₂ teaspoons baking soda	10²/₃ tablespoons butter, melted
1 teaspoon salt	1 tablespoon vanilla extract
2 eggs, beaten	1¹/₂ cups peanut butter

Combine the flour, sugar, baking soda and salt in a large bowl. Whisk the eggs and buttermilk in a large bowl. Add the pumpkin, melted butter, vanilla and peanut butter and mix well. Add the dry ingredients and stir just until combined. Fill greased muffin cups ³/₄ full. Bake at 425 degrees for 18 to 20 minutes or until a wooden pick inserted in the center comes out clean. Cool in the pan for 5 minutes. Remove to a wire rack to cool. Yield: 24 servings.

Patti McBride, Xi Lambda Zeta
Mt. Vernon, Missouri

RHUBARB MUFFINS

1¹/₄ cups packed brown sugar	1 teaspoon baking soda
¹/₂ cup vegetable oil	1 teaspoon baking powder
1 egg	¹/₂ teaspoon salt
2 teaspoons vanilla extract	1¹/₂ cups diced rhubarb
1 cup buttermilk	¹/₂ cup chopped nuts
2¹/₂ cups all-purpose flour	¹/₃ cup sugar
	1 teaspoon cinnamon
	1 tablespoon butter

Beat the first 5 ingredients in a large bowl. Stir in the flour, baking soda, baking powder and salt. Stir in the rhubarb and nuts. Fill nonstick muffin cups ³/₄ full. Mix the sugar, cinnamon and butter in a small bowl until crumbly. Sprinkle over the muffins and press gently into the batter. Bake at 350 degrees for 20 minutes or until a wooden pick inserted in the center comes out clean. Cool in the pan for 5 minutes. Remove to a wire rack to cool. Yield: 24 servings.

Sue Andersen, Alpha Psi
Sidney, Montana

SAUSAGE CHEESE MUFFINS

1 pound hot bulk pork sausage	¹/₂ cup milk
1 (10-ounce) can condensed Cheddar cheese soup	2¹/₂ teaspoons rubbed sage
	3 cups baking mix

Brown the sausage in a skillet, stirring until crumbly; drain. Whisk the cheese soup and milk in a bowl. Stir in the the next 3 ingredients just until moistened. Fill greased muffin cups ³/₄ full. Bake at 400 degrees for 15 to 20 minutes or until a wooden pick inserted in the center comes out clean. Cool in the pan for 5 minutes. Remove to a wire rack to cool. Yield: 24 servings.

Juanita Koehler, Xi Alpha Tau
Dandridge, Texas

TANGERINE AND BASIL MUFFINS

2 cups all-purpose flour	1 egg, lightly beaten
¹/₂ cup sugar	¹/₄ cup (¹/₂ stick) butter, softened
2 teaspoons baking powder	2 tablespoons low-fat milk
1 teaspoon baking soda	2¹/₂ tangerines
¹/₂ teaspoon salt	1¹/₂ teaspoons basil
1 cup low-fat vanilla yogurt	

Sift the flour, sugar, baking powder, baking soda and salt into a large bowl. Combine the yogurt, egg, butter and milk in a large bowl. Mix with a fork until smooth. Add the dry ingredients and stir to mix well.

Grate the zest from the tangerines and add to the batter. Peel the tangerines and chop. Stir the tangerines and basil into the batter. Fill paper-lined muffin cups with batter. Bake at 375 degrees for 18 to 20 minutes or until a wooden pick inserted in the center comes out clean. Cool in the pan for 5 minutes. Remove to a wire rack to cool. Yield: 9 to 12 servings.

Barbara Lockner, Alpha Upsilon Master
Palm Coast, Florida

WHOLE WHEAT MUFFINS

³/4 cup whole wheat flour	*1 tablespoon baking powder*
1 cup all-purpose flour	*¹/4 cup vegetable oil*
¹/3 cup sugar	*1 egg, lightly beaten*
1 teaspoon salt	*1¹/4 cups milk*

Mix the first 5 ingredients in a bowl. Add the oil, egg and milk and stir just until combined. Fill nonstick muffin cups ³/4 full. Bake at 400 degrees for 20 to 25 minutes or until a wooden pick inserted in the center comes out clean. Cool in the pan for 5 minutes. Remove to a wire rack to cool. Yield: 12 to 14 servings.

Neva R. Everly, Alpha Epsilon Master
Bethany, Missouri

MONKEY BREAD

3 (10-count) cans refrigerator biscuits	*¹/2 cup (1 stick) butter, melted*
¹/2 cup sugar	*³/4 cup packed brown sugar*
1 tablespoon cinnamon	

Cut each biscuit into quarters. Combine the sugar and cinnamon in a bowl and mix well. Add 8 to 10 biscuit quarters and toss to coat. Place in a greased bundt pan. Repeat with the remaining biscuit quarters. Mix the melted butter and brown sugar in a bowl. Pour over the top. Bake at 350 degrees for 40 minutes. Invert onto a serving plate and let cool. Yield: 30 servings.

Winnie Lee Fuller, Xi Epsilon Iota
Depew, Oklahoma

GORILLA BREAD

2 (10-count) cans refrigerator biscuits	*1¹/2 cups coarsely chopped walnuts*
¹/2 cup sugar	*¹/2 cup (1 stick) butter*
1 tablespoon cinnamon	*1 cup packed brown sugar*
8 ounces cream cheese	

Separate the biscuits and flatten each on a work surface. Combine the sugar and cinnamon in a bowl and mix well. Sprinkle ¹/2 teaspoon of the cinnamon-sugar onto each biscuit. Cut the cream cheese into 20 pieces. Place 1 piece of cream cheese on each biscuit.

Fold the dough over the cream cheese and pinch to seal. Sprinkle ¹/2 cup of the walnuts in the bottom of a bundt pan coated with nonstick cooking spray. Arrange ¹/2 of the filled biscuits in the prepared pan. Melt the butter and brown sugar in a saucepan over low heat, stirring frequently. Pour ¹/2 of the brown sugar mixture over the biscuits in the pan. Sprinkle with ¹/2 cup of the walnuts. Sprinkle with some of the cinnamon-sugar. Top with the remaining biscuits, brown sugar mixture, walnuts and cinnamon-sugar. Bake at 350 degrees for 50 minutes. Cool in the pan for 5 minutes. Invert onto a serving plate and let cool. Yield: 10 to 12 servings.

Janice Adams, Xi Alpha Upsilon
Evington, Virginia

BREAKAWAY VEGETABLE BREAD

8 ounces bacon	*3 (10-count) cans refrigerator buttermilk biscuits*
1 small onion, minced	
1 small green bell pepper, chopped	*¹/2 cup (1 stick) margarine, melted*
1¹/2 cups (6 ounces) shredded Cheddar cheese	

Fry the bacon in a skillet until crisp. Remove to paper towels to drain; crumble. Combine the bacon, onion, bell pepper and cheese in a bowl. Separate the biscuits and cut into quarters or halves. Place the melted margarine in a bowl. Roll the dough into balls and dip in the melted margarine. Arrange ¹/3 of the biscuit balls in a lightly greased bundt pan. Sprinkle with ¹/2 the bacon mixture. Top with ¹/3 of the biscuit balls and sprinkle with the remaining bacon mixture. Top with the remaining biscuit balls. Bake at 350 degrees for 40 to 45 minutes. Yield: 30 servings.

Ruth N. Burgess, Lambda Master
Muskogee, Oklahoma

PARMESAN PULL-APART BREAD

3 tablespoons margarine, melted	*1 (10-count) can refrigerator buttermilk biscuits, separated and cut into quarters*
¹/2 cup (2 ounces) grated Parmesan cheese	

Pour the margarine into a bowl. Place the cheese in a bowl. Dip each biscuit quarter into the margarine and coat in the cheese. Arrange in a greased 3×7-inch loaf pan. Bake at 350 degrees for 30 to 35 minutes or until golden brown. Invert the pan onto a serving plate. Let stand for 1 minute before removing the pan. Yield: 10 servings.

Marcia Herman, Laureate Alpha Lambda
Manhattan, Kansas

CARAMEL ROLLS

1/2 cup packed brown sugar	*2 (8-count) cans refrigerator crescent rolls*
1/2 cup (1 stick) butter or margarine, softened	*2/3 cup chopped pecans*
1/4 cup light corn syrup	*1/4 cup sugar*
	1 teaspoon cinnamon

Combine the brown sugar, butter and corn syrup in a bowl and mix well. Spread in the bottom of 2 greased 8-inch baking pans. Unroll the crescent dough on a lightly floured work surface. Press the seams to seal to form 1 large rectangle. Combine the pecans, sugar and cinnamon in a bowl. Sprinkle the pecan mixture over the dough. Roll up from the long side and pinch the edges. Cut into 16 slices. Place 8 slices, cut side down, in each prepared pan. Bake at 375 degrees for 13 to 17 minutes. Let cool in the pans for 1 minute. Invert onto serving plates. Yield: 6 to 8 servings.

Cindie Olson, Preceptor Eta Tau
Houston, Texas

CHEESE DANISH

2 (8-count) cans refrigerator crescent rolls	*1 teaspoon vanilla extract*
16 ounces cream cheese, softened	*1/3 cup sugar*
	1 teaspoon cinnamon
1 cup sugar	*1/4 cup (1/2 stick) butter, melted*

Unroll 1 can of crescent dough and fit in the bottom of a nonstick 9×13-inch baking pan. Press the seams to seal. Beat the cream cheese, 1 cup sugar and the vanilla in a bowl until smooth. Spread over the dough in the pan. Unroll the remaining can of crescent dough and press the seams to seal. Place the dough on top of the cream cheese mixture. Mix 1/3 cup sugar and the cinnamon in a bowl. Sprinkle over the dough. Drizzle with the butter. Bake at 350 degrees for 30 minutes. Remove to a wire rack to cool. Cover and chill. Yield: 12 servings.

Mary Beth (Betsy) Schmitz, Lauerate Zeta Beta
Fairview, Pennsylvania

BUTTERMILK BREAD

1 cup buttermilk	*5 to 6 cups all-purpose flour*
1 cup water	
1/4 cup (1/2 stick) butter	*3 tablespoons sugar*
1 teaspoon salt	*1/4 teaspoon baking soda*
1 envelope dry yeast	

Heat the first 4 ingredients in a saucepan over low heat just until lukewarm, stirring occasionally. Combine the yeast, flour, sugar and baking soda in a large bowl. Add the warm buttermilk mixture and stir until a dough forms. Knead the dough on a lightly floured work surface until smooth and elastic. Remove to a greased bowl and turn to coat. Cover and let rise in a warm place for 1 1/2 hours. Turn the dough out onto a floured work surface; shape into 2 loaves. Place in nonstick loaf pans and let rise in a warm place for 30 minutes. Bake at 350 degrees for 30 minutes. Remove to a wire rack to cool. Yield: 10 to 12 servings.

Carolyn Sepich, Kappa Master
Raleigh, North Carolina

PUMPKIN CRESCENT ROLLS

8 ounces cream cheese, softened	*2 tablespoons cinnamon*
1 (15-ounce) can pumpkin	*1 teaspoon pumpkin pie spice*
1 (14-ounce) can sweetened condensed milk	*1 cup finely chopped pecans*
2 tablespoons all-purpose flour	*4 (8-count) cans refrigerator crescent rolls*
	1/2 cup sugar

Beat the first 6 ingredients in a bowl until smooth. Stir in the pecans. Separate the crescent rolls on a work surface. Spread each roll with 1 1/2 tablespoons of the pumpkin mixture. Roll up and place on a greased baking sheet. Sprinkle with the sugar. Bake at 375 degrees for 11 to 13 minutes or until golden brown. Yield: 32 servings.

Rose Ann Abernathy, Preceptor Delta
Centralia, Illinois

CHEDDAR PEPPER BREAD

1 envelope dry yeast	*1 egg*
1/4 cup warm water	*1 cup all-purpose flour*
1 1/3 cups all-purpose flour	*1 cup (4 ounces) shredded sharp Cheddar cheese*
2 tablespoons sugar	
1 teaspoon salt	*3/4 teaspoon freshly ground pepper*
1 cup sour cream	

Dissolve the yeast in the warm water in a large bowl. Add 1 1/3 cups flour, the sugar, salt, sour cream and egg. Beat with an electric mixer at low speed for 30 seconds. Beat at high speed for 3 minutes. Add 1 cup flour, the cheese and pepper and stir to mix well. Pour the batter into 2 greased 1-pound coffee cans. Let rise in a warm place for 1 hour or until doubled in bulk. Bake at 350 degrees for 40 minutes. Remove the bread from the cans immediately to a wire rack. Let cool slightly before slicing. Yield: 16 servings.

Lou Distefano, Laureate Gamma Upsilon
Kansas City, Missouri

PLASTIC BOWL BREAD

1½ cups scalded milk
1½ cups cold water
4 eggs, beaten
²/₃ cup sugar
²/₃ cup nonfat dry milk
   powder
2 teaspoons salt
2 envelopes dry yeast
9 cups all-purpose flour
1 cup (2 sticks)
   margarine, melted

Combine the scalded milk and cold water in a bowl. Stir in the eggs, sugar, dry milk powder, salt and yeast. Place the flour in a 6-quart plastic bowl with a sealable plastic lid. Make a well in the center of the flour. Pour the milk mixture into the well, do not stir. Seal the bowl with the plastic lid and let stand. Add the melted margarine when the lid pops open. Stir until a dough forms. Knead the dough on a floured work surface until smooth. Return to the plastic bowl and seal with the lid. Let stand until the lid pops open. Turn the dough out onto a lightly floured work surface and shape into loaves. Place in greased loaf pans and let rise in a warm place for 20 minutes or until doubled in bulk. Bake at 400 degrees for 30 minutes or until golden brown. You may bake this as rolls instead of loaves and may also halve the recipe for a smaller amount. Yield: 36 servings.

Cindra Goodburn, Preceptor Delta Tau
Winterset, Iowa

BACON BEER BREAD

8 slices bacon
2 envelopes dry yeast
1 envelope dried onion
   soup mix
3³/₄ to 4 cups
   all-purpose flour
1 (12-ounce) can beer
¼ cup milk
1 tablespoon sugar
2 tablespoons yellow
   cornmeal

Fry the bacon in a skillet until crisp. Remove to paper towels to drain; crumble. Reserve 2 tablespoons of the bacon drippings. Combine the yeast, soup mix and 1³/₄ cups of the flour in a large bowl and mix well. Combine the beer, milk, sugar and reserved bacon drippings in a saucepan. Heat just until warm over low heat, stirring occasionally. Add to the dry ingredients. Beat with an electric mixer for 3 minutes. Stir in the bacon and enough of the remaining flour to make a moderately stiff dough. Knead the dough on a lightly floured work surface until smooth and elastic. Remove to a greased bowl and turn to coat. Cover and let rise in a warm place for 40 to 45 minutes or until doubled in bulk. Punch down and turn the dough out onto a floured work surface. Shape into 2 loaves or 16 rolls and place on a greased baking sheet. Sprinkle with the cornmeal. Let rise in a warm place for 25 minutes or until doubled in bulk. Bake at 375 degrees for 20 minutes. Remove to a wire rack to cool. Yield: 16 servings.

Marianna Spain, Laureate Beta Psi
Lansing, Kansas

WHOLE WHEAT ORANGE BREAD

3 envelopes dry yeast
³/₄ cup warm water
½ cup honey
4½ teaspoons grated
   orange zest
6 tablespoons
   shortening
4 cups water
7½ cups all-purpose
   flour
2 tablespoons salt
3 cups whole wheat
   flour

Dissolve the yeast in ³/₄ cup warm water in a large bowl. Add the honey, orange zest, and shortening. Beat with an electric mixer until combined. Beat in 4 cups water, 2 cups of the all-purpose flour and the salt. Beat in the remaining all-purpose flour and whole wheat flour 2 cups at a time. Knead the dough on a lightly floured work surface for 5 minutes. Remove to a greased bowl and turn to coat. Cover and let rise in a warm place until doubled in bulk. Turn the dough out onto a floured work surface and shape into 4 loaves. Place in greased 5×8-inch loaf pans and let rise in a warm place until doubled in bulk. Bake at 400 degrees for 30 to 40 minutes. Remove to a wire rack to cool. Yield: 48 servings.

Alice Dorene Prior, Laureate Alpha Alpha
Spokane, Washington

HONEY BREAD

1 envelope dry yeast
¼ cup warm water
1 cup hot water
½ cup (1 stick) butter
¼ cup honey
1¼ teaspoons salt
1½ cups all-purpose
   flour
2 eggs, beaten
1 cup rolled oats
1³/₄ cups all-purpose
   flour

Dissolve the yeast in ¼ cup warm water in a small bowl. Combine 1 cup hot water, the butter, honey and salt in a large bowl and mix well. Add 1½ cups flour and mix well. Stir in the yeast mixture. Add the eggs, oats and 1³/₄ cups flour. Stir to mix well. Cover and let rise in a warm place for 40 to 45 minutes or until doubled in bulk. Spoon into a greased 2-quart baking dish. Bake at 375 degrees for 45 minutes. Remove to a wire rack to cool. Yield: 8 servings.

Judy Ramer, Xi Beta Xi
North Little Rock, Arkansas

FINNISH COFFEE BREAD

3/4 cup milk	*1/2 teaspoon salt*
5 1/2 tablespoons butter, melted	*4 1/2 cups all-purpose flour*
2 cakes yeast	*1 egg white, lightly beaten*
1/4 cup lukewarm water	*beaten*
2 eggs, lightly beaten	*Sugar*
1/3 cup sugar	

Scald the milk in a small saucepan. Let cool to warm. Stir in the melted butter. Dissolve the yeast in the lukewarm water in a large bowl. Add the eggs, 1/3 cup sugar and the salt and stir to mix well. Stir in the milk mixture alternately with the flour to make a stiff dough. Knead the dough on a lightly floured work surface until smooth. Remove to a greased bowl and turn to coat. Cover and let rise in a warm place for 1 1/2 hours or until doubled in bulk. Turn the dough out onto a floured work surface and shape into 2 braids. Place on a nonstick baking sheet. Let rise in a warm place for 30 minutes. Bake at 350 degrees for 20 to 25 minutes. Brush the hot bread with egg white and sprinkle with sugar. Remove to a wire rack to cool. Yield: 12 to 16 servings.

Marge Fleming, Laureate Delta Upsilon
Canal Fulton, Ohio

SOPAPILLAS

1 1/4 cups milk	*1/2 teaspoon salt*
1 cake or envelope dry yeast	*1 tablespoon sugar*
yeast	*1 tablespoon shortening*
1/4 cup warm water	*Vegetable oil for frying*
4 cups all-purpose flour	*Confectioners' sugar or honey*
1 teaspoon baking powder	*honey*

Scald the milk in a small saucepan. Let cool to warm. Dissolve the yeast in the warm water in a small bowl. Stir into the warm milk. Let cool to room temperature. Combine the flour, baking powder, salt and sugar in a large bowl. Cut in the shortening with a pastry blender or fork. Stir in the milk mixture to make a stiff dough. Knead the dough on a lightly floured work surface 15 to 20 times. Let stand for 10 minutes. Roll out the dough to 1/4-inch thickness and cut into squares. Heat oil in a heavy saucepan or deep-fryer until hot but not smoking. Fry the dough squares in batches for 1 to 2 minutes. Remove to paper towels to drain. Sprinkle with confectioners' sugar or drizzle with honey. These can also be topped with cooked meat, beans, chili, cheese and avocado dip for a main dish. Yield: about 36 servings.

Dorothy Smith, Xi Beta Iota
Gallup, New Mexico

HAWAIIAN COFFEE RING

When our children were young, I made this for Christmas morning and we enjoyed it while opening presents. Our youngest son and his wife came from Michigan this past Christmas and I made this coffee cake for all or us.

1 envelope dry yeast	*1/2 cup evaporated milk*
1/2 cup warm water	*1/4 cup warm water*
1/4 cup (1/2 stick) butter, softened	*1 teaspoon salt*
softened	*3 1/2 to 4 cups all-purpose flour*
1/4 cup sugar	*purpose flour*
2 eggs	

Dissolve the yeast in 1/2 cup warm water in a small bowl. Beat the butter and sugar in a large bowl until light and fluffy. Beat in the eggs, evaporated milk, 1/4 cup warm water, the salt and yeast mixture. Beat in 1 1/2 cups of the flour. Cover and let rise in a warm place for 30 minutes. Stir in the remaining flour until a stiff dough forms. Knead the dough on a lightly floured work surface and shape into a ring. Place in a nonstick 9-inch ring mold. Let rise in a warm place for 30 minutes or until doubled in bulk. Bake at 350 degrees for 30 to 35 minutes. Remove to a wire rack to cool. Yield: 8 servings.

Ruth A. Rightmer, Laureate Beta Omicron
Mayer, Arizona

GOLDEN HONEY PAN ROLLS

1 cup lukewarm milk	*1 envelope dry yeast*
1 egg	*1/3 cup sugar*
1 egg yolk	*2 tablespoons butter, melted*
1/2 cup vegetable oil	*melted*
2 tablespoons honey	*1 tablespoon honey*
1 1/2 teaspoons salt	*1 egg white*
3 1/2 cups all-purpose flour	

Add the milk, egg, egg yolk, oil, 2 tablespoons honey, the salt, flour and yeast to the bread machine pan in the order recommended by the manufacturer. Set the machine on dough mode. Remove the completed dough to a lightly floured work surface. Punch down and cover. Let stand for 10 minutes. Shape the dough into 24 balls. Arrange in a greased 9×13-inch baking pan. Cover and let rise in a warm place for 30 minutes. Combine the sugar, butter, 1 tablespoon honey and the egg white in a small bowl. Drizzle over the rolls. Bake at 350 degrees for 20 to 25 minutes. Remove to a wire rack and brush with additional honey, if desired. Yield: 24 servings.

Phyllis Moore, Xi Delta Tau
Jonesboro, Louisiana

ENGLISH MUFFIN BREAD

1¹/₂ cups water
3¹/₂ cups bread flour
1 tablespoon sugar
1 teaspoon salt
1 teaspoon baking soda
¹/₄ cup nonfat dry milk
   powder
2 teaspoons dry yeast

Add the water, flour, sugar, salt, baking soda, milk powder and yeast to the bread machine pan in the order given. Set the machine on the basic white bread cycle with medium to normal color setting. Remove the baked bread from the pan to a wire rack to cool completely. Slice and toast the bread.
Yield: 1 large loaf.

Suzanne B. Long, Laureate Epsilon Rho
Carlisle, Pennsylvania

FLAT BREAD

1¹/₂ teaspoons dry yeast
1¹/₂ cups lukewarm
   water
1 teaspoon sugar
1¹/₂ teaspoons salt
3¹/₂ cups all-purpose
   flour
Salt
Favorite seasonings
   to taste

Combine the yeast, water and sugar in a large bowl. Let stand until the mixture begins to bubble. Stir in 1¹/₂ teaspoons salt and the flour gradually to make a stiff dough. Knead the dough on a lightly floured work surface until elastic. Shape into a log and cut into 16 pieces. Roll out each piece to a thin circle. Place on a floured baking sheet. Sprinkle with salt and favorite seasonings. Bake at 400 degrees for 10 minutes or until light brown, turning once during baking. Remove to a wire rack to cool.
Yield: 16 servings.

Carol Phillips, Preceptor Beta Iota
Quesnel, British Columbia, Canada

HAZELNUT POPPY SEED BREAD

This bread was sold at a special store before my husband and I were married. I lived in another state and he would bring me a loaf every time he came to visit. The bread is no longer sold, so I developed this recipe after my husband passed away four years ago.

2 cups white bread flour
1 cup whole wheat flour
3 tablespoons dry milk
   powder
3 tablespoons packed
   brown sugar
³/₄ teaspoon salt
¹/₂ cup ground hazelnuts
1¹/₄ cups water
4¹/₂ teaspoons poppy
   seeds
1 envelope dry yeast

Add the white bread flour, whole wheat flour, dry milk powder, brown sugar, salt, hazelnuts, water, poppy seeds and yeast to the bread machine pan in the order recommended by the manufacturer. Set the

machine on the whole wheat bake rapid cycle. Remove the baked bread from the pan to a wire rack to cool. Yield: 1 (1¹/₂-pound) loaf.

Shasta Hornack, Iota Master
Overland Park, Kansas

VANILLA BREAD OR BUNS

1 egg
1 tablespoon vanilla
   extract
¹/₃ cup vanilla yogurt or
   sour cream
1 tablespoon
   vegetable oil
¹/₂ cup hot water
3 tablespoons sugar
1¹/₄ teaspoons salt
3 cups all-purpose flour
2 teaspoons dry yeast
Melted margarine

Beat the egg in a small bowl. Stir in the vanilla, yogurt and oil. Pour into the bread machine pan. Add the hot water to the empty bowl and swirl. Add the hot water to the pan. Add the sugar, salt, flour and yeast to the bread machine pan. Set the machine on dough mode. Remove the completed dough to a lightly floured work surface and knead a few times. Shape into a loaf or rolls. Place the loaf in a nonstick loaf pan or the rolls on a nonstick baking sheet. Let rise in a warm place until doubled in bulk. Bake at 350 degrees for 20 to 25 minutes. Remove to a wire rack and brush the hot bread or rolls with melted margarine. Yield: 12 servings.

Diane Gladden, Xi Zeta
Brandon, Manitoba, Canada

WHOLE WHEAT ROLLS

My sister revised this recipe from an existing recipe. I revised it again to use cracked wheat and whole wheat flour. It may be kneaded by hand if one doesn't have a bread machine.

1 cup warm water
5 tablespoons margarine
¹/₃ cup sugar
¹/₄ cup instant potato
   flakes
³/₄ teaspoon salt
1 egg
2¹/₂ cups all-purpose
   flour
1 cup whole wheat flour
¹/₂ cup cracked wheat
2 teaspoons dry yeast

Add the warm water, margarine, sugar, potato flakes, salt, egg, all-purpose flour, whole wheat flour, cracked wheat and yeast to the bread machine pan in the order recommended by the manufacturer. Set the machine on dough mode. Remove the completed dough to a lightly floured work surface. Shape into rolls and arrange in a greased 9×13-inch baking pan. Let rise in a warm place until doubled in bulk. Bake at 350 degrees for 30 minutes. Yield: 20 servings.

Elaine L. Rowett, Preceptor Pi
Sturgis, South Dakota

GRANDMA'S HOMEMADE HOT ROLLS OR BREAD

This was my great grandmother's recipe and has been passed down. We use it for every family gathering.

2 cups warm water	1/4 cup vegetable oil
1/4 cup sugar	1 heaping teaspoon salt
1 envelope dry yeast	1 egg, beaten
3 cups (or more) all-purpose flour	

Combine the warm water and sugar in a large bowl. Stir until the sugar dissolves. Sprinkle the yeast over the top, do not stir. Let stand for 5 to 10 minutes or until the mixture begins to bubble. Stir in 1 1/2 cups of the flour. Stir in the oil, salt and egg. Stir in the remaining flour until the dough is no longer sticky. Remove to a greased bowl and turn to coat. Cover and let rise in a warm place until doubled in bulk. Punch down and turn the dough out onto a lightly floured work surface. Shape into rolls or 2 loaves. Place the rolls in 2 nonstick 9×13-inch baking pans or the loaves in 2 nonstick loaf pans. Let rise in a warm place until doubled in bulk. Bake at 350 degrees for 20 to 30 minutes for rolls and 50 minutes for loaves or until golden brown. This recipe can be doubled. Yield: 6 to 8 servings.

Marcella Swanson, Xi Delta Iota
Walsh, Colorado

FARMHOUSE ROLLS

1 1/2 cups boiling water	1 envelope quick-rising yeast
2/3 cup shortening	5 cups all-purpose flour
2 eggs, beaten	1/4 cup (1/2 stick) butter, melted
1/2 cup sugar	
1 teaspoon salt	

Pour the boiling water over the shortening in a large mixing bowl. Stir until the shortening melts. Let cool to lukewarm. Add the eggs, sugar, salt, yeast and 1 cup of the flour. Mix well, using the paddle attachment on an electric mixer. Mix in the remaining flour, 1/2 cup at a time, until the dough is too stiff for the paddle attachment. Replace the paddle with the dough hook or turn out onto a lightly floured work surface and knead in the remaining flour. Remove to a greased bowl and turn to coat. Cover with plastic wrap and let rise in a warm place until doubled in bulk. Punch down and turn the dough out onto a lightly floured work surface. Roll out the dough to 1/2-inch thickness. Cut into squares or cut into circles with a biscuit cutter. Brush the squares with the melted butter. Fold over and pinch the edges to seal. Arrange the rolls tightly in a lightly greased 9×13-inch baking pan. Cover and let rise in a warm place until doubled in bulk. Bake at 350 degrees for 20 minutes or until lightly browned. Yield: 32 servings.

Kay Dunning, Xi Delta Psi
Erie, Kansas

EGG BATTER BUNS

1 envelope dry yeast	1 egg, beaten
1 cup warm water	2 tablespoons shortening or softened butter
2 tablespoons sugar	
1 teaspoon salt	
2 1/4 cups all-purpose flour	

Sprinkle the yeast over the warm water in a large bowl. Stir until the yeast dissolves. Add the sugar, salt and 1 cup of the flour. Stir until smooth. Stir in the egg and shortening. Add the remaining flour and stir until smooth. Scrape down the sides of the bowl. Cover and let rise in a warm place for 30 minutes or until doubled in bulk. Stir the batter. Fill nonstick muffin cups 1/2 full. Let rise in a warm place until the batter reaches the top of the muffin cups. Bake at 400 degrees for 15 minutes. Cool in the pan for 5 minutes. Yield: 12 servings.

Cheryl Muse, Preceptor Beta Gamma
Augusta, Kansas

GRANDMA MCMAHON'S DINNER ROLLS

My grandma made these rolls almost every Sunday when we visited after church. This is just one of many wonderful things she did for her family.

1 envelope dry yeast	6 tablespoons sugar
1/4 cup warm water	1 egg, beaten
1 cup hot water	3 to 4 cups all-purpose flour
1 1/4 teaspoons salt	
1/2 cup shortening	

Dissolve the yeast in the warm water in a small bowl. Combine the hot water, salt and shortening in a large bowl. Stir until the shortening melts. Stir in the sugar and egg. Let cool to lukewarm. Stir in the yeast mixture. Stir in the flour until a stiff dough forms. Knead the dough a few times on a lightly floured work surface. Remove to a greased bowl and turn to coat. Cover and chill overnight. Shape the dough into balls and arrange in a greased 9×13-inch baking pan. Let rise in a warm place until doubled in bulk. Bake at 350 degrees for 20 to 25 minutes. Yield: 15 to 18 servings.

Melanie Payne, Preceptor Delta Tau
Gladstone, Missouri

FLUFFY ROLLS

1 cup milk	*1/2 cup vegetable oil*
1 envelope dry yeast	*1/2 teaspoon baking soda*
1/4 cup warm water	*2 eggs, beaten*
1/2 cup sugar	*5 cups all-purpose flour*
1 teaspoon salt	

Scald the milk in a small saucepan. Let cool slightly. Dissolve the yeast in the warm water in a large bowl. Add the scalded milk, sugar, salt, oil, baking soda and eggs and beat well. Beat in the flour. Cover and let stand at room temperature overnight. Turn out the dough on a lightly floured work surface and divide into 3 balls. Roll out each ball to the size of a pie crust, 1/2-inch thick. Cut into wedges. Roll up starting at the wide end. Place the rolls 1 inch apart on a greased baking sheet. Let rise in a warm place for at least 2 hours or all day. Bake at 350 degrees for 10 to 15 minutes. Yield: 24 servings.

Marlene Mallon, Mu Theta
Salina, Kansas

SOUR CREAM FAN ROLLS

2 tablespoons dry yeast	*1 1/2 teaspoons salt*
1 cup warm water	*1/2 cup sugar*
2 tablespoons sugar	*1/4 teaspoon baking*
2 cups sour cream,	*powder*
warmed	*7 to 8 cups all-purpose*
2 eggs, lightly beaten	*flour*
6 tablespoons butter,	
melted	

Dissolve the yeast in the warm water in a small bowl. Stir in 2 tablespoons sugar and let stand for 5 minutes. Combine the sour cream, eggs, butter, salt and 1/2 cup sugar in a large bowl and mix well. Stir in the baking powder, yeast mixture and 4 cups of the flour. Stir in enough of the remaining flour to make a soft dough. Turn out the dough onto a lightly floured work surface and knead for 6 to 8 minutes or until smooth and elastic. Place in a greased bowl and turn to coat. Let rise in a warm place until doubled in bulk. Punch down and turn out onto a lightly floured work surface. Divide the dough in half. Roll out each half to a 9×23-inch rectangle. Cut into 1 1/2-inch strips and stack 5 strips together. Cut the stacks into 1 1/2-inch lengths. Place, cut side up, in greased muffin cups. Let rise in a warm place for 20 minutes. Bake at 350 degrees for 20 to 25 minutes. Cool in the pan for 5 minutes. Yield: 30 servings.

Loy Valdez, Xi Phi
Roswell, New Mexico

ZWIEBACH

1 1/4 cups milk	*1 tablespoon dry yeast*
1/2 cup (1 stick) full-fat	*1/2 cup warm water*
margarine	*1/4 cup vegetable oil*
2 tablespoons sugar	*6 3/4 cups all-purpose*
1 tablespoon salt	*flour*
1/2 cup cold water	

Scald the milk in a saucepan. Pour over the margarine, sugar and salt in a large bowl. Stir until the margarine melts. Stir in 1/2 cold water and cool to lukewarm. Dissolve the yeast in 1/2 cup warm water in a small bowl. Let stand until the mixture begins to bubble. Stir into the milk mixture. Stir in the oil. Add the flour, stirring until smooth. Let rise in a warm place until doubled in bulk. Make 30 golf ball-sized balls of dough. Make 30 smaller balls of dough. Let the dough balls rise in a warm place until light. Arrange the large balls on a nonstick baking sheet. Dab water on the bottom of the small balls and place on top of the large balls. Bake at 425 degrees for 12 minutes. Yield: 30 servings.

Myrna Zielke, Xi Nu Omega
Aurora, Missouri

BUTTERY CRESCENTS

This recipe has never failed to produce soft, great-tasting homemade bread. I bake these for all family gatherings and to take to a sister's house as a comfort food. Everyone loves homemade bread!

1 envelope dry yeast	*1/3 cup sugar*
1/2 cup warm water	*1 egg*
1/2 cup warm milk	*3/4 teaspoon salt*
1/2 cup (1 stick) butter,	*4 cups all-purpose flour*
softened	

Dissolve the yeast in the warm water in a large bowl. Add the warm milk, butter, sugar, egg, salt and 2 cups of the flour. Beat for 2 minutes. Stir in enough of the remaining flour to make a soft dough. Place in a bowl coated with nonstick cooking spray and turn to coat. Let rise in a warm place for 1 hour or until doubled in bulk. Place 1/2 the dough on a work surface coated with nonstick cooking spray. Pat into a 15-inch circle. Cut into wedges. Roll up starting at the wide end. Place the rolls on a nonstick baking sheet. Repeat with the remaining dough. Let rise in a warm place for 30 minutes. Bake at 375 degrees for 12 minutes. Yield: 24 servings.

Emma Williams, Alpha Epsilon Psi
Linn, Missouri

Cakes

ALMOND JOY CAKE

1 (2-layer) package
    white cake mix
1 (14-ounce) can
    sweetened condensed
    milk
1 (8-ounce) can cream of
    coconut
1 (16-ounce) container
    frozen whipped
    topping, thawed
1 (14-ounce) can flaked
    coconut
1¹/₂ to 2 cups slivered
    almonds
³/₄ cup chocolate syrup

Prepare the cake mix using the package directions, baking in a 9×13-inch baking pan. Cool on a wire rack for 5 minutes. Poke holes in the top of the cake with a chopstick. Mix the sweetened condensed milk and cream of coconut in a bowl until smooth. Pour slowly and evenly over the cake. Chill, covered until cold. Spread the whipped topping over the cake. Sprinkle with the coconut and almonds. Drizzle the chocolate syrup over the top. Chill, covered, until ready to serve. Yield: 10 to 12 servings.

Diane C. Bush, Xi Beta Xi
Dublin, Georgia

SKILLET ALMOND CAKE

³/₄ cup (1¹/₂ sticks)
    margarine, melted
1¹/₂ cups sugar
2 eggs
Pinch of salt
2 teaspoons almond
    extract
¹/₂ teaspoon vanilla
    extract
1¹/₂ cups all-purpose
    flour
2 teaspoons sugar
2 tablespoons slivered
    almonds

Beat the margarine and 1¹/₂ cups sugar in a mixing bowl. Add the eggs 1 at a time, beating well after each addition. Beat in the salt, almond extract and vanilla. Add the flour and stir to mix well. Pour into a greased 8- or 9-inch ovenproof skillet. Sprinkle with 2 teaspoons sugar and almonds. Bake at 350 degrees for 35 to 40 minutes or until golden brown. Cool in the pan on a wire rack. Yield: 6 to 8 servings.

Jessie R. Neighbors, Xi Beta Chi
Alexander City, Alabama

APPLE CAKE

3 cups sifted all-purpose
    flour
1 teaspoon baking
    soda
1 teaspoon cinnamon
2 eggs
2 cups sugar
1¹/₂ cups vegetable oil
2 teaspoons vanilla
    extract
1 tablespoon grated
    lemon zest (optional)
2 tablespoons lemon
    juice
1¹/₄ teaspoons salt
3 cups chopped peeled
    apples
2 cups chopped pecans
Confectioners' sugar

Combine the flour, baking soda and cinnamon in a bowl and mix well. Beat the eggs in a mixing bowl. Beat in the next 6 ingredients. Add the dry ingredients gradually, beating constantly. Stir in the apples and pecans. Pour into a greased and floured 10-inch tube pan. Bake at 325 degrees for 1¹/₂ hours or until a wooden pick inserted in the center comes out clean. Cool in the pan for 15 minutes. Invert onto a cake plate and let cool. Dust with confectioners' sugar. Yield: 12 servings.

Madeline McMillan, Preceptor Gamma Pi
Newport News, Virginia

FRESH APPLE CAKE

3 cups all-purpose flour	1/4 cup fresh orange juice
1 teaspoon baking soda	1 tablespoon vanilla
1/4 teaspoon salt	extract
1 tablespoon cinnamon	3 cups finely chopped
2 cups sugar	peeled Granny Smith
3 eggs, beaten	apples
1 1/2 cups vegetable oil	1 cup flaked coconut
2 tablespoons grated	1 cup chopped pecans
orange zest	Buttermilk Sauce

Combine the flour, baking soda, salt and cinnamon in a bowl and mix well. Beat the sugar, eggs, oil, orange zest, orange juice and vanilla in a large mixing bowl. Stir in the dry ingredients. Fold in the apples, coconut and pecans. Pour into a greased and floured tube pan. Bake at 325 degrees for 1 1/2 hours or until a wooden pick inserted in the center comes out clean. Poke holes in the top of the cake with a wooden skewer. Pour the Buttermilk Sauce evenly over the cake. Cool in the pan on a wire rack for 1 hour. Invert onto a wire rack and cool completely.
Yield: 16 to 20 servings.

BUTTERMILK SAUCE

1/2 cup (1 stick) butter	1/2 cup buttermilk
1 cup sugar	1/2 teaspoon baking soda

Melt the butter in a large saucepan. Stir in the sugar, buttermilk and baking soda. Bring to a rolling boil, stirring constantly. Boil for 1 minute. Remove from the heat.

Sandy Helms, Laureate Beta
Longview, Washington

APPLE CREAM CAKE

1 (2-layer) package	1/2 cup chopped walnuts
yellow cake mix	1/4 cup sugar
3 cups thinly sliced	1 teaspoon cinnamon
peeled tart apples	1 cup heavy cream

Prepare the cake mix using the package directions. Pour into a nonstick 9×13-inch baking pan. Combine the apples, walnuts, sugar and cinnamon in a bowl. Toss to mix. Spoon over the cake batter. Pour the cream evenly over the apple mixture. Bake at 350 degrees for 60 to 70 minutes or until a wooden pick inserted in the center comes out clean. Serve warm with whipped cream or vanilla ice cream. Yield: 15 servings.

Linda Jackson, Preceptor Gamma Tau
Jacksonville, Florida

SPECIAL APPLE CAKE

6 McIntosh apples	1/3 cup orange juice
2 teaspoons cinnamon	2 1/2 teaspoons vanilla
5 tablespoons sugar	extract
3 cups all-purpose flour	1 teaspoon salt
3 cups sugar	1 cup raisins
1 cup vegetable oil	1 cup coarsely chopped
4 eggs	walnuts
1 tablespoon baking	Confectioners' sugar
powder	

Peel, core and thinly slice the apples. Mix the cinnamon and 5 tablespoons sugar in a large bowl. Add the apples and toss to coat. Combine the flour, 3 cups sugar, oil, eggs, baking powder, orange juice, vanilla and salt in a large mixing bowl. Beat until smooth. Pour 1/2 of the batter into a greased tube or bundt pan. Top with 1/2 of the apples. Sprinkle with 1/2 of the raisins and 1/2 of the walnuts. Repeat the layers. Swirl a knife through the batter. Bake at 350 degrees for 1 1/2 hours or until a wooden pick inserted in the center comes out clean. Cool in the pan on a wire rack. Invert onto a cake plate and dust with confectioners' sugar.
Yield: 10 to 12 servings.

Anita Guza-Mercado. Laureate Delta Rho
San Diego, California

OLD-FASHIONED FRESH APPLE CAKE

2 1/2 cups all-purpose	1 cup vegetable oil
flour	2 eggs
1 teaspoon baking	2 cups sugar
soda	3 cups chopped peeled
1 teaspoon baking	tart apples
powder	1 cup pecans or black
1 teaspoon salt	walnuts
1 teaspoon cinnamon	1 cup butterscotch chips

Combine the flour, baking soda, baking powder, salt and cinnamon in a bowl and mix well. Beat the oil, eggs and sugar in a large mixing bowl. Beat in the dry ingredients. Fold in the apples and pecans. Spread in a greased and floured 9×13-inch baking pan. Sprinkle with the butterscotch chips. Bake at 350 degrees for 55 to 60 minutes or until a wooden pick inserted in the center comes out clean. Cool in the pan on a wire rack. This cake is best if made 1 day before serving. Yield: 15 servings.

Frances Kay Adkins, Xi Gamma Mu
Gallipolis, Ohio

APPLE WALNUT CAKE WITH CREAM CHEESE FROSTING

2 eggs, beaten
1/2 cup vegetable oil
2 cups sugar
1/2 teaspoon salt
2 teaspoons baking soda
2 teaspoons cinnamon
2 cups all-purpose flour
4 cups diced peeled tart apples
2 cups chopped walnuts
Cream Cheese Frosting

Beat the eggs, oil and sugar in a mixing bowl until smooth. Beat in the dry ingredients. Fold in the apples and walnuts. Spoon into a lightly greased 9×13-inch baking pan. Bake at 350 degrees for 1 hour or until a wooden pick inserted in the center comes out clean. Cool in the pan on a wire rack. Frost the cake with the Cream Cheese Frosting. Yield: 20 to 24 servings.

CREAM CHEESE FROSTING

1/4 cup (1/2 stick) butter or margarine, softened
8 ounces cream cheese, softened
2 teaspoons vanilla extract
1 1/2 cups confectioners' sugar

Beat the butter, cream cheese, vanilla and confectioners' sugar in a mixing bowl until smooth.

Diane Thomsen, Preceptor Delta Kappa
Cedar Rapids, Iowa

FRESH STRAWBERRY CAKE

1 (2-layer) package strawberry cake mix
3 eggs
1 cup water
1/3 cup vegetable oil
8 ounces cream cheese, softened
1 cup whipping cream
2 cups confectioners' sugar
2 pounds strawberries, sliced
1 (13 1/2-ounce) container strawberry glaze

Combine the first 4 ingredients in a large mixing bowl and beat for 2 minutes. Divide between two 9×13-inch baking pans coated with nonstick cooking spray. Bake at 350 degrees for 23 minutes or until a wooden pick inserted in the center comes out clean. Cool completely on a wire rack. Beat the cream cheese in a mixing bowl until light and fluffy. Add the whipping cream and confectioners' sugar and beat until stiff peaks form. Spread the frosting over 1 of the layers in the pan. Remove the other layer from the pan and place on top of the frosting. Cover and chill for at least 2 hours. Mix the strawberries and glaze in a bowl. Spread over the cake. Spread with whipped topping, if desired. Yield: 16 servings.

Ann C. Winters, Laureate Beta Gamma
Kingman, Arizona

BOURBON CAKE

2 cups (4 sticks) butter, softened
1 cup sugar
9 egg yolks
2 tablespoons almond extract
2 tablespoons vanilla extract
1 teaspoon nutmeg
3 cups all-purpose flour
1/2 cup bourbon
1 cup walnuts or pecans, chopped
9 egg whites
1 cup sugar

Beat the butter and 1 cup sugar in a mixing bowl until light and fluffy. Add the egg yolks 1 or 2 at a time, beating well after each addition. Beat in the almond extract, vanilla and nutmeg. Beat in the flour alternately with the bourbon. Beat for 2 to 3 minutes. Stir in the walnuts. Beat the egg whites in a large mixing bowl until soft peaks form. Add 1 cup sugar gradually, beating constantly. Fold in the butter mixture. Pour into a greased and floured tube pan. Bake at 350 degrees for 1 1/2 hours or until a wooden pick inserted in the center comes out clean. Remove to a wire rack to cool. Yield: 12 to 15 servings.

Lillian Liliensteins, Laureate Alpha Iota
Shelby, North Carolina

BURNT SUGAR CAKE

2 1/2 cups all-purpose flour
2 teaspoons baking powder
1 1/2 cups sugar
1/2 cup shortening
2 eggs
1 cup cold water
1 teaspoon vanilla extract
3 tablespoons Burnt Sugar

Combine the flour and baking powder in a bowl and mix well. Beat the sugar and shortening in a large mixing bowl until light and fluffy. Beat in the eggs. Beat in the dry ingredients alternately with the cold water. Beat in the vanilla and Burnt Sugar. Pour into a 9×13-inch nonstick baking pan. Bake at 375 degrees for 40 minutes or until a wooden pick inserted in the center comes out clean. Cool in the pan on a wire rack. Yield: 15 servings.

BURNT SUGAR

2 cups sugar
1/2 cup hot water

Cook the sugar in a cast-iron skillet over medium-high heat until boiling, stirring constantly. Remove from the heat and stir in the hot water. Let cool.

Tamara Taylor, Alpha Eta Mu
Ennis, Texas

BUTTERSCOTCH NUT TORTE

6 egg yolks
1¹/₂ cups sugar
1 teaspoon baking
  powder
1 teaspoon almond
  extract
1 teaspoon vanilla
  extract

6 egg whites
2 cups graham cracker
  crumbs
1 cup chopped pecans
1 cup (or more)
  whipping cream
Butterscotch Sauce

Beat the egg yolks, sugar, baking powder, almond extract and vanilla in a mixing bowl. Beat the egg whites in a large mixing bowl until stiff but not dry. Fold in the egg yolk mixture. Fold in the graham cracker crumbs and pecans. Pour into a well greased 9×13-inch baking pan. Bake at 325 degrees for 30 to 35 minutes. Cool completely on a wire rack. Beat the whipping cream in a mixing bowl until soft peaks form. Spread over the cooled cake. Drizzle with the Butterscotch Sauce. Cover and chill. Yield: 12 servings.

BUTTERSCOTCH SAUCE

1 cup packed brown
  sugar
1 tablespoon all-
  purpose flour
¹/₄ cup (¹/₂ stick) butter

¹/₄ cup orange juice
¹/₂ scant cup water
1 egg, beaten
Vanilla extract to taste

Combine the brown sugar, flour, butter, orange juice, water, egg and vanilla in a skillet and mix well. Bring to a boil, stirring frequently. Remove from the heat and let cool.

Mary Rose Spore, Laureate Gamma Iota
Springfield, Missouri

OLD-FASHIONED CARROT CAKE

1¹/₂ cups all-purpose
  flour
³/₄ teaspoon salt
1¹/₄ teaspoons baking
  soda
2¹/₂ teaspoons cinnamon
1¹/₂ cups sugar
1 cup vegetable oil

1 teaspoon vanilla
  extract
3 eggs
2¹/₄ cups grated carrots
¹/₂ cup chopped nuts
¹/₂ cup raisins
Cream Cheese Frosting

Combine the flour, salt, baking soda and cinnamon in a bowl and mix well. Beat the sugar, oil and vanilla in a large mixing bowl. Beat in the eggs. Stir in the dry ingredients. Fold in the carrots, nuts and raisins. Grease the bottom of a 7×12-inch microwave-safe dish. Pour in the batter. Microwave on High for 14 to 16 minutes or until a wooden pick inserted in the center comes out clean, turning the dish every

4 minutes. Cool completely on a wire rack. Frost with the Cream Cheese Frosting. Yield: 8 to 10 servings.

CREAM CHEESE FROSTING

1¹/₂ to 2 cups
  confectioners' sugar
3 ounces cream cheese

3 tablespoons butter
1 teaspoon vanilla
  extract

Combine the confectioners' sugar, cream cheese, butter and vanilla in a 2-quart microwave-safe mixing bowl. Microwave on Low for 2 minutes or just until the ingredients are softened. Beat with an electric mixer until light and fluffy.

Lynette Hruzek, Preceptor Omicron Tau
Hallettsville, Texas

CARROT CAKE

4 eggs
1¹/₂ cups vegetable oil
1 teaspoon vanilla
  extract
3 to 4 drops black
  walnut extract
2 cups sugar
1 teaspoon cinnamon

2 cups self-rising flour
1¹/₂ cups shredded
  carrots
1 cup walnuts or pecans
¹/₂ cup buttermilk
1 cup sugar
¹/₂ teaspoon baking soda

Beat the eggs, oil, vanilla, walnut extract and 2 cups sugar in a large mixing bowl. Beat in the cinnamon and flour. Stir in the carrots and walnuts. Pour into a greased tube pan. Bake at 325 degrees for 1 hour and 15 minutes or until a wooden pick inserted in the center comes out clean. Cool in the pan for 10 to 15 minutes. Remove to a wire rack to cool completely. Combine the buttermilk and 1 cup sugar in a saucepan. Bring almost to a boil. Stir in the baking soda. Pour over the cooled cake. Yield: 16 servings.

Betty Collins, Preceptor Beta Tau
Newport News, Virginia

Ann Levingston, Theta Chi, Steinhatchee, Florida, makes a delicious **Coconut Cake** *from an ordinary yellow cake mix and a few other ingredients. She combines 1 cup sugar with 8 ounces sour cream and one 8-ounce package frozen flaked coconut in a bowl and mixes well. The coconut mixture is covered and chilled in the refrigerator overnight. The next day, she prepares and bakes the yellow cake mix using the package directions. When the cake has cooled, she combines the coconut mixture with 8 ounces whipped topping. The cake is frosted with the coconut mixture.*

COCONUT CARROT CAKE

2 cups all-purpose flour	3 eggs
2¹/2 teaspoons baking soda	1 (8-ounce) can crushed pineapple
2 teaspoons cinnamon	2 cups grated carrots
1 teaspoon salt	1¹/2 cups flaked coconut
3/4 cup vegetable oil	¹/2 cup chopped nuts
2 cups sugar	Cream Cheese Frosting

Combine the flour, baking soda, cinnamon and salt in a bowl and mix well. Beat the oil, sugar and eggs in a bowl. Add the dry ingredients and beat until smooth. Stir in the pineapple, carrots, coconut and nuts. Pour into a greased 9×13-inch baking pan. Bake at 350 degrees for 50 to 60 minutes or until a wooden pick inserted in the center comes out clean. Cool completely on a wire rack. Frost with the Cream Cheese Frosting. Sprinkle with additional coconut.
Yield: 15 servings.

CREAM CHEESE FROSTING

3 ounces cream cheese, softened	1 tablespoon milk
1/4 cup (¹/2 stick) butter, softened	¹/2 teaspoon vanilla extract
3 cups sifted confectioners' sugar	¹/2 cup flaked coconut

Beat the cream cheese and butter in a mixing bowl. Beat in the confectioners' sugar alternately with the milk and vanilla until smooth. Stir in the coconut.

Betty Storsberg, Alpha Omega Master
Longwood, Florida

3-DAY COCONUT CAKE

2 cups sour cream	1 (2-layer) package white cake mix
12 ounces flaked coconut	1¹/2 cups frozen whipped topping, thawed
1 cup sugar	

Combine the sour cream, coconut and sugar in a bowl and mix well. Cover and chill overnight. Prepare the cake mix using the package directions, baking in 2 round nonstick cake pans. Cool in the pans for 10 minutes. Remove to a wire rack to cool. Cut each layer with a serrated knife horizontally into halves. Reserve 1 cup of the sour cream mixture. Spread the remaining sour cream mixture between the cake layers on a covered cake plate. Combine the whipped topping and the reserved sour cream mixture in a bowl and mix well. Frost the top and side of the cake with the whipped topping mixture. Cover and chill for 3 days before serving. Yield: 16 servings.

Carol Kolb
Waco, Texas

RAVE REVIEWS COCONUT CAKE

1 (2-layer) package yellow cake mix	4 eggs
1 (3-ounce) package instant vanilla pudding mix	¹/4 cup vegetable oil
	2 cups flaked coconut
	1 cup chopped pecans
1¹/3 cups water	Coconut Cream Cheese Frosting

Combine the cake mix, pudding mix, water, eggs and oil in a large mixing bowl. Beat at medium speed for 4 minutes. Stir in the coconut and pecans. Pour into 3 greased and floured 9-inch cake pans. Bake at 350 degrees for 35 minutes or until a wooden pick inserted in the center comes out clean. Cool in the pans for 15 minutes. Remove to a wire rack to cool completely. Spread the Coconut Cream Cheese Frosting between the layers and over the top and side of the cake. Yield: 12 servings.

COCONUT CREAM CHEESE FROSTING

2 tablespoons butter	2 teaspoons milk
2 cups flaked coconut	3¹/2 cups sifted confectioners' sugar
8 ounces cream cheese, softened	¹/2 teaspoon vanilla extract
2 tablespoons butter, softened	

Melt 2 tablespoons butter in a skillet over low heat. Add the coconut. Cook until golden brown, stirring constantly. Remove to paper towels to drain. Beat the cream cheese and 2 tablespoons butter in a mixing bowl until light and fluffy. Beat in the milk. Add the confectioners' sugar gradually, beating constantly. Beat in the vanilla. Stir in 1³/4 cups of the toasted coconut, reserving ¹/4 cup to sprinkle over the frosted cake.

Mildred K. Loe, Gamma Theta Master
Houston, Texas

CHOCOLATE ANGEL FOOD CAKE

3/4 cup sifted cake flour	¹/4 teaspoon salt
3/4 cup plus 2 tablespoons sugar	1¹/2 teaspoons vanilla extract
¹/4 cup baking cocoa	3/4 cup sugar
1¹/2 cups egg whites, at room temperature	2 cups whipping cream
	¹/2 cup baking cocoa
1¹/2 teaspoons cream of tartar	1 cup confectioners' sugar
	Dash of salt

Sift the flour, 3/4 cup plus 2 tablespoons sugar and ¹/4 cup baking cocoa together 3 times. Beat the egg whites, cream of tartar, ¹/4 teaspoon salt and vanilla in large mixing bowl until foamy. Beat in 3/4 cup sugar, 2 tablespoons at a time, beating for 10 seconds after each addition. Beat until stiff peaks

form. Fold in the dry ingredients 3 tablespoons at a time; the mixture will be stiff. Spread in a ungreased 10-inch tube pan. Cut through the batter with a knife to remove air bubbles. Bake at 350 degrees for 40 to 45 minutes or until the top springs back when lightly touched. Invert on a funnel to cool completely. Loosen the cake from the side of the pan. Invert onto a cake plate. Combine the whipping cream, 1/2 cup baking cocoa, confectioners' sugar and a dash of salt in a chilled mixing bowl. Beat until thick enough to spread. Spread over the top and side of the cake. Chill until ready to serve.
Yield: 16 servings.

Tricia Bliss, Preceptor Tau
High River, Alberta, Canada

CHOCOLATE LOVERS' CAKE

1 (2-layer) package chocolate cake mix	1 cup chopped nuts
1 (3-ounce) package instant chocolate pudding mix	2 ounces unsweetened chocolate
1 cup milk	3 tablespoons butter
1/2 cup sour cream	1 1/2 cups sifted confectioners' sugar
4 eggs	2 to 3 tablespoons water
2 cups semisweet chocolate chips	1 teaspoon vanilla extract

Combine the first 5 ingredients in a large mixing bowl. Beat at low speed just until blended. Beat at high speed for 2 minutes. Stir in the chocolate chips and nuts. Pour into a greased and floured bundt pan. Bake at 350 degrees for 55 to 60 minutes or until a wooden pick inserted in the center comes out clean. Cool in the pan for 20 minutes. Remove to a wire rack to cool completely. Combine the unsweetened chocolate and butter in a saucepan. Cook over low heat until melted, stirring until smooth. Stir in the confectioners' sugar alternately with the water to make a glaze. Stir in the vanilla. Pour over the cooled cake.
Yield: 12 to 18 servings.

Sue Hughes, Xi Delta Eta
Delta, Colorado

DOUBLE CHOCOLATE CHOCOLATE CHIP CAKE

1/2 cup shortening	1/2 teaspoon salt
1/2 cup (1 stick) margarine	2 teaspoons vanilla extract
1/2 cup baking cocoa	2 eggs, beaten
1 cup water	1 cup milk
2 cups sugar	1/2 cup chocolate syrup
2 cups all-purpose flour	1 cup chocolate chips
1 teaspoon baking soda	Chocolate Frosting

Combine the shortening, margarine, baking cocoa and water in a saucepan. Bring to a full boil, stirring occasionally. Remove from the heat. Combine the sugar, flour, baking soda and salt in a large bowl and mix well. Add the shortening mixture and stir to mix well. Stir in the vanilla. Whisk in the eggs. Add the milk and chocolate syrup and stir to mix well. Pour into a greased 9×13-inch baking pan. Sprinkle the chocolate chips over the top. Bake at 350 degrees for 40 to 45 minutes or until the top springs back when lightly touched. Cool completely on a wire rack. Spread with the Chocolate Frosting. Sprinkle with additional chocolate chips, if desired. This cake may be baked in three 8-inch cake pans. Yield: 15 servings.

CHOCOLATE FROSTING

1/2 cup (1 stick) margarine, melted	1/2 cup milk
1/2 cup baking cocoa	1 (32-ounce) package confectioners' sugar
1 teaspoon vanilla extract	

Combine the margarine, baking cocoa, vanilla and milk in a large mixing bowl and mix well. Beat in the confectioners' sugar to a spreading consistency.

Susan McEvoy, Xi Beta Omega
Valentine, Nebraska

FAMILY FAVORITE FUDGE CAKE

2 1/4 cups all-purpose flour	1 cup buttermilk
1/4 teaspoon salt	1/2 cup (1 stick) margarine, softened
2 teaspoons baking soda	1/2 cup evaporated milk
1 scant cup water	3/4 cup baking cocoa
2 cups sugar	1 (16-ounce) package confectioners' sugar
2/3 cup shortening	Chopped walnuts
2 eggs	
1/2 cup baking cocoa	

Sift the flour and salt together. Dissolve the baking soda in the water in a mixing bowl. Combine the sugar, shortening and eggs in a bowl. Beat for 2 minutes. Beat in 1/2 cup baking cocoa. Beat in the dry ingredients alternately with the water mixture. Beat in the buttermilk. Beat for 3 minutes. Pour into two 9-inch nonstick cake pans. Bake at 350 degrees for 30 to 35 minutes or until the cake tests done. Cool in the pans for 10 minutes. Remove to a wire rack to cool completely. Combine the next 4 ingredients in a mixing bowl and beat until smooth. Spread the frosting between the layers and over the top and side of the cake. Sprinkle with chopped walnuts.
Yield: 12 to 14 servings.

Marjorie P. Ford, Alpha Gamma Alpha
Lakeland, Florida

CHOCOLATE FUDGE CAKE

2 cups semisweet chocolate chips	2 cups sugar
5 tablespoons water	6 egg yolks
2 tablespoons instant coffee granules	1 cup all-purpose flour
1½ cups (3 sticks) butter, softened	6 egg whites
	Confectioners' sugar

Combine the chocolate chips, water and coffee granules in a saucepan. Cook over very low heat until the chocolate melts, stirring occasionally. Remove from the heat and let cool to room temperature. Beat the butter in a mixing bowl until creamy. Add the sugar and beat for 5 minutes or until light and fluffy. Add the egg yolks 1 at a time, beating well after each addition. Add the flour gradually, beating constantly at low speed. Stir in the chocolate mixture. Beat the egg whites in a large mixing bowl at low speed until foamy. Beat at high speed until stiff but not dry. Fold in the chocolate mixture. Butter a 9-inch springform pan and wrap the outside securely with foil. Pour the batter into the prepared pan. Bake at 350 degrees for 60 to 65 minutes or until a wooden pick inserted 1 inch from the side comes out clean; the top of the cake may be cracked. Cool completely on a wire rack. Remove the foil. Cover and chill overnight. Loosen the cake from the side of the pan with a sharp knife and remove the side. Dust lightly with confectioners' sugar. Yield: 14 to 16 servings.

Betty P. Andrews, Beta Lambda
Virginia Beach, Virginia

DECADENT FUDGE CAKE

3/4 cup (1½ sticks) butter, softened	3 tablespoons vegetable oil
1½ cups sugar	3/4 cup chopped pecans
1 teaspoon vanilla extract	3 egg whites
3 egg yolks	1/8 teaspoon cream of tartar
1/2 cup all-purpose flour	1/8 teaspoon salt
1/2 cup baking cocoa	1 1/3 cups chocolate chips
3 tablespoons water	1/2 cup heavy cream

Beat the butter, sugar and vanilla in a large mixing bowl until smooth. Add the egg yolks 1 at a time, beating well after each addition. Stir in the flour, baking cocoa, water, oil and pecans. Beat the egg whites, cream of tartar and salt in a mixing bowl until stiff. Fold into the butter mixture. Cover the bottom of a 9-inch springform pan with foil. Butter the foil and side of the pan. Pour the batter into the prepared pan. Bake at 350 degrees for 45 minutes or until the top cracks. Place on a wire rack and let cool for 1 hour. Cover and chill. Loosen the cake from the side of the

pan with a sharp knife and remove the side. Place on a cake plate. Combine the chocolate chips and cream in a saucepan. Cook over medium heat until melted and smooth, stirring constantly. Remove from the heat and let cool slightly. Pour over the cake. Serve at room temperature. Yield: 12 servings.

Cathy Tucker, Xi Beta Upsilon
Kingsport, Tennessee

CHOCOLATE IGLOO CAKE

4 ounces German's sweet chocolate	3 egg whites
1²/3 cups milk	1/3 cup sugar
1/2 cup sugar	1 (8- or 9-inch) baked chocolate cake layer
3 egg yolks	1 cup whipping cream
1 envelope unflavored gelatin	
2 tablespoons cold water	

Combine the chocolate, milk and 1/2 cup sugar in a saucepan. Cook over low heat until the chocolate melts, stirring constantly. Beat the egg yolks in a mixing bowl for 1 minute. Stir a small amount of the hot chocolate mixture into the beaten egg yolks. Return to the saucepan and stir to mix well. Cook over medium heat for 5 to 7 minutes or until thickened, stirring constantly. Remove from the heat. Soften the gelatin in the cold water in a small bowl. Stir into the chocolate mixture. Pour into a bowl. Chill until beginning to set. Beat the egg whites in a mixing bowl until foamy. Add 1/3 cup sugar gradually and beat until stiff. Fold into the chocolate mixture. Pour into a deep bowl. Cover and chill overnight. Unmold the chocolate mixture onto the cake layer. Whip the cream in a bowl until stiff peaks form. Cover the chocolate mixture and the cake with the whipped cream. Chill until ready to serve. Yield: 12 servings.

Justine Duke, Alpha Master
Goodlettsville, Tennessee

ITALIAN LOVE CAKE

If you're Italian, food is love. No matter what your nationality, you'll love this cake!

1 (2-layer) package fudge marble cake mix	1 (3½-ounce) package instant chocolate pudding mix
2 pounds ricotta cheese	1 cup milk
4 eggs	1 (8-ounce) container frozen whipped topping, thawed
3/4 cup sugar	
1 teaspoon vanilla extract	

Prepare the cake mix using the package directions. Pour into a greased and floured 9×13-inch cake pan. Beat the ricotta cheese, eggs, sugar and vanilla in a mixing bowl. Spread over the batter. Bake at 350 degrees for 1 hour. Cool completely on a wire rack. Thaw the whipped topping. Beat the pudding mix and milk in a mixing bowl. Stir in the whipped topping. Spread over the cooled cake. Yield: 15 servings.

Linda Cozzi, Rho
Tucson, Arizona

FAVORITE CHOCOLATE CAKE

1/2 cup (1 stick) margarine, softened	1 teaspoon baking powder
1 cup sugar	1 1/2 cups miniature marshmallows
4 eggs	1 cup chopped pecans
1 (16-ounce) can chocolate syrup	Chocolate Sauce
1 cup all-purpose flour	

Beat the margarine and sugar in a large mixing bowl until light and fluffy. Add the eggs 1 at a time, beating well after each addition. Beat in the chocolate syrup. Beat in the flour and baking powder. Pour into a greased 9×13-inch baking pan. Bake at 350 degrees for 30 minutes or until a wooden pick inserted in the center comes out clean. Sprinkle immediately with the marshmallows and pecans. Cool completely on a wire rack. Pour the Chocolae Sauce over the cooled cake. Yield: 15 servings.

CHOCOLATE SAUCE

1/2 cup (1 stick) margarine	1 egg or an equivalent amount of egg substitute
2 tablespoons baking cocoa	1 1/2 cups confectioners' sugar
1 teaspoon vanilla extract	

Melt the margarine in a saucepan. Add the baking cocoa and stir until smooth. Remove from the heat and beat in the vanilla, egg and confectioners' sugar.

Jean Smith, Preceptor Kappa
Cicero, New York

---

*Gretchen Green, Upsilon Gamma, Wooster, Ohio, prepares a **Quick Caramel Frosting** by melting 1/2 cup (1 stick) butter in a skillet over low heat. She adds 3/4 cup packed brown sugar and cooks for 2 minutes, stirring constantly. She then adds 1/4 cup milk and brings the mixture to a boil. The mixture is removed from the heat and cooled. Two cups confectioners' sugar are gradually stirred into the cooled mixture.*

❖ CHOCOLATE BRANDY FUDGE MOUSSE CAKE

1 cup all-purpose flour	2 eggs
1/4 cup baking cocoa	1/2 cup milk
1 1/2 teaspoons baking powder	Brandy
	Chocolate Mousse
1/2 teaspoon salt	1 1/2 cups heavy cream
1 cup sugar	24 ounces semisweet chocolate, chopped
1/2 cup (1 stick) butter, softened	1/4 cup (1/2 stick) butter
2 teaspoons vanilla extract	1/4 cup light corn syrup

Combine the flour, baking cocoa, baking powder and salt in a bowl and mix well. Beat the sugar and 1/2 cup butter in a large mixing bowl until light and fluffy. Beat in the vanilla and eggs. Beat in the dry ingredients alternately with the milk. Pour into a greased 10-inch cake pan. Bake at 350 degrees for 20 to 25 minutes or until a wooden pick inserted in the center comes out clean. Cool in the pan for 10 minutes. Remove to a wire rack to cool completely. Split the cooled cake horizontally into 2 layers. Soak the cake layers with brandy. Place 1 layer on a cake plate. Spread the Chocolate Mousse over the layer. Top with the remaining layer. Chill until firm. Heat the cream in a saucepan to boiling. Remove from the heat and add the chocolate, 1/4 cup butter and corn syrup. Stir until melted and smooth. Let cool to room temperature. Pour about 1/3 of the chocolate mixture over the cake and down the side. Chill until firm. Repeat, using another 1/3 of the chocolate mixture and chilling the cake until firm. Repeat with the remaining chocolate mixture and chill the cake until firm. Yield: 16 servings.

CHOCOLATE MOUSSE

1 1/8 teaspoons unflavored gelatin	1 teaspoon vanilla extract
1/4 cup brandy	1 1/3 cups chocolate chips
1/4 cup sugar	2 cups whipping cream
1 cup sour cream	

Soften the gelatin in the brandy in a small bowl. Heat the sugar, sour cream and vanilla in a saucepan to boiling. Remove from the heat and add the chocolate chips. Stir until the chocolate melts. Add the gelatin mixture and stir until smooth. Let cool to room temperature. Beat the whipping cream in a mixing bowl until soft peaks form. Fold in the cooled chocolate mixture.

Sharon Womack, Preceptor Delta Upsilon
Webster City, Iowa

CHOCOLATE COCONUT RUM CAKE

1 cup chopped pecans
1 (2-layer) package
   devil's food cake mix
   with pudding
3 eggs

1/2 cup cold water
1/3 cup vegetable oil
1/2 cup coconut-flavored
   rum
Coconut Rum Glaze

Grease and flour a 10-inch tube pan or 12-inch bundt pan. Sprinkle the pecans over the bottom of the pan. Combine the cake mix, eggs, water, oil and rum in a large mixing bowl. Beat at medium speed for 2 minutes. Pour into the prepared pan. Bake at 325 degrees for 1 hour or until a wooden pick inserted in the center comes out clean. Cool in the pan for 10 minutes. Remove to a wire rack to cool completely. Place on a serving plate. Poke holes in the top and side of the cake with a skewer. Spoon the Coconut Rum Glaze over the cake slowly, allowing it to absorb before adding more. If you make this cake using a cake mix without pudding, use 4 eggs instead of 3 and use 1/2 cup of vegetable oil instead of 1/3 cup. Yield: 16 servings.

COCONUT RUM GLAZE

1/2 cup (1 stick) butter
1/4 cup water
1 cup sugar

1/2 cup coconut-flavored
   rum

Melt the butter in a saucepan. Stir in the water and sugar. Bring to a boil and cook for 5 minutes, stirring constantly. Remove from the heat and stir in the rum.

Susan M. Edwards, Preceptor Mu
Darlington, South Carolina

CHOCOLATE PRALINE LAYER CAKE

1/2 cup (1 stick)
   margarine
1 cup packed brown
   sugar
1/4 cup heavy cream
3/4 cup coarsely chopped
   pecans
1 (2-layer) package
   devil's food cake mix
   with pudding

1 1/4 cups water
1/3 cup vegetable oil
3 eggs
1 3/4 cups whipping
   cream
1/4 cup confectioners'
   sugar
1/4 teaspoon vanilla
   extract

Combine the margarine, brown sugar and 1/4 cup heavy cream in a saucepan. Cook over low heat just until the margarine melts, stirring frequently. Pour into 2 ungreased 8- or 9-inch cake pans. Sprinkle with the pecans. Combine the cake mix, water, oil and eggs in a large mixing bowl. Beat at low speed until moistened. Beat at high speed for 2 minutes. Pour into the prepared pans. Bake at 325 degrees for 35 to 45 minutes or until the top springs back when lightly touched. Cool in the pans for 5 minutes. Remove to a

wire rack to cool completely. Stack the layers praline side up on a serving plate. Beat 1 3/4 cups whipping cream in a mixing bowl until stiff peaks form. Blend in the confectioners' sugar and vanilla. Spread over the top and side of the cake. Chill until ready to serve. Yield: 12 servings.

Sharon Fennell, Mu Sigma
Plantation, Florida

CHOCOLATE MINT CAKE

1 cup sugar
1/2 cup (1 stick) butter,
   softened
4 eggs
1 (16-ounce) can
   chocolate syrup
1 cup plus 1 tablespoon
   all-purpose flour
1 teaspoon vanilla
   extract
2 cups confectioners'
   sugar

1/2 cup (1 stick) butter,
   softened
2 tablespoons milk
1 teaspoon peppermint
   extract
2 to 3 drops green food
   coloring
1 cup chocolate chips
6 tablespoons butter

Combine the sugar and 1/2 cup butter in a large mixing bowl. Beat until light and fluffy. Add the eggs, chocolate syrup, flour and vanilla. Beat for 2 minutes; the batter will be thin. Pour into a greased and floured 9×13-inch baking pan. Bake at 350 degrees for 30 minutes or until a wooden pick inserted in the center comes out clean. Cool completely on a wire rack. Beat the confectioners' sugar, 1/2 cup butter, milk, peppermint extract and food coloring in a mixing bowl until smooth. Spread over the cooled cake. Cover and chill. Combine the chocolate chips and 6 tablespoons butter in a saucepan. Cook over low heat until melted, stirring frequently. Let cool to room temperature. Spread over the iced cake. Chill until firm. Yield: 24 servings.

Marge Fye, Xi Iota Lambda
Dundas, Illinois

CHOCOLATE MINT RED VELVET CAKE

1 (2-layer) package red
   velvet cake mix
4 eggs
1 cup sour cream
1/3 cup canola oil
1/4 cup water
1 cup miniature
   chocolate chips

1/3 cup coarsely crushed
   candy canes
Cream cheese frosting
Additional coarsely
   crushed candy canes

Combine the cake mix, eggs, sour cream, canola oil and water in a mixing bowl. Beat at low speed until moistened. Beat at medium speed for 2 minutes. Stir in the chocolate chips and 1/3 cup crushed candy

canes. Pour into two 9-inch nonstick cake pans. Bake at 350 degrees for 25 to 30 minutes or until a wooden pick inserted in the center comes out clean. Cool in the pans for 10 minutes. Remove to a wire rack to cool completely. Place 1 layer on a serving plate. Spread with frosting and sprinkle with crushed candy canes. Top with the other layer. Frost the top and side of the cake with frosting and sprinkle with crushed candy canes. You may bake this in a bundt pan. Increase the baking time to 1 hour.
Yield: 12 servings.

Heather Murphy, Laureate Alpha Epsilon
Ottawa, Ontario, Canada

TIA MARIA CAKE

1 (2-layer) package devil's food cake mix	*1/2 cup Tia Maria liqueur*
1 (31/2-ounce) package instant vanilla pudding mix	*4 eggs, at room temperature*
1/2 cup water	*1/2 cup (1 stick) butter*
1/2 cup vegetable oil	*1 cup sugar*
	1/4 cup rum
	1/4 cup water

Beat the cake mix, pudding mix, 1/2 cup water, oil and liqueur in a large mixing bowl. Add the eggs 1 at a time, beating well after each addition. Pour into a bundt pan coated with nonstick cooking spray. Bake at 325 degrees for 1 hour or until a wooden pick inserted in the center comes out clean. Combine the butter, sugar, rum and 1/4 cup water in a microwave-safe bowl. Microwave on High until the sugar melts, stirring occasionally. Pour slowly over the hot cake. Let stand for 1 hour. Invert the cake onto a serving plate. Yield: 16 servings.

Mary Ann Kelley, Xi Alpha Gamma Epsilon
Longview, Texas

❖ TIRAMISU TOFFEE TORTE

1 (2-layer) package white cake mix with pudding	*1/3 cup chocolate syrup*
4 egg whites	*4 ounces cream cheese, softened*
1 cup strong brewed coffee, at room temperature	*2 cups whipping cream*
4 (11/2-ounce) toffee candy bars, chopped	*2 teaspoons vanilla extract*
2/3 cup sugar	*1 cup strong brewed coffee, at room temperature*

Combine the cake mix, egg whites and 1 cup coffee in a large mixing bowl. Beat at low speed until moistened. Beat at high speed for 2 minutes. Fold in the chopped candy. Pour into 2 greased and floured 8- or 9-inch cake pans. Bake at 350 degrees for 25 to 35 minutes or until a wooden pick inserted in the center comes out clean. Cool in the pans for 10 minutes. Remove to a wire rack to cool completely. Beat the sugar, chocolate syrup and cream cheese in a mixing bowl until smooth. Add the whipping cream and vanilla and beat until light and fluffy. Chill until ready to use. Cut each cake layer horizontally into halves with a serrated knife. Drizzle 1/4 cup of the remaining coffee over each layer. Assemble the cake, spreading the cream mixture between the layers and over the top and side of the cake. Garnish with chopped toffee bars or chocolate curls. Yield: 12 servings.

Linda Mann, Laureate Beta Rho
Cherokee, Iowa

TIRAMISU CAKE

1 (2-layer) package French vanilla cake mix	*1/4 cup sour cream*
1 pint coffee ice cream, melted	*3 tablespoons unsalted butter, softened*
3 eggs	*2 tablespoons coffee liqueur*
8 ounces cream cheese, softened	*11/2 cups confectioners' sugar*
	Baking cocoa

Combine the cake mix, melted ice cream and eggs in a large mixing bowl. Beat at low speed for 1 minute. Beat at medium speed for 2 minutes. Pour into a greased and floured bundt pan. Bake at 350 degrees for 35 to 40 minutes or until a wooden pick inserted in the center comes out clean. Cool in the pan for 20 minutes. Remove to a wire rack to cool completely. Combine the cream cheese, sour cream, butter and liqueur in a mixing bowl. Beat at medium speed for 1 minute. Beat in the confectioners' sugar at low speed. Beat for 1 to 2 minutes. Spread the frosting over the cake and dust with baking cocoa. Chill until ready to serve. Yield: 16 servings.

Marge Jewell, Laureate Gamma Omicron
Warren, Ohio

*JoAnn Panushka, Laureate Delta, Newport News, Virginia, makes an easy **Kahlúa Cake** by combining one 2-layer chocolate cake mix, one 4-ounce package chocolate instant pudding mix, 16 ounces sour cream, 1/2 cup Kahlúa, 1/4 cup vegetable oil and 2 eggs in a large mixing bowl. The mixture is beaten at medium speed for 2 minutes or until smooth. Twelve ounces chocolate chips are stirred in and the mixture is poured into a greased 9×11-inch baking pan. The cake is baked at 350 degrees for 45 to 55 minutes or until the layer tests done.*

TURTLE CAKE

Let this cake stand for several hours before serving.

1 (2-layer) package German Chocolate cake mix	1/2 cup evaporated milk
1/2 cup evaporated milk	1/4 cup (1/2 stick) butter or margarine
3/4 cup (1 1/2 sticks) butter or margarine, melted	1 cup chocolate chips
1 (14-ounce) package caramels	1 cup chopped pecans

Combine the cake mix, 1/2 cup evaporated milk and 3/4 cup melted butter in a large bowl. Beat at medium speed for 2 minutes. Pour 1/2 of the batter into a greased 9×13-inch baking pan. Bake at 350 degrees for 10 minutes. Combine the caramels, 1/2 cup evaporated milk and 1/4 cup butter in a microwave-safe bowl. Microwave on High for 2 minutes; do not overcook. Stir to mix well. Pour evenly over the hot cake in the pan. Sprinkle with the chocolate chips and pecans. Cover with the remaining batter. Bake at 350 degrees for 20 to 25 minutes. Cool on a wire rack. Yield: 18 to 20 servings.

Debbie Windmiller, Xi Mu Iota
Salisbury, Missouri

WHITE CHOCOLATE BANANA CAKE

I adapted this recipe from a standard banana cake recipe. It was a big hit at our granddaughter's wedding. I also make it for family and friends.

3 cups cake flour	2 eggs
1 teaspoon baking powder	3 ripe bananas, mashed
1/2 teaspoon salt	1 tablespoon vanilla extract
1/2 cup buttermilk	1/2 cup melted white chocolate
1 teaspoon baking soda	
2 cups sugar	Cream Cheese Frosting
1/2 cup shortening	

Sift the flour, baking powder and salt into a large bowl. Combine the buttermilk and baking soda in a small bowl and mix well. Beat the sugar and shortening in a large mixing bowl until light and fluffy. Beat in the eggs and bananas. Beat in the dry ingredients alternately with the buttermilk mixture. Stir in the vanilla. Fold in the white chocolate. Pour into 2 well greased and floured 8-inch cake pans. Bake at 350 degrees for 25 to 30 minutes or until a wooden pick inserted in the center comes out clean. Cool in the pans for 10 minutes. Remove to a wire rack to cool completely. Spread the Cream Cheese Frosting between the layers and over the top and side of the cake. Yield: 12 to 15 servings.

CREAM CHEESE FROSTING

1/4 cup (1/2 stick) butter, softened	1/2 teaspoon vanilla extract
8 ounces cream cheese, softened	3 1/2 cups confectioners' sugar
2 tablespoons milk	

Combine the butter and cream cheese in a mixing bowl. Beat until creamy. Beat in the milk and vanilla. Add the confectioners' sugar gradually, beating until smooth.

Yvonne M. Artz, Xi Delta Alpha
Greenville, Ohio

CHOCOLATE ZUCCHINI CAKE

2 1/2 cups all-purpose flour	2 cups sugar
1/2 cup baking cocoa	3/4 cup vegetable oil
2 1/2 teaspoons baking powder	3 eggs
1 1/2 teaspoons baking soda	2 teaspoons vanilla extract
1 teaspoon salt	2 cups grated zucchini
1 teaspoon cinnamon	3/4 cup buttermilk
	1 cup chopped nuts
	Vanilla Glaze

Combine the flour, baking cocoa, baking powder, baking soda, salt and cinnamon in a bowl and mix well. Beat the sugar and oil in a large mixing bowl. Add the eggs and beat well. Stir in the vanilla and zucchini. Stir in the dry ingredients alternately with the buttermilk. Stir in the nuts. Pour into a well greased and floured bundt pan. Bake at 350 degrees for 1 hour or until a wooden pick inserted in the center comes out clean. Cool in the pan for 15 minutes. Remove to a wire rack to cool completely. Drizzle with the Vanilla Glaze. Yield: 16 servings.

VANILLA GLAZE

2 cups confectioners' sugar	1 teaspoon vanilla extract
3 tablespoons milk	

Combine the confectioners' sugar, milk and vanilla in a mixing bowl. Beat until smooth.

Linda Rehmert, Xi Delta Tau
Dove Creek, Colorado

---

*Linda Gish, Laureate Beta Lambda, Topeka, Kansas, makes **Easy Lemon Icing** by combining 1/4 cup (1/2 stick) butter, softened, with 1 cup confectioners' sugar and 2 teaspoons lemon juice in a bowl. She beats the mixture until smooth and pours the icing over hot lemon cake.*

GRANDMA BERCHER'S CINNAMON CAKE

This was my grandma Bercher's favorite cake recipe. It has been made by family members all over the world. My cousin used to make it for the morning snack for her husband's company.

3 cups all-purpose flour	1/2 cup shortening
4 teaspoons baking powder	2 eggs
1 teaspoon salt	1 1/2 cups milk
1 1/2 cups sugar	Cinnamon Topping

Combine the flour, baking powder and salt in a bowl and mix well. Beat the sugar and shortening in a mixing bowl until light and fluffy. Beat in the eggs. Beat in the dry ingredients alternately with the milk. Pour into an 8×11-inch nonstick baking pan. Sprinkle with the Cinnamon Topping and press lightly into the batter. Bake at 350 degrees for 30 to 40 minutes or until a wooden pick inserted in the center comes out clean. Remove to a wire rack to cool. Yield: 8 to 10 servings.

CINNAMON TOPPING

1/2 cup sugar	4 teaspoons cinnamon
2 tablespoons all-purpose flour	1/4 cup shortening, melted

Combine the sugar, flour, cinnamon and melted shortening in a bowl. Stir until crumbly.

Jean Ann Roddy, Theta Epsilon
Fort Smith, Arkansas

GREEK CAKE

1 1/2 cups all-purpose flour	1 1/2 cups sugar
1 1/2 teaspoons baking powder	5 eggs, beaten
1 teaspoon cinnamon	1 1/2 cups chopped pecans
1/2 cup (1 stick) butter, melted	1 1/3 cups water
	1 cup sugar

Combine the flour, baking powder and cinnamon in a bowl and mix well. Beat the butter and 1 1/2 cups sugar in a large mixing bowl. Beat in the eggs and dry ingredients. Stir in the pecans. Pour into a buttered 9×13-inch baking pan. Bake at 350 degrees for 30 minutes or until a wooden pick inserted in the center comes out clean. Cool on a wire rack. Combine the water and 1 cup sugar in a saucepan. Bring to a boil and cook for 10 minutes. Pour over the cooled cake. Yield: 10 to 12 servings.

Mary Ruth Alexander, Gamma Sigma Master
Alice, Texas

CHRISTMAS CRANBERRY CAKE WITH HOT BUTTER SAUCE

2 cups all-purpose flour	1 teaspoon vanilla extract
1 tablespoon baking powder	1 cup milk
1/2 teaspoon salt	2 cups fresh cranberries
2 tablespoons butter, softened	1/2 cup (1 stick) butter
1 cup sugar	1 cup sugar
	1/2 cup evaporated milk

Combine the flour, baking powder and salt in a bowl and mix well. Beat 2 tablespoons butter and 1 cup sugar in a large mixing bowl. Stir in the vanilla. Beat in the dry ingredients alternately with the milk. Fold in the cranberries. Pour into a greased 9×13-inch baking pan. Bake at 400 degrees for 35 minutes or until a wooden pick inserted in the center comes out clean. Melt 1/2 cup butter in a saucepan. Stir in 1 cup sugar and evaporated milk. Simmer for 3 to 4 minutes, stirring occasionally. Cut the cake into squares and serve warm topped with the hot butter sauce. Yield: 15 servings.

Trish Morehead, Xi Xi Kappa
Allen, Texas

FRUITCAKE

2 teaspoons baking soda	1 cup chopped walnuts
9 figs, finely chopped	1 cup chopped dried pineapple
1/2 cup minced dates	1 teaspoon vanilla extract
1/2 cup raisins	3/4 teaspoon cinnamon
1 1/4 cup boiling water or juice	1 to 1 1/2 cups halved maraschino cherries
3 tablespoons shortening	3 cups all-purpose flour
1 3/4 cups sugar	1/2 teaspoon salt
2 eggs	

Sprinkle the baking soda over the figs, dates and raisins in a bowl. Pour the boiling water over the top. Let cool. Beat the shortening and sugar in a large mixing bowl until light and fluffy. Beat in the eggs. Add the walnuts, pineapple, vanilla and cinnamon and mix well. Add the fig mixture and stir until combined. Stir in the cherries. Sift the flour and salt together. Add to the fruit mixture and stir to mix well. Spoon into a nonstick tube pan. Bake at 325 degrees for 1 hour or until a wooden pick inserted in the center comes out clean. Cool in the pan for 20 to 30 minutes. Remove to a wire rack to cool completely. Cover and chill. Yield: 12 to 14 servings.

Sarah R. McCammon, Laureate Omicron
Terre Haute, Indiana

EGGNOG CAKE

This is our dessert along with a good cup of coffee after trimming the tree. I think this cake is the reason my family wants to help me trim the tree!

1/2 cup chopped walnuts or pecans	1/4 teaspoon nutmeg
1 (2-layer) package yellow cake mix	2 tablespoons rum or orange juice
1 cup eggnog	1 cup sugar
1/4 cup vegetable oil	1 cup water
3 eggs	3 tablespoons rum

Grease and flour a 10-inch bundt pan. Sprinkle the walnuts over the bottom of the pan. Combine the next 6 ingredients in a large mixing bowl. Beat at low speed for 2 minutes. Pour into the prepared pan. Bake at 325 degrees for 1 hour or until a wooden pick inserted in the center comes out clean. Cool in the pan for 15 minutes. Remove to a wire rack to cool completely. Combine the sugar and water in a saucepan. Bring to a boil, stirring occasionally. Remove from the heat and stir in 3 tablespoons rum. Let cool. Place the cake on a serving plate. Brush some of the sugar mixture over the cake every 15 minutes to saturate the cake. Yield: 8 servings.

Juanita Corkwell, Laureate Chi
Ellenton, Florida

EGGLESS, MILKLESS, BUTTERLESS CAKE

While growing up in Ohio, this was my favorite recipe to make and eat with my grandma. She had limited means but always had a box of raisins in the cupboard.

2 cups packed brown sugar	1/4 teaspoon nutmeg
2 cups hot water	Pinch of salt
1 box raisins	2 teaspoons baking soda
1/3 cup shortening	Hot water
2 teaspoons cinnamon	4 cups all-purpose flour
1 teaspoon cloves	1 teaspoon baking powder

Combine the first 8 ingredients in a saucepan and mix well. Bring to a boil and cook for 3 minutes, stirring occasionally. Remove from the heat and let cool. Dissolve the baking soda in a small amount of hot water and stir into the brown sugar mixture. Combine the flour and baking powder in a large bowl; stir in the brown sugar mixture. Pour into a greased 9×13-inch baking pan. Bake at 325 degrees for 1 hour or until a wooden pick inserted in the center comes out clean. Remove to a wire rack to cool. Yield: 15 servings.

Cecelia A. Shirley, Alpha Epsilon Omega
St. Charles, Missouri

PUMPKIN FRUITCAKE

1 package nut bread mix	1 (15-ounce) box raisins
1 (15-ounce) can pumpkin	1 or 2 jars maraschino cherries, drained
2 eggs	1 cup chopped dates
1 cup chopped nuts	

Combine the nut bread mix and pumpkin in a large bowl and mix well. Stir in the eggs, nuts, raisins, cherries and dates. Pour into a greased and floured tube pan. Bake at 350 degrees for 1 hour or until a wooden pick inserted in the center comes out clean. Cool in the pan for 20 to 30 minutes. Remove to a wire rack to cool completely. Yield: 20 servings.

Mildred Filius, Theta Master
Fairmont, West Virginia

SWEDISH GINGER CAKE

13/4 cups all-purpose flour	1 cup sugar
1 teaspoon baking soda	3 eggs
1/2 teaspoon salt	1 teaspoon cinnamon
1/2 cup (1 stick) butter, softened	1 teaspoon ginger
	1 teaspoon cloves
	2/3 cup sour cream

Sift the flour, baking soda and salt into a bowl. Beat the butter and sugar in a large mixing bowl until light and fluffy. Beat in the eggs, cinnamon, ginger and cloves. Beat in the dry ingredients alternately with the sour cream. Pour into a greased and floured bundt pan. Bake at 325 degrees for 18 minutes. Reduce the heat to 250 degrees and bake for 1 hour or until a wooden pick inserted in the center comes out clean. Cool in the pan for 7 minutes. Remove to a wire rack to cool completely. Yield: 16 to 18 servings.

Dayle L. Nelson, Beta Master
Cheyenne, Wyoming

MY FAVORITE GINGERBREAD

Being from Ohio, we had lots of snow during the winter months. My mom would have this gingerbread baked and ready to serve warm when we came in from an afternoon of snow sledding.

21/2 cups all-purpose flour	1/2 cup (1 stick) butter, softened
1 teaspoon baking soda	1 cup molasses
1 teaspoon cinnamon	1 cup boiling water
1/2 cup sugar	2 eggs

Sift the flour, baking soda and cinnamon into a bowl 3 times. Beat the sugar and butter in a large mixing bowl until light and fluffy. Beat in the molasses and boiling water. Beat in the dry ingredients and eggs. Pour into a nonstick 9×13-inch baking pan. Bake at

350 degrees for 35 to 40 minutes or until a wooden pick inserted in the center comes out clean. Remove to a wire rack to cool. Yield: 12 servings.

Virginia (Ginny) Tawzer, Laureate Mu
Lexington, South Carolina

AUNT DELLA'S GINGERBREAD

3³/₄ cups all-purpose
   flour
³/₄ teaspoon baking soda
³/₄ teaspoon salt
1¹/₂ teaspoons cinnamon
1¹/₂ teaspoons ginger
³/₄ teaspoon cloves
1¹/₂ cups hot water
1¹/₂ cups molasses
³/₄ cup (1¹/₂ sticks)
   butter, softened
³/₄ cup packed brown
   sugar
2 eggs
Lemon Wine Sauce

Combine the flour, baking soda, salt, cinnamon, ginger and cloves in a bowl and mix well. Combine the hot water and molasses in a bowl and mix well. Beat the butter and brown sugar in a large mixing bowl until light and fluffy. Beat in the eggs. Beat in the dry ingredients alternately with the molasses mixture. Pour into a greased 9×13-inch baking pan. Bake at 350 degrees for 35 to 45 minutes or until a wooden pick inserted in the center comes out clean. Cool on a wire rack. Serve with the Lemon Wine Sauce.
Yield: 15 servings.

LEMON WINE SAUCE

2 cups sugar
5 eggs
3 egg yolks
Grated zest of 4 lemons
Juice of 4 lemons
1 cup (2 sticks) chilled
   butter, cut into pieces
2 tablespoons (or more)
   white wine

Beat the sugar, eggs and egg yolks in the top of a double boiler. Stir in the lemon zest and lemon juice. Cook over simmering water until thickened, stirring constantly. Add the butter and cook until thickened, stirring constantly. Stir in the wine.

Frances C. Parks, Laureate Beta Sigma
St. Charles, Missouri

LEMON POPPY SEED CAKE

1 (2-layer) package
   lemon cake mix with
   pudding
3 eggs
¹/₃ cup vegetable oil
¹/₄ cup water
1 cup sour cream
¹/₃ cup poppy seeds
¹/₂ (16-ounce) can lemon
   frosting
¹/₄ cup sour cream

Combine the cake mix, eggs, oil, water and 1 cup sour cream in a large mixing bowl. Beat at low speed just until moistened. Beat at high speed for 2 minutes. Add the poppy seeds and beat at low speed

until mixed well. Pour into a greased and floured 12-inch bundt pan. Bake at 350 degrees for 45 to 50 minutes or until a wooden pick inserted in the center comes out clean. Cool in the pan for 20 minutes. Remove to a wire rack to cool completely. Place the frosting in a microwave-safe bowl. Microwave on High for 3 to 4 seconds. Whisk in ¹/₄ cup sour cream. Pour over the cooled cake. Chill until the frosting sets. Yield: 12 to 18 servings.

Carolyn Clemens, Xi Delta Eta
Eckert, Colorado

LEMON PUDDING CAKE

³/₄ cup sugar
¹/₄ cup all-purpose flour
1 cup milk
3 egg yolks
¹/₄ cup (¹/₂ stick) butter
   or margarine, melted
1 tablespoon grated
   lemon zest
¹/₃ cup fresh lemon juice
3 egg whites
¹/₈ teaspoon salt

Combine the sugar and flour in a bowl and mix well. Whisk in the next 5 ingredients. Beat the egg whites and salt in a small mixing bowl until soft peaks form. Fold ¹/₄ of the egg whites into the lemon mixture. Fold in the remaining egg whites. Pour into a greased 8-inch baking dish. Place the baking dish in a small roasting pan. Add enough boiling water to the larger pan to come halfway up the side of the baking dish. Bake at 350 degrees for 40 minutes or until golden brown. Remove the baking dish to a wire rack and let cool for 10 minutes. Serve warm. Yield: 6 servings.

Joanne Bowen, Xi Beta Rho
Shelbyville, Indiana

KEY LIME CAKE

1 (2-layer) package
   lemon cake mix
1 (3-ounce) package lime
   gelatin
4 eggs
²/₃ cup vegetable oil
²/₃ cup water
1 teaspoon lemon
   extract
2 cups confectioners'
   sugar
¹/₄ cup Key lime juice

Combine the first 6 ingredients in a large mixing bowl. Beat at medium speed for 2 minutes. Pour into a greased and floured 10-inch bundt pan. Bake at 350 degrees for 40 to 50 minutes or until a wooden pick inserted in the center comes out clean. Cool in the pan for 5 minutes. Invert onto a baking sheet. Mix the confectioners' sugar and lime juice in a bowl until smooth. Pour gradually over the cake, allowing the mixture to absorb before adding more. Bake for 5 to 8 minutes longer. Remove to a wire rack to cool. Yield: 12 servings.

Debbie Gwynn, Xi Delta Rho
Miami, Florida

OATMEAL CAKE

1½ cups boiling water	1 cup sugar
1 cup rolled oats	1 cup packed brown
1½ cups all-purpose	sugar
flour	½ cup shortening
1 teaspoon baking soda	2 eggs
½ teaspoon salt	Crunchy Topping
½ teaspoon nutmeg	

Pour the boiling water over the oats in a bowl. Let stand for 20 minutes. Combine the flour, baking soda, salt and nutmeg in a bowl and mix well. Beat the sugar, brown sugar, shortening and eggs in a large mixing bowl until light and fluffy. Beat in the dry ingredients alternately with the oatmeal mixture. Pour into a greased 9×13-inch baking pan. Bake at 375 degrees for 35 minutes or until a wooden pick inserted in the center comes out clean. Spread the Crunchy Topping over the cake. Broil until golden brown. Remove to a wire rack to cool.
Yield: 12 servings.

CRUNCHY TOPPING

½ cup (1 stick)	2 teaspoons vanilla
margarine	extract
½ cup half-and-half	½ cup crisp rice cereal
½ cup packed brown	½ cup chopped pecans
sugar	

Combine the margarine, half-and-half, brown sugar and vanilla in a saucepan. Cook over medium heat until thick, stirring frequently. Stir in the cereal and pecans.

Mitzie Seals, Xi Delta Eta
Eckert, Colorado

ORANGE SLICE CAKE

2½ cups all-purpose	1 cup all-purpose flour
flour	1½ cups chopped dates
½ teaspoon salt	2 cups chopped nuts
½ cup buttermilk	1 pound orange slice
1 teaspoon baking soda	candies, chopped
1 cup (2 sticks)	2 cups flaked coconut
margarine, softened	1 cup confectioners'
2 cups sugar	sugar
4 eggs	¼ cup orange juice
1 teaspoon vanilla	3 to 4 tablespoons
extract	lemon juice

Combine 2½ cups flour and salt in a bowl and mix well. Combine the buttermilk and baking soda in a small bowl and mix well. Beat the margarine and sugar in a large mixing bowl until light and fluffy. Add the eggs 1 at a time, beating well after each addition. Stir in the vanilla. Beat in the dry ingredients alternately with the buttermilk mixture. Combine 1 cup flour, dates, nuts and orange slice candies in a bowl. Toss to coat. Add to the batter and stir to mix well. Fold in the coconut. Pour into a nonstick bundt pan. Bake at 250 degrees for 3½ hours or until a wooden pick inserted in the center comes out clean. Cool in the pan for 20 minutes. Remove to a wire rack to cool completely. Beat the confectioners' sugar, orange juice and lemon juice in a bowl until smooth. Drizzle over the cooled cake. Yield: 12 servings.

Mary E. McCarty, Laureate Gamma
Dalhart, Texas

❖ GOLDEN COINTREAU CAKE

8 egg yolks	½ teaspoon vanilla
1½ cups sugar	extract
⅓ cup fresh orange	8 egg whites
juice	¼ teaspoon salt
1 cup all-purpose flour,	½ teaspoon cream
sifted twice	of tartar
1½ teaspoons Cointreau	Cointreau Frosting

Beat the egg yolks in a large mixing bowl for 8 minutes or until thick and pale yellow. Add the sugar slowly and beat until smooth. Beat in the orange juice. Sprinkle the flour over the egg yolk mixture and fold in gently. Stir in the Cointreau and vanilla. Combine the egg whites and salt in a mixing bowl. Beat for 2 minutes or until foamy. Add the cream of tartar and beat for 4 minutes or until stiff but not dry. Stir a few spoonfuls of the egg whites into the egg yolk mixture. Fold in the remaining egg whites. Spoon into an ungreased 10-inch tube pan. Bake at 325 degrees in the middle of the oven for 1¼ hours. Invert onto a funnel and let cool overnight. Loosen the cake from the side of the pan. Invert onto a cake plate. Frost with the Cointreau Frosting.
Yield: 12 to 14 servings.

COINTREAU FROSTING

½ cup (1 stick) butter,	1 egg yolk
softened	6 to 8 tablespoons
⅛ teaspoon salt	Cointreau
1 (16-ounce) package	
confectioners' sugar	

Beat the butter and salt in a mixing bowl until light and fluffy. Add the confectioners' sugar gradually, beating constantly. Beat in the egg yolk. Add the Cointreau gradually, beating constantly. Beat until smooth and thick. Note: If raw eggs are a problem in your area, use an equivalent amount of pasteurized egg yolk.

Sandra Lange, Laureate Gamma
Choteau, Montana

FUZZY NAVEL CAKE

1 (24-ounce) can peaches
1/2 cup peach schnapps
1 cup sugar
4 eggs
1 (3 1/2-ounce) package
  instant vanilla
  pudding mix

1 (2-layer) package
  yellow cake mix
1/4 cup orange juice
2/3 cup vegetable oil
1 cup chopped pecans
1 1/2 cups confectioners'
  sugar

Drain the peaches, reserving 1/2 cup of the juice. Chop the peaches. Mix the peaches, reserved juice, schnapps and sugar in a glass bowl. Cover and let stand at room temperature for 24 hours. Drain, reserving the liquid. Measure 1/2 cup of the liquid and pour into a large mixing bowl. Measure 1/2 cup of the remaining liquid and set aside. Add the eggs, pudding mix, cake mix, orange juice, oil, pecans and peaches to the liquid in the large mixing bowl. Beat to mix well. Pour into a greased bundt pan. Bake at 350 degrees for 40 minutes or until a wooden pick inserted in the center comes out clean. Cool in the pan for 15 minutes. Remove to a wire rack to cool completely. Combine the confectioners' sugar and 1/2 cup reserved liquid in a bowl. Stir until smooth. Drizzle over the cooled cake. Yield: 14 to 16 servings.

Susan Miller, Laureate Beta
Longview, Washington

PINEAPPLE-ORANGE SUNSHINE CAKE

My grandson loves this delicious cake. Last year we decorated the top with toy cowboys, Indians, and horses. This year it will be Star Wars action figures.

1 (2-layer) package
  yellow cake mix
1/2 cup vegetable oil
4 eggs
1 (11-ounce) can
  mandarin oranges
1 (20-ounce) can crushed
  pineapple

1 tablespoon sugar
3 (3 1/2-ounce) packages
  instant cheesecake
  pudding mix
1 cup sour cream
1 (8-ounce) container
  frozen whipped
  topping, thawed

Combine the cake mix, oil, eggs and undrained oranges in a large mixing bowl. Beat at medium speed for 1 to 2 minutes. Pour into 3 greased and floured 9-inch cake pans. Bake at 325 degrees for 15 to 20 minutes or until a wooden pick inserted in the center comes out clean. Cool in the pans for 10 minutes. Remove to a wire rack to cool completely. Combine the undrained pineapple, sugar, pudding mix and sour cream in a large bowl. Stir until thickened. Fold in the whipped topping. Spread between the layers and over the top and side of the cake. Garnish with additional mandarin oranges, if desired. Chill until ready to serve. Yield: 12 servings.

Patricia Gay, Preceptor Mu
Anchorage, Alaska

MANDARIN CAKE

2 (11-ounce) cans
  mandarin oranges
2 cups all-purpose flour
2 cups granulated sugar
2 teaspoons baking soda
2 teaspoons vanilla
  extract
2 eggs

1 teaspoon salt
1 cup chopped walnuts
3/4 cup packed brown
  sugar
3 tablespoons milk
3 tablespoons butter or
  margarine

Combine the undrained oranges, flour, granulated sugar, baking soda, vanilla, eggs, salt and walnuts in a large mixing bowl. Beat to mix well. Pour into an ungreased 9×13-inch baking pan. Bake at 350 degrees for 30 to 35 minutes or until a wooden pick inserted in the center comes out clean. Cool completely on a wire rack. Poke holes in the top of the cake with a fork or wooden pick. Combine the brown sugar, milk and butter in a saucepan and mix well. Bring to a boil, stirring occasionally. Pour over the cake. Yield: 15 servings.

Juanita Fleming, Preceptor Beta Mu
Prineville, Oregon

PIÑA COLADA CAKE

1 (2-layer) package
  yellow cake mix
1 (8-ounce) can crushed
  pineapple
3 eggs
1/3 cup canola oil
2 tablespoons rum or
  rum extract

1/2 cup flaked coconut
1 (8-ounce) container
  frozen whipped
  topping, thawed
1 cup (or more) flaked
  coconut, toasted

Combine the cake mix, pineapple, eggs, canola oil, rum and 1/2 cup coconut in a large mixing bowl. Beat to mix well. Pour into a greased 9×13-inch baking pan. Bake at 350 degrees for 34 to 38 minutes or until a wooden pick inserted in the center comes out clean. Cool completely on a wire rack. Spread the whipped topping over the cake. Sprinkle with 1 cup toasted coconut. Chill until ready to serve. Yield: 16 to 18 servings.

Eleanor B. Lombardi, Beta Master
Pocatello, Idaho

HUMMINGBIRD CAKE

3 cups all-purpose flour,
  sifted
2 cups sugar
1 teaspoon baking soda
1 teaspoon cinnamon
1/2 teaspoon salt
3 eggs, beaten
3/4 cup applesauce

1/4 cup sunflower or
  corn oil
1 cup crushed pineapple,
  drained
3 bananas, mashed
1 cup chopped pecans or
  walnuts
Cream Cheese Icing

Sift the flour, sugar, baking soda, cinnamon and salt into a large mixing bowl. Add the eggs, applesauce and sunflower oil and beat to mix well. Stir in the pineapple, bananas and pecans. Pour into 3 buttered and floured 8-inch cake pans. Bake at 325 degrees for 25 to 30 minutes or until the top springs back when lightly touched. Cool in the pans for 10 minutes. Remove to a wire rack to cool completely. Spread the Cream Cheese Icing between the layers and over the top and side of the cake. Yield: 12 servings.

CREAM CHEESE ICING

8 ounces cream cheese,
  softened
1/2 cup (1 stick) butter or
  margarine, softened
1 teaspoon vanilla
  extract

3 cups sifted
  confectioners' sugar
Pineapple juice, as
  needed

Beat the cream cheese, butter and vanilla in a mixing bowl until smooth. Add the confectioners' sugar gradually, beating constantly. Beat until smooth, adding pineapple juice to thin the mixture, if needed.

Vera Woronchanka, Xi Theta Alpha
Grimsby, Ontario, Canada

BUTTER NUT POUND CAKE

2 1/2 cups all-purpose
  flour
1/2 cup self-rising flour
1/4 cup (1/2 stick)
  margarine, softened
1 cup shortening
3 cups sugar
5 eggs

1 1/2 cups milk
4 1/2 teaspoons vanilla
  extract
4 1/2 teaspoons butter
  flavoring
4 1/2 teaspoons black
  walnut flavoring

Sift the all-purpose flour and self-rising flour together. Combine the margarine, shortening and sugar in a large mixing bowl. Beat for 10 minutes or until light and fluffy. Add the eggs and beat at high speed. Beat in the dry ingredients alternately with the milk. Beat at medium speed for 2 minutes. Beat in the vanilla, butter flavoring and walnut flavoring. Pour into a greased and floured 10-inch tube pan. Bake at 350 degrees for 1 to 1 1/2 hours or until a

wooden pick inserted in the center comes out clean. Let cool in the pan for 15 minutes. Remove to a wire rack to cool completely. Yield: 10 to 12 servings.

Beverly J. Phillips, Xi Eta
Sumter, South Carolina

COCONUT POUND CAKE

3 cups all-purpose or
  cake flour
1/2 teaspoon baking
  powder
1/4 teaspoon salt
1 1/2 cups shortening
2 1/2 cups sugar

5 eggs
1 cup milk
1 tablespoon coconut
  extract
1 cup flaked coconut
Buttermilk Glaze

Combine the flour, baking powder and salt in a bowl and mix well. Combine the shortening and sugar in a large mixing bowl. Beat at high speed for 10 minutes. Reduce the speed to low. Add the eggs 1 at a time, beating well after each addition. Beat in the dry ingredients alternately with the milk. Beat in the coconut extract. Fold in the coconut. Pour into a non-stick bundt pan. Place in a cold oven and set the temperature to 325 degrees. Bake for 1 hour and 25 minutes or until a wooden pick inserted in the center comes out clean. Remove to a wire rack. Poke holes in the top of the cake with a skewer. Pour the Buttermilk Glaze slowly and evenly over the cake. Yield: 16 servings.

BUTTERMILK GLAZE

1/2 cup (1 stick)
  margarine
1 cup sugar

2 tablespoons light corn
  syrup
1/2 cup buttermilk

Conbine all the ingredients in a saucepan and mix well. Bring to a slow boil, stirring occasionally.

Janetta Kunkel, Laureate Eta
Warner Robins, Georgia

SOUR CREAM POUND CAKE

1 cup (2 sticks) butter
  or margarine,
  softened
3 cups sugar
6 eggs

1 teaspoon vanilla
  extract
1/4 teaspoon baking soda
3 cups all-purpose flour
1 cup sour cream

Beat the butter and sugar in a large mixing bowl until light and fluffy. Add the eggs 1 at a time, beating well after each addition. Beat in the vanilla, baking soda and flour. Beat in the sour cream. Pour into a greased and floured 10-inch tube pan. Bake at 325 degrees for 1 1/2 hours or until a wooden pick inserted in the center comes out clean. Cool in the pan for 15 minutes.

Remove to a wire rack to cool completely. Serve plain or with ice cream or fresh fruit. Yield: 10 to 12 servings.

Sharon M. Ingram, Laureate Epsilon Theta
St. Petersburg, Florida

PUMPKIN HAZELNUT DATE CAKE

3¹/₂ cups all-purpose flour	*1 cup vegetable oil*
3 cups sugar	*1 cup water*
2 teaspoons baking soda	*4 eggs, beaten*
1¹/₂ teaspoons salt	*1 (8-ounce) package dates, chopped*
1 teaspoon cinnamon	*1 (16-ounce) can pumpkin*
1 teaspoon nutmeg	
1 cup chopped hazelnuts, toasted	

Sift the flour, sugar, baking soda, salt, cinnamon and nutmeg into a large bowl. Make a well in the center and pour in the hazelnuts, oil, water, eggs, dates and pumpkin. Stir to mix well. Pour into a greased and floured bundt pan. Bake at 325 degrees for 1 hour and 10 minutes or until a wooden pick inserted in the center comes out clean. Cool in the pan for 15 minutes. Remove to a wire rack to cool completely. Serve with whipped cream. Yield: 16 servings.

Ann Miles, Preceptor Epsilon Beta
Meriden, Kansas

PRALINE ICE CREAM CAKE

2 cups packed brown sugar	*1¹/₂ teaspoons vanilla extract*
1 cup sour cream	*1¹/₂ cups all-purpose flour*
4 teaspoons cornstarch	
¹/₄ cup (¹/₂ stick) butter	*1 cup graham cracker crumbs*
¹/₂ teaspoon vanilla extract	*²/₃ cup granulated sugar*
1 cup (2 sticks) butter, melted	*2¹/₂ teaspoons baking powder*
2 cups vanilla ice cream, softened	*¹/₂ cup chopped pecans, toasted*
2 eggs	

Combine the brown sugar, sour cream, cornstarch and ¹/₄ cup butter in a saucepan. Bring to a boil over medium heat, stirring constantly. Remove from the heat and stir in ¹/₂ teaspoon vanilla. Mix 1 cup butter and ice cream in a large bowl. Add the eggs 1 at a time, beating well after each addition. Stir in 1¹/₂ teaspoons vanilla. Combine the flour, graham cracker crumbs, granulated sugar and baking power in a bowl and mix well. Add to the ice cream mixture gradually, stirring constantly. Pour into a greased 9×13-inch baking pan. Drizzle with ¹/₂ of the brown sugar mixture. Bake at 350 degrees for 25 to 30 minutes. Cool slightly on a wire rack. Sprinkle with the pecans and drizzle with the remaining brown sugar mixture. Let cool completely. Serve with whipped cream. Yield: 15 servings.

Faye A. Magers, Alpha Upsilon Master
Chester, Illinois

RASPBERRY SOUR CREAM CAKE

1 (10-ounce) container frozen sweetened raspberries	*1 cup sour cream*
	¹/₂ cup vegetable oil
	4 eggs
1 (2-layer) package butter-recipe cake mix	*2 cups confectioners' sugar*
	¹/₄ teaspoon lemon extract
¹/₃ cup sugar	

Thaw the raspberries and drain, reserving ¹/₄ cup of the liquid. Combine the cake mix, sugar, sour cream, oil and eggs in a large mixing bowl. Beat at low speed until moistened. Beat at medium speed for 4 minutes. Pour ²/₃ of the batter into a greased and floured 12-cup bundt pan. Sprinkle the raspberries over the batter. Top with the remaining batter. Place in a cold oven and set the temperature to 325 degrees. Bake for 50 to 55 minutes or until a wooden pick inserted in the center comes out clean. Cool in the pan for 10 minutes. Remove to a wire rack to cool completely. Stir the reserved raspberry liquid gradually into the confectioners' sugar in a bowl. Add the lemon extract and stir until smooth. Spoon over the cooled cake. Yield: 20 servings.

Linda Wilmoth, Preceptor Gamma Xi
St. Petersburg, Florida

OLD-FASHIONED SOUR CREAM CAKE

1 cup (2 sticks) butter, softened	*¹/₄ teaspoon baking powder or baking soda*
3 cups sugar	
1 cup sour cream	*2 teaspoons vanilla extract*
6 eggs	
3 cups all-purpose flour	

Beat the butter and sugar in a large mixing bowl until light and fluffy. Beat in the sour cream. Add the eggs 1 at a time, beating well after each addition. Beat in the flour, baking powder and vanilla. Pour into a greased and lightly floured tube or bundt pan. Bake at 325 degrees for 1¹/₂ hours or until a wooden pick inserted in the center comes out clean. Cool in the pan for 15 to 20 minutes. Remove to a wire rack to cool completely. You may add 2 cups candied fruit and 1 cup pecans to make a fruitcake. Yield: 16 servings.

Linda Boekeloo, Xi Delta Sigma
Brunswick, Georgia

❖ BEE STING CAKE

1/2 cup (1 stick) butter	1/2 teaspoon salt
1/2 cup sugar	1/2 cup (1 stick) butter,
1 cup finely ground	softened
unblanched almonds	1/3 cup sugar
2 tablespoons milk	1 egg
2 teaspoons vanilla	2 tablespoons (or more)
extract	milk
2 cups all-purpose flour	1 cup raspberry jam
2 teaspoons baking	Butter Cream Filling
powder	

Combine 1/2 cup butter, 1/2 cup sugar, almonds, 2 tablespoons milk and vanilla in a saucepan. Bring to a boil, stirring frequently. Remove from the heat and let cool. Combine the flour, baking powder and salt in a bowl and mix well. Beat 1/2 cup butter and 1/3 cup sugar in a large mixing bowl until smooth. Beat in the egg. Beat in the dry ingredients alternately with 2 tablespoons milk. Pour into a well greased 8-inch springform pan. Pour the cooled almond mixture evenly over the top. Bake at 400 degrees for 25 minutes. Remove to a wire rack to cool completely. Loosen from the side of the pan with a sharp knife and remove the side. Heat the raspberry jam in a small saucepan. Pour through a wire-mesh strainer to remove the seeds. Let cool slightly. Cut the cake horizontally into halves to make 2 layers. Spread the Butter Cream Filling over the bottom layer. Spread the raspberry jam over the Butter Cream Filling. Replace the top layer. Sprinkle with sifted confectioners' sugar. Yield: 10 servings.

BUTTER CREAM FILLING

1/4 cup (1/2 stick) butter,	1 cup confectioners'
softened	sugar
1 egg yolk or an	1 teaspoon milk
equivalent amount of	1 teaspoon vanilla
egg substitute	extract

Beat the butter in a mixing bowl until smooth. Beat in the egg yolk. Add the confectioners' sugar, milk and vanilla and beat until smooth.

Margaret Anne Broscomb, Laureate Epsilon
Brantford, Ontario, Canada

STRAWBERRY NUT CAKE

1 (2-layer) package	1 cup flaked coconut
white cake mix	1 cup pecan pieces
1 (3-ounce) package	4 eggs
strawberry gelatin	1 cup vegetable oil
1 cup sliced fresh or	1/2 cup milk
frozen strawberries	Strawberry Frosting

Combine the cake mix, gelatin, strawberries, coconut, pecans, eggs, oil and milk in a large mixing bowl. Beat with an electric mixer at medium speed until well mixed. Pour into a greased and floured 9×13-inch baking pan. Bake at 350 degrees for 35 to 40 minutes or until a wooden pick inserted in the center comes out clean. Remove to a wire rack to cool completely. Frost with Strawberry Frosting. Yield: 12 servings.

STRAWBERRY FROSTING

1 (16-ounce) package	1/2 cup sliced fresh or
confectioners' sugar	frozen strawberries
1/2 cup (1 stick)	1/2 cup pecan pieces
margarine, melted	2 tablespoons milk
1/2 cup flaked coconut	

Combine the confectioners' sugar, margarine, coconut, strawberries, pecans and milk in a mixing bowl. Beat until well mixed.

Pam Williams
Cresson, Texas

TENNESSEE JAM CAKE

1 cup all-purpose flour	1 cup seedless
1 teaspoon baking soda	blackberry jam
1 teaspoon salt	1 cup buttermilk
1 teaspoon cinnamon	1 cup black walnuts
1 teaspoon nutmeg	1 teaspoon vanilla
3 eggs, beaten	extract
1 1/2 cups sugar	Buttermilk Sauce
1 cup vegetable oil	

Combine the flour, baking soda, salt, cinnamon and nutmeg in a bowl and mix well. Combine the eggs, sugar, oil, jam, buttermilk, walnuts and vanilla in a large bowl and mix well. Add the dry ingredients and stir to mix well. Pour into a nonstick 9×13-inch baking pan. Bake at 350 degrees for 40 minutes or until a wooden pick inserted in the center comes out clean. Remove to a wire rack. Poke holes in the top of the cake with a fork. Pour the hot Buttermilk Sauce over the hot cake. Let stand for at least 8 hours before serving. Yield: 16 servings.

BUTTERMILK SAUCE

1/2 cup buttermilk	1 tablespoon light corn
1 cup sugar	syrup
1 teaspoon baking soda	

Combine the buttermilk, sugar, baking soda and corn syrup in a saucepan. Cook until heated through, stirring constantly.

Shirley Shults, Tau Pi
West Carrolton, Ohio

Pies

CURRANT TARTS

1 cup packed brown
  sugar
1/4 cup cream or half-
  and-half
1 egg
1/4 teaspoon salt

1 cup currants, nuts or
  flaked coconut
1 teaspoon vanilla
  extract
Unbaked tart shells

Beat the brown sugar, cream, egg and salt in a mixing bowl. Stir in the currants and vanilla. Spoon into unbaked tart shells and place on a baking sheet. Bake at 350 degrees for 10 to 12 minutes or until the shells are golden brown and the filling is set.
Yield: 8 servings.

Aileen S. Johnston, Gamma Master
Victoria, British Columbia, Canada

CHOCOLATE CHIP WALNUT PIE

1/2 cup (1 stick) unsalted
  butter, softened
1/3 cup granulated sugar
1 cup packed brown
  sugar
2 eggs, at room
  temperature
1 teaspoon vanilla
  extract

1/2 cup all-purpose flour
1/4 teaspoon salt
2 tablespoons milk
1 cup semisweet
  chocolate chips
1/2 to 3/4 cup chopped
  walnuts
1 unbaked (9-inch) pie
  shell, chilled

Beat the butter in a mixing bowl with an electric mixer until light and fluffy. Beat in the granulated sugar and brown sugar. Add the eggs, 1 at a time, beating well after each addition. Beat in the vanilla, flour and salt. Beat in the milk; the mixture may be lumpy. Stir in the chocolate chips and walnuts. Pour into the pie shell and smooth the top. Bake at 350 degrees in the center of the oven for 25 minutes. Turn the pie from front to back and bake for 25 minutes longer or until golden brown and the filling is almost set. Remove to a wire rack to cool. Serve slightly warm or chill for 1 to 2 hours. Yield: 8 to 10 servings.

Doris J. Bain, Xi Epsilon
Chattanooga, Tennessee

GERMAN CHOCOLATE PIE

1 bar German's sweet
  chocolate
1/4 cup (1/2 stick)
  margarine
1 (12-ounce) can
  evaporated milk
1 1/2 cups sugar
3 tablespoons
  cornstarch

1/8 teaspoon salt
2 eggs, lightly beaten
1 teaspoon vanilla
  extract
1 1/3 cups flaked coconut
1/2 cup pecans
1 unbaked (9 or 10-inch)
  pie shell

Melt the chocolate and margarine in a saucepan over low heat, stirring until smooth. Pour into a bowl and stir in the evaporated milk. Combine the sugar, cornstarch and salt in a separate bowl and mix well. Add to the chocolate mixture and stir to mix well. Stir in the eggs. Fold in the vanilla, coconut and pecans. Pour into the pie shell. Bake at 375 degrees for 40 to 50 minutes. Cover the edges of the crust with foil while baking if the crust becomes too brown. Remove to a wire rack to cool. Yield: 6 to 8 servings.

Sylvia Lloyd, Preceptor Omicron Pi
China Spring, Texas

FUDGE PIE

1 ounce unsweetened chocolate	2 eggs, beaten
1/2 cup (1 stick) margarine	1 scant cup all-purpose flour
1 cup sugar	1 teaspoon vanilla extract

Melt the chocolate and margarine in a saucepan over low heat, stirring until smooth. Pour into a bowl and let cool. Add the sugar, eggs, flour and vanilla. Stir to mix well. Pour into a buttered 8-inch pie plate. Bake at 350 degrees for 20 to 25 minutes; the center will be soft. Remove to a wire rack to cool. Serve with whipped topping or ice cream. Yield: 6 servings.

Vicky Wiebe, Preceptor Beta Alpha
El Dorado, Kansas

JACK DANIELS CHOCOLATE PECAN PIE

3/4 cup sugar	2 tablespoons Jack Daniels
3 eggs	
2/3 cup light corn syrup	1 cup pecan halves
1 ounce semisweet chocolate	1 unbaked (9-inch) pie shell
51/3 tablespoons unsalted butter	

Combine the sugar, eggs and corn syrup in a bowl and mix well. Microwave the chocolate and butter in a microwave-safe container until melted. Let cool for 5 minutes. Stir into the sugar mixture. Stir in the Jack Daniels. Spread the pecans in the bottom of the pie shell. Pour the chocolate mixture over the pecans. Bake at 325 degrees for 1 hour. Cool on a wire rack. Yield: 8 servings.

Carol J. Johnson, Preceptor Alpha
Honolulu, Hawaii

MACADAMIA NUT CHOCOLATE PIE

3 eggs	11/2 to 2 cups chopped macadamia nuts
2/3 cup sugar	
1 cup light corn syrup	1/2 cup semisweet chocolate chips
3 tablespoons butter, melted	1 unbaked (10-inch) pie shell
1 teaspoon vanilla extract	

Combine the eggs, sugar, corn syrup, butter and vanilla in a bowl and mix well. Stir in the macadamia nuts. Sprinkle the chocolate chips in the bottom of the pie shell. Pour the sugar mixture carefully over the chocolate chips. Bake at 350 degrees for 45 minutes or until set. Remove to a wire rack to cool. Yield: 8 to 10 servings.

Cindy Simmons, Xi Sigma Omicron
San Antonio, Texas

MEXICAN KAHLÚA PIE

11/4 cups crushed chocolate sandwich cookies	1 teaspoon vanilla extract
6 tablespoons butter, melted	1/3 cup Kahlúa
	4 chocolate-covered toffee candy bars
1/2 cup chopped nuts	1 quart coffee ice cream, softened
2 cups whipping cream	

Combine the crushed cookies, butter and nuts in a bowl, stirring until crumbly. Pat into the bottom and up the sides of a greased 10-inch pie plate. Bake at 350 degrees for 10 minutes. Remove to a wire rack to cool completely. Beat the cream in a mixing bowl until soft peaks form. Fold in the vanilla and Kahlúa. Crush the candy bars and fold into the cream mixture. Fold in the ice cream. Spoon into the cooled pie shell; freeze until firm. Let stand at room temperature for 15 minutes before serving. Garnish with crushed double-stuffed chocolate sandwich cookies, whipped cream and chocolate curls. Yield: 8 servings.

Vera "Elaine" Swanner, Xi Tau Tau
Brazoria, Texas

PIXIE PIE

2 tablespoons butter, softened	3 egg yolks, lightly beaten
1 (4-ounce) package flaked coconut	3 egg whites
1 envelope unflavored gelatin	1/3 cup sugar
	1 teaspoon vanilla extract
1/3 cup sugar	Whipped cream
1/4 teaspoon salt	11/2 ounces unsweetened chocolate, melted
3/4 cup evaporated milk	
3/4 cup water	41/2 teaspoons light corn syrup
2 ounces unsweetened chocolate	

Spread the butter evenly in the bottom and up the sides of a 9-inch pie plate. Sprinkle with the coconut, pressing into the butter. Bake at 300 degrees for 15 minutes or until golden brown. Remove to a wire rack to cool completely. Combine the gelatin, 1/3 cup sugar and salt in a saucepan. Stir in the evaporated milk, water and 2 ounces chocolate. Cook over medium heat until the chocolate melts, stirring constantly. Do not boil. Remove from the heat and beat until smooth. Stir a few tablespoons of the hot chocolate mixture gradually into the egg yolks in a bowl. Return to the saucepan and stir to mix well. Cook over medium heat for 3 minutes or until thickened, stirring constantly. Remove from the heat and let cool for 15 minutes. Beat the egg whites in a large bowl until foamy. Beat in 1/3 cup sugar gradually.

Beat until soft peaks form. Fold in the chocolate mixture gradually. Fold in the vanilla. Spoon into the cooled crust. Chill until firm. Top with whipped cream. Mix 1 1/2 ounces chocolate and corn syrup in a small bowl. Drizzle over the whipped cream. Yield: 8 servings.

Paula Plath-Tanhaeff, Nu Lambda
Madrid, Iowa

TOFFEE BROWNIE PIE

1/2 cup (1 stick) butter, softened	1 1/2 cups semisweet chocolate chunks
3/4 cup packed brown sugar	1 cup almond brickle chips
3 eggs, at room temperature	1 unbaked (9-inch) deep-dish pie shell
1 teaspoon vanilla extract	1/4 cup semisweet chocolate chunks
1/4 cup all-purpose flour	1/4 cup almond brickle chips
1/4 teaspoon salt	
1 cup chopped pecans	1/4 cup chopped pecans

Beat the first 3 ingredients in a bowl at high speed for 1 minute. Beat in the vanilla. Mix the flour and salt together and add to egg mixture. Beat at medium speed to mix well. Stir in 1 cup pecans 1 1/2 cups chocolate chunks and 1 cup brickle. Pour into the pie shell. Bake at 350 degrees for 45 minutes. Mix 1/4 cup chocolate chunks, 1/4 cup brickle and 1/4 cup pecans in a small bowl. Sprinkle over the pie. Bake for 15 minutes longer. Cool on a wire rack. Yield: 8 servings.

Sandra Hall, Xi Alpha Rho
Harrodsburg, Kentucky

BASIC CREAM PIE

4 to 5 tablespoons cornstarch	1 1/2 tablespoons butter
Pinch of salt	1 1/2 teaspoons vanilla extract
1 3/4 cups sugar	1 baked (10-inch) pie shell
5 egg yolks	
3 cups milk, scalded	5 egg whites

Combine the cornstarch, salt and 3/4 cup of the sugar in a bowl. Beat the egg yolks and 1 cup sugar in a medium bowl. Stir in the cornstarch mixture. Stir in 1/2 of the hot milk gradually and beat until the sugar dissolves. Pour into a saucepan and stir in the remaining milk. Cook until thickened, stirring constantly. Remove from the heat and stir in the butter and vanilla. Let cool. Pour into the pie shell. Beat the egg whites in a bowl until stiff peaks form. Spread the egg whites over the filling, sealing to the edge. Bake at 350 degrees for 15 minutes or until golden brown. Cool on a wire rack. For **Chocolate Cream Pie**, add 3 tablespoons baking cocoa to the sugar. For **Coconut Cream Pie**, add 3/4 to 1 cup flaked coconut to the cooled filling. For **Banana Cream Pie**, slice 1 banana into the pie shell and add 1 mashed banana to the cooled filling. For **Butterscotch Cream Pie**, use brown sugar instead of sugar. For **Peanut Butter Pie**, add 3/4 cup creamy peanut butter to the hot filling. Yield: 8 servings.

Kayce L. Weber, Xi Alpha Eta
Torrington, Wyoming

COCONUT CREAM PIE

1 envelope unflavored gelatin	1 teaspoon vanilla extract
1/4 cup cold water	1 1/2 cups flaked coconut
3 eggs	1 cup whipped cream
2/3 cup sugar	1 baked (9-inch) pie shell
1/4 cup cornstarch	
2 cups milk	

Sprinkle the gelatin over the cold water in a small saucepan. Let stand for 5 minutes. Cook over low heat until the gelatin dissolves, stirring occasionally. Remove from the heat. Beat the eggs and sugar in a bowl. Whisk in the cornstarch. Whisk in the milk. Whisk in the gelatin mixture. Pour into a saucepan. Cook just until the mixture comes to a boil and thickens, stirring constantly. Remove from the heat and stir in the vanilla and coconut. Let cool to room temperature. Fold in the whipped cream. Spoon into the pie shell. Chill for 4 hours. Pipe or spoon sweetened whipped cream around the edge of the pie. Sprinkle with toasted coconut. Yield: 6 to 8 servings.

Louise Miskew, Laureate Xi
Toronto, Ontario, Canada

CUSTARD MERINGUE PIE

1 cup sugar	1 teaspoon cloves
1 cup half-and-half	2 tablespoons butter
1 cup milk	1 teaspoon vanilla extract
3 egg yolks, lightly beaten	1 baked (9-inch) pie shell
3 tablespoons cornstarch	
1 teaspoon cinnamon	3 egg whites

Combine the first 7 ingredients in a saucepan and mix well. Cook until thick, stirring constantly. Remove from the heat and stir in the butter and vanilla. Let cool to room temperature. Pour into the pie shell. Beat the egg whites in a bowl until stiff peaks form. Spread over the filling, sealing to the edge. Bake at 350 degrees for 10 minutes or until golden brown and the meringue is cooked through. Cool on a wire rack. Yield: 6 servings.

Rita Sellers, Preceptor Kappa Zeta
Anderson, California

GLUTEN-FREE KEY LIME PIE

½ cup white rice flour	*4 egg yolks*
6 tablespoons potato starch	*1 (14-ounce) can sweetened condensed milk*
3 tablespoons tapioca flour	*3 to 4 teaspoons Key lime juice*
3 tablespoons confectioners' sugar	*1 drop green food color*
½ teaspoon xanthum gum	*4 egg whites*
	⅓ cup sugar
½ cup (1 stick) butter	*½ teaspoon vinegar*

Combine the rice flour, potato starch, tapioca flour, confectioners' sugar and xanthum gum in a bowl. Cut in the butter with a pastry blender or fork until crumbly. Pat into the bottom and up the sides of a 9-inch pie plate. Bake at 350 degrees for 15 minutes. Combine the egg yolks and sweetened condensed milk in a bowl and mix well. Stir in the lime juice gradually. Stir in the food color. Pour the mixture into the pie shell. Bake at 350 degrees for 10 minutes. Combine the egg whites, sugar and vinegar in the top of a double boiler. Cook over hot water until the sugar dissolves, stirring constantly. Remove from the heat. Beat with an electric mixer at medium speed until stiff peaks form. Spread over the filling, sealing to the edge. Bake at 350 degrees for 10 minutes or until golden brown and the meringue is cooked through. Remove to a wire rack to cool. Yield: 6 servings.

Kathy Vine, Laureate Omega
Clear Lake, Iowa

LEMON MERINGUE PIE

1½ teaspoons unflavored gelatin	*1¼ cups hot water*
¼ cup cold water	*3 egg yolks, beaten*
¾ cup Splenda sweetener	*½ teaspoon grated lemon zest*
¾ cup sugar	*2 tablespoons butter*
3 tablespoons cornstarch	*⅓ cup fresh lemon juice*
	1 baked (9-inch) pie shell
3 tablespoons all-purpose flour	*3 egg whites*
	1 teaspoon lemon juice
	6 tablespoons sugar

Dissolve the gelatin in ¼ cup cold water in a small bowl. Mix the sweetener, ¾ cup sugar, cornstarch and flour in a saucepan. Stir in 1¼ cups hot water gradually. Bring to a boil, stirring constantly. Reduce the heat to medium and cook for 8 minutes, stirring constantly. Remove from the heat. Stir a small amount of the hot mixture gradually into the egg yolks in a bowl. Return the egg yolk mixture to the saucepan and stir to mix well. Cook over medium heat for 4 minutes, stirring constantly. Remove from the heat and stir in the gelatin mixture. Add the lemon zest, butter and ⅓ cup lemon juice. Stir gently to mix well. Let cool for 10 minutes. Pour into the pie shell. Beat the egg whites and 1 teaspoon lemon juice in a bowl until soft peaks form. Beat in 6 tablespoons sugar gradually until stiff peaks form. Spread over the filling, sealing to the edge. Bake at 350 degrees for 12 to 15 minutes or until golden brown and the meringue is cooked through. Remove to a wire rack to cool. Yield: 8 servings.

Lillian Cook, Upsilon Master
Matheny, West Virginia

PUMPKIN CREAM PIE

1 (8-ounce) container frozen whipped topping, thawed	*1 (3½-ounce) package instant vanilla pudding mix*
1 (29-ounce) can pumpkin	*1 cup milk*
	1 tablespoon pumpkin pie spice
1 (5-ounce) package instant vanilla pudding mix	*2 baked (9-inch) pie shells*

Combine the pumpkin, pudding mixes, milk and pumpkin pie spice in a large mixing bowl. Beat with an electric mixer at low speed for 1 minute or until well blended. Fold in ½ of the whipped topping. Spoon into the pie shells. Chill for at least 1 hour. Garnish with the remaining whipped topping. You may use graham cracker pie shells. Yield: 12 servings.

Margaret Parker, Rho Master
Raton, New Mexico

BUTTERSCOTCH APPLE PIE

2 cups quick-cooking oats	*Filling*
½ teaspoon cinnamon	*½ to ¾ cup whipping cream*
¼ cup packed brown sugar	*¼ cup crushed peanut brittle*
½ cup (1 stick) butter or margarine, melted	*½ teaspoon grated orange zest*

Combine the oats, cinnamon, brown sugar and melted butter in a bowl, stirring until crumbly. Pat into the bottom and up the sides of a 9-inch pie plate. Bake at 350 degrees for 15 minutes or until golden brown. Remove to a wire rack to cool completely. Spoon in the Filling and let cool. Whip the cream in a bowl until stiff peaks form. Fold in the crushed peanut brittle and orange zest. Spoon over the cooled filling. Chill until ready to serve. Yield: 8 servings.

APPLE FILLING

4 large cooking apples	*2 tablespoons cornstarch*
1/4 cup water	*1/2 teaspoon salt*
1/4 cup light corn syrup	*1/2 teaspoon cinnamon*
1/4 cup packed brown	*2 tablespoons butter or*
sugar	*margarine*

Peel, core and slice the apples. Combine the apples, water and corn syrup in a large saucepan. Cover and cook gently until the apples are tender-crisp. Drain, reserving 2/3 cup of the cooking liquid. Mix the brown sugar, cornstarch, salt and cinnamon in a saucepan. Stir in the reserved cooking liquid. Add the butter. Cook until thickened, stirring constantly. Remove from the heat and fold in the cooked apple slices.

Louise Baker, Theta Master
Raleigh, North Carolina

❖ CARAMELIZED DUTCH APPLE PIE

3/4 cup sugar	*2 tablespoons butter or*
1/4 cup all-purpose flour	*margarine*
1/2 teaspoon cinnamon	*1/4 cup cinnamon-sugar*
1/2 teaspoon nutmeg	*Caramel ice cream*
Dash of salt	*topping*
8 cups sliced apples	*1/2 cup packed brown*
1 unbaked (9-inch) pie	*sugar*
shell	*1 cup all-purpose flour*
1/2 cup chopped walnuts	*1/2 cup (1 stick) butter*

Combine 3/4 cup sugar, 1/4 cup flour, cinnamon, nutmeg and salt in a large bowl and mix well. Add the apples and toss to coat. Spoon into the pie shell. Sprinkle with 1/2 of the walnuts and dot with 2 tablespoons butter. Sprinkle with 1/2 of the cinnamon-sugar. Drizzle with caramel topping. Mix the brown sugar and 1 cup flour in a bowl. Cut in 1/2 cup butter with a pastry blender or fork until crumbly. Spoon over the top of the pie. Sprinkle with the remaining walnuts and cinnamon-sugar. Drizzle with caramel topping. Bake at 425 degrees for 40 minutes. Cover with foil and bake for 10 minutes longer. Remove to a wire rack to cool. Serve warm with ice cream. Yield: 8 servings.

Mary Carlson, Preceptor Alpha Delta
Burnsville, Minnesota

SWISS APPLE PIE

2 eggs, well beaten	*3/4 cup sugar*
1/2 cup all-purpose flour	*1 teaspoon vanilla*
1 teaspoon baking	*extract*
powder	*1/2 teaspoon cinnamon*
Pinch of salt	*1 heaping cup diced*
1/2 cup chopped walnuts	*peeled apples*

Combine the eggs, flour, baking powder, salt, walnuts, sugar, vanilla and cinnamon in a large bowl and mix well. Stir in the apples. Spoon into a greased 9-inch pie plate. Bake at 350 degrees for 30 minutes. Remove to a wire rack to cool. This pie freezes well. Yield: 6 servings.

Cheri Brown, Laureate Kappa
Fort Washington, Maryland

DELICIOUS FRUIT PIE

1 1/2 cups raspberries	*1 1/2 cups water*
1 1/2 cups sliced	*1 (3-ounce) package*
strawberries	*strawberry gelatin*
1 cup blueberries	*1 (8-ounce) container*
1 baked (9-inch) pie	*frozen fat-free*
shell	*whipped topping,*
3/4 cup sugar	*thawed*
3 tablespoons cornstarch	

Combine the raspberries, strawberries and blueberries in a large bowl. Toss gently to mix. Spoon into the pie shell. Mix the sugar and cornstarch in a saucepan. Stir in the water gradually until smooth. Cook over medium heat until the mixture comes to a boil, stirring constantly. Boil for 1 minute, stirring constantly. Remove from the heat and add the gelatin. Stir until the gelatin dissolves. Pour over the berries. Chill for 3 hours or until firm. Spread over the pie. Yield: 6 to 8 servings.

Helen A. Walkden, Laureate Epsilon Epsilon
Columbia Station, Ohio

FRESH BLUEBERRY PIE

Every year in late June, we take our grandsons blueberry picking. Then we go home and make this pie. What a wonderful summer treat!

1 cup sugar	*1 cup water*
3 tablespoons	*3 cups fresh blueberries*
cornstarch	*1 baked (9-inch) pie*
1/4 teaspoon cinnamon	*shell*
1 cup fresh blueberries	

Mix the sugar, cornstarch and cinnamon in a 3-quart saucepan. Stir in 1 cup blueberries and water. Cook until the blueberries pop and the mixture begins to thicken, stirring frequently. Remove from the heat and fold in 3 cups blueberries. Pour into the pie shell. Chill until firm. Serve with whipped cream. Yield: 8 servings.

Kathy Walker, Preceptor Epsilon Lambda
St. James, Missouri

APPALACHIAN CHERRY PIE

2 (16-ounce) cans pitted tart red cherries	1 tablespoon butter or margarine
3/4 cup sugar	4 drops almond extract
1/4 cup cornstarch	1 (2-crust) pie pastry
1/4 cup sugar	

Drain the cherries, reserving 1 cup of liquid. Mix 3/4 cup sugar and cornstarch in a large saucepan. Stir in the reserved cherry liquid. Cook over medium heat until thickened and bubbly, stirring constantly. Cook for 2 minutes, stirring constantly. Remove from the heat and stir in 1/4 cup sugar, butter and almond extract. Stir in the cherries and let cool slightly. Fit 1 pie pastry into a 9-inch pie plate. Pour in the cherry mixture. Cut the remaining pastry into strips. Arrange lattice-fashion over the pie. Cover the edges with foil. Bake at 375 degrees for 25 minutes. Remove the foil and bake for 25 to 30 minutes longer or until golden brown. Remove to a wire rack to cool. Yield: 8 servings.

Edna Klauck, Laureate Eta Beta
Laguna Woods, California

LEMON ORANGE PIE

2 large lemons	5 eggs, well beaten
1 large orange	1 (2-crust) pie pastry
2 cups sugar	

Score lengthwise 1 lemon and the orange. Cut off the ends and discard. Cut each into paper-thin slices. Remove the peel and white pith from the other lemon and cut into paper-thin slices. Combine the lemon slices, orange slices and sugar in a bowl. Toss to mix. Cover and chill overnight. Add the eggs to the fruit mixture and mix well. Fit 1 pie pastry into a 9-inch pie plate. Spoon in the fruit mixture. Cut the remaining pastry into strips. Arrange lattice-fashion over the pie. Bake at 450 degrees for 15 minutes. Reduce the heat to 375 degrees. Bake for 35 minutes. Remove to a wire rack to cool. Yield: 6 servings.

Doris K. Etherington, Omega Laureate Beta Epsilon
Newport, Oregon

MARVELOUS PEACH PIE

3 large peaches, peeled and sliced	3 tablespoons cornstarch
1 baked (9-inch) pie shell	1/2 cup water
2 peaches, peeled and mashed	2 tablespoons butter or margarine
1 cup sugar	1 teaspoon almond extract

Arrange the sliced peaches in the pie shell. Combine the mashed peaches, sugar, cornstarch and water in a saucepan and mix well. Cook over medium heat for

5 minutes or until thickened, stirring constantly. Remove from the heat and stir in the butter and almond extract. Let cool to room temperature. Pour over the peaches in the pie shell. Chill until firm. Yield: 8 servings.

Fluff Stephens, Laureate Iota Psi
Banning, California

PLUM CROSTADA

2 cups all-purpose flour	1/2 cup packed brown sugar
1/4 cup sugar	2 teaspoons grated orange zest
1/2 teaspoon salt	
1 cup (2 sticks) butter	1/4 cup orange juice
6 to 8 tablespoons cold water	Confectioners' sugar
6 ripe plums	

Combine the flour, sugar and salt in a bowl. Cut in the butter with a pastry blender or fork until crumbly. Stir in the water with a fork just until the dough holds together. Press or roll the dough out to a 14-inch circle on a baking sheet or pizza pan lined with parchment paper. Form a 2-inch rim around the edge of the dough. Prick the bottom of the dough with a fork. Bake at 400 degrees for 15 minutes. Pit the plums and cut into 1/8-inch slices. Arrange the sliced plums on the dough in a pinwheel pattern. Mix the brown sugar, orange zest and orange juice in a bowl. Drizzle over the plums. Bake at 400 degrees for 25 to 30 minutes or until golden brown. Remove to a wire rack to cool. Dust with confectioners' sugar. Yield: 10 servings.

Karol Holton, Gamma Omicron
LeMars, Iowa

RASPBERRY ALMOND TART

1 1/3 cups all-purpose flour	1 cup ground almonds
1 teaspoon baking powder	1/2 teaspoon almond extract
1/3 cup sugar	2 eggs
1/2 cup (1 stick) butter, softened	1/2 cup confectioners' sugar
1 egg, beaten	2 tablespoons milk
1/2 to 3/4 cup raspberry jam	1/2 teaspoon almond extract
2/3 cup sugar	1 to 2 tablespoons sliced or slivered almonds
1/2 cup (1 stick) butter, softened	

Mix the flour, baking powder and 1/3 cup sugar in a bowl. Cut in 1/2 cup butter with a pastry blender or fork until the mixture resembles coarse meal. Add 1 beaten egg and stir just until moistened. Press the dough into the bottom and up the sides of a 9 1/2 to

10¹/₂-inch tart pan. Spread ¹/₂ the jam over the dough. Cover and chill for 30 minutes. Beat ²/₃ cup sugar and ¹/₂ cup butter in a bowl until light and fluffy. Stir in the ground almonds and ¹/₂ teaspoon almond extract. Add 2 eggs, 1 at a time, beating well after each addition. Spoon the filling over the jam layer. Bake at 350 degrees for 45 to 50 minutes. Remove to a wire rack to cool completely. Spread the remaining jam over the cooled filling. Beat the confectioners' sugar, milk and ¹/₂ teaspoon almond extract in a mixing bowl until smooth. Drizzle over the top. Sprinkle with the sliced almonds before the glaze hardens.
Yield: 12 servings.

Valerie McArdle, Alpha Alpha Master
Grants Pass, Oregon

STRAWBERRY PIE

1 cup all-purpose flour
3¹/₂ tablespoons
confectioners' sugar
¹/₂ cup (1 stick) butter, softened
2 pints strawberries, sliced
1 cup sugar

3 tablespoons cornstarch
1¹/₂ cups water
¹/₄ cup light corn syrup
¹/₄ cup strawberry gelatin powder
2 drops red food color

Combine the flour and confectioners' sugar in a bowl. Add the butter and mix to form a dough. Press into the bottom and up the sides of an 8-inch pie plate or 8-inch baking pan. Bake at 350 degrees for 18 minutes. Remove to a wire rack to cool completely. Arrange the sliced strawberries on the cooled crust. Combine the sugar and cornstarch in a saucepan. Stir in the water. Bring to a boil and cook for 6 minutes, stirring often. Remove from the heat and stir in the corn syrup, gelatin powder and food color. Let cool. Pour over the strawberries. Cover and chill until firm. Serve with whipped cream. Yield: 8 servings.

Arlene P. Burton, Laureate Beta Omega
Allyn, Washinton

Helen Harry, Epsilon Master Chapter, Ashland, Kentucky, shared her technique for No-Weep, No Shrink Meringue. She combines 1 tablespoon cornstarch, 1 tablespoon sugar and ¹/₂ cup water in a saucepan and cooks over medium heat until the mixture is clear, stirring constantly. The mixture is removed from the heat and cooled. She whips 3 egg whites with a pinch of salt in a bowl until soft peaks form and pours the sugar mixture into the egg whites, beating until stiff peaks form. Six tablespoons sugar are gradually beaten into the egg white mixture until fluffy.

APPLE CRISP PIZZA

1 (1-crust) pie pastry
²/₃ cup sugar
3 tablespoons all-purpose flour
1 teaspoon cinnamon
4 baking apples
¹/₃ cup packed brown sugar

¹/₂ cup all-purpose flour
¹/₃ cup rolled oats
1 teaspoon cinnamon
¹/₄ cup (¹/₂ stick) margarine, softened
¹/₄ to ¹/₂ cup caramel ice cream topping

Roll out the pie pastry on a lightly floured work surface to fit a 12-inch pizza pan. Place the pastry in the pan. Fold under and flute the edges. Combine the sugar, 3 tablespoons flour and 1 teaspoon cinnamon in a large bowl. Peel and core the apples. Cut into ¹/₂-inch slices. Add to the sugar mixture and toss to coat. Arrange the apples in a circular pattern in a single layer on the pastry. Mix the brown sugar, ¹/₂ cup flour, oats and 1 teaspoon cinnamon in a bowl. Cut in the margarine with a pastry blender or fork until crumbly. Sprinkle over the apples. Bake at 350 degrees for 35 to 40 minutes or until the apples are tender. Remove to a wire rack and immediately drizzle with the caramel topping. Serve warm with ice cream. Yield: 12 servings.

Kim Florian, Xi Gamma Eta
Wilber, Nebraska

BANANA SPLIT BROWNIE PIZZA

1 (21¹/₂-ounce) package brownie mix
8 ounces cream cheese, softened
1 (8-ounce) can crushed pineapple, drained
2 tablespoons sugar

2 bananas, sliced
1 cup strawberries, sliced
¹/₂ cup nuts, chopped
¹/₄ cup chocolate ice cream topping

Prepare the brownie batter using the package directions. Cut a circle of parchment paper to fit a 15-inch baking stone. Spread the batter in a 14-inch circle on the parchment paper on the baking stone. Bake at 375 degrees for 15 to 18 minutes or until set; do not overbake. Remove to a wire rack to cool completely. Place the brownie on a large serving plate. Combine the cream cheese, pineapple and sugar in a bowl and mix well. Spread over the brownie. Arrange the bananas and strawberries on top. Sprinkle with the nuts and drizzle with the chocolate topping. Chill until ready to serve. Yield: 16 servings.

Marilyn Pettay, Iota Gamma
Kinsley, Kansas

FRUIT PIZZA

1 tube sugar cookie dough	*8 ounces cream cheese, softened*
1/2 cup orange juice	*1/2 cup sugar*
1/4 cup plus 2 tablespoons water	*1/2 teaspoon vanilla extract*
1/2 cup sugar	*Favorite sliced or chopped fresh fruit*
1 tablespoon cornstarch	
1/8 teaspoon lemon juice	

Pat the cookie dough into a lightly greased 12-inch pizza pan. Bake using the package directions. Remove to a wire rack to cool completely. Combine the orange juice, water, 1/2 cup sugar, cornstarch and lemon juice in a small saucepan. Bring to a boil, stirring constantly. Boil for 1 minute. Remove from the heat and let cool completely. Beat the cream cheese, 1/2 cup sugar and vanilla in a bowl until smooth. Spread over the cooled cookie. Arrange the fruit on the cream cheese layer. Spoon the cooled orange juice mixture lightly over the fruit. Slice into wedges. Yield: 10 to 16 servings.

Sally Bair, Iota Tau
Pryor, Oklahoma

MACADAMIA NUT PIE

3 eggs	*2 tablespoons butter, melted*
2/3 cup sugar	
1 cup light corn syrup	*1 teaspoon vanilla extract*
1 1/2 cups chopped macadamia nuts	*1 unbaked (9-inch) pie shell*

Beat the eggs, sugar and corn syrup in a bowl. Stir in the macadamia nuts. Add the melted butter and vanilla and stir to mix well. Pour into the pie shell. Bake at 325 degrees for 50 minutes or until the crust is golden brown and the center is set. Remove to a wire rack to cool completely. Cover and chill. Serve with whipped cream or vanilla ice cream. Yield: 8 to 10 servings.

Elizabeth White, Preceptor Zeta
Winchester, Virginia

NEW ORLEANS PECAN PIE

3 egg yolks	*3 egg whites*
1 cup granulated sugar	*1/4 teaspoon cream of tartar*
5 tablespoons cornstarch	
1 cup sour cream	*1/2 teaspoon vanilla extract*
1/4 teaspoon lemon extract	*2/3 cup packed brown sugar*
Pinch of salt	
1 baked (9-inch) pie shell	*1 cup pecans*

Combine the first 6 ingredients in the top of a double boiler. Cook over simmering water until thickened, stirring constantly. Pour into the pie shell. Beat the egg whites and cream of tartar in a mixing bowl until foamy. Add the vanilla and brown sugar and beat until stiff peaks form. Fold in the pecans. Spread over the filling, sealing to the edge. Bake at 350 degrees for 10 to 15 minutes or until golden brown and the meringue is cooked through. Remove to a wire rack to cool. Yield: 8 servings.

Lizette L. Pryor, Theta Master
Raleigh, North Carolina

SOUR CREAM RAISIN PIE

1 cup raisins	*Pinch of nutmeg*
3 1/2 cups water	*3 tablespoons warm water*
1 cup sugar	
3 tablespoons all-purpose flour	*1 1/2 cups sour cream*
3 egg yolks	*1/4 cup (1/2 stick) margarine, melted*
Juice of 1 lemon	*1 baked (9-inch) pie shell*
Pinch of salt	

Combine the raisins and 3 1/2 cups water in a saucepan. Simmer for 35 minutes. Remove from the heat. Beat the sugar, flour, egg yolks, lemon juice, salt, nutmeg and 3 tablespoons warm water in a mixing bowl until smooth. Stir into the raisin mixture. Fold in the sour cream and margarine. Return to the heat and cook until thickened, stirring often. Pour into the pie shell and let cool. Yield: 6 servings.

Connie Cook, Xi Lambda Tau
Urich, Missouri

PEANUT BUTTER PIE

1 1/4 cups chocolate cookie crumbs	*1 cup creamy peanut butter*
1/4 cup sugar	*1 tablespoon butter or margarine, softened*
1/4 cup (1/2 stick) butter or margarine, melted	*1 teaspoon vanilla extract*
8 ounces cream cheese, softened	*1 cup whipped cream*
1 cup sugar	

Combine the cookie crumbs, sugar and 1/4 cup butter in a bowl and mix well. Press into the bottom and up the sides of a 9-inch pie plate. Bake at 375 degrees for 10 minutes. Remove to a wire rack to cool completely. Beat the next 5 ingredients in a bowl until smooth. Fold in the whipped cream. Spoon into the cooled crust. Garnish with grated chocolate or chocolate cookie crumbs. Chill until ready to serve. Yield: 8 to 10 servings.

Carol Mangola, Epsilon Master
Atwater, Ohio

Cookies & Candy

CHOCOLATE ALMOND BISCOTTI

2¹/4 cups all-purpose
  flour
1 teaspoon baking
  powder
¹/4 teaspoon salt
¹/2 cup (1 stick) butter,
  softened
1¹/4 cups sugar
2 eggs

1 teaspoon almond
  extract
1 cup sliced almonds
1 cup semisweet
  chocolate chips
1 tablespoon shortening
1 cup white chocolate
  chips
1 tablespoon shortening

Mix the flour, baking powder and salt together. Beat the butter and sugar in a mixing bowl until light and fluffy. Beat in the eggs and almond extract. Beat in the dry ingredients gradually, the dough will be stiff. Stir in the almonds. Divide the dough in half. Shape each half with floured hands into a 2-inch diameter rectangular log, 11 inches long. Place 2 inches apart on an ungreased baking sheet. Bake at 350 degrees for 30 minutes or until set. Cool on the baking sheet for 15 minutes. Remove to a cutting board. Cut diagonally with a serrated knife into ¹/2-inch slices. Discard the end pieces. Arrange the slices, cut side down, closely together on an ungreased baking sheet. Bake at 350 degrees for 8 to 9 minutes. Turn the slices over and bake for 8 to 9 minutes longer. Remove to a wire rack and let cool on the baking sheet. Melt the semisweet chocolate chips and 1 tablespoon shortening in a small saucepan. Drizzle over the biscotti. Melt the white chocolate chips and 1 tablespoon shortening in a small saucepan. Drizzle over the semisweet chocolate. Yield: 3¹/2 dozen biscotti.

Holli Little, Preceptor Alpha Phi
Wendell, Idaho

BEST BISCOTTI

4¹/2 cups all-purpose
  flour
1 tablespoon baking
  powder
¹/2 teaspoon salt
4 eggs
2 tablespoons vanilla
  extract
¹/4 cup flavored orange
  or brandy liqueur

1 cup (2 sticks) butter,
  softened
1¹/2 cups sugar
Dried cranberries,
  chopped chocolate,
  candied fruit, chopped
  nuts, grated orange
  zest or lemon zest
  (optional)

Sift the flour, baking powder and salt together. Whisk the eggs, vanilla and liqueur in a bowl. Beat the butter and sugar in a mixing bowl until light and fluffy. Beat in the egg mixture gradually. Stir in the dry ingredients. Divide the dough into 4 equal portions and place in 4 bowls. Mix in ³/4 to 1 cup of desired additions to each bowl: dried cranberries, chopped chocolate, candied fruit, chopped nuts, grated orange zest or lemon zest. Shape each portion into 2¹/2-inch diameter logs, 12 inches long. Place 4 inches apart on a baking sheet lined with parchment paper. Bake at 325 degrees for 30 minutes or until golden brown and firm. Cool on the baking sheet for 15 minutes. Remove to a cutting board. Cut diagonally with a serrated knife into ¹/2-inch slices. Arrange the slices, cut side down, on a baking sheet lined with parchment paper. Bake at 325 degrees for 25 minutes or until golden brown and crisp, turning once during baking. Remove to a wire rack to cool completely. Drizzle with melted chocolate, if desired.
Yield: 5 dozen biscotti.

Gerda Charlton, Preceptor Gamma Nu
Guelph, Ontario, Canada

ITALIAN ANISE COOKIES

3 cups plus 2 tablespoons all-purpose flour	1/2 cup granulated sugar
4 teaspoons baking powder	3 eggs
3/4 cup (1 1/2 sticks) butter or margarine, melted	2 tablespoons anise extract
	Confectioners' sugar
	Water
	Food coloring

Combine the flour and baking powder together. Beat the melted butter and granulated sugar in a mixing bowl. Beat in the eggs and anise extract. Beat in the dry ingredients. Shape into balls. Arrange on an ungreased cookie sheet. Bake at 375 degrees for 8 minutes or until the bottoms are light brown. Cool on the cookie sheet for 1 minute. Remove to a wire rack to cool. Mix confectioners' sugar in a bowl with enough water to make a glaze. Stir in food coloring to desired hue. Dip the cooled cookies in the glaze to coat. Yield: 3 1/2 dozen cookies.

Kate Melton, Preceptor Kappa Epsilon
Fort Worth, Texas

BUTTERFINGER COOKIES

1 cup all-purpose flour	2 egg whites
1/2 teaspoon baking soda	1 1/4 cups chunky peanut butter
1/4 teaspoon salt	
1/2 cup (1 stick) butter, softened	1 1/2 teaspoons vanilla extract
3/4 cup granulated sugar	4 to 5 Butterfinger candy bars, chopped
2/3 cup packed brown sugar	

Mix the flour, baking soda and salt together. Beat the butter, granulated sugar and brown sugar in a mixing bowl until and light and fluffy. Beat in the egg whites. Beat in the peanut butter and vanilla. Stir in the dry ingredients. Stir in the chopped candy. Shape into 1 1/2-inch balls. Arrange on a baking sheet coated with nonstick cooking spray. Bake at 350 degrees for 10 to 12 minutes or until golden brown. Cool on the baking sheet for 1 minute. Remove to a wire rack to cool. Yield: 4 to 5 dozen cookies.

Mary Ann Miller, Laureate Lambda
Port St. Lucie, Florida

KAHLÚA CHOCOLATE CHIP COOKIES

2 1/4 cups all-purpose flour	1 egg
1 teaspoon baking soda	1 teaspoon vanilla extract
1 teaspoon salt	2 tablespoons Kahlúa
1 cup (2 sticks) butter, softened	2 cups chocolate chips
1 1/2 cups sugar	1 cup chopped pecans

Mix the flour, baking soda and salt together. Beat the butter and sugar in a mixing bowl until light and fluffy. Beat in the egg, vanilla and Kahlúa. Beat in the dry ingredients. Stir in the chocolate chips and pecans. Shape into 2-inch balls. Place 3 inches apart on an ungreased cookie sheet. Bake at 350 degrees for 12 to 13 minutes or until golden brown. Remove the cookie sheet to a wire rack and let cookies cool. Yield: 4 dozen cookies.

Dorothy E. Markham, Xi Gamma Theta
Casa Grande, Arizona

CHOCOLATE CARAMEL COOKIES

3 ounces unsweetened chocolate	1 teaspoon baking soda
1 cup (2 sticks) butter	1/4 teaspoon salt
1 cup sugar	Finely chopped pecans
1 egg	1 (14-ounce) package caramels
1 teaspoon vanilla extract	2 tablespoons milk
2 cups all-purpose flour	1 ounce semisweet chocolate, melted

Melt the unsweetened chocolate and butter in a large microwave-safe bowl in the microwave. Stir until smooth. Stir in the sugar. Stir in the egg and vanilla. Add the flour, baking soda and salt and stir to mix well. Chill for 30 minutes. Shape into 1-inch balls. Roll in pecans. Arrange on an ungreased cookie sheet. Make an indentation with your thumb on top of each ball. Bake at 375 degrees for 8 to 10 minutes. Cool on the cookie sheet for 1 minute. Remove to a wire rack to cool. Melt the caramels in a microwave-safe bowl in the microwave. Stir in the milk. Fill each indentation with the caramel mixture. Drizzle the melted semisweet chocolate over the cookies. Yield: 3 1/2 dozen cookies.

Cyndi Conley, Alpha Alpha Psi
Destin, Florida

MONSTER COOKIES

12 eggs	1 (16-ounce) bag "M&Ms" chocolate candies
2 pounds brown sugar	
4 cups granulated sugar	
1 tablespoon vanilla extract	1 large container quick-cooking oats
2 cups (4 sticks) margarine, softened	2 cups nuts (optional)
	1/2 cup light corn syrup
2 2/3 cups chocolate chips	1 (24-ounce) jar peanut butter
2 tablespoons plus 2 teaspoons baking soda	

Beat the eggs in a very large bowl. Add the brown sugar, granulated sugar, vanilla, margarine, chocolate chips, baking soda, "M&Ms," oats, nuts, corn syrup and peanut butter, stirring well after each addition. Drop by large scoops onto a cookie sheet, placing only 6 scoops per cookie sheet. Bake at 350 degrees for 12 to 15 minutes. Cool on the cookie sheet for 3 minutes. Remove to a wire rack to cool. Yield: 12 dozen cookies.

Sherry Long, Laureate Delta Psi
Lees Summit, Missouri

❖ S'MORE COOKIES

This recipe was inspired by the current s'more comeback. How difficult could it be to invent?

2 cups all-purpose flour	2 eggs
1/2 cup graham cracker crumbs	2 teaspoons vanilla extract
1 teaspoon baking soda	1 cup coarsely chopped unblanched almonds
1/2 teaspoon salt	
1 cup (2 sticks) butter, softened	11/2 cups chocolate chunks
1 cup packed brown sugar	11/2 cups miniature marshmallows
1/2 cup granulated sugar	

Mix the flour, graham cracker crumbs, baking soda and salt together. Beat the butter, brown sugar, granulated sugar and eggs in a large mixing bowl. Stir in the vanilla. Add the dry ingredients and mix well. Stir in the almonds, chocolate and marshmallows. Drop by scoops onto a nonstick baking sheet. Press the top of each cookie lightly with a fork dipped in water. Bake at 350 degrees for 12 to 14 minutes or until light brown. Cool on the baking sheet for 1 minute. Remove to a wire rack to cool. Yield: 3 dozen cookies.

Lenore Hamers, Preceptor Phi
Sv. Norglenwold, Alberta, Canada

CHERRY FUDGE DROPS

21/4 cups all-purpose flour	2 eggs
3/4 cup baking cocoa	21/4 teaspoons vanilla extract
1/4 teaspoon plus 1/8 teaspoon each baking powder, baking soda and salt	2 (10-ounce) jars maraschino cherries
	11/2 cups semisweet chocolate chips
3/4 cup (11/2 sticks) butter, softened	3/4 cup sweetened condensed milk
11/2 cups sugar	

Mix the flour, baking cocoa, baking powder, baking soda and salt together. Beat the butter and sugar in a mixing bowl until light and fluffy. Beat in the eggs and vanilla. Beat in the dry ingredients gradually. Shape into 1-inch balls. Place 2 inches apart on an ungreased cookie sheet. Make an indentation with your thumb on top of each ball. Drain the cherries and reserve 6 tablespoons of juice. Place 1 cherry in each indentation. Combine the chocolate chips and sweetened condensed milk in a microwave-safe bowl. Microwave on Medium until the chocolate melts. Stir in the reserved cherry juice. Spread 1 teaspoon of the chocolate mixture over each cherry. Bake at 350 degrees for 10 to 12 minutes or until the edges are firm. Cool on the cookie sheet for 1 minute. Remove to a wire rack to cool. Yield: 41/2 to 5 dozen cookies.

Laura Amundson, Xi Alpha Delta
Verona, Wisconsin

APPLESAUCE COOKIES

2 cups cake flour	1/4 teaspoon cloves
1 teaspoon baking powder	1/2 cup shortening
1/2 teaspoon baking soda	1 cup sugar
1/2 teaspoon salt	1 egg, beaten
1/2 teaspoon cinnamon	1 cup thick unsweetened applesauce

Sift the flour, baking powder, baking soda, salt, cinnamon and cloves together. Beat the shortening and sugar in a mixing bowl until light and fluffy. Beat in the egg. Beat in the dry ingredients alternately with the applesauce, beginning and ending with the dry ingredients. Drop by teaspoonfuls onto a greased cookie sheet. Bake at 375 degrees for 15 minutes. Cool on the cookie sheet for 1 minute. Remove to a wire rack to cool. Yield: 21/2 dozen cookies.

Pamella Carlson, Preceptor Xi Zeta
West Sacramento, California

CARROT-DATE COOKIES

11/2 cups chopped dates	1 teaspoon vanilla extract
1 cup grated carrots	11/2 cups sifted cake flour
1/2 cup nonfat plain yogurt	
1/4 cup packed brown sugar	1/4 cup Grape-Nuts cereal
2 tablespoons vegetable oil	1/2 teaspoon baking soda
	1/2 teaspoon salt

Combine the the first 6 ingredients in a large bowl. Let stand for 15 minutes. Mix the flour, cereal, baking soda and salt in a bowl. Add to the date mixture and stir to mix well. Drop by tablespoonfuls, 11/2 inches apart, onto a greased baking sheet. Bake at 350 degrees for 15 minutes or until the tops spring back when lightly touched. Cool on the baking sheet for 1 minute. Remove to a wire rack to cool. Yield: 21/2 dozen cookies.

Barbara Babb, Eta Master
Seattle, Washington

FROSTED PUMPKIN COOKIES

4 cups all-purpose flour
2 teaspoons baking soda
2 teaspoons cinnamon
2 cups sugar
2 cups (4 sticks) margarine, softened
2 eggs
1 (16-ounce) can pumpkin
2 teaspoons vanilla extract
2 cups nuts (optional)
4 ounces cream cheese, softened
1/2 cup (1 stick) margarine, softened
4 cups confectioners' sugar

Mix the flour, baking soda and cinnamon together. Beat the sugar and 2 cups margarine in a mixing bowl until light and fluffy. Beat in the eggs, pumpkin and vanilla. Beat in the dry ingredients. Stir in the nuts. Drop by spoonfuls onto a greased baking sheet. Bake at 375 degrees for 12 minutes. Cool on the baking sheet for 1 minute. Remove to a wire rack to cool. Beat the cream cheese and 1/2 cup margarine in a bowl until smooth. Beat in the confectioners' sugar. Spread on the cooled cookies. Yield: 4 to 5 dozen cookies.

Sandy Boos, Zeta Mu
Russell, Kansas

SANTA'S WHISKERS

1 cup butter-flavor shortening
1 cup sugar
2 tablespoons milk
1 teaspoon vanilla extract
2 1/2 cups all-purpose flour
3/4 cup red candied cherries, chopped
1/2 cup pecans, chopped
3/4 cup flaked coconut

Beat the shortening and sugar in a mixing bowl. Beat in the milk and vanilla. Stir in the flour, cherries and pecans. Divide the dough in half. Shape each portion into an 8-inch log. Roll the logs in the coconut to coat well. Wrap in waxed paper or plastic wrap. Chill until firm. Unwrap and cut into 1/4-inch slices. Arrange on an ungreased cookie sheet. Bake at 375 degrees for 12 minutes or until the edges are golden brown. Cool on the cookie sheet for 1 minute. Remove to a wire rack to cool. Yield: 5 dozen cookies.

Dot Clisby, Xi Beta Omega
Ray City, Georgia

HAWAIIAN SURPRISE COOKIES

3 1/2 cups all-purpose flour
1 teaspoon baking soda
1 teaspoon baking powder
1/2 teaspoon salt
1 cup (2 sticks) margarine, softened
1 1/2 cups sugar
3 eggs
1 cup crushed pineapple, drained
1 to 1 1/3 cups white chocolate chips
1 small jar macadamia nuts

Mix the flour, baking soda, baking powder and salt together. Beat the margarine and sugar in a mixing bowl until light and fluffy. Beat in the eggs. Beat in the dry ingredients. Stir in the pineapple and white chocolate chips. Coarsely chop the macadamia nuts and stir into the dough. Drop by teaspoonfuls onto a greased cookie sheet. Bake at 375 degrees for 15 minutes or until golden brown. Cool on the cookie sheet for 1 minute. Cool on a wire rack.
Yield: 3 to 4 dozen cookies.

D'Ila Rohm-Ritchie, Xi Beta Rho
Shelbyville, Indiana

ORANGE CRANBERRY COOKIES

2 1/2 cups all-purpose flour
1/2 teaspoon baking soda
1/2 teaspoon salt
1 cup granulated sugar
1/2 cup packed brown sugar
1 cup (2 sticks) butter or margarine, softened
1 egg
1 teaspoon grated orange zest
2 tablespoons orange juice
2 cups coarsely chopped fresh or frozen cranberries
1/2 cup chopped nuts (optional)
Orange Frosting

Mix the flour, baking soda and salt together. Beat the next 6 ingredients in a large mixing bowl until smooth. Stir in the dry ingredients. Stir in the cranberries and nuts. Drop by rounded tablespoonfuls, 2 inches apart, onto an ungreased cookie sheet. Bake at 375 degrees for 12 to 14 minutes. Remove to a wire rack and let cool on the cookie sheet. Frost the cooled cookies with Orange Frosting. Yield: 3 dozen cookies.

ORANGE FROSTING

1 1/2 cups confectioners' sugar
1/2 teaspoon grated orange zest
2 to 3 tablespoons orange juice.

Beat all the ingredients in a mixing bowl until smooth.

Donna Sisson, Delta Psi
Milan, Ohio

CHOCOLATE COCONUT MACADAMIA NUT COOKIES

2 1/4 cups all-purpose flour
1 teaspoon baking soda
1/2 teaspoon salt
1 cup (2 sticks) butter, softened
3/4 cup packed brown sugar
1/2 cup granulated sugar
2 teaspoons vanilla extract
2 eggs
2 cups chocolate chips
1 cup flaked coconut
1 cup macadamia nuts, chopped

Mix the flour, baking soda and salt together. Beat the next 4 ingredients in a mixing bowl until smooth. Beat in the eggs. Beat in the dry ingredients gradually. Stir in the remaining ingredients. Drop by spoonfuls onto a greased cookie sheet or ungreased baking stone. Bake at 350 degrees for 10 to 12 minutes. Cool on the cookie sheet for 1 minute. Remove to a wire rack to cool. Yield: 3 to 4 dozen cookies.

Suzann Alstrin, Laureate Alpha Psi
Colorado Springs, Colorado

WHITE CHOCOLATE MACADAMIA NUT COOKIES

3/4 cup packed brown sugar	*1 3/4 cups all-purpose flour*
1/2 cup granulated sugar	*1 teaspoon baking soda*
1/2 cup (1 stick) butter or margarine, softened	*1/2 teaspoon salt*
1/2 cup shortening	*1 1/2 cups white chocolate chips*
2 teaspoons vanilla extract	*1 (3 1/2-ounce) jar macadamia nuts, coarsely chopped*
1 egg	

Beat the brown sugar, granulated sugar, butter and shortening in a mixing bowl until light and fluffy. Beat in the vanilla and egg. Add the flour, baking soda and salt and stir to mix well. Stir in the white chocolate chips. Stir the macadamia nuts into the dough. Drop by tablespoonfuls, 3 inches apart, onto an ungreased cookie sheet. Bake at 375 degrees for 8 to 10 minutes or until golden brown. Cool on the cookie sheet for 1 minute. Remove to a wire rack to cool. Yield: 3 dozen cookies.

Janice Roth, Xi Epsilon Pi
Abilene, Kansas

LEMON MADELEINES

2 eggs	*1 cup all-purpose flour*
3/4 cup sugar	*1/2 cup (1 stick) butter, melted and cooled*
1/4 cup plain yogurt	*1/4 teaspoon salt*
1 teaspoon lemon extract	*1 teaspoon grated lemon zest*
1/2 teaspoon vanilla extract	*Confectioners' sugar*

Beat the first 5 ingredients in a mixing bowl with an electric mixer at high speed for 5 minutes. Add the flour, butter, salt and lemon zest and beat at low speed to mix well. Spoon 1 tablespoon of batter into greased madeleine molds. Bake at 400 degrees for 10 to 15 minutes. Remove to a wire rack to cool. Dust with confectioners' sugar. Yield: 2 dozen.

Kathryn Faye Weston, Alpha Gamma Alpha
Lakeland, Florida

RASPBERRY TASSIES

1/2 cup (1 stick) butter, softened	*1/2 cup almond paste, softened*
3 ounces cream cheese, softened	*2 egg yolks*
1 cup all-purpose flour	*3 tablespoons all-purpose flour*
1/4 cup seedless raspberry preserves	*2 tablespoons milk*
1/2 cup sugar	*1 tablespoon orange juice*

Beat the butter and cream cheese in a mixing bowl. Beat in 1 cup flour. Cover and chill. Divide into 24 portions and form into balls. Press over the bottom and up the side of nonstick miniature muffin cups. Spoon 1/2 teaspoon of raspberry preserves in each pastry shell. Beat the sugar and almond paste in a bowl. Add the egg yolks, 1 at a time, beating well after each addition. Beat in 3 tablespoons flour, milk and orange juice. Pour into the pastry shells. Bake at 400 degrees for 15 minutes. Remove to a wire rack and let cool in the pan. Yield: 2 dozen tassies.

Betty O. Savage, Beta Lambda
Portsmouth, Virginia

CHOCOLATE WAFFLE COOKIES

1/2 cup shortening	*2 1/2 cups all-purpose flour*
1/2 cup (1 stick) margarine	*1/4 teaspoon baking powder*
1/2 cup baking cocoa	*6 cups confectioners' sugar*
1 1/2 cups granulated sugar	*1/4 cup shortening*
4 eggs	*Few drops of cold water*
2 teaspoons vanilla extract	*Colored sprinkles*

Melt 1/2 cup shortening, margarine and baking cocoa in a saucepan, stirring until smooth. Remove from the heat and let cool. Beat the sugar, eggs and vanilla in a large mixing bowl. Stir in the chocolate mixture. Stir in the flour and baking powder. Drop by teaspoonfuls, 4 at a time, onto a hot waffle iron. Cook using manufacturer's directions or until the waffle iron stops steaming. Loosen the cookies carefully with a fork and remove to a wire rack to cool completely. Beat the confectioners' sugar, 1/4 shortening and water in a bowl until light and fluffy. Spread on the cookies and top with sprinkles.
Yield: 4 dozen cookies.

Lorna Wasson, Pi Master
Coeur d'Alene, Idaho

PECAN COOKIES

5 cups all-purpose flour
1 teaspoon baking soda
1 teaspoon salt
2 cups (4 sticks) butter
5 cups packed brown
  sugar
4 extra-large eggs, beaten
4 cups pecans

Mix the flour, baking soda and salt together. Beat the butter and brown sugar in a mixing bowl until light and fluffy. Beat in the dry ingredients alternately with the eggs. Stir in the pecans. Drop by teaspoonfuls onto a greased cookie sheet. Bake at 350 degrees for 8 minutes. Cool on the cookie sheet for 1 minute. Remove to a wire rack to cool. Yield: 7 dozen cookies.

Linda Norris, Xi Alpha Beta Eta
Seminole, Texas

PECAN CRESCENTS

1 cup (2 sticks) butter,
  softened
1/3 cup sugar
2 teaspoons vanilla
  extract
2 teaspoons water
2 cups all-purpose flour
1 cup finely chopped
  pecans
Confectioners' sugar

Beat the butter, sugar, vanilla and water in a mixing bowl until smooth. Beat in the flour. Stir in the pecans. Shape into crescents and arrange on an ungreased cookie sheet. Bake at 325 degrees until golden brown. Roll the hot cookies in confectioners' sugar and cool on waxed paper. Yield: 3 dozen cookies.

Shirley A. Swart, Laureate Kappa
Fayetteville, North Carolina

MEXICAN WEDDING COOKIES

My mother made these cookies all the time, especially at Christmas, when I was growing up. She made them for my wedding. I make them every year during the holidays.

1 cup (2 sticks) butter,
  softened
1/3 cup confectioners'
  sugar
1 1/2 teaspoons vanilla
  extract
2 cups all-purpose flour,
  sifted
1/2 teaspoon salt
1 cup chopped walnuts
Confectioners' sugar

Beat the butter, 1/3 cup confectioners' sugar and vanilla in a mixing bowl until smooth. Stir in the flour and salt. Fold in the nuts. Shape into walnut-sized balls. Arrange on an ungreased cookie sheet. Bake at 400 degrees for 10 to 12 minutes. Roll the hot cookies in confectioners' sugar and place on a wire rack to cool. Roll in confectioners' sugar again when cool. Yield: 2 dozen cookies.

Ruth Ann Branin, Xi Phi Sigma
Wake Village, Texas

SALTED PEANUT CRUNCHIES

2 cups sifted all-purpose
  flour
1 teaspoon baking soda
1/2 teaspoon salt
1/2 cup (1 stick) butter,
  softened
1 cup chunky peanut
  butter
1/2 cup shortening
1 cup granulated sugar
1 cup packed brown
  sugar
2 eggs
1 cup miniature
  chocolate chips
1 cup Spanish peanuts

Mix the flour, baking soda and salt together. Beat the butter, peanut butter and shortening in a large bowl until combined. Beat in the granulated sugar and brown sugar gradually. Add the eggs 1 at a time, beating well after each addition. Stir in the dry ingredients. Stir in the chocolate chips and peanuts. Drop by teaspoonfuls onto a greased cookie sheet. Bake at 325 degrees for 15 minutes. Cool on the cookie sheet for 1 minute. Remove to a wire rack to cool.
Yield: 12 dozen cookies.

Donna Durian, Laureate Epsilon Kappa
The Villages, Florida

LEMON OATMEAL COOKIES

1/2 cup all-purpose flour
1/2 cup quick-cooking
  oats
1/4 teaspoon baking
  powder
1/4 teaspoon baking soda
3/4 cup crisp rice cereal
1/3 cup shortening
1/3 packed brown sugar
1 egg
1 1/2 teaspoons grated
  lemon zest
1 tablespoon lemon
  juice
1/2 teaspoon vanilla
  extract

Mix the first 5 ingredients in a bowl. Beat the shortening in a large bowl until smooth. Add the brown sugar gradually and beat until light and fluffy. Beat in the last 3 ingredients. Stir in the dry ingredients. Drop by heaping teaspoonfuls onto an ungreased cookie sheet. Bake at 375 degrees for 8 to 10 minutes. Cool on the cookie sheet for 1 minute. Remove to a wire rack to cool. Yield: 2 1/2 to 3 dozen cookies.

Frances Kucera, Laureate Omicron
Eugene, Oregon

OATMEAL TREASURES

1 cup shortening or
  softened butter
1 cup granulated sugar
1 cup packed brown
  sugar
3 eggs
2 teaspoons vanilla
  extract
2 cups all-purpose flour
1 teaspoon baking soda
2 cups quick-cooking
  oats
1 cup raisins
1 cup sweetened dried
  cranberries
1 cup dried cherries
1 cup chocolate chips
1/2 cup chopped walnuts

Beat the shortening, granulated sugar and brown sugar in a mixing bowl until light and fluffy. Beat in the eggs and vanilla. Add the flour and baking soda and beat to mix well. Stir in the remaining ingredients. Drop by spoonfuls onto a nonstick cookie sheet. Bake at 325 degrees for 12 to 15 minutes or until golden brown. Cool on the cookie sheet for 1 minute. Remove to a wire rack to cool. Yield: 3 dozen cookies.

Luella Nelson, Zeta Master
Superior, Wisconsin

SLICE AND BAKE OATMEAL PECAN COOKIES

1¹/₂ cups all-purpose flour	1 cup granulated sugar
1 teaspoon baking soda	2 eggs
1/2 teaspoon salt	1 teaspoon vanilla extract
1 cup shortening	3 cups quick-cooking oats
1 cup packed brown sugar	2 cups chopped pecans

Sift the flour, baking soda and salt together. Beat the shortening, brown sugar and granulated sugar in a mixing bowl until light and fluffy. Beat in the eggs and vanilla. Beat in the dry ingredients. Stir in the oats and pecans. Shape into 2 logs and wrap in plastic wrap. Chill for several hours or overnight. Unwrap and cut into slices. Arrange on a nonstick cookie sheet. Bake at 350 degrees for 10 to12 minutes or until light brown. Cool on the cookie sheet for 1 minute. Remove to a wire rack to cool. Yield: 4 dozen cookies.

LaVonda Wentworth, Laureate Omega
Enid, Oklahoma

PEANUT BUTTER COOKIES

1¹/₄ cups all-purpose flour	1/2 cup shortening
3/4 teaspoon baking soda	1/2 cup peanut butter
1/2 teaspoon baking powder	1/2 cup granulated sugar
1/4 teaspoon salt	1/2 cup packed brown sugar
	1 egg

Mix the flour, baking soda, baking powder and salt together. Beat the shortening, peanut butter, granulated sugar, brown sugar and egg in a mixing bowl until smooth. Beat in the dry ingredients. Shape into 1¹/₄-inch balls. Place 3 inches apart on a lightly greased baking sheet. Flatten the cookies in a criss-cross pattern using a fork dipped in flour. Bake at 375 degrees for 7 to 10 minutes. Cool on the baking sheet for 1 minute. Remove to a wire rack to cool. Yield: 3 dozen cookies.

Sandi Wurster, Alpha Rho
Polk City, Iowa

TEA CAKES

Being our 75th anniversary lead me to remember these cookies my mom would make. She would have them waiting for my 6 siblings and me after school. They were so good.

3 cups all-purpose flour	1/2 cup shortening or softened butter
1 cup self-rising flour	
2 teaspoons baking powder	1 egg
1/4 teaspoon baking soda	1/2 cup buttermilk
1/2 teaspoon salt	Grated orange zest or flavoring of choice
1¹/₂ cups sugar	

Sift the all-purpose flour, self-rising flour, baking powder, baking soda and salt together. Beat the sugar and shortening in a mixing bowl until light and fluffy. Beat in the egg. Beat in the dry ingredients alternately with the buttermilk. Beat in the orange zest; the dough will be stiff. Roll out the dough on a floured work surface to 1/4-inch thickness. Cut with a floured cookie cutter. Arrange the cookies on an ungreased baking sheet. Bake at 400 degrees for 10 minutes. Cool on the baking sheet for 1 minute. Remove to a wire rack to cool.
Yield: 4 to 5 dozen cookies.

Yvonne Johnson, Preceptor Upsilon
Brantley, Alabama

SOUR CREAM TWIST COOKIES

1 cup shortening	1 cup chopped dates
2 eggs	1 cup ground walnuts
1 cup sour cream	1 cup sugar
1 teaspoon vanilla	1 cup water
1 cake yeast or 1 envelope dry yeast	Confectioners' sugar
	Beaten egg
1/2 teaspoon salt	
3¹/₂ cups all-purpose flour	

Beat the shortening in a large bowl until smooth. Beat in 2 eggs. Beat in the sour cream, vanilla, yeast and salt. Beat in the flour. Cover and chill overnight. Combine the dates, walnuts, sugar and water in a saucepan. Cook until thick, stirring often. Remove from the heat and let cool. Roll out the dough on a work surface dusted with confectioners' sugar. Cut into squares. Spoon the date mixture in the center of each square and roll up. Arrange on an ungreased baking sheet. Brush each with the beaten egg. Bake at 375 degrees for 10 minutes or until light brown. Cool on the baking sheet for 1 minute. Remove to a wire rack to cool. Yield: 3 to 4 dozen cookies.

Cheryol Miller, Xi Lambda Gamma
Mansfield, Ohio

SPRINGERLE COOKIES

Store these cookies for 3 weeks before eating. They will keep for about 3 months at room temperature in an airtight container. We could not keep them that long at our house.

Anise seeds	4 eggs
4¹/2 cups all-purpose flour	2¹/4 cups sugar
1 teaspoon baking powder	1 tablespoon grated lemon zest

Sprinkle anise seeds on a greased cookie sheet. Sift the flour and baking powder together. Beat the eggs in a mixing bowl until thick and pale yellow. Beat in the sugar and lemon zest. Beat in the dry ingredients. Chill for 1 hour or until the dough is easy to handle. Roll out on a lightly floured work surface to 1/2-inch thickness. Flour a springerle rolling pin or mold. Press firmly into the dough. Cut the designs apart. Place the cookies, 1/2-inch apart, on the prepared cookie sheet. Let dry overnight. Bake at 350 degrees for 13 to 15 minutes. Cool on the cookie sheet for 1 minute. Remove to a wire rack to cool.
Yield: 2¹/2 dozen cookies.

Janith K. Masteryanni, Preceptor Theta Theta
Port Charlotte, Florida

VIENNESE SUGAR COOKIES

1 cake yeast or 1 envelope dry yeast	1 cup (2 sticks) butter, softened
1/3 cup lukewarm water	2 cups all-purpose flour
	1 cup sugar

Dissolve the yeast in the lukewarm water in a small bowl. Beat the butter in a mixing bowl until smooth. Beat in the flour. Beat in the yeast mixture. Spread the sugar on a large plate or piece of waxed paper. Press walnut-sized pieces of dough into the sugar to coat on both sides. Arrange on a cookie sheet lined with parchment paper. Bake at 375 degrees for 15 to 20 minutes or until golden brown. Cool on the cookie sheet for 1 minute. Remove to a wire rack to cool. Store in an airtight container. Yield: 2 dozen cookies.

Arlene Poplewko, Laureate Alpha Epsilon
Longmont, Colorado

JAN HAGEL COOKIES

1¹/2 cups (3 sticks) butter, softened	3 cups all-purpose flour
1 cup packed brown sugar	1/4 cup granulated sugar
1 teaspoon vanilla extract	Sliced almonds or chopped walnuts

Beat the butter in a mixing bowl until smooth. Beat in the brown sugar and vanilla. Beat in the flour. Pat evenly into an ungreased 11×17-inch baking pan. Sprinkle with the sugar and the almonds, pressing the nuts gently into the dough. Bake at 350 degrees for 20 minutes for a soft cookie and 25 minutes for a firmer cookie. Cool in the pan for only 15 minutes. Cut into bars and remove to a wire rack to cool. Yield: 4 dozen cookies.

Gail Selent, Xi Lambda
Baton Rouge, Louisiana

CHINESE ALMOND COOKIES

Almond cookies will keep for at least a week in an airtight container or for months in the freezer. Chinese cookies are just right for a snack or after a big meal.

2 cups all-purpose flour	1¹/2 teaspoons almond extract
1 teaspoon baking powder	1 egg
1/2 teaspoon baking soda	36 whole blanched almonds
1/4 teaspoon salt	
1¹/4 cups shortening	1 egg yolk
1 cup sugar	1 egg

Mix the flour, baking powder, baking soda and salt together. Beat the shortening and sugar in a mixing bowl until light and fluffy. Stir in the almond extract and 1 egg. Add the dry ingredients and knead to form a dough. Shape into 1-inch balls. Place 2 inches apart on an ungreased cookie sheet. Press 1 almond gently into the top of each ball. Beat the egg yolk and 1 egg in a small bowl. Brush on the cookies. Bake at 350 degrees for 12 to 15 minutes. Cool on the cookie sheet for 10 minutes. Remove to a wire rack to cool. Yield: 3 dozen cookies.

Ruby Moone, Gamma Theta Master
League City, Texas

ST. NIKOLAS KOEKJES

4 cups all-purpose flour	2 cups (4 sticks) butter, softened
4 teaspoons cinnamon	
1 teaspoon cloves	2 cups sugar
1/2 teaspoon nutmeg	1/2 cup sour cream
1/2 teaspoon baking soda	1/2 cup pecans, finely chopped
1/2 teaspoon salt	

Sift the flour, cinnamon, cloves, nutmeg, baking soda and salt together. Beat the butter and sugar in a mixing bowl until light and fluffy. Beat in the dry ingredients alternately with the sour cream. Add the pecans. Knead the dough on a lightly floured surface and shape into logs. Wrap in waxed paper and chill overnight. Cut into slices and arrange on a nonstick baking sheet. Bake at 350 degrees for 10 to 12 minutes or until golden brown. Cool on the baking sheet for 1 minute. Remove to a wire rack to cool. Yield: 7 dozen cookies.

Margaret Miller, Eta Eta
Fredericktown, Missouri

APRICOT COOKIES

1 package dried
  apricots, ground
1 (14-ounce) can
  sweetened condensed
  milk

1 small can flaked
  coconut
1 (16-ounce) box
  confectioners' sugar

Combine the apricots, sweetened condensed milk, coconut and confectioners' sugar in a large bowl and mix well. Drop by teaspoonfuls onto waxed paper. Let stand overnight. Yield: 5 dozen cookies.

Jean Harris, Beta Master
Atoka, Tennessee

STRAWBERRY TEA CUPS

Leave the green top on the strawberries for a pretty look.

Melted butter
48 wonton wrappers
Milk

1 (6-ounce) package
  vanilla pudding mix
48 fresh strawberries

Brush miniature muffin cups with melted butter. Fit 1 wonton wrapper in each muffin cup. Bake at 375 degrees for 15 to 20 minutes or until golden brown. Remove to a wire rack to cool completely. Cook the milk and pudding mix in a saucepan using the package directions. Chill until cold. Fill each won ton cup with 1 tablespoon pudding and top with a strawberry. Yield: 4 dozen cups.

Melody Reasoner, Laureate Kappa
Clarksville, Arkansas

BROWNIES

These are a very rich, dark chocolate "comfort food."

5 ounces unsweetened
  chocolate
1/2 cup (1 stick) butter
4 eggs
2 teaspoons vanilla
  extract

2 cups sugar
1 cup all-purpose flour
1 cup chopped walnuts
  or pecans (optional)

Combine the chocolate and butter in a saucepan. Melt over low heat, stirring often. Remove from the heat and let cool. Beat the eggs, vanilla, sugar, flour and walnuts in a mixing bowl. Stir in the chocolate mixture gradually. Pour into a greased 9×9-inch baking pan. Bake at 350 degrees for 25 to 30 minutes or until the center is set. Remove to a wire rack and let cool slightly. Cut into squares and serve with whipped cream. Yield: 20 (2-inch square) brownies.

June Hamann, Laureate Beta Delta
Pasco, Washington

APPLE BROWNIES

2 cups all-purpose flour
1 teaspoon salt
1 teaspoon baking soda
1 teaspoon cinnamon
3 eggs
1³/4 cups sugar
1 cup vegetable oil
1 cup chopped peeled
  apples

2 cups chopped walnuts
1/4 cup (1/2 stick)
  margarine, softened
3 ounces cream cheese,
  softened
1 teaspoon vanilla
  extract
1³/4 cups confectioners'
  sugar

Mix the flour, salt, baking soda and cinnamon together. Beat the eggs, sugar and oil in a mixing bowl. Beat in the dry ingredients. Stir in the apples and 1 cup of the walnuts. Pour into a greased 9×13-inch baking pan. Bake at 350 degrees for 35 to 40 minutes or until a wooden pick inserted in the center comes out clean. Remove to a wire rack to cool completely. Beat the margarine and cream cheese in a mixing bowl until light and fluffy. Beat in the vanilla and confectioners' sugar until smooth. Stir in the remaining 1 cup walnuts. Spread over the cooled brownies. Yield: 16 brownies.

Mary E. Blanchard, Alpha Gamma Master
Gambier, Ohio

BITTERSWEET APRICOT BROWNIES

4 ounces bittersweet
  chocolate
1/2 cup (1 stick) unsalted
  butter
1/2 cup sugar
2 eggs, at room
  temperature

1/2 teaspoon vanilla
  extract
1/4 cup all-purpose flour
Pinch of salt
1/2 cup chopped dried
  apricots

Combine the chocolate and butter in the top of a double boiler. Melt over hot water, stirring until smooth. Remove from the heat and let stand for 10 minutes or until lukewarm. Whisk in the sugar. Whisk in the eggs 1 at a time. Stir in the vanilla. Add the flour and salt and stir just until blended. Stir in the apricots. Line the bottom of an 8×8-inch baking pan with waxed paper. Butter and flour the inside of the pan. Spread the batter evenly in the pan. Bake at 350 degrees for 20 to 25 minutes or until a wooden pick inserted 1 inch from the edge comes out clean and the center appears wet. Remove to a wire rack to cool. Yield: 16 brownies.

Helen Bixler, Xi Beta Epsilon
Watsonville, California

ORANGE BROWNIES

1½ cups all-purpose flour	1 teaspoon grated orange zest
2 cups sugar	1 cup confectioners' sugar
1 teaspoon salt	
1 cup (2 sticks) butter, softened	1 teaspoon grated orange zest
4 eggs	2 tablespoons orange juice
2 teaspoons pure orange extract	

Mix the flour, sugar and salt in a large bowl. Add the butter, eggs, orange extract and 1 teaspoon orange zest. Beat with an electric mixer until well blended. Pour into a greased 9×13-inch baking pan. Bake at 350 degrees for 30 minutes or until golden brown and set. Remove to a wire rack. Poke holes in the top of the cake with a fork. Whisk the confectioners' sugar, 1 teaspoon orange zest and orange juice in a bowl until smooth. Pour evenly over the cake. Let cool and cut into squares. Yield: 2 dozen brownies.

Donna Goodson, Preceptor Epsilon
Hot Springs, Arkansas

PUMPKIN BROWNIES

2 cups all-purpose flour	4 eggs
1 teaspoon baking soda	1 cup vegetable oil
1 teaspoon baking powder	2 cups sugar
1 teaspoon cinnamon	1 (15-ounce) can pumpkin
½ teaspoon salt	

Mix the flour, baking soda, baking powder, cinnamon and salt together. Beat the eggs, oil, sugar and pumpkin in a large mixing bowl. Add the dry ingredients and beat until smooth. Pour into a greased and floured 9×13-inch baking pan. Bake at 350 degrees for 30 minutes or until the top springs back when lightly touched. Remove to a wire rack to cool completely. Top with cream cheese frosting or whipped cream and sprinkle with chopped nuts. Yield: 2 to 3 dozen brownies.

Debra Paulsen, Laureate Gamma Mu
Victorville, California

CHIPPY BLOND BROWNIES

1 cup all-purpose flour	2 eggs
1 teaspoon salt	1 teaspoon vanilla extract
¼ teaspoon baking soda	
6 tablespoons butter, softened	1 cup semisweet chocolate chips
1 cup packed brown sugar	½ cup chopped pecans

Mix the flour, salt and baking soda together. Beat the butter and brown sugar in a mixing bowl until light and fluffy. Beat in the eggs 1 at a time. Add the vanilla. Beat in the dry ingredients. Stir in the chocolate chips and pecans. Spread in a greased 7×11-inch baking pan. Bake at 350 degrees for 25 to 30 minutes or until the brownies test done. Remove to a wire rack to cool. Yield: 2 dozen brownies.

Mary Caley, Laureate Kappa Nu
Laguna Hills, Califonia

CHOCOLATE CARAMEL BROWNIES

1 (2-layer) package devil's food cake mix	2 cups chocolate chips
¾ cup (1½ sticks) butter, melted	2 (14-ounce) packages caramels
⅓ cup heavy cream	⅔ cup heavy cream

Combine the cake mix, butter and ⅓ cup cream in a mixing bowl. Beat until smooth. Pour ½ of the batter into a nonstick 9×13-inch baking pan. Bake at 350 degrees for 6 minutes. Sprinkle with the chocolate chips and let stand until melted. Spread the chocolate evenly. Combine the caramels and ⅔ cup cream in a microwave-safe bowl. Microwave for 5 minutes or until melted, stirring occasionally. Stir until smooth. Pour evenly over the chocolate layer and let cool. Pour the remaining batter evenly over the caramel layer. Bake at 350 degrees for 18 minutes. Remove to a wire rack to cool completely. Yield: 15 brownies.

Bobbie Baker, Laureate Delta Psi
Independence, Missouri

DOUBLE DECKER CONFETTI BROWNIES

2¼ cups all-purpose flour	1 cup granulated sugar
2½ teaspoons baking powder	1 cup packed brown sugar
½ teaspoon salt	3 eggs
⅓ cup baking cocoa	1 teaspoon vanilla extract
1 tablespoon butter or margarine, melted	¼ cup all-purpose flour
¾ cup (1½ sticks) butter or margarine, softened	1 cup "M&Ms" chocolate candies

Mix 2¼ cups flour, baking powder and salt together. Combine the baking cocoa and 1 tablespoon melted butter in a small bowl. Beat ¾ cup butter, granulated sugar and brown sugar in a mixing bowl until light and fluffy. Beat in the eggs and vanilla. Add the dry ingredients and mix well. Remove ½ the dough to a bowl. Stir in the cocoa mixture. Spread in a lightly greased 9×13-inch baking pan. Stir ¼ cup flour and ½ of the "M&Ms" into the remaining dough. Spread

evenly over the cocoa dough layer. Sprinkle with the remaining "M&Ms". Bake at 350 degrees for 25 to 30 minutes or until a wooden pick inserted in the center comes out clean. Remove to a wire rack to cool completely before cutting into bars.
Yield: 2 dozen brownies.

Maxine Zawol, Epsilon Master
Flint, Michigan

PEANUT BUTTER-TOPPED BROWNIES

2/3 cup all-purpose flour	*2 eggs, beaten*
1/4 teaspoon baking soda	*1/4 cup (1/2 stick) butter,*
1/4 teaspoon salt	*softened*
1/2 cup sugar	*2/3 cup peanut butter*
2 tablespoons water	*11/2 cups confectioners'*
2 tablespoons butter	*sugar*
11/2 cups chocolate chips	*3 to 4 tablespoons*
1/2 teaspoon vanilla	*cream or milk*
extract	

Mix the flour, baking soda and salt together. Mix the sugar, water and 2 tablespoons butter in a saucepan. Cook over low heat to boiling, stirring occasionally. Remove from the heat and add the chocolate chips. Stir until the chocolate melts. Beat in the vanilla and eggs gradually. Add the dry ingredients and stir to mix well. Pour into a greased 9×9-inch baking pan. Bake at 325 degrees for 25 to 30 minutes or until the sides are beginning to pull away from the pan; do not overbake. Remove to a wire rack to cool completely. Beat 1/4 cup butter, peanut butter, confectioners' sugar and cream in a bowl until smooth. Spread over the cooled brownies. Drizzle a chocolate glaze over the top, if desired. Yield: 2 dozen brownies.

Terri Marada, Laureate Delta
Rio Rancho, New Mexico

RICH CHOCOLATE CHIP TOFFEE BARS

21/3 cups all-purpose	*1 cup coarsely chopped*
flour	*walnuts or pecans*
2/3 cup packed brown	*1 (14-ounce) can*
sugar	*sweetened condensed*
3/4 cup (11/2 sticks)	*milk*
butter, softened	*1 (10-ounce) package*
1 egg, lightly beaten	*English toffee bits*
11/2 cups semisweet	*1/2 cup semisweet*
chocolate chips	*chocolate chips*

Combine the flour and brown sugar in a large bowl. Cut in the butter with a pastry blender or fork until crumbly. Stir in the egg. Stir in 11/2 cups chocolate chips and walnuts. Remove and reserve 11/2 cups. Pat the remaining mixture in the bottom of a nonstick 9×13-inch baking pan. Bake at 350 degrees for

10 minutes. Pour the sweetened condensed milk evenly over the hot crust. Sprinkle with 11/2 cups of the toffee bits. Sprinkle with the reserved crumb mixture and 1/2 cup chocolate chips. Bake at 350 degrees for 25 to 30 minutes or until golden brown. Remove to a wire rack and sprinkle with the remaining toffee bits. Cool completely before cutting.
Yield: 4 dozen bars.

Shanda Dyke, Xi Lambda Tau
Garden City, Missouri

PEANUT BUTTER MARBLED BARS

I entered these brownies in a Mother's Day Bake Off, hoping to win a gift certificate to a local jeweler for my mom. I won, but my mom wouldn't accept the gift. She wanted me to use it to buy a birthstone ring, which I did. I still have the ring.

1 cup all-purpose flour	*3/4 cup packed brown*
1 teaspoon baking	*sugar*
powder	*3/4 cup granulated sugar*
1/4 teaspoon salt	*2 eggs*
1/2 cup chunky or creamy	*2 teaspoons vanilla*
peanut butter	*extract*
1/2 cup (1 stick) butter or	*2 cups chocolate chips*
margarine, softened	

Mix the flour, baking powder and salt together. Beat the peanut butter, butter, brown sugar and granulated sugar in a mixing bowl until light and fluffy. Add the eggs and vanilla and beat until smooth. Beat in the dry ingredients. Spread in a greased 9×13-inch baking pan. Sprinkle with the chocolate chips. Bake at 350 degrees for 25 to 30 minutes. Remove to a wire rack. Swirl a knife through the chocolate chips. Cool completely before cutting. Yield: 4 dozen bars.

Kristine A. DeMarinis, Xi Beta Xi
Herndon, Virginia

SCOTCHAROOS

1 cup light corn syrup	*2 cups chocolate chips*
1 cup sugar	*2 cups butterscotch*
1 cup peanut butter	*chips*
6 cups crisp rice cereal	

Bring the corn syrup and sugar to a boil in a saucepan. Remove from the heat and add the peanut butter. Stir until the peanut butter melts. Pour over the cereal in a large bowl. Stir to mix well. Press into a nonstick 9×13-inch baking pan. Melt the chocolate chips and butterscotch chips in a microwave-safe bowl in the microwave. Spread over the cereal layer. Cover and chill until firm. Yield: 2 to 3 dozen bars.

Trudy Adams, Laureate Beta Delta
Richland, Washington

CARAMEL ALMOND GRAHAM WAFERS

Graham crackers
1 cup (2 sticks)
  butter

³/4 cup packed brown
  sugar
¹/4 cup sliced almonds

Arrange the graham crackers in a single layer on a cookie sheet. Melt the butter in a saucepan. Stir in the brown sugar. Bring to a boil and boil for 3 to 4 minutes. Pour evenly over the crackers. Sprinkle with the almonds. Bake at 350 degrees for 5 to 8 minutes or until bubbly. Remove to a wire rack to cool completely. Yield: 3 dozen bars.

Gail Teslyk, Preceptor Alpha Epsilon
Vernon, British Columbia, Canada

CHOCOLATE DOUBLE GRAHAMS

13 whole graham
  crackers
¹/2 cup slivered almonds
¹/2 cup (1 stick) butter

¹/2 cup packed brown
  sugar
7 ounces semisweet
  chocolate, melted

Arrange the graham crackers in a single layer in a 10×13-inch baking pan. Sprinkle with the almonds. Combine the butter and brown sugar in a saucepan. Bring to a simmer and simmer for 1 minute, stirring often. Drizzle over the graham crackers. Bake at 350 degrees for 4 minutes or until bubbly. Remove to a wire rack and let cool slightly. Spread the melted chocolate over the top. Chill until cold. Break into pieces. Yield: about 8 dozen cookies.

Donna Moll, Delta Delta
Boyne City, Michigan

BROWNIE CHEESECAKE BARS

1 cup all-purpose
  flour
³/4 teaspoon baking
  powder
¹/4 teaspoon salt
³/4 cup (1¹/2 sticks) butter
³/4 cup baking cocoa
1¹/2 cups sugar
2 eggs
2 teaspoons vanilla
  extract
1 cup chopped pecans or
  walnuts

8 ounces cream cheese,
  softened
2 tablespoons butter,
  softened
1 tablespoon cornstarch
1 (14-ounce) can
  sweetened condensed
  milk
1 egg
1 teaspoon vanilla
  extract
2 ounces semisweet
  chocolate, melted

Mix the flour, baking powder and salt together. Melt ³/4 cup butter in a large saucepan. Remove from the heat and stir in the baking cocoa. Stir in the sugar, 2 eggs and 2 teaspoons vanilla. Add the dry ingredients and stir to mix well. Stir in the pecans. Spread in a greased 9×13-inch baking pan. Beat the cream cheese, 2 tablespoons butter and cornstarch in a mixing bowl until light and fluffy. Beat in the sweetened condensed milk gradually. Beat in 1 egg and 1 teaspoon vanilla. Pour evenly over the batter in the baking pan. Bake at 350 degrees for 40 minutes or until light brown. Remove to a wire rack to cool completely. Drizzle the melted chocolate over the top. Chill until firm. Cut into bars. Chill until ready to serve. Yield: 2 to 3 dozen bars.

Catherine Cox, Laureate Rho
Kindersley, Saskatchewan, Cananda

MERRY BERRY CHEESECAKE BARS

2 cups all-purpose flour
1¹/2 cups rolled oats
³/4 cup packed brown
  sugar
1 cup (2 sticks) butter or
  margarine, softened
8 ounces cream cheese,
  softened
¹/4 cup lemon juice from
  concentrate

1 (14-ounce) can
  sweetened condensed
  milk
1 (16-ounce) can whole
  cranberry sauce
2 tablespoons
  cornstarch
1 tablespoon packed
  brown sugar

Combine the flour, oats, ³/4 cup brown sugar and butter in a bowl and stir until crumbly. Remove and reserve 1¹/2 cups. Pat the remaining mixture in the bottom of a greased 9×13-inch baking pan. Bake at 350 degrees for 15 minutes or until light brown. Beat the cream cheese in a bowl with an electric mixer until light and fluffy. Beat in the lemon juice and sweetened condensed milk gradually. Beat until smooth. Spread over the baked crust. Combine the cranberry sauce, cornstarch and 1 tablespoon brown sugar in a bowl and mix well. Spoon over the cream cheese layer. Sprinkle with the reserved crumb mixture. Bake at 350 degrees for 45 minutes or until light brown. Remove to a wire rack to cool completely before cutting into bars. Yield: 1 dozen bars.

Debbie Meegan, Preceptor Beta Phi
Lemont Furnace, Pennsylvania

GOODY NUT BARS

1 cup butterscotch chips
1 cup chocolate chips
¹/2 cup peanut butter
1 cup dry-roasted
  peanuts
¹/4 cup (¹/2 stick)
  margarine
¹/4 cup milk

2 tablespoons vanilla
  pudding mix
1¹/2 to 2 cups
  confectioners' sugar
¹/2 teaspoon maple
  flavoring or vanilla
  extract

Melt the butterscotch chips, chocolate chips and peanut butter in a microwave-safe bowl in the microwave. Stir until smooth. Pour ¹/₂ of the melted mixture into a 9×13-inch baking pan lined with waxed paper. Freeze for 15 minutes. Stir the peanuts into the remaining melted mixture. Combine the margarine, milk and pudding mix in a saucepan. Bring to a boil, stirring often. Remove from the heat and stir in the confectioners' sugar and maple flavoring until smooth. Let cool to room temperature. Pour over the frozen layer. Top with the remaining melted mixture. Chill until ready to serve. Yield: 3¹/₂ dozen bars.

Linda Clemons, Theta Psi
Cookeville, Tennessee

PERSIAN BAKLAVA

While speaking on my life in Iran and how my family celebrates the Persian New Year, my Beta sisters enjoyed this baklava. I won for program of the year.

12 ounces shell-on pistachios	1¹/₂ cups sugar
¹/₂ cup slivered almonds, finely chopped	¹/₄ cup rose water
³/₄ cup sugar	¹/₂ package phyllo dough, thawed
1 teaspoon cardamom	1 cup (2 sticks) butter, melted
1 cup water	

Shell the pistachios and finely chop. Mix the pistachios, almonds, ³/₄ cup sugar and cardamom in a bowl. Combine the water and 1¹/₂ cups sugar in a saucepan. Bring to a boil over medium heat. Boil for 15 minutes, stirring occasionally. Remove from the heat and stir in the rose water. Cut the phyllo dough to fit a 9×13-inch baking pan. Brush the pan with some of the melted butter. Lay 1 sheet of phyllo in the pan and brush with melted butter. Top with another sheet of phyllo and brush with melted butter. Sprinkle with a thin layer of the nut mixture. Repeat the layers to use all of the phyllo, melted butter and nut mixture. Bake at 350 degrees for 20 to 30 minutes or until golden brown. Remove to a wire rack and immediately pour the sugar syrup evenly over the baklava. Let cool completely before cutting. Yield: 3 dozen baklava.

Kathy Leamer Dabestani, Xi Zeta
Twin Falls, Idaho

---

*Nancy Davis, Laureate Psi, Waupun, Wisconsin, prepares **Ting-a-Lings** by combining 16 ounces semisweet chocolate, melted, 2 cups cornflakes, 2 cups crisp rice cereal, 1 cup coarsely chopped walnuts or pecans and 1 cup coarsely chopped dates in a large bowl. She stirs to mix well and drops the mixture by teaspoonfuls onto waxed paper. The cookies are chilled until firm.*

CHERRY COCONUT BARS

1¹/₄ cups all-purpose flour	¹/₂ teaspoon baking powder
³/₄ cup confectioners' sugar	¹/₄ teaspoon salt
³/₄ cup (1¹/₂ sticks) margarine	2 eggs, lightly beaten
¹/₄ cup all-purpose flour	³/₄ cup finely chopped maraschino cherries
³/₄ cup sugar	¹/₂ cup flaked coconut
	³/₄ cup chopped pecans

Sift 1¹/₄ cups flour and confectioners' sugar into a bowl. Cut in the margarine with a pastry blender until the mixture resembles coarse crumbs. Reserve ¹/₄ cup of the crumb mixture. Pat the remaining crumb mixture into a nonstick 10×15-inch baking pan. Bake at 350 degrees for 10 minutes. Remove to a wire rack. Sift ¹/₄ cup flour, sugar, baking powder and salt into a large bowl. Stir in the eggs. Mix in the cherries, coconut and pecans. Spread over the baked crust and sprinkle with the reserved crumb mixture. Bake at 350 degrees for 30 minutes. Remove to a wire rack to cool completely before cutting into bars. Yield: 4 dozen bars.

Kathleen Radcliffe, Alpha Master
Lancaster, Pennsylvania

RAZZ-MA-TAZZ BARS

¹/₂ cup (1 stick) margarine	¹/₂ teaspoon salt
2 cups white chocolate chips	¹/₂ teaspoon almond extract
2 eggs	¹/₂ cup seedless raspberry jam
¹/₂ cup sugar	¹/₄ cup toasted sliced almonds
1 cup all-purpose flour	

Microwave the margarine in a microwave-safe bowl on High for 1 minute and stir. Add 1 cup of the white chocolate chips and let stand, do not stir. Beat the eggs in a bowl with an electric mixer. Add the sugar and beat for 5 minutes or until thick and pale yellow. Blend in the margarine mixture. Add the flour, salt and almond extract and beat at low speed just until combined. Spread ²/₃ of the batter into a greased and floured 9×9-inch baking pan. Bake at 325 degrees for 15 to 17 minutes. Remove to a wire rack. Microwave the raspberry jam in a microwave-safe bowl on High for 30 seconds and stir. Spread over the warm crust. Stir the remaining white chocolate chips into the remaining batter. Drop spoonfuls over the jam layer. Sprinkle with the almonds. Bake at 325 degrees for 25 minutes or until the edges are golden brown. Remove to a wire rack to cool completely. Yield: 1¹/₂ dozen bars.

Janice Wilson, Laureate Delta Delta
Oak Grove, Missouri

CRÈME DE MENTHE SQUARES

1 cup (2 sticks) butter
1/2 cup baking cocoa
1/2 cup confectioners' sugar
1 teaspoon vanilla extract
2 cups graham cracker crumbs
1/2 cup (1 stick) butter, melted
1/3 cup crème de menthe
3 cups confectioners' sugar
1/2 cup (1 stick) butter
1 1/2 cups chocolate chips

Heat 1 cup butter and baking cocoa in a saucepan until melted, stirring until smooth. Remove from the heat and stir in 1/2 cup confectioners' sugar and vanilla. Stir in the graham cracker crumbs. Press in the bottom of an ungreased 9×13-inch baking pan. Combine 1/2 cup melted butter and crème de menthe in a mixing bowl. Beat in 3 cups confectioners' sugar at low speed until smooth. Spread over the graham cracker layer. Cover and chill for 1 hour. Melt 1/2 cup butter and chocolate chips in a saucepan, stirring until smooth. Spread over the mint layer. Cover and chill for 1 to 2 hours. Cut into small squares and chill until ready to serve. Yield: 8 dozen squares.

Nancy Conlee, Preceptor Beta Mu
Prineville, Oregon

LEMON RASPBERRY CHEESECAKE SQUARES

1 1/4 cups all-purpose flour
1 cup rolled oats
1/4 teaspoon salt
3/4 cup shortening
1/3 cup packed brown sugar
1/2 cup seedless raspberry jam
32 ounces cream cheese, softened
1 1/2 cups granulated sugar
1/4 cup all-purpose flour
4 eggs
4 teaspoons grated lemon zest
1/3 cup lemon juice

Mix 1 1/4 cups flour, oats and salt together. Beat the shortening and brown sugar in a large mixing bowl until light and fluffy. Stir in the dry ingredients gradually. Press in the bottom of a greased 9×13-inch baking pan. Bake at 350 degrees for 15 to 18 minutes or until golden brown. Spread the raspberry jam over the crust. Beat the cream cheese, granulated sugar and 1/4 cup flour in a large mixing bowl until light and fluffy. Add the eggs, lemon zest and lemon juice and beat just until blended. Spread over the jam layer. Bake at 350 degrees for 30 to 35 minutes or until the center is almost set. Remove to a wire rack to cool completely. Cover and chill until ready to serve. Yield: 1 1/2 to 2 dozen squares.

Susan Bergman, Mu Theta
Paxton, Illinois

MARBLE SQUARES

1 cup plus 2 tablespoons all-purpose flour
1/2 teaspoon baking soda
1/2 teaspoon salt
1/2 cup (1 stick) margarine, softened
6 tablespoons brown sugar
6 tablespoons granulated sugar
1 teaspoon vanilla extract
1/2 teaspoon water
1 egg
1/2 cup chopped pecans
1 cup chocolate chips

Mix the flour, baking soda and salt together. Beat the margarine, brown sugar, granulated sugar, vanilla and water in a mixing bowl until light and fluffy. Beat in the egg. Stir in the dry ingredients. Stir in the pecans. Spread in a greased 9×13-inch baking pan. Sprinkle with the chocolate chips. Bake at 375 degrees for 1 minute. Swirl a knife through the dough. Bake for 12 to 14 minutes longer. Remove to a wire rack to cool completely. Yield: 2 dozen squares.

Sharon Peine, Pi Iota
Shawnee, Kansas

PUMPKIN PIE SQUARES EXTRAORDINNAIRE

This is best served warm with a dollop of whipped cream. This recipe is so good and easy and is always requested.

1 (2-layer) package yellow cake mix
1 egg, beaten
1/2 cup (1 stick) margarine, melted
3 cups canned pumpkin
2 eggs, beaten
1 1/2 cups sugar
2/3 cup milk
1 teaspoon pumpkin pie spice
1 teaspoon vanilla extract
1/4 cup sugar
1 teaspoon cinnamon
1/4 cup (1/2 stick) margarine, softened

Remove 1 cup of the cake mix to a bowl. Combine the remaining cake mix, 1 egg and 1/2 cup melted margarine in a large bowl. Stir to mix well. Press in the bottom of a greased 9×13-inch baking pan. Combine the pumpkin, 2 eggs, 1 1/2 cups sugar, milk, pumpkin pie spice and vanilla in a large mixing bowl. Beat at medium speed until smooth. Pour over the crust. Add 1/4 cup sugar, cinnamon and 1/4 cup margarine to the reserved cake mix. Stir until crumbly. Sprinkle over the pumpkin layer. Bake at 350 degrees for 45 to 50 minutes or until a knife inserted in the center comes out clean. Remove to a wire rack.
Yield: 4 dozen squares.

Virginia "Gina" Martin, Xi Eta Sigma
La Mesa, California

SEVEN LAYER COOKIES

1/2 cup (1 stick) butter, melted	*1 cup butterscotch chips*
1 cup crushed graham crackers	*1 (14-ounce) can sweetened condensed milk*
1 cup flaked coconut	*1/2 cup chopped pecans*
1 cup chocolate chips	

Spread the melted butter in the bottom of a 9×13-inch baking pan. Sprinkle with the crushed graham crackers. Sprinkle with the coconut. Sprinkle with the chocolate chips and butterscotch chips. Drizzle the sweetened condensed milk over the top. Sprinkle with the pecans. Bake at 350 degrees for 30 to 35 minutes. Remove to a wire rack to cool completely before cutting into squares. Yield: 3 to 4 dozen squares.

Donna J. Carlson, Preceptor Omicron Gamma
Salton City, California

WALNUT BROWN SUGAR SQUARES

1/2 cup plus 2 tablespoons all-purpose flour	*1 egg, at room temperature*
1/4 teaspoon baking soda	*1 teaspoon vanilla extract*
1/4 teaspoon salt	*1 cup chopped walnuts*
1 cup packed brown sugar	

Mix the flour, baking soda and salt together. Combine the brown sugar, egg and vanilla in a bowl. Beat at medium speed for 2 minutes or until smooth. Beat in the dry ingredients. Reserve 2 tablespoons of the walnuts and set aside. Stir the remaining walnuts into the dough. Press in the bottom of a lightly greased 8×8-inch baking pan. Sprinkle with the reserved 2 tablespoons walnuts. Bake at 350 degrees for 25 minutes or until the center is slightly soft; do not overbake. Remove to a wire rack to cool completely. Cover with plastic wrap and let stand overnight before cutting. Yield: 1 1/2 dozen squares.

Diane L. Pruett, Preceptor Alpha Upsilon
Tamaqua, Pennsylvania

ALMOND CRUNCH

2 cups (4 sticks) butter	*1/2 cup water*
2 cups sugar	*2 cups almonds*
1/4 cup corn syrup	

Melt the butter in a large saucepan. Add the sugar and cook until dissolved, stirring constantly. Increase the heat to high and stir in the corn syrup. Stir in the water. Stir in the almonds. Cook until the steam is gone and the mixture is starting to smoke, stirring constantly. Pour immediately onto a nonstick baking sheet and spread evenly. Break into pieces when cool. Yield: 12 servings.

Jocelynne Blais, Gamma Nu
Edson, Alberta, Canada

APRICOT CASHEW CLUSTERS

2 cups chocolate chips, melted	*1 cup chopped dried apricots*
1 cup chopped cashews	

Combine the melted chocolate, cashews and apricots in a bowl and mix well. Drop by teaspoonfuls onto waxed paper and let cool. Store in an airtight container in the refrigerator. Yield: 7 to 8 dozen candies.

Arlene Haldeman, Omicron Master
Granite City, Illinois

BUCKEYES

1 cup chunky peanut butter	*2 cups chocolate chips*
1/2 cup (1 stick) butter, softened	*2 ounces unsweetened chocolate*
2 1/2 cups confectioners' sugar	*2 tablespoons melted paraffin*
2 teaspoons vanilla extract	

Combine the peanut butter, butter, confectioners' sugar and vanilla in a bowl and mix well. Shape into 3/4-inch balls. Combine the chocolate chips, unsweetened chocolate and paraffin in the top of a double boiler. Cook over hot water until melted, stirring until smooth. Dip the balls in the chocolate and place on waxed paper to cool. Yield: 3 to 4 dozen candies.

Andrea Simmonsen, Beta Kappa
Kuna, Idaho

CAP'N CRUNCH CANDIES

1 (14-ounce) box Cap'n Crunch Peanut Butter cereal	*2 tablespoons peanut butter*
1 (16-ounce) jar dry-roasted peanuts	*4 cups white chocolate chips*

Combine the cereal and peanuts in a large bowl. Melt the peanut butter and chocolate chips in a saucepan, stirring until smooth. Pour over the cereal mixture and stir to mix well. Spread on a nonstick baking sheet. Freeze until firm. Break into pieces. Yield: 16 servings.

Marilyn Anderson, Preceptor Kappa Omega
Riverside, California

❖ CHOCOLATE TOFFEE CRUNCH SQUARES

4 cups milk chocolate chips	1 cup halved pretzel sticks
1 cup crushed toffee pieces or toffee bits	1/2 cup white chocolate chips
1 cup salted peanuts	1 teaspoon shortening
1/2 cup flaked coconut	

Place the milk chocolate chips in a large microwave-safe bowl. Microwave on High for 1 minute and stir. Microwave on High in 15 second increments just until the chocolate is melted and smooth when stirred. Add the crushed toffee, peanuts, coconut and pretzels immediately. Stir to mix well. Spread in a 9×9-inch baking pan lined with plastic wrap. Chill for 45 minutes or until firm. Melt the white chocolate chips and shortening in a microwave-safe bowl in the microwave, stirring until smooth. Drizzle with a fork over the milk chocolate mixture in the pan, making a zigzag pattern. Chill until firm. To make haystacks, drop heaping tablespoons of the milk chocolate mixture onto waxed paper and drizzle with the white chocolate when chilled. Yield: 3 dozen squares.

Norma J. Newmeister, Preceptor Lambda
Cedar Rapids, Iowa

COCONUT PEAKS

3/4 cup mashed cooked potatoes	1 1/2 teaspoons vanilla extract
4 cups confectioners' sugar	2 cups semisweet chocolate chips
4 cups flaked coconut	

Combine the potatoes and confectioners' sugar in a large bowl and mix well. Add the coconut and vanilla and stir to mix well. Drop by teaspoonfuls onto waxed paper. Let stand until slightly firm. Melt the chocolate chips in a microwave-safe bowl in the microwave. Dip the coconut peaks halfway into the chocolate and place on waxed paper to cool. Yield: 2 1/2 pounds candy.

Nancy Williams, Xi Alpha Delta Sigma
Fort Worth, Texas

COCONUT RUM BALLS

1 (12-ounce) box vanilla wafers	1 (14-ounce) can sweetened condensed milk
1 1/2 cups flaked coconut	
1 cup finely chopped walnuts	2 tablespoons confectioners' sugar
1/4 cup rum	

Crush the vanilla wafers to crumbs. Combine the vanilla wafer crumbs, coconut and walnuts in a large bowl. Add the rum and sweetened condensed milk and mix well. Cover and chill for 4 hours. Shape into 1-inch balls. Roll the balls in the confectioners' sugar. Store in an airtight container in the refrigerator. Yield: 8 dozen balls.

Lori Sadler, Preceptor Zeta Pi
Madison, Ohio

EZY-DO DIVINITY

2 cups sugar	1/2 cup chopped walnuts or pecans
1/2 cup water	1 teaspoon vanilla extract
Pinch of salt	
1 (7-ounce) container marshmallow creme	

Combine the sugar, water and salt in a saucepan. Bring to a boil. Cook to 250 to 268 degrees on a candy thermometer, hard-ball stage, stirring constantly. Place the marshmallow creme in a large bowl. Pour in the hot sugar, stirring until slightly stiff. Fold in the walnuts and vanilla. Drop by teaspoonfuls onto waxed paper. This divinity is not affected by humidity. Yield: 2 dozen candies.

Carol J. Neilson, Rho
Ponca City, Oklahoma

FOUR-CHIP FUDGE

3/4 cup (1 1/2 sticks) butter	1 cup butterscotch chips
3 tablespoons milk	1 (7-ounce) container marshmallow creme
1 (14-ounce) can sweetened condensed milk	1/2 teaspoon vanilla extract
2 cups semisweet chocolate chips	1/2 teaspoon almond extract
2 cups milk chocolate chips	1 cup chopped walnuts
2 cups peanut butter chips	1 1/2 teaspoons butter

Melt 3/4 cup butter in a large saucepan. Add the milk, sweetened condensed milk, semisweet chocolate chips, milk chocolate chips and peanut butter chips. Cook over medium heat until melted and smooth, stirring constantly. Remove from the heat and add the butterscotch chips, marshmallow creme, vanilla and almond extract. Stir until smooth. Stir in the walnuts. Butter a 9×13-inch baking pan with 1 1/2 teaspoons butter. Spread the fudge in the prepared pan. Chill for several hours before cutting into squares. Yield: 6 dozen squares.

Donna Sisson, Delta Psi
Milan, Ohio

MILLION DOLLAR FUDGE

1 (7-ounce) chocolate candy bar
2 cups chocolate chips
1 (10¹/₂-ounce) package marshmallows
1 ounce unsweetened chocolate
¹/₂ cup pecans or walnuts
4¹/₂ cups sugar
1 (12-ounce) can evaporated milk
¹/₂ cup (1 stick) margarine

Break the candy bar in pieces into a large bowl. Add the chocolate chips, marshmallows, bittersweet chocolate and pecans. Combine the sugar, evaporated milk and margarine in a saucepan. Cook until beginning to bubble, stirring occasionally. Boil for 8 minutes, stirring occasionally. Pour over the chocolate mixture. Stir until melted. Pour into a buttered 9×9-inch baking pan. Let cool before cutting into squares. Yield: 2 pounds fudge.

Melody Ruddell, Alpha Omicron
Lewiston, Idaho

WHITE FUDGE

3 cups sugar
6 tablespoons margarine
1 cup evaporated milk
6 squares white almond bark, broken
1 (7-ounce) container marshmallow creme
1 cup pecans

Mix the sugar, margarine and evaporated milk in a saucepan. Cook to 234 to 240 degrees on a candy thermometer, soft-ball stage, stirring constantly. Remove from the heat and add the almond bark and marshmallow creme. Stir until melted. Stir in the pecans. Pour into a buttered 8×8-inch baking pan. Chill before cutting into squares. You may add ¹/₂ box red candied cherries to make Christmas fudge. Yield: 3 dozen squares.

Janice Shahan, Preceptor Delta Tau
Winterset, Iowa

PEANUT BUTTER FUDGE

6 squares vanilla-flavored white chocolate coating
1 (14-ounce) can sweetened condensed milk
Dash of salt
¹/₂ cup peanut butter
¹/₂ cup chopped pecans
1 teaspoon vanilla extract

Combine the chocolate coating, sweetened condensed milk and salt in a large microwave-safe bowl. Microwave on High for an additional 1¹/₂ minutes and stir. Microwave on High for 1¹/₂ minutes and stir until smooth. Stir in the peanut butter until smooth. Stir in the pecans and vanilla. Spread in a foil-lined 9×9-inch baking pan. Chill until firm. Invert onto a cutting board and remove the foil. Cut into squares. Yield: 3 dozen squares.

Jan Freeby, Omicron Master
Manhattan, Kansas

PEANUT BUTTER TEMPTATIONS

1¹/₄ cups sifted all-purpose flour
³/₄ teaspoon baking soda
¹/₂ teaspoon salt
¹/₂ cup (1 stick) butter, softened
¹/₂ cup peanut butter
¹/₂ cup granulated sugar
¹/₂ cup packed brown sugar
1 egg
¹/₂ teaspoon vanilla extract
Mini chocolate-covered peanut butter cups

Sift the flour, baking soda and salt together. Beat the butter, peanut butter, granulated sugar and brown sugar in a mixing bowl until light and fluffy. Beat in the egg and vanilla. Beat in the dry ingredients. Shape into 1-inch balls and place in ungreased mini-muffin cups. Bake at 375 degrees for 8 to 10 minutes. Press a mini peanut butter cup into the center of each hot cookie. Cool in the pan for 10 minutes. Remove to a wire rack to cool. Yield: 3¹/₂ dozen cookies.

Ann Marie Phillips, Delta Gamma
Jamestown, New York

PECAN PIE COOKIES

1 cup packed brown sugar
¹/₂ cup all-purpose flour
2 eggs
10²/₃ tablespoons butter, melted
1 cup chopped pecans

Combine the brown sugar, flour and eggs in a bowl and mix well. Stir in the melted butter and pecans. Fill greased mini-muffin cups ²/₃ full. Bake at 350 degrees for 12 to 15 minutes.
Yield: 2¹/₂ to 3 dozen cookies.

Virginia Jean Cole, Laureate Theta Eta
Livingston, Texas

---

*Elaine Maynard, Xi Beta Zeta, Pacifica, California, makes **Easy Fudge** by cutting 1 cup (2 sticks) margarine into pieces in a bowl. She adds one 8-ounce jar marshmallow creme, 3 cups chocolate chips, 2 cups chopped walnuts and 2 tablespoons vanilla extract and mixes well. One 12-ounce can evaporated milk and 4¹/₂ cups sugar are brought to a rolling boil in a large saucepan, stirring constantly. The heat is reduced and the mixtures boils for 10 minutes, stirring constantly. The chocolate mixture is added and stirred until well blended. The fudge is poured into a buttered 9×13-inch baking dish and chilled until firm.*

PRALINES

My grandmother got this recipe from friends before I was born. It has been a Christmas tradition my whole 49 years.

2 cups sugar
1 cup buttermilk
1 teaspoon baking
   soda

1 teaspoon vanilla
   extract
1 cup pecans halves

Combine the sugar, buttermilk and baking soda in a large heavy saucepan. Cook slowly to 234 to 240 degrees on a candy thermometer, soft-ball stage, stirring constantly. Remove from the heat and add the vanilla and pecans. Stir until the mixture begins to crystallize. Drop by teaspoonfuls onto waxed paper or parchment paper and let cool. Store in an airtight container. Yield: 2 to 3 dozen candies.

Jane Jamis, Beta Beta
Bethany, Missouri

CANDIED PECANS

1/2 cup packed brown
   sugar
2 tablespoons orange
   juice

1 cup pecan halves

Combine the brown sugar and orange juice in a bowl. Add the pecans and toss gently to coat. Spread the pecans in a buttered 10×15-inch baking pan. Bake at 350 degrees for 10 to 12 minutes or until light brown, stirring once. Spread the pecans on a buttered sheet of foil and let cool completely. Break apart, if necessary. Yield: 8 servings.

Maria Kuhn, Kappa Chi
Woodstock, Georgia

BUTTER CRACKER COOKIES

When I make these for friends, they are surprised by the salty and sweet combination. These are great during the holidays when everything is sweet.

1 (14-ounce) can
   sweetened condensed
   milk
1 cup chopped dates
1 cup chopped walnuts
25 butter crackers
1/2 cup (1 stick)
   margarine, softened

3 ounces cream cheese,
   softened
1 teaspoon vanilla
   extract
1 1/2 cups confectioners'
   sugar

Combine the sweetened condensed milk and dates in a saucepan. Cook until thick, stirring often. Remove from the heat and stir in the walnuts. Spread on the crackers. Arrange on a baking sheet. Bake at 325 degrees for 8 minutes. Remove to a wire rack to cool completely. Beat the margarine, cream cheese, vanilla and confectioners' sugar in a mixing bowl until smooth. Spread over the crackers. Yield: 25 cookies.

Nancy Barton, Laureate Zeta Xi
Austin, Texas

DECADENT CHOCOLATE TRUFFLES

12 ounces semisweet
   chocolate
1/2 cup heavy cream
2 tablespoons sugar

1 tablespoon cognac
2 tablespoons unsalted
   butter
1/3 cup baking cocoa

Combine the chocolate, cream, sugar and cognac in the top of a double boiler. Cook over hot water until melted, stirring constantly. Add the butter and stir until melted. Chill for 2 hours or until firm. Scoop 1 to 2 ounces of the firm chocolate mixture and shape into a ball. Repeat with the remaining chocolate mixture. Roll the balls in the baking cocoa to coat. Chill until ready to serve. You may add chopped nuts to the mixture or roll the balls in chopped nuts instead of baking cocoa. You may use flavored liqueurs instead of cognac. Yield: 16 truffles.

Maryanne Denisi, Laureate Beta Psi
Mishawaka, Indiana

S'MORE BALLS

1 1/2 cups sugar
3 tablespoons butter
2 squares unsweetened
   chocolate
1 (5-ounce) can
   evaporated milk
1/2 teaspoon vanilla
   extract

28 to 30 whole graham
   crackers
4 cups miniature
   marshmallows
1 cup chopped pecans
   (optional)

Combine the sugar, butter, chocolate and evaporated milk in a 3-quart saucepan. Cook over low heat until melted and smooth, stirring constantly. Remove from the heat and stir in the vanilla. Let cool to room temperature. Crush the graham crackers. Reserve 3/4 cup of graham cracker crumbs and set aside. Mix the remaining graham cracker crumbs, marshmallows and pecans in a buttered 5-quart bowl. Add the cooled chocolate mixture and stir to mix well. Shape into balls with buttered hands and roll in the reserved graham cracker crumbs.
Yield: 1 1/2 dozen balls.

Connie Sue Schulenburg, Preceptor Alpha Nu
The Dalles, Oregon

Desserts

OLD-FASHIONED APPLE DUMPLINGS

This recipe was passed down from my mother-in-law from her mother. This was one of her favorite recipes for my family when the apples are ready in the fall.

2 cups all-purpose flour
1 tablespoon baking
    powder
1 teaspoon salt
2 tablespoons butter
3/4 cup milk
3 cups chopped apples

2 teaspoons cinnamon
1 tablespoon sugar
1 cup sugar
1 tablespoon all-
    purpose flour
1 cup water

Combine the flour, baking powder and salt and mix well. Cut in the butter until crumbly. Add the milk slowly, mixing with a fork until the mixture forms a ball. Roll the dough into an 8x10-inch rectangle, 1/2 inch thick. Spread the apples over the dough and sprinkle with the cinnamon and 1 tablespoon of sugar. Roll as for a jelly roll to enclose the filling. Cut into 1-inch slices. Arrange cut-side down in a greased 9×13-inch baking pan. Combine 1 cup sugar, flour and water in a medium saucepan and mix well. Bring to a boil over high heat. Cook until the mixture thickens slightly, stirring constantly. Pour the sauce over the dumplings in the pan. Bake at 375 degrees for 35 minutes. Yield: 10 to 12 servings

Joann Wirfel, Zeta Pi
Madison, Ohio

QUICK AND EASY APPLE DUMPLINGS

4 Granny Smith apples
2 (8-count) cans crescent
    rolls
1/2 cup (1 stick) butter

1 (20-ounce) can citrus
    soda
Cinnamon to taste

Peel, core, and cut each apple into quarters. Unroll the crescent roll dough and separate into triangles. Roll each apple piece with a crescent roll triangle. Melt the butter and pour into a 9×13-inch baking pan. Arrange the wrapped apple pieces over the melted butter in the pan. Pour the citrus soda over the apples. Sprinkle with the cinnamon. Bake at 350 degrees for 50 to 60 minutes. Yield: 16 small servings.

Kaye Stevens, Xi Alpha
Albuquerque, New Mexico

APPLE YULE LOGS

8 large cooking apples,
    peeled and cored
1/2 cup finely chopped
    seedless raisins
1/4 cup packed brown
    sugar

1 cup soft bread crumbs
1 to 2 tablespoons
    Scotch whiskey
1/4 cup light corn syrup
1/4 cup dark corn syrup
1/2 cup Scotch whiskey

Arrange the apples in 2 rows in a large baking dish. Combine the raisins, brown sugar, bread crumbs and 1 to 2 tablespoons whiskey in a large bowl and mix well. Spoon the bread crumb mixture into the apples. Combine the light and dark corn syrups and pour over the stuffed apples. Bake at 325 degrees for 30 to 40 minutes or until the apples are tender, basting frequently with the pan juices. Drain the syrup from the baking dish into a small bowl. Just before serving, warm 1/2 cup of the whiskey in a small saucepan over medium heat. Pour the warm whiskey over the apples and ignite with a match. Serve the apples immediately and drizzle with the additional sauce. Yield: 8 servings.

Sonya Lee, Xi
Jackson, Mississippi

BAKED PEARS WITH VANILLA CREAM

A special romantic dessert for two!

2 firm pears, peeled and
   halved
3 tablespoons sugar
1 teaspoon butter,
   melted

1/2 cup heavy cream
1/2 teaspoon vanilla
   extract

Arrange the pears cut side down in a 9×13-inch baking dish. Sprinkle with the sugar and drizzle with the butter. Broil 4 inches from the heat source for 8 to 10 minutes or until golden brown. Reduce the oven temperature to 375 degrees. Combine the cream and the vanilla in a small bowl and mix well. Pour the cream mixture over the pears. Bake for 20 minutes or until brown and bubbly. Serve immediately. Yield: 2 servings.

Nancy Yartz, Laureate Kappa Nu
Mission Viejo, California

VANILLA PEARS

3 firm pears
2 lemon wedges
4 cups water

3 tablespoons vanilla
   extract
2 tablespoons honey

Peel and core the pears, leaving the stems intact. Trim the bottom of the pears so they will stand upright. Rub the pear with the lemon wedges to prevent browning. Combine the water, vanilla and honey in a large saucepan and mix well. Bring to a boil over high heat. Reduce the heat and add the pears. Cover and cook for 15 to 20 minutes. Remove the pears from the liquid and cool slightly. Serve with a dollop of whipped cream. Yield: 4 servings.

Suzanne L. Harter, Preceptor Kappa
Charlotte, North Carolina

CREAM PUFFS

1 cup water
1/2 cup (1 stick)
   butter
1/4 teaspoon salt

1 cup sifted all-purpose
   flour
4 eggs, at room
   temperature

Bring the water, butter and salt to a boil in a medium saucepan over high heat. Reduce the heat and add the flour all at once. Stir quickly with a wooden spoon until the mixture forms a ball. Remove from the heat. Add the eggs one at a time, beating well after each addition using an electric mixer. The final mixture should be smooth, glossy, and pale yellow. Drop by rounded teaspoonfuls 3 inches apart on an ungreased baking sheet. Bake at 325 degrees for 45 to 50 minutes. Do not open the oven door during the first 15 minutes of baking. Cool for a few moments then remove to a wire rack to cool completely. Cut a roundslice off the top of each cream puff. Remove any soft dough inside and fill with desired filling. Replace the tops and dust with confectioners' sugar before serving. Yield: 1 dozen.

Betty Read, Preceptor Delta Epsilon
New Haven, Indiana

BIG TEX FUNNEL CAKES

Oil for deep-frying
1 egg, beaten
3/4 cup milk
1 cup all-purpose flour
1/8 teaspoon cinnamon

1/4 teaspoon salt
1 teaspoon baking
   powder
Confectioners' sugar

Pour the oil into a large heavy skillet to a depth of 1 inch and heat to 360 degrees. Whisk together the egg and the milk in a small bowl. Combine the flour, cinnamon, salt and baking powder in a bowl and mix well. Add the egg mixture to the dry ingredients and beat until smooth. Holding a finger over the funnel opening, pour 1/4 cup of batter into a funnel. Hold the funnel over the skillet and release the finger from the opening. Let the batter run into the hot oil, moving the funnel in circles to create a spiral shape. Fry the funnel cake for about 1 minute per side or until golden brown. Remove the cake from the oil with a slotted spatula and drain on paper towels. Repeat the process until all of the batter has been used. Sprinkle lightly with confectioners' sugar before serving. Stir in 1 or 2 tablespoons milk if the batter thickens while standing. The batter should be thin enough to flow freely through the funnel. Yield: 6 large funnel cakes.

Judy Knight, Epsilon Alpha
Mesquite, Texas

PUMPKIN BLAHCHINDY

This is a recipe that my German grandmother used to make. My mom made it for me and now I make it for my grandson and his friends at college.

2 1/4 cup all-purpose
   flour
1/2 teaspoon baking
   powder
1/2 teaspoon salt
2/3 cup butter
1/4 cup cold water

2 cups pumpkin
3/4 cup sugar
1/2 teaspoon salt
1/2 teaspoon cinnamon
1/4 teaspoon cloves
1/4 teaspoon allspice

Combine the flour, baking powder and 1/2 teaspoon salt in a bowl and mix well. Cut in the butter until crumbly. Stir in the water gradually with a fork until the mixture forms a ball. Wrap the dough in plastic wrap and chill in the refrigerator for 30 minutes. Combine the next 6 ingredients in a bowl and mix well. Remove the dough from the refrigerator. Divide the dough into 6 portions. Roll each piece of dough into a 7-inch round on a lightly floured surface. Place 3 heaping tablespoons of the pumpkin filling in the center of each pastry round. Fold the dough over the filling, sealing and crimping the edges. Place on a large baking sheet. Bake at 375 degrees for 50 minutes. Yield: 6 servings.

H. Joyce Johnson, Preceptor Beta Lambda
Broken Arrow, Oklahoma

AWESOME NUT ROLL

4¹/₂ cups sifted all-purpose flour	1 cup milk
2 tablespoons sugar	6 egg yolks, beaten
1 teaspoon salt	6 egg whites
2 tablespoons dry yeast	2 cups sugar
1³/₄ cups (3¹/₂ sticks) butter	5 cups ground walnuts
	1 teaspoon vanilla extract

Combine the flour, sugar, salt and yeast in a bowl and mix well. Cut in the butter until crumbly. Whisk together the milk and egg yolks in a separate bowl and add to the flour mixture. Beat at low speed until the dough pulls away from the side of the bowl. Divide the dough into 4 portions and wrap each in waxed paper. Chill in the refrigerator overnight. Beat the egg whites at high speed in a large mixing bowl until stiff. Combine the sugar, walnuts, and vanilla in a bowl and mix well. Fold the nut mixture into the egg whites gradually using a rubber spatula. Remove the dough from the refrigerator. Roll each portion of dough into a rectangle ¹/₄ inch thick on a floured surface. Spread the filling over the dough and roll tightly as for a jelly roll. Place on 2 ungreased jelly roll pans and let rise until doubled in bulk. Bake at 350 degrees for 45 minutes. Slice into ¹/₂-inch slices to serve. Yield: 50 or more servings.

Emily H. Larsen, Laureate Delta Kappa
N. Ridgeville, Ohio

APPLE CRISP

4 cups sliced apples	¹/₂ cup packed brown sugar
1 tablespoon lemon juice	¹/₂ teaspoon salt
¹/₂ cup all-purpose flour	1 teaspoon cinnamon
1 cup rolled oats	¹/₂ cup (1 stick) butter, melted

Place the apples in an 8x8-inch glass baking dish and sprinkle with the lemon juice. Combine the remaining 7 ingredients in a bowl. Crumble the mixture and sprinkle over the apples. Bake at 375 degrees for 30 minutes. Yield: 6 to 8 servings.

Donna Hart, Laureate Epsilon Beta
Lithia, Florida

MIXED BERRY COBBLER

6 cups mixed berries (blueberries, blackberries, raspberries)	2 teaspoons baking powder
1 tablespoon lemon juice	¹/₂ teaspoon salt
¹/₂ cup sugar	¹/₂ cup (1 stick) butter
1 tablespoon cornstarch	¹/₄ cup vegetable shortening
¹/₂ teaspoon cinnamon	¹/₃ cup plus 2 tablespoons milk
2 cups all-purpose flour	2 tablespoons sugar

Place the berries in a large bowl and sprinkle with the lemon juice. Combine ¹/₂ cup sugar, cornstarch and cinnamon in a bowl and mix well. Sprinkle the sugar mixture over the berries and stir to combine. Spoon the mixture into a 9×13-inch baking dish and cover with aluminum foil. Bake at 400 degrees for 15 minutes. Combine the flour, baking powder and salt in a large bowl and mix well. Cut in the butter and shortening until crumbly. Add ¹/₃ cup of the milk gradually, stirring until the mixture forms a slightly sticky ball. Roll the dough to ¹/₂-inch thickness on a floured surface. Cut the dough to desired shapes using a biscuit cutter. Place on top of the warm berry mixture. Brush the dough with the remaining milk and sprinkle with 2 tablespoons of sugar. Bake at 400 degrees for 10 to 15 minutes or until the biscuits are light brown. Yield: 10 to 12 servings.

Sharon Brunn, Laureate Gamma Delta
Yakima, Washington

BLACKBERRY COBBLER

2 quarts fresh blackberries	2 cups all-purpose flour
5 tablespoons tapioca	4 teaspoons baking powder
4 teaspoons butter, melted	1 cup milk
1 cup sugar	1 cup sugar
	¹/₂ cup water

Place the blackberries in a greased 9×13-inch baking dish. Sprinkle the tapioca over the berries. Combine the butter, 1 cup of sugar, flour, baking powder and milk in a bowl and mix well. Spoon the batter over the berries. Sprinkle 1 cup of sugar over the batter and pour ¹/₂ cup water over the top. Bake at 350 degrees for 1 hour. Yield: 12 servings.

Mary Ellen Grossman, Laureate Beta Nu
Laurenceburg, Indiana

CRANBERRY-APPLE COBBLER

3 cups chopped peeled
  apples
2 cups fresh cranberries
2 tablespoons all-
  purpose flour
1 cup sugar
3 (1⅝-ounce) packages
  cinnamon and spice
  instant oatmeal

¾ cup chopped pecans
½ cup all-purpose flour
½ cup packed brown
  sugar
½ cup (1 stick) butter,
  melted
Pecan halves
Fresh cranberries

Combine the apples, 2 cups cranberries and 2 table-spoons flour in a large bowl, tossing to coat. Add 1 cup of sugar and mix well. Place the fruit mixture in a 2-quart baking dish. Combine the oatmeal, chopped pecans, ½ cup flour and brown sugar in a bowl and mix well. Add the butter and mix well. Spoon the batter over the fruit mixture. Bake, uncovered, at 350 degrees for 45 minutes. Garnish with pecans and cranberries. Yield: 6 to 8 servings.

Angela Dwyer, Preceptor Zeta
Stephens City, Virginia

PUMPKIN COBBLER

½ cup (1 stick) butter
1 cup self-rising flour
1 cup sugar
1 cup milk
1 teaspoon vanilla
  extract
2 eggs, beaten

1 (5-ounce) can
  evaporated milk
1 (30-ounce) can
  pumpkin pie filling
Vanilla ice cream or
  whipped topping
  (optional)

Melt the butter in a 9×11-inch glass baking dish in a 350-degree oven. Combine the flour, sugar, milk and vanilla in a bowl and mix well. Spoon the flour mixture into the dish over the melted butter; do not stir. Mix the eggs, evaporated milk and pumpkin pie filling in a bowl. Spoon the pumpkin mixture over the crust mixture in the baking dish; do not stir. Bake at 350 degrees for 50 to 60 minutes or until the crust is a golden brown on top. Let the cobbler cool for 20 minutes before serving. Yield: 8 to 10 servings.

Betty Ducharme, Xi Master
Merritt Island, Florida

STRAWBERRY CRUNCH

1 cup sifted all-purpose
  flour
½ cup chopped pecans
⅓ cup packed brown
  sugar
½ cup (1 stick) melted
  butter

2 egg whites
⅔ cup granulated sugar
1 (10-ounce) package
  frozen strawberries,
  thawed
1 cup whipped cream or
  whipped topping

Combine the flour, pecans, brown sugar and butter in a bowl and mix well. Spread the mixture into a shallow baking pan. Bake at 350 degrees for 20 minutes, stirring occasionally until crumbly. Remove from the oven and cool slightly. Sprinkle ⅔ of the crumbs into a 9×13-inch baking pan, reserving the remaining crumbs. Combine the egg whites, sugar and strawberries in a large mixing bowl and beat at high speed until soft peaks form. Fold in the whipped cream. Spoon the strawberry mixture over the crumbs in the pan and top with the remaining ⅓ of the crumbs. Freeze overnight and cut into squares for serving. Yield: 10 to 12 servings.

Kathryn Barnett, Xi Lambda Tau
Urich, Missouri

BEST-EVER CHEESECAKE

1¾ cups graham cracker
  crumbs
½ teaspoon cinnamon
½ cup (1 stick) butter,
  melted
2 (8-ounce) packages
  cream cheese,
  softened

1 cup sugar
3 eggs, beaten
½ teaspoon salt
1½ teaspoons vanilla
  extract
½ teaspoon almond
  extract
2 cups sour cream

Combine the crumbs, cinnamon, and butter in a bowl and mix well. Press the mixture into the bottom of a 9-inch springform pan. Cream the cream cheese and sugar together in a bowl until light and fluffy. Add the eggs one at a time, mixing well after each addition. Add the salt and flavorings, beating until smooth. Blend in the sour cream and mix well. Pour the mixture over the crust. Bake at 375 degrees for 40 to 45 minutes or until set. If the top begins to brown, cover lightly with aluminum foil. Cool in the pan for 3 to 4 hours at room temperature. Cover with plastic wrap and refrigerate until ready to serve. Remove the side of the springform pan before serving. Yield: 10 to 12 servings.

Rosemarie Varner, Pi Upsilon
Odessa, Missouri

Helen Battershell Pretz, Alpha Nu Master, Ponte Vedra Beach, Florida, prepares **Instant Strawberry Ice Cream** *by processing 24 ounces slightly thawed frozen sweetened strawberries in a blender. She then blends ½ cup plus 1 tablespoon sugar and 1½ cups heavy cream in a small bowl. The mixture is added gradually to the blender container, stopping 3 or 4 times to stir and is then poured into a shallow pan. The pan is covered and placed in a freezer for 2 hours or until nearly frozen. To serve, the ice cream is scooped into bowls and garnished with fresh strawberries.*

OLD-FASHIONED CHEESECAKE

As a young bride I wanted to impress my family and in-laws with something a little different—"Cheese Cake." It's been on the menu every Christmas since 1946.

24 pieces zwieback toast, crushed	3/4 teaspoon vanilla extract
1 cup sugar	2 tablespoons lemon juice
1 teaspoon cinnamon	
1/2 cup (1 stick) margarine, melted	2 tablespoons grated lemon zest
4 eggs	1 cup evaporated milk
1 cup sugar	2 (8-ounce) packages cream cheese, softened
1/4 cup all-purpose flour	
1/4 teaspoon salt	

Combine the zwieback crumbs with 1 cup of sugar, cinnamon, and margarine in a bowl and mix well. Reserve 2/3 cup of the crust mixture; set aside. Press the remaining crust mixture onto the bottom and side of a 9-inch springform pan. Chill the crust in the refrigerator while preparing the filling. Beat the eggs in a large mixing bowl until thick and pale yellow. Add 1 cup sugar, flour, salt, vanilla extract, lemon juice and lemon zest and mix well. Beat the evaporated milk and cream cheese together in a mixing bowl until smooth. Combine the egg mixture with the cream cheese mixture and mix well. Pour into the chilled crust and sprinkle with the reserved crumbs. Bake at 325 degrees for 1 1/4 to 1 1/2 hours. Cool in the pan. Chill until ready to serve. Remove the side of the springform pan before serving. Yield: 10 servings.

Helen Heath, Laureate Alpha Kappa
Munice, Indiana

ALMOND CHEESECAKE

2 1/2 cups graham cracker crumbs	1 3/4 cups sugar
1/2 cup slivered almonds	3 tablespoons all-purpose flour
1/2 cup sugar	1/2 teaspoon almond extract
1/2 cup (1 stick) plus 1 tablespoon butter, melted	5 eggs plus 2 egg yolks
5 (8-ounce) packages cream cheese, softened	1/4 cup heavy cream
	3/4 cup sour cream
	1/4 cup slivered almonds for garnish

Combine the graham cracker crumbs, 1/2 cup almonds, 1/2 cup sugar and butter in a bowl and mix well. Press the mixture with a fork onto the bottom and side of a 10-inch springform pan. Bake at 375 degrees for 5 minutes. Remove from the oven and cool. Beat the cream cheese, 1 3/4 cups sugar, the flour and almond extract at medium speed until smooth. Beat in the eggs and yolks at low speed until smooth and creamy, gradually increasing to medium speed. Add the heavy cream and mix well. Pour the cream cheese mixture into the prepared crust. Bake at 450 degrees for 10 minutes. Lower the temperature to 250 degrees and bake for 1 hour or until center is set. Cool in the pan on a wire rack. Spread the sour cream on top and garnish with 1/4 cup slivered almonds. Chill in the refrigerator until ready to serve. Remove the side of the springform pan to serve. Yield: 16 servings.

Mary Long, Preceptor Omicron Epsilon
Manteca, California

APRICOT CHEESECAKE WITH FRESH STRAWBERRIES

1 cup dried apricots	3/4 cup sugar
Grated zest of 1 orange	4 large eggs
1 cup gingersnap crumbs	1/2 cup sour cream
3 tablespoons unsalted butter, melted	3 cups fresh strawberries, whole or sliced
3 (8-ounce) packages cream cheese, softened	1 tablespoon sugar
	2 tablespoons Triple Sec

Place the apricots in a small saucepan and add water to cover. Cover and simmer over low heat for 1/2 hour or until the apricots have softened; drain. Purée the apricots in a food processor until smooth. Pour the apricot purée into a small bowl; stir in the grated orange zest. Combine the gingersnap crumbs with the melted butter and mix well. Press onto the bottom and sides of a 9-inch springform pan. Cream the cream cheese and sugar together in a large bowl until light and fluffy. Add the eggs, one at a time, beating well after each addition. Gently fold in the sour cream and the apricot purée until well blended. Pour the cream cheese mixture into the prepared crust. Bake at 350 degrees for 50 to 60 minutes or until the center is set. Cool in the pan until room temperature. Chill, covered, in the refrigerator until ready to serve. Combine the strawberries, 1 tablespoon sugar, and Triple Sec in a large bowl and toss to combine. Chill, covered, in the refrigerator until ready to serve. Arrange the berries on top of the cheesecake and remove the side of the springform pan to serve. Yield: 12 servings.

Mary A. Courten, Laureate Beta Omicron
North Fort Myers, Florida

NEW YORK-STYLE CHEESECAKE

This is Paul Little's recipe. It is delicious plain or with a fruit topping.

1 cup graham cracker crumbs	3/4 cup sugar
3 tablespoons sugar	3 tablespoons cornstarch
3 tablespoons butter, melted	1 teaspoon vanilla extract
3 (8-ounce) packages cream cheese, softened	1 teaspoon lemon extract
1 cup sour cream	3 large eggs

Combine the graham cracker crumbs, 3 tablespoons sugar and butter in a bowl and mix well. Press evenly onto the bottom and sides of a 9-inch springform pan. Combine the cream cheese, sour cream, 3/4 cup sugar, cornstarch, vanilla and lemon extract in a bowl and blend well. Add the eggs 1 at a time, beating well after each addition until smooth. Pour the mixture into the crust. Bake at 350 degrees for 40 minutes or until golden brown. Let cool in a partially open oven. Chill, covered, in the refrigerator until ready to serve. Remove the side of the springform pan to serve. Yield: 12 to 16 servings.

Karen Little, Alpha Zeta Master
Chesterfield, Virginia

EASY PUMPKIN CHEESECAKE BARS

1 (2-layer) package yellow or white cake mix	1 teaspoon vanilla extract
1/2 cup (1 stick) butter, melted	1 (15-ounce) can pumpkin
4 eggs	1 teaspoon cinnamon
1 (8-ounce) package cream cheese, softened	1 teaspoon nutmeg
1 (1-pound) package confectioners' sugar	Whipped topping (optional)

Combine the cake mix, melted butter, and 1 egg in a bowl and mix well. Press the mixture into a greased 9×13-inch baking pan. Beat the cream cheese, 3 eggs, confectioners' sugar and vanilla in a separate bowl until smooth. Combine the pumpkin, cinnamon and nutmeg in a small bowl and mix well. Add the pumpkin mixture to the cream cheese mixture, stirring to combine. Pour the pumpkin cream cheese mixture over the cake mix in the pan. Bake at 350 degrees for 45 minutes. Cool and serve with whipped topping, if desired. Yield: 12 servings.

Jane Moyer, Xi Zeta Rho
Lamar, Missouri

SOPAIPILLA CHEESECAKE

2 (8-count) cans crescent rolls	2½ cups sugar
2 (8-ounce) packages cream cheese, softened	1/2 cup (1 stick) butter, melted
	1 cup sugar
	Cinnamon

Unroll one can of crescent rolls and spread over the bottom of a 9×13-inch baking pan. Cream the cream cheese and 1½ cups sugar in a bowl until light and fluffy. Spread the cream cheese mixture on top of the crescent rolls. Unroll the other can of crescent rolls and spread on top of the cream cheese mixture. Combine the melted butter and 1 cup sugar in a bowl, stirring until the sugar granules dissolve. Pour the butter mixture over the crescent rolls and spread evenly. Sprinkle the top with the cinnamon. Bake at 350 degrees for 30 minutes. Chill before serving. Yield: 12 servings.

Judy Miller, Preceptor Iota Eta
Ennis, Texas

GERMAN CHEESECAKE

1/2 cup sugar	1 cup sugar
1/2 cup (1 stick) unsalted butter, softened	1/2 cup (1 stick) unsalted butter
2 cups all-purpose flour	1 tablespoon lemon juice
1 egg yolk	1 teaspoon vanilla extract
1/2 teaspoon baking powder	5 egg yolks
1 Granny Smith apple, peeled and sliced	2 tablespoons cream of wheat
3 (8-ounce) packages cream cheese, softened	5 egg whites

Combine the sugar, butter, flour, 1 egg yolk and baking powder in a bowl, stirring with a fork until crumbly. Press 2/3 of the mixture onto a 9-inch springform pan, reserving the remaining mixture. Arrange the apple slices on top of the crust. Cream the cream cheese, sugar and butter in a large mixing bowl until smooth and creamy. Add the lemon juice, vanilla, 5 egg yolks and cream of wheat and mix well. Beat the egg whites in a separate mixing bowl until stiff and glossy. Fold the egg whites into the cream cheese mixture. Spoon the filling into the prepared crust and sprinkle with the reserved 1/3 of the crumb topping. Bake at 450 degrees for 20 minutes. Reduce the temperature to 200 degrees and bake for 1 hour. Cool before serving. Remove the side of the springform pan to serve. Yield: 12 servings.

Christa Tinlin, Preceptor Sigma
Daleville, Alabama

NO-BAKE LADYFINGER CHEESECAKE

2 (11-ounce) packages
   no-bake cheesecake
   mix
2/3 cup butter
   or margarine,
   melted
1/4 cup sugar
1 (3-ounce) package
   ladyfinger cookies

1 (8-ounce) package
   cream cheese,
   softened
3 cups cold milk
1 (12-ounce) carton
   frozen whipped
   topping, thawed
1 (21-ounce) can
   raspberry pie filling

Combine the contents of the crust mix packages, butter and sugar in a bowl and mix well. Press the crust mixture over the bottom of an ungreased 10-inch springform pan. Arrange the ladyfingers around the edge of the pan. Beat the cream cheese and 1/2 cup of the milk in a mixing bowl until smooth. Gradually beat in the remaining 2 1/2 cups milk. Add the contents of the cream cheese filling mix packages. Beat at medium for 3 minutes or until smooth. Fold in the whipped topping with a rubber spatula. Pour the mixture into the crust. Cover and refrigerate for 1 hour or longer. Top with the raspberry pie filling. Remove the side of the springform pan to serve. Yield: 12 servings.

Diane Paxin, Alpha Omicron Master
Palmdale, California

LINGONBERRY CHEESECAKE

1 1/4 cups graham cracker
   crumbs
1/2 cup finely chopped
   pecans
1/3 cup butter, melted
1 (14-ounce) jar
   lingonberry preserves,
   or 1 quart fresh
   lingonberries

3 (8-ounce) packages
   cream cheese,
   softened
3/4 cup sugar
1/2 teaspoon ground
   cardamom
1 1/2 teaspoons vanilla
   extract
3 eggs

Combine the graham cracker crumbs, pecans and butter in a bowl and mix well. Press the mixture over the bottom of a 9-inch springform pan. Bake at 350 degrees for 10 minutes; cool on a wire rack. Place the lingonberries in a small saucepan and heat over low heat until softened, stirring occasionally. Strain the syrup from the berries. Cover and reserve the syrup. Beat the cream cheese, sugar, cardamom and vanilla in a mixing bowl until smooth. Add the eggs 1 at a time, mixing well after each addition. Fold in the lingonberries, stirring until incorporated. Pour the cream cheese mixture over the prepared crust. Bake at 350 degrees for 40 to 45 minutes or until the edges are set. Cool for several hours at room temperature. Chill, covered, in the refrigerator for at least 4 hours before serving. Remove the side of the spring-

form pan to serve. Spoon the reserved syrup over each piece of cheesecake. Yield: 12 servings.

Dianne V. Berthe, Xi Alpha Sigma
Eagan, Minnesota

UPSIDE-DOWN STRAWBERRY CHEESECAKE

To cut down on calories, use light whipped topping instead of the whipping cream.

1 cup whipping cream
1 (8-ounce) package
   cream cheese,
   softened
1 (3-ounce) package
   vanilla instant
   pudding mix
1/2 cup milk

2 tablespoons sugar
1/2 teaspoon lemon juice
1 pint fresh
   strawberries, hulled
   and halved
4 graham crackers,
   crumbled

Beat the whipping cream to stiff peaks in a large bowl; set aside. Beat the cream cheese in a medium bowl until smooth and creamy. Add the pudding mix, milk, sugar and lemon juice and beat until smooth. Fold in the whipped cream gently. Place the strawberries in a 9-inch pie plate. Spoon the cream cheese mixture over the berries and top with the crumbled graham crackers. Cover and chill until ready to serve. Yield: 8 servings.

Mary M. Fronczak, Alpha Omega Master
Oviedo, Florida

CHOCOLATE-PEPPERMINT CHEESECAKE

1 1/2 cups crushed Oreo
   cookies
1 (8-ounce) package
   cream cheese,
   softened
1 (14-ounce) can
   unsweetened
   condensed milk

1/2 teaspoon peppermint
   extract
1/2 cup milk chocolate
   chips
2 cups whipped cream
1/4 cup crushed
   peppermint candy

Press the Oreo cookie crumbs in a buttered 8-inch springform pan. Bake at 375 degrees for 8 minutes. Cool on a wire rack. Beat the cream cheese in a mixing bowl on medium speed until light and fluffy. Add the condensed milk and peppermint extract and mix well. Fold the chocolate chips into the cream cheese mixture. Fold in the whipped cream gently. Spoon the filling into the prepared crust. Freeze, covered, for 2 hours or until set. Garnish with peppermint candy. Remove the side of the springform pan to serve. Yield: 8 servings.

Orine A. Wilson, Theta Master
Clarkston, Washington

❖ RED VELVET CHEESECAKE

1½ cups chocolate graham cracker crumbs	2 teaspoons vanilla extract
¼ cup (½ stick) butter, melted	1 teaspoon distilled white vingegar
1 tablespoon sugar	2 ounces red food coloring
3 (8-ounce) packages cream cheese, softened	3 ounces cream cheese, softened
1½ cups sugar	¼ cup (½ stick) butter, softened
4 eggs, lightly beaten	2 cups confectioners' sugar
3 tablespoons baking cocoa	1 teaspoon vanilla extract
1 cup sour cream	
½ cup buttermilk	

Combine the graham cracker crumbs, melted butter and 1 tablespoon sugar in a bowl and mix well. Press the mixture in the bottom of a 9-inch springform pan. Beat 24 ounces cream cheese and 1½ cups sugar at medium-low speed in a large bowl for 1 minute. Add the eggs, cocoa, sour cream, buttermilk, 2 teaspoons vanilla, vinegar and red food coloring, mixing on low speed until just combined. Pour the batter into the prepared crust. Bake at 325 degrees for 10 minutes. Reduce the temperature to 300 degrees and bake for 1¼ hours or until the center is set. Run a knife along the edge of the cheesecake. Turn off the oven and let the cheesecake sit in the oven for 30 minutes. Remove from the oven and cool on a wire rack for 30 minutes. Cover and chill for 8 hours. Beat 3 ounces cream cheese and ¼ cup butter at medium speed in a mixing bowl until smooth. Gradually add the confectioners' sugar and vanilla, beating until smooth. Spread evenly over the top of the cheesecake. Remove the side of the springform pan to serve. Yield: 8 to 10 servings.

Gayle Taylor, Zi Gamma Tau
King, Tennessee

WHITE CHOCOLATE MACADAMIA NUT CHEESECAKE

1½ cups graham cracker crumbs	4 eggs
½ cup chopped macadamias	½ cup (1 stick) butter, softened
¼ teaspoon cinnamon	¾ pound white chocolate, melted
½ cup (1 stick) butter, melted	1 tablespoon praline liqueur
4 (8-ounce) packages cream cheese, softened	2 teaspoons vanilla extract
¼ cup packed brown sugar	1 cup chopped toasted macadamias

Combine the first 4 ingredients in a bowl and mix well. Press the crumb mixture onto the bottom and partway up the side of a 9-inch springform pan. Bake at 375 degrees for 10 minutes; cool on a wire rack. Beat the cream cheese on medium speed until light and fluffy. Add the brown sugar and mix well. Add the eggs one at a time, beating well after each addition. Stir in the butter. Add the melted chocolate, praline liqueur and vanilla, mixing until smooth. Fold in the nuts. Pour the mixture into the prepared crust. Reduce the oven temperature to 350 degrees. Bake for 1½ hours or until the center is set. Cool completely on a wire rack. Cover and refrigerate overnight. Remove the side of the springform pan before serving. To serve, drizzle with semisweet chocolate and garnish with white chocolate leaves. Yield: 12 servings.

Beverly Harrell, Alpha Pi
Natchitoches, Louisiana

MINI CHEESECAKES

12 vanilla wafers	1 teaspoon vanilla extract
2 (8-ounce) packages cream cheese, softened	2 eggs
½ cup sugar	1 (21-ounce) can fruit pie filling

Line miniature muffin cups with foil liners. Place 1 vanilla wafer in each cup. Beat the cream cheese, sugar and vanilla on medium speed in a bowl until smooth and creamy. Beat in the eggs one at a time until smooth. Spoon the cream cheese mixture over the wafers, filling each muffin cup ¾ full. Bake at 325 degrees for 25 minutes. Cool on a wire rack. Remove from the pan when cool. Chill, covered, in the refrigerator. Top each with a fruit pie filling and garnish with fresh fruit, if desired. Yield: 12 servings.

Jeanette Osbotne, Xi Beta Chi
Eclectic, Alabama

BANANA SPLIT IN-A-PAN

2 cups graham cracker crumbs	7 bananas
1½ cups (3 sticks) margarine, melted	1 (20-ounce) can crushed pineapple, drained
2 cups confectioners' sugar	2 cups whipping cream or whipped topping
2 eggs	1 cup chopped pecans or walnuts
1 teaspoon vanilla extract	1 small bottle of maraschino cherries

Combine the graham cracker crumbs and 1 stick of the margarine in a bowl and mix well. Press the mixture in a 9×13-inch pan. Beat the remaining 2 sticks of butter and confectioners' sugar on medium speed in a bowl until light and fluffy. Add the eggs and vanilla and beat on medium speed for 10 to 15 minutes. Spread the mixture over the graham cracker crust. Cut the bananas in half lengthwise and place on top of the sugar mixture. Top with the crushed pineapple and spread with whipped cream. Sprinkle with pecans and maraschino cherries. Cover and chill, in the refrigerator, until cool. Yield: 12 to 15 servings.

Ann Matney, Laureate Eta Beta
Mission Viejo, California

CHOCOLATE ÉCLAIR DESSERT

1 (16-ounce) box graham
   crackers
2 (3-ounce) packages
   French vanilla
   instant pudding mix
3 cups cold milk
1 (8-ounce) container
   whipped topping
1/2 cup sugar
1/3 cup baking cocoa
1/2 teaspoon salt
1/4 cup milk
1/4 cup margarine
1 teaspoon vanilla
   extract

Cover the bottom of a greased 9×13-inch baking dish with whole graham crackers. Combine the pudding mix and the milk in a bowl and beat at medium speed with an electric mixer until well combined. Fold in the whipped topping. Pour half the mixture over the graham crackers. Add another layer of graham crackers. Pour the remaining pudding mixture over top and add another layer or graham crackers. Combine 1/2 cup sugar, the cocoa, salt and 1/4 cup milk in a saucepan and mix well. Bring to a boil over high heat, stirring constantly. Remove from the heat and stir in the margarine and the vanilla. Cool for 3 minutes and pour over the top layer of graham crackers. Cover and refrigerate overnight.
Yield: 20 servings.

Doris Blakeney, Delta Master
Greenville, South Carolina

COCONUT CREAM DESSERT

1 cup all-purpose flour
2 tablespoons sugar
1/2 cup (1 stick) butter,
   chilled
1/2 cup chopped
   pecans
1 (8-ounce) package
   cream cheese,
   softened
1 cup confectioners'
   sugar
1 (12-ounce) carton
   frozen whipped
   topping, thawed
4 cups cold milk
4 teaspoons coconut
   flavoring
3 (3-ounce) packages
   vanilla instant
   pudding mix
1/2 cup flaked coconut,
   toasted

Combine the flour and sugar in a bowl and mix well. Cut in the butter until crumbly. Stir in the pecans. Press the crust mixture in a greased 9×13-inch baking dish. Bake at 325 degrees for 20 to 25 minutes or until the edges are light brown. Cool on a wire rack. Beat the cream cheese and confectioners' sugar in a mixing bowl on medium speed until smooth and creamy. Fold in 1 cup of the whipped topping. Spread the mixture over the crust. Whisk the milk, coconut flavoring and pudding mixes together in a large bowl for 2 minutes or until well blended. Let stand for 2 minutes or until beginning to set. Spread the pudding mixture over the cream cheese layer in the pan. Top with the remaining whipped topping and sprinkle with the coconut. Refrigerate, covered, for 4 hours or overnight. Yield: 15 servings.

Diana L. Fernandez, Alpha Omicron Master
Pearblossom, California

LEMON PUDDING DESSERT

1 cup (2 sticks) butter or
   margarine, chilled
2 cups all-purpose flour
1 (8-ounce) package
   cream cheese, softened
1 cup confectioners'
   sugar
1 (8-ounce) carton
   frozen whipped
   topping, thawed
3 cups cold milk
2 (3-ounce) packages
   lemon instant
   pudding mix

Cut the butter into the flour in a large bowl until crumbly. Press the mixture in an ungreased 9×13-inch baking pan. Bake at 350 degrees for 18 to 22 minutes or until golden and firm. Cool on a wire rack. Beat the cream cheese and confectioners' sugar in a bowl on medium speed until smooth. Fold in 1 cup of the whipped topping. Spread over the crust. Beat the milk and pudding mix in a large mixing bowl on low speed for 2 minutes. Spread the mixture carefully over the cream cheese layer in the pan. Top with the remaining whipped topping. Refrigerate, covered, for 1 hour or more. Yield: 12 to 16 servings.

Linda Black, Xi Delta Eta
Cedaredge, Colorado

Lucy Eaton, Steeleville, Illinois, makes **Death by Chocolate Trifle** *by preparing and baking one 22-ounce box brownie mix according to the package directions. The brownies are then cut into 1/2-inch squares when cool. She combines two 6-ounce packages chocolate instant pudding and 2 1/2 cups cold milk in a large bowl and beats at medium speed for 4 minutes or until smooth and creamy. The brownies, pudding, one 12-ounce container whipped topping and one 8-ounce package toffee bits are layered in a large trifle bowl until all the ingredients are used, ending with the whipped topping and toffee bits.*

SEX IN A PAN

1/2 cup (1 stick) butter	*1 (6-ounce) package*
1 cup all-purpose flour	*instant pudding mix*
1/2 cup chopped pecans	*(butterscotch,*
1 (8-ounce) package	*chocolate, or pecan*
cream cheese,	*flavor)*
softened	*3 cups cold milk*
1 (12-ounce) container	*1 (3-ounce) milk*
whipped topping	*chocolate bar, shaved*
1 cup confectioners'	*1/2 cup chopped pecans*
sugar	*for garnish*

Cut the butter into the flour in a large bowl until crumbly. Stir in the pecans. Press the mixture in an ungreased 9×13-inch baking pan. Bake at 350 degrees for 15 minutes. Cool on a wire rack. Beat the cream cheese, whipped topping and confectioners' sugar on medium speed in a mixing bowl until smooth. Spread half of the cream cheese mixture over the prepared crust. Beat the pudding mix and milk together in a mixing bowl on medium speed until smooth and beginning to thicken. Spread the pudding mixture over the cream cheese mixture in the pan. Top with the remaining cream cheese mixture. Garnish with the chocolate shavings and chopped pecans. Chill before serving. This dessert also freezes well. Yield: 12 servings.

Lois L. Drobot, Delta Iota Greenwater
Porcupine Plain, Saskatchewan, Canada

STRAWBERRY PARFAIT

1 cup milk	*1 (3-ounce) package*
1 (3-ounce) package	*strawberry gelatin*
vanilla instant	*1 cup hot water*
pudding mix	*1 (16-ounce) package*
1 pint vanilla ice cream,	*frozen strawberries*
softened	
1 small prepared angel	
food cake	

Beat the milk and pudding mix in a mixing bowl on medium speed until smooth and thickened. Beat in the ice cream until smooth. Tear the angel food cake into bite-size pieces and place in a 9×13-inch baking dish. Pour the pudding mixture over the cake pieces. Chill, covered, in a refrigerator for 1 hour or until firm. Combine the strawberry gelatin and hot water in a bowl and mix well. Stir in the strawberries. Chill, covered, until slightly thickened. Pour the strawberry mixture over the pudding mixture. Chill, covered, for 2 more hours or until the topping has congealed. Yield: 12 servings.

Shelly Vandiver, Preceptor Zeta Beta
Shelbina, Missouri

WHISKEY ICE BOX DESSERT

2 (3-ounce) envelopes	*1 cup sugar*
unflavored gelatin	*1 teaspoon lemon juice*
1/2 cup cold water	*2 cups whipping cream*
1/2 cup boiling water	*6 egg whites*
6 egg yolks	*3 packages ladyfingers,*
1/4 cup whiskey	*split lengthwise*

Soak the gelatin in the cold water in a small bowl. Add the boiling water and stir until the gelatin is dissolved. Beat the egg yolks in a mixing bowl on medium speed until thickened. Add the whiskey slowly, beating on low speed constantly. Add the sugar and lemon juice, beating until smooth. Stir in the gelatin. Cover and chill for 10 to 15 minutes. Whip the cream until soft peaks form; fold into the chilled mixture. Beat the egg whites in a large mixing bowl until stiff; fold into the chilled mixture. Line the side and bottom of a 12-inch springform pan with split ladyfingers. Spoon 1/2 of the mixture into the springform pan. Arrange a layer of ladyfingers on top. Top with the remaining 1/2 of the mixture and arrange more ladyfingers on top. Cover and chill overnight in the refrigerator. Yield: 12 servings.

Barbara Reeves, Preceptor Kappa
Baldwinsville, New York

MONACO GRAPEFRUIT MOLD

1 large ruby grapefruit	*1/4 cup grenadine*
1 (6-ounce) package	*1 tablespoon honey*
orange gelatin	*1/2 cup orange juice*
Juice of 1 grapefruit	*3 tablespoons honey*
(approximately 3/4	*1/4 cup Grand Marnier*
cup)	*2 tablespoons orange*
4 mint leaves, chopped	*marmalade*

Peel the grapefruit and divide into sections. Place the sections in four 3/4-cup custard cups. Combine the gelatin and grapefruit juice in a small saucepan and heat over low heat until the gelatin melts, stirring constantly. Add the mint leaves, grenadine and 1 tablespoon honey and mix well. Pour the mixture over the grapefruit. Cover with plastic wrap and chill for 4 hours or until set. Combine the orange juice, 3 tablespoons honey, Grand Marnier and orange marmalade in a bowl and mix well. Unmold the congealed grapefruit on serving plates and surround with the orange sauce to serve. Yield: 4 servings.

Diane Alaman, Xi Beta Kappa
Pace, Florida

POINSETTIA CHARLOTTE

2 (12-ounce) packages pound cake mix, prepared	2 cups milk
1/2 cup seedless raspberry jam	1/2 tablespoon orange zest
4 (4-ounce) packages chocolate mousse mix	1 pint fresh raspberries

Trim the sides and top of the pound cakes. Slice each horizontally into 3 layers. Alternate layers of pound-cake and 2 tablespoons jam, beginning and ending with the pound cake. Cut the cakes into 1/2-inch slices. Line the side and the bottom of an 8-inch springform pan with the cake slices. Prepare the mousse using the package directions, using only 2 cups milk and adding the orange zest. Reserve 1 cup of mousse. Spoon the remaining mousse into the prepared pan. Top with the remaining cake slices, mousse and raspberries. Chill, covered, for 4 hours. Yield: 12 servings.

Carol Woodworth, Xi Alpha Omicron
Elkhart, Indiana

APPLE KUCHEN

1/2 cup (1 stick) butter or margarine, softened	2 1/2 cups sliced peeled apples
1 (2-layer) package yellow cake mix	1/2 cup sugar
1/2 cup flaked coconut	1 teaspoon cinnamon
	1 cup sour cream
	2 egg yolks or 1 egg

Combine the butter, cake mix and coconut in a bowl, stirring until crumbly. Press the mixture in an ungreased 9×13-inch baking pan. Bake at 350 degrees for 10 minutes. Arrange the apple slices on the warm crust. Sprinkle a mixture of the sugar and cinnamon over the apples. Whisk the sour cream and egg yolks in a bowl until smooth and drizzle over the apples. Bake at 350 degrees for 25 minutes or until the edges are light brown. Do not overbake. Serve warm. Yield: 10 to 12 servings.

Rita Cane, Preceptor Epsilon Lambda
Whitby, Ontario, Canada

BLUEBERRY DESSERT

1 cup all-purpose flour	1 cup crushed pineapple, drained
4 ounces flaked coconut	1 teaspoon vanilla extract
1/2 cup (1 stick) margarine	1 (8-ounce) carton whipped topping
2 bananas, sliced	1/2 cup chopped pecans
8 ounces cream cheese, softened	1 (14-ounce) can blueberry pie filling
1 cup confectioners' sugar	

Mix the flour and coconut in a bowl. Cut in the margarine until crumbly. Press the mixture in a 9×13-inch baking pan. Bake at 375 degrees for 15 minutes or until golden brown. Cool on a wire rack. Cover the cooled crust with the banana slices. Beat the cream cheese and confectioners' sugar in a mixing bowl on medium speed until smooth and creamy. Add the pineapple and vanilla and mix well. Fold in the whipped topping. Spread the cream cheese mixture over the bananas and sprinkle with the chopped pecans. Top with the blueberry pie filling. Cover and refrigerate 4 hours or overnight. Yield: 12 servings.

Joan E. Tebbenhoff, Alpha Delta Omicron
Bonne Terre, Missouri

PECAN PUMPKIN TORTE

2 cups crushed vanilla wafers	4 eggs
1 cup chopped pecans	3 cups confectioners' sugar
3/4 cup (1 1/2 sticks) butter, softened	1/2 cup (1 stick) butter, softened
1 (2-layer) package spice cake mix	6 ounces cream cheese, softened
1 (16-ounce) can pumpkin	2 teaspoons vanilla extract
1/4 cup (1/2 stick) butter, softened	1/3 cup caramel topping
	Pecan halves for garnish

Combine the crushed wafers, chopped pecans, and 3/4 cup butter in a large mixing bowl. Beat at medium speed for 1 to 2 minutes or until well combined, scraping the sides often. Press the mixture over the bottoms of 3 greased and floured 9-inch round cake pans. Combine the cake mix, pumpkin, 1/4 cup butter, and eggs in the same bowl. Beat at medium speed for 2 to 3 minutes or until smooth. Spread 1 3/4 cups of the pumpkin batter over the wafer mixture in each pan. Bake at 350 degrees for 20 to 25 minutes or until a wooden pick inserted into the center comes out clean. Cool for 5 minutes in the pans. Remove from the pans and cool on wire racks. Combine 1/2 cup butter, cream cheese and vanilla in a small mixing bowl. Beat at medium speed for 2 to 3 minutes or until light and fluffy. Place 1 cake crust nut side down on a serving platter. Spread with 1/3 of the cream cheese filling. Continue layering with the remaining 2 cake layers and 1/3 filling ending with a cake crust. Frost the sides of the torte with the remaining 1/3 filling. Drizzle the caramel topping over the torte. Garnish with pecan halves. Cover and refrigerate until ready to serve. Yield: 14 servings.

Geri Hetterich, Preceptor Lambda Kappa
Dallas, Texas

CREAM PUFF DESSERT

We love cream puffs at our house but not the fuss of making them. This is quick, easy and delicious!

1/2 cup (1 stick) butter
1 cup water
1 cup all-purpose flour
4 eggs
3 (4-ounce) packages
  vanilla instant
  pudding mix
2 3/4 cups milk

1 (8-ounce) package
  cream cheese,
  softened
1/4 cup milk
1 (8-ounce) carton
  whipped topping
2 ounces chocolate,
  melted

Bring the butter and the water to a boil in a saucepan over high heat. Add the flour all at once and stir vigorously until the mixture forms a ball. Remove from the heat. Add the eggs 1 at a time, beating until the mixture is smooth and glossy. Spread the mixture in a greased 9×13-inch baking pan. Bake at 375 degrees for 25 to 35 minutes. The mixture will puff up while baking; press down with a spatula to form a crust. Remove to a wire rack to cool. Beat the pudding mix and 2 3/4 cups milk in a mixing bowl on medium speed until smooth. Combine the cream cheese with 1/4 cup milk in a bowl and beat until smooth. Combine the pudding mixture with the cream cheese mixture and mix well. Spread the mixture over the cooled crust. Top with the whipped topping and drizzle with the melted chocolate.
Yield: 12 servings.

Cyndi Johnson, Preceptor Nu
Trenton, Missouri

CHOCOLATE CARAMEL CREAMY DELIGHT

1 (18-ounce) package
  devil's food cake mix
1 (12-ounce) can
  sweetened condensed
  milk
1 (10-ounce) jar caramel
  topping

1 (8-ounce) container
  whipped topping
1 (8-ounce) package
  chocolate-covered
  toffee bits

Prepare and bake the cake mix using the package directions for a 9×13-inch pan. Remove from the oven and immediately poke holes all over the cake using the handle of a wooden spoon. Combine the sweetened condensed milk and the caramel topping in a bowl and mix well. Pour the mixture evenly over the cake. Let cool on a wire rack. Combine the whipped topping with the toffee bits and mix well. Frost the cake with the whipped topping mixture and serve immediately. Yield: 12 servings.

Ada E. Fravel, Laureate Beta Omicron
Sioux Falls, South Dakota

MISSISSIPPI MUD

1 cup (2 sticks)
  margarine, melted
1 1/2 cups all-purpose
  flour
1/3 cup baking cocoa
2 teaspoons vanilla
  extract
1 cup chopped pecans
4 eggs
2 cups sugar

1 (7-ounce) jar
  marshmallow creme
1/2 cup (1 stick)
  margarine
1/3 cup baking cocoa
16 ounces confectioners'
  sugar
2 to 4 tablespoons milk
2 cups chopped pecans

Melt 1 cup margarine in a saucepan over medium heat. Add the flour, 1/3 cup cocoa and 1 teaspoon of the vanilla and mix well. Stir in 1 cup pecans. Beat the eggs and sugar at medium speed in a large bowl until light and fluffy. Stir the butter mixture into the egg mixture. Pour into a greased and floured 9×13-inch baking pan. Bake at 350 degrees for 30 minutes. Remove from the oven and spread with the marshmallow creme. Melt 1/2 cup margarine in a saucepan over medium heat. Add the remaining 1 teaspoon vanilla and 1/3 cup cocoa and mix well. Remove from the heat and add the confectioners' sugar, stirring until smooth. Add the milk if needed to thin the mixture. Stir in 2 cups pecans and spoon over the cake and mix with the marshmallow creme. Yield: 24 small servings.

Pamela S. Jones, Epsilon Alpha
Garland, Texas

BANANA PUDDING TRIFLE

1 (14-ounce) can
  sweetened condensed
  milk
1 1/2 cups water
1 (4-ounce) package
  vanilla instant
  pudding mix
2 cups whipping cream

1/2 cup sugar
1/4 cup amaretto
36 vanilla wafers
3 bananas, sliced and
  dipped in lemon juice
1 (12-ounce) package
  toffee bits

Combine the sweetened condensed milk and water in a large bowl and mix well. Add the pudding mix. Beat at medium speed for 4 minutes or until smooth and creamy. Chill, covered, for 5 minutes. Whip the cream and the sugar in a bowl until stiff peaks form. Fold the whipped cream and the amaretto into the pudding. Spoon 1 cup of the pudding mixture into a large trifle bowl. Top with 1/3 each of the wafers, bananas, pudding mixture and toffee bits. Repeat the layers twice, ending with the pudding mixture. Chill, covered, in the refrigerator until cool. Garnish with the remaining toffee chips . Yield: 12 servings.

Beverly Schwan, Preceptor Omicron Pi
Waco, Texas

STRAWBERRY TRIFLE

1 (18-ounce) package
yellow cake mix
1 (3-ounce) package
vanilla instant
pudding mix
4 teaspoons sherry
(optional)

1 (16-ounce) package
frozen strawberries,
thawed and drained
1 cup whipping cream
1/4 cup sugar
1 tablespoon slivered
almonds

Prepare and bake the cake mix using the package directions. Cool on a wire rack. Prepare the pudding mix using the package directions. Chill in the refrigerator until cool. Cut the cake crosswise in half. Cut 1 half into 8 pieces; split each piece in half. Arrange 1/2 of the cake pieces in a large glass serving bowl. Sprinkle with 2 teaspoons sherry. Cover with 1/2 of the strawberries and spread with 1/2 of the pudding. Repeat the layers, ending with the pudding. Beat the whipping cream and sugar in a mixing bowl until stiff peaks form. Spread the whipping cream over the trifle and sprinkle with almonds. Cover and refrigerate 1 hour or more. Yield: 14 servings.

Pat Ballard, Xi Gamma Nu
Grand Forks, British Columbia, Canada

CHOCOLATE BREAD PUDDING

1/2 loaf country white
bread, cubed
4 eggs
4 egg yolks
1 cup sugar

2 cups half-and-half
12 ounces bittersweet
chocolate, finely
chopped

Place the bread cubes into a buttered 9×13-inch baking dish. Beat the eggs, egg yolks and sugar at medium speed in a large bowl for 3 minutes or until smooth. Heat the half-and-half in a saucepan over medium heat until simmering; do not boil. Whisk the half-and-half into the egg mixture until well blended. Add the chocolate, stirring until smooth. Pour the chocolate mixture over the bread and stir gently. Bake, covered, at 325 degrees for 35 minutes. Cool slightly on a wire rack. Cut into squares and serve warm with vanilla ice cream. Yield: 12 servings.

Billy Jane Gabel, Xi Master
South Bend, Indiana

MAPLE DECADENCE BREAD PUDDING

1/2 pound sliced bread,
crusts removed
12 egg yolks

1 cup plus 2 tablespoons
maple syrup
4 cups heavy cream

Cut the bread into 1/2-inch cubes and toast until golden brown. Spread evenly in a 9×13-inch baking pan. Whisk the egg yolks and syrup together in a bowl until smooth. Heat the cream in a saucepan until hot; do not boil. Gradually whisk the hot cream into the egg mixture until well blended. Strain the mixture and pour over the bread cubes. Cover the pan with plastic wrap; press on the bread to submerge in the cream mixture. Let stand for 1 hour or until the bread is soaked. Remove the plastic wrap and cover with aluminum foil. Place the baking dish in a water bath. Bake at 350 degrees for 1 1/4 hours or until the custard is set. Drizzle with additional warm syrup and serve with vanilla ice cream.
Yield: 8 to 10 servings.

Paula Roberts, Laureate Epsilon Theta
St. Petersburg, Florida

BANANA PUDDING MADE FAMOUS

1 (14-ounce) can
sweetened condensed
milk
1 1/2 cups cold water
1 (4-ounce) package
vanilla instant
pudding mix

3 cups whipping cream
1 (12-ounce) package
vanilla wafers
4 cups sliced ripe
bananas

Beat the sweetened condensed milk and water at medium speed in a bowl for 1 minute or until blended. Add the pudding mix and beat for 2 minutes. Refrigerate, covered, for 3 to 4 hours or overnight. Whip the cream in a large bowl until stiff. Gently fold the pudding mixture into the whipped cream. Arrange 1/3 of the vanilla wafers in the bottom of a large glass serving bowl. Layer with 1/3 of the bananas and 1/3 of the pudding. Repeat the layers twice more, ending with the pudding. Garnish with additional vanilla wafers and wafer crumbs. Chill, covered tightly with plastic wrap, in the refrigerator for 4 to 8 hours. Yield: 12 to 15 servings.

Diane L. Pruett, Preceptor Alpha Upsilon
Tamaqua, Pennsylvania

RHUBARB PUDDING

4 cups chopped fresh
rhubarb
1 cup sugar
1 (6-ounce) package
strawberry gelatin

1 (18-ounce) package
white cake mix
1 cup water
1/4 cup (1/2 stick) butter,
melted

Arrange the rhubarb in a greased 9×9-inch baking dish. Sprinkle with the sugar, strawberry gelatin and cake mix. Pour the water over the dry ingredients and drizzle the top with the melted butter. Bake at 300 degrees for 1 hour. Yield: 9 servings.

Eda MacAulay, Alpha Eta Master
Guelph, Ontario, Canada

Metric Equivalents

A*lthough the United States has opted to postpone converting to metric measurements, most other countries, including England and Canada, use the metric system. The following chart provides convenient approximate equivalents for allowing use of regular kitchen measures when cooking from foreign recipes.*

Volume

These metric measures are approximate benchmarks for purposes of home food preparation.
1 milliliter = 1 cubic centimeter = 1 gram

Liquid	Dry
1 teaspoon = 5 milliliters	1 quart = 1 liter
1 tablespoon = 15 milliliters	1 ounce = 30 grams
1 fluid ounce = 30 milliliters	1 pound = 450 grams
1 cup = 250 milliliters	2.2 pounds = 1 kilogram
1 pint = 500 milliliters	

Weight

1 ounce = 28 grams
1 pound = 450 grams

Length

1 inch = $2^1/_2$ centimeters
$^1/_{16}$ inch = 1 millimeter

Formulas Using Conversion Factors

When approximate conversions are not accurate enough, use these formulas to convert measures from one system to another.

Measurements	Formulas
ounces to grams:	# ounces x 28.3 = # grams
grams to ounces:	# grams x 0.035 = # ounces
pounds to grams:	# pounds x 453.6 = # grams
pounds to kilograms:	# pounds x 0.45 = # kilograms
ounces to milliliters:	# ounces x 30 = # milliliters
cups to liters:	# cups x 0.24 = # liters
inches to centimeters:	# inches x 2.54 = # centimeters
centimeters to inches:	# centimeters x 0.39 = # inches

Approximate Weight to Volume

Some ingredients which we commonly measure by volume are measured by weight in foreign recipes. Here are a few examples for easy reference.

flour, all-purpose, unsifted	1 pound = 450 grams = 3¹/₂ cups
flour, all-purpose, sifted	1 pound = 450 grams = 4 cups
sugar, granulated	1 pound = 450 grams = 2 cups
sugar, brown, packed	1 pound = 450 grams = 2¹/₄ cups
sugar, confectioners'	1 pound = 450 grams = 4 cups
sugar, confectioners', sifted	1 pound = 450 grams = 4¹/₂ cups
butter	1 pound = 450 grams = 2 cups

Temperature

Remember that foreign recipes frequently express temperatures in Centigrade rather than Fahrenheit.

Temperatures	Fahrenheit	Centigrade
room temperature	68°	20°
water boils	212°	100°
baking temperature	350°	177°
baking temperature	375°	190.5°
baking temperature	400°	204.4°
baking temperature	425°	218.3°
baking temperature	450°	232°

Use the following formulas when temperature conversions are necessary.

Centigrade degrees x $9/5$ + 32 = Fahrenheit degrees
Fahrenheit degrees - 32 x $5/9$ = Centigrade degrees

American Measurement Equivalents

1 tablespoon = 3 teaspoons	12 tablespoons = ³/₄ cup
2 tablespoons = 1 ounce	16 tablespoons = 1 cup
4 tablespoons = ¹/₄ cup	1 cup = 8 ounces
5 tablespoons + 1 teaspoon = ¹/₃ cup	2 cups = 1 pint
8 tablespoons = ¹/₂ cup	4 cups = 1 quart
	4 quarts = 1 gallon

Merit Winners

Nancy AufDerHeide, page 138
Delicious Blueberry Zucchini Bread
Chris Boyd, page 114
Vidalia Onion Casserole
Marie Bray, page 135
Morning French Toast
Margaret Anne Broscomb, page 172
Bee Sting Cake
Mary Carlson, page 177
Caramelized Dutch Apple Pie
Joyce Cooper, page 77
Chipotle Pork Tenderloin
Gerda M. Cote, page 113
Baked Portabella Mushrooms
Zonna F. Craig, page 46
Chicken Caesar Salad Wraps
Sandi Davison, page 82
Ham and Artichoke Lasagna

Anne Elmore-DeVinny, page 47
Salpicon
Lynn Gustin, page 63
Grilled Tri-Tip Roast with Tequila Marinade and Cherry Tomato Relish
Lenore Hamers, page 183
S'More Cookies
Lilli (Gigi) Inness, page 19
Avocado and Shrimp Salsa
Sandra Lange, page 168
Golden Cointreau Cake
Linda Mann, page 163
Tiramisu Toffee Torte
Rosemary Marc-Aurele, page 107
Greek Spinach Pie
Jackie Ann Nelson, page 108
Parmesan Roasted Asparagus

Norma J. Newmeister, page 196
Chocolate Toffee Crunch Squares
Mary Elizabeth Reinhart, page 38
Spinach Salad with Caramelized Onion Dressing
Mickey Roberts, page 92
Grilled Chiles Rellenos
Gayle Taylor, page 206
Red Velvet Cheesecake
Pamela Thomas, page 98
Sizzle Salmon Steaks
Vickie Thomas, page 10
Mixed Olive Bruschetta
Lucille Wanee, page 124
Mushroom-Spinach Soufflé
Sharon Womack, page 161
Chocolate Brandy Fudge Mousse Cake

Honorable Mention

Alstrin, Suzann, 185
Beers, Patricia E., 123
Black, Kay, 12
Blane, Terri, 38
Blankenship, Marlene, 61
Bronowski, Dolores, 99
Byers, Claudia S., 89
Cain, Debbie, 33
Courten, Mary A., 203
Denisi, Maryanne, 198
Evans, Judy Ann, 121
Fields, Cherie, 135
Gardner, Kathy Jaske, 122

Hamilton, Kelli, 48
Harper, Carol, 141
Harrell, Beverly, 206
Haynes, Jeannette, 118
Head, Karen, 10
Hetterich, Gerri, 209
Holton, Karol, 178
Kubr, Marjorie, 64
Little, Holli, 181
Lockner, Barbara, 147
Magers, Faye A., 171
Mawyer, Carolyn S., 107
Mendiola, Gloria F., 44

Munger, Barb, 16
Neilson, Carol J., 196
Sharp, Mildred, 115
Swinhoe, Claire, 61
Switzer, Lavinia, 62
Thiems, Deb, 133
Tucker, Cathy, 160
Waller, Delma, 77
Weems, Gladys, 117
Wensel, Deborah, 30
Weston, Kathryn Faye, 185
Wright, Fawn, 133
Zawol, Maxine, 191

Index

To order additional copies of

75ᵗʰ Anniversary

call 1-800-251-1520